German Writers
in Soviet Exile,
1933–1945

David Pike

German Writers in Soviet Exile, 1933-1945

The University of North Carolina Press

Chapel Hill

Publication of this work has been made possible
in part by a grant from the Andrew W. Mellon Foundation.

Manufactured in the United States of America

Library of Congress Cataloging in Publication Data

Pike, David, 1950–

German writers in Soviet exile, 1933–1945.

Bibliography: p.
Includes index.
1. Authors, German—20th century—Political and social
views. 2. Germans—Soviet Union. 3. Authors, German—
20th century—Biography. 4. German literature—Soviet
Union—History and criticism. 5. Kommunisticheskaia
partiia Sovetskogo Souiza—Purges. 6. Terrorism—Soviet
Union.
I. Title.
PT405.P46   830'.9'00912 [B]   81-10394
ISBN 0-8078-1492-X   AACR2

For my parents

Contents

Preface

I began this study with expectations tempered by an awareness of the special difficulties that it would entail. The subject (as the Russian saying goes) was a book waiting for its author. But I knew that there would be no avoiding the problem of unpublished materials located, alas, in Soviet and East German archives. The political nature of the topic made it seem improbable that those in charge there would welcome me with a show of support for my research. In fact, little available evidence even pointed to the existence of important documents. I left for Moscow in August 1976, aware of an oblique reference in a Soviet archival guide to papers belonging to the German Section of the Soviet Writers' Union and to certain files from the exile monthlies *Internationale Literatur* and *Das Wort*. This was all I had to go on aside from a few cryptic archival signature numbers given in the annotation to another Soviet publication.

At the time, though, I regarded this information as a start. After all, Soviet archivists are more liable to allow a foreign scholar to read unpublished papers if their existence can be proven, usually by referring to the work of a Soviet scholar who documented his research with precise archival numbers. A Western researcher utilizing this approach may at least be given access to these materials, though he can be thankful if he sees any others. Because the *opisi* (bound guides listing all extant documents included in a certain *fond*) are essentially off limits, any further research in Soviet archives is often akin to working in a library without the benefit of a card catalog. The situation is similar in the German Democratic Republic (GDR), except that I found East German archivists more flexible and cooperative than their Soviet counterparts. Still, the rules for use of the archives run by the Akademie der Künste der DDR, for example, state that access to reference guides does not go along with permission to read unpublished papers

So the scholar finds himself in the hands of the archivist, who (if ill-willed) may bring any project to a dead stop if he chooses. Not that good intentions are a rarity, but even they fail to insure that the working relationship between Soviet archivist and Western scholar will not degenerate into a sort of blindman's bluff. The use of *opisi* that would permit the scholar himself to identify and file requests for precise materials is severely restricted. The archivist's own frequent unfamiliarity with the relevant material then compounds an already serious problem. Unable to gauge either the political sensitivity or the potential importance of documents that the scholar himself is prevented from choosing, the archivist may consequently decide that discretion is the better part of professional valor and opt to show him nothing. *Materialov po vashej teme net*—we have no material on your topic—is the customary straight-faced response.

Mindful of this posture, I was not confident at first that I could expand the project into a thorough account of the German Communist writers who thought they had found asylum from Hitler in Stalin's Russia. But as the months passed during my stay in Moscow, I gradually came across material that was essential to an unabridged treatment of the many facets of Soviet exile. Subsequently, I was able to round out my work in Soviet archives by going through the unpublished papers in the Academies of Art in both East and West Berlin, in Budapest's Georg Lukács Archivum, and in the Hungarian Academy of Sciences. A few unpublished memoirs and the score of interviews that I conducted from 1976 to 1980 supplied more information. I undertook to place it all in the proper context by drawing on rare published primary sources (many of them from Moscow's Lenin Library) and on secondary literature about the German Communist Party, the Communist International, the Soviet Union, and Soviet cultural politics. I confess that I was unable to illuminate all aspects of Soviet exile. The last remaining survivors are at least in their seventies; their memories, in many cases, are either failing or gone. Some, who still live in the Soviet Union or in East Germany (plus a few in western Europe) and who do remember well, would not speak candidly about their experiences. Much extant documentary evidence remains inaccessible in the GDR and the Soviet Institutes for Marxism-Leninism. (East Berlin's Institut für Marxismus-Leninismus granted me access to its holdings, but withdrew permission a week later.) So lacunae do exist. Nevertheless, I am optimistic that new information would not alter substantially the broader contours of my findings, only some details.

The twelve months that I spent in Moscow in 1976 and 1977 and the six months in East Berlin in 1979 were made possible by the International Research and Exchanges Board (IREX) and by Fulbright-

Hayes grants. In 1979 the National Endowment for the Humanities, in cooperation with the Hoover Institution's National Fellows Program, provided me with a fellowship for the academic year 1979–80. I owe the finished typescript to this year of uninterrupted writing and gladly acknowledge the generous assistance of the institution. Its staff, librarians, and curators, particularly Mrs. Agnes Peterson and Ms. Hilja Kukk, did everything possible to help me. Ms. Cheri Gross worked exhaustingly on the manuscript during the last hectic weeks of July 1980. I also express my gratitude to the archivists of the Akademie der Künste der DDR (East Berlin), to Professor Walter Huder of West Berlin's Akademie der Künste, and to the staff of the Hungarian Academy of Sciences and the Lukács Archivum és Könyvtár.

I am indebted to the following for information provided in letters and in interviews: Margarete Buber-Neumann, Martin Esslin, Marta Feuchtwanger, Walter Fischer, Lou Fischer, Hans Goldschmidt, Wieland Herzfelde, Hugo Huppert, Hans Kunzl, Mikhail Lifshits, Ruth von Mayenburg, Trude Richter, Igor Sats, Lotte Schwarz, George Steiner, and several persons in the USSR. Lev Kopelev, an exile himself now, allowed me to draw on his knowledge of the German community in Moscow; the same is true of W., who belonged to the colony of exiles. Lilli Beer permitted me to read her unpublished memoirs and took the time to answer many of my inquiries by mail. Finally, there are scholars and friends at the Hoover Institution and at Stanford University whose contribution to the completion of the book was equally important though perhaps less tangible: at the Hoover Institution, Lewis Gann and Sidney Hook; in the Department of Slavic Languages and Literatures, Edward J. Brown and William M. Todd; and in the German Studies Department, Galina Brunot and Gerald Gillespie. To all of them go my thanks. I owe an unrepayable debt of gratitude to Katharina and Momme Mommsen, from whose unselfish and never-ending support I benefited (and continue to benefit) so greatly.

David Pike
Stanford, 31 July 1980

Abbreviations

AdK (West Berlin)	Akademie der Künste (West Berlin)
BdO	Bund deutscher Offiziere (League of German Officers)
Becher-Archiv	Johannes-R.-Becher-Archiv (East Berlin)
BPRS	Bund proletarisch-revolutionärer Schriftsteller (League of Proletarian Revolutionary Writers)
Brecht-Archiv	Bertolt-Brecht-Archiv (East Berlin)
Bredel-Archiv	Willi-Bredel-Archiv (East Berlin)
Comintern	Communist International
ECCI	Executive Committee of the Communist International
GlavPURKKA	Glavnoe politicheskoe upravlenie raboche-krestjanskoj Krasnoj Armii (Central Political Administration of the Workers' and Peasants' Red Army)
IAH	Internationale Arbeiter-Hilfe (see IWR, MRP, and Mezhrabpom)
IBPL	Internationales Verbindungsbüro für proletarische Literatur (International Liaison Office of Proletarian Literature)
IBRL	Internationales Büro für revolutionäre Literatur (International Office of Revolutionary Literature)
INTERAPP	Internatsionalnaja assotsiatsija proletarskikh pisatelej (International Association of Proletarian Writers)

IRH	Internationale Rote Hilfe (see IRR and MOPR)
IRR	International Red Relief
IRTB	Internationaler revolutionärer Theaterbund (International League of Revolutionary Theaters)
IVRS	Internationale Vereinigung revolutionärer Schriftsteller (International League of Revolutionary Writers)
IWR	International Workers' Relief
KAPD	Kommunistische Arbeiterpartei Deutschlands (Communist Workers' Party of Germany)
KPD	Kommunistische Partei Deutschlands (German Communist Party)
KPOe	Kommunistische Partei Österreichs (Austrian Communist party)
LEF	Levyj front iskusstv (Left Front of Arts)
Lukács Archivum	Lukács Archivum és Könyvtár (Budapest)
MBPR	Mezhdunarodnoe bjuro svjazi proletarskoj literatury (see IBPL)
MBRL	Mezhdunarodnoe bjuro revoljutsionnoj literatury (see IBRL)
Mezhrabpom	Mezhdunarodnaja rabochaja pomoshch (see IWR and MRP)
MOPR	Mezhdunarodnaja organizatsija nomoshchi bortsam revoljutsii (see IRR and IRH)
MORP	Mezhdunarodnoe objedinenie revolju- tsionnykh pisatelej (see IVRS)
MORT	Mezhdunarodnoe objedinenie revolju- tsionnykh teatrov (see IRTB)
MRP	Mezhdunarodnaja rabochaja pomoshch (see IWR)
MTA	Magyar Tudományos Akadémia (Budapest)

Narkomindel	Narodnyj komissariat inostrannykh del (Peoples Commissariat for Foreign Affairs)
NEP	New Economic Policy
NKFD	Nationalkomitee Freies Deutschland (National Committee for Free Germany)
NKVD	Narodnyj komissariat vnutrennykh del (Peoples Commissariat for Internal Affairs)
NSDAP	Nationalsozialistische Deutsche Arbeiterpartei (National Socialist German Workers Party)
OMS	Otdel mezhdunarodnoj svjazi (International Liaison Office)
RAPP	Russkaja assotsiatsija proletarskikh pisatelej (Russian Association of Proletarian Writers)
SAP	Sozialistische Arbeiterpartei (Socialist Workers Party)
SDS	Schutzverband deutscher Schriftsteller (Association of German Writers)
SPD	Sozialdemokratische Partei Deutschlands (Social Democratic Party of Germany)
TsGALI	Tsentralnyj gosudarstvennyj arkhiv literatury i iskusstv (Moscow)
VAPP	Vsesojuznaja assotsiatsija proletarskikh pisatelej (All-Union Association of Proletarian Writers)
VEGAAR	Verlagsgenossenschaft ausländischer Arbeiter (Foreign Workers Cooperative Publishing House)
Weinert-Archiv	Erich-Weinert-Archiv (East Berlin)
WKKF	Weltkomitee gegen Krieg und Faschismus
Wolf-Archiv	Friedrich-Wolf-Archiv (East Berlin)

German Writers
in Soviet Exile,
1933–1945

Article 129 reads: "The USSR shall grant the right of asylum to foreign citizens persecuted for their defense of working-class interests, for scholarly activity, or because of national struggles for liberation." How bitter for all of us who wish to view the new Russian constitution as the instrument of an authoritarian democracy should this asylum actually turn out to be a prison cell!

Thomas Mann to
Mikhail Koltsov
1 August 1936

Chapter 1

The Political Legacy

Six weeks after Hitler took office, crushing the Communists, Leon Trotsky spoke of the "tragedy of the German proletariat." The German Communist Party was doomed, he charged, betrayed by the Stalinist policy of the Communist International, which had caused "historic positions" to be surrendered to fascism without a fight. Stalinism in Germany, Trotsky concluded, had had its August Fourth.[1] The policy Trotsky had in mind was the offspring of the ideological notions and Machiavellian *Realpolitik* blended together in what passed in the twenties as Marxism-Leninism. The doctrine came first: capitalism had reached its historical zenith, the day of reckoning with the proletariat was near, and local and international conflicts were soon to engulf the entire world in wars between the armies of socialism and capitalism-imperialism. The "Marxist-Leninist" parties,[2] which joined forces in 1919 in the Comintern to prepare the way for world revolution, would exploit the crises created by moribund monopoly capitalism at home and imperialism abroad to replace bourgeois dictatorship with the dictatorship of the proletariat.[3]

Czarist Russia had fallen to revolution in 1917; the old regimes of Germany and Austria had collapsed one year later; what the Comintern christened a "proletarian revolution" had put a council republic in power in Hungary—the Communists saw and imagined signs of revolution everywhere, and the final conflagration seemed only a matter of time. But even as they banded together and, in Germany, drew up

1. Trotsky, "The Tragedy of the German Proletariat: The German Workers Will Rise Again—Stalinism, Never!," in *The Struggle against Fascism in Germany*, pp. 375–84.
2. The Communist International and its sections were said to stand "wholly and unreservedly upon the ground of *revolutionary Marxism* and its further development, *Leninism*, which is nothing else but Marxism of the epoch of imperialism and proletarian revolution" (*Program of the Communist International*, p. 8).
3. Ibid., pp. 5–8; see also Weber, *Die Wandlung des deutschen Kommunismus*, 1:56. Unless otherwise indicated, all translations from the German are by the author.

a "theory of the revolutionary offensive," conditions in Europe stabilized and the post–World War I revolutionary wave receded. The Comintern just managed to nudge the German Communist Party (KPD) into a single insurrection in Saxony, the ill-starred 1921 *März Aktion*, before Lenin and Trotsky acknowledged the changed circumstances. Said Trotsky in 1921 at the Comintern's Third World Congress: "Now for the first time we see and feel that we are not so immediately near to the goal, to the conquest of power, to the world revolution. At that time, in 1919, we said to ourselves: 'It is a question of months.' Now we say: 'It is perhaps a question of years.' "[4] In response to the changed situation, pragmatism and expediency were now allowed to intrude into the sphere of ideology as Lenin and Trotsky came up with new tactics, the united front, to deal with the nonrevolutionary conditions of stabilized postwar Europe.

The new policy, which called for cooperation with socialists, was first tried out in Germany, where the return of normalcy had broken up the KPD's previously radicalized mass following.[5] Confronted with the choice of altering their activist tactics, which were geared to an immediate revolutionary or crisis situation, or watching the party degenerate into an ineffectual political sect, the German Communists accepted the united front over the opposition of those who loathed the thought of working with "social imperialists" and "social traitors." The party's left wing regarded the new line as a plain abnegation of principle and as a direct threat to the existence of Communism, asking why, if there ought to be collaboration with "reformists," Communism had split with Social Democracy to begin with.

But the opposition should have known that this was a simple matter of expediency, for Lenin had already divulged the quintessence of the united front maneuver in 1920, defining cooperation with socialists as being tantamount to "the support the rope gives to the hanged man."[6] Party principles were still clearly inviolable, for the new tactic of the united front was a mere political stratagem: since German communism lacked the power to make a successful revolution, the KPD would acquire strength by luring socialist workers to its side. Legal

4. Quoted from Carr, *History of Soviet Russia*, 3:385.
5. The party's membership, as a result of the March Action and the decrease in revolutionary fervor, plummeted from 350,000 to 180,443 by the summer of 1921. Angress, *Stillborn Revolution*, p. 168.
6. Lenin, " 'Left-Wing' Communism—An Infantile Disorder," in *Selected Works*, 3:346. Karl Radek remarked a few years later that the Communists did not want to merge with Social Democrats but to "stifle them in our embrace." Quoted in Degras, "United Front Tactics in the Comintern," p. 11.

activity in the trade unions and even participation in the bourgeois parliament were to expose to the socialist rank and file the limitations of the Social Democratic Party's (SPD) program of "partial demands" and the treachery of reformist leaders bent on venting working-class militancy only within the general capitalist system. By shelling socialist officials with proposals and demands that they were bound to reject,[7] the Communists imagined that workers could be turned away from their own party and convinced to join the ranks of the KPD.

This was the thrust of the call "to the masses" and the thinking behind the united front: political expediency was allowed to corrupt ideological purity, but only on the face of it. For *"the basic guarantee of orthodoxy"*[8] was the disingenuousness that informed the whole masquerade. Zinoviev categorized three kinds of united front ploys. A united front "from below," considered virtually "always necessary," connoted the "mobilization of all really revolutionary workers" by driving a wedge between them and their socialist party. A united front "from below and from above" admixted tactical overtures to the socialist leaders, though "safeguards" were built in to prevent a "method of *agitation and mobilization of the masses*" from developing into a political coalition with Social Democracy. The third possibility was a united front solely "from above," rejected regardless of circumstances.[9]

The new policy did not touch the original Marxist-Leninist credo: capitalism was still thought to be suffering from a terminal illness that would end in world revolution. Over this point there was never any debate, but conflicting attitudes toward the united front injected controversy of a different kind into the formulation of party policy—the notion of *deviation*. Henceforth Communist feelings toward socialists pendulated between the poles of cooperation (such as it was) and condemnation, and Moscow decided the direction in which the pendulum should swing. If for whatever reasons Soviet leaders ascertained that conditions in a given country were unfavorable for successful revolution, moderate united front tactics were employed. Radical activists who persisted in pushing revolutionary programs were then stigmatized as sectarians, ultraextremists, and "putschists." If, on the other hand, the Kremlin determined that the objective prerequisites for a victorious revolution were present in a given country, alliances

7. Cf. Zinoviev in 1923: "[The policy] consists in our appealing constantly to people who, we know in advance, will not go along with us" (Degras, "United Front Tactics," p. 13).
8. Borkenau, *European Communism*, p. 54.
9. *Protokoll: Fünfter Kongress*, pp. 80–81. The classifications were elaborated on and accepted in the Congress's theses. *Thesen und Resolutionen des V. Weltkongresses*, p. 26.

with socialists were proscribed[10] and right-wing Communists who appealed for moderation in dealings with them were baited as "opportunists," liquidators (who secretly sought amalgamation with Social Democracy), and bourgeois traitors of the working class. All factions within the Communist parties were thus well supplied with invective for use against each other in the upcoming party power struggles.

The Communists discovered fascism (the Italian brand first) in 1922 and defined it in terms that have remained unchanged down through the years. Comintern propagandists argued simply that, as Lenin had emphasized in 1919, "bourgeois" parliamentary democracy was devoid of any absolute value (it was a ruling-class instrument of dictatorship and nothing more) and that fascism was the means by which the bourgeoisie held its grip on power when it felt threatened by the revolutionary proletariat. Fascism and bourgeois democracy, or monopoly capitalism, or imperialism, were therefore all interchangeable terms. "Fascism represents a method by which the ruling class employs all the means at its disposal to perpetuate its rule," said the Italian Bordiga in 1922; "the party of the Fascisti . . . is the executory bourgeois state organ in the era when imperialism is on the decline."[11] German fascism was perceived no differently except that the Communists distinguished between National Socialism and fascism—the state itself. In the aftermath of the German October of 1923, the KPD's second major defeat in as many years, "Seeckt fascism" was said to be in control of the Reich.[12] "The November Republic has been handed over . . . to fascism," declared the party; "power is in the hands of the military, and the military has made a clear-cut decision to wage a war of destruction against the gains of the working class."[13] The real Fascists were accordingly the power-wielding German bourgeoisie, and in this scheme of things Hitler was a cipher. The ignominious end of his Beer Hall Putsch in November 1923 was regarded by the Communists as the demise of National Socialism. The "big capitalist aspect of fascism," they opined, had triumphed over its "petty bourgeois side." The Resolution on Fascism passed at the Comintern's

10. Except, of course, in a united front "from below."
11. Bordiga at the Fourth World Congress, quoted in Bahne, " 'Sozialfaschismus' in Deutschland," p. 216.
12. General Hans von Seeckt, chief of the Reichswehr, had been granted full emergency powers by Stresemann in early November 1923.
13. Quoted from the resolution adopted at a KPD conference held on 3 November 1923, reprinted in Pirker, *Komintern und Faschismus*, pp. 144–45.

Fifth World Congress in 1924 ratified the view of fascism as "one of the classic forms of counterrevolution during the era of capitalist disintegration and the age of proletarian revolution. . . . Fascism is a weapon employed by the grand bourgeoisie against the proletariat, whose subduel can no longer be achieved by utilization of legal methods of state power; fascism is the extralegal weapon which the bourgeoisie wields to erect and consolidate its dictatorship."[14]

Throughout the twenties, the topic of fascism was paramount at all Comintern and KPD meetings, conferences, and congresses; all proclamations, slogans, demands, and resolutions carried statements about fascism, and all Communist orators referred extensively to it. This theory of fascism was then rounded out with the notion of *social fascism*. Fundamental differences with "reformism" had, of course, led to the birth of Communist parties in the first place, whose hatred for Social Democracy was scarcely rivaled even by animosity toward the bourgeoisie. That capitalism decays and dies lay, after all, in the natural order of things; it was a predetermined historical process; the bourgeoisie merely carried out the role history assigned it. That Social Democracy, on the other hand, collaborated with the system and to all intents and purposes coalesced with it, this was not historic necessity but treachery. The logic was flawless: if capitalism had reached its highest stage of development, imperialism, then any party that fraternized and joined forces with it was likewise imperialist, including the SPD. But the theory began to go astray with the next deduction. The Communists dubbed Social Democracy the "main enemy" of communism, for without socialist support, as Lenin had already argued in 1921, "the bourgeoisie could not assert itself against the workers."[15] Though the debut of the united front policy in 1921 led to rhetoric softened in proportion to the value the Communists attached at any given time to cooperation with socialists, the underlying irreconcilability remained. The Theses on the Tactics of the Communist International passed in 1924 highlighted the belligerence: "All attempts to interpret this tactic [the united front] as a political coalition with counterrevolutionary Social Democracy are opportunism, which the Communist International repudiates." The united front had one purpose only, "to draw Social Democratic . . . workers gradually over to our side." By no means a program of alliance with reformism, the

14. *Thesen und Resolutionen des V. Weltkongresses*, pp. 121–23.
15. Lenin at the Second World Congress of the Comintern, quoted in Bahne, " 'Sozialfaschismus' in Deutschland," p. 213.

united front represented "a revolutionary strategic maneuver of the Communist vanguard in its struggle, above all else, against the traitorous leaders of counterrevolutionary Social Democracy."[16]

If the SPD had indeed "merged with bourgeois policy" (Lenin), how did Social Democracy and fascism stand in relation to each other? Responsibility for the "victory of fascism over bourgeois democracy" in late 1923, the Communists insisted, had to be borne by socialist leaders, for their policy of tolerance of the Reich government had paved the way for the triumph; the socialist "accomplices of fascism" had betrayed the gains of the proletariat to fascism and had lifted it (in the person of Stresemann and Seeckt) into the saddle. All that remained was a life-and-death struggle with socialist leaders.[17]

The bellicosity peaked in April 1924 when the KPD's left wing, headed by Ruth Fischer and Arkadij Maslow, assumed power in the aftermath of the October 1923 defeat. During its two-year reign, political union of any kind with "Fascist Social Democracy" was strictly prohibited and contacts with socialists limited to a united front "from below."[18] Social Democracy was now dubbed "the third bourgeois party" in Germany—a "wing of fascism"[19]—and the Fifth World Congress in 1924 passed resolutions and theses defining "fascism and Social Democracy as two sides of one and the same tool used by a big capitalist dictatorship."[20] The same year Stalin had the final say on the subject. "Fascism," he explained, "is a fighting organization of the bourgeoisie which counts on the active support of Social Democracy." His conclusion: "Social Democracy is objectively the moderate wing of fascism. . . . These organizations do not cancel each other out; rather the one complements the other; they are not antipodes but twins."[21]

The resolutions of the Fifth World Congress also carried one of the earlier charges that the "international policies" of Social Democracy manifested themselves in preparation for war against the USSR, a theme repeated regularly over the next ten years. The closer the end of capitalism and the more difficult and contradictory the predicament of the international bourgeoisie, the more probable it was that a direct military adventure on their part would be launched against the Soviet Union, stated the Theses on the Tactics of the Communist

16. *Thesen und Resolutionen des V. Weltkongresses*, pp. 25 and 27.
17. Pirker, *Komintern und Faschismus*, p. 146; Bahne, " 'Sozialfaschismus' in Deutschland," pp. 222–23.
18. Bahne, " 'Sozialfaschismus' in Deutschland," pp. 222–23.
19. Zinoviev at the Fifth World Congress. *Protokoll: Fünfter Kongress*, p. 67.
20. *Thesen und Resolutionen des V. Weltkongresses*, p. 121.
21. Bahne, " 'Sozialfaschismus' in Deutschland," p. 224.

International. The theses also added: "The counterrevolutionary leaders of Social Democracy, in their infinite hatred of Soviet power, will even decide upon military adventures more readily than many an outspoken bourgeois. . . . There is no doubt that precisely these leaders . . . will demonstrate the greatest zeal in the execution of preparation of even a direct campaign of international capital against the first proletarian revolution in the world."[22]

The Comintern and the KPD thus began to make lasting ideological mainstays out of a narrowly conceived understanding of fascism and social fascism as early as 1921, and these were the misconceptions that helped bring about the disaster of 1933. But what really contributed to the collapse of German communism was its subservience to the USSR, a subservience that began in the early twenties when Soviet political figures took the first steps toward total control of the KPD. This control allowed the manipulation of the party in the interests not of revolution but of Soviet domestic and foreign policy.[23] The process started almost imperceptibly, because the retreat in 1921 had been legitimate in terms of revolutionary logic—conditions in Europe had stabilized and the continuation of radical policies in Germany would have led nowhere. But there were other reasons for backing down. The Comintern's new tactical approach to world revolution was the "natural counterpart"[24] of a major change both in Soviet domestic and foreign policy. Soviet leaders in 1921, though for the first time since the revolution enjoying a relatively stable domestic atmosphere, nonetheless needed a further breathing spell to consolidate their grip on power and to recover from the ravages of civil war and war communism. The extreme policies in effect since 1917 were therefore discontinued and replaced by a form of private enterprise called the New Economic Policy (NEP). This was the Soviet domestic pendant to the Comintern's post-1921 deemphasis on world revolution.

There was likewise a profound shift in the nature of Soviet foreign affairs. In the years following the revolution, Soviet activity abroad had largely been the domain of the Communist International in its pursuit of world revolution; but now the Comintern had to give up some of its sovereignty and share power with the Commissariat for Foreign Affairs (Narkomindel), which sought normal diplomatic rela-

22. *Thesen und Resolutionen des V. Weltkongresses*, p. 15.
23. A detailed account of the first phase of the KPD's sovietization (1919–23) is found in Angress, *Stillborn Revolution*, (see his summaries on pp. 100–103, 193–95); the bolshevization and Stalinization of the party (1924–29) is dealt with exhaustively throughout Weber, *Die Wandlung des deutschen Kommunismus*.
24. Carr, *History of Soviet Russia*, 3:383.

tions and even trade agreements with capitalist states. Not that the Comintern now became inactive; it was just that Soviet foreign policy developed two prongs, because both the Comintern (indirectly and often unbeknownst to its own members) and the Narkomindel were employed to achieve Soviet objectives and protect Soviet state interests, however they happened to be conceived. A strange state of affairs thus ensued, where one of the main European nations "maintained trade and diplomatic relations with most other states and had a virtual alliance with one of them (Germany from the Treaty of Rapallo on), while at the same time it directed movements and activities within those countries designed ultimately to overthrow the existing governments."[25]

Soviet interest in the Western nations triggered a quick response from more radical Communists, who suspected that the USSR might allow the Narkomindel to take priority over the Comintern by putting Soviet state interests above those of world revolution. The Communist Workers' Party of Germany (KAPD), for instance, noted as early as 1921: "We do not forget for a moment the difficulties into which Russian Soviet power has fallen owing to the postponement of world revolution. But we also see the danger that out of these difficulties there may arise an apparent or real contradiction between the interests of the revolutionary world proletariat and the momentary interests of Soviet Russia."[26] The contradiction was already there, but in the very early twenties it could still be argued persuasively that with respect to the retreat of 1921 this was not a case of state interests overriding world revolution. The reappraisal of policy in the Comintern plainly corresponded to the "momentary interests" of Soviet Russia, which needed a period of normalcy in its relationship with the West; but by the same token the long-term interests of world revolution would not have been well served in the early twenties by revolutionary posturing, a point not lost on more realistically minded Communists, who saw no discrepancy in 1921 between the policies of the Narkomindel and the Comintern.[27]

With the passage of each year, however, the dichotomy of interests grew, and the cause of world revolution soon gave way to Stalin's call for the "construction of socialism in one country." In the process, the Comintern suffered the complete loss of its original raison d'être and took on new duties as an organization meant to attain foreign policy

---

25. Ulam, *Expansion and Coexistence*, p. 131.
26. Carr, *History of Soviet Russia*, 3:396.
27. Ibid., 3:397.

objectives by nondiplomatic means. This was only possible after the Kremlin had absolute dominion over foreign Communist parties, whose interests were from here on out only respected when they happened to conform to Soviet needs. In the case of the KPD, the spread of Soviet influence over German communism occurred in the context of the intraparty fights that broke out in 1923–24 in the Soviet Communist party and were copied in the KPD. As Stalin formed alternate alliances with elements of various wings of his party to defeat an opposing faction, following up each victory by arrogating the programs of his defeated opponents and then turning upon his most recent allies, he carried the entire process into the Comintern and the KPD. In this manner the Stalinization of the Soviet party was attended by the Stalinization of the KPD.

The whole process was exalted ideologically in the term "bolshevization," the irony being that its initial stage was carried out by political figures like Zinoviev and Ruth Fischer who soon after fell victim to it. "Bolshevization is the unshakeable resolve to fight for the hegemony of the proletariat," Zinoviev defined the program. "Bolshevization is flaming hatred of the bourgeoisie and of the counterrevolutionary leaders of Social Democracy. . . . Bolshevization is Marxism in action, loyalty to the concept of proletarian dictatorship and to the precepts of *Leninism*. Such is bolshevization: not mechanical imitation of the Russian Bolsheviki, but the acceptance of all that was and is immortal in bolshevism."[28] But who determined what was "immortal" in bolshevism? Who defined the "precepts of Leninism"? Stalin, of course, in ever-greater measure until Leninism and Stalinism became synonyms. The two main ideological dangers to Leninism, as Stalin now identified them, were the twin heresies of Luxemburgism and Trotskyism, and he called upon all believers to join the battle against the apostasies. The real motivation behind the struggle, though, was clearly not ideological at all but political.[29] The set of anti-Leninist ideas associated with Rosa Luxemburg was certainly disavowed in the KPD; but the underlying reason for the renunciation of "Luxemburgism" was simply that most of the early Spartacists and friends of Luxemburg had long been at variance with the KPD's ruling radical faction, which was now carrying out the bolshevization and using it to settle scores with its party foes.

In combating Trotsky and "Trotskyism" the KPD sided with Stalin for similar political reasons: the Fischer-Maslow leadership happened

28. *Protokoll: Fünfter Kongress*, p. 508.
29. Cf. Weber, *Die Wandlung des deutschen Kommunismus*, 1:89–98.

to be allied with Trotsky's enemies in the USSR, the so-called Stalin-Zinoviev left-wing bloc. Together they assailed Trotsky as a right-winger for his original advocacy of united front tactics in 1921 and for his support of the KPD's right wing, led by Heinrich Brandler, whom the left had made the scapegoat for the abortive German October. The point was entirely lost on the radical KPD leadership that positions had shifted. By late 1924 Stalin was arguing for the construction of socialism in one country, to which Trotsky opposed his theory of permanent revolution. Now Stalin was the moderate and Trotsky the radical. Put in those terms, the Stalin-Trotsky quarrel was of overriding importance to the KPD. Should revolution in Germany take precedence over the desiderata of the Soviet state? Or should foreign and domestic interests (socialism in one country) be given priority over the viability of the other Communist parties? This was the real issue, at least in theory, and the vitality of German communism was at stake. By throwing its allegiance to Stalin and Zinoviev, the Fischer-Maslow diumvirate contributed directly to the nullification of German communism's independence and revolutionary élan. The next stage in the Stalinization of the KPD came in 1925 when Stalin turned on Zinoviev. After his triumph over Trotsky, won with the aid of Zinoviev and other left Russian and foreign Communists, Stalin formed a bloc with his party's right wing and succeeded in stripping Zinoviev and the left of all power in the Soviet party and in the Communist International. Zinoviev's duties were then taken over by Bukharin. The entire process was duplicated in the KPD: German leftists were purged, Fischer and Maslow were replaced, and a new man, Ernst Thälmann, put at the head of the party.[30]

The KPD, with the radical Fischer-Maslow interlude behind it, then followed a moderate course from 1925 to 1928 corresponding to the calm of the NEP years in the Soviet Union. Socialists were no longer called "social fascists," at least not publicly, and the party readopted united front tactics. But in 1928 the Comintern abruptly lurched back to the left, in line with the end of NEP and the start of the First Five-Year Plan. The most radical phase of ultraextremism since the Comintern came into being now began. In 1928–29 as in 1925–26, the KPD followed suit and, as before, the introduction of the new line "was carried through in the context of the intraparty factional strug-

---

30. See Weber, *Die Wandlung des deutschen Kommunismus*, 1:120–86. Thälmann actually came from the party's left wing too, but he was a chameleon who allowed himself to be used in all party factional struggles by Soviet Stalinists.

gle in Russia, and in no other context whatsoever."[31] Shortly after
Stalin used Bukharin to outmaneuver Zinoviev and the party's left
wing in 1925–26 and after he replaced Fischer and Maslow with
Thälmann in the KPD, he began preparing Bukharin's elimination.
The "right deviation" was now proclaimed the "chief danger" to communism. By April 1929 Bukharin had been removed from his position in the Comintern, his expulsion from the Politburo following in
November. The right wing and moderate elements in the KPD, many
of them Bukharinists, were likewise singled out and forced to chose
between capitulation or expulsion. Thälmann, however, who played a
central role in the political purge, remained in power, but he was now
joined by Hermann Remmele and Heinz Neumann, the three men
who made up the Stalinist triumvirate.[32]

The switch to the left required ideological justification, a task that
devolved on the Sixth World Congress of the Comintern in 1928.
Since objective prerequisites (a crisis situation) had to be present to
warrant radical policies, the Communists preemptorily declared that
the "temporary stabilization of capitalism" was over and christened
the new era in postwar socioeconomic development the "third period," the first having been the time of unrest ending in 1923 and the
second the "temporary stabilization of capitalism" in 1923–28.[33] "This
[third] period," the Sixth Congress resolved, "is bound to lead . . . to
fresh convulsions of capitalist stabilization and to an extreme intensification of the general crisis of capitalism."[34] The upsurge of revolutionary unrest and the strength of the labor movement would result
in "gigantic class warfare,"[35] and a new phase of wars between the
capitalist states and of the capitalist states against the Soviet Union was
prophesied.[36]

---

31. Borkenau, *European Communism*, p. 72.
32. Cf. Weber, *Die Wandlung des deutschen Kommunismus*, 1:186–238.
33. The "temporary stabilization" had begun in 1921, but the Communists advanced
the date to 1923 in ex post fiasco justification for the German October.
34. *Protokoll des 6. Weltkongresses*, 4:14. The Great Depression of 1929 seemed to bear
out the forecast, but there is strong evidence that Soviet leaders did not anticipate the
end to economic stability in the West. Prophecies about the collapse of capitalism were
believed as much as the rhetoric about an impending "war of intervention" against the
USSR, and they served the same political purpose. See Ulam, *Expansion and Coexistence*,
p. 182.
35. *Protokoll des 6. Weltkongresses*, 4:14.
36. Stalin had already resurrected the "ghost of imperialist intervention" (Ulam) in
1927. Now as before, though, it was used for propaganda and as a weapon in the
factional struggles. Speaking in 1927 about the threat of war against the USSR, Stalin
had noted that "our task consists in strengthening the defensive capacity of our country,

All the radical shibboleths reemerged as the common currency from 1928 to 1934. The program of the Communist International adopted at the Sixth Congress outlined the situation: the general crisis of capitalism had rejuvenated the class struggle; its intensification had caused a "bankruptcy of parliamentarism." Police actions, antilabor ordinances, the curtailment and annulment of democratic liberties— all these "new" methods and forms of administration the bourgeoisie adopted in a process of fascistization meant to "stabilize and perpetuate its rule." Under special historical conditions, moreover, "the progress of this bourgeois, reactionary offensive assumes the form of Fascism."[37] Ernst Thälmann explained that there were only two camps: that of the bourgeoisie, turning fascist in its desperate bid to hold power, and that of the radicalized working class, led by its Communist vanguard and bent on revolution. It was "class against class," and National Socialism and Social Democracy were solidly on the side of the bourgeoisie, which (in Thälmann's words) "avails itself of two methods to suppress and subjugate the working class: *reformism* and *fascism* [here in the sense of nazism]."[38] Thälmann then followed through with the same type of deductions made in the early twenties. "The internal and external contradictions of relative stabilization," he expounded, "are likewise mirrored in the essence and development of Social Democracy," the transformation of reformism to "*social fascism,*" with which the only acceptable form of cooperation was the united front "from below."[39] Now not only had the "ghost of imperialist intervention" been resurrected, but also the notion that Social Democracy played the most important role in preparation of the new war against the Soviet Union. Thälmann intoned, "Everyone must recognize the fact that imperialism would be wholly incapable of unleashing war if Social Democracy did not support all the imperialist preparations for war." In Germany "Social Democracy . . . is the main factor in the line of war preparation against the Soviet Union."[40]

As in 1923–24, the Communists identified fascism with democracy.

---

raising its national economy, improving industry. . . ." And he concluded: "What can we say after all this of our wretched opposition and its new attacks on the party in face of the threat of a new war?" Quoted in Ulam, *Expansion and Coexistence*, p. 165. The war hysteria was fanned at the Sixth World Congress and remained high until 1933, after which the danger of an imperialist war was transmuted into the threat of a "Fascist war," that is, a Nazi war.

37. *Program of the Communist International*, p. 23.
38. *Protokoll des 6. Weltkongresses*, 1:304.
39. *Protokoll des 6. Weltkongresses*, 4:30: "The intensification of the struggle against Social Democracy puts the emphasis decisively on the united front *from below.*"
40. *Protokoll des 6. Weltkongresses*, 1:302.

In 1929 Thälmann called the Weimar coalition government headed by the Social Democrat Müller a "social-fascist dictatorship," following that up in early 1930 with the conclusion that "fascism is ruling in Germany" (by then Brüning's administration was in power).[41] Over the next two years Thälmann backed away only slightly from that hard line, without altering the basic premise that fascism and democracy were synonymous. In early 1931 he made this reference to Brüning's government: "We have a situation in Germany where a Fascist dictatorship is maturing but not yet fully matured. Brüning's administration, in the present stage of its development, represents a government there for the establishment of a Fascist dictatorship."[42]

Only after the elections of 1930 did the German Communists concern themselves with National Socialism, rethinking, however, none of their original suppositions. Thälmann reiterated what he had said at the Sixth Congress: finance capitalism made alternate use of both wings of fascism, the moderate wing of social fascism and the radical wing of Hitler fascism; and Social Democracy, the parliamentary basis of Brüning's government, had paved the way for National Socialism, which was the "extraparliamentary" mass basis of the bourgeoisie in its implementation of fascist dictatorship.[43] Communists were still called upon to focus their attention on Social Democracy, proclaimed in early 1931 by Dmitrij Manuilskij, who had followed Bukharin as head of the Comintern, to be the "main social pillar of the bourgeoisie."[44] The "chief enemy of the working class always has been, is, and will be the bourgeoisie," Manuilskij claimed, the "basic hindrance" to the revolutionary crisis being the fact that the mass basis of Social Democracy had not yet been "shattered";[45] he reaffirmed Stalin's 1924 definition of fascism and Social Democracy as twins and called for the "main blow" to be directed at the latter.[46]

With the Nazis the KPD chose to compete *ideologically*. The National Socialist mass following had to be shown that the KPD, not the NSDAP (Nationalsozialistische Deutsche Arbeiterpartei), best represented its nationalist interests. The party accordingly published a "Declaration for the National and Social Liberation of the German People"

---

41. Ernst Thälmann, "Gegen den Youngplan," (Rede im Reichstag), in Thälmann, *Reden und Aufsätze*, 2:304. See also Weingartner, *Stalin und der Aufstieg Hitlers*, p. 49.
42. Thälmann, *Volksrevolution über Deutschland*, p. 30.
43. Ibid., pp. 28–29.
44. Manuilsky, *The Communist Parties*, p. 62.
45. Ibid., p. 112.
46. These same notes were still heard in December 1933. See Pieck, *We are Fighting for a Soviet Germany*, pp. 54, 64–65.

in late summer 1930[47] and used it in the fall elections, but when the votes were tabulated, the Nazis had increased their contingent of Reichstag deputies from 12 to 107. The Communists too had won something of a victory, their deputation increasing from 54 to 77. The "losers" were the Social Democrats, whose numbers had fallen off from 153 to 143. This was all a significant victory, the Communists insisted, for Social Democracy was losing ground to Communism, while National Socialism had peaked. The *Rote Fahne* explained: "National Socialists are the paid agents of finance capital. . . . The Fascists . . . will not be able to avoid destroying the trust of their 6.4 million voters, disappointing their expectations and trampling their demands underfoot." The paper added: "That is why Hitler's victory in the elections—this is absolutely certain—carries with it the seeds of his future defeat. The fourteenth of September was the culmination of the National Socialist movement in Germany. What comes after can only be decline and fall."[48]

What bred the optimism? Many Communists, both rank and file and upper-level functionaries, actually believed that nazism was on the verge of disintegration. If the Nazi bosses were really little more than puppets of the bourgeoisie, as the KPD preached, then the National Socialist mass movement was bound to break up once it became clear to the individual members that the NSDAP did not have their interests in mind. The KPD's appeal to the nationalism and revanchism of the lower middle class was supposed to expedite this process of disillusionment. The optimism was further generated by the KPD's own revolutionary posturing, according to which Nazi terrorism, as well as the "fascistization" of the bourgeoisie, was no more than a sign of infirmity—the death throes of German capitalism. "As a counterresponse to the revolutionary upsurge during the [capitalist] crisis, there is occurring a crisis and fascistization of the bourgeois parties, including Social Democracy." This fascistization, in the words Thälmann used in early 1931, "is the antithesis of the dialectical process." But no real concern was warranted, for nothing pointed to the longevity of fascism in any of its manifestations. "If the German bourgeoisie is now on the verge of implementing a Fascist dictatorship, this is evidence not of bourgeois strength and proletarian weakness or defeat," Thälmann explained. "Rather, the opposite is true: the bourgeoisie reaches out for the supreme form of rule; it avails itself of fascism as a battering ram against the proletarian revolution."[49]

47. Reprinted in Thälmann, *Reden und Aufsätze*, 2:530–40.
48. Quoted in Pirker, *Komintern und Faschismus*, p. 156.
49. Thälmann, *Volksrevolution über Deutschland*, pp. 25–26.

Fascism was logically thought to be providing a stimulus to the revolutionary wave. Since the current "capitalist offensive" would have to be directed in time not only at the proletariat but at the lower middle class as well (the main backer of National Socialism), the petty bourgeois would eventually see through Hitler's demagogy and recognize their commonality of interests with the KPD. They would then form a sort of "rear guard" of the revolution to collaborate with the Communist "advance guard." It was all part of the dialectic, a historical necessity: the worse the capitalist crisis became, the more the bourgeoisie would resort to means of retaining power that would alienate and drive away its own supporters. The Communists carried the dialectic a step further. If all this was true, then fascism represented the transition to revolution and must precede it. The bourgeoisie would never relinquish power peacefully, resorting first to what Thälmann had styled its "supreme method of rule"—fascism. A Fascist dictatorship was accordingly the culmination of bourgeois rule in the era of imperialism. This analysis fostered the desire to advance the date of revolution by getting the preceding stage over with as soon as possible. If fascism was an unavoidable phase to be passed through before the revolution could occur, why not let the Nazis into power? They would then come to economic wrack and ruin all the sooner and drive their supporters into the ranks of the KPD. This dialectic, however, was getting out of hand, and Soviet leaders intervened, finding scapegoats for the excesses. Hermann Remmele and Heinz Neumann were relieved of their posts; Thälmann kept his job, however, even though his speeches show clearly that his views—in May 1931 he had made reference to the party's "brilliant general line"[50]—had not originally differed from those of the expelled.[51]

But the Comintern intervention was not intended to prompt a real reexamination of policies; nor did it signal a new awareness of the threat posed by National Socialism. Throughout 1932 the sanguine attitude toward Hitler continued, and the struggle against social fascism was reaffirmed. Thälmann wrote in October 1932 that the National Socialist movement "has in all probability reached its watershed" and that Social Democracy was still the "moderate wing of fascism," the principal social pillar of the bourgeoisie. What was needed was an "intensification of the united front from below in all its forms and

50. Thälmann, *Vorwärts unter dem Banner*, p. 14.
51. Neumann and his group were charged with "underrating fascism and weakening the basic struggle against Social Democracy" (the accusation was made by Thälmann in October 1932 and listed in the political resolutions of the party conference printed in *Im Kampf gegen die faschistische Diktatur*, pp. 25–28, 47). The charge of "underrating

methods," for "only when the main blow is struck at Social Democracy
. . . can the chief class enemy of the proletariat, the bourgeoisie, be
successfully defeated and crushed."[52]

Just a few months before Hitler took office, the KPD raised the
pitch of its invective against the Reich government even higher, referring to the Papen-Schleicher cabinet as a government of Fascist dictatorship.[53] But there was a danger within the KPD, Thälmann remarked, of an "exaggeration of fascism," a tendency to see Fascist
dictatorship as the consolidation of bourgeois class rule. Thälmann
informed his readers that "fascism, too, as a product of putrifying
monopoly capitalism, is subject to decomposition." He then proferred
a definition of bourgeois democracy and its relation to fascism that
showed the extent to which the Communists in the early thirties were
still harnessed to doctrines formulated almost a decade before: "*Bourgeois democracy represents the dictatorship of the bourgeoisie in its cloaked
form. Fascism is the open, undisguised dictatorship, which is erected as part of
the process of annihilation of the class organizations of the proletariat.*"[54] A
few months later Hitler was in power and Trotsky's words of 1931 had
come true: " 'Without a victory over the Social Democracy,' " he had
mocked the utterances of KPD leaders, " 'we cannot battle against
fascism!' say such terrible revolutionists, and for this reason . . . they
get their passports ready."[55]

----

fascism" stemmed from the argument that National Socialism would disintegrate as
time passed and that its following would defect to the Communist camp. The first half
of the accusation was not without basis, though Neumann and Remmele were by no
means the sole exponents of that view. But there was another phase of Neumann's
activity pertaining to the second charge. In 1932 Neumann and Remmele ceased
identifying fascism in its National Socialist manifestation with bourgeois democracy,
regarding it instead as an independent, lumpenproletarian movement at some variance with the bourgeoisie and out to replace it in power. The tactical conclusion of this
more realistic appraisal was the advocacy of a united front with socialists, or, as the
Communists put it, "weakening the basic struggle against Social Democracy." See Pieck,
We are Fighting for a Soviet Germany, p. 35.

52. Thälmann, *Im Kampf gegen die faschistische Diktatur,* pp. 15, 17, and 29. It is interesting to compare Thälmann's remarks with Lenin's comments of 1916: "The fight
against imperialism is a sham and a humbug unless it is inseparably bound up with the
fight against opportunism" (Lenin, *Selected Works,* 1:729). In October 1932 Thälmann
stressed the validity of Stalin's definition of Social Democracy and fascism as "twins" (*Im
Kampf gegen die faschistische Diktatur,* p. 16).

53. Remarks made at the ECCI's Twelfth Plenum, quoted by Thälmann in *Im Kampf
gegen die faschistische Diktatur,* p. 13.

54. Ibid., pp. 12–13.

55. Trotsky, "For a Workers' United Front Against Fascism," in *The Struggle against
Fascism in Germany,* p. 141.

The Communist response to National Socialism in the twenties and thirties was virtually foreordained by an ideology developed altogether independently of nazism. When Hitler and the NSDAP emerged as a robust political force, the Communists were already locked into an evaluation of the movement that was based on ossified concepts and premises woefully out of touch with the reality of the situation. But was ideology alone responsible for the disastrous misunderstanding of National Socialism? In a specific sense, it was. It bore sole responsibility for Stalin's failure to take another ideology—the irrationalism, racism, and antibolshevism of National Socialism—seriously. Stalin evidently assumed that, ideology or not, Hitler was a run-of-the-mill nationalist politician whose foreign policy, like that of other nationalist parties, could be counted upon to pursue revanchist goals antagonistic to the League of Nations. According to this line of thinking, the advent of Hitler would not necessarily herald a negative turn of events for the USSR as long as the Nazis continued the cooperation with the Soviet Union started in the early twenties with the Treaty of Rapallo.

The Treaty of Rapallo had molded German-Soviet diplomatic and economic relations ever since 1922. Throughout the twenties there had been an ongoing debate between supporters of a Western orientation in German foreign policy, sponsored by Social Democrats and various bourgeois parties, and proponents of economic (and military) cooperation with Soviet Russia, an Eastern orientation favored not only by radical leftists but by nationalists and many leading members of the German military caste as well. Junkers and old-line generals argued that Germany must focus on a settling of accounts with France. By helping Russia strengthen herself, Germany could improve her bargaining position vis-à-vis the West and assure the nation of a ready source of raw materials. A friendly Russia would permit Germany to withstand a possible Western blockade and avoid the possibility of a future two-front war. The Treaty of Rapallo had been the first step in this direction, a move that perturbed France and Great Britain, who saw it as a menace to the balance of power on the continent.

But leading Social Democrats, fearing the response of the Western nations and believing that bilateral agreements between Germany and Russia would inflict severe damage on Germany's efforts to rehabilitate herself in the eyes of her Western neighbors, continued to oppose rapprochement with the Soviet Union, supporting instead action that would alleviate tensions with the West. This led in 1925 to Germany's entry into the League of Nations, a movement toward Western alignment that the Russians looked upon as an ill omen. However, while refusing to forgo alliances with the West, Germany signed another accord with Moscow, the 1926 Treaty of Berlin, which continued the policy of Rapallo.

In 1928 the Social Democrats had once again entered the Reich government, a development taken by the Soviets as an augury of worsening German-Soviet relations. Because the Soviet Union regarded France as Russia's most dangerous European enemy from 1928 to 1933, the USSR was very uneasy about the prospects of improved Franco-German relations, which the Soviets fully expected German Social Democrats, as unstinting exponents of fulfillment with the Western powers, to pursue. Communist vilification of Social Democracy as social fascism in 1928–33 was thus a means of combating a political party in Germany whose foreign policy was pro-Western rather than pro-Soviet. In that sense it had nothing to do with ideology. As for the real Fascists, the Kremlin considered the growth of a strong revanchist "nationalist opposition" in Germany as a political force benefiting the Soviet Union by making it politically hazardous for any Reich government to pursue Franco-German accords. The KPD's Program for National and Social Liberation intentionally fanned German revanchism and nationalism as a means of keeping pressure on a Reich government that, the Soviets felt, was losing its interest in the relationship with Russia established at Rapallo. By fomenting anti-Versaille nationalism within Germany, the Comintern hoped to reduce the amount of maneuverability the Reich government had in exploring possibilities for rapprochement with France.[56]

This was the sense in which the mindless Communist policy toward Hitler and National Socialism resulted not from ideological but from reasonable diplomatic and political premises. Stalin and his Comintern puppets used ideology merely to focus the attention of the German Communists *on* Social Democracy, which was viewed in a diplomatic context, with justification, as Russia's main enemy, and *away* from National Socialism, which Stalin did not look upon as a direct threat to the vital interests of the Soviet Union. But Hitler was a menace to Russia, and the principal reason why Stalin misread the threat went back again to his own ideology. Pragmatically and politically, Stalin interpreted National Socialism in terms of the anti-Western influence it exerted upon the Reich government and in terms of the shape he expected its foreign policy to take should Hitler ever come to office. But ideologically he viewed the essence of the movement from his own Marxist-Leninist vantage point, which told him that Hitler was a

56. In *Stalin und der Aufstieg Hitlers*, Weingartner explores the relationship between Comintern ideology and Soviet *Realpolitik* in detail.

marionette of big business and that "fascism" was imperialist capitalism. National Socialist ideology thus had no independent significance whatsoever outside the realm of predictable monopoly capitalism, which Stalin felt could be dealt with by playing off one capitalist power against the other. Stalin failed to grasp the fact that Hitler in office would act according to an ideology none of the Communists really understood and that his actions would not be predicated on Marxist-Leninist notions of advanced, putrifying capitalism. He thus sensed no real danger in Hitler and did little to prevent his advent to power. In the process, by imposing the Comintern's extremist line upon the KPD, he saw to it that the German Communists followed his lead.[57]

57. Karl Radek is said to have remarked to a German Communist, while pointing to Stalin's office in the Kremlin, that "there sit those who bear the guilt for Hitler's victory." Zinoviev also said to Erich Wollenberg: "Apart from the German Social Democrats, Stalin bears the main responsibility to history for Hitler's victory." Both quoted in Isaac Deutscher, *The Prophet Outcast*, 3:166.

Chapter 2

The Literary International

While the Comintern manipulated foreign Communist parties in furtherance of Soviet state interests and the Narkomindel pursued normal relations with the West, a third dimension of Soviet activity abroad flourished during the twenties: the cultivation in Western progressive circles of solidarity, sympathy, and goodwill toward the Soviet Union. This promotion of a popularized pro-Sovietism came under the purview not of the foreign commissariat but of a semiautonomous branch of the Comintern, the International Workers' Relief or Mezhrabpom (MRP), founded by the German Willi Münzenberg in 1921 and headed by him ever since. In 1921 famine had broken out in the Soviet Union as one of the consequences of war communism and civil war, and Lenin personally asked Münzenberg to oversee the activities of an international relief agency created to combat the hunger. This was the MRP's original purpose, and among its charter members it boasted such names as Käthe Kollwitz, George Grosz, Bernard Shaw, Anatole France, Henri Barbusse, and Albert Einstein. The MRP thus became the prototype for virtually all ensuing Communist fronts—congresses, committees, agencies, and institutions—all of which drummed up sympathy for the USSR behind a nonpartisan facade of support for every thinkable progressive working-class cause. Within five years of the MRP's birth, Münzenberg boasted that "virtually all the left-oriented prominent writers, actors, and so on in Europe, along with their counterparts elsewhere, have without fail supported the various enterprises undertaken by the MRP."[1] Münzenberg had hit upon the secret of the success of pro-Communist mass organizations: the active participation in them of well-known non-Communist intellectuals and artists who made Western public opinion. These unwitting supporters were dubbed fellow travelers. Time and again over the next decade

---

1. Münzenberg, *Fünf Jahre Internationale Arbeiterhilfe*, pp. 27–28.

Münzenberg's use of the same propaganda techniques would win their backing of what counted as "progressive" causes.

By the mid-twenties the MRP had grown into a veritable worldwide propaganda empire. Often referred to as the Münzenberg Trust, the organization controlled a publications branch responsible for scores of worker-oriented books, pamphlets, dailies, and journals that flooded the market. In Berlin alone during the twenties and early thirties, Münzenberg published the *Arbeiter-Illustrierte Zeitung, Berlin am Morgen,* and *Welt am Abend,* all of which had mass circulations. The diversity of the MRP's enterprises defies description.[2] But whatever the nature of a specific action, there were always two objectives uppermost in Münzenberg's mind: working-class solidarity around the world and the popularization of the Soviet Union. "We exist for one purpose—to wage *the* broadest propaganda campaign for Soviet Russia," Münzenberg declared in 1923 during a private talk in front of Communist MRP functionaries.[3] But the key to the success of his operations in the twenties was the perpetuation of the myth that the MRP was not affiliated with the Comintern. Publicly Münzenberg scoffed at allegations that this was all a Communist enterprise; such claims were a "foolish fairy tale."[4] This brazen denial of the obvious—it was common knowledge that Münzenberg had entered the Reichstag as a Communist deputy in 1924 and from 1927 on sat on the KPD's Central Committee—worked, however, because intellectual sympathizers everywhere swallowed the lie. Of course the Communists ran the MRP, which unfolded its activities within the context of the united front in western Europe. "You realize that the Comintern, now that it is sure that the course of revolution has slowed down, is out to broaden its base in accordance with the slogan of the united front," Münzenberg said privately in 1923. "*The MRP can take steps in this direction which the political parties cannot,*" he added, but it was imperative that "we use all our ingenuity in resisting the charge that we are a purely Communist organization." He said in continuation:

> Now particularly we have to pursue new names and new
> groups. . . . The question of the Clubs for the New Russia

2. See Münzenberg, *Solidarität.* See also *Willi Münzenberg,* the biography by Münzenberg's widow, Babette Gross. A good capsule summary of Münzenberg's activities is in Arthur Koestler, *The Invisible Writing,* pp. 250–60.

3. *Die Dritte Säule,* p. 24. This pamphlet, containing sensitive material not intended for publication, was issued by the German Social Democratic Trade-Union Organization to expose the Soviet origin of the MRP and to discredit Münzenberg.

4. Münzenberg, *Fünf Jahre Internationale Arbeiterhilfe,* p. 27.

[miniature fronts] is of particular importance. . . . It is up to us to make inroads into the broadest social strata, winning over artists and professors and exploiting the theaters and movie houses. . . . We all understand that the MRP, which not only participates in these clubs but actually created them in the first place, must use them to fashion paths of understanding within broad bourgeois circles between these very elements and Russia. This will benefit us far more than if the Communist press writes continually about how well things are going in Russia.[5]

Münzenberg's "congresses" may have been his best idea. Every so often, generally from behind the scenes, he would convene a "world congress" to address some vaguely defined issue like antiimperialism, anticolonialism or, later on, antifascism. These international assemblies, whose executive boards or organizing committees always had well-known fellow-traveler personalities in prominent positions, were intended as exhibitions of the unity of all "antiimperialist and anticapitalist forces" and as illustrations of the identity of the working-class cause with the betterment of all mankind.[6] Münzenberg tampered with the strategy of the congresses very little down through the years, employing the same tactics in 1933 as he did in 1923, when he outlined privately this general strategy for a World Congress for Economic Assistance and Reconstruction of Soviet Russia. Some eighty representatives of German industry, engineers, entrepreneurs, scientists, artists, writers, and journalists would attend, Münzenberg explained, all of whom were grouped around the club "Friends of the New Russia." Münzenberg told his listeners: "We must make certain ahead of time that only certain speakers are given the floor; all political debates are to be avoided. The affair is to end in the acceptance of a resolution in which willingness is expressed to work for the reconstruction of Russia." Münzenberg continued: "We are to try and get the business men attending . . . to agitate and propagandize for Soviet Russia once they have returned to their factories and businesses. Above all else, everything must be done to see that the conference concludes on the same day; otherwise it will disintegrate by Monday. . . . The whole thing will come off with a bluff."[7]

---

5. *Die Dritte Säule*, pp. 11–12.
6. See Münzenberg, *Solidarität*, pp. 154–87, for the thinking behind the congresses and a list of those that took place between 1921 and 1927.
7. *Die Dritte Säule*, p. 13.

The idea of a Communist conglomerate working with non-Communists would have been unthinkable as long as revolution in the West was still considered imminent. But the New Economic Policy, the Comintern's adoption of united front tactics in the West, and Soviet eagerness for stable relations with the Western nations marked the onset of a new, pragmatic plan for the twenties, and Münzenberg's courting of European fellow travelers fit in perfectly with it. However, there existed parallels to the new cultural policy for western Europe in Soviet cultural life. Once the turbulence of 1917–21 abated, there had been a general renascence of Russian literature, as scores of literary groupings with more or less unique sets of literary-political principles sprang up. Two factions soon came to wield the greatest power and influence. One side was led by the critic Aleksandr Voronskij, who published in his journal *Red Virgin Soil* (*Krasnaja nov*) the works of non-Communist writers whom Trotsky christened fellow travelers.[8] The other group, which named itself "October," comprised proletarian writers who objected passionately to the very existence of "bourgeois writers" in a proletarian state and took the struggle for literary hegemony to be class warfare.[9] Voronskij, whose views essentially matched those of Trotsky, challenged the very raison d'être of a proletarian literature and refused to condone the proletarian idea that literature could or should serve direct political ends. He formulated a theory of literature that, though Marxist, put good art ahead of politics.[10] He also gave overwhelming preference in his journal to the talented fellow-traveler writers who, without embracing any specific ideology, were thought to have a generally sympathetic attitude toward the revolution. More importantly, Voronskij, rather than October, enjoyed party backing between 1921 and 1925.[11] Thus, there were analogies from the outset between Münzenberg's fellow traveler operations in the West and the official Soviet attitude toward fellow travelers in the USSR.

At a loss to believe that a proletarian dictatorship would submit to literary dominance by bourgeois writers, the Octobrists declared war

8. See Trotsky, *Literature and Revolution*, pp. 56–115. Trotsky's pamphlet was first published in 1924.
9. There are first-rate studies of both sides of the dispute. Robert A. Maguire, *Red Virgin Soil*, focuses on Voronskij and his journal, whereas Edward J. Brown, *The Proletarian Episode*, concentrates on the proletarian side of the dispute. Herman Ermolaev attempts more of a synthesis in *Soviet Literary Theories*.
10. See Maguire, *Red Virgin Soil*, especially pp. 188–259.
11. Ibid., pp. 3–35.

on "Voronskiism" and the fellow travelers—the class enemy.[12] They urged the Soviet regime to support a proletarian seizure of power in literature and clamored for official sponsorship of "On Guardism" against the encroachment of alien ideas into the Communist ideology of proletarian literature.[13] The clash of fellow travelers with proletarian "On Guardists," as they called themselves, was the outstanding Soviet literary debate of the twenties, and it naturally embroiled political figures in the controversy. Leon Trotsky and Nikolaj Bukharin were the chief spokesmen for the opposing viewpoints. Trotsky sided with Voronskij, impugning the underlying principles of "proletarian culture." He maintained that it could not exist, backing his argument with the contention that all past cultures had taken centuries to develop. Because the proletarian state in Russia was temporary and because the transition from a capitalist to a socialist order brief and sanguinary, there would not be ample time for a class culture of any sort to take root. He reasoned that Soviet art of the future would therefore not be proletarian at all, but socialist—classless. In the meantime, all Russian writers were to be given the opportunity to create freely; this freedom had certain limits, of course, for it was taken for granted that a writer with counterrevolutionary views had no place in Soviet literature. Trotsky's radical politics were thus significantly responsible for his broad-minded attitude toward literature.

The opposite was true of Bukharin, the leader of the party's right wing. He envisaged a slow, protracted transition from capitalism to socialism and was therefore more open to the notion of a proletarian culture. But he was never an unqualified exponent of the On Guardist movement, advocating instead peaceful competition between literary groups. With the introduction of NEP, a "dialectical change of functions in the class struggle" had taken place permitting cooperation between the bourgeoisie and the proletariat, Bukharin said, and this collaboration ought to be duplicated in dealing with fellow-traveler writers.[14]

Because of the intensity of the controversy, the party intervened in the dispute between Voronskij and the On Guardists in 1925, and the Resolution on Creative Literature passed that year reflected the prevailing power alignment within the Central Committee. Stalin was then allied with Bukharin against Trotsky, whose political career in the USSR was in eclipse, and the 1925 resolution thus contained Bu-

---

12. The fellow travelers represented the dominant force in Soviet literature and counted among their number the most talented writers in Russia.
13. Cf. Brown, *The Proletarian Episode*, p. 20.
14. See Ermolaev, *Soviet Literary Theories*, p. 46.

kharin's views on the major issues, which were less favorable to the fellow travelers than Trotsky's ideas. The importance of winning fellow-traveler support for the revolution was still acknowledged, the On Guardists being chastised for abusing them and obstructing their gradual acceptance of Soviet power. The resolution pressed the need for free competition between various literary groups and refused to acquiesce in the proletarian demand that the party decree the On Guardists the premier literary organization in the country. Still, the decision was anything but a resounding victory for the fellow travelers: the Central Committee endorsed the contention that a literary class war was raging, underscored the impossibility of "neutral art" in a class society, and accentuated the "great importance of the struggle for the ideological hegemony of the proletarian writers." The "conquest of positions in the field of belles-lettres," the resolution stated, "must . . . sooner or later become a fact."[15]

The decision afforded a measure of protection to the fellow travelers for a time, but it also inaugurated the rise to ascendancy of the All-Union Association of Proletarian Writers (VAPP), now representing the On Guardist movement. In early 1926 VAPP "moderates," led by Leopold Averbakh, banished the old On Guardist leadership, which had refused to abide by the 1925 resolution and its call for tolerance toward fellow travelers. The new VAPP, on the other hand, now bided its time, making a show of support for the Central Committee decision and acting with relative leniency in dealing with the fellow travelers.[16] But in 1928 and 1929 Stalin terminated NEP, began his campaign against Bukharin and the right wing of the party, and proclaimed the start of the First Five-Year Plan. The tolerance in literature called for by the 1925 decision began to disappear in the radicalized atmosphere as Soviet literary policy was gradually Stalinized. In the process, the party granted to VAPP in 1928 the monopoly in Soviet literature that a few years before had been denied any single group.

In these years, beginning in 1928, the Russian proletarians would have an impact upon proletarian literature in other countries as well through a "Literary International" patterned after the Comintern. The roots of this "International" went back to 1921, when Soviet proletarian writers, still in the person of the On Guardists, began to

---

15. The resolution is reprinted in Brown, *The Proletarian Episode*, pp. 235–40; the quotations here are from pages 236 and 238.
16. An ill omen, however, was the treatment of Voronskij, who lost his position as editor of *Red Virgin Soil* in 1927 and was expelled from the Communist party. He later disappeared in the purges. See Maguire, *Red Virgin Soil*, p. 33 and pp. 417–20.

think about duplicating the organizational structure of the Comintern by forming "something like a Litintern."[17] The idea was first broached at the Third World Congress of the Comintern, and again a year later, in 1922, at the Fourth, before the first concrete action was taken in 1924 at the Fifth World Congress in Moscow.[18] On Guardist officials appealed there to congressional delegates for their support in the creation of an international organization for proletarian literature existing as a subsidiary of the Comintern. The On Guardists of VAPP seem to have reckoned originally with the establishment of foreign associations patterned after VAPP; these would be answerable (much like the Communist parties to the Comintern) to a central International Association of Proletarian Writers, or INTERAPP, based in Moscow.[19] This plan, as well as other On Guardist designs, evidently aroused official opposition, and the concept of an INTERAPP was scrapped in favor of a less ambitious International Liaison Office of Proletarian Literature (MBPL), "affiliated with the Comintern." Joining several On Guardist VAPP figures on the executive board were Anatolij Lunacharskij, People's Commissar of Education, and Nikolaj Bukharin. The MBPL's goals for the immediate future included the establishment of ties with proletarian revolutionary writers and literary organizations around the world, coordination of work aimed at the creation of such associations, and preparatory work for a "Founding Congress of the International of Proletarian Literature."[20]

Since the On Guardists ran the MBPL, their quarrel with Voronskij and Soviet fellow travelers immediately found its way into the organization in the form of controversy about the MBPL's attitude toward Western liberal intellectuals. There were evidently two sides to the issue: one represented by On Guardist officials, whose attitude toward Western intellectuals was clear, and the other by Lunacharskij, who was apparently intensely displeased with the On Guardists for translating their scorn for Soviet fellow travelers into MBPL contempt for Western sympathizers (those personalities Münzenberg and the MRP were out to win over). But the On Guardists had the strength at the time to outvote Lunacharskij on the matter,[21] and the setting of MBPL policy remained the privilege of VAPP On Guardists until early 1926.

17. A. V. Lunacharskij, "Doklad o Mezhdunarodnom bjuro svjazi proletarskoj literatury," in *Iz istorii MORPa*, p. 38.
18. Ibid. There had been a precursor of sorts to a "Litintern" in the Provisional International Bureau of Proletkult.
19. N. A. Trifonova, "Lunacharskij i Morp," in *Iz istorii MORPa*, p. 32.
20. Lunacharskij, "Doklad," pp. 40–41.
21. Cf. Trifonova, "Lunacharskij i Morp," p. 34.

At a March 1926 plenum, though, the On Guardists lost their positions in the MBPL as a consequence of Averbakh's general purge of radical On Guardists from VAPP's executive board. From here on out, until 1932, Averbakh's VAPP administration retained control of the MBPL, whose policies were greatly influenced by Averbakh and VAPP.[22]

The events of February and March 1926—the exit of On Guardists both from VAPP and from the MBPL—led to a slight shift of emphasis in the MBPL stance regarding Western fellow travelers. The First International Conference of Proletarian Revolutionary Writers, which met in Moscow in November 1927, formalized the change. The MBPL now became the International Office of Revolutionary Literature (MBRL), the substitution of "revolutionary" for "proletarian" supposedly signaling an advance in the treatment of non-Communist but radical Western intellectuals. Lunacharskij pointed out that the Communists had now revised their tactics somewhat; they had begun to accept in their midst "revolutionary writers of the entire world" who had definitely cut their ties with the bourgeoisie; and they had established an Office of Revolutionary Writers. "Clearly," he pointed out, "we see nothing alluring in a writer who is an arch enemy of communism; but there are writers who, though they still have their differences with us, are ill-disposed toward the bourgeoisie."[23]

Here were the writers in whom the MBRL was now interested, yet this minor modification of attitudes still left the organization in a position very much at odds with the purpose of Willi Münzenberg's MRP. For the time being, though, from 1926 to 1928, the MBRL was not active enough abroad to pose any real threat to Münzenberg's work with Western fellow-traveler intellectuals and artists; in fact, not a single proletarian organization in the West even existed until October 1928, when German Communist writers founded the League of Proletarian Revolutionary Writers (BPRS).[24]

The decision to form a German proletarian literary association had been reached at the 1927 congress in Moscow after consultations

22. Ibid.

23. Lunacharskij, "Lektsija v Kommunisticheskom Universitete im. Ja. M. Sverdlova 9 Fevralja 1929 g.," in *Neizdannye materialy*, pp. 340–41.

24. Béla Illés wrote in 1928: "The first period of the office's existence, from 1923–26, was a time of wasted effort since the entire objective was false. The founders of the office . . . set themselves the goal of creating nothing less than a Literary International of On Guardists of all countries. But . . . at the time On Guardists were nowhere to be found in any of the capitalist countries" (Lunacharskij, "Doklad," p. 44).

"with the Russian comrades of VAPP . . . and of the International Office,"[25] though the actual creation of the BPRS was delayed for a year. In the meantime, VAPP was renamed the Russian Association of Proletarian Writers (RAPP), and in early 1928 RAPP theorists began formulating their ideas on literary and critical methods. These views would come to dominate not only the MBRL but, as time went on, the BPRS as well. RAPP's main concern was quality in literature, though the artistry had to be realized within the narrowly prescribed boundaries of RAPP's "dialectical materialist creative method." Toward groups that entertained divergent views RAPP behaved in a prescriptive, censorious, and often dictatorial fashion. RAPP waged its battles on two fronts. On the one hand, the 1926–28 lull in hostilities against Soviet fellow travelers gave way to a resurgence of belligerence as RAPP flayed Russian "bourgeois" writers for neglecting to apply conscious Marxism to their writing. On the other hand, RAPP was determined to discredit two specific literary strands within the proletarian revolutionary movement itself, the avant-garde revolutionary writers assembled around the Left Front of Arts (LEF) and the radical proletarian writers under the influence of the former hard-line On Guardist leadership of VAPP. These were RAPP's Marxist competitors, so to speak. RAPP officials were at variance with LEF for its endorsement of ultrarationalism in literature, that is, the rejection of creative literature in favor of "factography" (reportage, sketches, biographies of people and things, newspaper accounts, and so on); for its alacrity in responding to the "social command" by executing "literary tasks" dictated to the writers by the party; and for its disavowal of the literary heritage. RAPP remonstrated with the old On Guardists for reducing literature to agitation and propaganda for the state.

RAPP countered the above programs with its method of dialectical materialism in literature, translating materialism into literary realism and the dialectic into the literary embodiment of society's inherent contradictions depicted in accordance with Marxist historical laws.[26] The application of the dialectic to literature was expressed in the RAPP slogan "for the living man," a *plaidoyer* for a type of psychologism in literature (the "dialectic" of the human soul). RAPP stigmatized LEF principles, then, as an assault on imaginative literature altogether, while the importance the old-line On Guardists attached to an agitprop use of literature in the service of politics and ideology

25. "Bericht über die Tätigkeit des Bundes proletarisch-revolutionärer Schriftsteller im Jahre 1929," in *Zur Tradition der sozialistischen Literatur in Deutschland*, p. 164.
26. Cf. Brown, *The Proletarian Episode*, pp. 58–86, 132–45; and Ermolaev, *Soviet Literary Theories*, pp. 55–71.

RAPP treated as the reduction of creative writing to propaganda. "The slogan for the presentation of the 'living man' . . . expresses the necessity of struggle with stereotypes, with schematic portrayal, with 'bare poster art,' and of development in the direction of showing forth the complex human psyche, with all its contradictions, elements of the past, and seeds of the future," read a RAPP resolution passed in 1928.[27] True proletarian literature must not be permitted to varnish reality by giving one-dimensional portraits of human beings—the commissar, the Red Army man, the Bolshevik, the bourgeois, and so on; class warfare had to be represented, rather, at its basic level—within the human psyche. Patterned, tendentious plots, a trait of On Guardist writing, RAPP abhorred as propaganda. RAPP was thus thoroughly Marxist, but defended a higher quality of literature against ostensibly lower forms of art, whether their practitioners considered themselves Marxists or not. There were no more vicious literary-theoretical debates, in fact, than those over whose aesthetic position was truly Marxist.

But even as RAPP was defining its literary standards in 1928, radical changes were occurring in the Soviet Union: Stalin abolished NEP, eliminated Bukharin, and launched the First Five-Year Plan. In literary policy the party departed from the relative tolerance it had practiced since the 1925 resolution and now expected writers without exception to contribute to "socialist construction." All literature was to advance blatant political ends, and the party evidently assumed that RAPP would fulfill these demands by becoming the locus for organizing Soviet literature behind the goals of collectivization and industrialization. But the new emphasis on crude utilitarianism (Five-Year Plan literature) brought RAPP and its notion of literature into opposition with the party and offered encouragement to the LEFists and On Guardists, who had always pleaded for thoroughly politicized writing. RAPP's hegemony in Soviet literature began to come undone. In 1930 the first of many attacks on the RAPP leadership came in midyear when the Literary Front (LITFRONT), comprised primarily of the On Guardist opposition to RAPP, lashed out at the organization for its psychologism and for its slogan of "the living man." The LITFRONT, with strong Central Committee backing, contended that RAPP sacrificed the needs of the day for the depiction of the inner lives of its heroes. It rejected RAPP's "contemplative realism" in favor of a tendentious style of literature imbued with the revolutionary enthusiasm and proletarian class bias of Soviet authors. This time RAPP mus-

27. Brown, *The Proletarian Episode*, p. 78.

tered the strength to fend off the LITFRONT offensive, but the organization soon came under fire from other quarters.[28]

After a one-year gestation, the League of Proletarian Revolutionary Writers was formed in October 1928,[29] and the first issue of its publication, *Die Linkskurve*, appeared in August 1929. In spite of the familial relationship with the MBRL and, through it, with RAPP, the BPRS's earliest theoretical statements in *Linkskurve* bore little resemblance to the RAPP program; the Germans were far more radical. The BPRS differed with RAPP, for instance, on the meaning of the term "proletarian" writer and on the cultural past. Whereas RAPP regarded any writer who embraced Marxism as "proletarian," Andor Gábor, speaking for the BPRS, maintained that only writers of legitimate working-class origin had the inherent ability to represent truthfully the proletariat and its fight for liberation. Writers who sided with Marxism and the working class out of preference, but not by right of birth, were restricted to assisting in the formation of truly proletarian literary cadres.[30] Erich Steffen restated the same argument: "The proletariat alone can create the literature it needs."[31] The matter of the cultural heritage was likewise a point of contention between RAPP and the BPRS. RAPP, though it by no means extolled all past art, called for the "study of the classics,"[32] but Gábor ridiculed the notion that proletarian literature had anything to gain from the heritage. "Literary weapons for the class struggle are to be taken from venerable old arsenals?" he asked. "That is tantamount . . . to telling the proletariat to go to war against the tanks and flamethrowers of the capitalist armies with breech-loaders!"[33]

German proletarian radicalism was actually more akin to the pro-

28. Ibid., pp. 150–71. If the LITFRONT opposition was unscrupulous, RAPP was just as unprincipled in its defense and counteroffensive. RAPP linked "Litfrontism" with the "antiparty, double-dealing bloc of Syrtsov-Lominadze," thereby bringing the organization into discredit not so much for its literary program as for its alleged political one. See *Literaturnaja èntsiklopedija*, pp. 507–8.

29. The Sixth World Congress of the Comintern, which met in July-August 1928 and radicalized Communist thinking on all issues, seems to have given the writers involved the final impetus needed to proceed with the creation of the BPRS. See, for instance, Berta Lask, "Vorschläge zur Durchführung der Parteibeschlüsse," Becher-Archiv, BPRS-Materialien, no. 13.

30. Andor Gábor, "Über proletarisch-revolutionäre Literatur," *Die Linkskurve* 3 (1929): 3–5.

31. Erich Steffen, "Die Urzelle proletarischer Literatur," *Die Linkskurve* 2 (1930): 8–9.

32. See Brown, *The Proletarian Episode*, pp. 66–69.

33. Gábor, "Über proletarisch-revolutionäre Literatur," p. 5.

grams of RAPP's enemies—the On Guardists, LEF, and the remnants of the Proletkult—though the discrepancy between RAPP and the BPRS derived by no means from conscious noncompliance with RAPP's program. Rather, it was a simple matter of no information: the BPRS initially lacked any real direct line of communication with the MBRL and RAPP in Moscow. The MBRL, the "Literary International," though it fancied itself a cultural corollary to the Comintern, thus could not have issued binding directives to the BPRS in the way of the Comintern and the KPD even had it wanted to. But as visits to the USSR and increased mail contact raised the level of the German proletarians' awareness of RAPP's political and literary-critical policies, the RAPP program gradually took over the BPRS.

RAPP's literary politics (its stance with respect to the fellow travelers), rather than its creative method, had the greatest immediate impact on the young BPRS. In fall 1929 a German delegation including the BPRS chairman, Johannes R. Becher, and Andor Gábor, journeyed to Moscow. The Germans arrived in a keyed-up atmosphere. RAPP had just ended its second plenum, at which the tolerance of 1926–28 had all but disappeared; in its stead was an ever-widening rift between proletarians and fellow travelers. Relations had deteriorated that fall when two prominent fellow-traveler writers, Boris Pilnjak and Evgenij Zamjatin, were expelled from their writers' associations for publishing novels outside of the Soviet Union. The Soviet ill will toward fellow travelers promptly found its way into *Die Linkskurve* upon the German delegation's return to Berlin. Otto Biha lectured on the Pilnjak case in the December issue of the journal, pointing to "parallels outside of Russia" and demanding that a distinction be made between writers in the West who participated in the revolutionary class struggle and those who merely "went along" as critics of the bourgeois order without making common cause with the proletariat. Biha issued a strong note of warning against the sympathizers in the West, whose status as fellow travelers was often used as a "disguise . . . for a more dangerous enemy." He then closed his article by indicating that, "though we may yet lack the power to rid ourselves of the Pilnjaks among us, the least we can do is to expose them and divulge their true identity."[34]

The campaign was not confined to the fellow travelers proper but also took in those who practiced cooperation with them. Andor Gábor went after Henri Barbusse, the French representative in the MBRL secretariat, for publishing a journal, *Monde*, which carried contribu-

---

34. Otto Biha, "Der Fall Pilnjak und die Folgen," *Die Linkskurve* 5 (1929): 14–15.

tions from authors of whom Gábor strongly disapproved. Gábor denounced the entire undertaking as an "aquarium for the grand and petty bourgeoisie in which fishes, frogs, and shellfish of the worst ilk swim around in a muddy sauce that lacks even a pink tinge."[35] Ensuing issues of *Die Linkskurve* then baited and insulted writers like Alfred Döblin, Ernst Toller, Kurt Tucholsky, Theodor Plivier, and others. In January 1930 J. R. Becher himself appealed to his readers to "cut themselves off from the 'sympathizers,'" calling them "absolutely worthless in any confrontation that threatens their class."[36]

This first of two BPRS bouts with radicalism soon came under attack from the KPD. In March 1930 Josef Winternitz, writing as N. Kraus, published an article in *Die Linkskurve* criticizing Erich Steffen.[37] Winternitz disagreed with every major point raised in Steffen's article, including the point that proletarian writers must be of working-class origin and would come to literature from the worker-correspondent movement. Winternitz quoted Lenin's remark about appropriating all that was valuable in past cultures. He also noted that the BPRS, and particularly the party and other "mass organizations" (a code word for Münzenberg's fronts), should be assisting those writers who were "coming to the proletariat from the bourgeois camp."[38] The articles by Gábor, Becher, and others, which had been just as sectarian as Steffen's, were not mentioned, though Gábor lost his position as a *Linkskurve* editor.

This party intrusion into the affairs of the BPRS in early 1930 was the first clear sign of annoyance with the organization in the upper echelons of the KPD.[39] An influential group in the Central Committee seems from the very beginning to have had serious misgivings about the activities of the German proletarians. Back in 1927 Becher was already protesting diffidently about the party's "regrettable" do-nothing attitude toward proletarian literature.[40] Berta Lask put it blunt-

35. Andor Gábor, "Die bunte Welt des Genossen Barbusse," *Die Linkskurve* 5 (1929): 6.
36. Johannes R. Becher, "Einen Schritt weiter!," *Die Linkskurve* 1 (1930), pp. 2–3.
37. Winternitz was head of the agitprop division of the KPD's Central Committee. See Weber, *Die Wandlung des deutschen Kommunismus*, 2:345.
38. N. Kraus, "Gegen den Ökonomismus in der Literaturfrage," *Die Linkskurve* 3 (1930): 12.
39. No convincing case can be made in support of the contention that the LITFRONT controversy in the Soviet Union was the underlying cause of KPD action against the BPRS's radical elements, as Gallas argues (Gallas, *Marxistische Literaturtheorie*, p. 52). Though left-wing opposition to RAPP began to crystalize in early 1930, the LITFRONT did not get off the ground until that summer, whereas Kraus's article appeared in *Die Linkskurve* in March 1930.
40. Johannes R. Becher, "Die proletarisch-revolutionäre Literatur in Deutschland"

ly: "The party has to desist in its ambiguous attitude toward the writers, making it clear either that it does not need them, or, *if* it needs them, work to integrate them in a befitting and productive manner into the corpus of the party; it must make the correct political and organizational demands upon the writers, and it must answer to their needs."[41] What seems to have occurred is that influential men within the Central Committee, Willi Münzenberg probably at the forefront of the group, adopted in 1928–29 an initial posture of benign neglect toward the BPRS.[42] That Münzenberg was in fact involved in an anti-BPRS faction that became increasingly hostile is an assumption based on sketchy evidence, but the import of a variety of sources seems to support it. One of the first unpublished BPRS platform drafts appeals to the party, for instance, "to respect our literary activity and to take it seriously; [the KPD] should quit running after the literature of the sympathizers and half-sympathizers."[43] Münzenberg's name was not mentioned, but the proletarians undeniably felt that the party was slighting them in favor of the liberal intellectuals. A section entitled "Our Difficulties" in a BPRS report of its activities for 1929 discourses on what was bothering the proletarians:

> We sentence ourselves to impotence in the sphere of literature, and we blunt the edge of a useful weapon in the class struggle when we veil our own comrades in anonymity—writers who have risen from the ranks of their own class and, at one with it, devote the whole of their creative endeavors to its service—even as the party press propagandizes bourgeois and half-bourgeois writers (thereby unleashing them on the proletariat) to whom we often willfully assign the quality of "being sympathetic" but who invariably react negatively when the central question of the party is broached. Time and again we hear the—correct—argument that these "sympathizers" subvert the bourgeoisie and the lower-middle class; but the point is missed that it is up to us to utilize our own writers to

(Referat, gehalten auf der I. Internationalen Konferenz proletarischer und revolutionärer Schriftsteller), in *Zur Tradition der sozialistischen Literatur in Deutschland*, p. 75.

41. Lask, "Vorschläge zur Durchführung der Parteibeschlüsse."

42. This only stands to reason because the entire notion of proletarian culture and literature was by definition sectarian and thus in opposition to the purposes of Münzenberg's MRP. Münzenberg's widow-biographer, Babette Gross, writes that the "forced endeavors" of RAPP and its "German parrots" struck Münzenberg as ridiculous. See Gross, *Willi Münzenberg*, p. 213.

43. "Entwurf von Richtlinien für kommunistische Schriftsteller," Becher-Archiv, BPRS-Materialien, no. 9.

counteract the subversive effect that in all questions of substance the sympathizers naturally, in view of their own limitations, exert on our own comrades. We must not forget that if we make oracles of the Ossietzkys and the Tucholskys, then, on occasions like the first of May,[44] not only what they say against Zörgiebel but also their concurrent comments against the KPD will be taken as the statements of oracles. We cannot forget that the unabashed goodwill that the sympathizers harbor for Trotsky, for the right wing, for all of those whom the Comintern or the party has disciplined, has been a repeated source of trouble for us: even comrades who have been supplied in their party cells with the correct explanation for these events begin to vacillate in their feelings when they read these writers. This is all the fault of our veneration of *these* names and, in most instances, lack of esteem for our own writers.[45]

Münzenberg's name is conspicuously absent here and elsewhere in the published and extant unpublished BPRS documents. But because the BPRS directorate, Becher particularly, was irresolute and infirm in its dealings with the party on controversial policy issues,[46] and because Münzenberg, after all, was a powerful and imposing personality in the party, it could have been that BPRS officials were reluctant to take on Münzenberg directly, arguing against his views instead through indirection and insinuation. For example, many proletarian writers enountered real obstacles in having their works published. Berta Lask complained privately: "The Party must influence those newspapers and journals that have connections with us—*Welt am Abend, Welt am Morgen, AIZ, Magazin für Alle*—to refrain from patronizing every bourgeois writer who chances to come running along in favor of enlisting, sponsoring, and further educating the proletarian revolu-

---

44. That is, when the KPD chose to defy a ban on demonstrations in Berlin, and the Social Democratic police chief, Zörgiebel, ordered his men to disperse the crowd by force of arms.

45. "Bericht über die Tätigkeit des Bundes proletarisch-revolutionärer Schriftsteller im Jahre 1929," Becher-Archiv, BPRS-Materialien, no. 36.

46. See Berta Lask's report of 26 December 1929: "Yesterday evening, in front of representatives of all [party] cultural organizations, the representative of the central agitprop division mocked and spat upon the works of proletarian revolutionary literature. Three members of the executive board of the BPRS were present but failed to register even a cry of protest" (Berta Lask, "An die Arbeitsgemeinschaft kommunistischer Schriftsteller," Becher-Archiv, BPRS-Materialien, no. 47). See also Lukács's characterization of Johannes R. Becher, pp. 41–42.

tionary writers."[47] The publications Lask mentions were all products of the Münzenberg Trust.

After Winternitz's article appeared in *Die Linkskurve* in March 1930, the BPRS shifted its literary-political stance slightly to the right, and the next months were taken up with planning the Second World Congress of Revolutionary Literature, to be held in November 1930 in Kharkov. At this congress all outstanding issues, chief among them the question of the fellow travelers, were scheduled to be aired.[48] There it came out that Andor Gábor's censure of Henri Barbusse in *Die Linkskurve*, more than Steffen's article, had brought matters to a head in March. In Kharkov this BPRS "left extremism" was now said to be a thing of the past,[49] but the further development of the Barbusse affair actually illustrated that neither the MBRL nor the BPRS were yet capable of outlining an unambiguous set of principles regarding the Western intellectuals. For though Gábor had been sacrificed for his sectarianism with respect to Barbusse and others, the Kharkov congress still declared the French writer and his journal to be the "primary threat" after all, the "right" danger.[50] "Deviations" now became part of the MBRL, which went to great extremes to avoid adopting a clear position one way or the other: the congress proceeded to condemn *Monde* as reactionary and petty bourgeois[51] at the same time that it tongue-lashed the "left sectarians" and set out to bring Barbusse, a valuable man to the movement, back into an acceptable state of orthodoxy. Serafima Gopner, the representative of the Executive Committee of the Communist International (ECCI) at the congress, declared: "We regard Comrade Henri Barbusse's deviation as a right deviation. . . . But we must spare no effort in helping Comrade Henri Barbusse to get the better of his confusion. . . . That is why we say that the so-called left reaction with respect to Comrade

---

47. Lask, "Vorschläge zur Durchführung der Parteibeschlüsse."

48. Béla Illés, "Vor dem Plenum der internationalen proletarischen Schriftsteller," *Die Linkskurve* 9 (1930): 16; Béla Illés, "Otchet Sekretariata MBRL o podgotovitelnoj rabote k rasshirennomu plenumu MBRL," in *Iz istorii MORPa*, p. 54.

49. Illés, "Otchet Sekretariata MBRL," p. 54; Illés, "Vor dem Plenum," p. 16. Illés, the general secretary of the MBRL, remarked figuratively in October 1930 that Gábor's "ultra-left sectarian tendencies" had been corrected without "blood-letting."

50. Illés's confidential report refers to another right deviation: "After the victory over [Gábor's] ultraleft deviation, there appeared a right deviation that is significantly more dangerous since it is represented by [Franz Carl] Weiskopf, the editor of the literary section of a widely disseminated newspaper (*Berlin am Morgen*, published by Mezhrabpom)." Illés, "Otchet Sekretariata MBRL," p. 54. This is another of the oblique criticisms of writers and enterprises connected with Münzenberg.

51. See Klein, *Schriftsteller in der französischen Volksfront*, p. 32.

Barbusse, expressed in the existence of those who call for his political execution right here at the plenum, this, Comrades, is left radicalism, which resembles the right deviation like one drop of water the other."[52]

The legacy of Kharkov was therefore an ideological construct analogous to the situation in politics. All ascribed to a credo: "The epoch of imperialism is the epoch of the collapse and decomposition of bourgeois culture. . . . The proletariat represents the only force within modern society capable of bringing world culture up to new, unscaled heights." But there were polar views and thus possible deviations on tactics and strategy. On the one hand, the congress regarded the "right danger"—the attempt to entrust the construction of proletarian literature to the "petty bourgeois intelligentsia," that is, the fellow travelers—as the greatest threat to the proletarian literary movement. On the other hand, the Kharkov delegates resolved that the "no less pernicious deviation" of left opportunism hid its sectarian nature behind radical phrases and renounced the "leading role of the proletarian literary movement with respect to those revolutionary petty bourgeois writers who are drawing near the proletariat."[53]

The MBRL's uncertainty in the matter of the liberal intellectuals was doubtless caused by a dichotomy of opinion within the Comintern-KPD, for, however considerable Münzenberg's influence, there had always been a residue of opposition to him, and Münzenberg's detractors now found the atmosphere after the Comintern swing to the left in 1928 more congenial to their long-standing objections about the MRP. The resulting absence of consensus within high official circles on the question of fellow travelers was therefore clearly mirrored in the equivocal, noncommittal policy of the MBRL. The BPRS was equally unsure of itself in dealing with the fellow travelers, though the truly uncompromising sectarianism had almost disappeared. Only one BPRS member, Alfred Kurella, hazarded something of a theoretical statement on the issue. Kurella lodged the problem of "petty bourgeois writers" squarely within the context of the KPD's Program for National and Social Liberation, which had been adopted in the summer of 1930 for the fall elections.[54] Proletarian revolutionary lit-

52. See ibid., and F. S. Narkirera, "Ezhinedelnik 'Monde,' " in *Iz istorii MORPa*, p. 231. As it was, the Barbusse controversy wore on into late 1932 before the differences between Barbusse and the Comintern-MBRL were finally settled. For a more complete account of the matter, see Klein, pp. 22–36, and Narkirera, pp. 227–34.
53. "Resolution zu den politischen und schöpferischen Fragen der internationalen proletarischen und revolutionären Literatur," in *Zur Tradition der sozialistischen Literatur*, pp. 270, 281–82.
54. See the discussion of the KPD programs in Chapter 1, pp. 15–16.

erature, explained Kurella, was represented by writers who had parted company with the petty bourgeoisie and merged with the labor movement and by writers, such as the worker correspondents, who were of actual proletarian descent. As for sympathizers, these men, Kurella believed, ought to be regarded as possible "reserves," future allies of revolutionary proletarian literature and of the revolutionary working class. Kurella was adapting to literature the KPD's then prevailing view of the lower-middle-class role in the social alignment of forces: the petty bourgeoisie, as a transitional class situated between the proletariat and the bourgeoisie, was not historically bound to the ruling class, but gravitated instead to the class that exhibited the greatest initiative in converting petty bourgeois to its side. The proletariat therefore had to battle for the assistance of the lower middle class in a revolutionary cause or lose it to fascism.

This was Kurella's correct understanding of the 1930 KPD program, which sought to win converts to communism from the National Socialist lower-middle-class following and which provided for a sort of united front from below with it. Kurella applied this reasoning mutatis mutandi to literature. There were petty bourgeois writers, he argued, who were perfectly willing to act as fascist, social-fascist, and anti-Communist ideologues, but some of these selfsame writers were also open to the interests of the proletariat. There was a process of side choosing going on, and the proletarian revolutionary writers were duty bound to intervene actively with an eye to accelerating the reconciliation of petty bourgeois with proletarian revolutionary writers.

The petty bourgeoisie as a proletarian "reserve," as the "rear guard" of the proletariat—this was Heinz Neumann's invention. Another major point of Neumann's policies was the contention that, as National Socialism developed and resorted to increasingly violent means of maintaining its hold on power, the Nazis would *nolens volens* disperse their own mass following, which would then close ranks with the revolutionary proletariat against the bourgeoisie. The 1930 program was calculated to hasten the natural, dialectical process by exposing the Nazi demagogy that had enabled Hitler to gain petty bourgeois support in the first place. This program had been formulated at the initiative of Neumann and Willi Münzenberg, and Kurella now sought to apply it to literary politics. Incidentally, it may be significant that this article did not appear in *Die Linkskurve*, but in *Der rote Aufbau*, the organ of the central committee of Münzenberg's International Workers' Relief.[55]

55. Alfred Kurella, "Die Reserven der proletarisch-revolutionären Literatur in den

The failure of the Kharkov congress to formulate clear principles on the major issues permitted one last resurgence of left radicalism in the BPRS. In the summer of 1931 the leadership of Becher, Otto Biha, Karl Wittfogel, and Andor Gábor came under attack by the "left opposition," led by Aladár Komját.[56] In June 1931 Becher wrote the MBRL, which at Kharkov began calling itself the International League of Revolutionary Writers (IVRS or, in Russian, MORP), that the BPRS "left opposition" was "engaged in an intense . . . campaign from the left against me, Biha, Wittfogel, and the IVRS. . . . Komját has nominated himself to work out a platform for the BPRS, using that as a way of slipping into the . . . leadership."[57] Becher added that the leadership had mounted a counteroffensive with the aid of the party. But it was not long before Becher gave in to the leftists, writing Béla Illés of the IVRS that "the movement is a revolution, an eruption from below" and that the platform proposed by Karl Biro and Komját was essentially "entirely correct."[58] The mercurial Becher soon made another volte-face, however, and came out against the Komját-Biro opposition after all. In October 1931 he wrote the IVRS that the leftists' "draft program has been rejected by the . . . leadership. It has been ascertained that the draft is false in its basic line and that it represents a LITFRONT program."[59] A commission was formed to work out a new platform.

The KPD had just intervened in BPRS affairs for the second time in less than two years. This time the key role was played by Georg Lukács, who was sent from Moscow to Berlin in summer 1931. According to his own version of the events, Lukács asked his friend Leo Flieg[60]—together with Willi Münzenberg an advocate of an "antisec-

---

kapitalistischen Ländern," in *Zur Tradition der sozialistischen Literatur*, pp. 295–313. See Weingartner, *Stalin und der Aufstieg Hitlers*, p. 42, for information regarding Neumann's and Münzenberg's role in formulating the 1930 program.

56. Gábor, out of favor since March 1930, confessed the error of his ways and was taken back into the inner circle of BPRS leaders. See "Resolution der IVRS zur Erklärung des Genossen Gábor vom 9. 6. 1931" and the IVRS letter to the agitprop division of the KPD from 26 June 1931, MTA, Gábor Andor-Hagyaték, Ms. 4496/194–95.

57. Becher to the MBRL, 17 June 1931, in "Pisma i dokumenty iz fonda I. R. Bekhera (1931–1932)," in *Iz istorii MORPa*, p. 107.

58. Gallas, *Marxistische Literaturtheorie*, p. 59.

59. Becher to the IVRS, 12 October 1931, in "Pisma i dokumenty," *Iz istorii MORPa*, pp. 107–8. The unpublished twenty-four page "Entwurf einer Platform des Bundes proletarisch-revolutionärer Schriftsteller Deutschlands, ausgearbeitet von A. Komját und Karl Biro" is in the Becher-Archiv, BPRS-Materialien, no. 40.

60. Flieg, a close friend of Münzenberg and Heinz Neumann, was organizational secretary of the KPD Politbüro until 1932.

tarian line" in the BPRS—to intercede with Heinz Neumann, who condemned the proletarian radicals and afforded protection for Lukács, Gábor, Becher, and Wittfogel within the upper echelons of the KPD.[61]

There is no reason to suppose that Lukács's move from Moscow to Berlin at this critical juncture was happenstance. Lukács, of course, was a party member. From 1930–31, while in the USSR, he belonged to the Soviet Communist party. When he arrived in Berlin he carried a KPD card,[62] and he could scarcely have left Moscow for Berlin unless he had approval for the trip or was on a party mission of some sort. Upon his arrival in Berlin, Lukács was immediately "appointed by the KPD to head the Communist faction in the Association of German Writers [that is, the Schutzverband deutscher Schriftsteller, or SDS],"[63] a move that seems to have coincided with what Becher, in an August 1931 letter to Illés, referred to as a "reorganization of work on the front involving the intellectuals."[64] The reorganization, Becher said, had been completed with the assignment of Lukács to head the leadership of the Communist faction in the SDS and to direct work in the BPRS with the intellectuals.

Who sent Lukács from Moscow to Berlin? Without more information about his relationship with men like Flieg and Münzenberg, the answer remains a mystery. But if Münzenberg and Flieg, perhaps with Neumann's support, headed a faction within the KPD Central Committee that advocated a more pragmatic attitude toward the fellow travelers, it must have been obvious to them that Becher was not the man to institute clear-cut policies, especially since there was no high-level party unanimity.[65] Years later Lukács described the events of 1931–33 as a time when "there were constantly changing moods in the Central Committee. Sometimes the secretariat was for us, some-

61. See Gallas, *Marxistische Literaturtheorie*, pp. 56–64. Gallas received much of her information from Lukács.
62. Georg Lukács, "Autobiographie," Lukács Archivum.
63. Ibid. According to the information Lukács gave Gallas (*Marxistische Literaturtheorie*, p. 199), Leo Flieg assigned Lukács to work in the SDS, a fact Lukács omitted in his "Autobiographie" (which was written while Lukács was still in the Soviet Union) because Flieg had been arrested in 1937 in the purges.
64. Gallas, *Marxistische Literaturtheorie*, p. 199.
65. According to Lukács, Becher took a more radical attitude toward the intellectuals in the years before 1933 than Lukács. Cf. "Tonbandgespräch mit Prof. György Lukács, geführt von Frau Dr. Siebert am 10. 12. 1969," Becher-Archiv. This is borne out by some of Becher's writings. As late as April 1932, for instance, Becher published a scathing attack on Heinrich Mann. See Johannes R. Becher, "Vom 'Untertan' zum Untertan," *Die Linkskurve* 7 (1932): 1–5.

times against us, and so on." Whenever Becher and Lukács were called in to the secretariat of the Central Committee, Lukács explained, he had conversations beforehand in which Becher "would ask me what we should say if we were asked this or that. . . . He found it impossible to simply wait; his fantasy got the better of him, and he imagined the worse possible things, which inclined him from the outset to strike some sort of compromise."[66]

Looking back almost forty years later on his Berlin stay, Lukács referred to two problems within the proletarian revolutionary literary movement. With respect to the fellow travelers, Lukács felt that "the official line was often too far to the left; what was needed was a . . . closer relationship with left-oriented intellectuals." As for proletarian literature, Lukács spoke of "official aspirations" that concentrated exclusively on the "propagandistic content"; he had considered it his duty, he said in 1969, to assist the nascent literature in achieving a "legitimate literary niveau."[67] In Lukács's very first article in *Die Linkskurve*, he made an overture to fellow travelers, writing about George Bernard Shaw's recent trip to the Soviet Union and proclaiming that a new era was dawning in the "attitude of the western European intellectuals toward the construction of socialism."[68] Lukács said that Shaw belonged to a growing number of liberal intellectuals who were gradually freeing themselves from the shackles of "capitalist ideology." The duty of Communists was to help in broadening the rift. Lukács also had the chance to put his beliefs into practice as the vice chairman of the Berlin local of the SDS, organizing "among left-bourgeois, Social-Democratic, and Communist writers a united front movement that achieved the majority within the Berlin section of the organization."[69]

In his pursuit of "quality" in proletarian literature, Lukács published a series of articles in *Die Linkskurve* in 1931 and 1932 applying RAPP aesthetic criteria to German proletarian writing. Here he found serious fault with the books of two members of the BPRS, Willi Bredel and Ernst Ottwalt. He viewed them as practitioners of two related strands in German proletarian revolutionary literature, which he linked, without saying it in so many words, to RAPP's adversaries in

66. "Tonbandgespräch."
67. Ibid.
68. Georg Lukács, "Shaws Bekenntnis zur Sowjetunion," *Die Linkskurve* 9 (1931): 5.
69. Lukács, "Autobiographie." Communist strategy in the Berlin SDS adumbrated the tactics used after 1933. The Communists set out to establish a " *'Left Cartel'* of all progressive organizations in order to unleash nationwide a more powerful movement of the bourgeois intelligentsia, which is becoming radicalized, against the system of

the Soviet Union: the On Guardists, who wrote utilitarian propagandistic literature, and the LEFists, proponents of avant-garde revolutionary writing. Lukács regarded Bredel as something of a German On Guardist. His novels suffered from a malaise induced by the absence of "living people and their relations, which are in a state of flux, animate and changing."[70] The sickness was curable, however, though what was required was "dialectics," which would add some life to schematic, one-dimensional characters such as the "decent non-Communist who suddenly converts to communism." But without the mastery of materialist dialectics and the infusion of the insights it provided into character portrayal, the picture of the revolutionary process would simply not conform to reality. Nor were these faults restricted to Bredel, whose "mistakes" Lukács took to be "less individual errors than general shortcomings plaguing the entire literary movement."[71]

Lukács considered Ottwalt's novel likewise typical of an entire school —a specific creative method. But whereas Lukács was in general agreement with the "broad epic framework" of Bredel's novels, allowing as it did for the inclusion of "essential elements" and requiring only that the skeleton be fleshed out by means of dialectics, he was uncompromisingly antagonistic to Ottwalt's creative method. Lukács characterized it as reportage, although under that rubic he subsumed all types of modern avant-gardistic literary techniques, including Brecht's epic theater.[72] Reportage had evolved in opposition to the bourgeois novel, Lukács wrote, which, pervaded with psychological representations of private lives, was powerless to address the important issues of the present. But the exclusive concentration on the depiction of objective facts by means of reportage was no solution, for without the "dialectical interaction of subjective and formal elements," objective facts could not be adequately dealt with; and the subjective element

---

emergency decrees and the fascistization of intellectual life." The nucleus of the movement was to be either the SDS opposition or any other "bourgeois organization or a radical group therein" so long as the Communists were strong enough to take a leading role in influencing the movement. "Our experiences up till now have been favorable. By means of this movement we can approach circles and groups that were hitherto reachable only with great difficulty or not at all." The above quotations were taken from the confidential "Rundschreiben," 3 October 1931, published in *Aktionen Bekenntnisse Perspektiven*, pp. 376–77.
70. Georg Lukács, "Willi Bredels Romane," *Die Linkskurve* 11 (1931): p. 24.
71. Ibid., p. 26. For a more thorough treatment of the Lukács polemic with Bredel and Ottwalt, see the East German view: Ingeborg Münz-Koenen, "Die Debatte proletarisch-revolutionärer Schriftsteller mit Georg Lukács," in *Dialog und Kontroverse mit Georg Lukács*, pp. 105–52, and Gallas, *Marxistische Literaturtheorie*, pp. 64–69 and 119–164.
72. Ibid.

intruded itself anyway through the author's subjectivity. The result was "moralizing commentary and a superficial, coincidental characterization of figures who are not organically woven into the narrative." [73] A "form experiment," an attempt to rejuvenate the novel by means of publicism, was the outcome. A literature was created that suffered from an absence of individuals and their fates. These needed to be present, by complementing each other, to illuminate people and events from different angles and through the totality of the work to lend the entire creation the quality of being "typical."

This characteristic of totality was what Lukács missed in reportage. Whereas proletarian revolutionary writing, "employing dialectical materialism as the basis of its creative method, constantly has in mind the driving forces of processes in their totality," [74] writers such as Ottwalt, Lukács explained, choose to depict and expose details. This proclivity was the fault of their social origin. As Lukács saw it, these writers were all petty bourgeois who stood in opposition to capitalism; but they were not proletarian revolutionaries [75] and therefore not heirs to "dialectical-materialist knowledge about [capitalist] laws of development and their active contradictions." They were able to grasp only individual, isolated facts, or, at best, clusters of facts divorced from the pulsating, contradictory unity of the whole, and to "present *moral value judgments* about these facts." [76] Yet the representation of a "process in its totality" was the "prerequisite for correct composition in a novel," Lukács reasoned, adding that this was not the sole preserve of the class conscious but could also be realized by an author who suffered from a " 'false consciousness.' " For instance, such representation could be achieved by writers who, in spite of their approval of superseded, dying societies, nonetheless recognized the "driving forces" and correctly embodied them in their literature—what Engels called the "triumph of realism."[77]

But Lukács had left himself somewhat open to attack here, and Ottwalt went straight to what he saw as a contradiction: "Lukács has no qualms about granting Tolstoy, in *Resurrection,* for example, the right to address a 'series of decisive questions of his time'; he concedes

73. Georg Lukács, "Reportage oder Gestaltung," *Die Linkskurve* 7 (1932): 25.
74. Ibid. p. 28.
75. This only applied to Ottwalt; Bredel was a proletarian.
76. Lukács, "Reportage oder Gestaltung," p. 25.
77. Ibid., p. 29. The notion of the "triumph of realism" and Lukács's further development of it in Soviet exile became one of the chief points of controversy in 1939 when the Lukács-Mikhail Lifshits "New Trend" came under fire from an organized group of Soviet critics. See Chapter 10.

to him an 'instinctive dialectic' in his representation of these questions, only to reproach the proponents of reportage for their inability, as a mechanical inadequacy [one's class origin], to deal creatively with the 'totality of a process.' " The reportage form, Ottwalt maintained, accorded with the demands of the class struggle, inasmuch as proletarian revolutionary literature was not an end in itself, after all, but a contribution to changing reality. "It is not the duty of our literature to stabilize the reader's consciousness but to alter it," Ottwalt said. What ought to be investigated was not the creative method but the "functional significance" of a piece of writing, the role it played in the class struggle. Indeed, Ottwalt accused Lukács of advocating the creation of works of art that, complete in themselves, automatically turned the reader into an enjoyer who "draws no conclusions and is satisfied with things the way they are, happy to have read a good book."[78] This was the beginning of a fundamental, totally irreconcilable disagreement in opinion over the essence of art, a dichotomy of views that was the substance of every essay Lukács wrote in Soviet exile after 1933. Now Lukács touched only briefly on the questions to which he would later devote voluminous articles. He rejected completely Ottwalt's position, insisting that Ottwalt confined the functional significance of literature in the class struggle to the treatment of events and questions that had importance only in a day-to-day context. As for Ottwalt's desire to alter the reader's consciousness rather than stabilize it, Lukács broadened his attack: "Brecht too juxtaposed the 'unchangeable man' of the old theater with the 'changeable and changing man' of the new."[79] Lukács dismissed all this as "mechanistic" and "idealistic."

He also flayed Ottwalt for his attitude toward the literary heritage. Ottwalt readily admitted that the question of the heritage was not of central importance to him, explaining that the ideas to be inherited were still very much alive. The bourgeois ideologies of classicism and humanism daily confronted the proletarian revolutionary writer not as a dead heritage, but as a living element of reaction in the age of bourgeois decline. Lukács turned Ottwalt's formulation against him, accusing the writer of overlooking the fact that if Marx and Engels had followed his prescription, dialectical materialism would never have evolved, for the history of proletarian ideology had always been a struggle for those elements, tendencies, and accomplishments of bour-

78. Ernst Ottwalt, " 'Tatsachenroman' u. Formexperiment: Eine Entgegnung an Georg Lukács," *Die Linkskurve* 10 (1932): 22, 24–25.

79. Georg Lukács, "Aus der Not eine Tugend," *Die Linkskurve* 11/12 (1932): 18. Lukács's head-on confrontation with Brecht after 1933 is dealt with in Chapter 10. Cf. also Gallas, *Marxistische Literaturtheorie*, pp. 135–47.

geois thought that the proletariat brought to a higher dialectical plane. He insinuated that Ottwalt was interested in the heritage only after the proletariat had seized power, a line of reasoning that Lukács equated with Trotsky's position on literature. Lukács pointed out that the "uncle" whose death Ottwalt was awaiting in order to obtain his inheritance was in fact already dead as far as the *real* heritage was concerned—the legacy of the *revolutionary* bourgeoisie. Ottwalt, on the other hand, and those like him—who practiced the literary forms of reportage and montage and who resorted to avant-garde techniques— were entering into the inheritance of a different, still living "uncle," that of the decadent bourgeoisie of the imperialist epoch. Every essay Lukács later wrote in Soviet exile would drive home this theme.

Lukács concluded by saying that the "proletarian revolutionary movement in literature" had no intention of lowering its "theoretical niveau" because some comrades were turning their predicament (their class origin) into a virtue (a literary and creative method) and seeking to foist it upon other writers.[80] The public debate was cut short by Hitler's accession to power, but it recrudesced soon after in Soviet exile, when Lukács in 1933 began his assault on "decadent" forms of modern art with a thorough condemnation of expressionism.[81]

In April 1932 the Central Committee of the Soviet Communist party unexpectedly dissolved RAPP. Throughout 1931 complaints about the organization had grown more intense as it came under fire from a variety of quarters, and by the end of the year the party had joined in the chorus of criticism.[82] RAPP was accused of hindering the free development of other creative trends within the organization by treating all deviations from the dialectical materialist creative methods advocated by the Averbakh leadership as impermissible offences; in fact, those methods themselves were assailed, particularly the emphasis on psychologism and the application of the "dialectic" to the portrayal of characters. In the forefront among RAPP's detractors, apart from representatives of political bodies, was a group of radical proletarian writers who enjoyed strong party backing because of their willingness to lend their pens to the cause of "socialist construction."

80. Lukács, "Aus der Not eine Tugend," pp. 19–21, 24.
81. The essay was first published in July 1933 in Russian (*Literaturnyj kritik* 2 [1933]: 34–54); several months later, it appeared in German: " 'Grösse und Verfall' des Expressionismus," *Internationale Literatur* 1 (1934): 153–73. See Chapter 10 for additional discussion.
82. Cf. Brown, *The Proletarian Episode*, pp. 172–99, and Ermolaev, *Soviet Literary Theories*, pp. 89–118.

These writers were now the party's favorites, and when official calls were made for a "creative discussion" and for "freedom of groupings" within RAPP, the party clearly intended that RAPP should give a free rein to the literary method of the radical proletarians. RAPP's response to the criticism was quick. Averbakh, for instance, dubbed the opposition a recrudescence of the LEF and LITFRONT groups, which put agitation and propaganda ahead of true art.[83] In December 1931 a leading RAPP writer charged that "the ideas of the 'left vulgarizers' have arisen in proletarian literature before; the theory of the left opposition which would reduce all literature to propaganda and the contents of today's newspapers is, in essence, a theory for the liquidation of art."[84] But time had run out on RAPP, and the organization, along with all other Soviet literary groups, was dissolved by the April 1932 decree, which also announced plans for the formation of a single writers' union to incorporate all Soviet writers irrespective of their class.

The dissolution of RAPP occurred as part of a general ideological offensive against all organizations still enjoying a measure of independence from governmental control.[85] RAPP's demise was the last in a series of party-inspired "reorganizations" and dissolutions, the irony being that, before falling victim to changing party policy, RAPP had gladly let itself be used as a party instrument for traducing and liquidating other literary groupings.[86] For that reason, the party decree was thought by many writers to be a step in the direction of greater creative freedom in Soviet letters (and was welcomed as such) when it in fact signaled the end to that freedom and the emergence over the next several months of "socialist realism." Two primary reasons, both disingenuous, were given for RAPP's dissolution: "It was an impediment to the growth of literature," and its slogan "ally or enemy" (symbolizing its intransigence toward Soviet fellow travelers, who were now considered by the party to be "socialist" writers) was an "approach to the task of remaking and reeducating the fellow travelers" that contradicted the party line.[87] Both charges contained a kernel of truth. RAPP and the RAPP method were indeed impeding the "growth of

83. The organizations as such, however, had been formally disbanded by this time.
84. Brown, *The Proletarian Episode*, p. 197.
85. For more details, see ibid., pp. 200–218, and Ermolaev, *Soviet Literary Theories*, pp. 119–38.
86. See, for instance, RAPP's cynical behavior in the campaigns against Professor Pereverzev and against the Pereval group, which the party abolished with the help of RAPP (Ermolaev, *Soviet Literary Theories*, pp. 93–101).
87. The party resolution is reprinted in Brown, *The Proletarian Episode*, pp. 200–201.

literature," but it was the Five-Year Plan literature of the utilitarians being hampered. As for the charge of RAPP's mishandling of fellow travelers, which was also true enough and had carried over into the BPRS, it neglected to point out that the organization's policy on this issue was in complete harmony with the official line: no party objections from 1928 to 1932 had been raised about RAPP's maltreatment of fellow travelers in the USSR.[88] But now the party had ostensibly changed its policy and conveniently shifted the blame onto RAPP for past "errors" with respect to non-Communist writers.

In May 1932 Johannes R. Becher attended a conference of the IVRS secretariat in Moscow to discuss the impact of RAPP's demise on the International League, which, after all, had been dominated by Averbakh and RAPP.[89] Upon Becher's return to Berlin, the BPRS leadership formulated these criticisms of the IVRS in a letter to the organization:

> On the basis of documents available to us it is clear . . . that the attention of the IVRS has for years been brought to the need for changes in its work and working methods. . . . You are no longer up to the tasks that the problems of the present require of you. . . . There exists a danger that you will practice self-criticism but only in order to continue your accustomed methods, which have damaged our movement. . . . A number of German proletarian writers who have journeyed to the USSR, where they came into contact with the IVRS, have been drawn into a net of intrigues and thereby seriously impaired.[90]

Details of the differences between the BPRS and the IVRS that came to the fore in the aftermath of RAPP's disappearance are sparse, but it seems that the disunity was real and not merely an obligatory BPRS expression of dissatisfaction with an organization badly compromised by the party action against RAPP. In August 1932 a "reorganization" of the IVRS was announced,[91] and in October Hans Günther was dispatched to Moscow to act as the BPRS representative in the IVRS.[92]

---

88. Cf. Ermolaev, *Soviet Literary Theories*, p. 117.
89. Cf. Weiss, *Johannes R. Becher*, pp. 174–79.
90. "An die Mitglieder der kommunistischen Fraktion der IVRS" (3 June 1932), in *Iz istorii MORPa*, pp. 118–19.
91. See the documents in *Iz istorii MORPa*, pp. 120–24.
92. The absence of a BPRS delegate at the IVRS meetings discussing the League's reorganization had been a major complaint of the Germans. See ibid.

The liquidation of RAPP precipitated a modest liberalization of the policy toward Western sympathizers. Following the abolition of all literary groups in the USSR, an Organizational Committee held a series of plenary sessions to lay the groundwork for a unified Soviet Writers' Union and to define the new "creative method"—socialist realism. The first and most important session met in late October 1932 and was attended by Hugo Huppert, an Austrian who had been in the Soviet Union since 1928. He gave an official history of RAPP, reporting on the first plenum of the "Org-Committee," at a gathering of the German National Commission of the IVRS in Moscow on 17 December 1932. Huppert noted that the successes of RAPP throughout the twenties against all types of pernicious literary cliques and circles had been considerable. It had solidified the proletarian position in literature and acquired for it ideological hegemony. But RAPP had not understood that after 1930 the literary intelligentsia had switched to the side of the "Soviet régime, to the party, to socialism," and RAPP, therefore, out of step with developments, had to be liquidated. Huppert explained that the institution of fellow travelers had been thoroughly convulsed by the historical success of burgeoning socialism in the USSR. The "overwhelming majority of the nonparty mass of writers" had found its way into the "camp of the Soviet regime," a fact not grasped by RAPP, whose "either-or" attitude demanded from the nonproletarians that they declare themselves "as one of our number or we shall consider you our enemy." Such tactics were no longer called for since the majority of the writers had gradually come around to a position of full support of the Soviet government. Now there were no longer "'fellow travelers', but rather . . . a large united front of Soviet writers who were ready to take part creatively in the work of the socialist cultural revolution, in the construction of a classless society."[93]

On 25 December 1932 there was a follow-up meeting of the National Commission during which Huppert's presentation of the issues raised at the plenum were discussed in terms of their application to Germany.[94] At this session, Huppert made the point that proletarian literature had actually won ascendancy in the USSR; since all Soviet

---

93. Hugo Huppert, "Ergebnisse und Perspektiven der Literaturbewegung in der UdSSR," *Internationale Literatur* 1 (1933): 99 and 101.
94. There is a record of the meeting: *Internes Material der deutschen Länderkommission—* Protokoll zur Sitzung der erweiterten deutschen Länderkommission der IVRS am 25. Dezember 1932, TsGALI, holding 631, catalog 12, unit 50, pp. 1–11. Subsequent references give citations only by number.

writers were now socialist, RAPP had become pointless as a protective organization. The BPRS, on the other hand, had to be strengthened and its base broadened by the "incorporation of sympathetic writers" into its ranks. Huppert mentioned Lion Feuchtwanger and his novel *Erfolg,* noting that Feuchtwanger "has not, to be sure, adopted our class standpoint as his point of departure; but still, at times, he portrayed the class situation in Bavaria [in *Erfolg*] in a surprisingly accurate manner." Huppert maintained that all petty bourgeois oppositional writers contributed to the growth of culture and needed to be shown what was truly progressive and what was antiquated and obstructive in their writing.

Huppert's remarks were seconded by almost everyone present. Alexander Barta mentioned "past mistakes" in the attitude toward Barbusse, while Sergej Tretjakov agreed that the work of the BPRS among the sympathetic writers had been lacking. "For ten years," Tretjakov claimed, "we've been saying that Heinrich Mann belongs to us and that we ought to try and win him over; but the tendency has been instead to snub him. In any case, he is still not part of our movement." But some of those attending the meeting felt that the Communists had been intolerant of more than fellow travelers. Paul Dietrich[95] spoke of two camps within the BPRS: one including Lukács, Becher, and Gábor, the other, Brecht, Ottwalt, and Bredel. Dietrich noted the presence of "old sectarian tendencies," arguing that the Lukács faction had kept the other group away from BPRS work, perhaps intentionally. The LEFist Tretjakov, a friend of Brecht and Ottwalt, agreed, sharply criticizing Lukács for his position on Ottwalt's novels and insisting that the Communists should be appreciative of Ottwalt's work instead of falling upon him with lethal criticism. Hans Günther, however, defended the organization from charges of mistreating writers like Ottwalt and Brecht. The latter, Günther said, was "incorrigible in his personal views; Brecht takes the position that whatever he thinks is right." Much the same was true of Bernard von Brentano and Ernst Ottwalt. The BPRS had not isolated itself and had not behaved in a sectarian fashion toward these men, responded Günther. "We *did* invite Brentano and Ottwalt to work with us; but there was a certain amount of friction because both frequently pass themselves off as better Marxists, and at times go in for rather sharp attacks themselves, while Lukács, for example, has always acted in an extremely fair manner."[96]

95. Paul Dietrich in the late twenties was a member of the KPD's Central Committee and also a Reichstag deputy. See Weber, *Die Wandlung des deutschen Kommunismus,* 2:97.
96. *Internes Material,* TsGALI, 631/12/50/1–11.

In an article written at about the same time, Günther addressed himself to the changes made in the IVRS-BPRS in the wake of the dissolution of RAPP. It was now realized, he said, that, much like the fellow travelers in the USSR, who had been convinced by the "success" of Soviet power to lend their support to the régime, there had also been a drift toward the left in the Western petty bourgeois intelligentsia. These circles were now against the existing capitalist society and might well be won over ideologically and politically to the Communist cause. The IVRS's failure in this respect necessitated a change in the way it functioned. Time was of the essence: in Germany there had been an intensification of class warfare, which was rapidly assuming the proportions of civil war; Social Democracy had turned into social fascism; and the threat of an imperialist war against the Soviet Union was growing. To meet these challenges, an expansion of the Communists' ranks was needed—the incorporation of all oppositional elements into a "red, antifascist and antiimperialist united front."

This should prove possible, Günther reasoned, because of the catastrophic condition of bourgeois society, which was destroying the illusions of the non-Communist intelligentsia. However, the Communists must change their "antiquated methods and tactics" of left sectarianism in the field of literature. There would be those sure to interpret the new line as a sign that the Communists were prepared to make concessions, perhaps to adopt in part the ideology of the petty bourgeois intelligentsia or at least to tolerate it. Nothing was further from the Communists' minds, for not even tactical considerations would induce them to hide their Marxist-Leninist world view, said Günther. The Communists should declare themselves "satisfied" with the fact that the fellow travelers were proving their mettle in the struggle against reaction as "sincere antifascists, as adamant opponents . . . of war, as honest friends of the Soviet Union." This was all the Communists ought to ask for because the demand for a wholesale confession of faith in Marxism-Leninism and in Communist literary theories would represent the old sectarianism. But what they should not do, argued Günther, however much they desired a fighting alliance, was accept one that implied a "nonprincipled bloc" with concessions, even if they were made by both sides. "A common front with the left-wing writers against fascism, war, and reaction—yes, absolutely! But only if the ideological independence of proletarian revolutionary literature can be retained within this fighting alliance, with the goal, moreover, of working toward the hegemony of our literature." Calling for a "broad united front" in literature, then, Günther emphasized that the IVRS had to become a mass organization for all writers in the

West who were ready to battle the present danger of "fascism, imperialist war, and the threat of intervention."[97]

But to support the campaign against these perils, at least the way the Comintern defined them, was to place oneself squarely in the Soviet camp, for the Communists identified fascism with imperialist monopoly capitalism, which, they said, was preparing the "upcoming war" against socialism, against the Soviet Union. The overriding objective of all IVRS-BPRS attempts to arrive at a modus vivendi with the Western intellectuals was therefore to maneuver them into pro-Soviet positions by gaining their support against developments that were hard not to oppose—"fascism" and war. This is, of course, what Willi Münzenberg and the MRP had been doing throughout the twenties and into the thirties, and the history of the IVRS-BPRS is one of gradual adoption of Münzenberg's tactics. The surface tolerance toward fellow travelers, however, hid the old bedrock intransigence. In a fall 1930 issue of *Die Linkskurve*, for example, a series of questions were put to intellectuals of "various political groupings." This was one of the queries: "What position will you adopt in the upcoming war of the capitalist powers against the Soviet Union?"[98] *Die Linkskurve* published the responses of a number of non-Communist intellectuals, commenting: "We shall inexorably demand an answer: *for the workers' revolution or for fascism? For capitalist dictatorship or for the dictatorship of the proletariat?*"[99]

Dependent on the KPD for its understanding of fascism, the BPRS paid the same price as the party for misjudging the nature of National Socialism.[100] Caught totally unaware by Hitler's accession to power, many BPRS members, like KPD functionaries, fled for their lives.

97. Hans Günther, "Die nächsten Aufgaben der Internationalen Vereinigung Revolutionärer Schriftsteller," *Internationale Literatur* 1 (1933): 5, 8, 9–10. The article was written before Hitler's accession to power.

98. "Die Intellektuellen haben das Wort," *Die Linkskurve* 9 (1930): 4.

99. "Deutsche Intellektuellen wählen einen politischen Standpunkt," *Die Linkskurve* 10 (1930): 11.

100. There was no difference between the BPRS and the KPD in their assessment of Hitler. Angress deals with the reflection in *Die Linkskurve* of KPD attitudes towards nazism in Werner T. Angress, "Pegasus and Insurrection: *Die Linkskurve* and its Heritage," *Central European History* 1 (1968): 35–55. Ernst Ottwalt was an exception. In early 1932 he published a lengthy study of National Socialism; by arguing between the lines, he presented a theory of National Socialism and advocated a united front to prevent its assumption of power. His concept of a united front differed on key points with the Comintern-KPD position and actually seemed to advance Trotsky's arguments in favor of joint Communist-socialist action. The implications of Ottwalt's book were not recognized by the party, and it naturally had no effect on altering the line (Ottwalt, *Deutschland erwache!*).

Chapter 3

Exile

With Hitler in office the days of the KPD were numbered, but in spite of the party's imminent destruction, the leadership acted mindlessly: Walter Ulbricht and Werner Hirsch debated the nature of Hitler's dictatorship (pure fascism or not?), while Wilhelm Pieck sat in his office in the Prussian Diet as if he had nothing to fear, and Thälmann moved freely about Berlin.[1] A month later, though, everything changed when the Reichstag burned and the arrests began. The Gestapo, in fact, narrowly missed capturing the entire KPD Politburo the night of 27 February; the members escaped arrest only because they chanced to be away from their homes meeting in Berlin-Lichtenberg. But the police caught many other luckless Communists that night and during the next several weeks. By March 1933, between four and ten thousand middle- and lower-level functionaries throughout Germany had been taken into custody, among them Thälmann, whose carelessness cost him his freedom on 3 March; the Gestapo picked him up, along with Werner Hirsch and Erich Birkenhauer, in an apartment that Thälmann had used for years.[2] By the end of the year, between sixty and a hundred thousand German Communists were in Nazi prisons and concentration camps.[3]

Thälmann's arrest triggered a sordid power struggle within the party leadership. Ulbricht and John Schehr fought it out through March, when Hermann Schubert arrived in Berlin from Hamburg announcing himself as Thälmann's chosen successor. He then joined forces with Ulbricht, and the pair conspired to keep Schehr or anyone else from assuming power, dividing important party posts among

1. Wehner, "Erinnerungen," pp. 32–35.
2. Thälmann had evidently been betrayed by a Gestapo informant, Alfred Kattner, within the KPD. Birkenhauer and Hirsch were later freed from concentration camps and fled to Moscow, where they were arrested by the NKVD a few years later. They perished in Soviet camps.
3. Duhnke, *Die KPD von 1933 bis 1945*, p. 104.

their followers.[4] In the meantime, the KPD secretariat began sending politburo members abroad. Franz Dahlem and Wilhelm Florin left for Paris; Pieck, who was to head the party's foreign office in the French capital, followed in mid-May. Ulbricht for the time being remained in charge of KPD activity within Germany.[5] That summer, then, Schubert left for Prague on the way to Moscow, and Ulbricht arrived in the Czech capital in October. Schehr and Herbert Wehner were told late in the year to prepare to leave Germany, but before he could flee, Schehr was arrested.[6] That left Fritz Schulte as the only Politbüro member still in the country, and before the year was out he too had left for Moscow via Prague. The Politburo then took up headquarters in Paris until January 1935, when the KPD Central Committee and Politburo moved its base of operations to Moscow.

German Communists who fled to Soviet Russia in 1933 found several thousand of their countrymen already living there. These were the so-called specialists—technicians, skilled workers, engineers, and the like invited to Russia in the twenties and early thirties by the Soviet government. By the start of 1931 the number of engineers, foremen, and general employees active in branches of Soviet industry had reached four thousand. One newspaper reported that in the course of the coming year an additional thirteen thousand specialists, many from Germany, would be signed to contracts,[7] and their total number may eventually have topped eighteen thousand.[8] These men, of course, were not originally political refugees, though many did go to the USSR as Communists. The Soviet government, in fact, seems to have utilized the KPD to screen applicants politically for employment in the USSR, and many of the specialists joined the party (often the Soviet party) while working in Russia. These Germans were therefore by no means apolitical, and after 1933 many wished to remain in Russia; those who received permission in effect united with the German emigration.[9]

4. Pieck stayed out of the power struggle (Wehner, "Erinnerungen," p. 41). Ulbricht insisted that Wehner remove from the party's central apparat functionaries "who had been out getting drunk with Teddy [Thälmann]."
5. Cf. Duhnke, *Die KPD von 1933 bis 1945*, p. 110; see also Vietzke, *Die KPD auf dem Wege zur Brüsseler Konferenz*, p. 50.
6. Wehner, "Erinnerungen," p. 52.
7. Cited in Diezel, *Exiltheater in der Sowjetunion*, pp. 14–15.
8. Röder, *Sonderfahndungsliste UdSSR*, p. 12.
9. Little is known about the subject. These East German publications offer some information: Ursula Kretzschmar, "Die Hilfe deutscher Arbeiter und Wissenschaftler beim Aufbau des Sozialismus in der UdSSR 1921–1933," in *Die Grosse Sozialistische Oktoberrevolution und Deutschland*, 2:149–76; and Nikolaj Sharapov, "Die Teilnahme aus-

A number of German Communists were working in Comintern offices in Moscow before 1933, joined by a small band of literati and artists. Gertrud Alexander, a literary critic who wrote regularly for the *Rote Fahne* in the early twenties, began work in the women's secretariat of the Comintern in 1925. Hugo Huppert arrived in Moscow in 1928. Erwin Piscator, under contract to Münzenberg's Mezhrabpom film agency, arrived in the USSR in 1931 to film Anna Segher's *Revolt of the Fishermen of St. Barbara* with Paul Wegner, Lotte Lenya, Erwin Kalser, Heinrich Greif, and Lotte Loebinger. Piscator and Loebinger remained in the country after 1933; the others left, though Greif returned in 1935. In 1931 the agitprop troupe Kolonne Links, also under contract to Münzenberg's International Workers' Relief, won a trip to the USSR. During the group's absence from Germany, the authorities promulgated new laws restricting the activity of agitprop groups (in Berlin they were outlawed altogether), and the German section of the Comintern decided that the Kolonne Links should remain in the USSR to assume responsibilities for the "cultural supervision of foreign workers in the Soviet Union." [10] The decision was wired to Leningrad, but the message arrived too late and the actors of Kolonne Links heard the news only after their ship docked back at Hamburg. But they returned to Russia anyway. Helmut Damerius, the director, Kurt Arendt, Bruno Schmidtsdorf, Hans Hauska, Karl Oefelein, and Hans Klering journeyed back to the Soviet Union, traveling from Bremerhaven to Vladivostok by ship and from there on to Moscow by Transsiberian Express. They reached the Soviet capital in October 1931 after a trip lasting over four months. [11]

Other Germans living in Moscow before 1933 included Peter Kast, who had been jailed in Berlin in 1932 as editor of the *Rote Fahne* and who fled late that year to Prague on the way to the USSR; [12] Karl Schmückle and Alexander Barta; Bernhard Reich and his wife Asja Lazis; and the former editor of *Der Sturm*, Herwarth Walden, who emigrated in June 1932. Hans Günther arrived in Moscow in October 1932 to represent the BPRS in the IVRS secretariat.

The exodus of German Communist writers after 1933 duplicated the flight of KPD officials. [13] Johannes R. Becher made his way on 28

ländischer Arbeiter und Spezialisten am sozialistischen Aufbau im Ural (1930–1934)," in *Jahrbuch für Geschichte der UdSSR*, 11:255–74.

10. Damerius, *Über zehn Meere*, p. 239.

11. Damerius tells the story in detail in ibid., pp. 244–342.

12. *Lexikon sozialistischer deutscher Literatur*, p. 276.

13. See Walter, *Bedrohung und Verfolgung bis 1933*, 1:197–250, for a treatment of the German emigration in its entirety.

February to Czechoslovakia and on to Austria; by May he was in Moscow. Franz Leschnitzer followed the same route, and Andor Gábor arrived in March.[14] Friedrich Wolf left Stuttgart for Austria on 3 March and went from there to Zurich. He then spent several months in France, moving to Moscow in November 1933.[15] Gustav and Inge von Wangenheim reached Paris in March, switching their residence to Moscow in August,[16] while the KPD gave Georg Lukács "orders and the technical possibility to travel to the Soviet Union," where he arrived in March.[17] Ernst Ottwalt and Waltraut Nicolas evidently fled in mid-1933 to Denmark, staying there a few months with Bertolt Brecht and Helene Weigel as guests of Karin Michaelis.[18] In the fall of 1933, Ottwalt and Nicolas moved to Prague and then settled in Moscow in late 1934.

Not all of the writers got out of Germany safely. Willi Bredel, for instance, did not; police arrested him in Hamburg on 1 March 1933. Released from Fuhlsbüttel concentration camp a year later, Bredel received party orders to leave Germany; he fled to Prague in early summer and arrived in Moscow shortly after.[19] In January 1934 Alfred Kurella was called from Paris to Moscow.[20] Theodor Plivier and Adam Scharrer arrived in the capital as guests of the First All-Union Soviet Writers' Congress and ended up staying in Russia for the duration of the Hitler years. Julius Hay arrived sometime after the congress.[21] Erich Weinert, who was in Switzerland on a speaking tour in early 1933, heard in March that the Gestapo had ransacked his apartment four times. He applied for asylum in Zurich, but because of his political affiliation, the Swiss allowed him to remain only until mid-June 1933.[22] Forced to leave Switzerland, he went first to Strasbourg, then on to Paris, and in October 1934 to the Saar, remaining there until early 1935. Back in Paris, he waited for a Soviet visa from April to August 1935 before he could leave for Moscow via Leningrad.[23] Fritz

14. Andor Gábor, "An die Vertretung der KPD beim EKKI," 6 February 1936, MTA, Gábor Andor-Hagyaték, Ms. 4490/39.
15. Pollatschek, *Friedrich Wolf*, pp. 183–85 and 195–96.
16. Diezel, *Exiltheater in der Sowjetunion*, pp. 47–48.
17. Georg Lukács, "Autobiographie," Lukács Archivum.
18. Cf. Nicolas, *Viele tausend Tage*, pp. 187–88; Mytze, *Ottwalt*, pp. 44 and 49.
19. Hofer, *Willi Bredel*, pp. 42 and 45.
20. See Walter Benjamin's letter to Bertolt Brecht in January 1934: "Kurella had to relinquish the editorship of *Monde*—at least for the time being—and has left for Moscow to report" (*Zur Aktualität Walter Benjamins*, p. 33).
21. Hay, *Geboren 1900*, p. 42.
22. See Mittenzwei, *Exil in der Schweiz*, pp. 84–85.
23. Weinert (Paris) to Schmückle (Moscow), 1 August 1935, TsGALI, 631/13/49/40; Bredel (Moscow) to Peter Merin (Switzerland), 14 August 1935, TsGALI, 631/13/69/85.

Erpenbeck and Hedda Zinner fled to Prague in 1933, settling in late 1935 in the Soviet Union.

By late 1935 the Communist flight to the USSR was down to a trickle. The Kirov assassination in December 1934 had already led to immigration restrictions, and after the show trials began in August 1936, visas for German émigrés were seldom issued.[24] Much earlier, though, just a few months after Hitler's accession to power, Soviet immigration policies had sparked a debate in the German émigré press. In June 1933 the *Neue Weltbühne* came out with an anonymous article ("By a Communist") querying Soviet intentions with respect to the thousands of German refugees whose lives were in imminent danger. Well over one hundred days had passed since Hitler had come to office. Since 180 million persons lived within the boundaries of the Soviet Union, the journal asked, was "space not to be found for several thousand whose lives and liberty have yet to be saved from the grasp of fascism?" Was the roofless refugee to approach the portals of Western fascism with more hope than the red boundary markers of the Soviet Union? The *Neue Weltbühne* demanded the right of asylum "in the name of the prestige and dignity of the Republic of Peasants, Workers, and Soldiers."[25] This the Communists dismissed as so much "sentimentality." A "Friend of the Soviets" answered the *Neue Weltbühne*: "[Soviet leaders] loathe fascism no less than we; but they require German machines for socialist construction. And above all else

24. Heinrich Mann and his relatives were, in a sense, an exception. Worried about his first wife and daughter in Prague, Mann went through J. R. Becher in Moscow to get them both to the Soviet Union in mid-1938 (see the correspondence between Mann and Becher in Becher-Archiv, Sig. 63–65). The pair evidently returned to Prague and in 1939 again found themselves in danger (see the correspondence between Mann and T. Rokotov in TsGALI, 1397/662/72, 54, 100, 103, 108). The situation grew critical in March 1939, when Mann wrote Rokotov: "The worst thing is that my daughter and her mother are still in their apartment in Prague—yet at liberty I hope. My concern and uncertainty have led me to send Becher a letter with a request that he will pass on to you" (the letter is dated 28 March 1939, TsGALI, 1397/1/662/95). Becher answered Mann on 3 April 1939: "I have passed on the matter of your daughter and her mother to the responsible authorities, and I hope very much, together with you, that the problem can be resolved soon" (Becher-Archiv, Sig. 66). According to the letters to Rokotov on 4 April and again on 1 July 1939, Mann also intended to flee to the USSR. He evidently approached Willi Bredel in Paris, asking for political asylum in the USSR should war break out. Bredel passed his request on to Moscow, and Mann received a telegram from Aleksej Tolstoj and Aleksandr Fadejev informing him that he had been invited to come to the USSR; a visa awaited him in Paris. See T. L. Motyleva, "Genrikh Mann," in *Istorija nemetskoj literatury*, 5:506. Mann did not emigrate to the USSR, and his wife was eventually arrested in Prague and imprisoned in Theresienstadt. She died in 1947 from the effects of her stay there.

25. "Und die Sowjetunion?," *Die neue Weltbühne* 22 (1933): 673–75.

—this is wholly within all of our interests—they need a secure peace," explained the letter writer. "That is why they must retain good relations with their big and menacing neighbor in the West, even if their temperament actually compels them in the other direction. Such motives of *Realpolitik* are decisive, not sentimentalities."[26]

Der Gegenangriff, a Münzenberg journal, voiced similar arguments. What was the Soviet Union doing for German Communists and for the emigration? The journal expressed its amazement at the naiveté or "maliciousness" of the question. The Soviet Union had not hit Germany with a boycott of goods, nor had it staged any parliamentary debates about the horrors in Germany; the USSR had made none of the noncommittal gestures so characteristic of the "diplomatic maneuvers" of the imperialist powers. But, *Der Gegenangriff* asked:

> Isn't the existence of the USSR in itself a blow against fascism? Isn't the USSR the only genuine antifascist power next to the fighting proletariat in the capitalist countries? Isn't the Executive of the Communist International, the hated archenemy of capitalism and fascism, headquartered in Moscow? . . . The Soviet Union refuses to open its doors to the emigration as other countries do? What a childish question! Is the emigration an end in itself? The emigration is one sector of the battle front [between capitalism and socialism]. Nothing else. Questions of expediency alone determine when and where the strategic positions from within and without are changed. Strategic questions are not the kind to be settled with humanistic fatuousness. The whole world knows[27] that Communists stand in the most advanced line of the fire fight. This side or that side of a Soviet border encircled by imperialism— it is one and the same struggle. Everything is calculated according to the single criterion of revolutionary expediency.[28]

Actually, these explanations were completely in consonance with Soviet efforts throughout 1933 to reach an agreement with Hitler and save the Rapallo Treaty; such were the motives governing "expediency," not the revolutionary struggle. Whether Litvinov actually stated openly to the Germans, "We don't care if you shoot your German Communists," is immaterial, for Soviet actions throughout 1933 and much of 1934 indicated clearly that the Soviet government was at

26. "Antworten," *Die neue Weltbühne* 24 (1933): 755.
27. The expression "the whole world knows" ("alle Welt weiss") could indicate that the article in *Der Gegenangriff* was translated from a Russian draft.
28. Extract quoted in *Die neue Weltbühne* 27 (1933): 847.

pains to demonstrate to the Germans that ideological differences mattered little to the USSR in questions of foreign policy and that Moscow
was not unduly solicitous about the fate of German Communists.[29]

The controversy surrounding Soviet immigration policy continued
for several years. In 1934 Elena Stassova, general secretary of the
International Red Relief, explained to Kurt Grossmann of the League
for Human Rights that what mattered most was not sanctuary in the
USSR but "prying" the right of asylum from the "capitalist countries."[30] Wieland Herzfelde told Grossmann in 1938 that refugees
allowed into the "democratic countries" represented a thorn in the eye
of fascism there. Herzfelde asked: "Do you truly want to remove that
thorn by transferring them to the East? . . . I in any case am persuaded
that to the extent this is done Western and American readiness to help
out would decrease. The end effect would be not more assistance for
the refugees altogether, but solely a triumph of the enemy of democracy and socialism in the other countries."[31]

Procedures followed in emigrating to the Soviet Union are largely a
matter of conjecture. Ordinary German party members and functionaries who fled to the USSR must have been instructed to do so; in
those cases the Comintern took care of visa and registration formalities. The writers too must have had party approval for their flight to
the Soviet Union, though this can be documented only in a few instances. The KPD instructed Georg Lukács and Willi Bredel to emigrate.[32] Trude Richter, Hans Günther's wife, worked illegally in the
BPRS in Berlin until April 1934. After the Gestapo began tailing her,
she passed word to Günther that she would have to leave soon, and he
notified the Comintern. Richter traveled by train to Prague, where
she met Günther and picked up her Soviet visa (which had been
prepared at the request of the Comintern) at the Soviet embassy.[33]

29. Litvinov's alleged remark is quoted from Ulam, *Expansion and Coexistence*, p. 194.
What he did say definitely was this: "We certainly are sympathetic towards the sufferings
of our German comrades; but it is possible to reproach us Marxists least of all with
permitting our sympathies to rule our policy. All the world knows that we can and do
maintain good relations with capitalist governments of any regime, including fascist.
That is not what matters. We do not interfere in the internal affairs of Germany . . . and
our relations with her are determined not by her domestic but by her foreign policy."
Quoted from Litvinov's December 1933 speech in Moore, *Soviet Politics—The Dilemma
of Power*, p. 364.
30. Cf. Grossmann, *Emigration*, p. 105. See also Stahlberger, *Der Zürcher Verleger Emil
Oprecht*, p. 30.
31. Grossmann, *Emigration*, p. 106.
32. Hofer, *Willi Bredel*, p. 42; and Lukács, "Autobiographie," Lukács Archivum.
33. Personal information from Trude Richter.

Some remarks J. R. Becher made in a report to Moscow in late 1933 seem to reveal the existance of tension between Communist writers who fled the country and those who remained behind: "Among the writers who have remained in Germany there is a pronounced feeling against the comrades who emigrated, in which context it should be noted that so far as some comrades are concerned the reasons for their emigration are indeed not clear."[34] Whether this dissension derived from unhappiness with the party's choice of writers whose emigration was approved, or whether those remaining behind simply felt deserted is uncertain. Nor is it possible to say how many Communist literati (or functionaries, for that matter) refused to wait around for the bureaucracy to sanction their emigration and simply fled for their lives, generally to France, Czechoslovakia, or Austria. It seems highly improbable, though, that the "second emigration" to the USSR ever occurred without party permission, and the proper papers were no doubt issued only on the basis of official approval.

Short visits to the USSR by exiles who had found asylum elsewhere were made possible through official invitation. The IVRS was often the sponsoring agency, for instance, in the case of Theodor Balk or Hermann Budzislawski.[35] The IVRS's sister organization, the International League of Revolutionary Theaters (IRTB), backed Julius Hay's trip, and the Soviet Writers' Union invited Theodor Plivier, Adam Scharrer, and Albert Ehrenstein to attend the Writers' Congress in August 1934. Ernst Ottwalt also seems to have left Prague for Moscow at the invitation of the Soviet Writers' Union.[36] Some of those who initially received permission to visit the USSR because of invitations from Soviet agencies then applied for and were granted permanent asylum. Erich Weinert, on the other hand, owed his entry papers to the initiative of Willi Bredel, who worked through various powerful institutions to get Weinert into the USSR. In a letter to Hermann Schubert (Max Richter), German representative to the Comintern,[37] Bredel wrote: "According to my talk with Comrade Stetskij a decision was made to wire Weinert 150 gold rubles for travel costs. So far, though, I have received no definite word. Since Comrade Weinert's situation is quite precarious, speed is of the essence, and in the next

34. Johannes R. Becher, "Bericht über die Tätigkeit während meiner Reise vom 5. Juli bis 27. September 1933," Becher-Archiv, BPRS-Materialien, no. 41.
35. Cf. "Ausweis für Theodor Balk," 10 March 1935, TsGALI, 631/13/75/1; Ottwalt (Moscow) to Budzislawski (Prague), no date [ca. March 1935], TsGALI, 631/13/69/200.
36. Mytze, *Ottwalt*, p. 71.
37. Schubert replaced Fritz Heckert in that position shortly after Schubert's arrival in Moscow.

few days I intend to contact MOPR if in the meantime I don't hear from Stetskij. It would be good if you too could arrange to do what is necessary in this matter."[38]

Bredel was working here through three different channels: the agitprop division of the Soviet Central Committee, headed by Stetskij; the International Red Relief (MOPR);[39] and the Comintern's German section. This may in fact have been a typical course of action because there simply was no established procedure for gaining political asylum in the USSR. In April 1935 Bredel advised Weinert that approval of his trip was imminent, but Weinert still waited five months for his visa.[40] Bredel, incidentally, was displeased with the amount of assistance to "proletarian-revolutionary writers." In early 1935 Werner Türk pressed persistently for an invitation to visit the USSR, but in IVRS headquarters in Moscow Bredel opposed the trip, arguing that he was "against Türk's journey, especially for an unlimited amount of time, until the question of the *proletarian* writers in the emigration is resolved."[41]

Exiles in the West often beleaguered their counterparts in Moscow with pleas for help in obtaining Soviet asylum; in all but a few cases, though, nothing could be done, especially after the December 1934 killing of Kirov. Bredel wrote Balder Olden on 9 August 1935 about a proposed visit: "I promise to make the necessary inquiries as rapidly as possible since, according to the new regulations (in force, I am told, since December last), the trip over here is normally possible only with a passport that is in order and, as I gather from your letter, yours expires this month. That will cause certain problems."[42] Once the real terror began, asylum seems to have been granted rarely, even though, oblivious to what was going on in the country, plenty of German exiles longed for Soviet asylum. "Please bear in mind," wrote W. Hugo Schenk in a 1938 letter to Erpenbeck, "that those of us here [in the West] are all far from enjoying the amenities and . . . secure existence available to our colleagues in Soviet Russia." Schenk went on to bemoan the fact

38. Bredel to Richter, no date [ca. March-April 1935], TsGALI, 631/13/69/63.
39. The MOPR had a "Department of Political Émigrés" and fulfilled an important but little known function in overseeing the German emigration in the USSR.
40. Cf. Weinert to Schmückle, 1 August 1935, TsGALI, 631/13/49/40; Bredel to Peter Merin, 14 August 1935, TsGALI, 631/13/69/85.
41. Cf. Türk to Schmückle, 7 April 1935, TsGALI, 631/13/49/29. Bredel's remark was handwritten at the top of Türk's letter.
42. Bredel to Olden, 9 August 1935, TsGALI, 631/13/69/91. Bredel's remarks make it clear that he found out about these changes by word of mouth; nowhere were the exact conditions for the issuance of entry visas published.

that Soviet Russia, "'the fatherland of all proletarian fighters,' " kept its gates tightly closed. "I have never, anywhere, heard that the USSR has welcomed a single one of the many writers of the Union [BPRS] who are in truly desperate straits, not even for rest and recuperation." Schenk said that he was thinking of colleagues who, "in the truest sense of the word, are going to the dogs here, and these are old fighters whose seniority, in part, goes back to the Spartacus years." Schenk closed his letter by asking for asylum in the USSR for himself, but Erpenbeck informed him that he could do nothing in the matter. "The political situation is momentarily too tense, as you can see for yourself, and the lessons the Soviet Union was compelled to learn with the completely magnanimous help it rendered earlier were less than encouraging."[43] In other words, many of the German exiles in Soviet Russia had been "exposed" in the meantime as Gestapo agents.

A Soviet entry visa was not the same as a residence permit; the privilege of remaining in the USSR was granted separately after consultation with official organizations. This was the procedure followed in the case of four prominent writers, according to a letter from Bredel to Hermann Schubert in the Comintern: "Acting at the behest of Comrades Theodor Plivier, Adam Scharrer, Albert Ehrenstein, and Ernst Ottwalt I would like to ask you to attend our meeting of the 19th in the Metropol, room 592, at 8 P.M. The comrades intend to discuss their continued stay in the Soviet Union, and their plans for work, with the responsible representatives of the writers' organization." Bredel concluded: "It would be good if you too were informed about the talk. Should you be unable to attend yourself, please arrange to send another comrade whom you delegate to be present."[44] Scharrer, for one, evidently already had official approval of sorts. He justified his request to remain in the USSR by explaining his intention to write a "history of the German farmers in the USSR and the resolution of

---

43. Schenk to Erpenbeck, 4 May 1938, TsGALI, 631/12/141/69. Erpenbeck to Schenk, 22 August 1938, TsGALI, 631/12/141/61. Erpenbeck, as the de facto editor of *Das Wort*, which was widely disseminated in the western emigration, received frequent requests from German exiles in the West who desired asylum in the Soviet Union. His answer was always the same. In reply to Michael Flürschein, who had asked for Erpenbeck's assistance in settling in the Volga-German Republic or elsewhere in Russia, Erpenbeck answered: "There is only one way, which has to be strictly adhered to: by way of the official authorities. Moreover, the request for an entry visa has to be made personally from outside. Believe me, in such matters I am completely powerless" (Erpenbeck to Flürschein, 31 October 1938, TsGALI, 631/12/152/101). See also TsGALI, 631/12/154/62–63 for a similar request.

44. Bredel to Richter (Schubert), 17 January 1935, TsGALI, 631/13/69/8.

the 'peasant question' by means of collectivization." The plan, he said, had been given the "complete approval of the German [KPD] representation in Prague and in the Comintern (Comrade Heckert)."[45] All of the above writers ended up staying except Ehrenstein.

Permission to reside in the country seems to have been granted in the form of a "residence permit without citizenship" (*vid na zhitelstvo bez grazhdanstva*) or a "passport without citizens' rights."[46] Plivier, for one, received such a permit valid only for specified lengths of time, and he had to apply for a renewal, never approved immediately, every two months. Wehner reports waiting ten months on one occasion for the return of his extended residence permit.[47] The waiting in such cases was unavoidably nerve-racking, but it seems unlikely, as Wehner writes, that the passport without citizens' rights was a "document that discriminated more than it helped." The waiting time certainly was a "psychologically almost unbearable means of pressure," yet few probably realized at the time that those who had actually forsaken their German nationality (as many did) in favor of Soviet citizenship and a normal Soviet passport were in greater danger. Subject to Soviet laws, a naturalized German could more easily fall victim to the NKVD, the Soviet secret police.

Many of the less prominent exiles lived under the constant threat of deportation, which was tied in with the complex matter of citizenship. Beck and Godin wrote that "all political refugees were required formally to surrender their nationality and apply for Soviet citizenship" and that, after the purges began, arrested "foreigners who had not been granted Soviet nationality could at least hope to be expelled."[48] The second remark is true, but there seems never to have existed any *formal* requirement that all German political refugees in Soviet exile take Soviet citizenship. There was, though, unofficial pressure in that Soviet authorities gave many of the exiles the "choice" of applying for Soviet citizenship or leaving the country. Susanne Leonhard was told by the International Red Relief (MOPR) in the fall of 1935 that she should become a Soviet national. She declined, but was eventually informed that if she did not sign an already prepared application for citizenship, she would be expelled within twenty-four hours. In that

---

45. Scharrer to VEGAAR (Krebs), to the Westeuropäische Ländersektion der Komintern (Knorin), to the Politische Leitung der deutschen Zentralzeitung, and to the Sekretariat der IVRS, 25 February 1935, TsGALI, 631/13/69/32.
46. Walter, *Deutsche Exilliteratur*, p. 140; Wehner, "Erinnerungen," p. 156.
47. Wehner, "Erinnerungen," p. 156.
48. Beck and Godin, *Russian Purge and the Extraction of Confession*, pp. 48–49.

eventuality her son would not be allowed to leave since he *was* a Soviet citizen. She signed.[49]

Then there was the case of Hans Kunzl, who had worked since June 1932 for the Verlagsgenossenschaft ausländischer Arbeiter (VEGAAR). He wanted to stay in the USSR and had applied for citizenship.[50] But in 1938 Kunzl was suddenly given one week to leave the country. In February he asked Lilli Beer, a close friend, to denounce him to the NKVD as an enemy of the USSR. He would then be arrested, he hoped, his case would be investigated, and, with his innocence established, he would be released. In the meantime, his wife Sophie would be able to stay in the country with their daughter. Lilli Beer refused to go along with the scheme, and the Kunzls had to leave the country on 9 March 1938.[51] Ilona Donath, who worked on the editorial staff of the *Deutsche Zentral-Zeitung* and afterwards for the printing press Iskra revoljutsii, was denied a renewal of her residence permit and had to leave the country. Her application for Soviet citizenship had been rejected earlier because of her "unsuitable social background"—her father had not been a day laborer.[52]

Many of the specialists, the foreign workers, did leave the country beginning in 1935, most by deportation. Of the eighteen thousand said to have been in the USSR at one time, twelve thousand had been forced to leave by 1939.[53] This did not necessarily mean that their lives were in danger in Germany; those who had gone to the USSR before 1933 were, it seems, interrogated upon their return and then left alone.[54] Things were no doubt different for those with a Communist background in Germany or for post-1933 émigrés, but it is unclear to what extent the Soviet Union expelled these Germans as well. Many of these had probably taken Soviet citizenship.[55] Prominent KPD leaders and functionaries who worked in the exiled party apparat in Moscow or in the Comintern, as well as the German writers, plainly comprised a special category. The question of citizenship seems not to have been put to them as crassly as to the less prominent, though a

49. Leonhard, *Gestohlenes Leben*, p. 33.
50. Hans Kunzl in a letter to the author.
51. Beer, "Memoirs."
52. Ibid.
53. Röder, *Sonderfahndungsliste*, p. 12.
54. Dr. Hans Goldschmidt, who arrived in the USSR in 1932 to work in VEGAAR and who left of his own accord in 1937, attested to this in conversation with me. The interrogations were used by the Gestapo to compile an arrest list, the *Sonderfahndungsliste*, for possible future use.
55. There is some indication, however, that between 1939 and 1941 German exiles with Soviet citizenship were also forced to leave the country. See Chapter 11, p. 344.

number of the writers did become Soviet citizens; Hugo Huppert, for example, who also belonged to the Soviet Communist party, became a citizen. Trude Richter applied for citizenship in 1935 and probably received it.[56] Alfred Kurella was a Soviet citizen.

The naturalization process applied to prominent German writers can be documented only in the case of Friedrich Wolf. He filed for citizenship in September 1936, supporting his request with a testimonial written by his friend Vsevolod Vishnevskij, the Soviet playwright. The documents were presented to the presidium of the Central Executive Committee of the USSR,[57] but for unknown reasons the request was not acted on at the time. More information about official policy in the question of citizenship emerges from a 1936 letter that Wolf wrote his first wife Käthe in Switzerland concerning their son Lukas. Wolf noted that it would be impossible for Lukas to stay in the USSR without Soviet citizenship. "In fact," Wolf said, "I can get him over here only as my son and as an emigrant. Even that is not simple." Wolf explained:

Lately large numbers of teachers and intellectuals are arriving uninterruptedly through INTURIST; they then want to remain and all wish to become Soviet citizens because life and work for them is "hell" in Germania. . . . But I can do nothing for them, of course; the regulations here are now justifiably very strict. It is a real honor to be a Soviet citizen. [The authorities] now sift very carefully. But if I have Lukas come over as my son and then, of course, vouch for him . . . then it should be possible to persuade the German party and Red Relief authorities here to recommend his naturalization and Lukas will receive Soviet citizenship. . . . Lukas wrote that his German passport expires in December anyway. As my son he can never go to the embassy here, say, to have his passport extended—aside from the fact that as a German party comrade I cannot answer for that.[58] But what would happen after December, when Lukas's passport expires? Then he would have to accept the citizenship of his second fatherland.[59]

56. Personal information from Trude Richter. Damerius, *Über zehn Meere*, p. 420, writes that "most" of the members of the Kolonne Links, "just as the other foreign workers," took Soviet citizenship.
57. See Vsevolod Vishnevskij's "Kharakteristika," 26 September 1936 (Spravka dlja predstavlenija v Presidium TsIK SSSR dlja perekhoda v sovetskoe grazhdanstvo), Wolf-Archiv, Mappe 248/5–7.
58. See Chapter 11, p. 316, regarding the danger of visiting the German embassy.
59. Wolf to Käthe Wolf (Switzerland), 5 May 1936, Wolf-Archiv, Mappe 331/1.

Wolf's letter reveals that application for citizenship had to be approved by the party or the International Red Relief; in certain cases, approval by both may have been required. It would also seem that the question of citizenship became acute only after an exile's German passport expired or was invalidated by the German consulate.[60]

The daily needs of the prominent exiles were generally taken care of during the thirties in the Soviet Union (leaving aside, of course, the question of the terror), though the uncertainty of living conditions, the housing shortage especially, affected the writers as well. Many of them began their exile in Soviet hotels. Andor Gábor lived in the Grand Hotel,[61] while Hans Günther had a room in the Hotel Europa, sharing it with Trude Richter. In 1935 they received two rooms in the Hotel Kiev, where Ernst Ottwalt and his wife were living.[62] Willi Bredel was forced to stay in a hotel well into spring 1935, paying an exorbitant seven hundred rubles a month in rent; that summer he obtained a three-room apartment in the center of Moscow.[63] Friedrich Wolf spent his initial weeks in Moscow first with Sergej Tretjakov and then with Vishnevskij; in February 1934, Vishnevskij contrived to locate a private apartment for Wolf.[64] Adam Scharrer was forced to spend several months in an "outrageously expensive room in the Hotel Metropol."[65] J. R. Becher and Erich Weinert were given rooms in the high-rise building on Lavrushinskij Street belonging to the Writers' Union, a building opened for occupancy in 1937. Günther and Richter had also paid for rooms there,[66] but after November 1936 (the date of their arrest) they received NKVD accomodations.

Top KPD and Comintern officials occupied rooms in the infamous Hotel Lux.[67] Alfred Kurella, probably for only a brief period in 1934–

---

60. This must have happened to all the exiles at some point. Hans Günther, for instance, had his passport invalidated by the German consulate in Leningrad on 28 October 1935, though he was not deprived of citizenship until 26 July 1936, the same day on which Ernst Ottwalt was expatriated. See the correspondence between the German embassy in Moscow, the Gestapo, and the Ministry of the Interior in *europäische ideen* 14/15 (1976): 87–91. By early 1937 all of the following (and probably many more) had been expatriated: Becher, Bredel, Erpenbeck, Plivier, Weinert, von Wangenheim.
61. Richter, *Die Plakette*, p. 249.
62. Ibid., pp. 250 and 259.
63. Bredel to Krebs (VEGAAR), 21 March 1935, TsGALI, 631/13/69/54. Bredel to Peter Merin, 8 July 1935, TsGALI, 631/13/69/81; and Bredel to Egon Erwin Kisch, 8 October 1935, TsGALI, 631/13/54/8.
64. Pollatschek, *Friedrich Wolf*, pp. 195–96.
65. See note 45.
66. Personal information from Trude Richter.
67. There is a monograph devoted to the Hotel Lux: Mayenburg, *Hotel Lux*.

35, is the only writer known to have lived there before the war; he stayed there presumably as long as he worked for Dimitroff. The Hotel Baltchik likewise housed exiles, and there was a *Schutzbündler* home for many of the three-hundred Austrian *Schutzbündler* who emigrated to Russia en masse following the abortive rising in February 1934. In early 1936 the cooperative apartment house Weltoktober opened its doors. A number of the employees and editors of the *Deutsche Zentral-Zeitung* lived there, together with writers Georg Lukács, Franz Leschnitzer, and Karl Schmückle.[68]

Almost all the émigré notables lived in Moscow.[69] Theodor Plivier and Adam Scharrer, however, the only German writers in the USSR who did not belong to the KPD, were exceptions. Scharrer waited months for the opportunity to settle in a Soviet German region to work on his book about collective farms,[70] and by May 1935 he was living in a German-speaking region of the Ukraine, where he remained for over two years, returning to Moscow in February 1938.[71] In early 1935 Plivier moved to Leningrad in search of suitable living quarters, but he had as little luck finding housing inside the city limits in Leningrad as he had in Moscow until the Soviet Writers' Union helped him obtain two rooms. He remained in Leningrad until late August 1936, when he moved to a small village, Paulskoje, in the Volga-German Republic. Back in Moscow a few years later, Plivier was still unable to settle in Moscow proper, living first in Galitsino, an hour outside the city, and then in a dacha he built in Domodjedovo in early 1939. There he remained until the Germans arrived in fall 1941.[72]

Once asylum had been given, Soviet authorities severely restricted travel outside the country. Important KPD officials, of course, commuted regularly between Moscow, Prague, and Paris on party business. The few writers who left the USSR also did so in most cases either with Comintern approval or in carrying out a Comintern mission. Becher's travels during 1933 to 1935, for instance, were surely regarded as official business, and the party took care of his visa formalities.[73] In November 1935 Willi Bredel left for Prague and Paris

68. Beer, "Memoirs."

69. There were colonies of writers in Leningrad, Kharkov, and Engels, but they were populated almost exclusively by Soviet German writers (see Chapter 6).

70. See note 45.

71. "Adam Scharrer-Abend," *Deutsche Zentral-Zeitung*, 28 February 1938.

72. Cf. Bredel (Moscow) to Plivier (Leningrad), 9 March 1935, TsGALI, 631/13/69/45; Plivier (Paulskoje) to Bredel (Moscow), 23 October 1936, TsGALI, 631/12/143/481.

73. See Bredel to Max Reimann, 7 October 1935, TsGALI, 631/13/69/107.

"on the orders of the Comintern," returning to Moscow in April 1936.[74] An invitation from a Western organization occasionally sufficed to obtain an exit visa. Friedrich Wolf visited the United States in spring 1935 as a guest of the First American Writers' Congress.[75] He actually seems to have had fewer problems obtaining permission to leave the USSR than he had receiving an American entry visa, which the U.S. embassy in Helsingfors was loathe to give him as a Communist.[76]

In 1937 Becher attempted to leave the USSR to attend the Second International Writers' Congress for the Defense of Culture in Valencia. In early April he asked Heinrich Mann to press for his invitation to the congress, an invitation that Mann assumed "would be forthcoming anyway." But there seems to have been resistance to Becher's plans to leave the USSR. On 25 May 1937 Mann apprised Becher that he would continue to work for an invitation and, evidently at Becher's request, agreed to write Dimitroff about the matter. A few days later, though, Becher received this word from Lion Feuchtwanger, whom he had also approached: "In the meantime I have suggested in rather influential quarters that you be invited to Spain," wrote Feuchtwanger; "I was also told that my request would be considered, but, to tell the truth, I don't have the feeling that anything will come of it." Finally, in June, Mann notified Becher: "Someone who ought to know told me a short time ago: 'B. is not coming.' I was unable to find out how I am supposed to take that. . . . It seems more important to me that an influential personality from over there [Moscow] designate or suggest you."[77]

74. Bredel to Alexander Barta (Parteizelle MORP), 20 November 1935, TsGALI, 631/13/69/127; Bredel to Oskar Maria Graf (Czechoslovakia), 5 May 1936, TsGALI, 631/12/152/321. Bredel worked in the Thälmann-Komitee in Paris and would have returned earlier, but had to wait "weeks" for his Soviet entry visa (Bredel to Gustav Regler [Paris], 5 May 1936, TsGALI, 631/12/143/523).

75. Pollatschek, *Friedrich Wolf*, p. 211.

76. Ibid., p. 213. Wolf had also hoped to attend the 1939 Writers' Congress in the United States, but the American embassy in Paris denied him a visa because of his political affiliation (even though Wolf had been invited by the League of American Writers). He was told that inquiries first had to be made about his past life in Germany, and the embassy actually contacted Nazi authorities in Stuttgart for information about Wolf. It is interesting to note, on the other hand, that in 1935 and again in 1939 Wolf evaded questions about his party membership. To the question of whether he was "a Communist" Wolf replied: "Here abroad I belong to no political party, but solely to the Association of German Writers [SDS], to which Thomas Mann, Franz Werfel, Feuchtwanger, and others also belong" (Wolf-Archiv, Mappe 380/1). Of course Wolf was a party member.

77. Mann to Becher, 2 April 1937, Becher-Archiv, Sig. 57; Mann to Becher, 25 May

Others applied for trips through the KPD office within the Comintern's Executive Committee. Andor Gábor filed on 6 February 1936 for permission to visit Czechoslovakia, France, and Holland to write a book on the Reichstag fire.[78] He was apparently turned down. In late March 1937, through the foreign office of the Soviet Writers' Union, Friedrich Wolf requested authorization for a trip abroad to collect material for his literary work, to assist in preparation of the writers' congress in Valencia (Wolf had an invitation from René Blech),[79] and to negotiate with publishers and theaters in various countries regarding productions of his plays.[80] Wolf hoped to travel by 10 April 1937, explaining that his German passport expired in January 1938.[81] A month later he renewed his request in a letter to Wilhelm Pieck in the presidium of the Comintern, asking for a two-month trip to Stockholm, Copenhagen, London, and Paris.[82] His request was backed by a letter from Apletin of the foreign office, in which, among other things, Apletin informed Pieck that as far as the congress was concerned "the character of these preparations is known to us and we are of the opinion that Comrade Wolf's trip and his participation in the preparations are absolutely necessary."[83] Wolf was not allowed to leave until the start of the new year, and he arrived in Paris in early January.[84]

1937, Becher-Archiv, Sig. 59; Feuchtwanger to Becher, 27 May 1937, Becher-Archiv, Sig. 30; Mann to Becher, 7 June 1937, Becher-Archiv, Sig. 60. There is some indication that Becher, as early as December 1936, was thinking of leaving the USSR—and not just for a brief stay abroad. He received a letter from Klaus Mann in mid-December that contained this remark: "I have thought about what kind of possibilities there would be for you here. If you don't know English *fluently* it will be difficult. Lectures are the only possibility that one has as a writer, and they have to be given in decent English" (TsGALI, 631/11/410/13). One wonders if the refusal to allow Becher to attend the Writers' Congress in Spain was in some way connected with the apprehension that he might not return to the Soviet Union.

78. Andor Gábor an die Vertretung der KPD beim EKKI, 6 February 1936, MTA, Gábor Andor-Hagyaték, Ms. 4490/39.

79. Preparations for the congress were being made in Paris.

80. The letter made no mention of the Spanish civil war, as Pollatschek, *Friedrich Wolf*, p. 131, clearly implies, and it is not entirely certain that at this time Wolf indeed intended to go to Spain.

81. Wolf to the Deutsche Kommission im Sowjetischen Schriftstellerverband and to the Sektion Dramatik im Sowjetschriftstellerverband, 22 March 1937, Wolf-Archiv, Mappe 300 S.

82. Wolf to Pieck (Presidium Komintern), 22 April 1937, ibid. That Wolf applied only for a two-month trip would seem to indicate that he did not originally intend to go to Spain.

83. Apletin to Pieck, 22 April 1937, ibid.

84. On 31 December 1937 Wolf notified Leonard and Ann Mins that his *Politstelle* had

Instead of Becher, the Soviet Writers' Union chose Willi Bredel and Erich Weinert as delegates to the writers' congress in Valencia meeting in July 1937. Weinert left Moscow in February 1937, while Bredel departed at the end of May.[85] The pair spent most of June in Paris, reaching Valencia on 1 July 1937. After the congress Weinert and Bredel remained in Spain, in Bredel's (and probably Weinert's) case, "with the agreement of the German party and the representative of the Comintern."[86] Bredel joined the Thälmann Battalion of the International Brigades as war commissar at the end of July. In April 1938 he began efforts to return to the Soviet Union,[87] and after more than a year in Paris, he arrived back in Moscow in July 1939.

Obtaining a return visa to the USSR was invariably problematical. Long waits were usually involved, and in Weinert's case this might have cost him several months in a French concentration camp, where he was interned in February 1939. Weinert had applied for an entry visa in December from Spain, according to a letter he wrote in Barcelona to Alfred Kantorowicz in Paris: "My departure was not as rapid as Willi had imagined. It turned out that the friends [party officials] here did not even pass on my application for over there, which I filed in December. Now I hear from my wife that Wilhelm [Pieck] had heard not a word. He said that he would set everything in motion but that I would have to expect a wait of two to three months. Have fun! The situation is now this: the friends here say that the visa for over there is the concern of the friends in P[aris]. But in order to travel to P., it's necessary for me to have a brief, legal stay where you are."[88] In February 1939—the Spanish civil war was over and the International Brigades were dissolved—Weinert, still waiting for his visa, was placed in the French camp St. Cyprien, where he remained until his return to Moscow in the fall.

Wolf, on the other hand, never made it to Spain, and in late 1938

---

consented to his trip (Wolf-Archiv, Mappe 280/1/3). It is curious that approval of Wolf's journey came through just as his passport was about to expire. In the meantime, Wolf had evidently decided that, apart from his other business, he did in fact wish to reach Spain and work there as a doctor. He wrote the Mins on 2 October 1937: "I am working quietly alone on my novel, upset that I can't get to the land of oranges and work there as an old battalion doctor, helping my friends" (ibid.).

85. Willi Bredel, "Bericht" (probably to the Comintern), no date [summer 1939], Bredel-Archiv, Sig. 252/14; Preuss, *Erich Weinert*, p. 103.

86. Bredel, "Bericht," Bredel-Archiv, Sig. 252/14.

87. Bredel, *Spanienkrieg*, 2:371.

88. Weinert (Barcelona) to Kantorowicz (Paris), no date [early 1939], TsGALI, 631/13/63/16. Kantorowicz apparently forwarded the letter to Moscow.

he began thinking of a return to the Soviet Union.[89] A year later he had firm plans to depart for Moscow in October,[90] but on 3 September France declared war on Germany. A few weeks later Wolf, while waiting for his documents for Russia, was taken into custody by the French, who put him in the Le Vernet internment camp. Else Wolf wrote Leonard Mins in the United States: "Since 16 September I have no news of Wolf. His last short postcard said that the same day he was writing he, along with many other friends, had to enter 'un centre de rassemblement.' . . . Even though he had already applied [for a Soviet entry visa], he didn't have enough time anymore to make it back here. At first I tried to speed up the matter for a while. But now I've given it up since it could possibly do him more harm than good."[91]

Wolf remained in the camp through 1940. In the Soviet Union, Else Wolf, Vishnevskij, Pieck, Manuilskij, and Losovskij of the Soviet Foreign Ministry apparently began working in late summer 1940 on Wolf's Soviet citizenship as a means of getting him out of France and back to Russia. By early August 1940, a decision was reached to grant Wolf certain entry papers,[92] but the documents seem not to have included naturalization certificates, without which the French refused to allow him to leave the country. Wolf described the situation from Le Vernet on 27 August 1940: "In the meantime I received the (Soviet) visa. But yesterday I was told here officially that, according to the conditions of the cease fire, prisoners of German origin . . . are not allowed to leave France. Either they will be handed over [to the Germans] or kept further in the camp. Till war's end. That's how serious the situation is."[93]

A few months later, almost a year to the day of Wolf's internment,

89. See Wolf to Leonard Mins, 25 April 1938, Wolf-Archiv, Mappe 380/1/3; Wolf to Mins, 26 May 1938, ibid. In a 12 November 1938 letter to Mins, Wolf wrote: "The situation is thus: either I must soon return to Mecca (though I don't even have any papers for that, and the time it takes to get a visa is unforeseeable) or I want in the meantime to attend the Writers' Congress [in the United States]" (ibid.).

90. Wolf to Margret Strub, 27 August 1939, Wolf-Archiv, Mappe 332/1.

91. Else Wolf to the Mins, 22 October 1939, Wolf-Archiv, Mappe 280/1/1. See also her letter of 22 June 1940: "Unfortunately to the present day I have been unable to do anything for Wolf. I am very upset about that, but often one encounters difficulties where one doesn't expect them. In my letter I cannot explain it all to you. But as soon as I find out where Wolf is I'll start trying everything again" (ibid.).

92. Telegramm des Volkskommissars für Auswärtige Angelegenheiten der UdSSR an die Politische Vertretung der UdSSR in Vichy, 8 August 1940, Wolf-Archiv, Mappe 248/5–7.

93. Wolf (Le Vernet) to Strub (?), 27 August 1940, Wolf-Archiv, Mappe 332/1.

the Soviet Foreign Ministry urged that the question of Wolf's citizenship be put before the presidium of the Supreme Soviet. "Agreement has been reached," the foreign ministry wrote, "concerning the expeditious and simplified resolution of the matter of granting F. Wolf citizenship of the USSR."[94] The question was settled, and two weeks later Losovskij, in the foreign ministry, wired the Soviet legation in Vichy with these instructions: "Friedrich Wolf has been granted Soviet citizenship. Approach Boduin in the foreign ministry [of Vichy France] and demand the release of the Soviet citizen Friedrich Wolf and the necessary visas for his departure to the USSR. Give him his Soviet passport and send him by a southern route to Moscow."[95] The news reached Wolf within a week or so. On 7 October 1940 he was released from camp,[96] and several days later he wrote Margret Strub in Switzerland that as "homeward-bound Soviet citizens" he and a group of other repatriates were "in principle" free.[97] But not all of the obstacles had yet been cleared away, for the homeward-bound Soviet citizens were forced to wait in another French camp. In early December 1940 Wolf received his Soviet passport, but it lacked the necessary transit visas.[98] Now the days of waiting stretched into weeks as Wolf and ninety others—from Bessarabia, Lithuania, and Estonia (territories acquired by the Soviet Union while the German-Soviet Pact was in effect)—were forced to remain in a camp in Carpiagne and in Les Milles near Marseille, where conditions were not much improved over Le Vernet.[99] On 22 January 1941 Wolf wrote: "Yes, we are still here. Now the hunger is becoming downright agonizing. I can no longer do or think about anything worthwhile. . . . That is only to be expected from water soup and 300 grams of bread twice a day, especially during the last beastly cold spell. Before I was always one of the strongest and most healthy. For the first time in my life I now find myself getting dizzy frequently and weak-kneed."[100]

In early March (two hundred men were now in the group) the trip

94. Brief des Volkskommissariats für Auswärtige Angelegenheiten an die Abteilung für Visa und Registrierung der Hauptverwaltung RKM des Volkskommissars für innere Angelegenheiten, 11 September 1940, Wolf-Archiv, Mappe 248/5–7.

95. Telegramm des stellvertretenden Volkskommissars für Auswärtige Angelegenheiten der UdSSR, Losowski, S.A. an die Politische Vertretung der UdSSR in Vichy, 26 September 1940, ibid.

96. Emmi Oprecht to Leonard Mins, 8 October 1940, Wolf-Archiv, Mappe 380/1/1.

97. Wolf to Strub, 16 October 1940, Wolf-Archiv, Mappe 332/1.

98. Wolf (Camp Les Milles) to Lola Humm-Bernau, 2 December 1940, Wolf-Archiv, Mappe S 380.

99. Wolf (Les Milles) to Strub (?), 3 November 1940, Wolf-Archiv, Mappe 332/1.

100. Wolf (Les Milles) to Strub (?), 22 January 1941, Wolf-Archiv, Mappe 332.

back to the Soviet Union finally began by way of Italy, Yugoslavia, Hungary, and the Ukraine.[101] On 20 March Wolf wrote Strub: "It has now finally come true. I am home. The trip was more than interesting through all the countries. And now here! So much is new."[102]

101. In Italy Wolf was almost pulled from the train by the Italian police. See Pollatschek, *Friedrich Wolf*, p. 277.
102. Wolf to Strub, 20 March 1941, Wolf-Archiv, Mappe 332.

Chapter 4

The United Front Reborn, 1933–1935

The German Communists and the Comintern in the months follow-ing the events of January-February 1933 saw no reason to alter the line that they had pursued since 1929. Valdemar Knorin, in a speech given in December 1933 at the ECCI's Thirteenth Plenum in Moscow, insisted that "our analysis has been upheld from year to year; we have had to change nothing."[1] He conceded only that fascism had tempo-rarily gained the day in Germany; however, it represented nothing more than a piecemeal victory of reaction carrying within itself the seeds of its own demise. Reaffirming their belief that the contradic-tions of monopoly capitalism had impelled the bourgeoisie to hand over "governmental power to fascism"[2] and that various economic, social, and political ills would soon ravage the entire system, the Com-munists predicted that in accordance with immutable economic laws the entire capitalist world was approaching a "new phase of revolu-tions and wars." These events in Germany, said Fritz Heckert in early 1933, were "an important step in the maturation of a revolutionary crisis in the center of Europe and in the advent of definitive battles between labor and capital."[3] The "obvious" politics of the financial oligarchy on the eve of the new phase of revolution and war, Knorin reiterated, had to be fascism—"this last desperate attempt of the most reactionary, terroristic, nationalistic portion of the bourgeoisie to hold on to state power . . . this try at finding a way out of the crisis by way of heightened preparation for a new imperialist war" (9). Far from a

1. Knorin, *Faschismus, Sozialdemokratie, und Kommunismus*, p. 5. Subsequent page ref-erences appear in the text in parentheses.
2. Pieck, *We are Fighting for a Soviet Germany*, p. 6.
3. Fritz Heckert, *Was geht in Deutschland vor*, p. 3. Subsequent page references appear in the text in parentheses.

sign of strength, the present wave of fascism was a manifestation of vulnerability and decrepitude. What had transpired in Germany Heckert defined as the "dying quivers of capitalism, not its 'stabilization' " (14)

The KPD-Comintern emphasized adamantly that prior to 1933 everything in the Communists' power had been done to prevent fascism; but in view of the given alignment of class forces at the time of the takeover (Social Democracy had ruptured the proletariat) the Communists had simply lacked the power to challenge the Fascists openly in a bid for power through proletarian revolution. Because of the disadvantageous correlation of forces, events had culminated in what Heckert referred to as a "temporary setback of the proletariat," not a defeat, for the proletariat "has not capitulated and will not capitulate to fascism." Any talk of a defeat or of the extermination of the KPD Heckert branded the "gossip of philistines" (10–12).

Fascism had not been unavoidable; its victory, Knorin stressed, "is only unavoidable or possible in those instances where Social Democracy is successful in warding off its proletarian supporters . . . from forming a revolutionary united front with the Communists." Knorin held that fascism could not emerge victorious in a single country without the "direct subvention of Social Democracy, which has long split the proletariat in half" (10–11). But precisely because reformism had devitalized the proletariat, Heckert reasoned, a frightened German bourgeoisie, scared by the militant spirit of the Communist portion of the proletariat, had taken the chance to strengthen its political position by giving the reins of power to the NSDAP, the one party most hostile to the working class. Hence, the KPD had been unable to go for broke in a try for power during the critical years immediately preceding the Nazi takeover.

The Communists argued that Social Democrats bore sole responsibility for the disaster of 1933, for time and again the reformist party bosses had refused KPD united front entreaties. Knorin felt that in the struggle against the bourgeoisie and fascism a united front would now be created forthwith if only the Social Democrats had the will to fight against the Nazis. Indeed, the united front would be forged even against the desires of the socialist chiefs just as soon as the workers convinced themselves that their leaders had surrendered labor interests wholesale to the Fascists. Knorin also charged that "the positive aspect of our united front strategy in Germany has perennially been that our German comrades always told the Social Democratic workers the truth about their party and habitually pointed out correctly the right way to go" (28).

When the Nazis outlawed the SPD in the summer of 1933, the

Communists were forced to explain the fact that in Germany the SPD was likewise being repressed and that the KPD was not the only party to have a systematic campaign of terror waged against it. Heckert explained that Social Democratic *workers* were being persecuted, not leaders; if the party itself was made the object of persecution, he thought, then this was so only because it was being beaten like a "loyal but invalid dog," beaten for the simple reason that it was too weak to strike back. After the blows, however, it would be more pliant and ready to serve its master, the bourgeois dictatorship, even in its open Fascist form (27–28). Knorin said that, in order for the Fascists to suppress the workers, it had been necessary to come down hard on the Communist party. But in view of the acute situation in Germany, the SPD, and especially the reformist labor unions, had become a meeting ground for elements unhappy with fascism. That was why the Fascists had chosen to destroy Social Democracy (12).

The Communists now pressed ahead with their argument that the worsening conjuncture of capitalism in its Fascist form had spawned growing insurrectionary sentiment within the masses. The revolutionary tide in Germany, the party said, was rising, with Knorin insisting, "We are approaching the revolution" (25). Fascism was on the brink of economic collapse, and the NSDAP had nothing more to offer the masses. The overthrow of the Nazi regime hinged only on Communist success in destroying the last vestiges of reformist influence in Germany and on winning the majority of the proletariat. For only the consolidation of the workers as a revolutionary class power, Heckert stressed, would "accelerate the process by which these strata of the peasantry and the urban petty bourgeoisie are deserting fascism" (15). The disappointment of the masses and their abandonment of fascism was "unavoidable" (18).[4]

Concluding his report, Heckert summed up the Communist position in the twelve- to fourteen-month period following Hitler's assumption of the chancellorship. The views of the KPD had been altogether correct because first, the Communists had made ample allowances for the rapid rise of the Fascists and had mobilized the masses to meet the danger; second, they had steadfastly maintained a course aimed at drawing the broad masses of Social Democratic and nonparty workers into the anti-Fascist front; and third, under the new conditions of unprecedented Fascist terror, they had reorganized and regrouped with "comparatively minimal losses." The fighting spirit of the Com-

4. The official Communist view of developments in Germany during 1933 was now reminiscent of Heinz Neumann's opinions in 1931 and 1932.

munist party had not been broken, and under the banner of a united working class the Communists would lead the proletariat unwaveringly to final victory over fascism and capitalism. (36).[5]

In the course of 1934, the gradual realization that Nazi Germany posed a grave military threat to Russia finally precipitated a major reassessment of Soviet foreign policy and Comintern ultraextremism.[6] For most of 1933 the Soviets had done their best to persuade Germany's new rulers to continue the country's eastern orientation (the policy of Rapallo) that had been in force since 1922. Convinced that practical politics rather than ideological considerations would win out in Nazi foreign policy, the Soviets tended to take Hitler's revanchism with respect to the Treaty of Versailles and particularly France more seriously than his antibolshevism, refusing to believe in any case that German foreign policy could be both anti-Soviet and revanchist. A full year passed before Stalin, at the Seventeenth Party Congress, made his first public pronouncement on developments in Germany; he professed to see no cause for a change in the relationship that Russia had shared with Germany from 1922 to 1933. He stated plainly: "Some politicians say that the USSR has now taken an orientation towards France and Poland; that from an opponent of the Versailles treaty it has become a supporter of that treaty, and that this change is to be explained by the establishment of the fascist regime in Germany. That is not true. Of course, we are far from being enthusiastic about the fascist regime in Germany. But fascism is not the issue here, if only for the reason that fascism in Italy, for instance, has not prevented the USSR from establishing the best relations with that country."[7]

Germany ignored the bait, however, and Stalin, now persuaded that a deal with Hitler would not likely be struck at this time, presided over the first radical revision of Soviet foreign policy since Rapallo. As the German menace became clearer in the minds of Soviet leaders, Stalin, whose major consideration was the avoidance of Soviet entanglement in a war, directed efforts to end Russia's increasingly dangerous diplomatic isolation. In November 1933 the USSR gained diplomatic recognition from the United States; it established normal relations with Czechoslovakia, Rumania, and Bulgaria the next summer. Sep-

---

5. See also Weingartner, *Stalin und der Aufstieg Hitlers*, pp. 197–252, who places the ideological stance within the context of Soviet foreign policy.
6. Cf. Ulam, *Expansion and Coexistence*, pp. 183–234; Deutscher, *Stalin*, pp. 414–26; Weingartner, *Stalin und der Aufstieg Hitlers*, pp. 197–274.
7. Deutscher, *Stalin*, p. 415.

tember ushered in the most thoroughgoing change yet, Russia's entrance into the League of Nations. For years the Soviets had heaped abuse upon the League (Lenin called it the "Robbers' Den") as an organization dominated by Russia's two greatest "imperialist" enemies, Great Britain and France. The hope now, as Stalin remarked, was that the League might be useful as an impediment to aggression. During the next year, 1935, Soviet Russia completed its reorientation as Stalin became the prime advocate of collective security and pursued protective alliances with the Western nations, signing mutual assistance pacts with France and Czechoslovakia.

The Comintern, in compliance with the new Soviet foreign policy, introduced the most sweeping revision of its program since the organization came into being. The left-extremist verbiage of 1928–34 gradually faded away. It was replaced with a reborn united front policy enhanced by a new dimension—the united front of socialists and Communists was extended into an anti-Fascist popular front of all parties, organizations, and coteries opposed to Hitler. The new strategy received its primary stimulus in France, where in February 1934 Communists and socialists acted in unison to organize a strike and demonstration in protest against what was felt to be a rising right-wing threat in France. The new spirit of cooperation there continued through 1935, taking in the center party, and eventually crested in 1936 in the French *Front populaire* led by Léon Blum.[8] The initial success of the strategy in France in 1934 encouraged exponents of the new line in Moscow to push for its application elsewhere. Borkenau depicts Manuilskij as the chief behind-the-scenes advocate of a united front and primary intercessor with Stalin, and he deprecates the celebrated Dimitroff as Manuilskij's marionette. Ravines, on the other hand, contends that Manuilskij was phlegmatic about the new line and that Dimitroff was in fact the driving force behind the shift.[9] Whatever the precise nature of Manuilskij's role, Dimitroff seems to have been more than a lackey in designing and promoting the new strategy. A letter written to Henri Barbusse in May 1934 by Alfred Kurella, Dimitroff's secretary at the time, highlights Dimitroff's role in persuading Stalin of the advisability of the new tactics: "Quite an intimate relationship has developed between the professor [Dimitroff] and the patron [Stalin]. You'll have no trouble understanding the deeper significance of this fact, particularly after what I already told you about the growth of breadth and depth in his field of vision,

8. See Borkenau, *European Communism*, pp. 221–33.
9. Ibid., pp. 227–28; Ravines, *The Yenan Way*, pp. 113–16 and 145–46.

which the professor's affair provided him.[10] Presently the professor will again assume his place in our great university [the Comintern]. I haven't the slightest doubt that he will soon be the leading figure there. That too without comment. A new wind . . . and so on."[11]

But any final decisions about the application of the new line other than in France had to come eventually from Stalin, of course, who declined to commit himself in late 1934, preferring to await definite signs of success of the tactics in France before he became involved. In the meantime, uncertainty about Stalin's intentions created a rupture within the KPD leadership.[12] Advocates of the old radicalism (Wilhelm Florin, Hermann Schubert, Fritz Schulte, Fritz Heckert, and, at the beginning, Franz Dahlem) resisted the arguments of proponents of a policy shift[13] and in mid-October 1934 succeeded for one last time in openly attacking the new trend, the principal spokesmen of which were now Pieck and Ulbricht. In late October, however, the Comintern stepped in and quelled the opposition, calling for an end to its "left-sectarian" obstruction of a united front from above. By January 1935 the Ulbricht-Pieck forces had won the unconditional support of the Comintern, which directed the KPD to adopt the new course and make suitable united front overtures both to the Sopade (the new Social Democratic executive in Prague) and to left-wing socialist groups.

When the Seventh World Congress of the Comintern met with much fanfare in August 1935 in Moscow, followed by the KPD's "Brüsseler Konferenz" held on the outskirts of the Soviet capital in October, the united and popular front was officialized. How substantive were the changes in the Comintern program? Dimitroff's speech leaves little room for doubt about the Communists' ulterior motives. Granted, for the first time ever there was a professed appreciation for the "freedoms of democracy": Dimitroff announced that Communists would "defend in the capitalist countries every inch of bourgeois-democratic liberties, which are being attacked by fascism and bourgeois reaction."[14] Yet this by no means presaged a fresh approach to

---

10. This is probably a reference to Dimitroff's Leipzig trial, which had made him famous the world over and fashioned his name into a symbol around which all those opposed to Hitler could rally.

11. Klein, *Schriftsteller in der französischen Volksfront*, p. 55.

12. See Duhnke, *Die KPD von 1933 bis 1945*, pp. 145–50.

13. Wehner, "Erinnerungen," p. 79.

14. Georgi Dimitroff, "Die Offensive des Faschismus und die Aufgaben der Kommunistischen Internationale im Kampf für die Einheit der Arbeiterklasse gegen den Faschismus," in *VII Kongress der Kommunistischen Internationale: Protokoll*, p. 145.

democracy, for now as before the Communists regarded "Soviet democracy" as the only true democratic form of government. The Seventh Congress resolved that, in fighting for the defense of bourgeois-democratic liberties and the gains of the working class against fascism, the revolutionary proletariat would "gather its forces, consolidate its militant ties with its allies, and direct the struggle towards the goal of establishing the true democracy of the toilers—Soviet power." [15] The major "concession," such as it was, involved a postponement of proletarian dictatorship, which, the Communists now said, did not necessarily have to come on the heels of Hitler's collapse. But it was just a postponement. Dimitroff asked the socialists, "Are we offering you today a united front for the purpose of proclaiming the dictatorship of the proletariat? *We make no such proposal now.*" [16] For the purpose of gaining allies, the Communists insisted that this was not their concern—*for the moment.* [17]

Circumstances called urgently for a proletarian united front and its expansion into an anti-Fascist popular front to ward off the Nazi menace, the Communists argued. But not even for the sake of genuine cooperation were they willing to budge an inch from their real objectives. The "new" line called for Communists to join hands with socialists, but only on Communist terms. Said Dimitroff, "Only the Communist party is in the final analysis the initiator, the organizer, and the driving force of the united front of the working class." Social Democracy, after all, the Communists still maintained, was to be held fully accountable for Hitler since the Social Democratic leaders had "glossed over and concealed from the masses the true class nature of fascism." Therefore, said Dimitroff, they bore the "great *historical responsibility* for the fact that at the decisive moment of the Fascist offensive a large section of the working people of Germany . . . failed to recognize in fascism bloodthirsty, rapacious finance capital, their most vicious enemy, and that these masses were not prepared to resist it." [18]

Could united front action lead to some sort of united or popular

15. "Resolution zum Bericht Georgi Dimitroffs," ibid., p. 576.

16. My italics. Dimitroff, "Die Offensive des Faschismus," pp. 144–45.

17. Pieck said at the KPD's Brüsseler Konferenz in October: "If we undertake a turn, that does not indicate that we no longer propagate our revolutionary final objective; rather, it indicates that we make such proposals in our struggle for our partial objective, for the collapse of the Fascist dictatorship, suited to winning all those segments for the struggle which are not yet convinced of the correctness of the Communist program, indeed, which are perhaps even opposed to it." Pieck, *Der neue Weg zum gemeinsamen Kampfe*, pp. 132–33.

18. Dimitroff, "Die Offensive des Faschismus," p. 128.

front government? This was a possibility, explained Dimitroff, as a transitional phase climaxing in Soviet power. Yes, the Communists would support an anti-Fascist united front government, if such a government would "*really*" prosecute the struggle against the "enemies of the people and give a free hand to the working class and the Communist party." But Dimitroff was clear on the crux of the matter. "*Final salvation* this government *cannot* bring," he argued. "It is not in a position to overthrow the class rule of the exploiters, and for this reason cannot finally remove the danger of Fascist counterrevolution. Consequently, it is necessary *to prepare for the socialist revolution. Soviet power* and only *Soviet power* can bring salvation."[19]

In other words, the Communists would join in a post-Hitler united or popular front government formed through united action with socialists and anti-Fascists. But somewhere along the line the Communists could be relied upon to withdraw their support and to spare no effort to topple the very coalition government they helped set up in the first place as a means of gaining a toehold on power. Dimitroff did not indicate openly how the Communists would then treat erstwhile allies who resisted, but in private he remarked to Eudocio Ravines, "Remember that all our concessions are only temporary. Don't forget that we communists are fighting for the world revolution. When it triumphs the steel columns of communism will march over the bodies of those same people who now hasten to offer us their protection. It cannot be helped. It is an inescapable consequence."[20]

The whole of the Communist program of alliances was a simulacrum, as later developments would prove. The old tactics for a successful bid for power had foundered, so new stratagems were developed. But the same single-mindedness of purpose, arrogant sense of infallibility, and unyielding will to power remained ingrained in the party, coupled now (this was the only novelty) with a certain "realism." Dimitroff intoned, "We must learn to combine the great teachings of Marx-Engels-Lenin-Stalin *with Stalinist determination* in work and in battle; *with Stalinist irreconcilability of principle* toward the class enemy and renegades from the line of bolshevism; *with Stalinist intrepidity in the face of difficulties; with Stalinist revolutionary realism.*"[21]

How, in 1935, did the Communists define the nature of National Socialism? Had their perceptions of nazism undergone any meaning-

---

19. Ibid., p. 179.
20. Ravines, *The Yenan Way*, p. 161.
21. Georgi Dimitroff, "Für die Einheit der Arbeiterklasse gegen den Faschismus, (Schlusswort)," in *VII Kongress der Kommunistischen Internationale: Protokoll*, p. 376.

ful change as compared to 1933–34, or even 1931–32? The most extensive statement in these years about National Socialism, and one that best illustrates official thinking, came from the pen of Hans Günther. In 1935 he completed his book *Der Herren eigener Geist*[22] and submitted the manuscript to VEGAAR in Moscow, whose editors were reticent to assume responsibility for the book's publication. The manuscript passed from one authority to another until it finally crossed the desk of Dimitroff, who, as Trude Richter tells the story, read it from cover to cover in one night and penciled the remark in the margin, "Publish immediately in four languages."[23] The book came out in an enormous printing, apparently just in time for the Seventh World Congress.[24]

Günther takes the customary tack that capitalism in the nineteen-twenties had been racked by a series of acute worldwide economic cataclysms that portended its doom. The only way out of the crisis—this Günther identifies as one of two "dominant tasks of fascism"—was an economic-political crusade against the proletariat, not only within national boundaries, but also around the world in the confrontation between capitalism and socialism. The second task of fascism was preparation on an international scale for the impending "new world war as the bourgeoisie's 'way out' of the crisis of capitalism" (15). This was all a historical inevitability that could never have been averted by "democracy," for every form of state was wholly dependent on the economic conditions upholding it, and those conditions in the twenties in Germany had reached the stage of monopoly capitalism. In other words, advanced capitalism *was* reaction, and with the passage of time the reactionary transmutation of Weimar democracy became

22. Günther, *Der Herren eigener Geist*. Subsequent page references appear in the text in parentheses.
23. Richter, *Die Plakette*, p. 261.
24. The edition was for 14,500 copies. The stenographic report of the Seventh World Congress, for the purpose of comparison, had a printing of only 2,400. Richter claimed (in *Die Plakette*, p. 262, and in conversations with me) that Dimitroff referred to Günther's book during his speech at the Seventh World Congress. I have been unable to find any reference to Günther either in Dimitroff's major speech in the versions published before Günther's arrest in late 1936 or in any other speeches made in 1935 or 1936, though he perhaps made oral reference to the book during his speech in front of the assembly. In any case, there is little doubt that *Der Herren eigener Geist* was viewed as the Comintern's standard work on the subject of National Socialist ideology until Günther's arrest. That view, incidentally, was carried over to East German literary history: "[Günther's book] written as early as 1934, accorded with the demands of the Communist International made at the Seventh World Congress" (see *Lexikon sozialistischer deutscher Literatur*, p. 206).

identical with the process of its fascistization. Freedom and equality within the democracy deteriorated to mere decoration as the state apparatus was fascistized from within, the essential institutions of fascism taking shape long before the curtain lifted to reveal that all power had accrued to the representatives of the "most reactionary, chauvinistic, and imperialistic elements of finance capitalism" (25).

None of this differs from the standard party view of 1928–34. Nor does Günther in any way alter the common assessment of Social Democracy, to which he ascribed a major role in the fascistization of the republic. Since the reformist bosses were inextricably linked to the fate of decaying German capitalism and wedded to a democracy relentlessly being fascistized, the reformists unavoidably became the hirelings of fascism by performing their duties of breaking Social Democratic and Communist strikes, carrying out programs of wage reductions, suppressing the Communist press, and so on. These were the facts that gave the Communists every right to "distinguish sharply between the leadership and the following of the SPD" (29).

Certainly there was "*much* that separates Social Democracy from fascism," (30), Günther conceded, for reformism had at its behest an altogether different " 'clientele,' " the Social Democratic worker; but the SPD put this clientele indirectly into the service of the ruling class, and on it the pre-Hitler form of capitalist dictatorship based itself. Democracy and fascism were undeniably different, but they were really only two different forms of rule by the same bourgeoisie, and the fight between them was a struggle to stay in the good graces of the same master. It was not just that Social Democracy had capitulated to its Fascist rival, but to its own detriment it had even undertaken to keep its rival's real enemy, the legitimate revolutionary force in the country, off the back of the bourgeoisie. Social Democracy thus gave fascism an open field of activity and even delivered the proletariat into the hands of the Fascist dictatorship. To assert that the SPD and the NSDAP were not identical, Günther averred, stopped short of full disclosure of the truth, for "they were *not allowed* to resemble each other; they *had* to appear at sword's point, else they would not have been able to carry out the *same* class commission. The *semblance* of an underlying hostility was the most valuable aspect of the entire affair" (33).

If democracy was no less an instrument of power in the hands of trust capitalism than the later Fascist state, what induced the ruling class to change over to fascism? Hitler, Günther explained, was a nullity; what precipitated the transition from democracy to fascism was the existence of an "instigator," the Communist party, that forced the bourgeoisie to leave the grounds of democracy. The growth of the

KPD and its rising influence on Social Democratic workers and the response from them in fighting off the system of emergency decrees, wage reductions, and Fascist terror—all this forced the bourgeoisie to forgo democracy and reach for the whip: "Fascism is the whip against the rise of the proletariat. Fascism is preventative counterrevolution" (41). On the one hand, the Communist setback of early 1933 came as an outgrowth of the fact that the whole bourgeoisie, including the majority of the lower middle class, had closed ranks behind the leadership of the Fascists; on the other hand, the SPD had ruptured the proletariat, retaining a hold on the majority of the working class and hampering the battle against fascism. A Communist victory in Germany, Günther concluded, demanded that the traitors within their own ranks, the socialists, be neutralized.

In these elaborations there is absolutely nothing original; the novelty of Günther's book is that he proceeded to examine Nazi ideology closely from a party standpoint (for the first time, really), with the intention of tying it in through a basis-superstructure analysis with nazism's political goals. If the bourgeoisie had entrusted National Socialism with the subduel of the burgeoning revolutionary proletariat so as to help the big capitalists over hard times, Günther argued, then the ideological spirit of nazism had to serve an identical purpose; Nazi ideology had to have arisen in contradiction to Marxist tenets and must act to defame, suppress, and belittle Marx's teachings. *"The ideology of fascism is an anti-Marxist 'Weltanschauung,'"* claimed Günther, and *"in ideological terms too fascism is preventative counterrevolution"* (49). The genesis and evolution of Nazi thought therefore had to be seen in terms of its underlying class content; it had to be demonstrated that these ideas sprang " 'organically' from bourgeois, 'democratic liberalistic,' and Social Democratic thought" (50), just as the Nazi dictatorship was born of Weimar's parliamentary democracy. But the paradox encountered in coming to grips with the meaning of Nazi ideology (this is Günther's interpretation) was this: if its essence was procapitalist and anti-Marxist, then it could not possibly be in harmony with the interests of its own mass following. "A reign of terror [was] to be erected *against* the masses *with the help of the masses.* . . . *The victims were to be led astray by the monstrous use of deception"* (55).

Here Günther came across what remained an enigma through 1945 for most Communists, even those in the highest echelons of the party: as a representative of monopoly capitalism, Hitler protected the interests of a tiny minority; whence, then, came his capacity to hold power and attract the support of millions? Whereas most Communist leaders through the thirties—and to the day Hitler fell—

refused to confront squarely the issue of National Socialism's mass backing, attributing its staying power first and foremost to Gestapo terror wielded to subjugate the German people, Günther set out to show how nazism won the minds of the masses, how it succeeded in erecting a "reign of terror" against the masses *with the help of the masses.*" Nationalism and irrationalism, the two staples of Nazi ideology, played the key role in the treachery. Günther wrote that none of the movement's supporters really had anything to gain from Hitler's brand of nationalism; the Nazi promise of liberation from the yoke of Versailles had only one purpose: the elimination of foreign exploitation so as to improve the profit margins of Germany's own national finance capitalists. But under the present conditions of worldwide economic conflicts, spheres of interest, and opposing economic designs, Germany's liberation from Versailles could only be accomplished by imperialist war. National Socialist "liberation" of Germany ultimately came down to a redivision of Europe at the cost of the Soviet Union and other countries. The backbone of Günther's theory was that National Socialism came forth as a counterbalance to Communism, and within that context he determined that "nationalism is an ideological instrument of power in the hands of the trust magnates. Nationalism is the ideology of war" (64). Nazism thus exploited the nationalism of the masses for imperialist purposes. It then followed that the main objective of National Socialist aggression was Soviet Russia, because of its growing influence in all parts of the world and because of the threat that it posed to capitalism.

Günther identified the other keystone of Nazi thinking as the repudiation of rational scientific methods of inquiry and the attachment to irrationalism. He explained, however, that although scientific methods of investigation had to be disparaged, "finance capital" allowed the anathema of reason only with the understanding that the rational development and application of scientific tools would remain in force in the sphere of the natural sciences. For the success of industrial and war technology, productivity, and profits hinged on the effective employment of science. But science was banned from the terrain of the social world, and all scientific thought that sought to comprehend history was thrown out. This obsession with the importance of irrationality served direct political, that is, military ends. Günther cited Hitler: "How do we create the intellectual climate that makes a people willing and able to take up arms" (189)? Irrationalism was the answer —the "spirit of military preparation." Hitler averred that propaganda, used correctly, could convince the people of anything, and herein, Günther concluded, lay the real purpose of irrational Fascist ideology: "*to prepare the people for war on the basis of mass psychology; to rob them of the consciousness of being exploited even while exploitation was intensified; to convince them that 'hell is heaven and that the most miserable of existences is paradise'*" (190).

What indications are there in *Der Herren eigener Geist* of what Pieck called the Comintern's "abrupt turn" in 1935? As for Social Democracy, there is not a word in the book that is remotely placatory to the Sopade,[25] to the left-wing socialists, or to any other non-Communist group.[26] Had Günther at least given lip service to the fact that exiled Social Democracy, even the conservative and cautious Sopade, had undergone certain ideological changes and had he made the slightest acknowlegement of past KPD mistakes, then his disquisition on the failures of Social Democracy *before* 1933 would have been understandable. But in his book Günther was still pleading, in 1935, for a united front from below, claiming that in so doing the Communists were wholly within their rights as sole representatives of working class interests.

How little Günther's political perception of nazism (fascism) had changed from the pre-1933 line can be seen plainly in his fruitless attempt to argue against the deterministic theory of fascism that had paralyzed the Communists in 1931–33. Günther first attacked the spontaneity theory of "false Marxists" who felt that capitalist development in a period of increasing economic upheaval would lead automatically, spontaneously, to an eruption of popular discontent and dissatisfaction. Capitalist economics, said Günther, never led "mechanically and automatically" to changed political circumstances. But he then raised the question of fascism's role in the era of decaying capitalism, maintaining that Communists would be "fatalists" were they to see in fascism the " 'natural' or 'corresponding' " superstructure of monopoly capitalism and, as such, an unavoidable phase in history. Günther thus promptly found himself in the old snare; he was at a loss to explain what, other than fascism, might become the governmental superstructure of monopoly capitalism during the era of advanced capitalism and the advancing proletariat.

The economy at once created the objective conditions for the growth of reaction (capitalism *was* reaction, Günther had said) and for a revolutionary proletarian upsurge; the more acute the economic cri-

---

25. On two occasions Günther even made use of the epithet "social Fascist," by now ostensibly stricken from Communist parlance.
26. Günther's overtures to anti-Fascist intellectuals are discussed in Chapter 5.

sis of capitalism, the more pronounced the growth of reaction and the stronger the forces of fascism. But the more powerful, too, were the armies of communism, which had failed to prevail over fascism and the Fascist bourgeoisie only because of Social Democratic class betrayal. Had Social Democracy not existed, so the argument went, then the Communists would have smashed the Nazis on the way to revolution. But if fascism was not the final stage of capitalism, not its "natural or corresponding" superstructure, as Günther now contended, to whom would the ruling class have turned in order to maintain through violence its hold on power? If not to the National Socialists, the terror arm of the bourgeoisie, then to whom? If the bourgeoisie in the final, moribund stage of capitalism could not resort to a strong Fascist movement, would the system not have crumbled on its own in the light of its inner contradictions and economic upheaval and the solidification of Communist revolutionary resolve? Would capitalism not have disintegrated "spontaneously," given up meekly, without fascism? If not, how would it have resisted? Surely in the absence of fascism—if it was not the final expression of monopoly capitalism—not even Social Democratic class betrayal could have saved the bourgeoise. For the Communists, their dialectic was a *circulus vitiosus* from which they had as much trouble escaping in 1934 and 1935 as in the period between 1931 and 1933. The Communists seemed caught between a theory of spontaneity or a theory of inevitability. Günther rejected both, but offered no real alternative.

Perhaps Günther's most meaningful contributions to Communist thinking were his linkage of National Socialism (not the vague Fascist and capitalist imperialism of previous years) to military preparation against the Soviet Union and his treatment of the uses of Nazi ideology to incite antibolshevism in Germany. This is the original element in the book, for unlike the previous line, which saw France, Great Britain, and the League of Nations as Russia's greatest imperialist enemies, Günther isolated Nazi Germany as the supreme threat to the USSR. Günther and the Communists, then, could not help but see antifascism and the defense of the Soviet Union as one and the same thing; moreover, they demanded this identification unceasingly from all opponents of Hitler, for in the Communists' mind antifascism and anti-Sovietism canceled each other out. But the problem with the application of this equation to the Communist policy of alliances was that now (in late 1935), as in earlier times, the professed objective remained the revolutionary overthrow of Hitler and his replacement with a proletarian dictatorship; the defeat of Hitler and the formation of proletarian dictatorship (perhaps, as Dimitroff hinted, after a brief popular front interlude) were interchangeable goals. Fascist-imperialist politics, Günther quoted Stalin, "would undoubtedly unleash the revolution," to which Günther added: "The victory of the German working class, led by a Communist avant-garde and dressed in the panoply of Marxist-Leninist theory, is unavoidable" (217). The challenge would now be to win for the united and popular front converts who were not put off by these ultimate objectives.

Chapter 5

The Literary United Front

The 1932 reorganization of the International League of Revolutionary Writers, together with Hitler's assumption of the chancellorship a few months later, brought the "antiimperialist" era of Communist cultural politics to an end. During those years, 1921–32, the relationship between official communism and the fellow travelers had been highlighted by the Comintern's sponsorship of two organizations operating for several years at cross purposes: Münzenberg's International Workers' Relief, which since 1921 pursued a consistent policy of courting sympathetic intellectuals; and the IVRS, which from 1927 to 1932 shifted gradually from a sectarian position wholly at variance with the MRP on the question of fellow travelers to an outlook more attuned to the goals of Münzenberg's organization. The synchronization of IVRS and MRP activities was now to come, in 1933 to 1935, when antifascism (now meaning antinazism) replaced antiimperialism as the party watchword.

The MRP had successfully weathered the Comintern's left-extremist storm in 1928–33, indicating unmistakably that influential figures in the Communist hierarchy had little trouble separating the issue of fanatical sectarianism toward Social Democracy, a position defensible at the time both in ideological and foreign policy terms, from the matter of currying favor with liberal bourgeois sympathizers, a policy that ran counter to ideology but offered the Soviet Union and international communism tremendous practical advantages. Even so, there had been Communists who found it difficult to reconcile MRP operations with the radical political line adopted in 1928. Münzenberg, in fact, would have been an easy target in this respect had he not ardently backed the party's left-wing policies.[1] At the KPD's Twelfth

---

1. Münzenberg belonged to the Neumann faction. Münzenberg and Neumann were also bound by family ties of a sort—they had liaisons with sisters Babette Gross and Margarete Buber.

Congress in the summer of 1929 Münzenberg ridiculed his detractors and reaffirmed his political allegiance: "There are also individual comrades who say: for Willi Münzenberg to support the left party line and still head up the MRP and similar organizations, the policies of which are anything but radical, is a contradiction. These people are either very stupid or very superficial. . . . Such united front maneuvers are only practicable if the party adheres to a consistently revolutionary line. . . . The more active we are in the unions, cooperatives, in the MRP, and so on, the more unwavering and uncompromising we must be in complying with the party line."[2]

Having enjoyed high-level party and Comintern backing for his fellow-traveling ventures through the twenties and early thirties, Münzenberg went on to sponsor two congresses in 1932–33 that played a key role in executing the transition from the antiimperialist to the anti-Fascist phase of Communist cultural politics. The shift in emphasis was carried out in the following way. One of Münzenberg's most prominent organizations in the twenties was the League against Imperialism. It was founded in 1927 and served by Albert Einstein and Henri Barbusse as honorary presidents.[3] In 1932 it had been responsible for arranging a round of congresses, conferences, and rallies against "imperialist war," the most important being the Antiwar Congress that Münzenberg and the Comintern, using Romain Rolland and Henri Barbusse as front men, organized in Amsterdam in August 1932.[4] At the Amsterdam congress, attended by over two thousand delegates from twenty-nine different countries, a World Committee against War was set up.[5] This congress turned out to be the last great production of the antiimperialist era, for a few months later Hitler ensconced himself in power. Münzenberg, following consultations in Moscow in January 1933 with Comintern representatives about the future of his "mass organizations," then transferred his base of operations from Berlin to Paris.[6]

2. *Protokoll der Verhandlungen des 12. Parteitages*, p. 198.
3. Cf. Gross, *Willi Münzenberg*, p. 256, and Jorgen Schleimann, "The Organization Man: The Life and Work of Willi Münzenberg," *Survey* 55 (1965): 74.
4. According to Gross, *Willi Münzenberg*, p. 240, Münzenberg's apparat was responsible for $38,000 in costs for the congress. The bill was sent by courier to Moscow and given to Osip Pjatnitskij in the International Liaison Office (OMS) of the Comintern. If this is true, it indicates which branch of the Comintern had responsibility for Münzenberg.
5. Members of the committee included Heinrich Mann, Albert Einstein, and Georgi Dimitroff, who, together with Fritz Heckert, headed the "Communist faction" at the Amsterdam congress. See Langkau-Alex, *Volksfront für Deutschland?*, 1:58, and Klein, *Schriftsteller in der französischen Volksfront*, p. 218.
6. Gross, *Willi Münzenberg*, p. 251.

In the French capital he began laying the groundwork for a new, anti-Fascist congress, and in February 1933 the Comintern, through Communist trade unions, announced plans for this Anti-Fascist Workers' Congress. All labor organizations and individuals "who really want to fight for the cause of the working population against fascism" were invited to attend.[7] The new congress, which evidently lacked even the scanty nonpartisan camouflage of similar past masquerades, met in June 1933 in the Salle Pleyel in Paris and called into existence a Central Committee of Anti-Fascist Workers' Leagues in Europe. The merger a few months later of Amsterdam's World Committee against War with this Central Committee of Anti-Fascist Workers' Leagues to create a single World Committee against War and Fascism (WKKF),[8] commonly known as the Amsterdam-Pleyel movement, marked the transition from an antiimperialist and anticapitalist campaign against the Western powers to an anti-Fascist world crusade against Nazi Germany. Alfred Kurella, whom the Comintern had sent to the Amsterdam congress as a delegate[9] and who acted as secretary for the World Committee against War, served in the same capacity in the WKKF. Henri Barbusse was elected president.[10]

7. Langkau-Alex, *Volksfront für Deutschland?*, 1:57.

8. On the merger see Klein, *Schriftsteller in der französischen Volksfront*, p. 220, and Langkau-Alex, *Volksfront für Deutschland?*, 1:58–59 and 246; the coalescence of the two committees evidently did not go smoothly. Incidentally, Soviet scholars have lately made no secret of the fact that the WKKF was a child of the Comintern. The annotation to a volume of documents (many published for the first time) pertaining to the Seventh World Congress contains the remark that the WKKF worked "in close touch with the Comintern" (*VII kongress Kommunisticheskogo Internatsionala*, p. 521). The WKKF, however, would soon be subordinated to yet another Soviet-sponsored front, the so-called Rassemblement universel pour la Paix (RUP) formed in 1936 at Soviet instigation and with Münzenberg's help. In September some 5,500 delegates to a RUP congress, the World Peace Congress, met in Brussels to call for "peace through the League of Nations" and for "collective security"—all, of course, Soviet foreign policy objectives (see Gross, *Münzenberg*, pp. 296–98). Münzenberg's task, writes Gross, was to inform the "Communist faction" of the WKKF that RUP, not the world committee, was to become the paramount organization of the peace campaign. Gross's claim that the WKKF was told to subordinate itself to RUP is backed up by an internal Comintern resolution of November 1936 (first published in 1975). The WKKF should continue its activity "within the parameters of the general peace movement [RUP]," the Comintern resolved, but it was by no means to "set itself up in opposition to or competition with it." The Soviet commentators added that the WKKF was expected to "find its place" within the broader RUP organization. "Postanovlenie Sekretariata IKKI o Mirovom komitete borby protiv fashizma i vojny," in *VII kongress Kommunisticheskogo Internatsionala*, pp. 449–51, 521.

9. "Gespräch mit Alfred Kurella," pp. 228–9.

10. Kurella had been entrusted in October 1933 with the editorship of Barbusse's journal *Monde* in order to institute a "reorganization" intended to rid the journal of a "band of Trotskyist and Social Democratic journalists." See Kurella's correspondence

The Amsterdam-Pleyel movement soon gathered momentum as many liberal intellectuals disillusioned with the Western response to Hitler came to regard the Soviet Union as the only country ready to back the anti-Fascist front for which they all yearned. In early 1934 Barbusse voiced his hopes for the future of the organization: "The 'Amsterdam-Pleyel Movement,' as I call it, will bring together all who know the danger and who love freedom—socialists, communists, laborites, democrats, liberals, catholics."[11] Barbusse himself did not live to see what became of his vision. He died during a visit to Moscow in late 1935, and his responsibilities as president of the WKKF were assumed by Heinrich Mann.[12]

The birth of the Amsterdam-Pleyel movement coincided with the first steps taken by the International League of Revolutionary Writers toward setting up a united front of writers. From July to September Johannes R. Becher, leaving from Moscow, paid visits to several European cities where German writers were to be found in their new exile. The purpose of his trip was to gather facts, make a reconnaissance of the attitude and disposition of exiled German intellectuals, and evaluate prospects for organization of a "united front of writers." On 11 October 1933 he sent a report of his findings back to IVRS headquarters in Moscow, requesting that a response be formulated as soon as possible to the issues raised.[13]

Becher visited Prague first, he reported, where he discovered that the outlook for the use of united front tactics among German writers there was particularly good, "in spite of the rather strong influence of the *Weltbühne*."[14] As for the situation in Vienna, Becher upbraided the Austrian BPRS in his report for its dereliction in carrying out tasks that the IVRS had assigned it, for instance, for not including Oskar Maria Graf in its activity. Otherwise, Becher evaluated the situation in Vienna as "objectively very favorable for our work." In Swit-

with Gorky in *Perepiska A. M. Gorkogo*, pp. 199–200, and with Rolland in *Iz istorii MORPa*, p. 313. Kurella and Barbusse collaborated closely in a number of ventures. Kurella, as a matter of fact, is said to have ghost written Barbusse's Stalin biography. Cf. Sinko, *Roman eines Romans*, p. 185.

11. Ravines, *The Yenan Way*, p. 113.

12. Langkau-Alex, *Volksfront für Deutschland?*, 1:60.

13. "Johannes R. Becher, "Bericht über die Tätigkeit während meiner Reise vom 5. Juli bis 17. September 1933," in Becher-Archiv, BPRS-Materialien, no. 41, and *Zur Tradition der sozialistischen Literatur*, pp. 570–590.

14. The *Neue Weltbühne* was then edited by Willi Schlamm, who was sympathetic to the positions of Trotsky.

zerland he came upon an "extremely involved and confused situation." Bernard von Brentano was adamantly propagating the theory of a petty bourgeois victory in Germany, a view that was "upsetting" some and convincing other "proletarian comrades."[15] Worse still, Brentano was in close contact with Social Democrats and even on a very enthusiastic footing with Ignazio Silone. The difficulty of "maneuvering" in Switzerland could be seen in the fact that the *Arbeiter-Illustrierte Zeitung* (a Münzenberg journal) published Silone and accepted his novel *Fontamara* as a great piece of antifascist literature, even though, as Becher put it, Silone was in the forefront of Trotskyism in Switzerland. Trotskyism in general, Becher claimed, was particularly rampant among the intellectuals there; the League of Friends of the Soviet Union was composed of up to "eighty percent Trotskyists."

Problems were likewise surfacing in the Parisian branch of the newly exiled German BPRS.[16] Upon being forced out of Germany, the organization had experienced an influx of new members unfamiliar with the "literary-theoretical progress" made in recent years; these people, Becher said, must be brought up to date through the use of "working committees" meeting to discuss problems of literary theory and "the question of Trotskyism in literature." Becher also bewailed the fact that the party's only public polemics against Trotsky were Bruno Frei's in *Der Gegenangriff* against Willi Schlamm and *Die neue Weltbühne*; more needed to be done because there was now a tendency for the formerly pervasive "émigré panic to become subliminal, reappearing in the form of a Trotskyist way of asking questions." Becher simply meant to say that as the shock of sudden exile wore off, many expatriate Germans began asking unsettling questions about past party policies.[17] Becher's trip also served to bring home to him

---

15. The notion of the Nazi victory as a petty bourgeois revolution was generally ascribed to Trotsky, though Neumann and Remmele supported a similar interpretation.
16. There were, according to Becher, some "thirty comrades" in the Paris-based BPRS. See Becher, "Bericht über die Tätigkeit," p. 577. The following East German account gives a general impression of the underground activities of the BPRS in Germany, which continued to exist until late 1935: Hans Baumgart, "Die illegale Arbeit des Bundes proletarisch-revolutionärer Schriftsteller in Deutschland, 1933–1935," in *Literatur der Arbeiterklasse*, pp. 191–203.
17. Brentano's dissatisfaction, for instance, apparently derived from his disgust with the ingrained stupidity of the party leaders. He wrote Brecht: "In G [ermany] I joined the club [the KPD] and saw how poor the [*Rote*] *Fahne* was, how dumb the articles written for Teddy [Thälmann]; but I guess I believed like everyone else in the cause, in the proletariat, etc. Now one defeat follows another. I have been watching this here and see that all the errors are being repeated with remarkable precision. And that is when I ask: does it really make no difference what kind of people guide a party? Is it really unim-

the need for a foreign base of operations, an IVRS "strongpoint" in western Europe. This issue was raised in Paris in connection with discussion concerning the IVRS's poor liaison with its French section, which expressed its willingness during Becher's stay to help raise money to finance a western IVRS office. In Prague too interest was shown in forming a branch of the IVRS located in western Europe.

In his report Becher summed up his findings and made his recommendations: (1) the absolute necessity of a base of operations in western Europe for the organization of anti-Fascist elements in literature; (2) the immediate creation of a journal for anti-Fascist intellectuals to "combat Trotsky's arguments" and to provide a forum for different representatives of the exiled intelligentsia;[18] (3) fundamental reorganization of the marketing and distribution of the IVRS Moscow-based journal, *Internationale Literatur*; (4) need for the preparation of a "world conference of all anti-Fascist writers"; (5) more invitations to foreign writers to visit the USSR so as to answer the question "persistently raised by Trotskyists and Social Democrats, What is the Soviet Union doing for the émigrés?"; (6) creation of a "central ideological directorate of all [IVRS] sections." Becher insisted that this could "only be located in Moscow, where all the material and ideological prerequisites are present."

The IVRS and its German emissaries in the West took no further action that year in preparation for a Münzenberg-style "world conference of all anti-Fascist writers," but by mid-1933 it began to dawn on German Communist literati that the consistent application of Münzenberg's organizational and propaganda techniques to their literary-political ploys could pay handsome dividends in the growth of Communist prestige within the anti-Fascist movement at large. The point was first brought home to the Communists in the summer of 1933 when a group of writers, former members of the Communist-controlled SDS opposition in pre-Hitler Berlin,[19] reestablished the Association of

---

portant that the articles are miserable? Or is it possible that this 'quality' and the quantity of the defeat are connected with each other?" Quoted from Mittenzwei, *Exil in der Schweiz*, p. 108.

18. See Chapter 8 for the prehistory and creation of the journals *Die neuen deutschen Blätter* and *Das Wort*.

19. Alfred Kantorowicz, "Fünf Jahre Schutzverband deutscher Schriftsteller im Exil," *Das Wort* 12 (1938): pp. 61–62. In keeping with his post-1957 efforts to "de-communize" retrospectively all party-controlled organizations with which he was at one time connected, Kantorowicz claims just the opposite in his last book, *Politik und Literatur im Exil*, pp. 151–56. Kantorowicz's book must be used with extreme caution; see my review of it in *Internationales Archiv für Sozialgeschichte der deutschen Literatur* 6 (1981).

German Writers (SDS) in Paris and promptly turned it into a flourishing front.[20] Arthur Koestler later characterized the manipulation of SDS functions by a Communist governing body (a caucus) within the organization: "Officially, the Association was politically neutral except for its opposition to the Nazi regime; in fact it was run by the Caucus, a group of Communist writers who determined the policy of the Association, decided upon whom to invite as speakers, and steered the public discussion into the proper channels."[21]

In the meantime, Münzenberg was redoubling his efforts to organize Western antifascism. In early 1933 he founded the widely recognized World Relief Committee for the Victims of German Fascism, chaired by Lord Marley. Though the committee was ostensibly based in London, Münzenberg ran it from the Parisian secretariat, which worked out of offices at 83, boulevard du Montparnasse—the former cover address used by the MRP's French branch and, apparently, beginning in 1936, by the Committee for the Preparation of a German Popular Front.[22]

Though the International Workers' Relief, the MRP, continued to function, the World Committee now acted as the driving force behind Münzenberg's anti-Fascist crusade. It published the *Brown Book of the Hitler Terror and the Burning of the Reichstag*, for instance, which flooded the market with millions of copies in seventeen languages.[23] A Committee of Inquiry into the Origins of the Reichstag Fire came into being, staging the so-called Counter Trial; its hearings were held in London in September 1933 on the eve of the real Leipzig trial of Communists Georgi Dimitroff and Ernst Torgler. The committee's findings, which absolved the Communists of guilt and accused the Nazis of setting the fire, were disclosed on 21 September 1933, one day before the Leipzig trial was slated to begin. The Counter Trial

20. Not much is known about the very first months of the SDS, but it seems clear that Communists, or those accustomed to working closely with them, controlled the SDS from the outset. See J. R. Becher's report of July-September 1933: "In the matter of the Association of German Writers, we [the Communists] decided to reconstruct the Association of German Writers in Exile into an Association of German Writers (since that organization no longer exists in Germany), to arrange the board representatively" (in *Zur Tradition der sozialistischen Literatur*, p. 578).
21. Koestler, *The Invisible Writing*, p. 283.
22. Ibid., p. 242, and Langkau-Alex, *Volksfront für Deutschland?*, 1:53–55 and 240. Langkau-Alex assumes that the offices were rented by the Comintern.
23. Koestler, *The Invisible Writing*, pp. 237–45; Gustav Regler, *Das Ohr des Malchus*, pp. 213–16.

received so much worldwide publicity that the Germans were forced to deal with its accusations during court proceedings in Leipzig. Münzenberg's second *Brown Book* documented the Reichstag Fire Trial on the basis of "material collected by the World Committee for the Relief of the Victims of Fascism." Dimitroff, who had since been acquitted in Leipzig, flown to Moscow, given Soviet citizenship, and made the new secretary general of the Comintern, introduced the volume; the well-known British barrister and M.P. D. N. Pritt (who, after lending his judicial expertise to the Counter Trial, let himself be shamefully taken in by the Moscow show trials three years later) provided the foreword; and Lion Feuchtwanger added an appendix on "Murder in Hitler Germany."[24]

All the while anti-Fascist literature flowed from the presses of Münzenberg's newly founded Editions du Carrefour. The *Arbeiter-Illustrierte Zeitung* continued to appear in Prague and in Paris, joined by a weekly, *Der Gegenangriff*, and a journal, *Unsere Zeit* (the continuation in exile of the MRP's *Der rote Aufbau*). A Committee for the Release of Thälmann, founded by Münzenberg, came into existence and attracted much publicity, broadening its activities to include non-Communists like Carl von Ossietzky who were languishing in Nazi prisons and concentration camps.[25] On 10 May 1934, one year to the day after the Nazi book burnings and after several months of organizational planning, the German Freedom Library opened its doors in Paris with Heinrich Mann as president and Alfred Kantorowicz general secretary. Housed in rooms belonging to the French branch of the International Workers' Relief, the Library's initial holdings came from the archives collected in compiling the two *Brown Books*.[26]

By early 1934 Münzenberg men and IVRS German writers were frequently rubbing shoulders, applying everywhere to the anti-Fascist movement the methods of mass organization, mobilization of public opinion, and propaganda techniques developed by Münzenberg in the twenties and early thirties. But even as the IVRS strove to join interests with all oppositional writers, formulating tentative plans for a center of operations in western Europe and for a writers' conference, it began to be queried as a suitable agency to coordinate the writers' movement. An unpublished and undated draft, "On the Re-

24. Koestler, *The Invisible Writing*, p. 244.
25. Langkau-Alex, *Volksfront für Deutschland?*, 1:56–57.
26. Ibid., pp. 65–67, and Kantorowicz, *Politik und Literatur*, pp. 271–93; also see Koestler, *The Invisible Writing*, p. 258.

construction of MORP and the Reorganization of its Sections," reveals the IVRS in the midst of making plans for the immediate future.[27] "The changed political situation forces us to reevaluate our methods in the fight against fascism and the danger of imperialist war," the draft noted, raising these major points: (1) possibilities for the Communists' work had improved markedly, not just within the proletariat but especially among the lower middle classes and the intelligentsia; (2) the writers' movement was the most visible part of the "intellectuals' movement" in various countries, and advances in the area of literature would therefore lead to progress within the entire movement; (3) in spite of a good start in the use of "united front tactics," such as *Die neuen deutschen Blätter*[28] and the *Comité* (Amsterdam-Pleyel or WKKF), there was much still to be done; (4) investigation of shortcomings in application of the tactics of a united front showed that the "organizational form of an International League of *Revolutionary* Writers and its sections" was antiquated and no longer conformed to the tasks of the day; (5) the "*sole* directorate of an international writers' movement, for various reasons we don't want to go into here," ought not to be located in Moscow.[29]

Circumstances dictated that the following steps be taken in line with "rebuilding" the IVRS: (1) a league of anti-Fascist writers, based in Paris, was to be created. The IVRS would be "transformed and developed into an *invisible organization* [my italics], a bureau that would supervise matters by supplying theoretical material and maintaining the link with Russian writers and the relevant authorities [that is, the Comintern]";[30] (2) the statutes and the slogans of the new league would be formulated to attract "all honest" anti-Fascist elements in literature. Of the five slogans selected in 1930 at the Kharkov Congress of Revolutionary Writers (Struggle against Imperialist War, Struggle against Social Fascism, Struggle for the Defense of the USSR, Struggle against White Terror, and Struggle against Fascism), only the call for a "Struggle against Fascism and Imperialist War" could be retained; (3) a league of anti-Fascist writers should be created on the occasion of the "student congress" that was scheduled to be held in Paris and followed by a "writers' congress"; (4) plans were to be made now, either through the World Committee for the Struggle against

27. "Entwurf zum Umbau der MORP und zur Reorganisation ihrer Sektionen," TsGALI, 631/13/73/10–11.
28. See discussion of this journal in Chapter 8.
29. "Entwurf zum Umbau der MORP," TsGALI, 631/13/73/10–11.
30. Ibid.

Fascism and Imperialist War (WKKF) or through the Institut pour l'Etude du Fascisme,[31] to approach writers like Romain Rolland, André Gide, Heinrich Mann, Thomas Mann, and Lion Feuchtwanger, for their opinion on these matters; (5) an "internal discussion" of the issues should be held with foreign writers visiting Moscow for the All-Union Congress of Soviet Writers.[32]

An approximate dating of the draft is possible on the basis of internal evidence. The Soviet Writers' Congress met in Moscow in late August 1934, followed a few months later by the World Congress of Youth, which the International Workers' Relief convened in Paris.[33] Initial plans for "reconstructing" the IVRS by turning it into an "invisible organization" must have been discussed, then, in the first half of 1934, when the draft was evidently drawn up. No "writers' congress" met after the youth congress, though; nor was there a league of anti-Fascist writers founded at that time. In fact, from here on out until December 1935, there were palpable efforts, emanating from inside the Comintern, to slacken the forward momentum of the literary united front.

Though slowed somewhat, plans for a writers' congress and a writers' league (the western European bureau) nevertheless went forward. "Bourgeois" anti-Fascist writers were the targets of more overtures made in August 1934 at the Congress of Soviet Writers.[34] This congress formalized creation of the Soviet Writers' Union called for in connection with the abolition of RAPP. Sergej Tretjakov addressed the congress and called for a modification of tactics: "Our international writers' front is called a League of Revolutionary Writers. But we must ask whether or not that is putting things too narrowly. 'Revolutionary writer'—isn't that overly restrictive? Doesn't that establish a barrier in front of those writers who come to us in possession of great artistic (and overall) authority and see themselves relegated to the unpleasant

31. Another Münzenberg front. See Koestler, *The Invisible Writing*, pp. 296–307. Koestler worked in the INFA, as it was called.

32. One of the other suggestions indicates a curious parallel between literary strategy and Soviet foreign policy. It was recommended that the Soviet Writers' Union enter the PEN Club, or cooperate with it in forming an anti-Fascist writers' league; this corresponds to the Soviet foreign policy objective of getting Russia out of her isolation by joining the League of Nations and promoting the cause of collective security.

33. Michev, *Mezhrabpom*, pp. 284–85.

34. The congress was attended by a number of Germans, including F. C. Weiskopf, Willi Bredel, Wieland Herzfelde, Johannes R. Becher, Theodor Plivier, Ernst Toller, Friedrich Wolf, Adam Scharrer, Klaus Mann, Albert Ehrenstein, Oskar Maria Graf, Gustav Regler, and Alfred Kantorowicz.

position of a fellow traveler?" Tretjakov argued that a more effective strategy would be to promote the following slogan: "Struggle against the common foe—struggle against fascism in the name of the ideas of real humanity, which are advanced and defended solely by the proletariat."[35]

Johannes R. Becher tailored his comments to fit two writers whose support the Communists were particularly keen to win. The number of writers who, in the light of the upheavals in bourgeois society, were no longer willing to support the old system was on the increase, said Becher. "Those among them who, like Heinrich Mann and Lion Feuchtwanger, abhor fascism like the plague will, on the strength of the intense struggles of our day, be brought to the point where they begin to develop a sense for and perception of the genuinely progressive forces of our era."[36] Such writers, Becher emphasized, were the ones who understood that the age of capitalism was past and that new, militant, and invincible forces were developing in the womb of the old society.

Becher singled out Mann's recent volume of essays, *Hass,* and Feuchtwanger's anti-Fascist novels, *Die Gebrüder Oppenheim* and *Erfolg,* for illustration. In *Hass* Mann showed plainly that the Hitler dictatorship had emerged from the "intestines" of the bourgeois republic. But, Becher emphasized, Mann at times gave too much credence to the deceptive phrases of German Social Democracy and criticized communism. "We shall make no exception of Heinrich Mann," wrote Becher; "we shall say 'no' to some of his ideas and pronouncements, but we respect him and honor in him a brave antifascist soldier." Like Mann, Feuchtwanger had also done much to expose the real face of National Socialist dictatorship and of counterrevolution in Germany. But Feuchtwanger too had occasionally made immature remarks about the Communist movement. Becher pointed out that Feuchtwanger "has spoken of the proletarian revolution; but he still shies away from it, even though it alone is able to break the yoke of despotism." Similarly, Heinrich Mann was "still afraid of the violence of the revolution, which alone points the way to the future."[37]

Nonetheless, the Communists were persuaded that the anti-Fascist writers possessed the will to comprehend the events of the day and that this sincere desire for the truth, among writers like Heinrich

35. *Sozialistische Realismuskonzeptionen,* pp. 229–30.
36. Johannes R. Becher, "Das grosse Bündnis," in *Sozialistische Realismuskonzeptionen,* p. 253.
37. Ibid., pp. 253–54.

Mann, Lion Feuchtwanger, and many others who hated fascism, would culminate in their espousal of the cause of the revolutionary workers. Much was expected from their cooperation and from their professed readiness to enter into the arena of battle against war and against fascism with the power of the written word.

The speeches by Tretjakov and Becher make it clear that the Communists placed distinct demands on their new allies. The reprobation of Feuchtwanger's and Mann's timidity with respect to proletarian revolution illustrates that the Communists insisted upon a linkage between antifascism and official communism. Antifascism, it was assumed, the "sincere desire for truth," would naturally merge with support for the cause of the revolutionary workers, which is what eventually happened with a handful of men like Heinrich Mann and Feuchtwanger, fellow travelers who essentially became fellow comrades. This process was hastened by Becher's speech and the Soviet Writers' Congress. Feuchtwanger, for instance, wrote Karl Schmückle in Moscow: "I read J. R. Becher's speech with special joy. You know that many of us, however much we may sympathize with Soviet writers, have been put off by our apprehension that an overly severe Russian censorship might adversely affect the basic premise of all writing—the possibility for the individual writer to express himself and represent his view of the world in total freedom. It is good that Becher's warm and congenial talk tore down the last dike here."[38]

After the Soviet Writers' Congress, the itinerant Becher again left the Soviet Union on a tour of the same émigré centers he had called on in late 1933—Prague, Vienna, Zurich, and Paris. During this latest trip, in October-November 1934, Becher ascertained that Communist expectations for unity with exiled German writers had been too low: "We can take in far larger circles than we ever imagined." In Prague Becher found that the issue of the literary heritage was central to winning over both writers who already sympathized with the party and writers who were still reticent to join forces with the Communists. Becher reported that the "new" Communist stance on the issue of the literary heritage had been taken as a revelation during one meeting attended by politically unaffiliated writers and journalists like Kurt

---

38. Feuchtwanger to Schmückle on 28 October 1934, TsGALI, 1397/1/674/1. Becher too referred to the positive impact of the congress in a late 1934 report to the IVRS: "The Congress of Writers has had an extremely positive effect, loosening things up and preparing the way." Johannes R. Becher, "Bericht über eine Reise nach Prag, Zürich und Paris (Oktober/November 1934)," in *Zur Tradition der sozialistischen Literatur*, p. 669.

Hiller, Hermann Budzislawski, Manfred Georg, and Kurt Kersten. "That we are really *for* literature and not just for topical political poetry" pleasantly surprised the non-Communists, Becher said. At another meeting, during which Becher read some of his sonnets to illustrate the new Communist attitude, a discussion ensued in which Max Brod "adopted our standpoint almost without reservation and said that under those conditions it really was possible to combine forces."[39]

The Communist attitude toward the literary heritage also came as a surprise to Heinrich Mann, with whom Becher had recently talked. Mann enthusiastically favored consolidation of forces and promised to write an article for the *Weltbühne*[40] in support of making common cause against National Socialism. Moreover, he expressed to Becher his willingness (the Communists soon exploited it) to serve on the presidium of any such anti-Fascist coalition. In Zurich Becher talked with Thomas Mann, who had also been happy to hear of the new Communist respect for literature of the past. Becher added that it should be possible to "influence him." The Communists had hitherto been remiss in helping Mann resolve the doubt and confusion he was experiencing, said Becher, indicating that he held the severity of past Communist publicistic attacks on Thomas Mann by Alfred Kurella and Ernst Ottwalt to be unwarranted.

This was an understatement: the Communists had tongue-lashed Mann mercilessly. In early 1934 Alfred Kurella took him to task for the "mysticism" of his novel *Joseph* and for his unwillingness to avow publicly his support of the German emigration. Kurella baited Mann with the insinuation that his sympathy actually lay with the Nazis: "What is the itinerary, Herr Thomas Mann? From Berlin to Bandol [Mann's residence in Switzerland] or from Bandol to Berlin? Well, he can go to hell, it is tempting to say. . . . He can go wherever he wishes, even back to that hell."[41] Becher himself, though he neglected to mention it in his 1934 report, had matched Kurella's innuendos in a piece of doggerel published early that year:

Thomas Mann and Alfred Döblin
Sent off to Goebbels

39. Becher, "Bericht über eine Reise," p. 669.
40. The *Neue Weltbühne* was now no longer under the control of Schlamm; it had been entrusted instead to Hermann Budzislawski, who, though very much pro-Communist, was not quite an unequivocal advocate of the official Communist line.
41. Alfred Kurella, "Die Dekadenz Thomas Manns," *Internationale Literatur* 2 (1934): 155–59.

A telegram to tell him
Herr Goebbels was falsely informed.
Their names had been wrongly mentioned
In the journal called *Die Sammlung.*
By their actions they've emasculated themselves.
Their publisher, though, will applaud them.[42]

Thomas Mann's "itinerary" soon proved of interest to the Communists after all, who approached him through his son. In July 1934 Hans Günther wrote Klaus Mann, apologizing somewhat for past attacks and explaining the Communist attitude toward Thomas Mann. Because of Hitler's dictatorship and Fascist terror in Germany, the Communists were intensely interested in keeping watch on the attitude of great writers toward German fascism. "And it may be true," the letter stated, "that some of us, who had expected to hear a meaningful and resolute word from Thomas Mann too about the monstrous cultural barbarism of fascism, tended to let our criticism go too far out of a sense of disappointment." As proponents of socialist realism, Günther explained to Klaus Mann, the Communists were persuaded that the search for truth would sooner or later lead every writer who hated fascism and "capitalist predatory war," believed in the cultural ascent of humanity and the power of reason, and lent his pen to the cause of "civilized progress" into the camp of men who tied the future of culture and humanity to the "unremitting struggle of the proletariat for liberation."[43]

The substance of the letter highlights changes that had occurred in the IVRS since the days of the proletarian emphasis. Then the Communists had argued that class warfare was raging between proletarian and bourgeois writers; because bourgeois culture served the interests of the ruling class, it would share the fate of putrifying capitalism, and only the proletariat would be capable of scaling new heights of culture. Now that Hitler had triumphed in Germany, fascism (capitalism in its final stage) had launched a war of annihilation against culture. The Communists contended that this was all historically foreseeable. Down through the ages cultural expression had always given

42. Becher, *Deutschland*, p. 157. Ernst Ottwalt was more discriminating in his judgments and more polite. See Ernst Ottwalt, "Der Turm zu Babel," *Die neuen deutschen Blätter* (December 1933): 253–58.
43. Günther, "Brief an Klaus Mann (Disposition—Hauptpünkte)," TsGALI, 1397/1/663/1. Günther's letter came in response to Klaus Mann's complaints about Kurella's article in *Internationale Literatur*, of which Günther was then editor. See also Thomas Mann's diary comments in his *Tagebücher, 1933–1934*, p. 489.

voice to mankind's progressive aspirations; therefore, real culture was bound to clash with the ruling class when, finally and irrevocably devoid of its once progressive proclivities, the bourgeoisie entered into its ultimate, arch-reactionary state before disappearing forever from the world arena. Progressive bourgeois culture had to break with the fascistized culture of the dying ruling class, for the two were inimical. All true cultural values were now to be found in the antithesis to fascism, the socialist humanism of communism. The times thus presented bourgeois writers with a life-and-death choice: they could ally themselves with the only bearers of true culture, the proletariat (and its Communist advance guard), or with the bourgeoisie, in which case the writers would consign themselves to oblivion. With those who chose the first path the Communists professed their readiness to work together to defeat the cultural barbarism of fascism and to build a new socialist-humanist culture that accorded with the forward march of history.

This was the import of Günther's letter to Klaus Mann. It was vitally important, the letter went on to say, that eminent writers who were "driven by hatred for fascism and for imperialist war" deal with questions like mankind, humanity, culture, standards of civilization, reason, and reality in a new way—as inalterably hostile antitheses to fascism. "Freedom, humanity, reason—these are not hollow phrases, even if they have been insidiously misused a thousand times over by the annihilators of all culture." The Communists viewed the question of mysticism in this context, Günther explained, which accounted for their uneasiness with respect to "mystic tendencies" in Thomas Mann's recent writing. However, the Communists made "no apodictic pronouncements about the development and work of a writer who enjoys our highest esteem." They were merely searching for common ground with all "honest adversaries of fascism," for the camp of fascism's opponents had to be made as capacious as possible. The letter closed with this suggestion: "Shouldn't we be thinking about the 'organizational' question of forming a large-scale league of anti-Fascist writers?"[44]

44. Günther, "Brief an Klaus Mann," TsGALI, 1397/1/663/1. Günther's letter evidently placated Klaus and Thomas Mann. The latter noted in his diary for 31 July 1934: "Klaus reported a Moscow critique of *Joseph* that denigrated the book as following Klage's suit. Klaus wrote a letter of protest to the editor, who by and large renounced the critique" (*Tagebücher, 1933–1934*, p. 489). Klaus Mann, in his 31 July 1934 reply to Günther's letter, defended "the mythical" against its "misuse" in Germany. He wrote: "I am no materialist. But I am firmly persuaded that one can be a consistent anti-Fascist nonetheless, indeed, that one can even be a genuine friend of necessary socialism." As

In his October-November report to Moscow in 1934, J. R. Becher called for strengthening the IVRS by intensifying its work, and he came out strongly against all talk of a possible dissolution of the IVRS "during this time of transition." This would be a mistake, he argued, since at the moment there was no institution that could replace the IVRS. Moreover, he emphasized, its location in Moscow, "in spite of the fact that this acts, on the one hand, as an impediment, serves on the other hand as an ever-growing source of attraction; what comes from there possesses a certain authority."[45] Becher was probably aware of specific plans to disband the IVRS in the immediate future because rumors were apparently circulating concerning the liquidation of the IVRS in favor of a more broadly based organization headquartered in western Europe. The 1934 draft on the reconstruction of the IVRS had, after all, stated that the "*sole* directorate" of the international writers' movement could not be located in Moscow and had called for turning the IVRS into an "invisible organization." Romain Rolland evidently got wind of these rumors and fired off a clearly worded missive to Maxim Gorky:

> Barbusse tells me that the International League of
> Revolutionary Writers (IVRS) has been disbanded, to be
> replaced with a more broadly accessible organization based
> primarily in Paris. I regret this. As I wrote Barbusse, "the soil
> of Paris is of poor quality. Sooner or later it spoils everything
> it brings forth." Moscow, in my opinion, must remain the
> center of the great new movement. The gaze of all free and
> intrepid minds the world over is fixed . . . on Moscow.
> Tomorrow the wave of fascism . . . can envelop France. The
> International of Revolutionary Writers will not find the solid
> support [in Paris] that it has in the USSR. And I'm not really
> much of a supporter of the diffusion of cadres. We live in a
> period of crisis, in conditions that make it imprudent to
> weaken markedly the firmness of our position. . . . No, the
> time is not right for tolerance.[46]

---

for Günther's call to unity, Klaus Mann was all for it. "This topic is large," he closed his letter; "I am answering your summarizing remarks in a similar abridged style. I too find the will to unity, which you expressed and which seems to me to accord with the call of the day—and not just the present or the next day—more important at the moment than this fragmentary discussion" (Klaus Mann, *Briefe and Antworten*, 1:194–95).

45. Becher, "Bericht über eine Reise," pp. 682–83.
46. Rolland to Gorky, 28 December 1934, *Perepiska A. M. Gorkogo*, pp. 353–54.

But the IVRS had not in fact been dissolved just yet, and confusion plagued the formulation of strategy.[47] The troublemaker seems to have been the Comintern, which procrastinated on the important issues. In early March Willi Bredel, in Moscow, complained to Otto Biha (Peter Merin): "Believe me, the entire situation disagrees with me too but I am truly not at fault and am still unable to send you and Hans [Becher] precise information. Believe me, though I have the best possible connections with our friends in the C [omintern] (and I have them now more than ever), I can't get anything concrete out of them. All I ever hear is: 'Wait! Don't rush things! Wait!' " The same day, Bredel informed Alfred Kantorowicz that he had read the reports filed by Kantorowicz concerning "work" in England and Spain and that he was pleased that "we are making progress everywhere. Unfortunately," Bredel lamented, "I cannot support you from here, as you had hoped, because an altogether unclear stance has been adopted here in all critical questions."[48]

Still, plans for a writers' congress went forward. During a meeting of four hundred SDS members in Paris, the Communists seem to have asked Anna Seghers beforehand to make the "spontaneous" suggestion in front of the mixed assembly that the association undertake steps in preparation for a "conference of all progressive elements in literature to be held within the foreseeable future in western Europe."[49] Heinrich Mann and Lion Feuchtwanger were to be incorporated into the SDS executive board as soon as possible, and the association would soon be approaching the IVRS and Russian "friends" (as Becher phrased it), the French section of the IVRS, and prominent liberal writers like Barbusse, Malraux, Dreiser, Shaw, and Wells. A date was tentatively set for the conference, May or June 1935, when it would coincide with a series of anti-Fascist demonstrations and exhibitions in Paris.[50]

47. See, for instance, Klein, *Schriftsteller in der französischen Volksfront*, p. 79.

48. Bredel to Merin, 7 March 1935, TsGALI, 631/13/69/42; Bredel to Kantorowicz, 7 March 1935, TsGALI, 631/13/63/7.

49. Johannes R. Becher, "Brief aus Paris (15 December 1934)," in *Zur Tradition der sozialistischen Literatur*, p. 684. The meeting must have been staged. The Communists had been planning a congress since at least mid-1933 and probably worked things out ahead of time so that Anna Seghers would make the seemingly spontaneous proposal in front of an audience that was not composed exclusively of Communists.

50. The announcement of the congress was made in the French press in April 1935 and read: "A number of writers, in view of the dangers which in a number of countries are threatening culture, have grasped the initiative to convene a congress in order to consider and discuss the means of the defense of culture. They desire to arrive at a

Most of the organizational planning was indeed entrusted to the French,[51] but the men involved were mainly writers who had in the past worked frequently in Münzenberg's operations, and they were assisted by Becher, Gustav Regler, and Alfred Kantorowicz.[52] Becher was entirely satisfied both with the program worked out for the conference and with the methods used to prepare it. He wrote "Friends in Moscow" that the program was extremely satisfactory and, most important, produced by the mutual labor of "no doubt the most important French friends." He had seen the view confirmed that a real consolidation could only transpire when "the friends" involved participate in the work; this was an indication of how things needed to be done in the future. "We can't win these friends by presenting documents of whatever sort, which they, as objects, are to sign, but must awaken their interest in working and involving themselves significantly in producing the documents."[53]

In the interim, the IVRS was active elsewhere. The secret designs for work in Austria, for instance, show that rather crass schemes for assuming control of nonparty anti-Fascist organizations hid behind the facade of tolerance and cooperation. An unpublished IVRS letter to Ernst Fischer on 10 April 1935 throws light on the nature of the ploys. The IVRS told Fischer that the Austrian BPRS had shown itself incapable of producing the effort needed to create a worthwhile anti-Fascist united front of writers and artists. "The comrades in the Bund have demonstrated that they are unable to exploit organizationally the widespread sympathy for the anti-Fascist struggle present among writers and artists."[54] The IVRS noted that the Austrian BPRS had degenerated into a state of sectarian isolation that kept it from satisfactorily fulfilling its task in the service of an anti-Fascist united front. Fischer was asked for his help in "reorganizing" and revamping the work in Austria.

The IVRS proposed that the Communists reestablish the disbanded Austrian Social Democratic Union of Socialist Writers; once it was viable again, the Austrian BPRS, the Communist group, would be "dissolved." For the strategy to work, however, it was "imperative that

---

precise formulation of the conditions for literary work and the relationship of the writers to those for whom they write." Klein, *Schriftsteller in der französischen Volksfront*, p. 82.

51. Ibid.

52. See Kantorowicz's account in *Politik und Literatur*, pp. 205–24.

53. Becher to "Friends in Moscow," on 11 March 1935, cited in Baumgart, *Der Kampf der sozialistischen deutschen Schriftsteller*, p. 191.

54. IVRS secretariat to Ernst Fischer, 10 April 1935, TsGALI, 631/13/69/65–66.

a number of sympathizers be brought into the executive of the organization [that is, the resurrected "socialist" union], but we have to be absolutely certain to work it so that we secretly and cleverly keep the leadership firmly in our hands." Moreover, Fischer was told, "trustworthy members should also be sent wherever possible into opposing literary organizations, where they can use their criticism in a clever, ostensibly loyal fashion to undermine [the opposing organization] and to bring the vacillating elements closer to our position."[55] Where the availability of documents permit it, scrutiny of all anti-Fascist organizations in which Communists were active confirm that the above modus operandi was universally applied.

Having been planned since 1933, the International Writers' Congress for the Defense of Culture finally met in Paris on 21–25 June 1935. The program had already been set in April: talks were organized around the topics of cultural heritage; the role of the writer in society; the individual; humanism; nation and culture; problems of creation and the dignity of thought; and the defense of culture. All these topics were selected to offer a broad forum with ample opportunity for writers of various political persuasions to speak on tame subjects that could easily be reduced, and generally were, to the antithesis Moscow-Berlin.

This was not the congress for strident pro-Sovietism. Neither the Soviet writers present nor the Communist German or French literati made loud demands for support of the USSR. No ultimatums were issued, and, generally speaking, no one presented arguments that came right down to an identification of antifascism with a pro-Soviet stance. The USSR certainly was spoken of in glowing terms by many of the delegates; and most of those who lionized the Soviet regime were not Communists. But this was precisely the Communists' intent and achievement at the congress. Party members did not have to make propaganda for the party; the fellow travelers did it for them. The 1934 Draft had noted that, of all the slogans formulated in 1930 in Kharkov, only the appeal for a struggle against "fascism" and "imperialist war" could be considered acceptable at the upcoming congress; even the slogan for defense of the Soviet Union (a staple in all Communist propaganda at least since 1928) was dropped, though it was easy enough to argue around that self-imposed limitation by simply supporting the "defense of culture" and, in the next breath, contrasting decadent Western and Fascist German culture with Soviet culture. The task of forming the nexus between defense of culture (antifascism) and support of the USSR fell to the non-Communist audience, which made the connection with alacrity.

The German Communists themselves actually went to great lengths to avoid proselytizing openly for Russia. Becher, for instance, interlarded his speech with vague references to humanism, the abhorrent situation in Germany, and to the might of the proletarian German writers. He spoke only briefly of the "construction of socialism in the Soviet Union."[56] Such was also the case with the other German Communists, who were determined to keep out of the limelight. Gustav Regler's speech, however, seems to have struck Becher as coming dangerously close to destroying the precautions that the Communists had taken to give the affair a nonpartisan facade. In a demonstrative gesture, Regler closed his speech by turning to André Gide and Barbusse, sitting on the platform, and, referring to the Gestapo informant everyone assumed was seated in the hall, announced grandly that the Nazis had been unable to keep men like Gide and Barbusse from the camp of the anti-Fascists, whereupon—this is how Regler told the story in his 1958 memoirs—the entire hall rose to its feet and began singing the "Internationale." Off to the side of the stage Becher waved Regler over to him and the following dialogue supposedly ensued:

> "Are you out of your mind!" he [Becher] hissed.
> "Don't you hear what they're singing!" I said; my voice was animated from excitement.
> "But that's exactly it!" he roared, his voice hidden by the powerful chorus now swelling. "You've ruined everything, you've unmasked us. This is now no longer a neutral congress. All that money! . . . You'll be kicked out of the party."
> "They'll hear that clear across the Rhine," I said emotionally.
> "You're a saboteur," said Johannes R. Becher, the poet, in a hoarse voice."[57]

According to Regler, his party cell met four days later, and he was raked over the coals for his actions. "It is not up to individual comrades to decide when the Internationale is to be sung, especially now, when we are obliged to restrain ourselves because of the popular front," the party representative told Regler. In response to Regler's answer that the singing had come spontaneously from the hearts of

56. Johannes R. Becher, "Im Zeichen des Menschen und der Menschheit," in *Zur Tradition der sozialistischen Literatur*, p. 689.
57. Regler, *Das Ohr des Malchus*, pp. 316–17.

the assembled, Anna Seghers told Regler, "That is a bunch of sentimental garbage; we are speaking here of a question of tactics." Alexander Abusch had the final word on the subject: "We are in a period of camouflage. Anyone who exposes our cover is a counterrevolutionary."[58]

But the success of the congress for the Communists lay in the fact that they had little to fear from such demonstrations; the fellow travelers were solidly behind them. Widespread sympathy for and support of the USSR among the liberal Western intelligentsia was by now simply a natural part of things. Edouard Dujardin, speaking of the cultural heritage, said that a society's culture was the sum total of fraternal cooperation between all races and all workers. "And that, for the first time, has been accomplished in the Soviet Union, where a new, all-embracing culture is emerging on the ruins of bourgeois culture."[59] Other non-Communists lent their voices to the chorus of praise. Max Brod had this to say: "Today the Russian proletariat has become the standard bearer of the cultural heritage of the ages. When I, a non-Marxist, returned from the USSR, I returned with great hope, ·for I had discovered that the Soviet Union was on the right road" (812). Some other pronouncements: Paul Nizan said that "in the Soviet Union the new human race is awakening" (816); Chamson, "Only in the Soviet Union is the true meaning of nationalism real-

---

58. Ibid. Regler's memoirs must be used critically. He was one of a number of former party partisans, such as Koestler and Kantorowicz, who later turned their backs on Communism and then inveighed against the "God that failed." Of the memoirs written by these three men, Koestler's alone is generally reliable. Regler, for instance, reports private conversations in August 1936 with Lev Kamenev concerning a proposed Regler biography of Loyola. But Kamenev, who from 19 to 24 August 1936 was tried in the first Moscow show trial, had been in prison since the Kirov murder in December 1934. In the matter of Regler's speech, however, there is outside evidence that it did indeed get him into hot water with the party. Willi Bredel, writing to Peter Merin from Moscow on 14 August 1935, asked: "What do you have to say about the P. [aris] congress? What do you think of Hans' [Becher's] speech or even of Gustav's? The latter caused quite a scandal, which, in my humble opinion, came as no surprise whatever to me" (in TsGALI, 631/13/69/85). In an article written for the *Pariser Tageblatt* of 30 June 1935, Heinrich Mann mentioned the singing of the Internationale: "While we were standing there once [at the congress], the Internationale was started up in the gallery, even though it was immediately broken off. The honor was too great: we aren't that far along yet" (Mann, *Verteidigung der Kultur,* p. 139).

59. The *Rundschau* carried a detailed report of the congress's proceedings in issue 28/29 (1935). The report is reprinted in *Zur Tradition der sozialistischen Literatur,* pp. 802–39, to which I refer here. Dujardin's remark is on p. 805. Further page references are given in the text in parentheses.

ized" (820); Heinrich Mann, "The development of the Soviet Union
. . . has led to extraordinarily good results" (826).[60]

Many of the Communist speakers went no further in extolling the
Soviet Union; many stopped far short, for instance, of Malraux's exuberance: "We want partnership with the Soviet Union, where the entire nation is experiencing together this great act of creation. . . . Let
us close ranks in preparation for the final battle in support of the
Soviet Union, for the new Man" (811). Speeches containing such appeals demonstrate why the Communists were in no danger of threatening the "front" character of the congress; there was scarcely any
front left to it, for the fellow travelers had relieved the Communists of
the need to protect the nonpartisan exterior of the assembly.

The congress did not come off without a hitch, however, and the
case of André Gide augured ill for the future of the Communists'
united and popular front. The anonymous commentator in *Rundschau*
wrote that on the subject of "The Individual," Gide, "France's most
representative novelist, gave the keynote address and was received
with a veritable storm of applause. His report, perfect in form and a
highpoint of the congress, developed into a broad attack of bourgeois
culture and into a confession of belief in communism and its culture"
(809). At the congress Gide had indeed made perhaps his clearest
expression to date of support for communism. For a number of
years, though, in his *Journal,* Gide had expressed privately his attraction to the Soviet Union. As early as 13 May 1931, Gide stated that
"above all else I should like to live long enough to see Russia's plan
succeed and the states of Europe obliged to accept what they insist on
ignoring. . . . Never have I bent over the future with more passionate
curiosity. My whole heart applauds that gigantic and yet entirely human
undertaking." A few months later, on 27 July 1931, he penned these
words: "I should like to cry aloud my affection for Russia; and that my
cry should be heard, should have importance. I should like to live
long enough to see the success of that tremendous effort; its realization, which I wish with all my soul and for which I would like to work."
Again on 23 April 1932: "In the abominable distress of the present
world, new Russia's plan now seems to be salvation. . . . And if my life
were necessary to ensure the success of the USSR, I would give it at
once."[61]

These remarks, made originally in the privacy of his journal, were

---

60. Heinrich Mann called the Russian writers the "aristocrats of the congress" (Mann,
Verteidigung der Kultur, p. 138).
61. Gide, *The Journals of André Gide,* 3:160, 180, 232.

published in the *Nouvelle Revue Française* in July 1932 and again in September. They were Gide's first public avowal of communism, which, however, stopped short of unqualified support; some of the other diary entries, in fact, betrayed the presence in Gide's mind of considerable doubt about the USSR. In the course of the next few years, he participated in a variety of protest actions, lending his voice to expressions of solidarity with Dimitroff and Ernst Thälmann, but he was not yet wholeheartedly sold on the idea of communism and its attitude toward the writer. In December 1932, for example, he refused to join the Association des Ecrivains et Artistes Révolutionnaires (AEAR), the French section of the IVRS, fearing that "the clearest result of such an engagement would be to keep me from writing anything at all." He went on to say that "I have declared as strongly and as clearly as I can my sympathy for the USSR and for all it represents in our eyes and to our hearts, in spite of all the imperfections that opponents bring up."[62] But he wanted to have no truck with a Communist literary organization.

Gide's history of admiration for the USSR reached something of a high watermark at the Paris congress in 1935. He proclaimed there that what had bothered him earlier, the conflict between the individual and communism, as well as his concern that there was no place in communism for any type of nationalism whatever or love of one's country, seemed to him to be resolved in Russia. "As far as I am concerned," Gide stated in his speech in Paris, "I would like to affirm that I feel free to consider myself in a profound sense to be an internationalist without ceasing to look upon myself as a Frenchman; in much the same way I affirm that I may remain very much an individual human being in complete accord with communism and while doing my part to aid it."[63] Gide added that what was true for the individual was true for an entire people. "Nothing excites me more about the USSR than the care with which the peculiarities, the essence of each small state that is united in the great Soviet Union, is preserved and respected." He went on to say that only detractors of communism could see in it the drive to uniformity. "What we expect from the USSR and what it is beginning to exhibit, following a difficult period of struggles and temporary deprivations and constraints leading to more thorough liberation—this is the social construct, which makes possible a more perfect growth of each human being."[64]

62. Cited in March, *Gide and the Hound of Heaven*, p. 328. Also in Gide, *Litterature engagée*, pp. 17–19.
63. Gide, *Litterature engagée*, p. 85; also see *Mezhdunarodnyj kongress*, p. 174.
64. *Mezhdunarodnyj kongress*, p. 181; Gide, *Litterature engagée*, p. 95.

The Communists represented Gide's espousal of communism in Paris as one of the greatest triumphs of their cause, and yet at the congress there were adumbrations of coming controversy, where discordant voices could be heard speaking of the lack of freedom in the USSR and, specifically, of the case of the imprisoned and banished Victor Serge.[65] The first to cause a scene was Gaetano Salvemini of Italy, who remarked that after listening to Gide's talk he could not help asking himself whether the USSR was truly such an individualistic communistic paradise. "I have the impression," he remarked, "that the Soviet regime is not viewed as an instrument for the construction of the communist society but as a state that has already reached its ideal. But we know not only of the existence of a Gestapo; there is also a Cheka, and there is a Victor Serge imprisoned in Siberia" (825). The *Rundschau* noted that Salvemini's talk resulted in some writers applauding "with the intention of disrupting; but the large majority of the participants at the Congress protested loudly against this attack on the Soviet Union" (826).

According to Serge's later memoirs, however, none other than Gide himself was "amazed" at efforts to hush up the Serge matter and insisted that the question be ventilated. Eventually, Malraux, the chairman on the particular day, allowed Magdalena Paz, a friend of Trotsky's, to speak.[66] She too demanded that the congress take up the case of Serge in conjunction with the topic "Freedom of Thought." Her speech was supported by Charles Plisnier; Henry Poulaille "demonstrated in the hall."[67]

Answering Paz was the Soviet writer Nikolaj Tikhonov, who noted that Serge was being "well-treated" but that he was guilty of helping prepare Kirov's assasination.[68] Brazenly ignoring the fact that Serge had been arrested two years *before* Kirov's murder, Tikhonov stated: "I, as a nonparty member, tell you that among the enemies of the Union there are none worse than the oppositionists and the Trotskyists."[69] Ilja Ehrenburg joined the protests against Paz's elaborations, hinting darkly that she too might be a Trotskyist. Other voices were

---

65. See Serge's account of the congress in Serge, *Memoirs of a Revolutionary*, pp. 317–19. While a few of the pro-Serge comments found their way into the *Rundschau* report, the Communist journal gives no true indication of how pervasive the issue of Serge's freedom was.
66. *Rundschau* report of the 1935 congress, p. 825; Serge, *Memoirs of a Revolutionary*, p. 318.
67. Serge, *Memoirs of a Revolutionary*, p. 318.
68. Ibid., p. 319.
69. *Rundschau* report of the 1935 congress, p. 832.

raised in support of Serge. One representative "of the Trotskyists," as the *Rundschau* put it, "read a resolution calling for either an official trial for Serge or his release abroad, as well as for asylum for Trotsky."[70] Anna Seghers lent her voice to the moral indignation of the Communists at the mention of Serge's name. The case of Victor Serge "has no place here," she insisted; ". . . at a time when we are fighting fascism, the exaggeration and false exploitation of a case that deeply concerns some of those here who pretend to defend the revolution can only have a counterrevolutionary effect!" (832). In other words, the Communists regarded advocacy of freedom and justice in the USSR as tantamount to the support of fascism. This was an equation the Communists had hitherto avoided in Paris; but now the slightest criticism brought the identity of anti-Sovietism with profascism rapidly to the surface. Seghers insisted: "Let us speak, instead, of Ossietzky and Renn!" (832). Vladimir Kirshon also maintained that to protest against a case like Serge's and to "say nothing" about Thälmann or the anti-Fascist prisoners was to use words as bullets shot at the best "of our leaders" (833). It was a classic double standard that, within eighteen months, would rend the ranks of the German emigration.

Gide finally closed the discussion on Serge with the remark—this is how it was reported by the *Rundschau*—that "in Serge's case we are dealing with the Soviet Union, which has won our love and admiration. The success of the USSR is more important to us than anything else. One must understand that in this case our trust is the greatest proof of our love that we can give" (833). Gide was answered with a "standing ovation." But that was not the end of the Serge affair. Without taking up the matter of the Russian's guilt or innocence (the two men had never met), Gide wrote a letter to the Soviet ambassador to France. He expressed no personal opinion but simply asked him to bear in mind that if the case were not handled with the appearance of justice there would be an adverse propaganda effect in western Europe.[71]

Notwithstanding these portents of a future explosion (Gide was soon to "cry aloud," all right, but it would not be his affection), the International Writers' Congress for the Defense of Culture was a victory for the IVRS in its efforts to set in motion a broad literary united

---

70. Ibid. Further page references given in the text in parentheses. Trotsky was denied political asylum by a number of different countries.
71. Cf. Gide, *Litterature engagée*, pp. 96–99. Serge was eventually released through Romain Rolland's direct intervention with Stalin. See Serge, *Memoirs of a Revolutionary*, p. 319.

front crusade against fascism. This was not affected by the fact, or perhaps it was due to it, that the resolutions accepted at the close of the congress were so innocuous. The most substantial of them merely expressed the commitment on the part of the writers to be ready at all times to fight in the area of culture "against war, fascism, and any other kind of danger threatening civilization."[72] Who could not support such aspirations? It was also decided to create a bureau of 112 writers from thirty-nine countries to guide a new International Writers' Association for the Defense of Culture. A presidium of twelve was selected: E. M. Forster, Aldous Huxley, Bernard Shaw, André Gide, Selma Lagerlöf, Valle Inclán, Heinrich Mann, Thomas Mann, Maxim Gorky, Sinclair Lewis, Romain Rolland, and Henri Barbusse. The congress, moreover, agreed to meet again "as soon as it was considered necessary."[73] That time came two years later when the Second International Writers' Congress met (at the peak of the Spanish civil war and in the shadow of the Moscow show trials) in Valencia, Madrid, and, on the last day, in Paris. The atmosphere of the 1937 congresses— the nexus between antifascism and pro-Sovietism, and even more the equation of anti-Sovietism with fascism, served as the keynote—accented the nature of the next phase of Communist cultural policies in 1936–39.

In the aftermath of the Paris congress, Becher passed on to Moscow his "preliminary assessment" of the assembly, characterizing it as a "great and, to some extent, unexpected success." Through the emphasis on humanism and the cultural heritage, Becher predicted, the Communists could succeed "in linking openly the best elements in literature with the labor movement." But Becher also complained about the "danger of a *slide to the left*," which had already manifested itself at the congress. He warned: "It must be avoided at all cost that the congress, along with the organization formed there, can be denounced as Communist." He went on to say that "in several cases we have made it unnecessarily easy for our opponents to disseminate such denunciations." Finally, Becher proposed the formation of what he called a "more select directorate." He evidently had in mind a close-knit body of loyal party literati and functionaries who would seek to pull the strings of the 112-member bureau and of the presidium of twelve. "Needless to say," he concluded, "in view of the complicated nature of the work, such a directorate is an absolute necessity."[74]

72. *Mezhdunarodnyj kongress*, p. 488.
73. Ibid.
74. Johannes R. Becher, in *Zur Tradition der deutschen sozialistischen Literatur: Kommentare*, pp. 394–97.

Whether such a group was ever put together or, indeed, how it might have functioned within the International Writers' Association for the Defense of Culture is unknown; in fact, very little at all has come to light about the writers' association apart from the simple fact that it was still operating well into 1938.

Organization of a writers' conference, formation of a league of anti-Fascist writers, reduction of the five Kharkov slogans to "Struggle against Fascism and War," and mobilization of anti-Fascist elements— these were the goals the Communists set themselves in 1933–34, and all were met by the end of 1935. What accounts for the success? The promotion of "socialist-humanist culture" rather than the "proletarian culture" of the Weimar era helped, but was plainly not the primary inducement for large numbers of intellectuals to fall in line ·behind a movement that, anti-Fascist or not, clearly backed the Soviet Union. For in essence the Communists expected no less from intellectuals in 1935 than they had during the proletarian heyday of the IVRS-BPRS. The head of agitprop in the Comintern's executive committee, Serafima Gopner, proclaimed at the Seventh World Congress of the Comintern in August 1935: "The moment has come when life itself demands categorically from the intellectuals the choice between *fascism* and *communism*."[75] So if there had not been a genuine change in the Communist position, what made so many willing to join a movement almost as unstinting in its lionization of the USSR as in its anathematization of Nazi Germany? In the twenties a large store of goodwill and sympathy for the USSR, far more perhaps than even Soviet leaders realized at the time, had accumulated in Western liberal circles. For much of it the USSR had Willi Münzenberg to thank. The conversion of this reservoir of benevolence into an active, influential force was primarily the achievement of Soviet ingenuity, which was reinforced by Western equivocation toward Nazi Germany. The Soviets managed to make plausible the contention that communism was the antithesis of fascism, that while fascism was the ultimate manifestation of a dying political, social, and cultural order, Soviet-styled socialism represented the wave of the future. Shaken by the triumph of National Socialism, the intellectuals searched the world for a power willing to stand up to Hitler and found, so they thought, only one.
But if the fellow travelers had not succumbed to wishful thinking and had taken instead a probing look at Soviet antifascism and the Communist concept of alliances, they would have found the same old

75. *Protokoll des VII. Weltkongresses*, 2:681.

obduracy. Hans Günther's *Der Herren eigener Geist* exemplifies the immutability of the "new line." Günther inserted the main text of his book (a study of National Socialist ideology) between a fictitious discussion carried on by two intellectuals, an anti-Fascist non-Communist writer (an unnamed Heinrich Mann) and a Communist litterateur, and a concocted letter from the Communist to the anti-Fascist.[76]

The anti-Fascist began by confessing his inability to fathom the justification for continued Communist criticism of writers such as Heinrich Mann, Lion Feuchtwanger, Arnold Zweig, Klaus Mann, Hermann Kesten, and Ludwig Marcuse. In spite of their opposition to nazism, the Communist press and Communist literary and political circles continually made them the butt of ideological criticism. Günther, the Communist writer, answered that these left-wing writers were implacably hostile to Hitler; the Communists recognized this, and it was, after all, precisely this commitment that made allies of them all. Because of this mutual animosity toward National Socialism, the Communists were striving "truly, seriously, and practically" for unity in the struggle against Hitler. The Communists' refusal to soften their criticism of the non-Communists, however, was the result of their belief that it was pointless to cover up differences of opinion. What the Communists really wanted was "*joint discussion*," not "*mutual criticism*," for such talks could only have a "salutory effect" on the common struggle.

Günther then put these words into the mouth of his anti-Fascist: "Our differences concern problems of the *ultimate objective*. You [the Communists] are fighting for: violent overthrow, proletarian dictatorship, a Soviet Germany, coercion!, party dictatorship" (6). These goals, the anti-Fascist said, non-Communists could simply never embrace as the precondition of a common struggle against Hitler. He proposed instead that the question of the final objective be put off until such time as the present "murderous regime has given way to some kind of reasonable, peaceful order" (6). But Günther rejected postponement of the ultimate goal. Both sides were clear as to the common enemy; that was true, Günther conceded. But how to wage the fight against nazism was another matter altogether, for "you cannot separate the ultimate objective from the day-to-day struggle" (6). Differences of opinion about the future social order "also touch on our opposition to fascism, on our perception of its essence and its function" (6).

The anti-Fascist responded that the Communists seemed willing to

76. Günther, *Der Herren eigener Geist*, pp. 5–9 and 218–23. Further page references are given in the text in parentheses.

form a united front only under the condition that non-Communists accept a revolutionary path to defeating Hitler. But Günther insisted that this assessment would be correct only if the Communists made a united front incumbent upon acceptance of such a precondition, which, he said, they did not. The non-Communists were avowed enemies of "fascism and of imperialist war"; they were sympathetic to the cause of the Soviet Union, and that was ample agreement for a start; the Communists "'demanded'" nothing more (9). Günther added jokingly that both he and his anti-Fascist friend would have time enough, "when we are sixty or seventy years old and living in a Soviet Germany" (218), to compose a couple of thick volumes on the history of philosophy in the age of imperialism. (Günther's life ended at the age of thirty-nine in a Soviet transit camp in Vladivostok.) But for now the Communists would not be "upset" if anti-Nazis declined to accept the whole of the Communists' estimation of Fascist ideology. If the advocates of proletarian dictatorship had the slightest thing in common with fascism, Günther stressed, they would force their allies at gunpoint to accept the Communist stance. But "ultimatism has no place in our program" (219).

That brought Günther to the "thorniest question" raised by the anti-Fascist writer—dictatorship. Günther explained the difference in totalitarian rule. The non-Communist, while admiring the achievements of the USSR in the First Five-Year Plan, suggested that things would be infinitely better in Russia were it not for the fact that the country was "in the iron chains of a dictatorship" (220). Günther replied that the working class had one real strength, namely, a fundamentally different approach to the question of violence and terror, as compared with the Nazis. The beasts of prey of finance capital did not intend to roll over and let the Communists assume and hold power; in the Soviet Union there were "even today scattered remnants of the bourgeois and grand bourgeois class enemy" (221). To protect the young Soviet republic and to preserve the gains of the revolution from such elements, "that is the reason, the only reason, we call for the use of force. That is the reason for proletarian dictatorship" (221). Günther used his appraisal of the role of brute force in the USSR to add that the German Communists too would apply force to the class enemy only to the extent that it was necessary to defeat him; on the other hand, the Communists would seek to "persuade" their "natural allies." But no ultimatums would be issued, nor was acceptance of the Communist world view demanded as a precondition for a united front; the Communists were satisfied, said Günther magnanimously, with manifestations of an honest will to fight.

This should all have been casuistry of a fairly transparent nature: today's ally was tomorrow's class enemy. The Communists were only willing to form a united front in which they had the upper hand; they balked at any situation where total organizational control was denied them, knowing full well that once the organizational question had been resolved in their favor ideological problems could be taken in stride. They also refused to believe—ever—that one could be anti-Soviet and anti-Fascist. To say under those circumstances that the proposed members of a united and popular front did not have to "accept" the Communist view was hollow talk. Günther ended his book on a note that, in the light of what he really said, bordered on mockery: "We shall continue to discuss the issues. But that is really not so important. In closing, let us reach consensus on what is most important: *we shall continue to fight—and we shall fight together!*" (223).

What surprises about Günther's elaborations is not his glibness in putting the same old wine into new wineskins, but the fact that men like Heinrich Mann drank it and mistook it for something new. In an August 1935 letter to Günther, Mann reacted to *Der Herren eigener Geist*, a copy of which Günther had sent him. Mann wrote: "It exhibits great erudition and a straightforward spirit that appeals to me. The issues you raise are good and well-taken; from that standpoint you get at the enemy better. In fact, it is the only standpoint that, by simple means, overcomes the foe." As for the section pertaining to him personally and to the "anti-Fascist writer," Mann added:

> You have favored me by referring to my person—sometimes critically, mostly as an ally. I am in complete agreement with that. You sense that I do not reject consistent socialism in any of its essential components. My desire to be truthful precludes me from rejecting it and, in practical terms, it would be folly to "reject" a world power. What I can impart in my literary endeavors is merely supplementation; this springs from a *romancier* who with the passage of time has learned much about human nature. One does what one can. If I often fail to mention scientific facts I nonetheless accept their validity no less than you.

Mann closed his letter: "A great deal would be gained if all polemics with ideological allies were carried out as tactfully as they are in your book."[77]

77. Mann to Günther, 21 August 1935, TsGALI, 1397/1/662/7.

Bitter dissension would rack the popular front several months later in the aftermath of the first Moscow show trial; during the remainder of 1935, however, there were only a few isolated disputes. In 1935 Friedrich Wolf's drama *Floridsdorf* came out in the Soviet Union and in Switzerland. Wolf's unflattering depiction of Otto Bauer, the Austrian Social Democrat, and his interpretation of Austrian Social Democracy in the context of the events of February 1934 prompted Oskar Maria Graf to fire off a furious letter to Karl Schmückle of the German Commission in the IVRS. Graf was appalled at the play, bemoaning the fact that it had appeared at the precise moment when "broad efforts are underway to create a united front, if not a united party! This is what is most upsetting about the disgusting concoction! . . . It has put a crimp again in efforts for a true united front." Graf indicated that he and others sympathetic to the cause of unity had every right to ask about the purpose of the writers' congresses and the Seventh World Congress if such "foolish nonsense" was going to be published. He told Schmückle: "If this was the point of the congresses, then leave me out. It is high time, once and for all, to express the frankest criticism and to use that criticism to put in their place such maudlin scribblers who endanger the united front movement with their inability and imprudence. 'Herr Comrade Wolff' [sic] ought to stick to medicine if he can do no better than to fabricate the likes of this."[78]

Wolf responded immediately with letters to Willi Bredel and Schmückle in the IVRS and to the Austrian and German sections of the Comintern. Claiming that Graf's letter was a virtual carbon copy of the article on *Floridsdorf* carried in Otto Bauer's journal, *Der Kampf*, he made it clear that a different understanding of the united front was at fault. The Social Democratic criticism of *Floridsdorf*, Wolf insisted, was a political ploy. "The apologists of Otto Bauer's tactics all invoke the united front movement as a smoke screen to forbid categorically, once and for all, any criticism of the reasons for the February 1934 defeat." These reasons Wolf saw as the actions of the Austrian Social Democratic Party. The Otto Bauer group interpreted the united front, said Wolf, as a "passport for the falsification of history . . . to shirk their historical responsibility and to kick sand anew in the eyes of the workers." Wolf went on to say that *Floridsdorf* was particularly unpleasant to the Bauer group, which was why they appealed suddenly to the united front and tried with all the means at their disposal to torpedo the play.

78. Graf to Schmückle, 27 September 1935, TsGALI, 631/13/49/52.

In his letter to the Comintern, Wolf asked: "Is a supporter of the united and popular front from now on truly not allowed to exercize criticism of the past mistakes of Social Democracy? . . . Am I to be prohibited from depicting the historical role of Bauer in a realistic play?" If the Bauer perception of the united front was correct, Wolf concluded, then a realistic playwright could no longer deal with topics associated with political life in the West.[79]

In retrospect it is clear that this whole grand scheme of alliance was doomed to disintegrate sooner or later, for the simple reason that the Communists never aspired to genuine cooperation. The eventual breakup would perhaps have come somewhat later than it did had Stalin not hastened the process by staging the first show trial in August 1936, but the breach would have occurred nonetheless. For even ingenuous Communists approached all forms of joint action with the overriding certainty that their understanding of National Socialism and no other conformed to reality. As Günther had pointed out in *Der Herren eigener Geist*, the Communists stood on the basis of Marxism-Leninism and were hence in a position to understand history correctly, for the interests of the working class were in absolute harmony with the objective, real tendencies of human social development. Because the Communists were able to delve correctly into social problems, Günther had said, they could be justifiably proud of the "scientific nature" of their view of the world and of fascism.[80] The intention of the Communists had never been any other than to "persuade" their allies of the truth of Marxism-Leninism-Stalinism and its estimation of Hitler; to call this cooperation, then, was a misnomer from the very beginning. The underlying attitude of Communists to the fellow travelers, even in the most halcyon days of the popular front, was never anything but condescending and school masterish.

The Communists' faith in the infallibility of their world view created a conflict even for the most honest of them in the matter of joint work with the intellectuals. This conflict invariably impinged on what was necessary for genuine cooperation. In November 1935 Alfred Kantorowicz submitted for publication in *Internationale Literatur* an article about Romain Rolland, a perennial fellow traveler with whom Kantorowicz had collaborated closely in such ventures as the German

79. Wolf to Bredel and Schmückle ("MORP"/Deutsche Sektion), 18 October 1935; Wolf to the Comintern (Austrian and German sections), 9 November 1935; both in Wolf-Archiv, Mappe 202.
80. Günther, *Der Herren eigener Geist*, pp. 219–20.

Freedom Library. He received in reply a letter from Willi Bredel that betrays Kantorowicz's attitude toward a fellow traveler. But the letter also exhibits Bredel's sincere desire to have done with unnecessary and counterproductive sectarianism, even as it demonstrates his own ingrained rigidity:

> We prefer not to publish your article . . . for the following reasons: your "Differences with Romain Rolland" [the title, evidently, of the article] are purely external. In discussions with anti-Fascist bourgeois writers we must not make assertions to the effect that concepts such as culture, humanity, and justice are "words of yesterday." . . . A differentiation can consequently occur only by our *proving* convincingly the validity of our standpoint, not in emphasizing differences of opinion. The method of using a man on the one hand, while setting him up as a fool on the other hand, is unacceptable. . . . We have to be continually aware of the fact that the battle waged by the eminent liberals against the Fascists is beyond any doubt a genuine "battle," the profound effects of which are obvious. We should thus not be searching for theoretical differentiations in such discussions but for questions of expediency.[81]

The Paris congress left important organizational questions unresolved —the IVRS had not yet become "invisible." That final step, the dissolution of the International League of Revolutionary Writers, was taken only after a six-month delay caused, it seems, by the Comintern. Certainly Becher and his associates would never have pushed forward with their united front initiative in the absence of general high-level approval from Moscow, and yet there had been puzzling indications all along that some Comintern influentials had reservations about the forward momentum of the literary united front. At the heart of the uncertainty probably lay two related concerns. First, the movement might have been retarded by apprehension within some Comintern quarters that the "new line" would prove unsuccessful and be scrapped after all or that it could fall victim to a sudden switch back to radical policies that would badly compromise its proponents. This had definitely been a problem in preparing the new *political* line—few were willing to assume responsibility for it without a policy statement from Stalin—and there is no reason to think that similar worries were

81. Bredel to Kantorowicz, ca. November 1935, TsGALI, 631/13/63/17.

absent in planning cultural policies. The result could have been the noncommittal, play-it-safe attitude that Bredel had lamented in his letters of 7 March 1935.[82] Of course Becher did not stage the Paris congress of his own volition; as a matter of fact, he seems to have received a last-minute go-ahead in Moscow shortly before the congress.[83] Still, even as late as mid-August, long after the Paris congress was over and a few weeks before the Seventh World Congress of the Comintern was called to order in Moscow, there were tensions of some sort between Becher and the Comintern. Bredel hinted at them in a letter to Otto Biha (Peter Merin) on 14 August 1935: "Hans is in real hot water. He certainly shares responsibility for his predicament, but in spite of this and other things I am doing for him what I can; after all, every blow that hits him strikes us too. But it is my opinion that things cannot go on the way they have, and I hope that our influential club friends [in the KPD or Comintern] will take the time to deal seriously with these questions, those of personnel as well. [Becher] continually sends me long wailing and grumbling letters. I have been running around everywhere, and, as soon as Hans's name comes up, I get a 'very cool reception.' "[84]

The second Comintern consideration perhaps at the heart of the delay in disbanding the IVRS may have been the worry that the literary front had outstripped the political united and popular front. This explanation gains credibility in light of the fact that cultural and political strategy did in fact merge in the first months of 1936 in the popular front, even though the policy of alliances with non-Communists in the area of literature had been kept somewhat separate from the political line through 1935. The Comintern may simply have waited six months to liquidate the IVRS in order to allow the nascent political popular front to get off the ground.

However that may be, the following facts can be pieced together about the last months of the IVRS. In early August, before the Seventh World Congress, the Comintern's Executive Committee (ECCI)

---

82. See note 48.
83. Willi Bredel in Moscow wrote Kantorowicz in Paris on 20 June 1935, the day before the congress opened: "You say you're not sure if Hans [Becher] will tell you everything with the necessary clarity. How am I to take that? If there is not even clarity between you two, how is there supposed to be understanding between us, separated by thousands of kilometers? Hans was here for only a few days, but I think he saw everything here he needed to see with the necessary clarity. I have to keep my ears open around here for a few days before I can tell you how things stand, and I'll let you know anything important immediately" (Bredel to Kantorowicz, 20 June 1935, TsGALI, 631/13/63/8).
84. Bredel to Merin, 14 August 1935, TsGALI, 631/13/69/85.

held a series of meetings to discuss ways of better integrating the International Workers' Relief (MRP) into efforts for an anti-Fascist popular front. On 2 October 1935, five weeks after the Seventh World Congress, the ECCI secretariat met again to discuss the MRP and decided to "reorganize" its executive board into an "internal" commission based in Paris and directly subordinate to the Comintern. The MRP's publishing house and its journals and newspapers, as well as the "Anti-Fascist Archive,"[85] were to be absorbed by the World Committee against War and Fascism. In line with these decisions, the Moscow bureau of the *Arbeiter-Illustrierte Zeitung* was also reorganized, that is, placed under the direct control of the ECCI.[86] Evidently, these were the first of many steps that the Comintern was taking to coordinate the work of the "mass organizations" in the anti-Fascist campaign and to harmonize their activities with Comintern policy and Soviet promotion of collective security. The "reorganizations" of late 1935 thus ushered in the 1936–39 phase of Communist cultural politics in the West. By contrast, all previous fronts, whether created by Münzenberg or by the IVRS, took their place within the general popular front movement. The dissolution of the IVRS should be seen in this context.

In early November 1935 Bredel notified Wilhelm Pieck that Becher, who had been "working on the cultural front in Paris," was back in Moscow and desired a conference with Pieck and any other of the party's Politburo members who chanced to be in Moscow at the moment.[87] The subject of the meeting was to be the most important questions concerning strategy in the cultural arena. The dissolution of the IVRS was probably discussed at this meeting, though no final decision seems to have been reached yet. In any case, the letter indicates the level at which planning was occurring, and there can be no doubt that the final verdict on the IVRS was reached in the Comintern.[88] The dissolution came abruptly and with no publicity on 19 December 1935.[89] *Internationale Literatur*, for instance, made no note of the decision; in fact, the move became apparent only after it

85. This collection of material became the German Freedom Library.
86. Michev, *Mezhrabpom*, pp. 290–99.
87. Bredel to Pieck, 4 November 1935, TsGALI, 631/13/69/124.
88. Michev (*Mezhrabpom*, p. 298), who had access to documents in the Soviet Central Party Archive, attributes the "liquidation" of the IVRS to the Comintern.
89. That the decision itself was taken rapidly is confirmed by the fact that Sergej Tretjakov, writing to Oskar Maria Graf, failed to mention the abolition of the organization in a letter of 17 December, but informed Graf of the end of the IVRS four days later, on 21 December 1935. Graf, *Reise in die Sowjetunion 1934*, pp. 173–75.

dropped the subtitle "Organ of the International League of Revolutionary Writers" in its December issue (which probably did not go to press until well into January). The unpublished Resolution of 19 December announcing the end of the IVRS stated that the "secretariat of the IVRS welcomes the 'International Association for the Defense of Culture,' which was created in Paris at the International Congress, and views it as an organization that is in harmony with the interests and endeavors of the widest circles of writers in their struggle for the defense of culture." The secretariat resolved that "the IVRS, as an organization whose limitations under the present conditions restrict the struggle instead of furthering it, shall be considered liquidated." It called upon writers, organizations, and groups belonging to the IVRS to "join without exception the International Association of Writers for the Defense of Culture, which is located in Paris," and to "appeal to those writers, who are not organizationally bound to the IVRS but who sympathized with and struggled for the realization of its goals, to make their way into the broad front of the struggle for the defense of culture, which is directed by the International Association."[90]

Copies of the resolution seem to have been distributed to various Communist writers who had been active in the IVRS, Martin Andersen Nexö, for instance, though the form of the letter was slightly different. The introductory paragraphs noted that the "secretariat of the IVRS has decided to liquidate the IVRS so as to support the development of the new organization for the defense of culture. A rapid decision was called for in order to avoid any type of parallelism. When we came to this conclusion, we were convinced that you would be in agreement."[91] Dated 31 December and signed by Mikhail Apletin, the communication went on to repeat the proposals contained in the resolution of 19 December. But there had certainly been nothing "rapid" about the decision to avoid "parallelism" because it took the Comintern six months to "dissolve" the organization.

The resolution had spoken of the liquidation of the IVRS. Was it really dismantled in any way, though, or merely turned into an "invisible" operation? The IVRS was undoubtedly abolished in name forever; once the new literary organization had been founded in Paris, the party "dissolved" the IVRS. But the Soviet Writers' Union created in 1934 following RAPP's demise had a "foreign office," a department charged with responsibility for literary affairs abroad, and one of its

90. "Beschluss," TsGALI, 631/13/69/137.
91. Apletin to Andersen Nexö, 31 December 1935, TsGALI, 631/13/69/144.

separate branches was the "German Section." The new foreign office simply rehired members of the IVRS staff, and the German Commission of the former league became the German Section within the foreign office. The people involved were the same as those in the IVRS, while the building out of which the league had worked, Kuznetskij most 12, remained the headquarters of the editorial staff of *Internationale Literatur*, with letters still being sent to and received from writers abroad at the same address well into 1939. The IVRS had become "invisible."

Chapter 6

The German Section of
the Soviet Writers' Union,
1933-1940

In Soviet exile the Germans first organized their activities in the IVRS German National Commission, which was probably created by Hans Günther in October 1932. Evidently identical with the later "Moscow local branch" of the BPRS founded on 14 June 1933,[1] the commission[2] continued to operate after 1933 as the German division of the IVRS until the league was dissolved in December 1935, after which the writers continued their work as the German Section of the Soviet Writers' Union.

The years 1933–34 were still comparatively quiescent for most of those writers already in the USSR, but three members of the IVRS German Commission were already at work in another organization "for the study of Soviet-German literature." This group was formed in 1933 as part of the Org-Committee of the Soviet Writers' Union.[3] This Soviet-German Commission had begun activity in the two main Russian-German population centers: Engels, the governmental seat of the Volga-German Autonomous Soviet Socialist Republic (ASSR), and the Ukrainian capital of Kharkov. Little is known about literary affairs among Soviet Germans. According to the 1934 *Literary Encyclopedia*, Soviet-German literature had grown and consolidated itself "in battle with the old traditions of kulakist-papist nationalistic literature, as one

1. An East German scholar mentions the existence of this Moscow branch of the BPRS but fails to give the source of her information (Jarmatz, *Exil in der UdSSR*, p. 261).
2. The "German National Commission" and the "German Commission" seem to have been interchangeable terms.
3. The Org-Committee, composed after the dissolution of RAPP, was preparing the ground for the new Soviet Writers' Union.

of the branches of Soviet literature." Currently, Soviet-German writing was said to be benefiting from the "achievements" of German revolutionary literature and was under the strong influence of German proletarian writing through the activity of several Germans living in the USSR: Hugo Huppert, Gustav Brand, Josef Schneider, Hermann Paul, and S. Gles.[4] At any rate, Soviet-German writers were first provided with a regular forum when two literary journals began publishing in the early thirties: *Der Sturmschritt* appeared in Kharkov from 1930 to 1935 as the official organ of the "German Section of the Pan-Ukrainian Union of Proletarian-Peasant Writers 'Pflug,'"[5] and *Der Kämpfer* was published from 1933 to 1938 as the official organ of the Union of Soviet Writers of the Volga-German ASSR.[6] Starting in 1926, the *Deutsche Zentral-Zeitung*, a sort of German-language *Pravda*, appeared in Moscow for the benefit of German-speaking Soviet citizens, though from 1935 to 1939 the newspaper rarely carried belles-lettres by Soviet-German authors.[7]

In late 1933 or early 1934 the Soviet-German Commission convened two conferences, the first in Engels and the second in Kharkov, followed a few months later by the First Union Conference of Soviet-German Writers. The meetings, or so the explanation went, were to review the current status of Soviet-German literature, its "successes and achievements, to further the future political and creative development of this literature through the mutual exchange of experiences, and, concurrently, to contrast the vast opportunities for development of the literature of all peoples of the Soviet Union with the . . . growing decline of culture and literature in Fascist Germany."[8] "Brigades" of writers, comprised of Huppert, Gábor, Barta, Hans Gün-

4. *Literaturnaja èntsiklopedija*, pp. 880–88. The *Literary Encyclopedia* provides some biographical information about Gustav Brand (born 1902 in Teplitz-Schönau), who had worked for several years in a "mirror factory" in the Ukrainian Soviet Socialist Republic. The identity of S. Gles, who lived in Leningrad, is a mystery. Josef Schneider, a political commissar under Max Hölz during the 1921 *März Aktion*, had fled to the USSR after the uprising. Hermann Paul was a Communist Sudeten-German writer who sometimes went by the pseudonym Catilina.

5. *Der Sturmschritt* had a circulation between 700 and 1,500. Cf. *Bulletin* (Nr. 1 Mai 1934), herausgegeben von der Kommission zum Studium der sowjetdeutschen Literatur beim Organisationskommittee des Unionsverbandes der Sowjetschriftsteller in Moskau (Redakteur Barta), TsGALI, 631/12/56/8.

6. I had access only to the few scattered issues of these two periodicals on file in the Lenin Library in Moscow.

7. I was able to draw on issues of the *Deutsche Zentral-Zeitung* for the years 1935 to 1939.

8. "Kommission zur Organisierung der Konferenz wolgadeutscher Schriftsteller in Engels und der sowjetdeutschen Schriftsteller in Charkow," TsGALI, 631/12/87/1.

ther, Franz Leschnitzer, and J. R. Becher, were dispatched to Kharkov, Engels, and Leningrad to supervise preparations for the conferences.[9]

The first of the assemblies, for Volga-German writers, met in Engels on 13 or 14 January 1934 with a program including presentations on the significance of the plenum of Soviet Russian writers[10] and on the upcoming meeting of Soviet-German writers in Kharkov (a talk by Barta). Other presentations included one on the international situation (Günther), one on Soviet Russian literature (Leshnev), and one on fascism and literature (Gábor).[11] At the end of the Volga-German Conference, "two or three comrades (BARTA and others)" were instructed to depart immediately for Kharkov to "organize the Conference of Soviet-German Writers in close collaboration with local German comrades and with the support of the Kharkov Org-Committee." The Kharkov conference was slated for middle or late February with "Reich German writer-comrades currently residing in the Soviet Union and several prominent Soviet Russian writers" scheduled to be in attendance. The program resembled that of the Engels conference; speeches were to be given by Barta (general report), Huppert (Soviet-German literature), and Becher (international report), with talks by representatives of Volga-German writers and German literati from Leningrad also on the program.[12]

The First Union Conference of Soviet-German Writers met in Moscow on 21–26 March 1934 with thirty-five delegates present: twelve from the Volga-German ASSR, seven from the Ukraine, five from Leningrad, and eleven from Moscow.[13] The gathering, which opened in the Foreign Workers' Club with an evening meeting attended by five hundred guests, including party and government representatives Fritz Heckert and Pavel Judin, heard speeches containing information about the recent "brigade" visit of Barta, Gábor, and Huppert to Kharkov. It seems that the three men, to judge from the speeches, had initiated a purge of sorts of Ukrainian-German writers associated with the journal *Der Sturmschritt.*

9. A small colony of local and exile German "writers" also made their home in Leningrad.

10. The Org-Committee was holding a series of plenary sessions in preparation for the new Soviet Writers' Union.

11. Hugo Huppert claims to have given the main address in Engels, but appears to be confusing his talk with one he gave in Kharkov. Huppert, *Wanduhr mit Vordergrund*, p. 491.

12. "Kommission zur Organisierung der Konferenz," TsGALI, 631/12/87/3–4.

13. "Über die erste Unionskonferenz sowjetdeutscher Schriftsteller," *Bulletin* (Nr. 1), TsGALI, 631/12/56/28.

Soviet literature in the Ukraine, Alexander Barta said in his conference speech, had made great strides forward; *"but the 'Sturmschritt,' as
well as the Kharkov group of writers, have committed a series of literary-
political errors that are naturally reflected in the journal and in literature
proper."* It was common knowledge that in recent times nationalist,
chauvinist, counterrevolutionary elements had set out in the cultural
arena in the Ukraine to organize "their counterrevolutionary machinations and gain influence." Many of these elements were the instru-
ments and accomplices of the interventionists. But the counterrevolutionary elements had been crushed and destroyed by the party and
the organs of proletarian dictatorship. Barta asked, "What should
have been the task of Soviet-German literature during this time of
intensified class warfare?" Its most important and preeminent job
should have been to thrust itself actively into the battle against counterrevolutionary elements. "The writers should have placed themselves
in the forefront of the ideological struggle." But had *Der Sturmschritt*
understood the response demanded of it? "I don't think it did!" Barta
complained. "No, comrades! The group of Kharkov writers and the
journal committed a number of errors, and the group *behaved passively
during a decisive time of class warfare in the Ukraine.* There were, to be
sure, a handful of articles published against fascism, but a systematic
journalistic line of opposition to fascism and cultural fascism was nowhere to be found. As regards class vigilance, the comrades have
made serious errors."[14]

Whether the outcry about *Der Sturmschritt* came in the wake of a
political or an actual blood purge is a matter of some uncertainty,
though blood purges had begun early there in connection with Ukrainian
nationalism. The Ukrainian-German writer Beiser alluded quite clearly
to an assault of sorts on a "group of wreckers." He said in his speech at
the conference, "I would like to speak of individual comrades in the
Ukraine, for instance, of Comrade Fichtner, who has no Marxist background.[15] Why? Because the Org-Committee took too little interest in
the German group; because after the wreckers' clique was crushed, no
one was concerned about the ideological strengthening and consolidation of the German group."[16]

The major address dealing with *Der Sturmschritt* was given by the
journal's editor, David Schellenberg, who spoke of the visit to Kharkov

14. Barta's speech is in *Bulletin* (Nr. 1), TsGALI, 631/12/56/8.
15. Fichtner, at least in 1930, was the secretary of the German section of the Pan-
Ukrainian Union of Proletarian-Peasant Writers "Pflug."
16. Beiser's comments are in *Bulletin* (Nr. 1), TsGALI, 631/12/56/17.

of a "brigade of the Org-Committee consisting of comrades Barta, Gábor, and Huppert. The brigade," Schellenberg explained, "imparted to our literature the knowledge of what it was doing—brought it to its senses. The brigade showed us what Bolshevist self-criticism looks like, something we had failed to understand in the years that lie behind us." The brigade had straightened out the Soviet-German Kharkov group insofar as it now saw the political tasks before it with crystal clarity. Political conditions in the Ukraine were troublesome; particularly disturbing was the increasing severity of class warfare in that portion of the Soviet Union that the Fascists and the foreign interventionists, particularly Germany, had an eye on. These serious situations should have had certain repercussions on the German literature of the Ukraine (if it had been correctly guided), in the sense that the writers' battle against fascism in the German village [in the Ukraine] should have been strengthened with respect to literature as well. But the response had been insufficient, Schellenberg confessed to his listeners; in *Der Sturmschritt* there had been an unacceptably low level of class vigilance. What had been at stake was not merely "one kulakist counterrevolutionary such as Jansen, who cleverly managed to sneak into our publication." Rather, "as Comrade Barta remarked," the image of the journal was in peril; there had been a wholesale lack of organization among the group of writers and lowered class vigilance. "What we wrote in 1933 was insufficiently anti-Fascist, though we were conscious of the fact that a battle against fascism should have been waged in the German village. The brigade held the opinion, and I share it, that in the political struggle against fascism the writers [must] recognize this danger and portray it in their writing."[17]

Schellenberg mentioned some of the "Fascist agents" by name. A certain Mikwitz, who worked as a professor of literature in Odessa, was "consciously involved in sabotage." He had wittingly left uncorrected the language of his students, "the awkward German of the colonists." He did this for the purpose of releasing the graduates back to the villages with the same low linguistic level with which they had come to his institute. At Mikwitz's side stood A. Ström, who formulated the theory, said Schellenberg, that posited the existence of a special Soviet-German language, the "German language of the kulaks in the former czarist villages." A. Mueller, who was "later unmasked as a spy," and S. Nickel, the editor of the pedagogical journal *Kom-*

---

17. These references to "fascism" and class warfare with respect to the German villages in the Ukraine are oblique but recognizable allusions to Russian-German resistance to forced collectivization during the First Five-Year Plan.

munistische Erziehung, had provided Ström with the opportunity to thwart past criticisms of his activity. In his closing remarks, Schellenberg thanked Barta personally for his help in rooting out the enemies. "With a highly developed political intuition he went after all our literary and political weaknesses and uncovered much that would have otherwise gone unnoticed, the poem by Jansen and a number of other shortcomings."[18]

As for Soviet-German literature in general, the conference resolved that the organization of the writers begun by the brigade would continue under the auspices of a German "subsection" within the Org-Committee of the Soviet Writers' Union. This subsection would establish contact with Soviet-German literary groups; sponsor creative and critical exchanges between the various groups of Soviet-German literature; keep the Soviet-German literary movement apprised of the status of German revolutionary literature in the capitalist countries; dispatch during the year "several comrades" from Moscow to the different Soviet-German groups to hold consultations, direct educational courses, and give talks; supply the German-language newspapers and journals with literary material; prepare future meetings and conferences of Soviet-German writers; and publish a monthly journal in Moscow. Finally, the notion of guardianship, which the Moscow group of writers had "introduced by assuming these duties with respect to Volga-German literature," would be broadened. The German writers in Moscow, the exiles, were to establish and actively pursue "personal guardianship" over all Soviet-German writers.[19]

Hugo Huppert, in his address, then shifted the emphasis of the conference somewhat, trying to define more specifically the role of the exiled German writer in the Soviet Union. Without losing contact with the revolutionary, anti-Fascist literary movement abroad, the "immigrant" proletarian writers had "more or less rapidly, more or less intensely" involved themselves in the "all-encompassing process of socialist construction." Huppert told the audience that the immigrant writers were "engaged in work among the masses in factories and collective farms." They were reaching, individually and in brigade groups, into the most remote construction sites of socialist industry and were working together with the indigenous German literary forces to fulfill a specific dual task: "to link correctly the struggle

18. David Schellenberg, "Über die Fehler des 'Sturmschritt,' " *Bulletin* (Nr. 1), TsGALI, 631/12/56/23–24.
19. "Beschlüsse der Konferenz," TsGALI, 631/12/56/26–27.

against fascism and Fascist cultural reaction in the capitalist world and against counterrevolutionary nationalism and national-democratic deviations in the Soviet Union with propaganda and popularization of the work of socialist construction and with cultural revolution in the Soviet Union." But the exiled Germans had not been active enough, "neither in the *exploitation of their Soviet experience* for the revolutionary literary movement abroad, nor in their depiction of Soviet subject matter in their creative work." They had put themselves insufficiently in touch with Soviet-German regions and their "literary cadres."[20]

Huppert then set forth his definition of exiled and local German writers. It would be "artificial and pernicious," he said, to separate in any methodological or literary-political sense "the 'local' and the 'immigrant' in literature." The decisive knots had long since been tied between the two groups, Huppert explained, "and the tasks of every Soviet-German writer [that is, exile and local alike], regardless of where he came from, have become clear in their characteristic duality." These two tasks were first, the depiction of the capitalist world and second, depiction of the socialist world. "Two irreconcilable worlds—the capitalist and the socialist—stand opposite to each other; it is the historic job of every Soviet-German writer, whether his crib was here or over there, to depict this conflict from the writer's standpoint in a realistic fashion. Without the correct understanding of this (I would like to say organizational) dual task, *socialist realism* is unthinkable for us."[21]

Huppert regarded the Reich German writers not as exiles at all, then, but as *immigrants,* as Soviet-German writers. This notion was rarely so plainly spelled out, and yet most of the exiled Germans would have accepted the general validity of the view. Willi Bredel, to take an example from another context, put it a bit differently, but the meaning was the same: the USSR was less a place of exile than a homeland. "Many Germans found asylum in other countries following the establishment of Fascist barbarism in Germany," he said; "but

---

20. An undated fragmentary document from the "Kommission zum Studium der sowjetdeutschen Literatur, unter Führung von Gen. Alexander Barta" (TsGALI, 631/12/1/1) mentions the following "literary gatherings" organized in collaboration with VEGAAR and the Library for Foreign Literature: an evening with old Bolsheviks (Gábor, Hotopp, Germanetto); two evenings in Kuntsevo (Hotopp, Leschnitzer); an evening in "Serp and Molot" (evidently a factory) in Pavshino (Bredel) and in Moscow at watch factories (Hotopp, Gábor); and an evening for Moscow construction workers (Leschnitzer, Scharrer, Hotopp, Bredel, Plivier, and Emma Dornberger).

21. "Rede von Hugo Huppert," *Bulletin* (Nr 2, Juni 1934), hg. von der Kommission zum Studium der sowjetdeutschen Literatur, TsGALI, 631/12/56/44.

only those who entered the land of socialism became state citizens with full rights, and those who are now working enthusiastically on socialist construction found a new home."[22] He himself had not, in this sense, located a new homeland, a new fatherland; rather, "the Soviet Union has always been the fatherland of my choice, my only true fatherland, long before the advent of the Hitler dictatorship. . . . Thus, I enjoy the great good fortune of living and working in the fatherland that, since it came into existence, has been the fatherland of my choice."[23]

The German Commission of the IVRS had met often in late 1932 and early 1933.[24] Still, apart from work with Soviet-German literature, principally the concern of Barta, Gábor, and Huppert, the writers seem not to have organized well until late 1934 and 1935, by which time most of the Germans had reached the Soviet Union. On 2 April 1933, shortly after his arrival in the USSR, Becher had talked to the German Commission about future plans for writers in the USSR,[25] and on 10 May 1933 discussion groups were set up, headed by Becher (poetry), Gábor (narrative prose), and Hans Günther and Paul Reimann (theory and criticism). Two meetings of the poetry section were held in June and July 1933, but gatherings of the other groups are recorded only for late 1934, 1935, and 1936.[26] The commission seems to have done little else in 1933 and early 1934.

The German Commission began displaying greater activity in the course of 1935. A work plan for February–March 1935 speaks of "organizing the German Commission," the activity of which was to be "intensified" by following through on a proposal "made several months

22. This remark indicates that Bredel counted himself among those who had assumed Soviet citizenship.
23. "Wahre Heimat," in Bredel-Archiv, Sig. 221/2 (732).
24. There were several meetings in December 1932 and in the first three months of 1933.
25. Cf. Jarmatz, *Exil in der UdSSR*, p. 256.
26. Ibid., pp. 256–57. Some examples from 1934–35: On 25 November Andor Gábor chaired a "working group" for narrative prose. Emma Dornberger, Hans Klemm, and Franz Leschnitzer also read poetry, and Gustav Brand gave a report on "Language and Style." At another meeting, Paul Reimann spoke on "Methods in Researching the Heritage." In January 1935 Georg Lukács spoke on the subject of one of his major essays, "Erzählen und Beschreiben." Leschnitzer reported: "With the most exact arguments he provided proof of why the typical in a prose work of art must not be identified with the 'day-to-day.' Hopefully these comments (and many others) in his excellent talk will provide his listeners with the stimulation they so badly need!" Fragment in TsGALI, 631/12/2/1–4.

earlier" to constitute a "German Commission" that would assemble monthly.[27] The anonymous author of the work plan suggested as members of the commission Ottwalt, Schmückle, Gábor, Günther, Scharrer, Plivier, Lukács, Piscator, Wolf, and Bredel.[28] Another work plan (fragmentary and anonymous) provides some details about the commission in October 1935: "For several weeks now there exist extremely good contacts with the German party leadership. Comrade Heinrich Most [Heinrich Meyer] has made it possible for the German writers in Moscow to contribute regularly to the illegal press."[29] The German Commission—Schmückle, Ottwalt, Lukács, Gábor, Weinert, Erpenbeck, Günther, and Bredel—had reconstituted itself and resolved to gather twice a month. Furthermore, "the comrades in the German Commission of MORP [IVRS] are to a large extent working actively in the Soviet Writers' Union[30] in planning the literary foregatherings of the foreign bureau of the Soviet Writers' Union and in establishing closer contact with Russian writer-comrades."[31]

Work with Soviet-German writers also continued as a top priority; for the first half of 1935, a variety of activities were scheduled for what this work plan now called in Russian a "Commission of German Writers within the Soviet Writers' Union."[32] These activities included: (1) publication of a monthly bulletin with information about questions of literary theory, German proletarian and Fascist literature, the work of individual groups of German writers in the USSR, the work of the Soviet Writers' Union leadership; also with "consultations,"[33] publica-

27. There is considerable confusion in the use of the term "German Commission"; it was evidently applied as a general designation for the German Commission of the IVRS as well as, more specifically, for the governing body of that Commission, a more select group.

28. "Plan für die Arbeit in der deutschen Kommission der IVRS—Februar–März 1935," TsGALI, 631/13/73/4–5.

29. Evidently, this meant contributions to illegal editions of papers like the *Rote Fahne* appearing sporadically inside Nazi Germany.

30. At this time there still seems to have been a distinction, though it was now beginning to blur, between the German Commission of the IVRS and German émigré work under the aegis of the Soviet Writers' Union. See note 32.

31. "Deutsche Kommission der IVRS (Oktober, 1934 [*sic*])," TsGALI, 631/12/50/1.

32. This document (see Note 38) refers unmistakably to a "Commission of German Writers within [*pri*] the Soviet Writers' Union of the USSR." It seems unlikely that there were now two separate German Commissions, one within the IVRS and the other within the Soviet Writers' Union, but, for whatever reason, the commission was now going by two different names and apparently existed somehow or other under the roofs of two different parent organizations.

33. "Consultations" were literary evaluations made by more "experienced" writers in the fashion of criticism and self-criticism among "party comrades".

tion of criticism and surveys of the production of Soviet-German literature, a chronicle of Soviet-German literature, and a survey of translations of creative literature from the German;[34] (2) organization of "creative gatherings" of German-Soviet writers (presided over by Bredel, Huppert, and Wolf); (3) creative gatherings for the benefit of German writers arriving from abroad;[35] (4) trips by separate "comrade-writer-critics" to provide assistance and literary consultations for separate groups of Soviet-German writers;[36] (5) plans for the work of future literary gatherings of foreign workers in factories and clubs;[37] (6) organization of a large anti-Fascist meeting attended by German, Russian, Ukrainian, Belorussian, Jewish, and other writers "opposed to fascism and Fascist culture"; (7) discussion of *Der Sturmschritt, II. (Internationale Literatur)*, and *Der Kämpfer*; (8) collection of informational and creative material for German radio broadcasts in Moscow; (9) plans for visits of German writers in factories in Moscow; and (10) discussion of the translations of German literature into Russian and of Soviet literature into German.[38]

The plan for the second half of 1935 was much the same, including more "business trips" to Engels and the Ukraine to benefit local groups of German writers. New on the agenda, though, was the preparation of an All-Union Meeting of Soviet-German Writers in Moscow. Another work plan for 1936 listed the same objectives and mentioned again an upcoming All-Union Meeting of Soviet-German writers.[39]

34. The "monthly bulletin," which never appeared monthly, was now put out by a different group. The first two had been edited by the "Kommission zum Studium der sowjetdeutschen Literatur beim Organisations-Kommittee des Unionsverbandes der Schriftsteller in Moskau." The third issue (I have seen a total of six) was put out by the "Deutsche Kommission des Verbandes der Sowjetschriftsteller in Moskau." Evidently, then, there was a German Commission of sorts, at least in name, formed within the Soviet Writers' Union shortly after the union was created, though the German Commission of the IVRS continued to function.

35. This sentence is inked out in the handwritten draft.

36. Trips were mentioned to Engels (fourteen days), Kharkov (ten days), and Leningrad (five days).

37. There were visits by Berta Lask, Albert Hotopp, Gábor, and Friedrich Wolf to various factories.

38. "Plan raboty Komissii nemetskikh pisatelej pri SSP SSSR na 1935 god," TsGALI, 631/12/84/4–5.

39. The congress seems to have met. A financial report of expenditures by the German Commission in the Soviet Writers' Union for 1935 reports an outlay of 6,850 rubles out of an annual 1935 budget of 23,910 rubles for "organization of the All-Union Congress of German Writers in Moscow lasting four days, with invitations to writers from Engels, Leningrad, Kharkov, Odessa—in all fifteen people." "Skhema raskhodov nemetskoj komissii pri SSP na 1935 god," TsGALI, 631/12/84/11–12.

Through most of 1935, the duties as head of the German Commission were discharged by Willi Bredel, whose correspondence casts some light on the atmosphere that year within the commission. "As a writer I am now being ground under by the conditions here," he complained in March 1935 to Otto Biha. "I don't intend to put up with it much longer; one of these days I am going to clear out of here." Bredel said that at the moment he was sitting in the IVRS all alone and with an enormous workload in front of him. "The only help is Comrade P. Karl [Schmückle] is dropping out. Don't be taken unaware if you hear something surprising from me one of these days." A few weeks later he wrote Biha again, mentioning that he was up to his neck in the "dirt of trifling matters" and often worn down by the most "ridiculous problems in the world." His plans for the future, he added, "are firm and they have precious little to do with the IVRS." Bredel wanted to leave for the West. In June he sent Hermann Schubert in the Comintern the addresses of "both comrades who could be considered as my successor in the IVRS," Biha and Kurt Kläber, both of whom were then living in Switzerland. In July Bredel informed Biha that the suggestion to bring him to the USSR was still under consideration; "the responsible authorities [the Comintern] will make the decision." But things evidently changed after the Paris Writers' Congress. Bredel wrote Biha that, on the one hand, they would have to wait and see what developed, and, on the other hand, "Hans [Becher] is returning, and, as far as I'm concerned, can have his old chair back; that would solve the 'chair question' he once wrote me about." None of this affected Bredel's plans to sever his ties with the IVRS. In October 1935, just a few weeks before the IVRS ceased its existence, he again wrote Biha, telling him that he had renewed the struggle for his "free time" from the IVRS with increased vigor. In November Bredel finally left "under Comintern orders for several months abroad."[40]

The BPRS had been riddled with personal and professional rivalries throughout its life; Lukács' criticism of Brecht, Bredel, and Ottwalt and other internal disagreements had done much to contaminate the atmosphere within the organization, some of whose members remained at each others' throats later in Soviet exile. That personality

40. Letters from Bredel to Otto Biha (Peter Merin), 7 and 8 July, 14 August, and 8 October 1935; Bredel to Hermann Schubert (Max Richter), 21 June 1935; Bredel to Alexander Barta (Parteiorg. der Parteizelle MORP), 10 November 1935. TsGALI, 631/13/69/42, 57, 80, 81, 85, 110, 127.

conflicts, bickering, and jealously plagued the émigrés may not have
been all that unusual in itself. In exile, however, some of these men
lost their composure completely, so that if the writers had been anything but close-knit prior to 1933, cliques formed and old ones re-
formed within a short time after beginning their Soviet exile. As a
result, duplicity, intrigues, and conspiracies began to dog the German
Section; and once the great terror was in full swing, small differences
of opinion among men who tended to distrust each other from the
outset were frequently magnified into political confrontations, the
arguments used being designed only to discredit and defame politically by innuendo, insinuation, and outright slander. Some of the literati in the German Section became past masters at the art of calumni-
ating through "literary criticism."

When altercations occurred among the literati, the cause was not
always immediately apparent. As often as not the real reason sprang
from some distant dispute in the past, though, on the other hand,
many of the quarrels and feuds happened to be conflicts with no real
cause, generated by minor differences of opinion or by personality
clashes that would have been easily resolved under conditions other
than those of the Soviet Union during the thirties. But the keyed-up
atmosphere of the times tended to blow completely out of proportion
insignificant disagreements and misunderstandings. Consequently, these
often grew into no-holds-barred "political" debates. The case of S.
Gles in 1935 is one of the instances where fellow exiles managed a
public attack on a German writer, and an explanation for the nastiness
of the criticism is hard to come by. In Soviet exile Gles published two
volumes of short stories and a play. One of the volumes, *Deutschland
erwacht!*,[41] drew the ire of Otto Bork, head of VEGAAR's German
section. Bork attacked Gles in the *Deutsche Zentral-Zeitung*, charging
that the volume, which contained stories about the illegal activity of
Communist workers in Hitler's Germany, was "bloody dilettantism."
Bork maintained that two of the stories were particularly blatant instances of "how little" Gles tried to make use of the lessons learned at
the Soviet Writers' Congress. "He fabricates a story; and if reality is
different, that's too bad for reality. Gles imposes a conflict on his
stories and generally solves it with some type of 'happy end.' The
people in these stories are depicted like lifeless models. . . . They
speak in the language of editorials and party theses."[42] Bork also used

---

41. Gles, *Deutschland erwacht!*
42. Otto Bork, *"Deutschland erwacht!," Deutsche Zentral-Zeitung*, 26 November 1935.

the opportunity to give the publisher in Engels a tongue-lashing for printing the book in the first place.

After Bork's upbraiding, the subject rested for five months, at least in the press, until the *Deutsche Zentral-Zeitung* published a short letter from A. Loos, head of the Deutscher Staatsverlag in Engels, announcing that Gles's book had been withdrawn from sale.[43] A few days later, Erich Weinert penned a long article for the paper entitled "A Blemish on German Literature," in which he scored Gles's drama *Verboten,* a play about the 1 May 1929 events in Berlin. In view of the attacks on Gles's earlier book, said Weinert, it had been hoped that he would exercise the necessary self-criticism and that it would have dawned on him that "he owes the publication of his literary blunderings solely to the circumstances that there are publishing firms that look upon him as a German writer."[44] Weinert also chastised the Staatsverlag für nationale Minderheiten der USSR in Kiev, charging that Gles lacked creative talent, responsibility, and diligence. Weinert flung one epithet after another, calling Gles an illiterate and insisting that only the very best anti-Fascist literature should be published by Soviet houses; and, he added, it generally was. But when that did not happen, readers were duty-bound to defend themselves against books such as those by Gles. Weinert also reproached MORT, the International League of Revolutionary Theaters, for printing its recommendation of the play in the foreword to *Verboten.*

A short time later the *Deutsche Zentral-Zeitung* published a response from the "repertory commission of MORT." The commission stated that its recommendation had been written in 1933 and that it intended for the play to be performed only in theater circles and by agitprop groups. MORT had been aware of the play's weaknesses and explained that it had opposed VEGAAR's publication when Gles sought to have it accepted there; it also had advised against publishing it in Engels, but Gles had then gone to the Kiev firm behind the back of MORT.[45] The denouement to the affair came in the fall, after the first Moscow show trial, when the *Deutsche Zentral-Zeitung* announced Gles's expulsion from the Soviet Writers' Union. The articles by Bork and Weinert had led to an "investigation by the Leningrad secretariat of the Soviet Writers' Union," which sent the *Deutsche Zentral-Zeitung* this resolution:

43. Ibid., 8 May 1936.
44. Erich Weinert, "Ein Schandfleck der deutschen Literatur," *Deutsche Zentral-Zeitung,* 24 May 1936.
45. Ibid., 27 May 1936.

S. Gles, candidate for membership in the Union of Soviet
Writers, was expelled from the union at a meeting of the
secretariat of the Leningrad chapter of the Union of Writers.
The reasons:

(1) For the publication of politically harmful trash.

(2) Because in his literary activity he has behaved like a
third-rate scribbler.

(3) For greed and a series of acts unworthy of a candidate
for membership in the Soviet Union of Writers.[46]

When and under what circumstances Gles may have met his end is
not known, but nothing more was heard from him.

Most of the cabals within the German Section were spun by the
coterie of literati that grouped itself around Georg Lukács and continued the literary theoretical debates of the BPRS. The activist role in
the campaign within the German Section to "improve" proletarian
literature was played less by Georg Lukács himself, though his views
served as inspiration, than by his lieutenant, Andor Gábor. In German Section meetings Gábor battled stereotyped, unimaginative proletarian literature. On the other hand, Lukács waged war, in one
form or another, in all of his essays against the "modern" writing
practiced outside Soviet exile by Brecht and other avant-gardists, whose
literary praxis was supported in theoretical statements by, among others, Eisler, Bloch, and Benjamin. Fritz Erpenbeck and Alfred Kurella
joined the fray later when the entire group stage-managed the expressionism debate in 1937. Gábor's behavior was particularly unsa-
vory. Whipped once by party discipline in 1930 for his dogmatic and
narrow insistence that *only* proletarian-born writers could create true
proletarian literature, Gábor learned never to buck the tide again;
after his volte-face of 1931, he threw in his lot with the Lukács group
and in Soviet exile turned his vulgarized version of Lukács's aesthet-
ics into an utter obsession, lashing out constantly at the "errors" being
made in literature by "political functionaries" who had taken up the
pen.

For Willi Bredel Gábor had a special animus. In early 1935 he
wrote in a review of Bredel's *Die Prüfung* that Bredel's other novels
contained an unintentional and unconscious mirror image of the political niveau of the writer who was first and foremost a political functionary. Bredel was typical, Gábor contended, of those who had found
their way to literature from the ranks of party cadres; they represented

---

46. "Der Fall S. Gles," *Deutsche Zentral-Zeitung*, 3 September 1936.

a new type of writer who created a kind of literature "either praised to high heaven for propagandistic reasons as party literature . . . or dismissed . . . with an arrogant wave of the hand." Only a few had taken the trouble ("especially Georg Lukács in the *Linkskurve*") to subject this literature and its practitioners to a Marxist critique. Bredel was one of the "best representatives" of this literature, said Gábor; he was the new type of writer "who was more a party functionary than an artist." But, he continued, "his initial artistic niveau matched exactly that of a party functionary of the times." He did know his class, but, as a representer of this "valuable material," he did not do justice in his first two novels to the demands that this material made upon the writer. "He remains dry and colorless, drawing silhouettes and contours rather than human beings, giving finished political results rather than the living process. These are the shortcomings, drawn together in a literary work, of the party functionary of the time."[47]

Such criticism does not sound unreasonable, but as time went on Gábor became more and more dictatorial and prescriptive. The archives in Budapest and East Berlin are full of his "consultations"— vicious, narrow-minded exposés of other writers' work. There was always, to be sure, a kernel of truth in Gábor's criticism; he was not being critical of good literature, but he did lash out at the hackneyed political tractates created by writers who began their careers within the proletarian literary movement of the twenties. But his vindictiveness was bound to insult writers who were time and again the targets of his nasty strictures, even had he not tried his own hand at creative writing. In Soviet exile, though, he himself published two lengthy volumes of short stories; these were not only inferior to most of what Bredel wrote, but also as banal, uninspired, and vapid as the lowest-grade proletarian writing. Yet this arrogant factionist nonetheless mandated himself to tell others how to write.

In early 1937 he published one of his volumes of short stories about the illegal Communist underground in Germany. Herbert Wehner (writing under the pseudonym Kurt Funk) read the book, and, aware of the true situation in the country, objected to the inaccuracy of Gábor's portrayal, bringing what he thought to be a purely literary matter to the attention of Walter Ulbricht and Philipp Dengel. He also discussed it with Julja Annenkova, who asked him to write an article about Gábor's book for the *Deutsche Zentral-Zeitung*. When the review was published,[48] Lukács and Gábor reportedly construed it as a de-

47. Andor Gábor, "Bredel: *Die Prüfung*," MTA, Gábor Andor-Hagyaték, Ms. 4479/87.
48. Herbert Wehner [Kurt Funk], "Gábors *Die Rechnung*," *Deutsche Zentral-Zeitung*, 22 March 1937.

nunciation and demanded an airing of the affair in a writers' meeting. According to Wehner, Lukács and Gábor had the idée fixe that, spurred on by Annenkova, he was being misused to "destroy" Gábor. Lukács and Gábor also linked Wehner to Willi Bredel[49] and Hugo Huppert, who were seen as allies of Annenkova.[50]

The way Julius Hay tells the story, Walter Ulbricht took Wehner's article and indeed tried to make a political case of it.[51] He initiated "disciplinary action" against Gábor, who, along with Lukács, visited Wehner in the Hotel Lux and made it clear to him what was possibly at stake. Wehner then managed to squelch further measures. But Ulbricht refused to let the matter lie. When Wehner left for illegal work in Germany, Ulbricht brought it up again, calling for a "literary discussion." There he sought to picture the writing of Gábor's book as a sinister falsification of reality. During the course of the discussion, Ulbricht began to threaten not only Gábor but *all* the "Hungarian writer-comrades." Things eventually came to a head when Ulbricht questioned whether the "damage" caused by the Hungarian writers was at all reparable, at which time he was called out of the meeting for a few minutes. When he came back in the company of Wilhelm Pieck, the latter told the writers in a jovial tone of voice to work diligently instead of squabbling among themselves, and the meeting was adjourned. Eugen Varga had evidently gotten wind of what was going on and went directly to Dimitroff; with a note from him, Ulbricht was reined in.[52] This was still not the end of the altercation. Shortly after the above affair ended, Gábor began planning revenge against Bredel, and differences between the leadership of the German Section and the *Deutsche Zentral-Zeitung* eventually culminated in an NKVD raid on the paper.[53]

German actors and actresses given asylum in the Soviet Union found work from 1933 to 1937 with four stage companies: the German Theater "Kolonne Links," the German Regional Theater in Dnjepropetrovsk, the German Collective Farm Theater in Odessa, and the German State Theater in Engels.[54]

49. Bredel had in fact backed Funk's harsh but fair criticism of Gábor.
50. Wehner, "Erinnerungen," pp. 137–38.
51. Hay, *Geboren 1900*, pp. 219–21.
52. It is not entirely clear from Wehner's account whether he ever knew about the continuation of the debate.
53. Virtually every member of the editorial staff was arrested. See the discussion in Chapter 11.
54. Most of my comments about German actors and actresses in the USSR are drawn from Diezel's excellent *Exiltheater in der Sowjetunion*.

As early as 1933, steps had been taken in Moscow to base a German exile theater permanently in the Soviet capital. The man behind the project was Erwin Piscator, who spoke in mid-1934 of the need for a resident German theater in the Soviet Union, one that would not only demonstrate the continuity of German culture, preserved by Communists rather than by Goebbels, but would "also assure the existence of German theatrical culture till the day for which we are preparing—the day of the revolutionary triumph over fascism."[55] Two agitprop groups, the Kolonne Links, which was already in the Soviet Union, and Gustav von Wangenheim's Truppe 1931, which needed to be brought to the USSR, were to merge in creating the new exile theater. Since its emigration to Russia in late 1931, the Kolonne Links had been busy performing programs designed to appeal to the foreign worker population in the USSR. After some initial success, though, the troupe had fallen on hard times, which caused it to be put under the supervision of the International League of Revolutionary Theaters (IRTB, or MORT). The new director, Arthur Pieck, had taken over and approached Wangenheim about a possible merger of his Truppe 1931 with the Kolonne Links as a preliminary move toward the establishment of a German theater in Moscow.

After the Nazis had outlawed it in March 1933, the Truppe 1931 had emigrated collectively to Paris. There initial plans were to turn it into an anti-Fascist traveling theater performing in France, the Saar, Switzerland, and Austria. But after several setbacks, the decision was made instead to move the Truppe 1931 to Moscow, a transfer to be made in separate stages because of visa and hard currency difficulties. In August 1933 Wangenheim and Ingeborg Franke (Inge von Wangenheim) arrived in Moscow and assumed the artistic management of the new German Theater "Kolonne Links." Arthur Pieck was to handle the business end of the venture. From the Kolonne Links Kurt Arendt, Karl Oefelein, Hanni Schmitz (Rodenberg), Bruno Schmidtsdorf, Albert Wolff, and Hans Hauska remained, joined by Curt Trepte and Luisrose Fournes from the Truppe 1931. Others scheduled to join the company were Steffie Spira and Günter Ruschin, but the project fizzled out before they reached Moscow. Rudolf Nehls (Fischer), who had been under contract to the Engels Volga-German State Theater from 1932 to 1933, and Sylta Reismann-Busse did sign with the new theater, which debuted in February 1934 in the Foreign Workers' Club with Wangenheim's *Helden im Keller*, Demjan Bednyj's

---

55. Ibid., p. 32.

Brak!—Brak! (reworked by Wangenheim), and Brecht's *Die Ballade vom Reichstagsbrand* in Ernst Ottwalt's adaptation.

The troupe soon set off on a two-week tour of the Donets Basin, performing in front of Russian and foreign workers; the trip was followed by one-week stands in Rostov-on-the-Don and Kharkov and by an August–September stay in the Volga-German ASSR. New, talented actors and actresses—Carola Neher, Lotte Loebinger, and Heinrich Greif—were then signed to contracts, and during a summer 1934 trip through Poland, Czechoslovakia, Austria, and Switzerland Wangenheim received tentative contract agreements from Alexander Granach, Erwin Geschonneck, and the scenic designer Teo Otto. The German Theater "Kolonne Links" set itself two major goals. The company planned to stage productions dealing with political problems, customs, and life in the West at the same time that it acted as an intermediary between the foreign workers in the USSR and "Soviet reality" by performing suitable plays about Soviet life. The theater also wanted to function as a "tribune for suppressed revolutionary dramaturgy of the West, with special consideration given to the German poets Brecht, Wolf, etc."[56] But the plans proved overly ambitious; financial limitations put a severe crimp on the project, and a permanent stage in Moscow failed to materialize. As an interim solution, it was tentatively agreed upon to make the transition gradually from a traveling company to a permanent one, but the troupe began to fall apart when Greif and Robert Troesch left for engagements in Switzerland, Neher and Loebinger fell ill, and the Wangenheims refused to perform as actors on a traveling basis. Gustav von Wangenheim also resigned his duties as artistic manager as long as the company's existence remained provisional. Thereafter, the members of the ensemble went their separate ways.

There had existed a "German sector" in the Technical Institute for Music and Theater in Dnjepropetrovsk since 1931, but over the next few years demand grew for the creation of a professional German regional theater. In 1934 Gustav Fischer suggested that a German producer be hired to prepare actors for professional careers, and soon after the Dnjepropetrovsk regional party committee began planning seriously for a professional German theater to begin work in May 1935. The ubiquitous Piscator was asked to take over "artistic guardianship" of the fledgling theater, and he sent off Curt Trepte and Missia Bönsch to Dnjepropetrovsk on an information-gathering trip.

---

56. Ibid., p. 63.

Their positive impressions prompted Luisrose Fournes, Karl Oefelein, Sylta Reismann-Busse, Hans Hauska, Erwin Geschonneck, and Trepte himself to move to Dnjepropetrovsk. Dora Dittmann-Wolff and Mischket Liebermann were also brought from Moscow, followed somewhat later by Hans Drach. Piscator hired Maxim Vallentin, then living in Prague, as artistic manager of the German Regional Theater. By July 1935 the company was ready for its first tour of the countryside, performing plays dealing with "socialist competition." By the close of the first season, the theater had made three trips through the Halbstadt, Rot Front, Vyssokopolje, Stalindorf, Zaparozhje, and Melitopol regions, appearing in seventy-one different localities and giving 102 performances in front of 24,600 spectators.[57]

By December 1935 five new actors and actresses had arrived from abroad in Dnjepropetrovsk: Hermann Greid, Amy Frank, Friedrich Richter, Gerhard Hinze, and Leo Bieber. In spring 1936 the theater again set out on an extended six-week tour through the Zaporozhje, Vyssokopolje, and Stalindorf regions, where some 12,400 collective farm workers sat through forty performances.[58] But the German Regional Theater had only a brief run. It was dissolved as a sort of "preventative measure" when the terror began in connection with the first show trial in late summer 1936. The management reportedly disbanded the company to avoid "any complications that might arise because of the strong concentration of foreigners."[59] Hermann Greid returned to Sweden; Hinze, Geschonneck, and Bieber joined the ensemble of the German Collective Farm Theater in Odessa; and Vallentin, Richter, Frank, and Trepte began work with the German State Theater in Engels.

The German Collective Farm Theater in Odessa existed as an amateur troupe performing mostly one-act and agitprop plays until the summer of 1935 when Ilse Berend-Groa took over duties as artistic director.[60] During her stay in Odessa, until 1939, the company staged productions of Molière, Kornejchuk, Shakespeare, Friedrich Wolf,

---

57. Ibid., p. 103.

58. Hermann Greid gives a first-hand description in his unpublished memoirs ("Als Fremder drei Jahre," pp. 63–66).

59. Diezel, *Exiltheater in der Sowjetunion*, p. 110. There must have been more to it than that. Whether some arrests had already taken place among the actors is unknown, but it seems unlikely that as early as summer 1936 the management or anyone else was anticipating that "concentrations" of foreigners would be potentially dangerous.

60. Berend-Groa, originally from Kassel, had been living in the Soviet Union since 1931. She later married the Hungarian philospher Béla Fogarasi.

Schiller, Mdivani, Gorky, Wangenheim, and Brecht.[61] Under Berend-Groa's direction the theater also put on a series of children's performances of Grimm and started a puppet theater in 1939 (the painter Heinrich Vogeler designed the puppets). In 1937 the company began performing anti-Fascist plays with greater regularity, Wolf's *Das trojanische Pferd,* for instance, with the leading roles given to former Dnjepropetrovsk actors Hinze, Bieber, and Geschonneck. The last play in which the exiled actors performed was *Konfrontation,* by the brothers Tur and Lev Scheinin, which dealt with the "topical matter of a case of espionage and its exposure by the organs of the NKVD, backed by the cooperation of the entire people."[62] Erwin Geschonneck took the role of the NKVD "judge," Hinze directed, and Bieber designed the sets, but ironically this was the swan song for all three—they were expelled shortly thereafter from the Soviet Union.

The German State Theater in Engels (in the Volga-German ASSR) was founded in summer 1931 and soon sought to attract talented actors from Germany as a "temporary" measure to help the theater make the transition from an amateur company to a professional one. Rudolf Nehls explained later, "People were needed who could not only provide examples on stage but who were also pedagogically talented. Russian artists could only be considered for this task to an extremely limited extent, and there was no other alternative but to bring in Reich German proletarian actors as 'specialists.'"[63] Nine actors voiced their willingness to move to Engels, but only Adolf Fischer (who stayed just a few weeks), his brother Rudolf Nehls, Karl Weidner, Herbert Prigann and his wife Lilli Towska, and Ulla Wimmler stuck by their promise. After the first successful winter season, cooperation between Reich German actors was dubbed a success, but there were already ill omens. An atmosphere of "petty bourgeois cliquism and nationalistic tension" reportedly thrived because of local antagonism toward the Reich German actors. By the end of the 1933 season, only Karl Weidner remained, and the German State Theater in Engels deteriorated.

In late 1935 the company revived when the regional committee of the Volga-German ASSR sent the entire ensemble to Moscow for four months of professional study and approached Erwin Piscator with

61. The performance of Brecht's *Die Gewehre der Frau Carrar* in Odessa remained until 1957 the only Soviet production of a full-length Brecht play.
62. Diezel, *Exiltheater in der Sowjetunion,* pp. 99 and 156.
63. Ibid., p. 167.

specific requests. Karl Weidner later said of these first measures taken to resurrect, with Piscator's help, the idea of a theater based on cooperation between émigré and local actors: "When Erwin Piscator . . . was in Engels making preparations for his film on the Volga Germans, representatives of the ASSR government asked for his advice and suggestions concerning the reorganization of the German Theater." In response Piscator made "extensive and far-reaching proposals pertaining not only to the development of the theater but to the establishment of a German Cultural Center for the Soviet Union. Theater, film, and literature are given elaborate consideration in his project."[64]

Piscator then pursued his notion of a "cultural center . . . a cultural combine" with the Comintern, to whose representatives he explained that two paramount problems could be solved by the realization of his plans. First, lagging Volga-German cultural development could be speeded up, and, second, a number of émigré writers, actors, and producers without work in their fields of expertise could find employment. Piscator accordingly envisioned the combination of local German actors in Engels with new German actors and actresses already living in the Soviet Union (Ernst Busch, Carola Neher, Alexander Granach, Heinrich Greif, and so on). This number was to be augmented by other anti-Fascist German emigrants brought in from other countries of exile. The result would be a "German theater of high quality and niveau." To use the talents of all concerned to the best advantage, a film agency was also to be established in Engels, producing a yearly four or five films. Piscator explained his vision to Comintern officials: "The Comintern [would] at this early date be able to build up good, strong cadres of artists for work in Germany," and, by creating such a cultural center, it would have the most "persuasive form of proof in hand that in socialism too German culture especially is growing and acquiring strength, while fascism is powerless to create a new culture and destroys existing works of culture and cultural values."[65] Piscator suggested the names of some twelve actors and producers, six of whom would need to be brought to the USSR.[66]

But Piscator had ignored the theater's past experience in Engels from 1932 to 1933. The artistic standards were set so high that Piscator and Bernhard Reich, after watching the Volga-German actors at work in Moscow, concluded that at best five of the twenty were usable

64. Ibid., p. 172.
65. Ibid., p. 174.
66. Those then living outside the USSR included Leon Kupfermann, Helene Weigel, Jo Mihaly, Leonhard Steckel, Wolfgang Langhoff, and Erwin Kalser.

in minor roles.[67] Friction was therefore bound to arise in Engels between the local actors, who felt that their theater was being taken over, and their colleagues from abroad; in fact, the locals back in Engels got the impression that Piscator made his participation incumbent on the presence of only German émigré actors "in his theater." Even if this was not formally the case—Reich later said that this rumor was spread to discredit the exiles politically[68]—the effect of Piscator's plans would have amounted to the same thing: the virtual exclusion of Volga-German actors from their own theater. Nonetheless, local officials approved the plan. Then, just as the project was scheduled to begin, the Comintern sent Piscator, as president of the IRTB, out of the country on official business in the summer of 1936.[69] His duties in Engels were to be temporarily taken over by Reich, but the atmosphere in Engels rapidly worsened as "denunciations of foreign producers piled up."[70]

Unaware of the deteriorating domestic scene following the August show trial, Piscator had every intention of returning to follow up on his plans in Engels until Wilhelm Picck "got rid"[71] of him by writing that he "didn't need to return" to the USSR: "In the meantime, you will have received my telegram from Elise to the effect that the job you

67. Reich, *Im Wettlauf mit der Zeit*, p. 351.
68. Diezel, *Exiltheater in der Sowjetunion*, p. 181.
69. Piscator was sent abroad in connection with Comintern efforts to bring the IRTB into line with the popular front movement. Cf. ibid., pp. 201–17. The IRTB, like the IVRS, was eventually dissolved. Wilhelm Pieck wrote Piscator in October 1936: "There are differing opinions about the further development of work in this area [the IRTB], and we must think over carefully how the work can be cultivated in the most expeditious and rational manner. This is, of course, closely tied in with the work of the established World Committee against War and Fascism, with the peace movement altogether. Any parallelism in the work (or work at cross purposes) must be avoided at all cost. . . . Since a genuine international organization of MORT [IRTB] with administration, board of directors, and apparat can scarcely be continued—the work being nationalized and backed only by an international bureau—tying you down to organizational problems associated with MORT is not justified." Pieck told Piscator that "the comrades" were of the opinion that Piscator need not return to Moscow. Pieck to Piscator, 8 October 1936 (original in Special Collections: Erwin Piscator Papers, Morris Library, Southern Illinois University; copy in Erwin Piscator Center, AdK [West Berlin]). Bernhard Reich wrote later of the dissolution of MORT: "It was said that several foreigners (our guests and correspondents, whom we valued for their upright anti-Fascist stance) had been exposed as spies. International organizations such as MORT allegedly gave the enemies of the Soviet Union good opportunities, in cases where political vigilance had tapered off, for infiltrating spies." Reich, *Im Wettlauf mit der Zeit*, p. 349.
70. Diezel, *Exiltheater in der Sowjetunion*, p. 190.
71. Erwin Piscator, "Tagebuch Nr. 23," Erwin Piscator Center, AdK (West Berlin).

took over for Engels can not be carried out for the time being," Pieck explained, "partly because of uncompleted renovations [on the theater], but in part as well because the prerequisites for the start of your work are lacking." Pieck spelled out his position: "If Wächter[72] nonetheless wired you to come—Reich too likely sent such a telegram—that is evidently the result of a certain over-zealousness with which they probably want to force the Engels matter." But Pieck had made precise inquiries and was adamantly opposed to Piscator's returning under those conditions. "New problems would arise," he added. "Therefore, in agreement with the responsible authorities [the Comintern], I am telling you that you don't need to return and for the time being there is no possibility for the realization of the Engels job."[73]

Pieck's letter put an effective stop to plans for an Engels cultural center, even though the German State Theater performed on a modest scale in 1936 and 1937. Bernhard Reich, Amy Frank, Friedrich Richter, Curt Trepte, and, beginning in early February 1937, Maxim Vallentin were still in Engels. They were joined by Li David-Nolden, who was married to the director of the Volga-German State Choir. They staged productions of Davurin's *The Volkov Family* and Shakespeare's *As You Like It* (the two plays that had been rehearsed in Moscow). The first new productions included the premiere of Wolf's *Das trojanische Pferd* and Ibsen's *Nora*. The last performances involving émigrés in the German State Theater came during a three-week tour of the Volga-German canton capitals Seelmann and Balzer in July 1937.

In September the final curtain fell when the contracts of all émigrés were suddenly canceled in the face of published and unpublished denunciations of the exiles as Fascists; the Volga-German actors had found an effective means of ridding their theater of foreign competition. Vallentin then set out for Moscow, where he obtained a "rehabilitation" document from Dimitroff for himself, Frank, Richter, and Trepte. Back in Engels he read the document in front of a meeting of the entire ensemble, but the Comintern nonetheless advised Frank, Richter, and Trepte to leave the country (fortunately they possessed valid passports, Czech in the case of Richter and Frank). Vallentin returned to Moscow for good. Karl Weidner, however, had disappeared; so, for a time, had Hans David.[74] Li David-Nolden left the Soviet Union, whether "voluntarily" or by deportation is not clear.

72. Wächter was head of the Volga-German Art Committee.
73. Pieck to Piscator, 8 October 1936 (see note 69 above).
74. See Chapter 11 for more on David's fate.

Other German actors swept away by the terror, though not necessarily just in Engels, included Hans Drach and Rudolf Nehls. Bruno Schmidtsdorf, Kurt Arendt, Karl Oefelein, and Helmut Damerius were all arrested; Damerius survived fifteen years in the camps, the others disappeared for good. Carola Neher, of course, became a prominent victim. Hans Hauska was merely expelled from the USSR, while Bernhard Reich began an odyssey of imprisonment and banishment; his wife Asja Lazis, likewise arrested, was not released from the camps until well after the war.

In March 1938, in the wake of the dispute between the German Section and the *Deutsche Zentral-Zeitung* that climaxed in the February NKVD raid on the paper, another of the periodic "reorganizations" of the section took place. A new bureau, which included Becher (president), Lukács, Scharrer, Erpenbeck, and Olga Halpern-Gábor (secretary), was elected and "all work had to be restructured and rejuvenated." During the remainder of the year, eight meetings of the section and ten of the bureau were held. These meetings dealt with such issues as work on *Internationale Literatur* and *Das Wort*, "cooperation" with the *Deutsche Zentral-Zeitung*, greater stress on the "topicality" of works by the émigré writers, German radio broadcasts, improvement of publication opportunities, living conditions and a higher standard of living, and personal matters (membership in the Soviet Writers' Union). It was decided to hold consultative meetings between the German Section and representatives of the KPD in the Comintern. Theodor Plivier, Julius Hay, and Klara Blum joined the Writers' Union, and an anti-Fascist publishing house was set up under the aegis of Mezhdunarodnaja kniga.[75]

Eight bureau and two plenary sessions, together with seven meetings to discuss literary work, were held in 1939 until the Soviet-German Pact of Nonagression in August abruptly halted the "anti-Fascist" activity of the writers.[76] Informational gatherings nonetheless continued during the beginning of 1940 with speeches by Walter Ulbricht and Herbert Wehner. On 26 March 1940, a plenum of the German Section again juggled the leadership and elected a "new" bureau headed by Lukács and comprised of Becher, Halpern-Gábor,

---

75. "Rechenschaftsbericht der Deutschen Sektion des Sowjetischen Schriftstellerverbandes für das Jahr 1938," reprinted (in a German translation from the Russian) in Barck, *Johannes R. Bechers Publizistik*, pp. 242–45.
76. "Rechenschaftsbericht der Deutschen Sektion für das Jahr 1939," in ibid., pp. 245–47.

Scharrer, and Bredel. Four writers (Dora Wentscher, Gregor Gog, Alfred Durus, and Hans Rodenberg) who had applied for membership in the Writers' Union were turned down for lack of a sufficient number of publications. On the other hand, Ernst Fabri was expelled from the union for "complete literary passivity" and Klara Blum was removed from the German Section "for lack of discipline and for hysteria"; she remained, however, a member of the Soviet Writers' Union.[77]

That October Andor Gábor rejuvenated his feud with Bredel during a meeting of the German Section. Gábor began the meeting with the request that there be a discussion of his critical article about Bredel's *Dein unbekannter Bruder*, a critique whose publication Bredel, with the help of the KPD, was said to have blocked three years earlier. Bredel explained what had happened.[78] In spring 1937 the Soviet Writers' Union chose him and Erich Weinert as delegates to the Second International Writers' Congress for the Defense of Culture, meeting in Valencia. With Comintern approval both remained in Spain afterwards; there Bredel served as a commissar in the Ernst Thälmann Battalion of the International Brigades. At the front word reached him that Gábor was planning to publish an article in *Internationale Literatur* addressing the question of Bredel's "'sectarian deviation'" in *Dein unbekannter Bruder*. Bredel took up the matter with Franz Dahlem, then visiting the brigade in Spain, who suggested that Bredel apprise the party in Moscow of the situation and let it make the decision to publish the article or not. This is what Bredel did, and Philipp Dengel in Moscow withdrew Gábor's critique.[79] Now, three years later, Gábor suddenly surprised the section with the demand that his article be discussed because he had since been "incapable of

77. "Protokoll der Plenartagung der Deutschen Sektion vom 26. März 1940," in ibid., pp. 247–49.
78. Willi Bredel, "Bericht über die Aussprache über die in deutscher Sprache nicht erschienene Kritik des Genossen Andor Gábor an dem Roman 'Der unbekannte Bruder' von Willi Bredel," Bredel-Archiv, Sig. 439/7.
79. Bredel wrote in his report, "I was in Spain, no longer attending congresses or working peacefully in the hinterlands, but (here I want to make this clear) literally as a soldier in battle, in foxholes. Such was the situation when I learn that in Moscow in *Internationale Literatur* a long article by Andor Gábor about my novel *Der unbekannte Bruder* is to appear, intended as a 'discussion article' and dealing with my 'sectarian deviations.' . . . I had the greatest possible mistrust of the critic, doubted that in such a critique certain politically defamatory undertones would be missing. I spoke with Comrade Franz Dahlem about the matter, who at the time was visiting the brigade, and he advised me to write the party in Moscow and let it decide. That's what I did" (ibid.).

working as a critic." Gábor and Bredel presented their arguments, rested their cases, and the discussion began.[80]

The section immediately split down the middle. Alfred Kurella said that Gábor's article, rather than Bredel's novel, was "decidedly sectarian," and he approved of the method of resolving the issue by leaving it to the party. There were dirtier means of hindering criticism, he said. Adam Scharrer, on the other hand, defended the criticism and called Bredel's behavior "peculiar." On it went: Hugo Huppert supported Bredel and called Gábor's article a "time bomb"; Fritz Erpenbeck, Julius Hay, and Hedda Zinner took Gábor's side (Zinner found "nothing wrong with the critique and explains that she fails to understand what all the talk is about"). Georg Lukács likewise had no quarrel with Gábor's arguments; the article should have been published, he said. But in the course of the "discussion" it became clear that more had been at stake in 1937 than a critical article. Gustav von Wangenheim pointed out that Gábor's criticism betrayed a malicious undertone that he, Wangenheim, took as Gábor's response to the fact that in 1937 Bredel had come out against his volume of short stories. He then mentioned a key point: Gábor had written his article at the same time that a friend of Bredel's, Heiner Most, a Comintern functionary, had been arrested. The timing of Gábor's article, then, along with its insinuations, reveals clearly that Gábor was bent on casting political aspersions on Bredel. Nor was this by any stretch of the imagination a harmless game. In 1937 Gábor's innuendos were tantamount to a political denunciation, and the alacrity with which some section members expressed their support of Gábor's intrigue gives some indication of the level to which their sense of ethics had sunk.

But the debate had not ended. Erich Weinert took the floor and said that the atmosphere in general within the German Section was

80. There is little point in dwelling on the specific "arguments" set forth in Gábor's article. He put Bredel in a hopeless situation, chastising him for not depicting the sectarian, left-extremist traits in his Communist characters (the novel is set in the years prior to the Seventh World Congress), evidence of Bredel's sectarian deviations. But Gábor knew perfectly well that it was impossible to write frankly of past Communist "mistakes," though this is what he assailed Bredel for not doing. Gábor's critique also contained other innuendos, for instance, that Bredel evidently felt it superfluous, when presenting Fascist arguments through Nazi characters, to give counterarguments. Gábor: "Let us assume that this is only [!] a literary defect." He then added that the "psychologically most interesting figure" in the book was a Nazi. In the atmosphere of 1937 any one of those accusations could have caught (or been brought to) the attention of the NKVD. A copy of the review is in the Bredel-Archiv, Sig. 439/6 (Andor Gábor: "Dein unbekannter Bruder").

impossible, mentioning a 1937 meeting during which Friedrich Wolf had been baited and vilified. In response to a question as to who had wanted to "destroy" Wolf, Weinert replied that "Comrade Becher told me later on that Friedrich Wolf ought to be slaughtered (Becher does not dispute having said this)."[81] Bredel's report continued: Shortly after the evening on which Wolf had been criticized, Bredel left for Spain. Right away there had been talk within the section that the "two least suited comrades had been sent (Gábor confirms this by furiously nodding his head.)" A few months after Bredel's departure, as he explained it, "my former friend H. Most" was arrested in Moscow. Shortly thereafter Gábor wrote an article in which he purported to show that "a comrade was allowed to travel to Spain who (1) was a sectarian . . . and (2) failed to recognize, or did not 'want to recognize' the problems that had been dealt with at the Seventh World Congress." Bredel's intuition had not misled him, he reported, when he suspected machinations of that sort without having seen Gábor's article. Bredel went on:

> Comrade Kurella has referred to the . . . tone of the beginning of the article and called it ambiguous. I would like to mention that in the Russian translation this portion has been changed. (Furious objections by Olga Halpern, Julius Hay, and Gábor: "That's a vulgarity! That's a fabrication! The beginning is identical! This is an outrage!" and so on.) I

81. Wolf was something of an outcast in the German Section throughout his years in Soviet exile. A few months after arriving in the USSR, Wolf complained to the secretariat of the IVRS and its German Section that he had not been invited to a series of IVRS meetings. He noted that he had been asked to work with the IVRS and that he had forwarded to the organization a manuscript of his new play, *Doktor Mamlocks Ausweg*. A scene was selected for publication, but time and again the publication had been delayed. Much the same had happened to some of his other plays. Not a single scene from any of them had been printed, and the IVRS had ignored them. Wolf argued: "Comrades, I don't need to assure you that I am not concerned about 'seeing myself in print.' But I have to make it clear that *I am not the one* who is isolating himself; rather it is you who (perhaps unintentionally) are driving me into isolation. . . . Again, I myself want to work with the MORP [IVRS], but with the boycott you have applied to my work you so far haven't made it easy for me" (Wolf to Sekretariat/MORP—Deutsche Sektion/MORP, Wolf-Archiv, Mappe 300/6). After his return to Moscow in spring 1941, Wolf addressed a letter to Aleksandr Shcherbakov in the Soviet Central Committee telling him that he had hoped to continue his previous work as a playwright but that the art committee kept putting him off, leaving his letters unanswered and refusing to meet with him. He pointed out that his plays were performed the world over, but that as a "new Soviet citizen and much performed dramatist just back from French internment camps he had found it impossible to have a talk with the Soviet art authorities." Wolf complained bitterly: "I feel obligated to bring to your attention, my dear Comrade Shcherbakov,

continued: I am imputing nothing . . . (Increasing furious
outcries: Julius Hay jumps up, translates the beginning of
the Russian and Hungarian versions of the article and shouts,
pounding the table with his fist: "What bastard has the
audacity to claim that these words are intended to refer to the
Soviet Union!")[82] (General tumult. The meeting is on the
verge of disintegrating. Gábor declares that he has no
intention of staying to give his closing remarks and begins
collecting his papers.) I stopped talking, and Olga Halpern,
Hay, and Gábor calm down. Lukács gives Gábor the
floor for his closing remarks. Andor Gábor's closing words
oscillate between insults of me and references to the basic
arguments. He calls me a "functionary who also writes" and
Kurella my "shyster lawyer." . . . In closing he quotes from my
novel to prove how loyal he had been in his criticism. But the
passages he cites are designed to show how I recreate the
words of praise coming from the mouth of a Nazi and how
miserably I fail to represent a Communist talking about
the goals of Communism.[83]

When he finished, there was general "disorganization among the
comrades." Becher then took the floor and resigned all responsibilities as chairman of the section; Lukács likewise intended to relinquish his office. There followed talk of dissolving the section, but

---

that after twenty-two years of not exactly unsuccessful activity as a dramatist it is impossible for me to find work in the Soviet Union as a playwright" (Wolf to Genosse Tscher-
bakow (ZK/WKPb), 9 June 1941, Wolf-Archiv, Mappe 300/9S). Bernhard Reich gives
some of the background to Wolf's problems in Soviet exile, which, at least in part, were
caused by the Lukács coterie. See Reich, *Im Wettlauf mit der Zeit*, pp. 313–38 (especially pp. 318 and 330–31).
82. Gábor's opening words were, "In countries passing through difficult crises the
usual questions such as How are you? What are you up to? How is your family? can
become tormenting interrogations. For if one wants to answer the question sincerely,
then one has no choice but to speak of one's deepest and most difficult experiences."
Kurella hinted that Gábor had intended those lines to apply to the Soviet Union.
Bredel (he had initially supported Kurella's remark) later disavowed that charge.
83. Bredel, "Bericht über die Aussprache," Bredel-Archiv, Sig. 439/7. The final sentence in this extract is a classic example of political denunciation disguised as "loyal"
literary criticism. Ironically, Lukács, who approved of Gábor's tactics, was constantly
bemoaning the existence of *skloki* (intrigues) in the German Section and came out
strongly on at least one occasion against criticism-cum-denunciation. In 1940 he had a
bitter falling out with Béla Balázs, a friend since the early twenties. In their caustic
exchange of letters, Lukács wrote: "There was once a time when slander campaigns
ran unchecked; the party has since condemned this severely. At that time there were
also 'codes' in your style. For instance in this manner: Comrade, you say it rained

Erpenbeck called on everyone to "sleep on the matter. Hay likewise. Gábor too insisted that there should be no hasty decisions." Bredel then suggested that a mutual exchange of views within the German Section about all "secretly and publicly made calumnies" be held in the presence of a party representative, a discussion Gábor declined to attend. If the party were disciplining him, he said, then he would attend; otherwise, he would have nothing to say in the presence of the writers so long as a party representative were there. With that the meeting adjourned.

Afterwards, Bredel asked Walter Ulbricht to investigate all charges raised against him both at the two section meetings and in a private conversation between the two Gábors and Erich Weinert. He explained in his report that the day before the first meeting the Gábors called on Weinert in order to "clear the air of all existing differences and to improve the atmosphere among the writers." But they had told Weinert, "Bredel is an intriguer. Since he returned to Moscow [from Paris in summer 1939], there has been discord and dissension among the writers." Bredel had "intrigued" against Julius Hay, ostensibly managing to have the Hungarian section of Mezhdunarodnaja kniga dissolved. He spread "gossip and twaddle everywhere," the Gábors said, adding for good measure that Hugo Huppert had falsified his membership in the Soviet Communist party.[84] So the pair set out to "combat intrigues and calumny," Bredel said, concluding that Gábor was a "disruptive element" among the writers. With his "deep pessimism" he adversely affected everyone. "Dozens of examples could be adduced to prove that Gábor, with his cynical, derogatory, thoroughly unpedagogical and profoundly pessimistic attitudes in the editorial collective of *Internationale Literatur* and in the meetings of the section, has had not a constructive, creative, forward-moving impact but a pernicious effect."

Thus it was that some of the BPRS differences of 1931 and 1932 transformed themselves after 1933, in the Moscow atmosphere of show trials, spy hysteria, and mass terror, into cynical misrepresenta-

---

yesterday. You mean to imply that Moscow is a dirty city. Did you know that in a recent article Otto Bauer [the Austrian Marxist] wrote about the dirt in Moscow? Do you regard Otto Bauer as a Marxist authority?" (Lukács to Balázs, 31 January 1940, MTA, Balázs Béla-Hagyaték, Ms. 5018/180). Lukács made the remark about ten months before he backed Gábor in criticism of Bredel, criticism that contained the same type of denunciatory "code."

84. Huppert was a genuine member of the Soviet Communist party, a fact that aroused the jealousy of more than just the Gábors in the German Section.

tion and political defamation thinly disguised as literary criticism. This last controversy, fortunately, occurred at a time when the terror had abated somewhat, and nothing more seems to have come of the matter.[85]

85. The German Section, by the way, was not dissolved.

Chapter 7

The Popular Front and the Moscow Show Trials, 1936–1938

At the Seventh World Congress of the Comintern, Walter Ulbricht called the goal of Communist politics "the establishment of a Soviet Germany." He added, however, that so long as the particular power alignment barred installation of a Soviet system, then the formation of an "anti-Fascist popular front government was possible." Such a post-Hitler government, though, would exist to create "better conditions for the establishment of Soviet power" and allow the Communists to make "better preparations for the struggle for proletarian dictatorship."[1] Not surprisingly, remarks of this sort failed to spark enthusiasm within the SPD executive for the "new" Communist policy of united and popular fronts. *Neuer Vorwärts*, the official SPD organ, drew an unflattering analogy in response to the Seventh World Congress. The entire business was said to smack of a united front between a coachman and his horse: the driver cracked his whip at the horse pulling the cart.[2]

The new policy approved at the world congress and the KPD's Brussels conference spawned only one encounter between the SPD and KPD, Friedrich Stampfer and Hans Vogel representing the Socialists and Ulbricht and Franz Dahlem speaking for the Communists. The talks, held in November 1935, went nowhere.[3] Stampfer and Vogel voiced their grave doubt that the Communists had out-

1. *Protokoll des VII. Weltkongresses,* 2:518.
2. "Der Kongress der Komintern," *Neuer Vorwärts,* 8 September 1935.
3. "Besprechung zwischen Vertretern des Parteivorstandes der SPD und des Zentralkomitees der KPD in Prag," in Matthias, *Mit dem Gesicht nach Deutschland,* pp. 241–50.

grown the "*Zinoviev* period of 'united front maneuvers using all means possible' " and were genuinely bent upon honoring eventual inter-party agreements. Vogel reminded Ulbricht and Dahlem (accurately) that the principle of proletarian dictatorship was still firmly embedded in the resolutions of the Seventh World Congress, which lent substance to apprehensions that Communist concern for "bourgeois-democratic liberties" was a mere tactical trick. Once "bourgeois-democratic liberties" were reestablished in Germany, what then? "Will that be time for a new tactical change?" asked Vogel. The speeches of the world congress pointed in just such a direction. In response, Ulbricht and Dahlem provided explanations; these, however, were unable to put to rest fears that the Communist party leaders had not had a sincere change of heart. When—after giving the impression that they would issue only a brief communique mentioning the talks—the Communists proceeded to publish a slanted rendition in which nine-hundred lines went to the utterances of Ulbricht and Dahlem and sixty to Stampfer and Vogel, the "proletarian united front" was still-born.

Thus ended all high-level contacts between the two parties; later KPD united front blandishments the Sopade either rejected or ignored.[4] But even though a united front formed by the two workers' parties had always been viewed as a prerequisite to an extension of the front further to the right, the Communists now pressed ahead anyway with efforts for a popular front, joining in the work that Willi Münzenberg had been doing in Paris since fall 1935 with a group of exiled writers and politicians.[5] This was the origin of the German popular front, that phase of Communist cultural politics during which the KPD-Comintern synchronized its efforts to fashion unity among exiled German Communists and non-Communists by fusing the literary or cultural front with the political united and popular front.

On 1 February 1936, representatives of the German "Marxist" parties (the KPD, SPD, Socialist Workers' Party [SAP], and the Revolutionary Socialists) gathered to hold preliminary talks; their meeting was followed the next day by the first full-scale popular front conference convened "at the behest" of Heinrich Mann and the Social Democrat Max Braun.[6] No less than 118 personalities attended, among

4. Cf. Sywottek, *Deutsche Volksdemokratie*, p. 62.
5. Münzenberg's widow writes that he returned to Paris following the Seventh World Congress with instructions from Dimitroff to begin working for cooperation between Social Democrats and members of the bourgeois emigration. Gross, *Willi Münzenberg*, p. 289.
6. Now and in the future individual Social Democrats would take part in the popular

them writers Heinrich Mann, Klaus Mann, Emil Ludwig, Lion Feuchtwanger, Ernst Toller, and Ludwig Marcuse; journalists Leopold
Schwarzschild, Victor Schiff, and Georg Bernhard; Social Democrats
Rudolf Breitscheid, Alexander Schifrin, and Paul Hertz; and KPD
upper-level officials Willi Münzenberg, Franz Dahlem, Hermann
Matern, Peter Maslowski, and Alexander Abusch. A Declaration to
the German Nation was passed and published in Schwarzschild's influential *Neues Tage-Buch,* which greeted the declaration as the first
step in the right direction.[7] The manifesto called for unity in the fight
against Hitler and announced formation of a committee for the preparation of the popular front; this committee was chaired by Heinrich
Mann, who was joined by Münzenberg, Breitscheid, and Bernhard.
The committee was empowered to work out a "platform for the concentration of all oppositional groups," a program which would lay the
foundation for the new Germany.

In reporting the results of the unsuccessful November talk between
SPD and KPD representatives, the Communists had complained that
the socialists put too high a premium on the issue of democracy, that
is, the nature of the government to follow Hitler, instead of concen-
trating on "concrete matters related to the next steps in the struggle
against fascism."[8] But now the Popular Front Committee likewise
brushed aside suggestions that concern for the new German state
should be secondary to the adoption of immediate measures aimed at
toppling Hitler. This issue proved to be the major stumbling block
throughout much of 1936, as the committee struggled without suc-

---

front meetings, but never as official representatives of their party, which refused to
participate as an organization.

7. "Ein Manifest," *Das neue Tage-Buch,* 15 February 1936, pp. 151–52. It was important
that Schwarzschild published the "Declaration," for the Communists were keenly interested in gaining his support because of his ties to conservative oppositional circles in
Germany. As early as August 1935, Schwarzschild had acknowledged the need for a
German organization in exile that would render assistance to the anti-Hitler opposition
within Germany and prepare for the takeover of power following Hitler's collapse. It
was time to form a "center," he had written, a coalition of exiled opponents of nazism,
for the very existence of such an organization abroad would act as a stimulus to those
within Germany who hoped for Hitler's fall but feared the chaos that might follow the
end of his rule ("Eine Aufgabe wird sichtbar," *Das neue Tage-Buch,* 3 August 1935, p.
730). In publishing the February 1936 "Declaration," the *Neues Tage-Buch* commented
that it was important to assure those in the Reich that there was a force, an organization,
which would see to it that Hitler's fall from power created neither a vacuum nor gave
rise to a new outbreak of terror "from a different source," a not so vague reference to
the Communists.

8. Quoted in Sywottek, *Deutsche Volksdemokratie,* p. 62.

cess to work out a popular front platform acceptable to all. Then, in mid-1936, the KPD took a major step toward what the party hoped would break the deadlock, which was caused largely by past Communist adherence to the idea of proletarian dictatorship as the only long-term solution to Germany's problems. After a Central Committee meeting in June 1936, the KPD issued a proclamation calling for a "popular revolution" in Germany leading toward the defeat of Hitler and the formation of a "democratic republic."[9] Gone now, for the first time since the KPD began its existence, was the insistence on proletarian dictatorship as a more or less immediate solution. No fewer than two and a half years earlier Wilhelm Pieck's speech at the ECCI's Thirteenth Plenum was titled "We are Fighting for a Soviet Germany"; now the KPD announced, *We Communists are fighting for a democratic republic.*[10]

In August 1936 Pieck published a clarification of the party's position. The KPD put at the center of united efforts to defeat Hitler "the *demand for democratic rights and liberties* with the goal of overthrowing the Fascist dictatorship and forming a democratic republic."[11] Communists were convinced that the fall of Hitler demanded a united and popular front movement from both within and outside Germany, but the central issue debated at the February meeting in Paris, which created the Popular Front Committee, had concerned the post-Hitler government. This, said Pieck, was no accident, for, whereas the creation of a front without Communists was unthinkable, Communists solidly favored proletarian dictatorship as the sole means to realize socialism, while all other parties interested in creating fronts rejected it. This made "*clarification of the question as to what regime will replace the Hitler dictatorship an essential prerequisite for the realization of the united and popular front.*"[12] The urgent necessity of forming alliances, as well as KPD "experience" since the Brussels conference, had precipitated a change in thinking; the Communists had now defined "more concretely and plainly, as an immediate goal of the struggle for the collapse of the Hitler dictatorship, the establishment of a *democratic republic.*" This was no maneuver, Pieck assured his readers, and he announced that Guidelines for a Political Platform of the Popular

9. Kundgebung des ZK der KPD, "Volksfront gegen die Kriegspolitik Hitlers, für die Erhaltung des Friedens und für ein demokratisches Deutschland," *Rundschau*, 23 July 1936, pp. 1340 and 1357.
10. Ibid.
11. Wilhelm Pieck, "Der Kampf um Demokratie," *Die Internationale* 4/5 (August 1936): 2.
12. Ibid.

Front had been prepared for submission to the preparatory Popular
Front Committee in Paris.[13]

Still, Pieck's remarks indicate that little of substance had changed in
terms of ultimate solutions. Pieck explained that in the democratic
republic "*all* partners of the popular front [government] can propagate their particular goals." The Communists would practice openly
and freely their agitation among the working people for socialism and
"for the only road which leads to it—proletarian dictatorship." But
the "establishment of Soviet power" was possible only through the will
of the great majority of the working people, and the policies of the
party were to help the people "draw the correct conclusions" more
rapidly and clearly, because the "democratic republic cannot bring
them socialism and liberation from capitalist exploitation." As long as
the Communists failed to win the support of the majority of the
German people, Pieck promised, the party would "have to take this
fact into consideration."[14]

It is impossible to speculate about the success the Communists might
have had with this new "democratic" tack had the German popular
front not been thoroughly convulsed by the dramatic August announcement in Moscow that Zinoviev, Kamenev, and several other influential Soviet party figures, many of them long-time associates of Lenin,
would presently stand trial on charges of organizing the 1934 murder
of Sergej Kirov under the direction of Leon Trotsky and planning the
assassination of top Soviet leaders, including Stalin. Scarcely half a
year old, the German popular front was dealt a fatal blow by the very
powers that had called it into existence. The Communist press overflowed with banner headlines, full-page articles, announcements, and
editorials about the upcoming trial. The *Rundschau* dealt with the
forthcoming proceedings in its 20 August issue in a large special supplement full of *Pravda* press releases, analyses, and favorable comments culled from the western pro-Soviet press. During the first trial
against Zinoviev and Kamenev,[15] their *moral* and *political* responsibility for the murder of Kirov had been established.[16] But the investigation had meanwhile continued and revealed far broader findings.

---

13. The guidelines were first printed in the Parisian *Deutsche Volkszeitung*, the KPD
paper in France ("Vorschläge zur Schaffung einer Volksfront," *Deutsche Volkszeitung*,
15 November 1936). The committee rejected them.
14. Pieck, "Der Kampf um Demokratie," pp. 6–8.
15. The two had already been arrested following Kirov's murder.
16. The pair had been found guilty of "moral complicity" in the crime, that is, their
ideas were said to have inspired the murderer to shoot Kirov.

The murder of Kirov had been not only directly contrived (politically and ideologically), but also *technically* and *organizationally* planned and executed under the direct supervision of Trotsky, Zinoviev, and the "Trotsykist-Zinovievist Center." Further assassination attempts on "leaders of the Soviet people" had been in the final planning stages when the terroristic bands, under the *"direct guidance* of Trotsky and the immediate control of the Trotskyist-Zinovievist Center," had been uncovered in the USSR. The *Rundschau* added that, though it was not mentioned in the official indictment, numerous articles in the Soviet press left no room for doubt that the Trotskyist-Zinovievist terrorists were "intimately associated" with Hitler's Gestapo.[17]

In the German-language Soviet press the atmosphere for the announcement was being readied in early August. On 9 August the *Deutsche Zentral-Zeitung* came off the press with a long, front-page editorial, "Learn to Unmask the Enemy."[18] This editorial demanded heightened vigilance in view of the fact that, for want of watchfulness, "the villainous enemy" (sometimes lurking behind party membership cards) had been successful in working against the party and "our great homeland." The murder of Kirov had uncovered the "true face of this counterrevolutionary, terrorist Trotsky-Zinoviev-Kamenev band." Five days later there appeared another article, "Raise the Level of Revolutionary Vigilance,"[19] in which the commentator noted that the enemies of the Soviet Union had been crushed and defeated but that contemptible remnants of oppositional forces were engaged in desperate attempts to impede the forward march of socialism. The same issue reprinted an editorial from *Pravda,* "Clever Maneuvers of the Class Enemy," which focused on the case of a traitorous party secretary in the Volga-German ASSR. A "Trotskyist" had managed to work his evil for many years, in collusion with the party secretary, before he was eventually uncovered. Another brief notice in the *Deutsche Zentral-Zeitung* commented on yet another discovery—a "Trotskyist editor" in the Donets region and the expulsion from the party of a former leader of a Trotskyist-Zinovievist group in a candy factory.

The next day, 15 August 1936, the *Deutsche Zentral-Zeitung* published the curt indictment of the sixteen accused. The edict was issued by the office of the state public prosecutor and mentioned only that during the course of 1936 a number of terrorist Trotskyist-Zinovievist groups had been uncovered; these groups, supervised from abroad by Trotsky and controlled by the "United Center of the Bloc of

17. *Rundschau,* 20 August 1936, p. 1509.
18. "Lernt den Feind entlarven," *Deutsche Zentral-Zeitung,* 14 August 1936.
19. "Höher die revolutionäre Wachsamkeit," *Deutsche Zentral-Zeitung,* 14 August 1936.

Trotskyists-Zinovievists" (founded in 1932), had been preparing a series of terrorist acts against Soviet leaders. Moreover, Trotsky had personally dispatched a number of terrorists into the Soviet Union to carry out his orders. The sixteen defendants were listed by name, the investigation was declared closed, and the start of the trial announced for 19 August.[20] The very next issue of the *Deutsche Zentral-Zeitung* carried expressions of workers' "outrage" at the news about the "United Center."[21] The trial lasted five days, and the Communist press, both within and outside the Soviet Union, devoted whole issues to verbatim transcripts of the proceedings. To a man the accused admitted their crimes, going to great lengths individually to picture themselves as even more vile and contemptible than their codefendants. No evidence to speak of was introduced, and, in the absence of anything resembling genuine proof or documentation of the alleged crimes, the convictions were based solely on the "confessions" of the accused. On 24 August the *Deutsche Zentral-Zeitung* published the official verdict and sentence on its front page: guilty and execution by shooting.[22]

The German popular front movement was staggered by the news coming out of Moscow. Social Democrat Rudolf Hilferding remarked tersely in a letter to Friedrich Stampfer, "The effect of the Moscow trial was catastrophic and has badly compromised the popular front."[23] One of the first published responses to appear in the German exile press came from the pen of Leopold Schwarzschild, who let it be known that the trial had severely shaken the credibility of the Soviet Union. Schwarzschild saw the executions as a pure power ploy designed to establish Stalin as the undisputed leader in the USSR. For the accused, though, he had little sympathy. "If [with their admissions] they spoke the truth, then in a legal sense nothing more can be said in their favor. If they falsified their statements, if, as former political leaders, they hid their true opinions in the hope of begging for mercy by humbling themselves, then nothing more can be said for their character." The "confessions" at the trial were not something new to Soviet jurisprudence, wrote Schwarzschild; during the Ramzin trial in 1930 there had been a similar scenario in which the chief defendant willingly besmirched himself with his admissions. The anom-

20. *Deutsche Zentral-Zeitung*, 15 August 1936.
21. "Keine Gnade den Feinden der Heimat: Sturm der Empörung unter den Moskauer Werktätigen," *Deutsche Zentral-Zeitung*, 16 August 1936.
22. "Urteil," *Deutsche Zentral-Zeitung*, 24 August 1936.
23. Hilferding's letter is published in Matthias, *Mit dem Gesicht nach Deutschland*, p. 285.

aly this time around was the monstrous attempt to denounce Trotsky, Zinoviev, and Kamenev, "founders and cofounders of the Soviet state," as paid agents of the Gestapo. That was the specific nuance of this trial, said Schwarzschild.[24]

The trial should never have taken place, he continued, and certainly not in the manner in which it was staged; those who had always spoken highly of the need for partnership with Russia were justified and obliged to say that loud and clear, for they had been wronged by the events in Russia. Just when others were so energetically pitting western Europe *against* bolshevism, Moscow staged a "performance" that supplied grist for the mill of such anti-Soviet propaganda. Schwarzschild warned that the trial would prove unsettling to those circles that had been on the verge of opting for "Moscow instead of Berlin, though no one knew how heavily that would weigh."

Similar concern about the effect of the trial on the popular front was voiced by Hermann Budzislawski in his *Neue Weltbühne*,[25] but while he rejected the "form" of the Moscow trial, the "political content" was another matter. Too much was at stake in the popular front to react hastily, he wrote, adding that "even in light of undesirable events in the camp of our partners we must not lose our nerves. For come what may, the Soviet Union is allied with anti-Fascist Europe, and the program of a popular front remains the correct policy." That was precisely the type of reasoning that the Communists hoped would win out in the end.[26] Heinrich Mann argued along the same lines. He had been asked repeatedly to protest against the executions that followed the trial, but wrote in the *Neue Weltbühne* that he could express only regret—the same regret, he assumed, felt by many in Moscow. "The Moscow trial and the death by shooting of sixteen old revolutionaries have hurt [the prestige of the USSR]. . . . But when conspirators emerged to do damage to the revolution they had to be done away with for the good of the revolution, quickly and thoroughly."[27]

Internationale Literatur in Moscow gave one of the many official accounts, choosing Hugo Huppert to write it. The tenor of the entire

24. Leopold Schwarzschild, "Der Gestapomann Trotzki," *Das neue Tage-Buch*, 29 August 1936, pp. 825–28.

25. Hermann Budzislawski, "Machtpolitik," *Die neue Weltbühne* 36 (September 1936): 113–16.

26. The article was not welcomed wholeheartedly in Moscow. Willi Bredel wrote Budzislawski that he had "several critical comments" to make about Budzislawski's response to the trial. Bredel to Budzislawski, 13 September 1936, TsGALI, 631/12/141/187.

27. Heinrich Mann, "Die Revolution," *Die neue Weltbühne* 39 (September 1936): 1212–16. Mann's article was well received in the USSR. Becher told him: "I can assure you in the

article was determined by one line taken from Zinoviev's "confession": "Trotskyism is a species of fascism; Zinovievism is a species of Trotskyism." Huppert had no doubt whatsoever that Trotsky stood behind the acts of terrorism and assassination and that the Zinovievists were all motivated by anger at having been proven wrong in their forecasts that socialism could not be built in a single country. "The construction of socialism in one land has proved possible; what is more, socialism has been triumphantly successful in this country," wrote Huppert.[28] For the simple reason that events in the USSR had proven them wrong, the Trotskyists and Zinovievists plotted revenge; and "no means were too malevolent, no partner too disreputable," not even the Gestapo, to use for carrying out their vindictive acts. This simply marked the "closing of the circle."[29]

One of the rare lucid and accurate descriptions of the background to the trial was written by A. Rudolf, who, like Schwarzschild, saw immediately from the statements made at the trial that Trotsky was intended to be the main defendant.[30] Also like Schwarzschild, Rudolf sought to understand the "confessions" by harking back to earlier trials, the Shakhtyj trial of 1928 and the Ramzin affair in 1931, where confessions had also served as the sole means to convict the accused. Rudolf claimed that confession offered the only chance, however slight, by which the defendants might survive. He spoke of the cases of a Yugoslavian and a young German Communist who had been detained for five months in prisons in Leningrad and Moscow. From these two eyewitnesses, said Rudolf, information had become available on the methods used to extract confessions—torture. Rudolf was sure that

---

name of all our friends that this essay is excellent and serves as a dignified and suitable answer to certain people. . . . Evidently you also have the impression that history tests us from time to time. This trial was just such a test. And, naturally, those who felt themselves directly or indirectly affected by the trial have put everything in motion to falsify the clear and unobjectionable result. Your imperturbability and calm behavior in this question is for me a sign that there is an uncorruptible force at the head of our German anti-Fascist literature" (Becher to Mann, 15 October 1936, Becher-Archiv, Sig. 56). Note the insinuation: those who protested against the trials did so, according to Becher, because they felt themselves "directly or indirectly affected," that is, incriminated.

28. Hugo Huppert, "Der Kreis ist geschlossen," *Internationale Literatur* 9 (1936): 129.

29. Ibid., pp. 130–31. See also the responses in the *Deutsche Zentral-Zeitung;* for instance, Willi Bredel, "Tod den Agenten der Gestapo—der Trotzki-Sinowjew-Meute! Rede des Genossen Willi Bredel in der Versammlung des Verbandes der Sowjet-Schriftsteller am 21. August 1936," *Deutsche Zentral-Zeitung,* 23 August 1936. Bredel was calling for death for the defendants even before they had been found guilty.

30. Rudolf, *Der Moskauer Prozess.* Rudolf, the pseudonym used by Raoul László, spent thirty-nine months working in the USSR, at least some of the time on the editorial staff of the *Rote Zeitung* in Leningrad. Little else is known about him.

men like Zinoviev, Kamenev, and others, who had made the Soviet state, were aware of these methods and knew the futility of denying anything. As to the charges leveled at Trotsky, Rudolf believed none of them. Stalin had expatriated Trotsky but was still deathly afraid of him. "In conjunction with every domestic and foreign-policy measure taken by Stalin, Trotsky has raised his . . . voice. Trotsky's articles came out in all the languages of the world. . . . With every step that Stalin took . . . he was given a bill of goods by Trotsky, accused of betraying the heritage of Lenin." That was the reason why Trotsky had to be destroyed, at least morally; the only thing that went wrong, according to Rudolf, was that attempts to "prove" the charges at the trial were clumsy beyond description. With respect to the effect of the trial abroad, Rudolf had this to say: "The realization has penetrated deeply into the masses of the Social Democratic parties and other socialist groups that the Comintern understands by 'united front' subjugation to its will, a renunciation of any criticism of the Soviet government."[31]

"It was the steepness of your bluff which made the downfall of my confidence, my admiration and my joy so severe and so painful," André Gide would confess at the beginning of *Back from the USSR*, which he wrote upon his return from a conducted tour of Russia in summer 1936. The Soviets had miscalculated badly when they invited Gide to visit the Soviet Union. Ever since his earliest expressions of support for the USSR had been published, the Soviet press had carried frequent laudatory articles about Gide and even unabashed encomiums. During his stay in Russia, the press overflowed with such tributes. The *Deutsche Zentral-Zeitung* treated Gide's arrival as front-page news, and Alfred Kurella wrote a long article in which he cited Gide's early diary entries concerning his admiration and love for the Soviet Union.[32] But Gide arrived in the Soviet Union, looked, and left—bitterly disillusioned. In late fall of 1936 he "cried aloud" in the foreword to a book of impressions that left no room for doubt about his changed view of Russia. When word leaked out about the nature of the forthcoming book, the Communists made a considerable effort to stop its publication. Ilja Ehrenburg had somehow managed to read the manuscript after it had been entrusted to the printer with strict orders to keep it secret, and Gide soon received a telegram from

31. Ibid., pp. 16 and 18. Thomas Mann too recorded his reservations about the trial, calling it and related developments "ugly riddles" (Thomas Mann, *Tagebücher 1935–1936*, pp. 358–59).
32. "André Gide in Moskau," *Deutsche Zentral-Zeitung*, 18 June 1936; Alfred Kurella, "Begegnung mit André Gide," *Deutsche Zentral-Zeitung*, 18 June 1936.

"militiamen on the Madrid front" asking him not to publish a book that would be a "mortal blow" to them.[33] The book came out in late 1936.

What is striking about *Back from the USSR* and the response it evoked among the Communists is the fact that, although Gide's criticism was blunt, the book was nevertheless written by one who cared a good deal about the future of the Soviet Union and who had not yet given up on the country. The following remarks, taken from various sections of the book, give some idea of the worst animadversions that Gide expressed:

> In the USSR everybody knows beforehand, once and for all, that on any and every subject there can be only one opinion. . . . What is discussed is whether such-and-such a work, or gesture, or theory conforms to this sacrosanct line. And woe to him who seeks to cross it! . . . I doubt whether in any other country in the world, even Hitler's Germany, thought be less free, more bowed down, more fearful (terrorized), more vassalized. . . . Stalin's effigy is met with everywhere; is it adoration, love, or fear? I do not know; always and everywhere he is present. . . . It is undeniable that there has been a divergence from the first ideal. . . . In the USSR, however fine a work [of art] may be, if it is not in line, it scandalizes. Beauty is considered a bourgeois value. However great an artist may be, if he does not work in line, attention will turn away—will *be* turned away— from him. What is demanded of the artist, of the writer, is that he shall conform; and all the rest will be added to him.[34]

Upon his return from Russia, Gide had read many of the latest accounts of life in the USSR by writers like Citrine, Trotsky, Victor Serge, and A. Rudolf; and, in response to the insults, accusations, and obloquy that greeted the publication of his book, Gide wrote a sequel. He now put more distance between himself and the Soviet Union, writing that "from month to month the state of the USSR gets worse. It diverges more and more from what we had hoped it was—it would be."[35] In *Afterthoughts* Gide is far more specific in his strictures, addressing himself to such problems as education and labor and citing

---

33. Cf. Serge, *Memoirs of a Revolutionary*, pp. 334–35.
34. Gide, *Back from the USSR*, pp. 44–45, 48, 60, 63, 66, 69.
35. Gide, *Afterthoughts*, p. 6.

statistics and facts culled from the Soviet press itself to prove his points. He put more effort into depicting the nature of the Soviet police state and the privileged status of the party's upper crust, writing that "the proletariat has been swindled" and comparing some of Lenin's arguments and proposals (in *State and Revolution*) with the reality of Stalin's rule. With respect to a passage where Lenin had spoken of Karl Kautsky, Gide asked "which of the two, whether Lenin or him [Kautsky], would Stalin today imprison or shoot." References to the trials are sparse, probably because Gide viewed them as mere excrescences on a body racked with severe internal illness. As to Stalin's attacks on Trotsky, Gide wrote that "Trotsky, for having denounced this compromising policy, is declared to be a public enemy, whereas he is only the enemy of Stalin's compromises, and is thus identified with fascism—which is really a bit too simple." Gide went on to say that Trotsky "is far more the enemy of fascism than is Stalin himself, and it is as a revolutionary and anti-fascist that he denounces Stalin's compromises."[36]

Following on the heels of the show trials, Gide in his books did as much to accelerate the process of disintegration of the popular front as any one single person. The effect of *Back from the USSR* was instantaneous. From Paris Maria Osten wrote to Moscow, "The atmosphere here among the intellectuals is quite confused. Three days ago Gide published . . . the foreword to the book about Russia. It is absolutely unheard-of—it is no less than the confession of a Trotskyist."[37] Those who heaped the vilest abuse upon Gide all seemed determined to outdo each other. *Pravda* set the example, publishing a sordid article entitled "The Laughing and Weeping of André Gide"; it was reprinted in the *Deutsche Zentral-Zeitung*. "André Gide writes that he 'made a mistake.' Now he is making another. He thinks—after mixing tears and laughter of enthusiasm with the poisonous venom of calumny— that he can retain the glorious name of friend of the USSR. But he is already being welcomed as a like-minded thinker in the camp of Trotskyists and Fascists."[38] There was the response for all to see: criticize the Soviet Union and you are no better than a Fascist.

The *Deutsche Zentral-Zeitung* followed that nauseous article with a "letter" to Romain Rolland from the "foreign workers" at a Magnitogorsk factory called "Stalin."[39] The workers asked Rolland to publish in the

36. Ibid., pp. 32–33, 46, 50, 57, 117.
37. Osten to Bredel, 8 November 1936, TsGALI, 631/12/143/413.
38. "Lachen und Weinen André Gides," *Deutsche Zentral-Zeitung*, 4 December 1936.
39. "Der Falschmünzer André Gide: Ein Brief ausländischer Arbeiter an Romain Rolland," *Deutsche Zentral-Zeitung*, 22 December 1936.

French press a "message" that they had sent him expressing their outrage at Gide's "Judas role."[40] It was a palpable Soviet attempt to get at Gide through Rolland, but Rolland balked at first. He did not want "to appear to be hiding behind the workers to attack Gide," Rolland wrote in his journal.[41] Instead, he told them to publish their protest themselves, but also enclosed a copy of his own letter of 5 January 1937, which was essentially identical to the one he published on 18 January 1937 in *L'Humanité*. It was published in the *Deutsche Zentral-Zeitung* first, where Rolland said in his "Reply to the Foreign Workers of Magnitogorsk": "It is an evil book and, in addition to that, medio-cre, astonishingly poor, superficial, childish and contradictory. . . . The rabid hatred of our enemies and the bankruptcy of our friends who are too weak to follow us should not be allowed to affect us."[42]

In the meantime, the *Pravda* article had infuriated not only Gide's supporters, but many who were simply insulted by the overall mali-cious tone of the remarks. On 26 December 1936 the *Neues Tage-Buch* commented on the *Pravda* denunciation, pointing out that the article had been intended to determine the unanimous Soviet-Russian judg-ment of the man and poet André Gide. Within the USSR *l'affaire Gide* was finished; the question now, the *Neues Tage-Buch* wrote, was whether the stigmatization of Gide as an incorrigible "White Guardist" would also become "obligatory outside of Russia, especially for those western European writers and former admirers of Gide who . . . desire to bear the 'glorious name of friend of the Soviet Union.'"[43]

Contrasted with *Pravda*'s invective and Rolland's opprobrium, Lion Feuchtwanger's objections—he visited the Soviet Union in December 1936 and January 1937—were comparatively mild. Feuchtwanger remarked with archetypal fellow traveler thinking that Gide had ob-served with an "overly critical eye the thousands of tiny imperfections, instances of tastelessness, lack of comfort; he failed to see the . . . grand methodicalness of the whole." Noted Feuchtwanger, the Soviet Union was so strong that a pronouncement about the country said

40. Cf. also Harris, *André Gide and Romain Rolland*, pp. 158–59.
41. Ibid.
42. *Deutsche Zentral-Zeitung*, 12 January 1937. In response to Rolland's words, Gide wrote at the beginning of *Afterthoughts*: "The publication of my book *Back from the USSR* brought me a great many insults. Romain Rolland's gave me pain. I never cared much for his writings, but at any rate I hold his moral character in high esteem. The cause of my grief was the thought that so few men reach the end of their life before showing the extreme limit of their greatness. I think the author of *Au-dessus de la Mêlée* would pass severe judgment on the Romain Rolland of his old age. This eagle has made his nest; he takes his rest in it."
43. *Das neue Tage-Buch*, 26 December 1936, p. 1230.

more about the observer than about what was being observed. "André Gide has lived for a long time in the ivory tower of the pure aesthete. . . . Then he left his ivory tower because he was bored and wanted to stretch his legs a bit. Now he's gone back to his tower. We hope he is comfortable there."[44] Feuchtwanger's contribution to the polemics injected a new ingredient into the Gide controversy, namely, Feucht-wanger's stance, which in the ensuing months became the focal point of as much bitterness as had Gide's book.

In 1937 Kurt Hiller wrote an article entitled "Gide and the Popular Front" in which he praised the "very critical enthusiasm" of Gide's book and spoke of the "(exemplary, noncontradictory) yes-no" of *Back from the USSR*. The very fact that Gide had both criticized *and* championed the Soviet Union could only be obfuscated, wrote Hiller, by the "tendentious manner in which those party-true critics of his critique turned items of secondary importance into the main content" of the book. Hiller compared such tactics to those of the Nazi press. He charged that *Pravda* "did not respond to the reservations of a convinced socialist, an honest . . . friend of the Soviet Union with counter arguments . . . but by flinging filth," and he went on to broach the subject of the popular front. *Pravda* had to be asked whether the way it reacted to the "honest and important criticism of a socialist comrade" was considered agitation and propaganda for the popular front. "Does a popular front mean uncritical adulation of one of the factions by all the others? Does a popular front mean the exclusion of discussion among those who form it? Does a popular front mean heightened stupefaction of the participants?" Hiller concluded that "evidently, from *Pravda*'s side of things, cooperation is only possible if the parties submit blindly. If someone refuses, he turns himself into a 'bourgeois,' an 'individualist,' a 'counterrevolutionary,' and may be slandered or shot." As for Feuchtwanger, Hiller said that he belonged "to the level of intellects whose members are not even worthy of cleaning Gide's typewriter."[45]

The *Neue Weltbühne* tried to give both sides of the controversy. Hermann Budzislawski refused to go into the actual merits of the case itself, leaving that to Klaus Mann. What bothered Budzislawski, though, was the fact that the " 'debate among friends' " had turned into a furious campaign and that Gide's friends had been just as insensitive to criticism as the Communists. Budzislawski lamented that individual phrases had been torn out of Feuchtwanger's article in *Das Wort*

44. Lion Feuchtwanger, "Der Ästhet in der Sowjetunion," *Das Wort* 2 (1937): 88.
45. Hiller, "Gide und Volksfront," in *Profile*, pp. 127–32.

and that Gide's defenders were thus using the same methods against Feuchtwanger that the French novelist's enemies had used against him. Indeed, "they surpass these critics and cover Feuchtwanger . . . with filth." The controversy connected with Gide, wrote Budzislawski, "has turned into a controversy within the German emigration."[46] Klaus Mann's article followed Budzislawski's, and Mann too decried the level to which the debate had sunk. He found all of the attacks on Gide from the left and in *Pravda* difficult to understand in view of the fact that Gide's book contained many enthusiastic pages. It was the lack of debate, of sober discussion, of serious attempts to come to terms or to understand or to reconcile on the part of the Communists, among them Feuchtwanger, that was disquieting to Klaus Mann. As far as he was concerned, the Gide affair was no longer related to whether or not he might be justifiably criticized for his book but "to the manner, to the . . . condemnatory, flippant, proscriptive way sincere criticism is dismissed."[47]

These words were a tailor-made description of Alfred Kurella's ex officio pronouncements in *Internationale Literatur.* Kurella came to the conclusion that the book, taken as a whole, put André Gide on the same level as regular enemies of the Soviet Union. Kurella, who had earlier been vocal in his praise of Gide, felt called upon not only to dissociate himself from his article in the *Deutsche Zentral-Zeitung* but to point out that even then he had referred to some of Gide's ideas as potentially "dangerous." Kurella did not call Gide a Trotskyist, but the hint was there: "The political debts owed to Trotsky, which . . . are unmistakable throughout Gide's book, have caused him to do things that are inconsonant with the 'honesty' he proclaims with such pathos in the foreword."[48] Kurella too brought up the question of the popular front, only from an understandably different viewpoint; he asked why Gide was so quick to get the book on the market "at the very moment of a crisis in the popular front" (Kurella omitted mention of who was responsible for the crisis).[49] Those were considerations of which Gide, "for all his apoliticality," was "aware." Nonetheless, he rushed to get the slanderous book out, even though he had been told of the objective effect his "berserk act" would have.

What was Kurella really saying? He charged Gide with damaging

46. Hermann Budzislawski, "Unsere Wahrheitssucher," *Die neue Weltbühne* 7 (February 1937): 189.
47. Klaus Mann, "Der Streit um André Gide," ibid., p. 207.
48. Alfred Kurella, "Schlechte Nahrung: Der Irrtum André Gides und seine Folgen," *Internationale Literatur* 1 (1937): 132.
49. Ibid., p. 133.

the popular front, at least objectively. How? By attacking the Soviet Union in his slanderous Trotskyist book. The official Communist denunciation of Gide's *Back from the USSR* had largely avoided calling him a Trotskyist; that would perhaps have been too much at this time, since being a Trotskyist in the eyes of the Communists was tantamount to being a Fascist, and in Gide's case the preposterous was even more preposterous. But Kurella nonetheless exhibited a proclivity that was presently to make itself strongly felt among Communists in the popular front: to be less than unflinching in one's support of the Soviet Union was to be an enemy of the popular front; to be an enemy of the USSR and the popular front was the action of a Trotskyist, and, "as the whole world knew," Trotsky had sold his soul to the Fascists. Gide's book and the trials had forced the issue, compelling the Communists, for whom any criticism of the USSR was utter anathema, to harden their attitudes within the popular front. More and more in the passing months the Communists began to demand from adherents of the popular front their full approval of domestic affairs in the Soviet Union (for example, the purge trials), because *any* expression of anti-Sovietism was synonymous with fascism.

By the end of 1936 the German popular front had been so thoroughly undermined that nothing could have saved it, even though it led a hamstrung existence for another year or so. The first important proponent to drop his support in the wake of the August trial was Leopold Schwarzschild. In November 1936 the *Neues Tage-Buch* reacted to the Soviet announcement of a trial of saboteurs and wreckers taking place in Novosibirsk by writing that "in spite of the numerous Soviet-Russian trials against 'saboteurs and wreckers,' only one legal procedure, unfortunately, is urgently called for: one against the practitioners of Soviet justice, who continue to sabotage the foreign policy of their land, harm the prestige of the Soviet Union and its government, trip up her foreign friends and allies and—last but not least—do much to help the Third Reich as unconscious and unwitting allies of Hitler."[50]

Just a month later, the *Neues Tage-Buch* came to the conclusion that the whole idea of a popular front had been a mistake. The most instructive lesson learned from the "German edition of the popular front experiment" had been that the notion of "combining *old, already existing* groups so as to amount to more than each represented by itself has proven illusory." The *Neues Tage-Buch* added that the combination

50. "Die Saboteure von Nowosibirsk," *Das neue Tage-Buch*, 28 November 1936, p. 1134.

resulted not in "*more* but in even *less* than the individual parts" and proposed that the emigration begin "'tabula rasa'";[51] an altogether new movement was called for, one that had no links with earlier groups whose only concern was their own further existence. The news that Karl Radek had been arrested and would be tried presently, along with sixteen others, gave the final fillip to the *Neues Tage-Buch*'s break with the Soviet Union. From here on out Schwarzschild's approach to all matters involving the USSR was "red equals brown." "All arguments break down when confronted with the parallelism," wrote the journal; "the recognition—fostered by the impressions left behind by these dramatic productions [the trials]—that the one dictatorship is a twin brother of the other will spread with growing rapidity throughout Europe."[52]

The Communists did what they could to lessen the harm done by Gide's book and the Moscow trials. In Prague, for instance, what seems to have been one of many "Gide discussions" was held; Wieland Herzfelde reported to Bredel on one in particular: "The Gide discussion, by the way, was well attended and, though an organized opposition was there, successful. . . . Feuchtwanger's utterances on the subject are very gratifying, as is Romain Rolland's letter to the workers in Kuznets. You can't imagine the far-reaching effect of Gide's book and how our opponents use the press to exploit it—distorting his criticism because it is evidently not crude enough." Herzfelde also complained cryptically about the aftermath of the first trial: "I don't know if you have noticed over there [in Moscow] to what extent formerly neutral or even ostensibly well-disposed circles have started to work against us again as of the last six months."[53] In early 1937 the verbatim transcript of the first trial was published in a number of languages; it was welcomed by Herzfelde in Prague, who wrote Bredel that the protocol of the trial was widely disseminated in Prague and had had an extraordinarily positive effect. "It is really marvelous that it was done so thoroughly and came out so soon."[54] (Ironically, the ostracized Heinz Neumann, together with his wife Margarete Buber-Neumann, were to thank for that. They had been assigned the task of translating into German for VEGAAR the mammoth six-hundred-page document. Its publication was made more ironic by the fact that Neumann was arrested in Moscow two months later.)[55]

51. "Lehren aus einer Erfahrung," *Das neue Tage-Buch*, 26 December 1936, p. 1231.
52. "Radeks Schicksal," *Das neue Tage-Buch*, 9 January 1937, p. 28.
53. Herzfelde to Bredel, 13 January 1937, TsGALI, 631/12/143/51.
54. Herzfelde to Bredel, 6 March 1937, TsGALI, 631/12/143/36.
55. Cf. Buber-Neumann, *Von Potsdam nach Moskau*, pp. 439, 443–44.

In January 1937 the second group of prominent Bolsheviks, this time alleged members of the Anti-Soviet Trotskyist Center, went on trial in Moscow; the response in the German exile press to the second trial fell into now predictable patterns. Joseph Bornstein, writing in the *Neues Tage-Buch* under the pseudonym Erich Andermann, prompted a debate when he attempted to account for the confessions of the accused. He began by comparing the medieval witch trials with the events in Moscow, the difference being, he said, that "in Stalinist Russia the devil bears the name 'Trotskyism-fascism.'"[56] Andermann wrote at length of the discrepancies in the confessions in order to show that, once the inconsistencies and errors were removed, the entire framework of the trial would collapse. He concluded that the "confessions" of all the defendants were utterly false, which confirmed for him the correctness of Hitler's adage that the larger and cruder a lie the better chance it has of being believed. The only way to account for the confessions, Andermann argued, was that the accused and the witnesses had had their admissions dictated to them by the GPU-NKVD.

Most perplexing was the willingness of the defendants to play along with the charade. Andermann suggested torture as one explanation, but discarded it. He also discarded the notion that chemical preparations had been used, settling finally on hypnosis as at least a possibility. But these were all secondary issues, and Andermann closed his article by raising an important question—the real purpose and meaning of the trials. He came as close as anyone did at the time to guessing the real motivation behind the purge. "In 1924," Andermann wrote, "some fifty prominent members of the old Bolshevik guard signed a document at the Communist party congress in which they declared themselves against Stalin's dictatorship and for reconciliation with Trotsky. The list of signatories of this document is virtually identical with the list of the accused in the Zinoviev and Radek trials."

Andermann's article triggered several replies. S. Aberdam took issue with the theory that hypnosis was used to gain the confessions, but agreed otherwise with everything Andermann had said.[57] Shortly thereafter, an unsigned letter from an "outstanding chemist" appeared in the *Neues Tage-Buch*. He argued that there was no mystery to the confessions. Hypnosis was out as an explanation, for the behavior of · the accused contradicted that interpretation. Rather, everything pointed

56. Joseph Bornstein [Erich Andermann], "Hexenprozess in Moskau," *Das neue Tage-Buch*, 8 February 1937, p. 133.
57. S. Aberdam, "Hypnose in Moskau?" in *Das neue Tage-Buch*, 13 February 1937, p. 162, and Andermann's reply, pp. 162–63.

to the use of a narcotic gas, probably "mescalin." [58] But then a certain Dr. Marcel Strauss, "former head of the Strasbourg University Clinic," wrote a letter to the *Neues Tage-Buch*, which Schwarzschild published. Strauss explained that on the basis of recent research hypnosis did indeed provide the solution to the mystery, adding that in 1934 several well-known psychiatrists had been called into the NKVD for the purpose of "scientific work."

Strauss's letter was a fake. It had been written by the Communists in an attempt to discredit Schwarzschild by linking him and his journal with Goebbels and Trotsky. No sooner had Schwarzschild published the Strauss letter than the Communist *Deutsche Volkszeitung* in Paris plastered its pages with astounding and sensational accusations. These bore the title "Goebbels in the 'Neues Tagebuch': A Crass Case of Trotskyist-Fascist Conformism—Hypnotized by Trotsky, Employed by Hitler." The *Deutsche Volkszeitung* (Bruno Frei was the author) explained that Marcel Strauss used sentences in his article identical with remarks found in the Nazi press; thus, there was not only "complete conformity between the editorial board of the 'Neues Tagebuch' and Goebbels's press in slandering the Soviet judiciary, but both also avail themselves of the same sources and articles." The *Deutsche Volkszeitung* issued this serious accusation "in front of the entire emigration, in front of those working illegally in Germany, and presents its proof."

The *Neues Tage-Buch* had systematically continued its defense of "counterrevolutionary Trotskyist criminals and agents of Hitler fascism," an egregious instance of the cooperation of Hitler agents and Trotskyists. What was at stake, the *Deutsche Volkszeitung* insisted, was less the cases of Schwarzschild and Andermann, who had already unmasked themselves completely, than the "purity of the emigration, vigilance vis-a-vis the machinations of the Gestapo, and the purging of anti-Fascist ranks of Trotskyist elements." The *Neues Tage-Buch*, the *Deutsche Volkszeitung* continued, had become a central organ of the Trotskyists! The *Neues Tage-Buch* was pursuing, and the Strauss matter proved it, "a premeditated, malicious, persistent disruption of united and popular front efforts in the German anti-Fascist camp." These political liaisons had to be understood in order to recognize certain facts. With the help of the Trotskyists, not only had a Fascist concoction (the Strauss letter) found its way into an émigré journal, but a disruptive force beneficial to Hitler fascism had been created in Paris within the German emigration. The *Deutsche Volkszeitung* closed

58. "Das Rätsel des Moskauer Prozesses," *Das neue Tage-Buch*, 28 February 1937, pp. 174–75.

piously: "By making available to the public our discovery and proof, we hope that responsible men in all parties and groups will draw the consequences."

But the Communists had outsmarted themselves: the entire "scandal" had come to light, the *Deutsche Volkszeitung* explained, when the Communists had ascertained that no such "Marcel Strauss" existed in Strasbourg "at the given address." However, the *Neues Tage-Buch* had not printed the address typed at the top of the original letter; it had printed only the comments Strauss made in it. The Communists, who had invented the name and address in the first place, failed to notice the *Neues Tage-Buch*'s omission of the address, and Schwarzschild caught them red-handed. "That's the method! That's the shoddy method of the 'accusations' [in the trials] that are raised with the help of material that the accuser himself, full of pathos and rolling his eyes, fabricated out of nothing," wrote Schwarzschild.[59]

The Communists greeted the trial of Radek and his codefendants with cheers. The *Deutsche Zentral-Zeitung* was full of applause, the titles of the articles reproducing the content entirely: Willi Bredel, "Pitiful Creatures"; Julius Schaxel, "Extermination of the Pernicious Foreign Substance"; Julja Annenkova of the *Deutsche Zentral-Zeitung*, "Handed Over";[60] Ernst Busch, "There Was Never a More Just Verdict"; Johannes R. Becher, "Three Defeats: After the Trial of the Anti-Soviet Trotskyist Center and the Anniversary of the Fascist Takeover of Power on 30 January 1933."[61] Lion Feuchtwanger's comments were carried on the front page of the *Deutsche Zentral-Zeitung* (he was in Moscow at the time), and Hugo Huppert waxed poetic.[62]

But of far more use to Moscow were the expressions of support from quarters not directly linked to the party. Ernst Bloch, for instance, took umbrage at the "exotic" interpretations of the trials published in the *Neues Tage-Buch*. For him it was all quite simple, and he "fired a torpedo at Schwarzschild,"[63] as he expressed it by letter to

59. "Hypnose in Moskau?," *Das neue Tage-Buch*, 27 February 1937, pp. 205–6. "Ein Presseskandal—Enthüllungen zum Moskauer Prozess. Goebbels im 'Neuen Tagebuch': Ein krasser Fall des trotzkistisch-faschistischen Konformismus—Hypnotisiert von Trotzki, engagiert bei Hitler," *Deutsche Volkszeitung*, 7 March 1937. Leopold Schwarzschild, "Ihr Milljöh," *Das neue Tage-Buch*, 13 March 1937, pp. 249–52.
60. The Bredel, Schaxel, and Annenkova articles appeared in the *Deutsche Zentral-Zeitung*, 28 January 1937.
61. The Busch and Becher articles appeared in the *Deutsche Zentral-Zeitung*, 1 February 1937.
62. See Feuchtwanger in the *Deutsche Zentral-Zeitung*, 30 January 1937, and Huppert's "poem," "Die Abstimmung," in the *Deutsche Zentral-Zeitung*, 1 February 1937.
63. Bloch to Bredel, 3 March and 20 March 1937, TsGALI, 631/12/141/152 and 148.

Moscow, in an article appearing in the *Neue Weltbühne*.[64] Poking fun at "exegetes" who looked for interpretations in such motives as Stalin's revenge and in the use of drugs or hypnosis for the purpose of forcing confessions, Bloch wrote that "bizarre explanations should only be given after the reasonable ones have been . . . exhausted." He then proceeded to employ the precise rationale welcomed in Communist circles: "Even if the emigration's right-wing bourgeois editors 'have as little respect for the current leaders of bolshevism as they do for the ones who were deposed yesterday,' " Bloch reasoned, "the Soviet Union remains the mainstay of the entire anti-Fascist front."[65]

For Bloch there was no doubt that Trotsky's hatred had driven him to an alliance with fascism, and he argued that Trotsky's bitterness and frustration had led him to a standpoint from which toppling Stalin's regime was justified by any means. But the final effect of Trotskyist activity would not be world revolution, which Trotsky wanted at any cost, Bloch thought, but the reinstitution of capitalism in Russia; the aftermath would be "German fascism in Moscow," and it would truly have been hard to believe that "the Gestapo and Trotskyism had not joined up in mutual hatred, even if they both intended, in the final analysis, to deceive the other." Bloch concluded by maintaining that "the anti-Fascists had reason enough to understand the cause of the Moscow trial," which was not in the "interest of antifascism" to obscure; it was inappropriate for anti-Fascists to use "their journal" to

---

Bloch added: "It ought to be clear why I avoided the total use of standard party language—in this case and for this purpose—in coming out in support of the party's cause. My attack and my commitment would otherwise have lost its impact in the eyes of many readers. . . . What needed to be said was still said, and the attack should have consequences."

64. Ernst Bloch, "Kritik einer Prozesskritik: Hypnose, Mescalin und die Wirklichkeit," *Die neue Weltbühne* 10 (March 1937): 294–99.

65. Ibid., p. 295. Lukács explained this sort of reasoning many years later: "On the one hand, it shouldn't be forgotten that men from Zinoviev and Bukharin to Trotsky actually represented an opposition in the twenties; and, having been brought up in the traditions of the French Revolution, in viewing the great trials we very often thought of the trials against the Girondists and Dantonists; there too not all forms were observed and we were nonetheless on the side of Robespierre against the Dantonists. This analogy played a large role, on the one hand, and, on the other hand, one shouldn't forget that this occurred in the Western emigration as well—think only of Ernst Bloch in America—where people who privately would have condemned much of what was happening in the USSR told themselves, 'I can't write a syllable that could be interpreted in Europe as support of Hitler against the Soviet Union.' The situation of the foreign writers in Moscow was supported not only by the pressure of Stalinism but also by motives of this kind, which in my opinion were thoroughly legitimate" (Georg Lukács, "Tonbandgespräch," in Becher-Archiv).

engage in miniature crusades, for "the trials have not been harmful, but this mysterious type of publicism has." Bloch suggested that anti-Fascists adopt the approach he had taken, borrowing from Socrates: "'What I have understood is excellent. From which I conclude that the rest, which I do not understand, is also excellent.'"[66]

Throughout the first six months of 1937 the *Neues Tage-Buch* followed events in the USSR closely. On 10 April the journal commented on the arrests of Rakovskij and Jagoda (the former head of the NKVD) and on the pretrial press campaign against Bukharin and Rykov, who would be the next old Bolsheviks to appear in the dock.[67] On 19 May 1937 the *Neues Tage-Buch* wrote of the arrests and of the anti-Trotskyist crusade within the Soviet Academy of Science,[68] and one month later Schwarzschild published a long article on the arrests and executions of Tukhachevskij and seven other Soviet generals.[69] Throughout the year the *Neues Tage-Buch* was full of comments and lengthy articles by Schwarzschild on other developments in Russia. The *Neue Weltbühne*, on the other hand, published apologias for these developments.[70] The lines were drawn: the *Neues Tage-Buch* had turned unreservedly anti-Soviet, while the *Neue Weltbühne* increasingly lent its backing to the USSR. This was highlighted by Schwarzschild's publication of an excerpt from Gide's *Back from the USSR* and Budzislawski's selection of passages from Feuchtwanger's *Moscow 1937.*[71]

After Feuchtwanger's eventful two-month visit to the USSR—he sat in on the January trial and was received in the Kremlin by Stalin—he left the country announcing grandiloquently: "I came, I saw, I shall write."[72] No sooner had Feuchtwanger arrived in the West, though, than he was widely denounced by those upset by his remarks about Gide and the second Moscow trial. Writing to Moscow, Feuchtwanger reported: "As you may have heard, I have been subjected to much abuse because of *Wort* [where he published his attack on Gide]; the especially clever ones suspect that I only stood up for the Soviet Union

66. Bloch, "Kritik einer Prozesskritik," pp. 296–99.
67. Cf. *Das neue Tage-Buch*, 10 April 1937, pp. 339–40.
68. *Das neue Tage-Buch*, 19 May 1937, p. 581.
69. Leopold Schwarzschild, "Hinrichtung," *Das neue Tage-Buch*, 19 June 1937, pp. 584–88.
70. Hermann Budzislawski, writing under the pseudonym Hermann Eschwege, "Moskauer Prozesse," *Die neue Weltbühne* 6 (February 1937): 170–73; and "Die Verschwörung von Moskau," *Die neue Weltbühne* 25 (June 1937): 765–72.
71. *Das neue Tage-Buch*, 10 July 1937, pp. 664–65 and *Die neue Weltbühne*, nos. 14, 25, 26, and 27 (1937).
72. See his remarks in the *Deutsche Zentral-Zeitung*, 6 February 1937.

so warmly because I was given the opportunity to edit *Das Wort*."[73] A few weeks later Feuchtwanger wrote Bredel:

> As I said before, I have been denounced from many
> different sides since my return from the USSR. Virtually
> all the Norwegian writers signed an open letter, which came
> out in most of the Scandinavian and many of the English
> papers and showed up in portions of the émigré press. My
> positive stance with respect to the Moscow trial caused an
> extraordinary amount of controversy. In the Prague press,
> especially in Social Democratic papers, a large number of
> vicious attacks on my person were published on the occasion
> of the prohibition of my Prague lecture. My article on
> Gide and the few words I wrote about the trial were particular
> bones of contention. Kurt Hiller was especially active in
> the entire affair.[74]

The bitterness of the attacks led to Feuchtwanger's decision to write a booklet about his travel impressions "somewhat more detailed than Gide's book." He announced that he had been working on it for ten days but that he could not be sure yet whether it would turn out to be publishable. In early May 1937 Feuchtwanger wrote that the book was finished and that it would appear, at the latest, in early July, but there had been some difficulty in finding a publisher. It had not been easy to have the book accepted by western publishers, Feuchtwanger remarked, since they, of course, had "reservations about publishing a pro-Bolshevist book." But Querido in Amsterdam had taken the manuscript and the type was already set. Feuchtwanger went on to say that he "only hoped that no one will get upset at me in the Soviet Union for the few critical comments I have made, without which the book would surely have no affect in the West at all."[75]

In the Soviet Union *Moscow 1937* met with a divided response.[76] It was promptly translated into Russian and published in a gigantic

73. Feuchtwanger to the editors of *Das Wort*, 27 February 1937, TsGALI, 631/13/87/82.

74. Feuchtwanger to Bredel, 8 March 1937, TsGALI, 631/13/87/85.

75. Feuchtwanger to Bredel, 2 May 1937, TsGALI, 631/13/87/100. Feuchtwanger's intentions had evoked some consternation in Moscow. Bredel wrote Feuchtwanger that he found the idea of composing a book about his travel impressions excellent (Bredel to Feuchtwanger, 17 March 1937, TsGALI, 631/13/87/86); however, because of the recent Gide affair, Bredel said to Maria Osten that Feuchtwanger "intends to write a book about his impressions (I get gray hair at the thought)" (Bredel to Osten, 17 March 1937, TsGALI, 631/12/143/415).

76. Personal information from Lev Kopelev and others, who recalled the reception afforded *Moscow 1937*.

edition of two hundred thousand copies.[77] At a time when the USSR was under intense fire from many quarters because of the bad publicity associated with Gide and the show trials, Feuchtwanger did the Soviet Union an enormous favor by publishing his apologia—the work of a "non-Communist" writer with a worldwide reputation. Yet *Moscow 1937* contained some passages, particularly those critical of the Stalin cult, that actually enlightened some of its readers in the USSR. Upon the book's publication, those who knew or suspected the truth about what was going on in the Soviet Union read Feuchtwanger's book and interpreted it as a betrayal, a sellout. Those who were confused or uncertain about the real meaning of events in the country, on the other hand, were made aware of the truth about some of these things by reading *Moscow 1937*. That the book sold out in a few weeks testifies to the fact that it was not being used and read just as propaganda.[78] Lev Kopelev remembered that, after a year or so, *Moscow 1937* was removed from the libraries—another indication that the authorities were aware of the effect of some of Feuchtwanger's "critical" remarks. The book was never republished.

Outside the Soviet Union there was also a twofold response. In late August Feuchtwanger wrote Maria Osten from his home in southern France that he was particularly pleased "to be able to do much for the *défense de la culture*. For my booklet *Moscow 1937* seems to have had a serious impact, and I hope to have repaired a substantial portion of the damage done by Gide." He had received convincing letters from all parts of the world, Feuchtwanger said; "even papers decidely hostile to the USSR, such as the *Times* or the *Manchester Guardian*, conclude that the persuasive power of many of my arguments cannot be ignored." But Feuchtwanger had also been sharply criticized: "I should have told myself ahead of time that I would stir up a storm of protest with the book. Our friend Schwarzschild has again distinguished himself with particular vehemence; he has already written three large articles against *Moscow 1937* and a fourth has been announced. His 'review' will thus be substantially longer than the book itself."[79]

The steepness of the "bluff" that led to Gide's disappointment with the USSR did not faze Feuchtwanger; apart from a handful of critical remarks, he wrote an apologia for all aspects of Soviet life—the status of the workers, living conditions, the happy life of Soviet citizens, and so on. On virtually every major point Feuchtwanger's opinion coin-

77. Timofej Rokotov to Lion Feuchtwanger, 14 December 1937, TsGALI, 1397/1/674/12. Feuchtwanger, *Moskva 1937*.
78. Mikhail Koltsov to Feuchtwanger, 11 March 1938, TsGALI, 631/12/87/153.
79. Feuchtwanger to Osten, 24 August 1937, TsGALI, 631/13/87/2.

cided with the official Soviet view of things, and he concluded: "It does one good after all the compromise of the West to see an achievement such as this, to which a man can say yes, yes, yes with all his heart."[80] But although he had ostensibly undertaken to write a pure travelog and description of the country and its inhabitants, he went far beyond that. He took up the major Soviet *political* controversies, rebutting Gide along the way and investigating the conflict between Stalin and Trotsky and the motives behind the "Trotskyist trials."

Indicative of the extent to which Feuchtwanger had been deluded by what he saw and was told is his attempt to dismiss hostile interpretations of the show trials: "The reason [for the trials], the opponents assert, is Stalin's ruthless despotism, his delight in terror. It is quite obvious: this man Stalin, with all his feelings of inferiority and boundless lust for power and revenge, wants to wreak vengeance on all those who have at any time injured him and all who might be dangerous to him in any way." "Like Hitler," Feuchtwanger said, attributing this argumentation to anti-Soviet observers, "he wants to shoot a clear space all around him."[81] Now as clear-sighted an explanation as that is, for Feuchtwanger it represented the opposite of the truth (though it was the publication of such passages—left intact in the Russian translation—that *nolens volens* opened some eyes in the Soviet Union).[82] Feuchtwanger insisted that "such nonsense betrays an ignorance of the human soul and a lack of discernment. Read any book or any speech of Stalin's, look at any portrait of him, think of any measure which he has taken for the purposes of construction," Feuchtwanger enjoined his readers; "it at once becomes as clear as daylight, that this modest, impersonal man cannot possibly have committed the colossal indiscretion of producing with the assistance of countless performers so coarse a comedy, merely for the purposes of holding a sort of

80. Feuchtwanger, *Moscow 1937*, pp. 138–39. Just a few years earlier, Feuchtwanger had not been able to say "yes, yes" to judicial practices in the USSR. In his novel *Erfolg* he had written in a chapter devoted to justice throughout the world in the twenties, "In Russia Bolshevist judges executed supporters of the Tsarist regime for acts of espionage of which they were presumably innocent in order to intimidate opponents" (Feuchtwanger, *Erfolg*, p. 36). That sentence, by the way, fails to appear in East German editions of Feuchtwanger's 1930 novel. See Feuchtwanger, *Erfolg* (Berlin: Aufbau-Verlag, 1973), p. 28.
81. Feuchtwanger, *Moscow 1937*, pp. 138–39.
82. The same can be said of Feuchtwanger's disapproval of Stalin-worship, of "distasteful . . . idolatry," comments that, ironically, may be as critical as anything ever published in Stalinist Russia. Cf. ibid., pp. 68–70.

festival of revenge with Bengal lights to celebrate the humiliation of his opponents."[83]

Elisabeth Poretsky, wife of the Soviet agent Ignace Reiss assassinated in Switzerland in 1937 by the NKVD, makes an interesting claim about Feuchtwanger and *Moscow 1937*. Basing her comments on the report of a close friend who allegedly acted as the translator at Feuchtwanger's talk with Stalin, Poretsky writes that, after the handshake and exchange of amenities with Stalin, Feuchtwanger courageously told the general secretary that he was shocked at the adulation of Stalin's person. Stalin reportedly grew angry, remarking tersely that it was not his fault if his own people saw him in this light, thus breaking off the interview. Feuchtwanger left the Kremlin "pale and shaken." That story supposedly made the rounds of the party, followed shortly thereafter by this verse:

> And there he appeared at the door
> With an odd expression on his face.
> Oh, let us hope that this one Jew
> Does not turn out to be a Gide.[84]

Poretsky contends that there was actually a *second* interview between Feuchtwanger and Stalin that went more smoothly than the first. During their second talk, Feuchtwanger is said to have agreed to write an apologia for the trials, asking in exchange that the lives of Karl Radek and the other *Jewish* defendants in the January 1937 trial be spared; *Moscow 1937* was to be written in return for the lives of the Jews among the accused![85] It is true that all those who received "mere" prison sentences at the trial were Jews, while the others were sentenced to death. But there is scarcely any truth to the story as a whole, though it is more than understandable that rumors of that sort circulated. It was, after all, difficult for intelligent Soviet citizens to look at the visit of Gide and Feuchtwanger (and the literary "outcomes") without becoming suspicious. The Feuchtwanger visit and the publi-

---

83. Had Feuchtwanger only known of one of the uses to which *Moscow 1937* was put: Bukharin's interrogators, in preparing the third show trial, gave him a copy of the book in order to convince him that he had no chance of secretly communicating the falsity of the charges lodged against him. See Cohen, *Bukharin and the Bolshevik Revolution*, p. 376.
84. Feuchtwanger was Jewish. The untranslatable pun is that "Gide," or in Russian "Zhid," means "Yid." Poretsky, *Our Own People*, pp. 176–77.
85. Ibid., pp. 198–99. Marta Feuchtwanger, unaware of Poretsky's charge, told me that her husband was received by Stalin only once.

cation of *Moscow 1937* smacked too much of Soviet orchestration, even if this time it was not.

The poem, however, is another matter; it is authentic in one version or another. Ivanov-Razumnik tells the story of a man arrested on a charge of embezzlement who, when the verse was found in his possession, was sentenced instead for counterrevolutionary activity.[86] The defendant got three years in a Kazakhstan concentration camp for his love of poetry. Ivanov-Razumnik, by the way, claims that Feuchtwanger was paid a "handsome sum" to write his book, a rumor that evidently enjoyed widespread currency in Moscow. But it too is untrue; there was no need to bribe a man to voice sentiments that he felt in the depths of his heart.

The response to *Moscow 1937* was predictable. In the USSR portions were carried in the *Deutsche Zentral-Zeitung*;[87] in the West, as already mentioned, *Die neue Weltbühne* published passages. Ernst Bloch also wrote a flattering review contrasting Feuchtwanger's account with that of another "well-known writer," praising Feuchtwanger's portrayal of Stalin and the effect the book would have in balancing the viewpoints and in easing the shock caused by the trials. Bloch also used the occasion to attack Schwarzschild's equation of Nazi and Soviet dictatorships.[88] But the attacks on Feuchtwanger came just as quickly. Kurt Hiller published a denunciation in his *Profile* that harked back to Feuchtwanger's censure of Gide. Quoting some of Feuchtwanger's remarks, Hiller commented that "here this anti-aesthete begins to smell abominably. . . . If such behavior vis-a-vis a lesser writer would be disgraceful, with respect to Gide it is disgusting and can scarcely be characterized in written words. . . . And Querido, the most 'distinguished' publishing house of the German émigrés, puts out such garbage."[89]

Leopold Schwarzschild kept the level of his remarks about Feuchtwanger generally high, using the latter's case to discuss the "psychosis" he felt afflicted countless opponents of Hitler. As Feuchtwanger had said, Schwarzschild did deal with *Moscow 1937* at great length, devoting no fewer than four long articles to the subject, the first two directly related to Feuchtwanger, the last two expanded to take in issues more

86. Ivanov, *The Memoirs of Ivanov-Razumnik*, pp. 311–12. The words of the poem printed by Ivanov-Razumnik, which he claims was circulating in Moscow, are a bit different: Lion Feuchtwanger with his friends so true / Sits happily in Moscow as he's bid. / I fear, however, that this Jew / May also prove to be a Gide.
87. *Deutsche Zentral-Zeitung*, 9 August and 5 December 1937.
88. Ernst Bloch, "Feuchtwangers *Moskau 1937*," *Die neue Weltbühne* 30 (July 1937): 934–36.
89. Hiller, *Profile*, p. 134.

broadly applicable to the anti-Hitler emigration at large. Russia, wrote Schwarzschild, as even Feuchtwanger and others like him admitted, was a dictatorship, which meant that in at least certain essential features it was akin to another dictatorship, one the German exiles rejected. Feuchtwanger, being one of the eminent, internationally known spokesmen of those who disdained Nazi dictatorship, had been among the first to write at length about a "foreign dictatorship," and that raised serious questions. For Feuchtwanger's case involved much more than just "a book about Russia. It is a literary-political case par excellence within the complex of Germany."

What particularly bothered Schwarzschild was that, although *Moscow 1937* purported to be a travelog, something like reportage, Feuchtwanger had chosen to take a very biased stand on such issues as the Stalin-Trotsky feud and the trials of the old Bolsheviks. Commented Schwarzschild, "The subject of Stalin-Trotsky is alien to a book that sets out to discuss the results of one's own experiences. A trip to Moscow does not give someone the increased authority to write about that issue." In this and other cases, the best that could be said for Feuchtwanger, Schwarzschild charged, was that he lacked the knowledge that might invest his opinions about Russia with a certain credibility. But Schwarzschild refused to go beyond that, for he claimed to have found passages where Feuchtwanger made statements whose falsity was not to be accounted for by mere ignorance.

There was a pattern of *willful* misinterpretation and falsification in *Moscow 1937*, claimed Schwarzschild. For instance, Feuchtwanger deprecated Trotsky and extolled Stalin. In support of what he wrote, Feuchtwanger adduced Lenin's "Testament" so as to discredit Trotsky, selecting one of Lenin's remarks in particular—"Trotsky's non-Bolshevist past is no accident." What upset Schwarzschild was this: by quoting from Lenin's "Testament," Feuchtwanger disclosed his familiarity with a document whose very existence had been steadfastly denied in Russia, a document whose overriding meaning pointed to Lenin's general admiration for Trotsky and animus for Stalin. That told Schwarzschild that Feuchtwanger had ceased to be an honest, impartial observer. "This is the instance where Feuchtwanger cannot even be excused by pleading ignorance."[90] The hint was clear: Feuchtwanger had deliberately doctored his account in the interests of Soviet Russia.

Schwarzschild's second article analyzed Feuchtwanger's discussion of the current standard of living in Russia. According to Schwarz-

90. Leopold Schwarzschild, "Feuchtwangers Botschaft," *Das neue Tage-Buch*, 30 June 1937, pp. 730–32.

schild, Feuchtwanger (and those who thought like him) reduced the question of the Soviet Union and the existence of a dictatorship to whether or not certain freedoms might be abridged so that the masses might immediately have "more bread, butter, and meat." In other words, social and economic conditions became the touchstone by which everything was justified (not that Schwarzschild agreed with Feuchtwanger's roseate assessment of the Soviet economy). The "Feuchtwangers" were willing to accept the necessity of dictatorship so long as material progress was being made. Thus, for the sake of the standard of living, Feuchtwanger was "cheerfully" willing to sacrifice "values— I'll subsume them under the three concepts Magna Carta, Bill of Rights, *Droit de l'homme*—for which generation after generation has fought for centuries." At this point, Schwarzschild explained, the question of knowledge or ignorance ceased to play a role. "Here something more serious begins, something that bears witness to the wide dissemination of a psychosis that has taken hold of far too many shell-shocked minds."[91]

Schwarzschild's next articles dealt with that psychosis, examining why so many anti-Hitler German exiles were perfectly willing to champion the Soviet Union, a dictatorship that, in Schwarzschild's mind, differed little from the regime in Germany. Schwarzschild could not understand why, during their "war" against Hitler, when they suddenly found themselves in close proximity to Stalin, these people immediately began praising him and swearing eternal fealty. How was that possible, asked Schwarzschild, "as long as they are enemies of despotism?" By reducing categories such as freedom, law, human rights, and humanity to affairs of "second, third, fifth, and seventh" magnitudes of importance, Schwarzschild explained, the Feuchtwangers were capable of "lashing out at dictatorship in Berlin even as they praised dictatorship in Moscow." In no time at all things had gone so far that "the sum total of monstrosities and abominations that are united in the concept of 'dictatorship' are accepted—more than that, they are praised, just so long as they represent means employed in the service of a pretended higher end.

This was the quintessence of the complex "Russia-Germany." Schwarzschild argued that because both were dictatorships there could be no confession on the subject of Russia that was not concurrently a confession on the question of Germany. For every spokesman of the German opposition who "joins the ranks of Stalin's foreign legion . . .

91. Schwarzschild, "Feuchtwangers Botschaft," *Das neue Tage-Buch*, 7 August 1937, pp. 752 and 759.

participates, perhaps unknowingly, in ravaging, undermining, and eventually bursting both spiritual and very tangible positions vis-à-vis the Third Reich." Freedom and human rights must not be discarded for pretended higher goals, pleaded Schwarzschild; the standard of living or any other alleged exalted objectives must not be seen as the all-important touchstone. For "people are strangled by dictatorship per se; it is the lack of freedom, law and order, human rights, and humaneness . . . that oppresses them, and their absence can not be bargained away by a living standard. Partisanship for Moscow . . . which attaches no independent significance to the nature of dictatorship, reducing everything instead to a standard of living, moreover, to a level that has not been achieved—that partisanship . . . is destroying the core of our position as Germans."

Schwarzschild went on to say that these conditions in the USSR, "in which human beings . . . are persecuted and destroyed—these conditions are hallmarks of dictatorship, heightened despotism, terrorism." These were the events that showed Soviet Russia as a "naked dictatorship." Whoever said " 'yes, yes' " to it approbated the same decisive characteristics that marked Nazi Germany,[92] for the reality of the Soviet Union was the reality of Hitler's Reich and a yes to the one carried in it an unavoidable yes to the other. How was it possible, Schwarzschild asked, for one to "scream 'brutality' at the one and 'bravo! bravo!' at the other?"[93]

As for alliances against Hitler, the decision was quite simple: whether anti-Nazis chose to further the chance that Hitler's regime would be followed by Stalin's rule. Schwarzschild suggested that everyone give a great deal of thought to whether "it was desirable to replace party rule with the hegemony of another single party; Hitler Youth with Comsomol; Gestapo with GPU; Reichsschrifttumskammer with Writers' Union." Each individual should ponder whether he wanted to help bring "the hour closer . . . when something could happen that would be irrevocable for years—the substitution of Red Fascists for Brown Fascists; Bolshi-terror for Nazi terror; Comintern for Nazi-intern." Yes, Schwarzschild said to the Communists, he would cooperate in the anti-Hitler struggle, but he would see to it that they, the Communists, remained just a "part of the struggle and were denied the opportunity to take it over in its totality, either spiritually or literally." He would do

92. Leopold Schwarzschild, "Zwei Despotien," *Das neue Tage-Buch*, 21 August 1937, p. 801–2, 805.
93. Schwarzschild, "Zwei Despotien," *Das neue Tage-Buch*, 29 August 1937, p. 825.

everything possible to see that they failed at that, "for if what really matters is merely exchanging terror for terror, Hitler's dictatorship for Stalin's dictatorship, it wouldn't be worth lifting a finger."[94]

Against the backdrop of show trials, terror, exposés, denunciations, and counterdenunciations at both ends of the political spectrum, the German popular front ran its course. In December 1936 the Popular Front Committee in Paris decided to make an outward show of unity by publishing an Appeal for the German Popular Front, yet scarcely had it been printed than some of the signatories either dissociated themselves from it or denied ever having signed it. In April 1937 the committee convened a Popular Front Conference that was attended by three hundred participants. But nothing of substance was achieved at this assembly either, and from there on out the popular front went downhill rapidly.

What the Communists did to Willi Münzenberg proved terribly upsetting to many committee members who had come to trust him alone among the Communists.[95] In October 1936 Münzenberg was ordered to Moscow and asked to stay there, ostensibly to assume control of the Comintern's Agitprop Department; the real purpose was to cut him off from his activities in Paris. While in Moscow Münzenberg was brought before the Comintern's International Control Commission and examined inquisitorially about his work in France, especially about alleged sinister political dealings on the part of his staff. Münzenberg barely managed to escape Moscow under the pretense of settling his affairs in Paris before returning to take the Comintern post. But back in France he refused to return to Moscow in spite of repeated orders to answer the charge of "Trotskyism." An emissary, Grete Wilde, was even sent to Paris to investigate Münzenberg's secretary Hans Schulz for attending an anniversary celebration of the Youth International in 1934 held at the German Club in Moscow, where "some critical remarks" were made.[96]

Münzenberg's differences with the party seem to have been generated by his view of the popular front as a sort of counter-German government, an end in itself; Walter Ulbricht and other Communist

---

94. Ibid., pp. 830–31.
95. See, for instance, a letter from Victor Schiff to Ernst Reuter (both Social Democrats), of 7–10 January 1936: "We have made a fair amount of progress recently, and *Willi* M. especially . . . has given us the impression that he has an honest interest in reaching an understanding minus party maneuvers." In Matthias, *Mit dem Gesicht nach Deutschland*, p. 255.
96. Gross, *Willi Münzenberg*, p. 303.

policy makers, as Wehner put it, thought of the committee instead as a "'nonpartisan' executive organ of the Communist party leadership."[97] Still, the Communists were not yet ready to discipline Münzenberg and remove him from the committee, where he continued to work well into the spring of 1937. But in May Ulbricht notified Heinrich Mann that Münzenberg would not be taking part in the committee's work "because of a lengthy absence from Paris";[98] Ulbricht and Paul Merker replaced him, and the progress of the committee ground to a halt. The beginning of the end came for Münzenberg in fall 1937 when a party circular informed the Communist faction of the committee that "investigative proceedings" had been instituted against Münzenberg on charges of holding talks with conservative bourgeois circles without party approval. Another circular followed on 27 October 1937 with the secret news that Münzenberg had been expelled from the party.[99] When the Popular Front Committee got wind of these developments, Rudolf Breitscheid and other Social Democrats threatened to pull out of the organization, but Münzenberg could no longer be saved.[100] Nevertheless, the Comintern did not slacken its efforts to entice Münzenberg back to Moscow. Dimitroff wrote conciliatory letters, and an agent named Belitskij was sent off to Paris to persuade Münzenberg that he had nothing to fear in Moscow. Who decided Münzenberg's fate, after all, Dimitroff or the NKVD? asked Belitsky, who said he "knew" that Ezhov was on Münzenberg's side. Münzenberg refused to take the bait.[101]

In May 1938 the KPD published a resolution in the party paper in Paris publicly announcing Münzenberg's expulsion from the party for "continuing his intrigues against the party leadership and its popular front policy."[102] Münzenberg responded to the charges of wrong-

97. Wehner, "Erinnerungen," p. 114.

98. Walter Ulbricht to Heinrich Mann, 25 May 1937. Letter printed in *Beiträge zur Geschichte der deutschen Arbeiterbewegung* 1 (1963): 83.

99. Gross, *Willi Münzenberg*, p. 314.

100. Sywottek, *Deutsche Volksdemokratie*, p. 81.

101. Gross, *Willi Münzenberg*, pp. 314–15. He seems to have had little doubt about what awaited him in Moscow; he also knew that his brother-in-law Heinz Neumann had been arrested in April 1937.

102. "Beschluss des ZK der KPD über W. Münzenberg," *Deutsche Volkszeitung*, 22 May 1938. Throughout 1938 there were repeated attempts to persuade Heinrich Mann, who had a friendly relationship with Münzenberg, to sever his ties with him (in spring 1937 Münzenberg mounted a campaign to have Mann awarded a Nobel Prize [see Mann's letters to Becher, 2 April and 10 May 1937 in Becher-Archiv, Sig. 57–8]; Becher was also involved in this, though it is unclear whether the original idea of promoting Mann was his or Münzenberg's). Kurt Kersten ("Das Ende Willi Münzenbergs," *Deutsche*

doing in an article not published until several months later. He fixed responsibility for the failures of the popular front solely on the Communists. The contradictory policies of the party, which spoke of new tasks in empty words without really changing tactics or the character and language of its propaganda; the ambiguity of its goals in appealing for a "'democratic people's republic'" without repudiation of single-party dictatorship; the duplicitous application of united front tactics in which the Communists called for creation of a single workers' unity party but persisted in policies condemned at the Seventh World Congress—all these had conspired to ruin the trust in socialist and democratic circles necessary for unity.[103] Münzenberg announced that, without forming a separate political faction, he would nonetheless not cease working toward formation of a large united party and a broad popular front movement powerful enough to bring down Hitler and create a new Germany.[104]

To move the Popular Front Committee off dead center, the KPD had virtually banned from its official propaganda all talk of proletarian revolution and dictatorship, substituting instead the slogan "democratic republic" as a means of prodding the socialists into support of a popular front and in the hope of preventing Communist isolation within the committee and within the mainstream of the nonsocialist anti-Hitler opposition. This was of paramount importance to the Communists, for one of their prime objectives all along was to band together somehow with conservative, bourgeois anti-Nazi circles. They wished to join these circles if for no other reason than to prevent just

---

Rundschau 5 [1957]: 491–92) claims that Wilhelm Pieck journeyed to Nizza and persuaded Mann to dissociate himself from Münzenberg, though it is doubtful whether it was really all that simple. This seems to have happened in 1938 (Kersten gives no date), and yet Mann's opinion of the Communists at this time had sunk to its lowest level. In any case, by March–April 1938 Mann had still not broken with Münzenberg. In a letter to Maria Osten, Feuchtwanger wrote: "I have been told you made a bet that you would separate Heinrich Mann from Münzenberg. Let me tell you as an old friend that I see little point in such bets. I think Münzenberg's case is far too important, and it is in all of our interest to settle it amiably." Feuchtwanger to Osten, 25 March 1938, TsGALI, 631/13/87/4. In a later letter Feuchtwanger refused to tell Osten the source of his information (7 April 1938, TsGALI, 631/13/87/5). Mann also wrote for the first few issues of Münzenberg's independent journal *Die Zukunft* in late 1938, and, though he failed to contribute to later issues, never announced publicly that he had broken with Münzenberg.
103. Willi Münzenberg, "Alles für die Einheit," *Die Zukunft*, 10 March 1939.
104. Ibid.

such groups, who were thought to possess ties to the Reichswehr and other supposedly powerful non-Communist anti-Hitler factions in Germany, from overthrowing Hitler themselves and setting up a conservative, Weimar-style republic without KPD participation. As an offshoot of such thinking, the Communists also worried that the Social Democrats resisted united front blandishments precisely because they had secret aspirations toward an anti-Hitler coalition (minus Communists) with bourgeois anti-Nazis.[105]

But their staunch espousal of democracy brought the Communists trouble from a different source, the Socialist Workers' Party (SAP) in the Popular Front Committee. The SAP took strong exception to the slogan "democratic republic," claiming that the Communist program signaled a "renunciation of the class struggle and the battle for socialism"; although the support of the intermediate classes had to be sought, the SAP refused to discuss the possibility of any alliance with bourgeois organizations that "rejected socialism." It insisted that the program for a "free, socialist, republican Germany" had to be realized without the help of liberal, capitalist, catholic, or other nonsocialist groups—precisely the circles in which the Communists, at least behind the scenes, were most interested.[106] The KPD met this left-wing challenge to its program with political denunciation. The impediment to further progress within the Popular Front Committee, Ulbricht wrote Heinrich Mann, was the position of the SAP, which was said to be pulling out all stops to combat the "only feasible popular front slogan—struggle for a democratic republic—and advocates . . . proletarian dictatorship so as to repell all participants save the most progressive segments of the working class." He who renounced the slogan of a democratic republic fought against the unification of the toiling masses and the people against Hitler, said Ulbricht, who went on to identify the SAP with the "Trotskyist" Spanish party POUM,

---

105. Ulbricht had written in his 25 May 1937 letter to Mann: "In the circles of the democratic bourgeoisie as well a certain relaxation is manifesting itself and in capitalist circles too fear of the consequences of Hitler's war politics is increasing. For that precise reason those elements disquieted by the growing popular front atmosphere in Germany and speculating in line with the old coalition politics on certain Reichswehr circles and big capitalist elements are becoming more active" (Ulbright to Mann, 25 May 1937, in *Beiträge zur Geschichte der deutschen Arbeiterbewegung* 1 [1963]: 82). Herbert Wehner writes that Ulbricht wanted to use the Popular Front Committee as a center for gaining influence over bourgeois oppositional currents inside Germany and that he viewed Leopold Schwarzschild as an "influential exponent" of those forces in Germany such as the leader of the Stahlhelm, Düsterberg (Wehner, "Erinñerungen," p. 114).
106. Duhnke, *Die KPD von 1933 bis 1945*, p. 248.

which had "given the call for resistance" to the Spanish popular front government and thereby aided Franco.[107]

In September 1937 Wilhelm Pieck spelled out the Communist position. After paying lip service to the progress of the Popular Front Committee,[108] he again brought up the issue of the SAP, whose goals "were anything but to promote the work of the committee."[109] SAP leaders were in actual fact "sabotaging" that work; their policies were no more than "water on the mill of fascism," and the committee ought to decide whether SAP representatives should continue to have the opportunity to sabotage the committee's efforts. Pieck then attacked SAP arguments, noting that the party had succeeded in winning the backing of some Social Democratic members of the committee for the campaign against a democratic republic. Instead of supporting a post-Hitler popular front government, the SAP stood firm in urging that "'socialism and, in putting it into effect, proletarian revolution must follow Hitler.'"[110] This was all hopelessly inopportune, wrote Pieck; it was self-deception to believe that the majority of the working class, the middle class, and the farmers were prepared to fight for "Soviet power." But another danger loomed large; there had been recent attempts, under the "pretense" of broadening the popular front, to "hinder or destroy it." Although Pieck mentioned the name of Otto Strasser and linked him to the newly formed Deutsche Freiheitspartei in Paris, he had in mind any joint venture by anti-Nazis that excluded the Communists and was aimed at marshalling forces against Hitler. "A popular front without Communists would be a knife without a blade," Pieck declaimed; "without Communists the united front is impossible, and without a united front there can be no popular front."[111]

There matters stood in fall 1937: the situation in the Popular Front Committee had deteriorated beyond repair. At three committee meetings in June and September, there were acrimonious exchanges between the Communists and committee members. Largely as a result of these three gatherings and the behavior of the Communists outside of the committee, the other members called upon the KPD Central

107. *Beiträge zur Geschichte*, p. 83.
108. Actually, in early 1937 the Communists had mulled over the idea of pulling out of the Popular Front Committee altogether. See Sywottek, *Deutsche Volksdemokratie*, p. 81.
109. Wilhelm Pieck, "Fragen der Volksfront in Deutschland: Klarheit tut not!," in *Gesammelte Reden und Schriften*, 5:473.
110. Pieck, "Fragen der Volksfront in Deutschland," pp. 479–81.
111. Ibid., pp. 483–84.

Committee to end the "intolerable conditions that, because of the KPD representation in the Popular Front Committee, have gotten worse and worse."[112] In a letter dated 1 October 1937, the committee expressed blunt criticism of Ulbricht and Merker, the Communist representatives, and recapitulated the "disloyal activity" of the Communists at the September meeting, where Georg Bernhard spoke of Communist "deception" and Max Braun of their "attempts to deceive." Signed by Heinrich Mann, Bernhard, Braun, and two other committee members, Denicke and Jacob Walcher, the letter made note of similar acts of disloyalty at the June meetings, and pointed out that afterwards the Communists promised to rectify the situation but had in fact done nothing.

On 25 October Mann wrote to Braun: "Your letter of the 23rd convinces me that Ulbricht does indeed want to engineer a popular front that is subordinate to him. As little as I want to view members of the German opposition as enemies, some of them evidently want it no other way. For that reason I am opposed to a meeting of the entire committee so long as U. is allowed to appear as the chief representative, or, for that matter, even as a representative of his party."[113] A few days later, the committee received an answer to its letter of 1 October. The response was written not by the Central Committee, to whom the letter had been sent, but by Ulbricht himself, who saw to it that his "private" letter first circulated freely among Communist and socialist committee members.

In his reply Ulbricht launched another passionate appeal for democracy, which must have struck those who recalled his equally passionate 1935 defense of the Communist goal of a Soviet Germany as less than persuasive. Ulbricht now announced with a straight face, "We Communists are serious about the struggle for socialism." Precisely for that reason, they rejected the SAP demand for socialism as a popular front slogan. To put forth "socialism" as a rallying cry would accentuate the dichotomy of opinions, enlarge the differences among many of the "Social Democratic comrades," and drive away middle-class masses and farmers. These people, said Ulbricht, were simply not yet ready to "give their lives" for proletarian dictatorship and socialism. The popular front movement had thus far been seriously impaired by the unwillingness of even the Social Democratic members and representatives of the "German bourgeoisie" in the Popular

---

112. Popular Front Committee to the Central Committee of the KPD, 1 October 1937, in "Ulbricht und die Volksfront," p. 151.
113. Mann to Braun, 25 October 1937, in "Ulbricht und die Volksfront," p. 151.

Front Committee to "stand up" for the slogan of a democratic republic.[114]

The committee seems simply to have compared such talk about democracy with Communist actions; on 13 November 1937 it answered Ulbricht in a letter whose tone was blunt by any standards. The committee members laid responsibility for the failures of the popular front squarely at the door of the Communists, who "stuck steadfastly" to their standpoint and "wholly ignored" requests for an airing of all differences of opinions and for the reestablishment of a basis for trust. The Communists hence took upon themselves a grave responsibility, for they were obstructing the preparation for a German popular front. The letter went on:

> You [the Communists] are discrediting the united and popular front movement in which, until the summer of this year, the KPD represented a very active group. You are strengthening in the proletarian camp the position of those who, for left-sectarian reasons or for reasons hostile to the popular front, refuse a united front with you by basing their stance, supported by the experience of earlier years, on the argument that comradely and beneficial cooperation is impossible with the Comintern and its sections. You are encouraging countless enemies by your attitude and are weakening the popular front movement at a time when its establishment within and outside Germany is more necessary than ever before.[115]

Were the Communists to persist in attempts to "form a popular front, so to speak, with [themselves]," such a beginning was bound to meet with a dire end. The committee accused the Communists of trying to create "parallel popular front organizations" behind the committee's back and of being interested only in a popular front "guided and directed solely by the Communist party." The committee did in fact have grave reservations about KPD seriousness with respect to democracy, pointing out that a recent Communist article had called for "'the preparation of revolutionary socialism by way of proletarian dictatorship under the guidance of the Communist party.'"[116] Moreover, the committee protested specifically against Ulbricht's attempt

114. Sywottek, *Deutsche Volksdemokratie*, pp. 82–83.
115. Popular Front Committee to the Central Committee of the KPD, 13 November 1937, in "Ulbricht und die Volksfront," p. 151.
116. The article had appeared in the 7 November 1937 issue of the *Deutsche Volkszeitung*.

in his letter of 26 October to blame all popular front problems on the non-Communist members who allegedly allowed themselves to be manipulated by "'dark powers and backers' or by 'Social Democratic enemies of unity.' " Ulbricht had accused these non-Communists of working toward a "united front with 'big bourgeois circles, right-wing catholic leaders, and Reichswehr generals.' " But the committee stated bluntly, "If these personal calumnies . . . and political flights of fancy represent the sole answer of the Central Committee of the German Communist Party to the serious charges raised by Heinrich Mann and the non-Communist members of the committee, then the KPD itself must be determined to impress upon us the impossibility of further cooperation."

The truth of the matter was, the letter went on, Ulbricht himself and Communist members had opposed during committee meetings all appeals for nationalization and socialization in post-Hitler Germany "so as to keep the road to Düsterberg and big capitalist circles open," a road the Communists had hoped to travel through the "mediation" of Schwarzschild (this was still in 1936). It was, in fact, Ulbricht and none other who had proposed the *inclusion* of Otto Strasser and his group in the popular front, a move opposed by Breitscheid and his Social Democratic colleagues, whom Ulbricht thereupon slandered as "allies of Strasser." Moreover, Ulbricht had recently suggested a "secret conference of 'genuine anti-Fascist leaders,' " to be attended not by leading members of the Popular Front Committee, whose names were missing from Ulbricht's invitation list, but by men whom Ulbricht had publicly characterized a short time before as "'representatives and agents of the Reichswehr, the big bourgeoisie, and National Socialism'"; and now the Communists insinuated that other members of the committee actually wanted to betray the Communists and themselves "form a coalition with right-wing bourgeois circles." The letter also pointed out that the activity of the SAP in the committee had not been disruptive, as the Communists claimed, but helpful, and closed by stating that work toward a united and popular front had been seriously hampered by the Communists in the committee, which refused to shoulder the blame for the continued passivity of its work.[117]

What followed was anticlimactic. Little more was heard from the paralyzed Popular Front Committee, though the Communists never officially severed their ties with it or backed completely away from

117. Popular Front Committee to the Central Committee of the KPD, 13 November 1937, in "Ulbricht und die Volksfront," pp. 152–53.

calls for united and popular fronts and establishment of a post-Hitler democratic republic. As for the grave charges contained in the letter of 13 November, the committee was told that the Communists wished to reestablish the basis for trust but that this was impossible at the moment because it would require a full meeting of the Central Committee, which did not gather for several months.

In the interim, the third batch of "traitors and spies," Nikolaj Bukharin among them, stood trial in Moscow on charges of murdering Kirov, planning the assassination of Stalin, and (this was new) killing Maxim Gorky.[118] In spite of the disastrous effects upon the popular front of three public show trials and secret proceedings, followed by the executions of top Red Army generals, the Communists still maintained that these had been blows against fascism and that the Soviet Union remained a mighty anti-Fascist bulwark. Mikhail Koltsov, the *Pravda* editor so deeply involved with the German emigration in the Soviet Union and in western Europe, voiced these sentiments in a letter to Lion Feuchtwanger in March. His work had just been interrupted, he said, by the trial of the " 'Right-Trotskyist Bloc.' " For an entire week he had sat in the courtroom, "rendered speechless by the mountain of filth and crime, speechless before the shocking tragedy of the murder of our mutual friend Maxim Gorky." Koltsov told Feuchtwanger that it was now time to fight against the "imminent danger of military aggression, against the Fascist attack on the Soviet Union," which had been proven beyond doubt by the discovery of the Trotskyist-Bukharinist-Jagoda conspiracy. "All progressive elements, all honest thinkers in the whole of Europe and the world must unite in the defense of the only true anti-Fascist fortress—the USSR."[119]

Two months later, on 14 May 1938, the KPD Central Committee met to discuss the popular front. Announcing the Central Committee resolution in a letter to the chairman of the Popular Front Committee, Heinrich Mann, Wilhelm Pieck said that the creation of a popular front, based on a united working class, was the most important task of

---

118. For the responses of German writers in Moscow to these charges, see, for instance: J. R. Becher, "In Namen des Friedens," *Internationale Literatur* 4 (1938): 4–8 (Gorky's alleged murder); Becher, "Dieser Prozess," *Deutsche Zentral-Zeitung*, 11 March 1938; "Keine Gnade," a statement signed by Becher, Alexander Barta (who himself disappeared a few months later), and Fritz Erpenbeck for the German Section of the Soviet Writer's Union, *Deutsche Zentral-Zeitung*, 12 March 1938; Adam Scharrer, "Abgrund menschlicher Verworfenheit," *Deutsche Zentral-Zeitung*, 14 March 1938. Hugo Huppert was unable to write any poetic laudatios as he had done in response to the second trial because he himself had recently become an enemy of the people.

119. Koltsov to Feuchtwanger, 11 March 1938, TsGALI, 631/13/65/153.

"all anti-Fascists"; he called for an end to the committee's passivity and issued another warning against all attempts to exclude the Communists from a popular front with an eye toward winning more easily the support of "bourgeois partners."[120] Neither Pieck's letter nor the resolution had anything to say about the substance of the committee's letter of 13 November 1937. Instead, the resolution reaffirmed the party's commitment to a democratic republic: "In the democratic republic the German people themselves will decide questions about their way of life and relationships with other peoples; they will exterminate fascism root and branch and deprive it of its material base through expropriation of Fascist conspirators among the big capitalists and large land owners." The democratic republic would differ from the earlier Weimar Republic insofar as it would not be based on the hegemony of the bourgeoisie, nor on the coalition of bourgeois parties with segments of the working class, parties that acted to subjugate working class and peasant interests to the interests of big capital and large land holders. The republic would be based instead on the popular front. "And the popular front," the resolution continued, "is an alliance of a united working class with farmers, the middle class, and the intelligentsia in representing the interests of working people and thereby representing the interests of the German nation." The democratic republic would assure peace, based on a strong people's army, by establishing friendly relations with other peoples and by friendly cooperation with the Soviet Union.[121]

As for the current popular front, "Trotskyism" was said to be preventing its formation. Hitler fascism, the resolution insisted, was doing its level best to obstruct the creation of a united front alliance and had "found willing accomplices among the Trotskyists who serve it as informers and provocateurs against the working masses." The Trotskyists sought to work their way into the organizations of the SPD and the KPD and to use their "pseudo-radical phrases" to confuse the workers, hinder unification, disintegrate workers' organizations, and by acts of provocation betray the most active elements of the proletariat to the Gestapo. "Their hostile activity is manifestly evident in the struggle of the Trotskyist group within the SAP against the popular front." The Moscow trial against the bloc of Rightists and Trotskyists, the uprising of the POUM in Barcelona, the provocations of the Trotskyists in China, the "undeniable" collaboration of German Trotskyists with the Gestapo and with Franco in Spain—all these proved that

120. Pieck to Mann, 16 May 1938, in Pieck, *Gesammelte Reden und Schriften*, 5:517–25.
121. *Resolution der Maitagung 1938 des Zentralkomitees der KPD*, p. 22.

Trotskyists throughout the world had become agents of fascism and that Hitler was using them as tools for his preparation for war. *"The unification of the forces of the working class in the struggle against fascism demands the extermination of Trotskyism, of Trotskyist influence on the labor movement, and the banishment of Trotskyist criminals from its ranks."* [122] There things remained throughout the next fifteen months, the popular front effectively crippled, until the Hitler-Stalin pact silenced all talk of unity. [123]

By summer 1939 the situation was just as bleak in the area of Communist cultural politics. [124] Returning that summer to Moscow after spending the previous year in Paris, Willi Bredel filed a long report, probably with the Comintern or with his own party, about the plight of "anti-Fascist German literature, particularly the predicament of Communist and other writers who back the popular front." Dangers had recently arisen that not only threatened the anti-Fascist struggle but also were potentially capable of undoing the years of tedious work done to win over bourgeois writers. The problem was the lack of publication opportunities. *"Today,"* said Bredel, *"not a single leftist-oriented literary German publishing firm remains in operation,"* and this was adversely affecting anti-Fascist German cultural politics. A few years ago, Bredel explained, there had been a number of publishers, the Malik-Verlag and the Editions du Carrefour, for instance, along with the bourgeois houses Querido and Allert de Lange. Only the latter two were still functioning. Editions du Carrefour had been replaced by Münzenberg's new enterprise, the Sebastian Brant-Verlag, "whose production is hostile to the party and to the Soviet Union." [125]

While in Paris Bredel had tried to alleviate the situation. Upon his arrival there from Spain in July 1938, he had received permission from the KPD Politburo to write Mikhail Koltsov, then head of the foreign bureau of the Soviet Writers' Union, with the proposal that the Writers' Association for the Defense of Culture organize a small publishing operation to print the works of German Communist and popular front writers and to "undermine the Münzenberg house." Koltsov

122. Ibid., p. 25.

123. See Sywottek, *Deutsche Volksdemokratie*, pp. 89–97, for a more detailed treatment of the Communists' policy during these intervening fifteen months.

124. The journal *Das Wort*, for instance, had been discontinued in March 1939; see Chapter 8 for more discussion. The SDS and the Deutsche Freiheitsbibliothek had also reached crisis points. See Kantorowicz, *Politik und Literatur im Exil*, and my review of Kantorowicz's book in *Internationales Archiv für Sozialgeschichte der deutschen Literatur* 6 (1981).

125. Willi Bredel, untitled and unsigned fragment in Bredel-Archiv, Sig. 252/14.

had agreed and made ten thousand francs monthly available to the Writers' Association, which used the Russian money to form the Verlag 10. Mai. After discussing the matter with the "comrades of the KPD's Politburo," Koltsov had also approved the selection of eight books for publication, the first two of which were Heinrich Mann's *Mut* and Bredel's *Begegnung am Ebro*.[126] The Soviet subvention was to continue for one year, by which time the Verlag 10. Mai would be self-supporting. Louis Aragon nominally headed the operation, which was registered in Paris under his name, while Bredel, at the request of the KPD, worked as an editor. Maria Osten, Koltsov's common-law wife ("whom he placed in the Association," said Bredel), assisted in technical matters. But then came Koltsov's "demotion," as Bredel delicately put it. He disappeared forever in Moscow on 12 December 1938; the Russian money was then withdrawn, and the Verlag 10. Mai promptly folded.

Bredel went on to explain that the demise of the Russian-sponsored operation had effectively eliminated the last publishing possibility for Communist and leftist writers, who now had to consider the wishes of bourgeois publishers if they wanted to see their writing in print. The problem was also compounded by the absence of literary journals. Communist writers, Bredel wrote, were enormously hindered in their ideological influence on sympathetic bourgeois authors by the fact that they did not have a single, well-paying periodical at their disposal,[127] whereas the "bourgeois and Trotskyist groups" sponsored several journals and papers. "For Communist and sympathetic writers in the emigration there is *to all intents and purposes no chance to publish;* they are gagged," Bredel complained. "Several writers who to date have strongly sympathized with us—Lion Feuchtwanger, Oskar Maria Graf, Alfred Döblin, Thomas Mann, and others—*have therefore been writing actively recently for Willi Münzenberg's journal 'Die Zukunft.'* Thomas Mann, moreover, contributes to the anti-Bolshevist weekly 'Das neue Tage-Buch,' published by Schwarzschild." The political dangers inherent in the situation were obvious, said Bredel, and "writer-comrades" who were growing increasingly irritated and depressed by the circumstances might begin to vacillate in their political stance.

Bredel suggested that the "bourgeois and Trotskyist" journals be countered by at least *"one German literary journal that represents our*

126. The other books were Anna Seghers's *Das siebte Kreuz*, Hans Marchwitza's *Der Vikar*, Hermann Kesten's *Das Donauschiff*, Arnold Zweig's *Erzählungen*, F. C. Weiskopf's *Erzählungen aus der Tschechoslowakei*, and Egon Erwin Kisch's *Briefe aus Versailles*.
127. *Das Wort* had ceased publication in March (see Chapter 8).

political and cultural political line and defends the position of the Soviet Union." Financial backing for the Verlag 10. Mai should be reinstituted. "Through more active, well-planned, and, above all, sensible literary politics and with a fairly modest amount of help, the Communist writers, together with all honest writers of goodwill who support anti-Fascist unity, could work with considerably more success to counter Münzenberg's policy of divisiveness, Trotskyist calumnies, and bourgeois indifference"; the writers could represent an even more important factor in establishing unity between Communists and Social Democrats in the formation of a German anti-Fascist popular front.[128]

But Bredel had no idea that Stalin was about to pull out the rug from Soviet-sponsored antifascism. Shortly after the above report was filed, Ribbentrop arrived in Moscow to sign the Pact of Nonaggression; this ushered in a two-year period of dormancy for virtually all Communist-backed anti-Fascist publishing firms and periodicals.

128. Bredel, untitled and unsigned fragment, Bredel-Archiv, Sig. 252/14.

Chapter 8

The Literary Popular Front, Part I: *Das Wort*

As the literary united front began to unfold in 1933, the Communists soon recognized the need for a broadly based "intellectuals' journal." *Internationale Literatur,* published since 1931, was regarded as a "useless undertaking" that at best had appeal for only a few writers and "could not approach reaching anything resembling a larger circle of readers."[1] As it happened, though, neither Becher nor the IVRS grasped the initiative and started a journal themselves; the preliminary work was conveniently done for them. Visiting Prague in late 1933, Becher got wind of Wieland Herzfelde's preparations for a literary journal, *Die neuen deutschen Blätter,* and leaped at the chance to get in on the project. Becher passed this report on to Moscow: upon his arrival in Prague, he had heard of plans by both Klaus Mann and Willy Haas to publish literary journals. "Since at the same time the influence of Trotsky was already showing up among writers whom we consider our allies," Becher wrote, "I decided to take the initiative with respect to a journal—one of the most important (!) organizational moves of anti-Fascist forces in literature." Becher then contacted Herzfelde and discussed his attitudes toward the KPD and its politics. After reassuring himself that Herzfelde was "wholly on the side of the party's line and that he regretted certain earlier vacillations," Becher, so he said, brought up the question of a journal. Herzfelde was all for it and sure that he could interest a number of financial backers. These patrons stipulated later, however, that their support would hinge on whether or not the editors came up with the money for the first three issues. Since Becher at the time saw no other possibility of starting a

1. Becher, "Bericht über die Tätigkeit während meiner Reise vom 5. Juli bis 27. September 1933," in *Publizistik I,* pp. 394 and 400.

journal, "the necessity of which has become clearer to me with each passing day,"[2] he took it upon himself to guarantee the first three numbers of the *Neue Deutsche Blätter* by drawing up a contract between Herzfelde and the IVRS. Such was Becher's rendition of events.

The actual stipulations of the contract are unclear, for an infusion of funds from Moscow seems not to have been part of the agreement. In fact, a scandal ensued once word leaked out about one of the sources of money. My conversations with Herzfelde revealed that in 1933 he had drawn up plans for a worldwide publishing house for anti-Fascist literature and had solicited funds from a number of governments unsympathetic to Hitler.[3] Herzfelde's requests struck a responsive chord with the Czech government, and he was put in touch with Masaryk's secretary, a man named Skrach, who seems to have provided money not just for the proposed publishing concern but for the *Neue Deutsche Blätter* as well. When party functionaries found out about this, they exploded,[4] evidently calling Herzfelde and Becher on the carpet for taking money from a bourgeois government (for permitting themselves to be "bought" by the Czechs, to use Herzfelde's phrase). Becher's 1933 report alludes to the controversy. The evening of the day he arrived, as he was about to enter the press office with Herzfelde and Hans Günther, he ran into "Comrade Hugo" [Eberlein, presumably]. "Comrade Herzfelde showed Comrade Hugo a letter," Becher explained, "a copy of which Wieland Herzfelde handed over to me as well and in which for the first time I learned of the name Skrach along with the intermediaries or source of money. Upon reading the letter, in which the money was returned to Skrach, Comrade Hugo declared the matter closed."[5] Adding that a contract had been signed by "Hugo, Günther, and Wieland" and that the first issue of the journal would soon appear, contingent on "several changes in its contents," Becher closed his report on the *Neue Deutsche Blätter* by calling it a "breakthrough to a united front movement of all anti-Fascist forces of German literature." But he warned that Herzfelde had strong proclivities toward "opportunistic distortions of our line" and that the IVRS should establish some "guarantees" that the "mar-

2. Ibid., pp. 402–3.
3. Herzfelde's remarks are drawn from his 1979 conversations with the author in East Berlin.
4. From Becher's account it appears that both the Czech and the German parties were upset (Becher, "Bericht," pp. 404–5).
5. Ibid.

shalling of all anti-Fascist forces in literature, to which this journal can make an extraordinary contribution, proceeds in our direction."[6]

Becher failed to spell out the form these "guarantees" would take, but, using Hans Günther as the hatchet man and, it would seem, with party backing, he tried to put teeth into them. Herzfelde explained to me that plans for the journal, which were drawn up by Herzfelde and his brother John Heartfield, were under way well before Becher turned up in Prague; his involvement in the journal, in fact, was a successful "attempt to intrude." Then, after initial discussions between Herzfelde and Becher were over, Hans Günther was sent to Prague to help get the journal off the ground. His duties, though, evidently called for a different sort of action. Whether on Becher's specific orders or at the behest of the party (perhaps through Eberlein), Günther barged into the printing shop as the first issue of the *Neue Deutsche Blätter* rolled off the press and ordered the machines shut down. The journal, he said, needed new masthead editors. Becher, according to Herzfelde, was dissatisfied with the too liberal editorial board of Herzfelde, Anna Seghers, O. M. Graf, and Jan Petersen—three party members and a confirmed fellow traveler![7] When Herzfelde ignored Günther's order to shut off the presses, Günther assaulted him, and the machines were turned off. Since Günther was unable to suggest a different editorial board, rectangular pieces of paper were printed up with a general list of the journal's contributors and pasted over its cover, concealing the names of Herzfelde, Graf, Seghers, and Petersen's three asterisks. Then the programmatic introductory article, written and signed by Herzfelde as one of the editors, was partitioned into two sections and reset in type, leaving the first half of Herzfelde's original article, now signed only "The Editors," and an ordinary "article" of equal length written by Herzfelde as a normal contributor. The first three issues thus carried no mention of the actual editors, whose names only began to appear in the fourth issue.[8]

To what extent any other "guarantees" were enforced (whether there was substantial outside interference in the journal's editorial practices) is a subject of conjecture. There seems to have been some. Long after the *Neue Deutsche Blätter* was dead and buried, Herzfelde, in Moscow preparing the first number of *Das Wort*, made vague allu-

6. ibid., pp. 405–6.
7. Still living in Berlin, Petersen signed in the *Neue Deutsche Blätter* with three asterisks.
8. This perhaps coincided with the expiration of the contract signed by the IVRS and Herzfelde for the first three issues of the *Neue Deutsche Blätter.*

sions to impediments that he encountered in publishing the *Neue Deutsche Blätter*. *Das Wort*, Herzfelde told Stefan Heym, would be "something like what I had originally hoped to do with the *NDB*—that is, unite all anti-Fascist writers." The implication was that he had been prevented from doing so in the *Neue Deutsche Blätter*. And in summer 1936 Herzfelde remarked to Bredel, one of *Das Wort*'s editors, that he had been "unable" to publish many articles by "friends," which "you are allowed to—and should—print today."[9]

Not that heavy pressure was put on the *Neue Deutsche Blätter*; in all likelihood this was not the case, nor would it have been necessary. Herzfelde, as a party member of long standing, was certainly sufficiently attuned to policy to adhere to whatever limitations in publishing non-Communists that he felt the party desired in 1933 and 1934. At any rate, the *Neue Deutsche Blätter* did its duty well enough to inspire Becher's willingness to keep it in the black. In late 1934 Becher again met with Herzfelde, who had just returned from London after an unsuccessful trip to locate financial support for the *Neue Deutsche Blätter*. Becher reported to the IVRS: "For us, of course, this is an extremely serious matter; the existence of the *NDB* must not be endangered."[10] But there were other signs that, whatever function the journal was thought to be fulfilling, it was not regarded as the "intellectuals' journal" originally envisaged. The 1934 draft on the reconstruction of the IVRS [MORP], for instance, contained the proposal that *Internationale Literatur* serve as the publication of the anti-Fascist writers' league (then in planning) until such time as a "literary journal" in the West was founded.[11] It was as if the *Neue Deutsche Blätter* did not exist. The remark is even stranger because the draft referred to the *Neue Deutsche Blätter* elsewhere as part of the "good start" in the use of united front tactics.

Whatever the reasons, once the journal's market began to dwindle in 1935, a conscious decision was made to allow the *Blätter* to founder financially. Herzfelde insisted in our talks that he never received a "penny" from the Comintern to publish the *Neue Deutsche Blätter*; that would have entailed a "certain subservience," he said.[12] But un-

9. Herzfelde to Heym, 11 April 1936, TsGALI, 631/12/143/199; Herzfelde to Bredel, 31 July 1936, TsGALI, 631/12/143/105.
10. Becher, "Bericht über eine Reise nach Prag, Zürich und Paris," in *Publizistik I*, p. 447.
11. "Entwurf zum Umbau der MORP und zur Reorganisation ihrer Sektionen," TsGALI, 631/13/73/10–11.
12. Herzfelde did indicate to me that he might have received support from the Soviet Union in a different sense; a sizable number of copies of the *Neue Deutsche Blätter* ("a

published correspondence tells a somewhat different story. The *Neue Deutsche Blätter* was indeed privately financed; but with the journal on shaky ground, Herzfelde went to Moscow to ask for money. In March 1935 Willi Bredel passed the word to Serafima Gopner in the Executive Committee of the Comintern that Herzfelde would be unable to publish the *Neue Deutsche Blätter* should financial assistance from Soviet sources not be forthcoming. "Up till now he has kept [the *Neue Deutsche Blätter*] above water completely for almost one and a half years on his own and independently out of his private funds, or with the funds of the Malik-Verlag." But with the elimination of Austria, Spain, and the Saar, his marketing difficulties had increased enormously, and he needed help if the journal was to continue. "As it is," Bredel explained, "the circulation today is still 4,000 and the necessary assistance comparatively minor since [the journal] is almost self-supporting."[13] Bredel added that he had spoken with Valdemar Knorin in the Comintern, who would most likely not be in a position to proffer any assistance. Things were so bad that "Herzfelde has ceased publication of the *NDB*"; but he would be arriving in Moscow presently to speak "with the relevant authorities." Indeed, the *Neue Deutsche Blätter* had stopped publishing with the February 1935 issue, but Herzfelde apparently got help of some sort in Moscow. In May 1935 Bredel wrote Graf: Herzfelde's "concern, I believe, has been taken care of to his and everyone's satisfaction."[14]

Even so, the *Neue Deutsche Blätter* did not appear again until June and then, for the last time, in August. Evidently, all support for Herzfelde's journal was terminated in connection with preliminary discussions at the June 1935 writers' congress in Paris concerning publication of a literary journal *in Moscow,* the pages of which would be open to anti-Fascist intellectuals in the West.[15] The move did not set well with Bredel. In August 1935 he complained to Jan Petersen that, though the entire affair had already been settled politically and the *Neue Deutsche Blätter* would probably cease publication, he planned on continuing the fight—"as I've fought up to now"—for its continuation. "Unfortunately," Bredel went on, "our friends are not at one on this question; Hans [Becher] and Kantor [owicz] have a different

---

few hundred," Herzfelde thought) were regularly sent to the Soviet Union, for which Herzfelde was paid not in hard currency but with credits he used to have Malik-Verlag books set and printed in the USSR. He could not recall whether the Soviet order for the *Neue Deutsche Blätter* was ever cancelled.

13. Bredel to Gopner, 26 March 1935, TsGALI, 631/13/69/55.

14. Bredel to Graf, 4 May 1935, TsGALI, 631/12/152/12.

15. Herzfelde told me that he had not been invited to Paris.

opinion than you or I. Nonetheless, I am not giving up the fight." He had no knowledge of what was planned in Paris, he said; "but I know the *NDB,* and you know the saying about the bird in the hand being worth two in the bush. Of course the *NDB* would have to broaden its base. . . . It seems to me that not all these questions have been fully resolved and until they are I plan on continuing to fight."[16]

But they had been resolved, and the *Neue Deutsche Blätter* was allowed to expire, as it were, so that *Das Wort* could be born.[17] One of the *Neue Deutsche Blätter*'s former editors, Oskar Maria Graf, had no illusions on this score. In response to a March 1936 letter in which Becher had alluded to *Internationale Literatur* as the only literary anti-Fascist journal remaining,[18] Graf vented his anger:

> That's painfully obvious, especially since, for reasons that
> were never understood by us anti-Fascist writers outside
> [of the USSR], the *NDB* was allowed to go under pathetically.
> We were hounded to death with resourcefulness and with
> a certain serenity; there was never any real effort to grasp our
> difficulties, and we were not supported in the least. As a
> result, a very necessary journal, built upon the broadest
> anti-Fascist foundation, went under, the Malik-Verlag
> almost along with it; this to all appearances for the sole reason
> that there was no interest in building up, and keeping
> afloat outside of the Soviet Union, a cultural and literary
> journal that was anti-Fascist in a more topical sense than
> the *IL* is or ever can be. . . . With the *NDB* much greater
> advances could have been made, much greater![19]

16. Bredel to Jan Petersen, 20 August 1935, TsGALI, 631/13/69/93.
17. Herzfelde accepted this more or less philosophically. He told Graf in discussing *Das Wort:* "Of course I would have preferred that the *Neue Deutsche Blätter* hadn't gone under, but on the other hand the economic prerequisites are much better here. The domestic market alone should assure [*Das Wort*'s] appearance" (Herzfelde to Graf, 3 April 1936, TsGALI, 631/12/141/326).
18. Klaus Mann's *Die Sammlung* had also discontinued publication in August 1935. There had earlier been some talk of a joint Mann-Herzfelde venture, but "nothing came of Klaus Mann's and my plan." Cf. Herzfelde to Leonhard Frank, 2 April 1936, TsGALI, 631/12/139/163.
19. Graf to Becher, 28 March 1936, Becher-Archiv, Sig. 38. Graf had much more to say: "By the way, Wieland is now over there; he can certainly pass along a variety of complaints [about the *Internationale Literatur*]. Let's hope you'll have the backbone this time really to stand by him. . . . If we are to contribute *anything* at all as writers to the struggle, then the least that can be expected is: absolute camaraderie! Unfortunately the clique sometimes appears to be much more important! It's outrageous and makes one want to vomit."

Once the question of a new literary journal had been broached in Paris, several months passed before Mikhail Koltsov, his companion Maria Osten, and J. R. Becher took any concrete measures.[20] In late January 1936 Koltsov and Becher asked Heinrich Mann and, through him, Thomas Mann to serve as editors. The response was not encouraging. His brother, Heinrich Mann replied, would be unable to participate, and though he himself would look forward to contributing to the journal, editing it was a different matter. Were he to act in that capacity, he said, German radio would shout it to the four corners of the world and say that "I had become a party Communist." That would be to no one's advantage, for he was of value only as an independent personality. On the other hand, he said, "I have to be on my guard not to create grounds here [France] for attacks (expulsion). My major conditions for collaboration in the journal are hence that I am not prominently mentioned anywhere. You would simply publish my contributions."[21]

In the meantime, Becher had received an answer from Lion Feuchtwanger, who had also been asked to edit the journal. Feuchtwanger was pleased that a new journal, "replacing *Die neuen deutschen Blätter* and *Die Sammlung*," was to appear, and "in principle" he was prepared to work on the editorial board. But he insisted that what the German emigration lacked most was a "literary organ of some caliber" (*Die neue Weltbühne* and *Das neue Tage-Buch* being more political in character), and he suggested strongly that the new journal publish primarily creative literature and literary criticism. After proposing a

---

20. Little is known about the discussions held in Paris. Fritz Erpenbeck's remarks in the afterword to the East German reprint of *Das Wort* contain some information but are generally misleading and often deliberately mendacious (*Das Wort: Registerband*, pp. 5–8). Huppert's account is also inaccurate and untruthful (*Das Wort: Bibliographie einer Zeitschrift*, pp. 5–22). That Gorky had any personal involvement with the creation of *Das Wort*, as Trude Richter (*Die Plakette*, p. 277) claims, strikes me as unlikely. Petrova writes that, even before the Parisian congress, Becher had taken up the matter of a journal with Fadejev, head of the Soviet Writers' Union, who then lent his assistance to Koltsov, the man in charge of the union's foreign bureau (Petrova, "Zhurnal—*Das Vort*," p. 49).

21. Heinrich Mann to Becher, 16 February 1936, Becher-Archiv, Sig. 54. Mann offered to write a monthly article for the journal in return for 76 gold rubles a piece; together with monthly payments of 124 rubles from Goslitizdat for Soviet editions of his writings, Mann expected a regular salary of 200 gold rubles a month for his collaboration with *Das Wort*. Incidentally, permission to publish the journal came several days after Mann and others were approached; it was officially granted by the RSFSR People's Commissariat of Education, and *Das Wort* was to appear as the organ of the German Section of the Soviet Writers' Union, though it was never so characterized (Petrova, "Zhurnal—*Das Vort*," pp. 50–51).

number of possible titles for the monthly, among them the name eventually adopted, *Das Wort*, Feuchtwanger backed away from his offer to act as an editor, pleading lack of time for his own creative work.[22] Nonetheless, Maria Osten took Feuchtwanger's letter as a commitment, and in April she gave Feuchtwanger the news that Bertolt Brecht had also consented to work as an editor. She added that if neither Heinrich Mann nor Thomas Mann could be pursuaded to join in, then Brecht, Feuchtwanger, and Willi Bredel (who seems to have been called back to Moscow from Paris to work on the journal) would make up the final editorial board.[23]

In mid-April Feuchtwanger set forth in detail some of the conditions he expected to be met should he participate in an editorial capacity after all. He reiterated his underlying readiness to join the board of *Das Wort*, but could see no way of surmounting the "technical difficulties" created by the distance between western Europe and Moscow. "Under no circumstances do I wish to be responsible for something I haven't seen," Feuchtwanger explained to Osten. "Please bear in mind that I am at the focal point of German polemics and that I am not especially highly thought of among the reactionary writers and newspapers in the Anglo-Saxon countries and in the rest of the world either." If he became part of *Das Wort*'s editorial board, his detractors would enjoy making him responsible for everything that appeared in its pages. "I must at least have a chance to see everything that is printed there beforehand."[24] One suggestion Feuchtwanger made after discussing the matter with Brecht in London was that editorial obligations be split up, with Brecht, for instance, assuming responsibility for poetry and Feuchtwanger for creative literature. But the modus operandi eventually agreed upon was Osten's idea of sending each editor a typescript of an issue on the day that it was set in

22. Feuchtwanger to Becher, 10 February 1936, TsGALI, 631/13/65/7.

23. Maria Osten to Feuchtwanger, 1 April 1936, TsGALI, 631/13/65/10. Efforts to win Thomas Mann had not been dropped. In April 1936 Wieland Herzfelde asked Mann, also on behalf of the publisher Mikhail Koltsov, to help "realize the plan of the journal by joining the editorial board" (Herzfelde to Thomas Mann, 1 April 1936, TsGALI, 631/12/143/341). Mann, in his reply, welcomed the appearance of the new journal, but turned down the request to edit it, explaining his unwillingness to be responsible for an undertaking in which he was not genuinely involved and pleading a heavy work load. Contributions were another matter, though, and he promised to write occasionally for the journal (which he did not). Thomas Mann to Herzfelde, 9 April 1936, TsGALI, 631/12/143/340. Evidently as part of the effort to win Mann for *Das Wort*'s editorial board, Mikhail Koltsov invited him to visit Moscow (Mann, *Tagebücher 1935–1936*, p. 238).

24. Feuchtwanger to Osten, 13 April 1936, TsGALI, 631/13/65/11.

type. The editors were then to telegraph or airmail their approval or disapproval.[25] This was the procedure Feuchtwanger and Brecht seem to have followed.

By mid-April Feuchtwanger had managed to persuade Heinrich Mann to commit himself after all, passing Mann's conditions on to Osten in Moscow. "I share your reservations," Mann had told Feuchtwanger. "The technical problems can become political at any moment. At a suitable opportunity German radio would cry out that we are involved with a Communist paper and making propaganda against our host country [France]. The denunciation of a French Fascist would suffice." Mann wrote that he would join the board only if the journal proclaimed itself an organ of "free German literature" and then acted accordingly. "Personally," he added, "I approve of Communist democracy, such as that practiced in the Soviet Union. For Germany we need a simple struggle for freedom—without doctrine. That comes later and will naturally be socialist."[26] If he was still wanted under those conditions, Feuchtwanger was to pass Mann's consent on to Moscow. Bredel promptly wired Mann that these demands were definitely acceptable, and he asked for written confirmation of Mann's consent. Bredel received it on 29 April.[27] But Mann had added to his list of conditions a request that he be paid a monthly salary of three hundred rubles in hard currency. In return he would write regularly for *Das Wort*.[28] Much as Mann's editorial participation was desired, this evidently went too far (neither Feuchtwanger nor Brecht, it seems, were to be paid for their work). Whether the salary question was the deciding factor or not (the correspondence contains no hint of other disagreements), Mann not only failed to sign as editor, he steadfastly refused to write for the journal.[29]

So Feuchtwanger, Brecht, and Bredel it remained, although the work was by no means evenly divided. Feuchtwanger and Brecht were largely figurehead editors all along, while the task of preparing the first issue of *Das Wort* fell to Osten, Bredel, and, starting in late March, Wieland Herzfelde, who worked on the journal in Moscow for nine weeks. Announcements of the forthcoming publication and requests for contributions went out in March and April to some sixty German

25. Osten to Feuchtwanger, 19 April 1936, TsGALI, 631/13/65/18.
26. Feuchtwanger to Osten, 18 April 1936, TsGALI, 631/13/65/17; the portion of Mann's letter sent by Feuchtwanger is TsGALI, 631/12/143/320.
27. Bredel to Mann, no date, TsGALI, 631/12/143/319.
28. Mann to Bredel, 29 April 1936, TsGALI, 631/12/143/322.
29. With one exception. His review of Becher's *Der Glücksucher* appeared in *Das Wort* 10 (1938): 103–4.

writers in exile, almost all of whom consented to contribute; by mid-April articles had been submitted by Alfred Döblin, Ludwig Marcuse, Arnold Zweig, Bodo Uhse, Anna Seghers, O. M. Graf, and others.[30] From the very beginning, *Das Wort* claimed to be "the most representative German journal"; strictly "non-partisan," it aspired "to provide a forum for all anti-Fascist forces on the German cultural front," preserving the "meaning of the popular front" and uniting "all anti-Fascist writers."[31] Herzfelde made a more elaborate statement of principle in his letter to Thomas Mann: "The journal will unite all German writers who with an honest heart would subscribe to those beautiful and decisive words with which you close your response to Korrodi.[32] The journal is to be called *Das Wort*. Its one-hundred-page size and monthly appearance should presumably make it possible to contribute to the existence of a free German literature and of its creators. The editorial board . . . must not represent a group or trend but all groups and trends united in the affirmation of humanity and in the struggle against those who glorify war and abnegate culture."[33]

Das Wort did not have an auspicious beginning. Technical problems of every imaginable sort, the slipshod and inept practices of the Soviet printers and exporters, and the passivity of Feuchtwanger and Brecht—all these provided an abundant supply of problems, which redounded on Bredel after Herzfelde and Osten left for the West. Herzfelde, embittered by the waste of time and energy he had expended on the journal and appalled at the inefficiency of Mezhdunarodnaja kniga, the Soviet marketing agency, complained bitterly to Bredel in July 1936 that "everything I discussed there went down the tube. The start, the advance propaganda, the press notices"—these, said Herzfelde, had been undertaken in an unexampled dilettante and ineffectual fashion. In Vienna, for instance, no one had heard a word about *Das Wort*. "Book dealers with whom I spoke asked me whether the journal would be obtainable through the book trade, what the terms were, and so on (I couldn't even answer them since I don't know the terms either, discount, etc., commission, and so on)." Herzfelde had no idea

---

30. Osten to Feuchtwanger, 19 April 1936, TsGALI, 631/13/65/18.
31. Feuchtwanger to Osten, 4 June 1936, TsGALI, 631/13/65/30; Bredel to Fritz Brügel (Prague), 5 May 1936, TsGALI, 631/12/139/160; Bredel to Bruno Frei (Prague), 11 May 1936, TsGALI, 631/12/139/184; Herzfelde to Leonhard Frank, 2 April 1936, TsGALI, 631/12/139/163.
32. The reference is to Mann's reply to the Swiss literary critic, Eduard Korrodi; Mann's letter is generally considered to have marked his public break with Nazi Germany.
33. Herzfelde to Thomas Mann, 1 April 1936, TsGALI, 631/12/143/341.

what Kniga was up to and saw no way for *Das Wort* to benefit from the "substantial experience" gained in marketing *Die neuen deutschen Blätter*. Herzfelde ended his letter: if *Das Wort* was not provided with its own marketing agent, with whom one could correspond on an individual and punctual basis and who could guarantee that he wanted to make use of the material sent in to him, and was able to, and who was sufficiently empowered to grant the sort of elastic conditions that conformed to the special and difficult marketing conditions of the foreign book trade in journals, then *Das Wort*, "however colorful the editorial board may be, will never achieve the circulation it could. When I think of that my blood boils."[34]

But all this was out of Bredel's hands. He had absolutely no control over Mezhdunarodnaja kniga,[35] and the mounting problems underscored his determination to rid himself of the editorial duties he had never wanted in the first place. Soon after his arrival in Moscow from Paris in April 1936, he had written Ludwig Renn that he was "only editor with an 'unfortunately,' "[36] and, before the first issue of *Das Wort* rolled off the press, Bredel began looking for ways to sever his ties with the journal. He first thought of bringing Kurt Kersten to Moscow as his replacement and planned on discussing the matter with Koltsov, who had the last word in such matters.[37] In mid-July 1936—*Das Wort* had reached a crisis point—he told Herzfelde that he had held a "lively discussion with our friend K. [oltsov]" and had begged him to find someone else to do his, Bredel's, job. "In all seriousness I have had enough of not only putting these volumes together virtually singlehandedly but of shouldering all the technical burdens as well."[38] Nor was there any improvement once the first issue, after numerous delays, came out on 21 July. Again Bredel poured out his heart to Herzfelde. "What turmoil, what struggles, what effort it takes here to bring out the journal," he lamented. These were all problems that Herzfelde had not encountered in Prague with the *Neue Deutsche Blätter*, the publication of which had been an "edi-

---

34. Herzfelde to Bredel, 1 July 1936, TsGALI, 631/12/143/127.
35. This never changed. Fritz Erpenbeck, after he had replaced Bredel as de facto editor in Moscow, complained to Graf: "You mustn't forget that virtually the only control we have over the marketing [of the journal] is precisely the letters of our friends. Moreover—and this complicates matters even more, but can't be altered—not *we* but a special different organization is the one which manages foreign business affairs: Mezhdunarodnaja kniga" (Erpenbeck to Graf, 11 October 1937, TsGALI, 631/12/141/253).
36. Bredel to Ludwig Renn, 20 May 1936, TsGALI, 631/12/143/538.
37. Bredel to Herzfelde, 11 June 1936, TsGALI, 631/12/143/141.
38. Bredel to Herzfelde, 16 July 1936, TsGALI, 631/12/143/112.

torial idyll." Bredel had the impression that friends who had seen with their own eyes the difficulties in Moscow forgot them straight away once they again had Western air about their nostrils. Herzfelde was no exception. "You pose questions in your letter and are amazed at certain things, an attitude which can only amaze me. Your questions make it seem as if you had never been here and had never experienced the upheaval that results from this type of editorial work."[39]

But technical hurdles were by no means the only source of difficulty. Bredel actually had to struggle in the first few months to fill up the pages of the journal. In early July he had reason to worry because he was far short of enough material for no. 3 of *Das Wort*. He had "virtually nothing," he said, adding a few days later that no. 3, still without sufficient creative literature, book reviews, and marginal notes, would be going to press in two days. No one cared about the journal, Bredel complained: "Unfortunately not a thing has thus far come of all the suggestions. No one has written, neither has anyone declared his willingness to contribute, and I have no alternative but to fill the issues with the work of local comrades [the Germans in Soviet exile]—this is the most unpleasant aspect." Bredel looked forward to the upcoming visit of "our Parisian friends" (Alfred Kantorowicz and Gustav Regler arrived in Moscow on 7 August 1936), hoping that talks with them would lead to better cooperation from the German writers living in Paris.[40] Bredel admitted that he was "very disappointed" with the support of friends outside of the USSR. "To tell the truth, I had imagined that things would be different."[41] Herzfelde thought that the reason for the apathy among German Communist writers toward *Das Wort* was the popular-front nature of the journal. "More time must pass before the old sectarian wounds among us are healed. I think we have to be patient here."[42]

Problems, of course, were compounded by the editorial situation—Bredel lived in Moscow, Feuchtwanger in Sanary, and Brecht in Denmark. Apart from occasional suggestions by Feuchtwanger, in fact, the latter two had comparatively little involvement with *Das Wort*. Brecht initially did nothing. He never contacted Bredel personally,

39. Bredel to Herzfelde, 21 July 1936, TsGALI, 631/12/143/108.
40. Bredel to Graf, 8 August 1936, TsGALI, 631/12/141/305.
41. Bredel to Herzfelde, no date, TsGALI, 631/12/143/121.
42. Herzfelde to Bredel, 31 July 1936, TsGALI, 631/12/143/105. Herzfelde was unwilling to accept any blame if *Das Wort* went under, which he thought it was almost bound to do after the "unhappy start. I tell various authors that I can only accept contributions for the October volume up to 10 August, but they laugh in my face and ask where the July issue is" (Herzfelde to Bredel, 25 July 1936, TsGALI, 631/12/143/90).

issuing instead periodical directives through Maria Osten, who was with him frequently in Denmark. Bredel's patience finally wore thin, and he told Osten:

> Certain things strike me as extraordinarily odd. You pass along directives: print this immediately—Bredel should read it. Period. Matter closed. In another letter I read: should be published, Brecht says so. Period. End. Can you have forgotten on your trip that I am an editor too and not just an executive organ (to avoid using a stronger expression)? I want our friend Brecht to collaborate actively very much. Unfortunately he has yet to send me a single line concerning the material to the different issues. . . . It would have been good had you been able to persuade Brecht to send along some of his own work. Our friend Feuchtwanger is, it must be said, extremely conscientious in these matters and so far has sent me his opinion about every issue.[43]

In late 1936 things finally took a turn for the better, and Brecht began displaying a greater interest in *Das Wort*. Within a few months everything was going smoothly, so much so that in a moment of exuberance Bredel told Osten in Paris that Feuchtwanger was writing pleasant letters on a frequent basis, while "editor no. 2 [Brecht] has grown very friendly, participating quite intensively in *Wort*, writing very nice letters, making suggestions, and so on. If all three [editors] resided in a single city the journal would be excellent."[44] Even so, Bredel still wanted out. In late 1936 he was planning to be in Prague by the end of November or by December.[45] But somewhere along the way Kurt Kersten either withdrew himself or was dropped from consideration as a possible replacement for Bredel, and that delayed his departure.[46] Ludwig Marcuse, who arrived in Moscow with Lion

---

43. Bredel to Osten, 26 July 1936, TsGALI, 631/12/143/411.
44. Bredel to Osten, 17 March 1937, TsGALI, 631/12/143/415. Herzfelde had already asked in December: "What is new to me is that you are not doing 99 percent of the work. Since when is Br.[echt] so active?" (Herzfelde to Bredel, 23 December 1936, TsGALI, 631/12/143/56). By late September 1936 *Das Wort* had a printing of seven thousand and soon went up to ten thousand (Bredel to Graf, 27 September 1936, TsGALI, 631/12/141/297, and Bredel to Gerhard Hinze (Dnjepropetrovsk), no date, TsGALI, 631/12/143/208). Petrova claims that the edition finally reached twelve thousand (Petrova, "Zhurnal—*Das Vort*," p. 64).
45. Bredel to Herzfelde, 4 September 1936 and 3 November 1936, TsGALI, 631/12/143/77 and 66.
46. In July Brecht had evidently thought of going to Moscow and assuming editorial

Feuchtwanger in November 1936, was also suggested as a temporary replacement. Maria Osten told Bredel that Marcuse should stay over the winter, "working mainly on *Wort,* since he knows everyone well personally. . . . You can take a breather and get your book done quickly."[47] Marcuse did in fact stay the winter, though he was not involved with the journal. In any case, he would have been considered only as a temporary replacement because Bredel's plans at the time envisioned only a brief stay abroad.

Bredel was still searching for a substitute in March 1937, telling Feuchtwanger that he could not leave until the matter of a replacement was settled.[48] Finally, in late April, Bredel left for a vacation in the Volga-German Republic after compiling the material for no. 6 of *Das Wort.* His duties were taken over by Fritz Erpenbeck. Then, in late May, Bredel departed for the Second International Writers' Congress for the Defense of Culture in Valencia, Spain. However, because he was evidently expected back shortly, Erpenbeck's job remained only temporary; he did not become the de facto editor of *Das Wort* until the August issue, when Bredel decided, or was asked by the Comintern, to stay in Spain. Erpenbeck continued to discharge these duties until the journal was discontinued in March 1939, although Bredel remained one of the three editors and, after he arrived in Paris from Spain in summer 1938, kept in touch with Erpenbeck on editorial matters.[49]

No less than the popular front movement in the West, *Das Wort* was severely hamstrung by the Moscow show trials, the first of which began only one month after *Das Wort* saw the light of day. Controversy initially broke out around Ignazio Silone, for a decision was evidently taken to engage him in a public debate about the political ramifications of his novel *Bread and Wine,* which was published prior to the August trial and unfavorably received in Russia. Ernst Ottwalt was delegated to write a critique of the work for *Das Wort,* but Bertolt Brecht opposed any kind of polemic with Silone, and Maria Osten, in a letter to

---

responsibilities, at least for several months (Bredel to Osten, 26 July 1936, TsGALI, 631/12/143/411).

47. Osten (Paris) to Bredel, 8 November 1936, TsGALI, 631/12/143/413. Bredel was trying to complete his novel *Dein unbekannter Bruder.* See Marcuse's version of events in *Mein 20. Jahrhundert,* p. 221.

48. Bredel to Feuchtwanger, 17 March 1936, TsGALI, 631/14/65/86.

49. Erpenbeck to Graf, 25 July 1937, TsGALI, 631/12/141/260; Erpenbeck to Felix Langer, 26 July 1937, TsGALI, 631/12/143/281; Erpenbeck to Graf, 11 October 1937, TsGALI, 631/12/141/253; Wolf Frank to Erpenbeck, 12 December 1936, TsGALI, 631/12/154/72.

Moscow, promised an "uproar" if Ottwalt's criticism was published. By the time Osten's letter reached the Soviet Union, however, Ottwalt had already written Silone a private letter, and the latter had agreed to reply; both letters would then be printed in *Das Wort*.[50]

Before Silone could respond officially to Ottwalt, the first show trial of Zinoviev and Kamenev was staged. Silone then composed an entirely different statement, which he forwarded to *Das Wort* and published in the *Arbeiter-Zeitung* in Basel.[51] Silone minced no words. He had received Ottwalt's letter, and he had indeed prepared an answer; but in view of "recent events" in Moscow, the trial, he had decided not to send along his original remarks because he no longer wanted his name to appear in *Das Wort*, "not even as that of an occasional contributor." There followed a scathing attack on the trial of the "oppositionists," in which Silone charged that the "'confessions'" of the old revolutionaries had been extracted by clever and barbaric torture. But Silone went much further than mere criticism of the court proceedings; he drew parallels between justice in the Fascist countries and justice in the Soviet Union. After the events of August, the Communists had lost their moral right to protest against Fascist police actions and Fascist court procedures, wrote Silone, in spite of the fact that the Communists claimed for themselves the leading role in the anti-Fascist resistance.

Silone rejected everything associated with the trial. "As long as we are talking about an entire political school represented by men who spent their lives fighting czarist absolutism and the international bourgeoisie; as long as we are talking about men whose names are Trotsky, Zinoviev, Kamenev, Radek, and Bukharin,[52] no amount of propaganda will be able to argue persuasively that the whole affair is a mere moral purge connected with a band of criminals." Silone considered his protest a "necessary act of anti-Fascist consequence." If he were to remain silent now, he would "no longer have the courage to write a single line against Fascist dictatorship." He concluded his letter by stating that he "refused to become a Fascist, not even a red Fascist."[53]

50. Osten to Ljudmilla Shejnina, 19 July 1936, TsGALI, 631/12/143/424; Shejnina to Osten, undated letter and letter from 25 July 1936, TsGALI, 631/12/143/431 and 423. Ottwalt's letter to Silone has been reprinted in *europäische ideen* 45/46 (1979): 84–88.
51. Ignazio Silone, *Arbeiter-Zeitung* (Basel), 24 September 1936. It was claimed in *Das Wort* that no letter from Silone arrived at *Wort*'s editorial office (*Das Wort* 6 [1936]: 111).
52. Radek and Bukharin had been "implicated" in the first trial, though the former did not appear in the dock until the second trial in early 1937 and the latter until the third a year later.
53. Silone, *Arbeiter-Zeitung* (Basel), 24 September 1936.

Silone's letter had an impact in the West and helped begin the disintegration of the popular front. In early November 1936, for instance, Osten informed Bredel that Silone's letter to *Das Wort* had been republished in all the newspapers; a day later Wieland Herzfelde told Bredel that he could scarcely imagine how "much more difficult the Silones make our work."[54]

There was an epilogue to the whole affair. Ernst Bloch was "commissioned" to answer Silone's "open letter" in *Das Wort*, and he in fact wrote his reply, but it was never published. Herzfelde, who was in touch with Bloch in Prague, asked Bredel repeatedly in December why Bloch's article was still unpublished, remarking: "It's embarrassing to me that Bloch has yet to receive an answer from you. I can more or less imagine the reasons, but still: you can't work like this if you attach any importance to not upsetting Bloch." On 4 January 1937, Bredel finally told Herzfelde what had happened. "Something stupid came up in connection with Bloch," Bredel explained; "he quoted too much, and that is not acceptable here; but I don't know how to explain that to him. Since he sent in the piece late, it would have to come out late. And who is interested in stirring up the old attack, except Ignatz, if it can only take place a few months later. Try and explain that to Bloch."[55]

The Silone controversy was not an isolated incident. The Swiss literary critic R. J. Humm likewise asked for the removal of his name from the list of contributors to *Das Wort*. His request was answered in a cryptic note at the end of the October 1936 issue. *Das Wort* wrote that Humm, who had "presented himself before the highest court of the Union of Soviet Socialist Republics as the defender of terrorist murderers condemned to death," had also sent copies of his letter to *Das Wort* and to four political dailies in Switzerland, thus proving that his main purpose had been a political manifestation against the "land of Soviets and its leaders." Humm, *Das Wort* said, "'would not have

54. Osten (Paris) to Bredel, 8 November 1936, TsGALI, 631/12/143/413; Herzfelde to Bredel, 9 November 1936, TsGALI, 631/12/143/63.
55. Herzfelde to Bredel, 23 and 28 December 1936, TsGALI, 631/12/143/56 and 55; Bredel to Herzfelde, 4 January 1937, TsGALI, 631/12/143/53. There were other similar instances of this type of censorship. Hans Altmann in early 1937 had a piece accepted by *Das Wort* called "Schillerszene," which evidently dealt with the treatment of Schiller in Nazi Germany. He told Bredel that he had used "unchanged Nazi terminology and original quotes." Several months later, Erpenbeck told him that "the reasons why your article was withdrawn are not technical; I can't, unfortunately, tell you any more by letter" (Altmann to Bredel, 18 February 1937, and Erpenbeck to Altmann, 28 June 1937, TsGALI, 631/12/139/15 and 7).

dreamt that it would ever be necessary to draw a line between himself and Soviet Russia.' He has drawn the line, and it's clear now to whom he feels an allegiance and what the nature of his 'humanism' is."[56]

The trials were not the only event adversely affecting *Das Wort*. In November 1936 the burgeoning purge of Germans struck the journal. Hans Günther and Ernst Ottwalt disappeared. With them went their names from the cover of the December issue. Wieland Herzfelde noticed the gaps and promptly commented to Bredel: "Of course I couldn't help noticing that the list of contributors in no. 6 lacks two names that appeared in no. 5. What a shame that one is so seldom mistaken about other human beings."[57]

Das Wort had been backed into a cul-de-sac: conceived as the literary voice of the German anti-Fascist emigration and of the popular front, it was now compelled to uphold the verdicts in the trials, verdicts that were convulsing the popular front. *Das Wort*'s defense of the trials, more than anything else, destroyed the myth of its nonpartisanship, although apologias in its pages by no means flowed solely from the pens of Germans in Soviet exile. In March 1937 Feuchtwanger concluded, "There can be no doubt that the guilt of the accused has been clearly proven. Those who are not of ill will must in addition concede that the ideological and, for the most part, the actual inspiration for their deeds stems from Trotsky."[58] Note the choice of words: Feuchtwanger held men who disagreed with his analysis to be of "ill will." Willi Bredel likewise linked Trotsky to fascism, explaining that the German Fascists only dared to be so impudent and aggressive toward the USSR because they knew the Trotskyist conspirators and traitors,

---

56. *Das Wort* 4 (1936): 112.

57. Herzfelde to Bredel, 23 December 1936, TsGALI, 631/12/143/56. Herzfelde should not be judged too harshly for his cynical remark; he had no idea what was really happening, and his experiences with both Günther and the semialcoholic Ottwalt had not been pleasant. A few weeks later, Herzfelde wrote Bredel again about the Ottwalt matter (13 January 1937, TsGALI, 631/12/143/51): "The case of Ottwalt is also an instrument [used against the Communists]. Enclosed is an excerpt from the Prague *Montag*. . . . An even more incredible account is given in the *Česke Slovo* by Borin, till May one of our most prominent Czech friends. According to this O. spent only six weeks in the ČSR, arriving from the Third Reich penniless and exhausted and living near Prague; he was in town on only three occasions to pick up 100 Czech crowns each time. How they all claim to know what O. has been accused of, only the devil can say. It would help our situation a lot if something authentic would be sent us so that we could combat these fabrications. There are even a few tactful people who place value publicly in mentioning my name clearly in connection with the affair. What can one do?"

58. "Eine neue Barriere gegen den Krieg: Zum Moskauer Prozess gegen die Trotzkisten," *Das Wort* 3 (1937): 100.

as accomplices and organizers, to be at their side. Bredel declaimed: "The Soviet Union—the name lights up the eyes of repressed peoples the world over. Organization of the united front, the popular front, the struggle for democracy and against fascism, the guarantee of peace—everywhere it is the Soviet Union which fills the masses with enthusiasm, raises their will to fight, strengthens their confidence in victory. . . . The land of the Soviets does not intend to allow itself to be laid waste by Fascist hordes of mercenaries; no conspirators and bandits sent by Trotsky and the Gestapo shall lay a hand on socialist property and on the accomplishments of the October Revolution."[59]

Das Wort, of course, staunchly endorsed the third trial of Bukharin and others in March 1938, where the leitmotif was that Maxim Gorky had "died at the hands of a murderer." The trial had been a blow against fascism and its war of conquest. Humanity had triumphed in the courtroom by "exterminating inhumanity," *Das Wort* opined. "*Peace* prevailed. . . . Once again. At the last minute." But Gorky, "the friend of Stalin and his policies, our friend, as well as a literary example for most of us and a human example for all of us, has fallen on behalf of peace. . . . Let us learn a hard lesson from this for our human, literary, and political stance with respect to fascism and the Trotskyism it supports: to be harder, more courageous, more vigilant."[60]

The trials, of course, inflicted the severest damage on Communist efforts to ensconce themselves in the moral forefront of the battle against Hitler, and they were a real blow to *Das Wort*'s prestige as well. But the series of farces in Moscow was not the only setback to *Das Wort* and its claim to be the voice of the literary popular front. Perhaps the greatest failure of the journal was its inability to prevail upon Heinrich Mann to write for it. More than any other personage, he embodied the notion of a popular front as the Communists conceived it. After the plan to engage him as an editor fell through, Bredel tried unsuccessfully during the rest of 1936 to obtain contributions from him, using Lion Feuchtwanger and Bruno Frei as intermediaries.[61] These

59. Ibid., pp. 102–3. The more complete text of Bredel's elaborations, for those who care to read it, is in the *Deutsche Zentral-Zeitung* for 28 January 1937 ("Erbärmliche Kreaturen: Handlanger und Spiessgesellen deutscher und japanischer Faschisten"); Feuchtwanger's text was likewise carried in the *Deutsche Zentral-Zeitung* for 24 January 1937.
60. "In memoriam Maxim Gorki," *Das Wort* 4 (1938): 2–4.
61. Feuchtwanger to Bredel, 31 August 1936, TsGALI, 631/13/65/55; Bredel to Heinrich Mann, 6 October 1936, TsGALI, 631/12/143/316; Feuchtwanger (Moscow) to Mann, 15 January 1937, TsGALI, 631/12/143/315. Mann's answer was generally always the

efforts continued well into 1937 as it gradually became obvious that Mann's refusal to write for *Das Wort* was actually something of a boycott. In early April 1937 Bredel wrote Feuchtwanger that Mann had responded neither to Ludwig Marcuse's letter nor to his own. "This is the more depressing since Heinrich Mann, after all, contributes to almost all other German-language periodicals and newspapers."[62] The solicitations went on after Bredel left for Spain. Erpenbeck tried his hand at it by approaching Mann through Hermann Budzislawski of the *Neue Weltbühne*.[63] Since Budzislawski worked continually with Mann, Erpenbeck wondered if Budzislawski could not encourage him to "write an article for us on some cultural question he deems important." If Budzislawski could manage that, he would be doing not only Erpenbeck but "'WORT' as well, and with it the popular front, a real service."[64]

Budzislawski passed on Erpenbeck's request, with no luck.[65] Later, he guessed at the reason for Mann's reticence to contribute to *Das Wort*: "That Heinrich Mann has yet to write for you probably has to do with certain dissension within the Parisian popular front."[66] After several months had passed Erpenbeck tried again on his own. "Please do not look upon these lines as one of the certainly all too numerous requests for contributions that some ambitious young editor makes of you," Erpenbeck wrote, explaining:

> Please don't look upon them either as simply the wish of a stranger who sincerely respects you; try instead to understand them politically as well. Our journal has lately taken a promising turn upwards: we are now reaching—our correspondence shows it—circles that until now have remained distant from or at least indifferent to the popular front. And here your word especially would carry particular weight. . . . Your participation, even if it were only seldom as a result of your extraordinary work load, would act after all against the

---

same. He told Bruno Frei: "Unfortunately I have to tell you that I cannot undertake any larger projects at all this winter; I am obligated to complete my novel" (Mann to Frei, 4 October 1936, TsGALI, 631/12/139/175).

62. Bredel to Feuchtwanger, 3 April 1937, TsGALI, 631/13/65/92.

63. For which Mann wrote extensively, a fact that doubtless galled Erpenbeck.

64. Erpenbeck to Hermann Budzislawski (Prague), 22 October 1937, TsGALI, 631/12/141/175.

65. Budzislawski to Erpenbeck, 27 October 1937, TsGALI, 631/12/141/174.

66. Budzislawski to Erpenbeck, 3 December 1937, TsGALI, 631/12/141/172. The date, of course, corresponds with the serious disagreements that had come up in the Popular Front Committee.

exceedingly unpleasant process of disintegration and division within the literary emigration: your name is, more than any other, a point of crystallization; a large number of the writers who thus far, because of a certain uneasiness, have not wanted to risk publishing in an organ that comes out over here would consider it an honor to be printed in the same publication as you. . . . So you see, my esteemed Heinrich Mann, my request is not only a personal wish but, far beyond that, the result of important political motives that you can certainly appreciate.

Erpenbeck closed by asking if Mann had any particular reasons for singling out *Das Wort* as a journal for which he did not wish to write. "If that is the case, then these reasons should absolutely be cleared away in the interest of the struggle that binds us all together." Mann still refused to contribute.[67] Was it really his unhappiness with dissension in the Popular Front Committee in Paris, as Budzislawski had suggested? Mann's dissatisfaction with Ulbricht and other Communists in the committee did not prevent him from associating with any number of other Communist-sponsored ventures, and there is no reason to think that his disappointment with the committee led to his boycott of *Das Wort*, a boycott that, after all, had lasted since 1936. His withdrawal of support for the journal was more likely caused by a very mundane reason: Mann was very sensitive about financial matters; on several occasions he had been easily offended by what he considered degrading or insulting treatment with respect to his Soviet royalties, even though he probably received more hard currency for Russian and German editions of his writings than any other German author. The most probable cause of his refusal to write for *Das Wort* was a feeling that the journal's editors had not considered him important enough to pay him the salary he had asked for in early 1936, when he made two separate offers to write for the journal and also to edit it. Although Mann's boycott was scarcely politically inspired, it nonetheless did severe damage to the political prestige of *Das Wort*, for without Heinrich Mann's name it was difficult to argue that the journal expressed the hopes and aspirations of the popular front.

In early 1937 the editors had new grounds to fear that the journal's exclusive role as a forum for popular front literati was in jeopardy. Word reached Bredel that the publication of a new periodical edited

67. Erpenbeck to Heinrich Mann, 20 January 1938, TsGALI, 631/12/151/9; Mann to Erpenbeck, 3 February 1938, TsGALI, 631/12/151/8.

by Thomas Mann was imminent. He informed Feuchtwanger immediately of this "extraordinarily important matter" of a "literary bimonthly in German, published by Oprecht and edited by Thomas Mann and Dr. Lion, which will in every respect represent a sort of competition for us."[68] Bredel apprised Feuchtwanger that he had gone promptly to the head of the publishing house in Moscow and had won for *Das Wort* "an improved technical makeup (better covers, better binding, and the like)." He had also discussed an improvement of the journal's contents with the director, though it is not clear from Bredel's letter what he thought could be done about that in Moscow. He did, however, ask Feuchtwanger to be more active in soliciting quality contributions from abroad. Bredel wrote to Wieland Herzfelde that the appearance of the bimonthly was a serious matter: "For you can imagine who the contributors will be, namely, Brentano, Glaeser, both Kessers, Silone of course, etc. And this will naturally be the journal that represents the right wing of the German emigration, thereby marking *Das Wort* even more as a Communist journal." Bredel asked Herzfelde and his friends in Prague to come up with suggestions and practical assistance in response to the new journal, which came out between 1937 and 1940 under the title *Mass und Wert*.[69] Bredel's concern was prompted by the same old Communist fear of isolation in the anti-Fascist front.

Ironically, after all the effort invested in putting out a journal based in Moscow, its geographical and political location was primarily responsible for most of its problems and its final demise. The Communists had attached great significance to publishing *Das Wort* in Moscow, but in late 1937, with contributors' complaints about technical matters mounting, they were compelled to reverse the process and move a portion of their operations out of Moscow and back to the West. But the Communists had to be nudged into it, for the establishment of a Parisian branch office of *Das Wort* resulted from a virtual ultimatum from Feuchtwanger and Brecht. In August 1937 Feuchtwanger told Maria Osten that unhappiness caused by inefficiency in marketing *Das Wort* was growing; from all quarters, he lamented,

68. Bredel to Feuchtwanger, 3 April 1937, TsGALI, 631/13/65/92.
69. Bredel to Herzfelde, 27 March 1937, 631/12/143/29. Becher was also worried about the impact of *Mass und Wert* on his *Internationale Literatur* and asked Heinrich Mann, among other things, whether he thought his journal would be adversely affected. Mann replied that *Internationale Literatur* should simply retain its commitment to internationalism and things would be all right (Mann to Becher, 2 April 1937, Becher-Archiv, Sig. 57).

contributors were turning to him with complaints about technical matters of which he had no knowledge.[70] Then, in October 1937, Feuchtwanger and Brecht insisted that changes be introduced and made their further work as editors incumbent upon them.

The pair came up with two suggestions. First, they proposed that the journal be issued on a bimonthly basis with twice as many pages; that way longer articles could be included, and Brecht and Feuchtwanger would have more time to examine the proposed material for each issue instead of sending off "our opinion about the current contributions, as before, in two or three days." The second proposal called for a "sort of intermediary office in western Europe"; the job of the editor there would be to resolve all preliminary problems, solicit new contributors, and take care of initial preparation of the material on time. Feuchtwanger and Brecht pointed out that frequently western European contributors turned to them about minor technical disagreements. These were all doubtless problems created by "the distance between Moscow and western Europe." The letter continued: "You will remember countless cases where writers who basically had every good intention of supplying desirable contributions on time were unable to do so since they were requested too late. All this could be avoided if a capable editor in western Europe took over such matters." This editor would have to be someone well acquainted with literary circumstances in western Europe and above all else with the personal situations of individual writers. He would relieve Feuchtwanger and Brecht of all superfluous technical work and, particularly, would look over the material sent in from western Europe before passing it on to Moscow and to the editors. "Needless to say, final decisions cannot of course be taken by this western European editor. It is also clear that, naturally, if political reservations are raised from over there [Moscow], this would under all circumstances be decisive." Brecht and Feuchtwanger emphasized that they saw no real possibility of continued productive work if these proposals were not considered. The next day Feuchtwanger asked Maria Osten if she would be willing to assume the duties as western editor.[71]

Six weeks passed before Erpenbeck was able to bring up the matter with Koltsov; following their discussion, Erpenbeck reported to Feuchtwanger that his and Brecht's desire for a Parisian editor would be met. Maria Osten had probably already contacted Feuchtwanger, wrote

70. Feuchtwanger to Osten, 24 August 1937, TsGALI, 631/13/87/2.
71. Brecht and Feuchtwanger to "Freunde," 18 October 1937, TsGALI, 631/13/65/131; Feuchtwanger (Paris) to Osten (Paris), 19 October 1937, TsGALI, 631/13/87/1.

Erpenbeck; "we are sending her a long letter today, and we would like you to inform her of all wishes, complaints, etc., as well as further suggestions. I think that, once this new office has been established, both of us will be rid of a lot of minor irritations; above all, many of the (technical) shortcomings and misunderstandings will be taken care of." As for the other suggestions, Erpenbeck explained to Feuchtwanger that it was not a good idea to appear only bimonthly; that would give the impression of a "retreat." Instead, beginning with the first issue of 1938, *Das Wort* would be increased in size by one-third while still selling at the same price. "We thereby have the chance to publish longer pieces without changing the actual nature of the journal." Erpenbeck had also managed to win from the Soviet publishers a higher quality cover and better paper.[72]

Erpenbeck wrote to Maria Osten that the main problems she would face as Paris editor involved complaints about manuscripts and honorariums. As a rule, these misunderstandings came up because of the great distance: manuscripts were not acknowledged swiftly enough or the honorariums, as Erpenbeck claimed, did not arrive because the authors, without notifying anyone, moved away.[73] Another of Osten's responsibilities would be to peruse the manuscripts, particularly those from France, and send all the useless ones back with a "few polite words." In that way the author would be "less upset than if his work journeys from country to country for months on end and is finally rejected anyway." Then there were numerous manuscripts that "were basically good or usable if minor emendations could be made."[74] Often

72. Erpenbeck did not explain why he thought publishing longer works bi-monthly would change the nature of *Das Wort* (Erpenbeck to Feuchtwanger, 30 December 1937, TsGALI, 631/13/65/148).

73. Erpenbeck to Osten, no date [early 1938], TsGALI, 631/12/143/412. This is not an accurate picture of the problems, most of which arose in connection with the sloppiness of Mezhdunarodnaja kniga. It is worth pointing out—since East German scholars, as well as Huppert and Erpenbeck (see note 20), blame most of *Das Wort*'s problems on the mail—that postal difficulties were comparatively rare. Letters in both directions, to judge by *Das Wort*'s extant files, regularly reached their destinations without delay—as fast or faster, actually, than today's mail. *Das Wort* was in any case not shut down because of interrupted correspondence.

74. This might be a good point to comment on censorship. *Das Wort* was given a fairly wide latitude; though each issue had to be read and approved by a Soviet censor (see Erpenbeck's portrayal in *Das Wort: Registerband*, pp. 12–13), there seem to have been few instances of direct interference. Here are some: Béla Balázs submitted several short stories to *Das Wort*, which Erpenbeck wanted to print. But, as he told Balázs, "during my discussion with the responsible Russian comrade (only for this case, for this issue), it turned out that he rejected every one of the stories. (Justification: that is not the way it is, that would create a false impression abroad, etc.)" (Erpenbeck to Balázs,

only a single passage was unacceptable, Erpenbeck explained. "If that could be discussed with the author, it would be a minor matter; if it has to be handled by mail (without, perhaps, being able to make the arguments clear), then we have preferred in the past to send the entire manuscript back, and that is too bad, not only with respect to literature. You get the point."

An editorial branch office in Paris also provided a greater opportunity to exert political leverage on particular authors. Erpenbeck explained this explicitly to Osten:

> Furthermore—and this is of the utmost importance for a literary journal like ours, in other words, urgent: we would like to have a lengthy report on events in the SDS. It is interesting to us to know *which* authors side with the one and which with the other view, as well as who simply goes along here or there. For we get contributions pretty much from all of them. For example, [Ludwig] Marcuse is currently writing for the *Tage-Buch*. This has made an exceedingly poor impression here: [he writes] for an organ that is waging a smear campaign in a despicable manner against the Soviet Union. Marcuse has to be told openly that it is impossible for one of our contributors to dance along in the rows of our most malicious enemies. If he lacks the political insight, he has

---

22 November 1937, TsGALI, 631/12/139/68). Censorship of a different sort was Erpenbeck's refusal to print an article by Ludwig Marcuse on Wagner and by Hans Natonek on Nietzsche. Erpenbeck told Natonek that "we cannot agree with your introductory assessment of Nietzsche. . . . We do indeed see in Nietzsche (considering his entire work) the father of Nazi philosophy" (Erpenbeck to Ludwig Marcuse, 16 May 1938, TsGALI, 631/12/151/20; Erpenbeck to Natonek (Prague), 10 February 1938, TsGALI, 631/12/151/80). Natonek was given a particularly hard time. In April 1938 a story of his was rejected by Erpenbeck "because we are of the opinion that, even if it was patterned after a true event, it would result in a false picture of the great historical truth, in a word, it isn't realistic enough." In July a story was turned down because its content could be "completely misunderstood," and in October another fell victim to the protestations of "two of our editors. They had historical and political reservations" (Erpenbeck to Natonek, 27 April, 28 July, and 1 October 1938, TsGALI, 631/12/151/77, 69, and 67). Other examples of censorship: Radek's or Bukharin's name had to be removed from Balder Olden's article, "Anno vierunddreissig in der UdSSR," *Das Wort* 2 (1938): 68–78. Erpenbeck wrote: "I had to remove a name whose bearer in the meantime—the proof is incontrovertible—has been exposed (to say the least) as a political imposter." Erpenbeck likewise cut some comments from Olden's "Schriftsteller Goebbels," *Das Wort* 1 (1938): 92–95. (Erpenbeck to Olden, 11 November 1938, TsGALI, 631/12/151/188).

to be shown that a question of tact is also involved. Please write him as soon as possible and find out what he says to this. I have several pieces from him, some set in type and others commissioned. But I cannot publish them until I hear his reaction. We have been asked to have you discuss the matter with Feuchtwanger.[75]

Like any other Communist-sponsored popular front venture, *Das Wort*'s "nonpartisanship" came to a stop when a contributor either adopted a critical stance toward the USSR or, like Marcuse, associated with those who had. Feuchtwanger was indeed asked his opinion, and, ever the compliant fellow comrade, agreed wholeheartedly with Erpenbeck. He informed Osten that "in a journal . . . issuing from Moscow, we cannot print the same authors who show up now and then in a journal [*Das neue Tage-Buch*] that uses the dirtiest means to oppose the Soviet Union."[76] Osten reported that, though Feuchtwanger had been a personal friend of Leopold Schwarzschild, "he has broken off all relations with him." She then went on to give this report:

We had a meeting [in Paris] attended by a representative of the German party. The following was decided: we cannot merely tell these authors, "We aren't going to publish you anymore." That would just lead to new discussions, cause new attacks. We decided—and writers in attendance like Seghers, Bruno Frei, etc. concurred—that we should try and pry these authors away from there [the *Tage-Buch*] by working on them personally, by keeping them busier. This has become easier lately because the *Deutsche Volkszeitung* is published now in Paris; what is more, it is published in an augmented edition, that is, each issue has weekly almost an entire page for literature. We are also convinced that we will succeed here since Klaus Mann has already told us that, of course, once he found out the nature of the organization, he had long since left it.[77] The two others involved are, as we

75. Erpenbeck to Osten, no date [early 1938], TsGALI, 631/12/143/412.
76. One cannot help wondering what Feuchtwanger thought of the fabricated letter the Communists had sent to the *Neues Tage-Buch* in order to accuse Schwarzschild of secret links with Goebbels and Trotsky.
77. Schwarzschild had formed, as a sort of counterorganization to the Communist-run SDS, a Bund Freie Presse und Literatur in June 1937, and Klaus Mann, among others, had joined it. Heinrich Mann eventually talked his nephew into severing his ties with the organization. See the documents in Klaus Mann, *Briefe und Antworte*, pp. 396–98, and Klaus Mann's correspondence with his uncle and with Schwarzschild, ibid., pp. 308–14.

mentioned, in dire financial straits.[78] It was decided, so as not
to injure the nature of the popular front (which *Das Wort*,
after all, is to preserve) [that] we cannot at the moment reject
the participation of these three since their contributions are
politically indifferent anyway. . . . With the bank account in
Paris, it is understood that payments [for articles in *Das Wort*]
shall be made more punctually. It would also be a good idea
in handling the authors, in order to consolidate them and lead
them into the desired political line, if we were in a position to
give an advance for an occasional commissioned article.[79]

Das Wort, which had helped more than one indigent author in exile
by paying handsome honorariums in hard currency, was now using
financial pressure to coerce authors who needed money and could not
always publish elsewhere into towing a political line.[80] Several months
elapsed before final permission was granted in Moscow for the Parisian office.[81] As late as May 1938, Feuchtwanger asked Koltsov to
expedite the "decision about the Parisian editorial office of 'WORT'
and the publishing house to be established within the framework of
the association."[82] By late 1938 the office was evidently functioning.
Contributions were forwarded to Paris first, then on to Moscow; and
issues of *Das Wort* arrived in large numbers in bulk shipments at the
Paris office for dissemination in the West.[83]

On 12 December 1938 Mikhail Koltsov disappeared without a trace
in Moscow, and his arrest set in motion the chain of events that ended
with the discontinuance of *Das Wort*. Koltsov's arrest had immediate
repercussions. The December issue seems not to have been sent off,
and scores of letters soon flooded the office in Moscow complaining
about the lost issue. Nor did the single large shipment of copies reach

---

78. Marcuse was evidently the second of the three; who the third writer was is unclear.
Perhaps it was Alfred Döblin.

79. "Beilage zum Brief Feuchtwanger/Osten vom 19. Februar 1938," TsGALI,
631/13/65/157.

80. The potential was there for a subtle but very effective sort of pressure: any author in
need of money would have to think twice, if he wanted his honorarium from *Das Wort*,
about what he wrote. It is, of course, impossible to say how many authors bore this in
mind in writing for the journal.

81. Feuchtwanger to Osten, 25 March 1938, TsGALI, 631/13/87/4.

82. Feuchtwanger to Osten, 10 May 1938, TsGALI, 631/13/87/6. The reference is to
the Verlag 10. Mai.

83. Hilde Leschnitzer (Moscow) to Lene Reiner, 3 November 1938, TsGALI, 631/12/
151/182; Karl Obermann to Erpenbeck, 28 January 1939, TsGALI, 631/12/154/213.

the branch office in Paris. Some subscribers were even missing the January and February numbers.[84] Why was *Das Wort* withheld? The December issue carried an article by Alfred Kantorowicz dealing with the SDS in Paris. In it, speaking of the solidarity of Soviet writers and the emigration, Kantorowicz mentions two who were on countless occasions "in our midst," Ilja Ehrenburg and Mikhail Koltsov.[85] The article was obviously written, submitted, and printed before Koltsov's arrest. So, when news of his disappearance made the rounds, Erpenbeck and his colleagues no doubt feared that if *Das Wort* were sent out with the name of an enemy of the people mentioned in its pages, the editors in Moscow would be held accountable. The delay in the arrival of the journal—copies finally reached their destinations in the West by late January and February—probably occurred as Erpenbeck awaited high-level approval to send out the issue.

The January and February numbers appeared with no apparent problems. Why Koltsov's arrest did not precipitate the journal's immediate liquidation is hard to say, though many contributions for the January and February issues had surely already been accepted at the time of his disappearance; sudden cessation of *Das Wort* would have been exceedingly awkward. Business apparently went on normally until 3 March 1939, when correspondence from Moscow ceased; after 3 March most letters to *Das Wort* simply went unanswered, while other contributors were told that Erpenbeck was on vacation and would reply upon his return.[86] The decision to "liquidate" *Das Wort* was then taken between 3 and 31 March, though it is unclear who had ultimate responsibility for the final action.[87] Letters notifying various contributors of *Das Wort*'s demise first went out on 31 March, the explanation generally being repeated in all the notices. Stefan Heym was told: "It has become necessary to meld our journal with the *IL* [*Internationale Literatur*]. Since the *IL* will in addition receive our hard currency fund, it will be in a position to broaden its circle of contributors

---

84. Obermann to Erpenbeck, 28 January 1939, TsGALI, 631/12/154/213; Wolf Frank to Erpenbeck, 14 March 1939, TsGALI, 631/12/154/70.

85. Alfred Kantorowicz, "Fünf Jahre Schutzverband Deutscher Schriftsteller im Exil," *Das Wort* 12 (1938): 168.

86. Hilde Leschnitzer to Paul Friedländer (Paris), 3 March 1939, TsGALI, 631/12/154/76.

87. Becher evidently sensed what was coming. On 14 March 1939 he asked Heinrich Mann to join the editorial committee of *Internationale Literatur*. "The journal," he explained, "is to be enlarged and made more representative." Mann agreed immediately (he harbored no ill will toward the *Internationale Literatur*). He also seems to have been promised regular payment. Becher to Mann, 14 March and 3 April 1939, 18 April 1944, Becher-Archiv, Sig. 65, 66, 195.

significantly. Erpenbeck is joining the *IL* and requests that from now on you devote your efforts completely to the *IL* and support it energetically with contributions."[88]

Occasional contributors and prominent writers—all received the same cryptic announcement. Nor were the three editors given the courtesy of a truthful account of the situation. Obviously the events surrounding the arrest of Koltsov could not have been elaborated upon in a letter from Moscow,[89] but neither was there any cause to prevaricate as the letter to Feuchtwanger, Brecht, and Bredel did. It read: "After a thoroughgoing examination of the possibility for better dissemination of the journal *Das Wort*, especially after the occupation of Austria and Czechoslovakia, and also in regard to marketing difficulties in other countries, the publishers felt compelled to ask serious questions about the matter of [the journal's] profitability. They arrived at the decision to merge the journal, beginning with no. 4, with the German edition of *Internationale Literatur*."[90] This was all eyewash: the journal had not been hamstrung by the loss of Austria and Czechoslovakia in 1938; even if it had, *Das Wort*, which was never intended to be "profitable," would have been worth continuing as a voice of the popular front. The demise of the journal was really just another signal that the Communists had given up on the movement. The show trials, Heinrich Mann's boycott of *Das Wort*, the appearance of Thomas Mann's *Mass und Wert*, Schwarzschild's campaign against Soviet totalitarianism, bitter dissension in the Parisian Popular Front Committee—everything conspired to undermine *Das Wort*'s claim to be "the representative German literary journal" and provided the major inducements to do away with it. Koltsov's arrest then set the final, overall review of the journal's worth in motion.[91]

The letter to Feuchtwanger, Brecht, and Bredel sought to reassure them; *Internationale Literatur*, "of course," would be restructured. "It was suggested to the *IL* that it not only maintain the ties with *Wort*'s permanent circle of contributors but that it also expand that circle." The "material basis" of *Internationale Literatur* was to be strengthened,

---

88. Erpenbeck to Stefan Heym (New York), 31 March 1939, TsGALI, 631/12/154/117.
89. Brecht had heard immediately of Koltsov's arrest, noting in his journal for January 1939, "Koltsov too arrested. My last Russian connection over there" (Brecht, *Arbeitsjournal: 1938 bis 1942*, p. 36. But he seems not to have connected Koltsov's arrest with the liquidation of *Das Wort*.
90. The letter to the three editors is neither signed nor dated, but seems to have been sent off on 31 March (TsGALI, 631/13/69/188).
91. The Hitler-Stalin pact, signed in August 1939, had nothing to do with *Das Wort*'s demise.

and *Das Wort*'s hard currency fund placed at its disposal. The letter then dismissed the three editors with this platitude: "In thanking you for your valuable participation, we hope that you will react positively to these necessary organizational measures and will support us in the future as well with your valuable contributions." This too was a falsehood: the nature of *Internationale Literatur* did not change, and Becher's journal seems never to have seen a cent of the hard currency.[92]

The announcement caught all three editors by surprise. Willi Bredel in late May 1939 still hoped to "save the journal, discontinued without his knowledge."[93] Brecht recorded his and Feuchtwanger's reaction to the journal's liquidation in a July 1939 missive to Erpenbeck. Complaining angrily about the meager payment for two scenes from *Furcht und Elend* and a translation by him and Margarete Steffin of Andersen Nexö's memoirs, Brecht fulminated: "Originally you said that accepted (and commissioned) pieces would definitely be paid for and if at all possible should be published as well." Erpenbeck's handling of Andersen Nexö's memoirs (only a portion of them were published in *Internationale Literatur* and only the few pages paid for) Brecht called "the shabbiest thing I have thus far experienced with any journal in 15 years of literary activity." He asked Erpenbeck: "Is it really necessary to follow up the crude and insulting manner in which the editors were 'informed' of the liquidation of the journal (Feuchtwanger wrote me a very peeved letter about it) with an even shabbier and undignified epilogue?"[94] Bredel too spoke of the "liquidation" of *Das Wort*. In his summer 1939 Comintern report he had argued that a German literary journal that "would represent *our political and cultural-political line* and defend the position of the Soviet Union" was absolutely necessary. He added: "Until now, *Das Wort* appeared monthly in Moscow, with Brecht, Feuchtwanger, and Bredel signing as editors. Since Koltsov's demotion, this journal was liquidated."[95]

92. In May 1939 Becher complained to Aleksandr Fadejev that *Das Wort*'s hard currency fund had not been transferred to *Internationale Literatur* and that articles originally accepted for the April issue of *Das Wort* could not be paid for, as Feuchtwanger, Brecht, and Bredel had been promised (Barck, *Johannes R. Bechers Publizistik*, pp. 64–65).
93. Walter, *Deutsche Exilliteratur, 1933–1950*, 4:502.
94. Brecht to Erpenbeck, 25 July 1939, Bertolt-Brecht-Archiv, Sig. 911/69. Brecht also complained that he had not even received reimbursement (which he had earlier been paid every year) for the money he spent on postage, typing, and so on, and that his honorarium for recent contributions was much less than for previous ones. It just may be that this—and the cardinal reason why *Das Wort* ceased publication—was connected with a cutoff of hard currency funds, such as happened with the Verlag 10. Mai.
95. Bredel-Archiv, Sig. 252/14.

Chapter 9

Literature in Exile

For thirteen years, from 1919 to 1931, political material in foreign languages had been published by the Zentral-Völker Verlag.[1] After the firm was disbanded in 1931, the Verlagsgenossenschaft ausländischer Arbeiter (VEGAAR) began publishing, joined in the next few years by five other German-language houses.[2] Of them all, however, VEGAAR remained the largest publisher of German material, although it housed, in addition to the "German sector," first twenty-eight and later a total of forty different "national sections." The few statistics available concerning the size of the operation vary; Goldschmidt[3] puts the number of Germans working in VEGAAR at twenty-five or so, whereas another former editor, Hans Kunzl,[4] estimates that some forty Germans and a total of two hundred workers were in VEGAAR's employ.

The firm was first charged with the task of providing the foreign-worker population in the Soviet Union with reading material: "to familiarize German workers and specialists in the Soviet Union with the theoretical foundation, the political and economic problems, the day-to-day life . . . in the country toward whose construction they are helping."[5] That basic responsibility was still the same in 1934, when one of the German émigrés, a certain Lieben, wrote that VEGAAR brought out literature for workers involved in the "gigantic project of socialist construction." Foreign workers and specialists from the capitalist industrial countries of Europe and America were active in all areas of the Soviet Union, he said, and "all of them are to be familiarized in their own language with the written word, with the most important literature. Above all the classics of Marxism-Leninism." They themselves, claimed Lieben, "demand this literature."[6]

1. Jarmatz, *Exil in der UdSSR*, p. 231.
2. Erich Wendt and Fritz Schälicke, according to what former editor Hans Goldschmidt told me, had been charged with responsibility for organizing VEGAAR.
3. Personal information from Hans Goldschmidt.
4. Personal information from Hans Kunzl.
5. Jarmatz, *Exil in der UdSSR*, p. 233.
6. Lieben, "Autor, Verlag und Buch," in *Bulletin* Nr. 2 (1935), hg. von der Kommission

But soon after its inception, VEGAAR took on added responsibilities—the publication in several languages of Comintern proceedings, ECCI protocols, major addresses (such as speeches given at the Seventh World Congress), translations of official Soviet documents, Stalin's pronouncements, and other pamphlets and propaganda connected with the Soviet Union and international communism. Some of these same materials also appeared in VEGAAR's camouflaged western branches, the Ring-Verlag in Zurich and the Editions Prométhée in Strasbourg. Not only did VEGAAR publish for the Comintern, in many cases it seems to have answered directly to it, even though, ironically, a significant number of its full and part-time employees, as a former editor put it, were "ostracized Comintern big wigs" who had lost their previous positions.[7] Heinz Neumann, for instance, Felix Wolf (Rakov), the former secret Comintern emissary,[8] and Erich Wollenberg worked for a time in VEGAAR. A few other employees whose names are known include Rose Wittfogel, Elinor Lipper, Ernst Noffke, Anne Bernfeld-Schmückle, Vali Adler (the daughter of Alfred Adler), and Hilde Angarova. Later on, perhaps only after VEGAAR had vanished in 1938 and reappeared as the Verlag für fremdsprachige Literatur, Otto Braun, Otto Winzer, and Wilhelm Zaisser joined the staff.

Richard Krebs, a Soviet national,[9] managed the entire house, assisted until 1936 by Erich Wendt. The German sector of VEGAAR was evidently first headed by a Swiss named Egli, who left for Sweden, however, at the beginning of 1933.[10] Otto Bork (Unger), a Communist from Hamburg, then took over, and VEGAAR soon began publishing the works of German exiles, principally, but not only, those living in the Soviet Union. VEGAAR was eventually shut down in 1938, probably in connection with the purges, which had decimated its staff, but it had still managed in eight years of existence to put out some 118 books. After VEGAAR was liquidated, the German Section of the Soviet Writers' Union reportedly asked the press department of the Soviet Central Committee and Georgi Dimitroff to set up a new

---

zum Studium der sowjetdeutschen Literatur beim Organisationskomitee des Unions-verbandes der Schriftsteller in Moskau, TsGALI, 631/12/56/67.

7. Information from private source.

8. For Wolf's earlier role in the Comintern, see Lazitch and Drachkovitch, *Lenin and the Comintern*, 1:150.

9. According to Goldschmidt, Krebs (who reportedly had connections with Osip Pjatnitskij) was a Jew from the Caucasus. Another editor thought he was of Baltic, Czech, or Sudeten German extraction (information from private source).

10. Personal information from Hans Goldschmidt.

publishing operation. The formation of Mezhdunarodnaja kniga resulted, which brought out some forty-six books, largely in 1939 through 1941. Another venture, the Verlag für fremdsprachige Literatur, seems to have been launched in 1939 to fill the void left by VEGAAR; it printed around forty-five books, most of them after 1942. Two provincial houses also specialized in exile literature: the Staatsverlag der nationalen Minderheiten in Kiev and Kharkov (thirty-six books, the bulk of them in 1935 to 1939, though the firm had operated at least since 1932) and the Deutscher Staatsverlag in Engels (twenty-six books between 1933 and 1938, with a few publications during 1939).[11]

The internal editorial practices of these houses remain something of a mystery. Only VEGAAR's performance record can be looked at in terms of the treatment accorded Oskar Maria Graf and Willi Bredel. In summer 1934 Graf completed his novel *Der Abgrund*, and in November Wieland Herzfelde took the manuscript for publication by the Malik-Verlag. Problems arose, however, because Herzfelde had many of his books printed in the Soviet Union by contract with VEGAAR; part of each edition was then bound and released for sale in the USSR under the VEGAAR imprint while remaining copies (frequently unbound) were shipped to Herzfelde in Prague. He then prepared them for sale as Malik products. The procedure ran into trouble in the case of Graf's novel when Comintern-KPD watchdogs, whose approval of VEGAAR books was evidently mandatory, objected to extensive passages in *Der Abgrund*; Graf resisted the changes, and publication of the novel was held up for the ensuing sixteen months. Finally, in April 1936, Herzfelde, in Moscow at the time, was given to understand that everything was finally in order and that the book would be printed in the course of the month. This is what he then reported to Graf.[12]

The apparent breakthrough probably occurred because Graf had given in to the pressure. He later told Bredel that he had expressed his "assent to all changes."[13] If that was the case, then the final obstacles the book still faced were technical rather than political. In early May Herzfelde wrote Graf from Moscow that printing was scheduled

11. Bibliographical information is taken from Halfmann, "Bibliographien und Verlage der deutschsprachigen Exil-Literatur 1933 bis 1945," 4:189–294, especially pp. 236–38 and 282. There is a partial bibliography of Russian translations of German exile literature in Motyleva, *Nemetskaja literatura v borbe protiv fashizma*.
12. Herzfelde to Graf, 3 April 1936, TsGALI, 631/12/141/326.
13. Graf to Bredel, 1 July 1936, TsGALI, 631/12/141/307.

for completion by the fifteenth; most of the book, in fact, was already set in print, but the edition could not be shipped to Prague, Herzfelde reckoned, until late June.[14] This was only the beginning of new delays. On 7 June Graf asked Bredel sarcastically if the Stakhanov system of shock workers had not yet been introduced into VEGAAR,[15] and a few weeks later he lost his temper completely. Herzfelde wrote Bredel at the time that it was "scandalous that the book is still nowhere to be seen. It was to have been printed on the fifteenth of May; six weeks have passed since. . . . You want to scream when you see how none other than the most decent people are treated."[16] The same day Graf sent a furious letter to Moscow, telling Bredel that he had gradually become thoroughly annoyed over the matter. After he had consented to all changes in the text, he said, Herzfelde had been given the assurance that the book would be printed up and could appear at the end of June. "Since then Wieland and I have been writing VEGAAR uninterruptedly; but the press simply doesn't respond and is doing nothing. . . . And then it's expected that I preside here over the popular front committee! I, who am being treated like this! I cannot understand the tricks being played on me and Wieland by VEGAAR."[17] The next day Graf vented his anger again in a letter to Becher:

> Since VEGAAR, in spite of its solemn promise to supply
> Wieland with fair proofs of *Abgrund* by mid-May, has again
> sent nothing and again refuses to answer urgent letters, I am
> gradually beginning to discern a pattern. I can no longer
> put up with the damage being done to me; nor do I intend to
> be treated any longer as a shoe-shine boy. I am finally going
> to raise hell. First and foremost I am going to tell the whole
> story to Heinrich and Thomas Mann, Bruno Frank, Feucht-
> wanger, and others so that the public finally learns how an
> honest anti-Fascist writer is treated in the context of the
> popular front. I am supposed to act here in the ČSR, so to
> speak, as the chairman of popular front work and come out
> in favor of it even as my own people make a liar of me and
> provoke me to rage. I've had just about all I'm going to
> take.[18]

14. Herzfelde to Graf, 5 May 1936, TsGALI, 631/12/141/320.
15. Graf to Bredel, 7 June 1936, TsGALI,631/12/141/314.
16. Herzfelde to Bredel, 1 July 1936, TsGALI, 631/12/143/127.
17. Graf to Bredel, 1 July 1936, TsGALI, 631/12/141/307.
18. Graf to Becher, 2 July 1936, TsGALI, 631/12/66/1.

The book eventually did come out; at the end of October 1936 Graf reported that the Malik-Verlag edition had been published. Had the final set of obstacles from April to October involved only technical matters? Whatever changes Graf made in his manuscript evidently failed to go far enough to satisfy the censors in Moscow, for he apparently had insisted all along that some objectionable passages be left alone,[19] which may well have caused the last seven-month delay.[20] This appears the more likely in view of the expurgation of the Russian version. Graf was surprised in May 1936 to hear rumors that a translation of *Abgrund* had already come out in print, and he asked Bredel to inquire about it. Bredel had not heard anything about a translation either, but he soon discovered that *Der Abgrund* had indeed been translated and published *in 1935*.[21] This had all been done behind Graf's back, one assumes because the Goslitizdat Russian version revealed deleted passages that had been construed as offensive or unflattering to Communists or communism.[22] With an expurgated text, the Russians ran into no difficulty getting the book out in less than a year, including translation time.

No sooner had the *Abgrund* controversy died down than the whole business started anew with Graf's *Anton Sittinger*, a novel he had finished before the publication of *Abgrund*. In February 1937 Graf told Bredel that *Sittinger* was in the VEGAAR offices and that VEGAAR had not answered any letters for ages.[23] A few months later he wrote, "VEGAAR is again leaving us completely up in the air."[24] This time it seems that Herzfelde, after trying the procedure followed with *Abgrund* once more, had somewhere along the way given up when it became obvious that VEGAAR was again dragging its feet. So he went ahead and had the edition printed in the West, from which VEGAAR ordered three thousand unbound copies for distribution in the USSR. Then, in September 1937, Graf wrote Mikhail Apletin, the assistant to Koltsov in the foreign office of the Soviet Writers' Union, that VEGAAR had

19. Herzfelde to Graf, 5 May 1936, TsGALI, 631/12/141/320.
20. One wonders if the censors were not trying to force Graf indirectly to withdraw the manuscript and publish it elsewhere.
21. Bredel to Graf, 20 May 1936, and Graf to Bredel, 7 June 1936, TsGALI, 631/12/141/318 and 314.
22. One small example. This sentence was deleted from the translation: "In the Communist party he met strange people, hardened, irreconcilable haters of Social Democrats with whom one couldn't talk" (Graf, *Der Abgrund*, p. 195).
23. Graf to Bredel, 9 February 1937, TsGALI, 631/12/141/282.
24. Graf to Ljudmila Schejnina and Bredel, no date [ca. April 1937], TsGALI, 631/12/141/280.

acknowledged its order of three thousand copies but had afterwards fallen silent again and not paid Graf his royalties.[25] Apletin responded that he had "intervened," clearing up the problem, and that Graf could hear of the results "from Wieland."[26] Again, nothing happened, and Graf told Apletin in another letter that Herzfelde had not heard a word from VEGAAR. Furthermore, in spite of his many reminders and regardless of the fact that the three thousand unbound copies of *Sittinger* had long since been sent, Herzfelde had no idea where he stood. Graf too had written VEGAAR, imploring them to fill him in on what was happening and to send him his royalties. "So far everything has been in vain. I am genuinely speechless to characterize that kind of behavior by VEGAAR. . . . The affair has gone on for almost half a year; in the course of that much time you can lose your mind."[27] *Anton Sittinger* eventually came out in 1937 in the Malik-Verlag edition, but there never was a VEGAAR version, and it is unclear what became of the three thousand unbound copies.[28]

In the case of *Anton Sittinger*, the content of the book was probably not the cause of the problems; these difficulties and others in 1937 and 1938 far more likely resulted directly and indirectly from the purges. By 1937 these were in full bloom, with VEGAAR having become something of a prime target for the NKVD. Otto Bork, according to Hans Goldschmidt,[29] was a nervous and timid sort, and there seem to have been delays and other instances of inefficiency in VEGAAR for the simple reason that no one was willing to accept responsibility for final decisions. Today's VEGAAR author could too easily become tomorrow's enemy of the people, leading to charges of insufficient vigilance or, far worse, charges against individual VEGAAR editors. Vali Adler reportedly told Susanne Leonhard about work in VEGAAR, "Keep your hands off; it is like dancing on eggs."[30] She was right. Adler disappeared in February 1937, the year that brought the arrests of many others, including VEGAAR chief Krebs and German sector head Bork.[31]

Others suffered from VEGAAR's slipshod editorial practices. Willi Bredel, for one, complained in a letter to Krebs that his concentration

---

25. Graf to Apletin, 17 September 1937, TsGALI, 631/12/66/13.
26. Apletin to Graf, 27 September 1937, TsGALI, 631/12/66/14.
27. Graf to Apletin, 4 October 1937, TsGALI, 631/12/66/11.
28. A Russian translation appeared in 1939.
29. Personal information from Hans Goldschmidt.
30. Leonhard, *Gestohlenes Leben*, p. 61.
31. See Chapter 11, p. 324 for more on arrests within VEGAAR. An example from a different but related context of the dangers involved in the publishing business:

camp account *Die Prüfung* was appearing six months behind sched-
ule.[32] In Bredel's case VEGAAR's sheer ineptitude, rather than political problems of the type Graf encountered, was probably at fault.[33]
Nevertheless, his experience, combined with what he knew about *Der
Abgrund*, led Bredel to look elsewhere to publish his new novel, *Dein
unbekannter Bruder*. In June 1936 he explained to Herzfelde that his
pamphlet *Edgar André* had still not seen the light of day, even though
it had been tagged as a top-priority item in VEGAAR. He could howl
with rage, he said, asking: "What's going to happen when I finish my
book at the end of the year, with twenty times the number of pages. . . .
Under no circumstances will I allow dozens of authorized and unau-
thorized people to tamper with it before printing." He explained to
Herzfelde, "After thorough consultation with you, I want to confront
all the others with a 'fait accompli'; otherwise I'll go crazy before it has
been pushed through everywhere." By no means did he want to wait
two years for its publication. Bredel had an explanation for the difficulties
in VEGAAR: "I have the impression that something is not in order
there. Some sort of strange friends are at work. But, as I say, that is
purely my own personal opinion; I haven't the slightest concrete bit of
evidence."[34] On one point he was clear: the novel was to appear out-

---

writing on 27 August 1936 in the *Literaturnaja gazeta*, I. Bespalov, head of the State
Publishing House (Goslitizdat), called for vigilance in all Soviet publishing firms. Occurrences of the following nature had to be avoided: in Henri Barbusse's book on Stalin the
word "many" (*mnogo*) had surreptitiously been changed to "few" (*malo*), giving the
entire phrase a "counterrevolutionary meaning." In such a manner the "masked enemies" tried to achieve their goals, and vigilance was called for to prevent it (I. Bespalov,
"Bditelnost v izdatelstvakh," *Literaturnaja gazeta*, 27 August 1936). No doubt some
poor typesetter disappeared, as did Bespalov, by the way, some time later. Incidentally,
Barbusse also included this comment in his book: "By means of machinations, trickery,
corruption, or else by secret service and crime . . . or by killing one's enemies in bed at
night (two at a time), one might become, and remain, king or emperor, or duce, or
chancellor—one might even become Pope. But one could never become Secretary of
the Communist Party by any such methods" (Barbusse, *Stalin*, p. 148).
32. Bredel to Krebs, 21 March 1935, TsGALI, 631/13/69/54. Andor Gábor termed the
delay in the publication of the Russian translation of *Die Prüfung* "strange," not the
result of " 'objective difficulties,' " and hinted that there had been sinister reasons for it
(MTA, Gábor Andor-Hagyaték, Ms. 4479/87).
33. Though, on the other hand, the second edition of *Die Prüfung* had been truncated
voluntarily by Bredel at the request of Hermann Schubert (Max Richter). "Enclosed
find the second edition of *Prüfung*. All the passages you objected to have been changed"
(Bredel to Richter [Vertreter der Deutschen Sektion in der Komintern], 21 June 1935,
TsGALI, 631/13/69/80).
34. Bredel to Herzfelde, 25 June 1936, TsGALI, 631/12/143/133. Herzfelde disagreed.
"By the way," he answered Bredel, "I don't believe in the presence and activity of any
'friends.' A good publisher can only do a certain quantity of work; if he is given more,

side of Russia by the next summer. He did not "give a damn," he said, about VEGAAR's promises and obligations and had not the slightest desire to become "the second *Abgrund*." He could not work that way, he finished, and the *André* matter had driven him to the brink of insanity.[35]

Herzfelde accepted the plan; he had no intention of having a manuscript printed in the Soviet Union again, and he told Bredel that he would try to get *Dein unbekannter Bruder* published as rapidly as possible. He also advised Bredel, "If you consider a political check necessary, try to get it there while you write the book, independently of V[EGAAR]."[36] This advice Bredel heeded, telling Herzfelde that he would have the novel checked out through his connections with "local friends," that is, in the Comintern; what he simply did not want was the VEGAAR route.[37] In November 1936 Bredel notified Herzfelde that the manuscript would be sent soon since "our political club friends, the most important, will have read it in a few days."[38] As things eventually turned out, though, VEGAAR somehow found out about the novel anyway and wanted, or so the press told Bredel, to print a huge edition and send some of the copies to Herzfelde. Bredel was not impressed. "VEGAAR's promises, as firm as they may be, and made by the new directorate,[39] don't move me any longer," he told Herzfelde.[40] But an agreement was evidently reached after all, for in 1937 the novel was copublished in London by Malik and in Moscow by VEGAAR.

What VEGAAR put Graf and Bredel through seems to have been fairly typical. In April 1937 Erich Barlud (Ludwig Barta) complained that he had sent the press a manuscript a year earlier; its arrival had been acknowledged, but he had since heard nothing.[41] A year or so later, F. C. Weiskopf wrote Apletin to tell him: "It is absolutely scandalous how poorly this house [VEGAAR] operates. It could do so much toward supporting writers, in dire straits, who have not cast their lot with the Nazis. It does nothing. Worse than that, it angers,

---

the quality, speed, etc. suffer automatically" (Herzfelde to Bredel, 1 July 1936, TsGALI, 631/12/143/127).

35. Bredel to Herzfelde, 25 June 1936, TsGALI, 631/12/143/133.

36. Herzfelde to Bredel, 1 July 1936, TsGALI, 631/12/143/127.

37. Bredel to Herzfelde, no date, TsGALI, 631/12/143/121.

38. Bredel to Herzfelde, 25 November 1936, TsGALI, 631/12/143/62.

39. Such references to "new directorates" usually meant that the previous heads had been picked up by the NKVD. This may also have just happened to VEGAAR; the months from August 1936 to January 1937, in any case, had witnessed many waves of arrests everywhere.

40. Bredel to Herzfelde, 4 January 1937, TsGALI, 631/12/143/53.

41. Barta to Bredel, 1 April 1937, TsGALI, 631/12/139/83.

discourages, drives them away by not answering, by breach of contract, and by lack of understanding, etc."[42] By this time, however, VEGAAR was nearing the end of its existence. In the course of 1938, reports claimed that VEGAAR had given up publishing just belles lettres;[43] but toward the end of the year (the precise date cannot be pinpointed), VEGAAR was dissolved completely under circumstances that probably paralleled those of the closing of other German organizations such as the Karl Liebknecht School and the Ernst Thälmann Club.[44]

Most of the fiction published in the Soviet Union between 1933 and 1939[45] by German émigrés living there depicted a Germany that the party thought existed in the years 1933 to 1935. Even the occasional stories set in Nazi Germany during later years, say 1936 to 1939, correspond by and large with the party's unjustifiably sanguine view of the situation during the first two or three years of Hitler's rule, that is, before the Comintern and the KPD generally overcame the illusion that National Socialism was going to crumble overnight. But even after the party had disavowed the notion of a "crisis of fascism," the émigré writers continued to portray a Germany on the brink of collapse. Their literary output, in fact, can be reduced to illustrations of a pair of related, illusory concepts defined by Ernst Thälmann back in the pre-Hitler thirties and by Comintern theoretists during the first few years after Hitler came to office: the idea, on the one hand, of the capitalist offensive, and, on the other hand, the notion of a proletarian revolutionary upsurge after several years of the "temporary stabilization of capitalism." This was the dialectic that begot "fascism," as Thälmann had explained in early 1931; that this scheme, concocted back in 1928 and 1929, made little allowance for "Hitler

---

42. Weiskopf to Apletin, 7 May 1938, TsGALI, 631/12/75/12. Martin Andersen Nexö had also complained angrily: "For two years VEGAAR drew things out, which was clear sabotage since we had firm agreements.... I had then hoped that VEGAAR's successor [Mezhdunarodnaja kniga] would get things moving, but I hear nothing from them. What can be done? Can't the foreign commission [foreign office] invoke its authority?" (Andersen Nexö to Apletin, 18 November 1938, TsGALI, 631/12/66/21).

43. For instance, Apletin to Martin Andersen Nexö, 4 September 1938, TsGALI, 631/12/66/19.

44. Erpenbeck/Hilde Leschnitzer to Jan Petersen, 31 March 1939, TsGALI, 631/12/154/214. See Chapter 11 for additional discussion.

45. Émigré writing during 1941 to 1945 is treated in Chapter 12; for reasons of space, any discussion of the handful of novels by Bredel, Scharrer, or others written and published in the USSR has been omitted; there is little in them anyway that differs from the points made about the other fiction.

fascism" did not change Communist thinking in the least after 1933. Past misconceptions and errors of judgment were simply ignored, and the party line was altered just enough to represent Hitler's accession to power as a logical continuation of the pre-1933 situation. The Communists now claimed to have warned the Germans unceasingly about the possible consequences of this situation in the years leading up to 1933. As Becher wrote many years later, addressing the Germans:

> I can say: nothing was left undone
> To forewarn you, to beseech you:
> "Keep away from disaster! Don't yield to your delusions!"
> But your ears were deaf to the truth.[46]

Thälmann had emphasized in 1931 that, "as a counterresponse to the revolutionary upsurge during the [capitalist] crisis, there is occurring a crisis and fascistization of the bourgeois parties, including Social Democracy." This fascistization, Thälmann had said, was the "antithesis of the dialectical process." But he had added—and this is the notion embodied in some form or other in practically every story published in Russia by the émigrés—that "if the German bourgeoisie is now on the verge of implementing a Fascist dictatorship, this is not an indication of bourgeois strength, nor of proletarian weakness or defeat." He had concluded that "a certain historical process manifests itself here, that the revolution, with its forward development, produces simultaneously a higher stage of counterrevolution, and, if it can overcome [the counterrevolution], may ripen into its most mature expression of strength."[47] The writers took this dictum and wrapped it in fictional garb, picturing inside Germany the crisis of fascism (decaying imperialist monopoly capitalism) and the imminence of proletarian revolution. It was as if the writers were heeding the admonitions of socialist realism to depict "reality in its revolutionary development."[48] "The Reds are coming" now became the clarion call of an upbeat (that is, Stalinist), happy-ending literature that evoked impressions of a country about to collapse as Communists waited in the wings.

The writers and the politicians never really grasped the nature of Hitler's mass backing. Nor could they, really, given the abstract, theoretical schemata within which every phenomenon connected with "fas-

---

46. Becher, *Die hohe Warte*, pp. 61–63.
47. Thälmann, *Volksrevolution über Deutschland*, pp. 25–26.
48. The replacement of RAPP's "dialectical materialist creative method" by the emergence of "socialist realism" is treated in Chapter 10.

cism" had been pigeonholed. Party theorists all wrote for the official Communist press the required disquisitions on the class nature of National Socialism, bending the truth of the real situation (when they knew what it was) to fit the theory or, in the absence of accurate information from inside the country, merely writing blind analyses that had to accord with the facts as their theories told them. Illusions were bred from one article to another as the general theory was allowed to develop only within a closed circle of givens. After their emigration to the USSR, the writers' understanding of events in Germany was thus the product of this theory, what they read in their own party press. Without any other source of information, they went on to create a literature that did little more than fictionalize leading articles, party decrees, resolutions, theses, and theoretical explanations of National Socialism, and none of these fathomed what had actually transpired in Germany. Shut off from fresh infusions of unbiased information, which might have induced them to think more independently, the writers were bound to produce "realistic" fiction as hopelessly out of touch with reality as the party was itself.

But this is not to say that in cases where a particular writer knew or suspected that things were different he would not willingly mold his writing to conform to the official view. The émigrés were not ones to let reality stand in the way of a good theory, and theory had it that National Socialism and Hitler were representatives and marionettes of big business, of monopoly capitalism. Theoretically, then, there was nothing to worry about, at least not in the long run. Since the NSDAP acted patently against the interests of the masses, it only stood to reason that the party's petty bourgeois backers, eventually realizing the nature of the "capitalist offensive" directed at them, would desert the NSDAP, join the ranks of class-conscious masses hitherto held in check only by Nazi terror, and overthrow the Fascists. There were really two Germanies, thought the Communists, Hitler's Germany and the anti-Fascist Germany being restrained solely through unbridled terror. Broadly based support of Hitler, adulation of the Führer, enthusiasm for the new Germany, total consolidation of Hitler's power, a strong nation unified and mobilized behind its leaders—none of these existed in theory so they could not exist in reality.

The literature of the émigrés therefore never went beyond the 1933–35 party proclamations of a "new phase of revolutions." To these writers fascism remained now and throughout the coming years nothing but an expression of ruling-class vulnerability, "the dying quivers of capitalism," as Fritz Heckert had seen it, "not its 'stabilization.'" Yes, there had been a "temporary setback of the proletariat," but the workers had "not capitulated and will not capitulate to fascism." The Communists, even in the face of unparalleled Fascist terror, had reorganized and regrouped with "comparatively minimal losses"; the party's fighting spirit had not been broken, and the Communists would lead the proletariat on to final victory over fascism and capitalism. "We are approaching the revolution," said the Communists.[49] This is the tenor of émigré fiction, and most of the stories fit the pattern with essentially interchangeable plots.

In *Januar 1933 in Berlin*, Berta Lask (writing under the pseudonym Gerhard Wieland) pictures the spontaneous formation of a united front between rank-and-file Communists and socialists. The front handily disrupts and disperses a Nazi demonstration shortly before Hitler comes to office.[50] In fact, Berlin is a city where storm troopers dare show their faces only in company with city police, who protect them from hostile proletarians. "Show them a bit of a united front," says one worker, "and the entire Nazi specter evaporates" (11). In another scene Lask characterizes a Nazi rally: "The National Socialist leaders gave their speeches at Bulowplatz. They made it quick; the atmosphere was too threatening. Their speeches were continually interrupted by the loud strains of the Internationale and cries of Red Front" (46). How strong Hitler's opponents are, writes Lask; the streets overflow with workers, Communists, Social Democrats, Reichsbanner members, independents. What are the Social Democratic leaders waiting for? asks a socialist worker. Why can they not seize the chance, take over power, and send the reactionaries to hell? "When will the signal come to attack?" (47). But Social Democratic leaders lack the will to fight, and the Nazis take over, or so writes Lask. But no need to worry. Lask has a scene in her story where Ernst Thälmann says in a speech: "We are witnessing a shift in the balance of class power in favor of proletarian revolution" (62). The party is growing, Lask concludes, the number of those demanding and reading illegal Communist newspapers is so high it is hard to imagine. "If the Gestapo knows it, they must be scared to death" (81).

Gustav von Wangenheim, who used the pseudonym Hans Huss, wrote a one-act play, *Helden im Keller*, that incorporates the same message:[51] The German proletariat and its avant-garde the Communist party were fighting heroically, regardless of persecution and cas-

49. See the discussion in Chapter 4.
50. Lask [Gerhard Wieland], *Januar 1933 in Berlin*. Subsequent page citations appear in the text in parentheses.
51. Von Wangenheim [Hans Huss], *Helden im Keller*. Subsequent page citations appear in the text in parentheses.

ualties. "Time and again the cry resounded: 'The Reds are alive!'" (5). Leaflets were being disseminated, the *Rote Fahne* published, spot demonstrations staged. The "party of the class-conscious proletariat" found hundreds of ways to approach the masses of workers, the petty bourgeoisie, even proletarians in SA uniforms. Wangenheim's play is set in a tavern where storm troopers drink and argue on the ground floor while arrested Communists are tortured in the cellar below. All talk revolves around the question of the "Reds." "The Reds are everywhere" is the general assumption. The SA too abounds with discontented elements; one character remarks, "It's only a matter of luck when you encounter an SA proletarian who has not deserted to the Reds" (62).

The proletarian class knew that it would emerge triumphant, wrote Albert Hotopp. "In spite of unprecedented terror and cruel repression, the battle will never let up." There would be victims, of course, but the German proletariat was fighting "uninterruptedly under the leadership of the glorious German Communist Party against the bourgeoisie." The Hitler regime would never succeed in destroying the party, for the working-class will to victory surmounted all obstacles. "The KPD is alive and will continue to live"; hundreds of thousands were organized fighters. "The party is anchored in the masses. Millions sympathize with the party. The influence of the party is growing. The masses will fight and the party will lead them on to victory."[52] Nor were these "millions" comprised solely of proletarians; "the majority of the population was with the Communists."[53]

The party had suffered only a temporary setback, explained S. Gles, telling of a "comrade" being sent abroad because the Gestapo was on to him. "It was damned difficult to leave the comrades. I don't want to say that our morale was low. We were making an organized retreat, but a retreat nonetheless."[54] All the writers admitted that the party had suffered blows, but none of them even hinted at the crippling effect of the party's losses. Hotopp "quotes" this compliment paid the Communists in the Nazi press: "There is no doubt," read Hotopp's article, "that the Communists have managed to create a new directorate from fresh functionaries as yet unknown to the police. They've changed their methods; they are entirely new. The police have proof that . . . entire local cells of Communists are intact."[55]

52. Hotopp, "Signal zum Gefecht," in *Die Unbesiegbaren*, pp. 2–5.
53. Hotopp, "SA-Mann Neidel," in ibid., p. 27.
54. S. Gles, "Bis zur letzten Minute," in *Deutschland erwacht!*, p. 39.
55. Hotopp, "Genosse R.", in *Die Unbesiegbaren*, p. 33.

When they did speak of the arrest of Communists, the writers often did so in conjunction with depictions of staunch party men resisting horrible beatings in Nazi cells and concentration camps. None of these arrests, torturings, murders, and so on, however, signaled to the émigrés a consolidation of Nazi power. "Today the brown beasts were still stronger. Today! But tomorrow?" asked Helmut Weiss (using the pseudonym Hans Wendt) in a story about a young man who refuses to provide the Gestapo with the name of his party contact and is supported in his heroic resistance by his politically immature mother.[56] Positive that nazism must surely collapse and communism triumph, the émigrés put the same conviction into the minds of the Nazis. Says one Gestapo officer to his informant: "Always another Communist taken care of. Always one more. Can a government remain in power that way? Can we wipe them all out? Be honest, you don't believe it any more than I; you'd have to shoot or imprison virtually every worker." The SS man lowers his voice and whispers, "Tell me, do you believe a worker today who cries out 'Heil Hitler?' I still say that Communism . . . is unavoidable; the stupidity and greed of the capitalists will see to that."[57]

Three or four years after Hitler's accession to power, the KPD was still intact and operating smoothly, damaged at times but never prostrated by the secret police. One of Fritz Erpenbeck's fictional Communists returns promptly to underground activity upon his release from a concentration camp. Back in the fold, he thinks to himself: "It filled him with pride and joy that in the third year of Hitler's dictatorship the illegal party work had been firmly reestablished and had reached into such important enemy strongholds."[58]

Although most of the émigré fiction underscores the imminence of Hitler's fall and a Communist takeover, virtually none of the writers make any statement about the Communist government expected to follow. This had nothing to do with any consideration for non-Communist opponents of Hitler, nor was it the writers' way of supporting the party's post-1936 slogan for a "democratic republic." None of this thinking and, with few exceptions, very little about a united or popular front finds a way into the émigrés' writing. The expectation that Hitler would soon be toppled and a Communist proletarian dictatorship installed (Soviet power) was still so much a part of the writers' understanding of the situation that it never occurred to them to spell

---

56. Weiss [Hans Wendt], "Die Mutter," in *Heer im Dunkeln*, p 65.

57. Bredel, "Der Spitzel," in *Der Spitzel und andere Erzählungen*, p. 44.

58. Erpenbeck, "Der Fingerabdruck," in *Deutsche Schicksale*, p. 68.

out what the party planned for Germany after Hitler's downfall. It was not a question of intentional deception of popular front partners; rather, the émigrés seemingly saw no cause to mention the obvious: Hitler's demise would come through proletarian revolution and his dictatorship would give way to the dictatorship of the proletariat. J. R. Becher, by way of exception, did utter the phrase otherwise conspicuously absent in the prose. His poem "Traum von Räte-Deutschland" describes a dream:

> In all these days
> I've thought only of Germany
> And in the dead of night I dreamt,
> Awakening in the heart of Germany.

Of what did he dream? The Communist liberation of Germany from Nazi rule and Ernst Thälmann's trimphant entry into a Berlin purged of the Nazi plague:

> Comrade Thälmann poised,
> Uplifted by our cries,
> We carried him on our shoulders
> Into the Reich Chancellery.
>
> .   .   .   .
>
> Thus I awoke one night in a dream
> In the heart of Germany
> And saw in my vision
> THE FORMATION OF GERMAN SOVIET POWER.[59]

The collapse of fascism was only a matter of time, the exiles believed. "The Third Reich, regardless of its loud talk of prosperity," wrote Andor Gábor, "is a sick body: wherever your finger presses, it's sensitive."[60] Imagining Germany as the party visualized it, the émigrés believed firmly in the existence inside the country of the two sociopolitical phenomena that did not genuinely exist, namely, the revolutionary upsurge and the crisis of capitalism. Nazism, the émigrés thought, was being undermined by subjective and objective factors. The subjective element, of course, was the presence of a powerful KPD dealing blow after blow to the Fascist edifice. Émigrés concentrated on the subjective element, and the depiction of illegal

---

59. Becher, "Traum von Räte-Deutschland," in *Der Mann, der alles glaubte*, pp. 116–27. Neither here nor elsewhere do I make any attempt to capture whatever poetic qualities émigré poetry might evince.
60. Gábor, "Im Wäldchen abends," in *Die Topfriecher und andere Erzählungen*, p. 106.

Communist underground activity and KPD opposition is the most common theme in their fiction. Supposedly life-threatening to fascism, Communist opposition and resistance is made up of various kinds of political vandalism and agitprop activity: painting slogans and graffiti on walls, printing and circulating leaflets, publishing illegal newspapers, staging spot demonstrations that dispersed before the police arrived, inserting slips of paper with such slogans as "Long Live the KPD" into cigarette packages sold to the populace, and so on ad infinitum. These were the expressions, according to the exiles, of KPD might and of the menace it posed to National Socialism.

Helmut Weiss characterized the act in which rhymed propaganda verses are slipped into cigarette packages. "The three poems were known by every child in the tenement housing of the proletarian quarter. They had a greater effect than many a long leaflet. . . . They hit the mark. The party was able to advance forward."[61] Another of Weiss's stories concerns smuggled newspapers, papers that would "make their way from hand to hand, would clear up unclear minds, make fighters of them. Everything hinged on the papers."[62] The simplest slogans, for instance, "The Fascists Are the Paid Agents of Monopoly Capitalism," were suddenly able to open eyes, win converts, solidify resistance. Somewhere in Germany the name Lenin is suddenly spotted on five kites flying high in the sky.[63] Gles, writing about a Nazi labor camp, has the inmates paint "Long Live Lenin" on a wall.[64] One of Hotopp's Communists carves "Free Thälmann" on the soles of his shoes, painting them somehow so that he leaves the words stamped all over the pavement.[65] Gábor thought of an unusual twist for one of his stories. An SS man comes across the phrase "The KPD is Alive" painted on a building in a proletarian section of town. When a worker chances to emerge from the building, the Nazi forces him to clean up the mess. But several other proletarians come across the scene and capture the Nazi, whom, of course, they do not murder—that would be individual terror, proscribed by the party. He is undressed and tied up instead. When the SS man, who soon unties himself, sees the police approaching, he flees out of embarrassment. But the police, assuming that he is responsible for the slogan on the wall, shoot him down. One less Communist, they say.[66]

61. Weiss [Hans Wendt], "Zigaretten," in *Heer im Dunkeln*, p. 49.
62. Weiss [Hans Wendt], "Weg über die Grenze," in ibid., p. 32.
63. Weiss [Hans Wendt], "Ostwind," in ibid., pp. 155–56.
64. Gles, "Antreten," in *Deutschland erwacht!*, p. 47.
65. Hotopp, "Auf sprechenden Sohlen," in *Die Unbesiegbaren*, p. 44.
66. Gábor, "Die Treppe," in *Die Rechnung und andere Erzählungen*, p. 50.

There were frequent witnesses to Communist bravery, ordinary Germans who could only shake their heads in amazement and admiration. "Those guys are something else," say some bystanders in an S. Gles story, watching Communists hand out leaflets in broad daylight; "no Hitler will get the best of them!" Gles concluded: "They know: the Red Front is alive and fighting!"[67] Hotopp portrays Communists handing out leaflets in a moving train. "In the car there were vocal discussions about the courage and inventiveness of the Communists and about the political situation."[68] In another story, Hotopp pictures several young Communists as they sing the Internationale at a train station, disappearing before the police arrive. Onlooking citizens remark, "Those are Communists, of course; they're quite courageous."[69] The Gestapo, on the other hand, is comprised of bumbling idiots. In the darkness of an air-raid practice the words WITH THE KPD AGAINST HITLER AND WAR are scrawled on a door. "The Nazis raved in impotent rage. The proletarians looked at the writing on the wall. As yet they were still silent. But the silence was a danger. A threat. Like a clenched fist."[70]

Nothing fazed Communists. Those thrown into concentration camps and released a few years later invariably return to pick up their illegal activity where they had left off. In a story by Erpenbeck, Wilm Nedderfehn arrives back in his home village after three years in a camp to discover that with few exceptions the entire village was anti-Nazi and that conditions for farmers in the Third Reich had become unbearable.[71] Wilm then assists in an open and successful act of rebellion against the small band of Nazi officials in the village.[72] To the terror ordinary Communists respond with raw courage and indomitable spirits. An old Communist shouts "Long Live the Party" as storm troopers barge into his apartment and, in front of his wife, throw him from the window to his death below.[73] In Bredel's "Das Experiment," a high Nazi official, visiting a concentration camp, admires a young Communist who stands by his convictions. His release is ordered as an "experiment," whereupon the young man promptly returns to his

67. Gles, "Schichtwechsel," in *Deutschland erwacht!*, p. 122.
68. Hotopp, "Bolschewistische Bazillenträger," in *Die Unbesiegbaren*, p. 38.
69. Hotopp, "Genosse R.," in ibid., p. 35.
70. Weiss [Hans Wendt], "Die Parole," in *Heer im Dunkeln*, p. 42.
71. Erpenbeck explained that the farmers in Nazi Germany were forced to deliver their products to the state at fixed state prices. His knowledge of how things were done on Soviet collective farms was evidently deficient.
72. Erpenbeck, "Heimkehr," in *Deutsche Schicksale*, pp. 173–233.
73. Hotopp, "Das Ende eines Kämpfers," in *Die Unbesiegbaren*, p. 42.

home and reorganizes the local Communist group in his street. Soon "the party cell of the [Communist] Youth League was alive, active, and growing."[74] The man is eventually re-arrested, and this time the Nazis murder him.

In émigré fiction the presence in the party of paid agents, Gestapo informants who had infiltrated the KPD, presents no insurmountable difficulties. Story after story sets forth in detail the ingenuity of Communists in ridding their ranks of police agents. Erpenbeck writes about a Communist who is ordered by the party to arrange a secret high-level meeting of KPD functionaries in the office of a sympathetic confectioner. After the Communist arranges for the meeting, he talks with the confectioner and it dawns on him that the man is a plant, a police agent. But the Communist cannot warn the party because he meets only at predetermined times with one other Communist, and the next contact is scheduled for after the conference. So he places an ad in the paper, in the name of the confectioner, announcing the availability of jobs; prospective workers were to appear for interviews the same day and time of the KPD conference. Because most of Berlin was unemployed, or so Erpenbeck thought, a huge crowd looking for work naturally gathered at just the right time, providing the cover for Communist officials to escape the police trap.[75]

Bredel also wrote about an informant, but varied the stock interpretation. Under the influence of his study of Marx, Engels, and Lenin, this particular agent develops sympathies for the aspirations and goals of communism, even though he lacks the courage to break with the NSDAP and to disclose his past role as an informant to the party he now admires. After Hitler comes to office, many of the Communists whom the agent Petzold had befriended are arrested and some murdered. Driven to suicide by his bad conscience, he leaves behind a note addressed both to his Nazi superiors and to his party comrades. To the former Petzold writes: "You have done me a great service. I have come to recognize that Communists are not criminals, subhumans, but rather the only ones who . . . fight for the happiness of working people." To the latter he says: "Comrades, you are stronger than you yourselves can imagine, you will triumph."[76]

Communists in prison or concentration camps displayed raw courage. Dora Wentscher, in *Die Schule der Grausamkeit*, tells of a young SA man who beats a Communist in an SA jail and puts out one of his

74. Bredel, "Das Experiment," in *Der Spitzel*, p. 56.
75. Erpenbeck, "Ein Mann allein," in *Deutsche Schicksale*, pp. 3–35.
76. Bredel, "Der Spitzel," in *Der Spitzel*, p. 49.

eyes. Several years later the SA man, now an important SS official, crosses paths with the man in a Nazi courtroom, where he holds forth bravely about the inevitability of a Communist victory over fascism.[77] Gábor went a step further with this particular theme and contrasted Communist fortitude under pressure with Social Democratic weakness. In one story he sketches an SA beating of an imprisoned Communist Youth League member caught handing out leaflets, a beating the young man endures heroically.[78] He follows it up with a long story about the arrest and internment in a concentration camp of an elderly SPD functionary wholly incapable of any resistance whatsoever. He manages only one act of opposition when, broken in spirit and released from camp, he kills the camp commander, who was trying to bilk him out of his life savings. But the Social Democrat no longer possesses the strength to take the struggle further and capitulates by committing suicide. Although he had established contact with Communists, taking the first step, so to speak, on the road to a genuine anti-Fascist position, he was powerless to follow it any further.[79]

Hans Günther also wrote about a Social Democrat, though in a different situation. He chronicles the successful transformation of a passive socialist worker, who is molded by experienced, patient Communists into an active anti-Fascist ready to make common cause with Communists. Bertram, the socialist, is evicted from his apartment when he falls behind in rent. Communists and socialists immediately rally to his aid in a united front demonstration, but a big capitalist has the smaller entrepreneur responsible for Bertram's eviction arrested in a demagogic show of the new "socialism." Back in his apartment, Bertram falls for the trickery, believing that there is something to the notion of *Volksgemeinschaft* after all. A few weeks later, however, he receives a letter from the big capitalist ordering him to pay his rent within three weeks or face eviction. Now Bertram finally sees the light, grasps the fact that there was nothing to the Nazi talk of a commonality of interests among the people, and joins up with the Communists. He has learned his lesson: "That us Social Democratic workers got to hold together, do or die, with you Communists. That's our only hope."[80] Together, in a united front from below, Communists and socialists plan a strategy to fight Bertram's upcoming eviction.

All these stories characterize the subjective threat to fascism, the

77. Wentscher, *Die Schule der Grausamkeit*.
78. Gábor, "Ein Glas Wasser," in *Die Rechnung*, p. 132.
79. Gábor, "Die Rechnung," in *Die Rechnung*, pp. 142–200.
80. Günther, *In Sachen gegen Bertram*, p. 70.

revolutionary upsurge. The objective danger, as the exiles saw it, was the Nazis' utter failure to manage the country's economy. The Germany portrayed in the émigré fiction is a country caught in the throes of a profound economic crisis, the crisis of capitalism. Widespread unemployment, absence of goods in the stores, hunger, suicide, bankruptcy for small merchants and store owners, wage reductions in the factories (contrasted with higher prices for food, housing, and transportation)—all these conspired to turn the population against the Nazis. Here too theory supplanted reality: the émigrés simply could not conceive of a Germany where anyone other than a handful of party bosses, big capitalists, or bank financiers had any hope of a decent existence. Fascism was moribund monopoly capitalism, the final stage of a system disintegrating due to internal contradictions. Economic prosperity or even modest upturns had no place in this scheme of things, and given such unheard-of economic conditions, there could be no mass support or popular enthusiasm for Hitler.

Because Hitler and the NSDAP did the bidding of the big bourgeoisie, there had to be "two Germanies," one of them Nazi, the other opposed to fascism and suppressed by the Gestapo. Helmut Weiss describes a street scene: "Enthusiasm was nowhere to be seen; no one had any. The street was gray and embittered. . . . All the suppressed bitterness of two years surfaced." He writes elsewhere: "Everything was so expensive; groceries grew scarcer, the money didn't stretch far enough. . . . The street was a raging sea. Resentment. Supressed rage. Fiery eyes that expressed the inarticulate—what could cause heads to roll and people to be thrown into Gestapo cellars."[81] Even terror, in the final analysis, was of no avail. An SS division arrives to quell a disturbance, "but they couldn't close mouths, couldn't smother the hate of the proletariat" that burned like a fire which "no brown hangmen could any longer extinguish."[82]

Writing in 1941, Wentscher speaks of concentration camps not capacious enough to take in all the arrested "resisting" elements. "The Gestapo worked feverishly, but those who were dissatisfied and spiteful spoiled everywhere the pasted-on facade of a 'happy Germany.'"[83] Wentscher goes on to characterize the scene in front of a courtroom in which sixteen Communist workers are being tried. The crowd outside mills about. "Their number, which reached into the thou-

81. Weiss [Hans Wendt], "Zwirn," in *Heer im Dunkeln*, pp. 108 and 114.
82. Weiss [Hans Wendt], "Ein paar Schuhe," in ibid., pp. 127–34.
83. Wentscher, *Die Schule der Grausamkeit*, p. 38. Subsequent page citations are in parentheses.

sands, looked for all the world like a demonstration directed against the regime" (39). These were by no means just workers. An onlooking SS man remarks, "The enemies of the Third Reich are in all segments of the population" (47). Inside the courtroom one of the workers, whose eye the SS man had put out five years earlier, is allowed to speak: "The German people cannot budge because they are trapped between guns everywhere." To the Nazis who fill the room he says: "You won't hang on to power. You know that yourselves. . . . After the sixteen of us, more will rise up, smarter, cleverer, sixteen more perhaps, then hundreds and hundreds of thousands and finally everyone— the millions of repressed!" (52–54).

The factories too are full of opposition to fascism; every factory described by the émigrés possessed its smoothly functioning Communist cell, illegal newspaper, and ubiquitous worker solidarity. The employees in one of Gábor's factories commit small acts of sabotage to persuade (successfully) the directors to force an SA man in the factory to remove his offensive uniform.[84] Hotopp tells of a strike in reaction to wage reductions and the arrest of a worker. The previous wage scale is then reinstituted and the "arrested shop foreman" released.[85]

In the cities and towns it is the factory, in the countryside the village that is a breeding ground for antinazism. In "Ein Dorf steht auf" Berta Lask depicts a farming community that, as a result of the government's disastrous, exploitative agricultural policies, musters the will to resist. The people are spurred on by a class-conscious farmer from a neighboring village, who tells the farmers: "It's good that you want to fight, but the farmers can't do it alone. We have to join together with the workers."[86] In June 1934 the village rises in rebellion. When an SS detachment arrives to put down the resistance, it is greeted with the demand for a "free workers' and peasants' government" (38). The SS men open fire, and the farmers charge the police vehicles, putting the police to flight. The thought begins to spread, writes Lask in conclusion, of "fighting alliances throughout the land" (38).

As if all this were not enough to bring Hitler's dictatorship tumbling down, the NSDAP was also threatened by internal disintegra-

---

84. Gábor, "Die Uniform," in *Die Topfriecher*, p. 12. Subsequent page citations are in parentheses.
85. Hotopp, "Solidarität," in *Die Unbesiegbaren*, pp. 52–55.
86. Lask [Gerhard Wieland], "Ein Dorf steht auf," in *Ein Dorf steht auf*, p. 23. Subsequent page citations are in parentheses.

tion: the proletarian elements within the SA were gradually coming to their senses, realizing that they were on the wrong side. Even after the Röhm purge, which seemed to support the notion, many stories continued to reflect the myth of a grave threat to the Nazi regime emanating from within the SA. Gábor came up with a story of a concentration camp prisoner, scheduled to be "shot while escaping," who is escorted from his camp to a different locality by the storm trooper ordered to murder him. Along the way, though, the man confesses, "I am a proletarian," and allows the Communist to make good his escape.[87] Georg Born,[88] in his *Das Tagebuch des SA-Mannes Willi Schröder*,[89] devoted an entire book to an SA story, the complete content of which is summarized in the foreword: a young Berlin worker, unemployed, chances to attend a Hitler rally in 1932 and becomes a storm trooper. At this point, on 5 March 1932, the "diary" of Willi Schröder begins, revealing the "hopes, illusions, and confusion of working people in the Fascist camp, the growing contradiction between their anticapitalist attitudes and the policies of Hitler fascism— the bestial rule of the finance oligarchy." Fortunately, Willi Schröder possesses a sound proletarian instinct, and he grasps the fact that fascism is the deadly enemy of working-class interests and communism their best exponent. As a result of Communist informational work within the SA, Willi Schröder "finds his way to the fighting party of the proletariat." Shot by the Gestapo in December 1934, Willi "dies as a Communist, as one of thousands of heroes of the working class."

The persecution of the Jews is one prominent feature of life in Nazi Germany that rarely shows up in émigré fiction. The few stories written on the subject, though, somehow surpass the quality of the other writing. Erpenbeck's "Gehetzt," for instance, relates how a Jewish woman manages to pass herself off as an Aryan. But during a scene in which Erpenbeck describes the torching of a Jewish home for the aged, she is found out and forced to flee for her life. Only the

---

87. Gábor, "Die Eskorte," in *Die Rechnung*, pp. 107–12.
88. The identity of Georg Born is a mystery. Evidently a pseudonym, Born published two novels as books in Russian (translation?), serialized two others in Soviet periodicals, and saw *Tagebuch des SA-Mannes Willi Schröder* pass through two editions in Russian along with the German version. Who was he? He may perhaps have been a Soviet writer using Born as a pseudonym and writing "anti-Fascist novels." But the manuscript of *Tagebuch* submitted to VEGAAR was an original, not a translation, and the VEGAAR editors who prepared it for publication also puzzled over Born's identity (information from private sources). All that is known for sure is that Born was later denounced in the press and arrested. See Chapter 11 for further discussion.
89. Born, *Tagebuch des SA-Mannes Willi Schröder*.

ending of the story is somewhat forced. Having reached the countryside, she is discovered unconscious by a farmer who takes her in and
hides her from the SA, the hint being that the local population did
not go along with Nazi anti-Semitism.[90] Popular solidarity with the
Jews is only marginally present in Gles's story "Pogrom," which deals
with an SA attack on a Jewish-owned shop, the beating of its owner,
and the murder of his son. While a few workers happen to come by
the scene and show through their facial expressions their objection to
what they see, Gles is otherwise clear about local sentiment: "The
narrow-minded citizenry strolling by . . . sense . . . the need for this
courageous action of scrawling 'Jewish swine' on the store owned by
Moses Kahlmann and for having their national interests defended by
heavily armed storm troopers."[91] The onlookers react to the SA attack: "The public encouraged the fight in front of the store: 'Jewish
swine!'—'Beat him!'—'Croak, Jew!' . . . 'What do the bastards want in
Germany!?' 'Go to Jerusalem!' " (43).

Bredel's "Der Tod des Siegfried Allzufromm" is the best short
piece of fiction he would write in Soviet exile. It is a tale free of any
political message. He tells the story of a middle-aged Jew who com-
mits suicide in the hopes of lessening persecution and improving the
prospects for a bearable future life for his non-Jewish wife and for
their children, who, as half-Jews, he thought, might have an easier
time if they went by their mother's maiden name. After his death his
wife asks: "Why, why? What is the reason for all this?. . . The senselessness, the pointlessness. . . . That's what I don't understand."[92] For
once Bredel offered no pat answers.

Rarely did the writers attempt to capture in their fiction the psychology of a particular Nazi. An exception is Adam Scharrer's *Der
Landsknecht*,[93] a very good story marred only slightly by a few sentences that read as if they had been lifted from a political editorial. The
key to Scharrer's success in drawing a pyschologically persuasive portrait of the farm laborer Joachim, a "Nazi," is the absence of any
notable authorial analysis or intrusion. Joachim's personality and character are not described but characterized by his day-to-day behavior
and by his own spoken and unspoken thoughts in response to events
around him. Scharrer avoids the need to politicize the man by making him, in a certain sense, a nonpolitical person. Joachim is a hateful,

90. Erpenbeck, "Gehetzt," in *Deutsche Schicksale*, p. 171.
91. Gles, "Pogrom," in *Deutschland erwacht!*, p. 41. Subsequent page citations are in
parentheses.
92. Bredel, "Der Tod des Siegfried Allzufromm," in *Der Auswanderer*, p. 35.
93. Scharrer, *Der Landsknecht: Biographie eines Nazi*.

criminally inclined, stupid psychotic who attempts, clumsily, to hide his own meanness and greed behind the occasional Nazi phrase, which he generally does not comprehend. He cares for no one but himself and is thoroughly opportunistic, although his National Socialism is by no means "insincere." He simply lacks the intelligence to feign sincerity for anything. He identifies with National Socialism's message of hate and brutality, and those attributes coincide perfectly with his own private resentments and distrust of others, whom he paranoically assumes are scheming against him. The eternally malcontent, lazy, and jealous Joachim intuitively learned to use National Socialism to his best advantage. He was willing to murder and cheat unscrupulously to satisfy his own needs, convinced that this was in consonance with the spirit of the times. Having spent his entire life in his own inner world of hatred and paranoia, he loses all control of himself when war breaks out a few years later and he is sent to the Eastern front. The story concludes with Joachim murdering Russian civilians at will; their faces remind him of various members from his village who, he thought, had always had it in for him. A Russian bullet eventually does away with him.

Dora Wentscher, in *Die Schule der Grausamkeit*, also undertook something of a psychological portrayal of a Nazi; her portrayal, however, leads nowhere. The original concept had possiblities: it told the story of two seventeen-year old storm troopers learning their trade beating prisoners and Communists and coming to terms with their bad consciences. But here the story becomes muddled because Wentscher is too unskilled to characterize the nature of the doubts and reservations that the young men supposedly experience. She fails even more in explaining the pair's divergent development. As a result of a nighttime conversation, both are arrested and sent to concentration camps. One of them dies from beatings incurred because of his newly found opposition to nazism; the other adapts to the situation and, convincing the authorities of his complete conversion to the cause, manages his own release from camp. He then rises in the ranks of the SA and eventually takes command of a concentration camp himself, now as an SS officer. Wentscher continues in her efforts to recreate the man's thought processes and personal motivation, to separate genuine conviction from careerism. But the story, apart from the standard message of widespread popular opposition to Hitler, makes little sense.

The Soviet Union was dealt with mostly in the poetry,[94] where the

94. Huppert did publish a collection of short stories, sketches, and reportage as a "small

themes of banishment and asylum occasionally find reflection. In Becher's "Der Bericht," for instance, he writes: "Among brave and believing men / I fought to preserve freedom in the Reich. / The German calling I considered deliverance from the evil which threatened the land. / But there came to power the force of evil, / and I was banished from the Reich."[95] In "Dank an die Freunde," Becher couples his exile with an expression of gratitude for the reception given him in the Soviet Union: "Like a brother you took me in, / Gave me everything to assure that my poetry / Would live on. Dark powers wrestled / Me to the ground. They did not prevail, / and I owe this to you."[96] The notion of Soviet Russia as a home, a fatherland, also highlights the poetry. In "Mein Vaterland," Franz Leschnitzer explains that, though he was born in Germany, the country was not his fatherland, at least not yet, and that he would not consider it so until the day "its tormentors" were ousted and it emulated the fatherland in which he now lived. The poem continues:

This Soviet land, it became my fatherland,
This Soviet land, it is my fatherland,
This Soviet land, shall remain my fatherland,
My second, no, my first fatherland.

He concludes that Russia would remain his fatherland even after Germany was free, when "Germany, *you too* are my fatherland!"[97]

Much time and effort was spent writing paeans of praise to the Soviet Union. Becher extolled the USSR as a "human fortress" in the "storm of barbarism,"[98] to take just a few examples, while Weinert lauded the "Fortress of Freedom and Peace," the torch bearer of human rights.[99] Weinert declaimed in another poem:

Workers, peasants of all continents!
Were you to see this work with your own eyes,
Grasp it with your own hand,
You would become a mighty force, and your foot would trample
The weak foundations of world fascism.

---

contribution to the publicistic-literary appreciation of Stalin's Second Five-Year Plan," something of a sequel to his *Sibirische Mannschaft*, which had dealt with the "heroic realization of the First Five-Year Plan" (Huppert, *Flaggen und Flügel*, pp. 378–79).
95. Becher, *Die hohe Warte*, pp. 61–63.
96. Becher, "Dank an die Freunde in der UdSSR," in *Gedichte 1936–1941*, p. 787.
97. Leschnitzer, *Verse*, pp. 8–9.
98. Becher, "Hymne an die UdSSR," in *Gedichte 1936–1941*, pp. 800–801.
99. Weinert, "Lenins Werk," in *Rot Front*, pp. 200–201.

Nothing greater has been done in the world
Than what Lenin's people knowingly created,
Giving life to Stalin's clear plan of construction!
Socialism is alive![100]

The exiles gave orations on the Soviet Union in unison with tributes
to Stalin. Weinert compiled an entire collection of Stalin poems translated from various languages of the Soviet Union. He added a few
hymns of his own to the samplings from the other exiles and dedi-
cated the volume "To the Genius of Freedom," the title of his introductory poem. Another of Weinert's panegyrics pictures the Kremlin
at nighttime as, one by one, the lights go out, leaving only one window
lit. "Late at night I lay down my pen / As dawn is breaking through
the clouds. / I look over at the Kremlin. The country sleeps peacefully. / Its heart stayed awake. There is still light in the Kremlin."[101]
Hedda Zinner concocted an unbelievably nauseous piece of Stalin
worship, a conversation between the great leader and an ordinary
worker who explains to the *Vozhd* that he was now able to buy things
he could not afford before. He had recently acquired a piano! Asks a
fatherly Stalin, "Can you play it yet?" And the worker answers him,
"Not yet, Comrade Stalin, but I shall!"[102] Elsewhere Zinner puts into
poetry a simple letter of thanks written to Stalin by "hundreds of
peasants": "Comrade Stalin, our land / Yielded an unprecedented
harvest. / Because we followed your directions. / Comrade Stalin, we
thank you! / Now we are rich."[103]

Stalin was also eulogized as Lenin's legitimate successor, the one
man called to continue Leninist ideas and ideals. "Lenin's fire blazes
in Stalin's steel!" exalted Leschnitzer,[104] and Huppert rejoiced, "Yet,
one from among the people, Stalin, / Is the image of that singular
one."[105] The dialectical materialist Becher cloaked his emotions in
quasi-religious terms, telling of a mother imploring her son to heed
the words of his dead father, who had often told how "Lenin fought
with the power of evil" to "deliver the souls of us all." Becher went on
to write: "And Lenin died. But as you know / Lenin did not give up
the spirit. / Lenin lived forth in Stalin's spirit, / And arose within him
to eternal life."[106]

100. Weinert, "Der Sozialismus lebt," in *Rot Front*, pp. 203–4.
101. Weinert, "Im Kreml ist noch Licht," in *Gedichte 1933–1941*, p. 473.
102. Zinner, "Neue Menschen," in *Geschehen*, pp. 15–16.
103. Zinner, "Zwei Briefe," in *Unter den Dächern*, pp. 63–64.
104. Leschnitzer, "Armee aus Feuer und Stahl," in *Verse*, p. 12.
105. Huppert, "Standbild Lenins im Kremlsaal," in *Vaterland*, pp. 66–67.
106. Becher, "Mütterlicher Befehl," in *Die hohe Warte*, pp. 17–18.

All the people's achievements, the social progress, prosperity, peace, happiness—socialism: all these were threatened by enemies of the people, by fascism, and by Trotsky. Trials, espionage, sabotage, and the machinations and intrigues hatched by unscrupulous enemies working their evil throughout the land provided the émigrés with ample subject matter for their poetry. In a long poem, "Der Volksfeind," Becher put his artistry to work describing a trial of enemies who allied themselves with fascism and sought to obstruct the progress of the country:

> It was mistaken to think that
> The enemy, once openly subdued, would relent.
> He changes positions; instead of appearing
> In the open he cleverly renders himself invisible.
> He feigns loyalty, approval,
> Crawls on his belly into the party, thus encircles
> Insidiously the best comrades,
> And lies in wait. . . .
>
> .   .   .   .
> So poisoned by hate he
> Wants most to murder the entire people
> And joins up with any enemy who
> Longs like him for the destruction of these people.

Thus it was that he had gunned down Kirov with a shot that seemed to strike directly at the heart of the people's happiness. But no, he had miscalculated—the result was only outrage. The people saw all the clearer where the real enemy was. "Rabid with despair, united with any scum," he now had no other goal but to kill, and so he aimed at the masses:

> Enemy of the people, wrecker, lunatic, he
> Creeps into the mine shafts and factories,
> Damages the machines to stop the work.
> Yes, he allows gas to collect
> In the tunnels, happy when the workers
> Collapse, poisoned, or when the
> Tunnels explode.

But there they now stood, the murderers, in front of a court, and in the meantime the people had "given themselves" a constitution—"new humanity" expressed in words.[107] Weinert explained that fascism re-

107. Johannes R. Becher, "Der Volksfeind," *Deutsche Zentral-Zeitung*, 17 January 1937.

quired accomplices to carry out murder in the "land of freedom" and to "weaken its strength with poison and injury." Yet even the blackest imagination could not have foreseen that there would be one willing to serve fascism in this way. But Trotsky, no longer a name but a "curse," had sent his "best team," bandits, to betray their own country. "The bankrupted formed a united front. . . . In blood they formed a front of baseness."[108] Hitler or Trotsky, there was no difference between the two. Leschnitzer wrote: "A scoundrel too the scoundrel's partner: / One rotten egg resembles the other. / The bastard Trotsky and like assassins / They deserve each other's company."[109] The murderers, the enemies of the people, the spies, however, had been soundly defeated. Huppert, yet to be "unmasked" himself, wrote in 1936:

> There lies the murderer's severed hand—
> Rigid, motionless; and still it grasps the dagger!
> With clammy fingers, cold and smooth, reptilelike
> It holds the handle of the murder weapon.
>
> From afar he had sent them out, groping:
> Spies, slavetraders, lookouts, hoodlums,
> Hired hagglers and bloodhounds, men
> Devoid of honor, without a fatherland.
>
> . . . There lies the hand—impotent monster,
> Harmless now, yet dreadful still
> In the haze and shadow of dark deeds.[110]

Huppert and Julius Hay both looked to other genres to call for vigilance against saboteurs and spies. Huppert recounts the story of Nastja, whose boyfriend Andrej had just graduated from school in Moscow and gone to work as a station chief at a new train depot in the Urals. While visiting him, Nastja discovers that Andrej's assistant Umorov is sabotaging the efficiency of the station. Further investigation proves that Andrej too is implicated—he is cowardly, afraid of Umorov. Nastja implores him to inform the party, but he will not listen, so she wires the fateful telegram to the regional party committee in Sverdlovsk: "Send immediately commission of inquiry to Bury Bor. Abuse by station head Andrej Kovrin and assistant Umorov."[111]

Hay wrote *Tanjka macht die Augen auf*,[112] a play about the family of

108. Weinert, "Trotzki," in *Gedichte 1933–1941*, pp. 352–53.
109. Leschnitzer, "Antifaschistische Akrosticha," in *Verse*, p. 30.
110. Huppert, "Die Abstimmung," in *Vaterland*, p. 120.
111. Huppert, "Bury Bor," in *Flaggen und Flügel*, pp. 72–81.
112. Julius Hay, *Tanjka macht die Augen auf, Das Wort* 11 (1937): 59–107.

Wiegand, a German architect working in Moscow. Wiegand is a skilled specialist who "opposes fascism" and has left Germany. He has been entrusted with the planning for a state archive under construction in Moscow.[113] One portion of the blueprints, for Wing D, was especially secret; according to Silentsev, Wiegand's supervisor, it will hold top secret material, documents the "enemy" especially wants to see. The architect is assigned an engineer to assist him, Erich Wohlgemuth, who makes his appearance in the company of a young woman, Anne-marie Reinartz, on the same day that Wiegand's daughter locates a maid—a young peasant women, Tanjka, from the countryside. She is totally ill at ease in the Wiegand's apartment, but she possesses "sound peasant reason" and immediately senses that something is not right with Wohlgemuth and Reinartz. However, they fear Tanjka and plant a stolen necklace on her. Tanjka is found out and excluded from family affairs, though she continues to live in a room in the apartment. With Tanjka out of the way, Wohlgemuth locates and begins copying the plans for Wing D one evening when Wiegand's apartment is empty. Fortunately, Tanjka comes home and discovers the Nazi spies. All ends happily with their arrest and the removal from the People's Commissariat for Internal Affairs of the Soviet official who had sent them in the first place.

Klara Blum wrote two unusual poems that belong to the body of writing dealing with the purges, but do not follow the same general pattern. In "Die Verleumdung," which talks of a flourishing Soviet economy in town and country, Blum warns that the enemy is lurking and implores "my Soviet land" to destroy him. For he manages to work his evil through slander, and suddenly some innocent citizen finds himself alone, cast out, ignored. With just a few words, the enemy has wrecked a part of the country's "wealth," a productive farmer or worker.[114] The long poem *Mit meinem Trotz* is patently autobiographical. Blum first describes herself "among comrades" in the Soviet Union; she then writes:

> But among them
> There sat the wrecker, the secret Trotskyist,
> Sat there arrogantly with his sly bald head.
> He looked me over with the sharp gaze of a spy,
> Let me feel his cleverly procured power.

---

113. Actually, all foreign architects had been excluded from work on municipal projects in early 1936 (Jarmatz, *Exil in der UdSSR*, p. 345).
114. Blum, "Die Verleumdung," in *Wir entscheiden alles*, pp. 35–36.

A curt wave of his hand: exclude her from everything.
And he ordered: no work for her.
He warned maliciously: something is not right.
He smiled: don't feel sorry for her.
And then he screamed: *I* am the party.[115]

Blum goes on to describe how she was ostracized; wherever she went, conversation promptly died down to a whisper. When she asked why, the response was in keeping with the wrecker's orders: "You've not been excluded, no, you are dreaming. / You can't get work? That's simply bad luck. / Everything else is hallucination. / You are clearly suffering from a persecution complex" (44). She then wrote "long letters" to the authorities accusing the wrecker and including, as she put it, "proof and evidence." For an interminable time she received no answer, but, on the verge of despair, she realized that she was in her "own land" and that the party and the people would protect her. One day she hears the news from a friend:

"He's been arrested, yes, an hour ago,
His diabolic game has finally been uncovered.
Many an honest comrade
He baited, slandered, tortured half to death
And reported to his masters: 'It's working!
Where *I* show up, well-trained,
No red cadres will grow. Heil!' " [46]

But calmly, politely, and unshakably, "they" had come to pick him up: "He'll harm no one else" (46). As if by magic, Blum is welcomed back into the fold, cleansed of the false suspicions, and able to find her niche in a happy Soviet society. Blum had in fact been expelled sometime in 1939 from the German Section for "lack of discipline and for hysteria."[116] Her poem *Mit meinem Trotz* evidently deals with that occurrence.

Finally, there were books that never made it into print. Herwarth Walden wrote two plays, "Krisl: Zeitdrama aus Berlin 1930" and "Kulaken: Zeitdrama aus der Sowjetukraine 1930"; "Zwischen den Klassen" ("Berliner Novellen"); and a two-volume novel, "Die Neutralen,"

115. Blum, *Mit meinem Trotz*, in *Die Antwort*, p. 44. Subsequent page citations appear in parentheses or brackets.
116. "Protokoll der Plenartagung der Deutschen Sektion vom 26. März 1940," in Barck, *Johannes R. Bechers Publizistik*, p. 248.

all of which, one assumes, disappeared along with him. The Russian translation of Georg Lukács's *Der historische Roman* had been accepted by a Russian firm and was also submitted for publication in the original German. His *Der junge Hegel*, for which he received a Soviet doctorate, also remained unpublished at the time, as did two lengthy studies of fascism, one written in 1933 and the other in the early forties. A monograph on Goethe fell victim to the NKVD and was confiscated at the time of Lukács's arrest.[117] Other unpublished novels included one by Klara Blum about ancient "feudal China," one by Dora Wentscher about Wilhelminian Germany, one by Andor Gábor about "the mennonites," as well as those by Berta Lask ("Atlantis Calls"), Hans Rodenberg ("Bankruptcy" and "Blind Mirror"), Alfred Kurella ("Das Kraut Moly"), and Maria Osten ("Kartofellschnaps"). Osten had begun her novel in Paris and intended to complete it by March 1941. Her arrest three months later evidently decided its fate. Hedda Zinner also planned a novel scheduled for completion by the end of 1941.[118] There is little reason to suppose, however, that any literary masterpiece perished in the Gulag or disappeared into some desk drawer.

117. See Chapter 11 for additional discussion.
118. For Walden's plays and "Berliner Novellen," see "Walden (Für den ukrainischen Staatsverlag)," TsGALI, 631/12/86/9; the other information is in "Plan" (in Russian), TsGALI, 631/12/86/27. Lukács's diploma (*doktorskaja stepen*) for *Der junge Hegel* is in his Budapest archive.

Chapter 10

The Literary Popular Front, Part II: Lukács

When the party set out in 1932 to replace RAPP's discredited dialectical materialist method with a new "creative method," Soviet literary officials had certain objectives in mind: the new program needed to diverge from RAPP's openly Marxist literary prescriptions, which had called for mastery of dialectical materialism, but it could not permit the relaxation of state control of literature. The phrase describing the new method, "socialist realism," was first coined shortly after RAPP's demise, on 20 May 1932, when *Izvestija* editor Ivan Gronskij lashed out at the keystone of RAPP's literary theory: he reversed the RAPP program by stating that a knowledge of dialectical materialism was not a prerequisite for creative writing. "The basic demand which we make on a writer is to write the truth, to portray truthfully our reality that is in itself dialectic. Therefore, the basic method of Soviet literature is the method of socialist realism."[1] Within several months, popular legend had it that Stalin was the inventor of the formulation "socialist realism."

The call to depict reality, after several years of RAPP's insistence on dialectical materialism, impressed many Soviet writers as a move toward greater artistic freedom. Of course it was clearly understood that a solid foundation in Marxism-Leninism would always benefit Soviet writers, who were enjoined to study Marxism. But the party's spokesmen in literature stressed that above all else a thorough knowledge of life itself was necessary for a truthful rendition of reality, for knowledge of life inevitably led to the figuration of the dialectic in any artistic creation. Stalin remarked in October 1932 that if an artist

---

1. Ermolaev, *Soviet Literary Theories, 1917–1934*, p. 144. I have relied heavily on Ermolaev's treatment of the emergence of socialist realism.

"truthfully depicts our life, he cannot but notice and depict in it that which leads to socialism. This exactly will be socialist art. This exactly will be socialist realism."[2] It all sounded far less odious to the writers than the RAPP demand for dialectical materialism; writers simply had to mirror reality, to capture truth. "You must understand that if a writer frequently and honestly reflects the truth of life he cannot fail to arrive at Marxism,"[3] explained Stalin.

This was all a hoax for the obvious reason that writers knew beforehand what would be recognized as truth and what would not. Soviet literature now became absolutely Stalinized, and socialist realism—literary Stalinism—developed devoid of meaning in any artistic sense. That dozens of Soviet critics, philosophers, politicians, and writers stepped forward to waste gallons of ink in "definitions" of socialist realism did not alter the fact that the new "creative method" was just what the party wanted it to be at any given moment and nothing else. Soon virtually every political pronouncement of Stalin's was thought relevant to Soviet literature; excerpts of his speeches were "concrete examples of socialist realism." To take Stalin's report to a joint plenum of the Central Committee and the Central Control Commission and translate it into literary images created art, because the "basic laws, basic forces, basic premises, and basic results" of life were all embodied in his speech.[4]

All the while the myth was upheld that no ideological constraints were being put upon the writer. "We do not make the demand that people apply the dialectical materialist method or other highly complicated scientific mechanisms," said Aleksej Stetskij, head of the Central Committee's agitprop department; "we demand that a writer see our reality in its revolutionary development . . . that his work inspire the fight for a new order, that he affirm this order in the consciousness of the people."[5] The statutes of the new Soviet Writers' Union passed at the 1934 congress contained the official definition of the new creative method: "Socialist realism, being the basic method of Soviet imaginative literature and literary criticism, demands from the artist a truthful, historically concrete description of reality in its concreteness" of the artistic depiction of reality had to be combined with the "task of ideological molding and education of the working people in the spirit of socialism."[6]

2. Ibid., p. 145.
3. Ibid., p. 167.
4. Ibid., p. 163.
5. Ibid., p. 168.
6. Ibid., p. 197.

Not that there were no disagreements over the meaning of socialist realism. A major dispute broke out in 1933 between two schools of thought, each battling to have its interpretation of socialist realism accepted as definitive. The argument focused on a key issue: was an artist's world viewpoint (his class upbringing and background, his political bias and ideology) "identical" with the literature he produced, with his "method," or could a contradiction exist between an author's subjective class viewpoint and the reflection in his writing of objective reality? Each side was persuaded that it alone represented the Marxist-Leninist standpoint in literature.

Mark Rozental, writing in a new journal of criticism and theory, *Literaturnyj kritik*, challenged the notion that a writer's class background, his viewpoint, was identical with the literature he produced. This outlook, charged Rozental, meant that a "Soviet fellow traveler" who lacked a Marxist-Leninist world view and consequently practiced an inadequate literary method, could never produce "a valuable and useful artistic work reflecting our reality." Such an insinuation was a roundabout way of saying that a Soviet fellow traveler must first change his world view and only then write. Rozental identified the argument as a restatement of RAPP's old dialectical materialist creative method. He made it clear, however, that his own position did not reject the value of a "proletarian world view" for Soviet writers if they were to render Soviet reality accurately. What, though, was to be done with writers who desired to participate in socialist construction and could create high-quality literature, but who still lacked a background in Marxism-Leninism? How should these writers go about overcoming the handicap of old world viewpoints and acquiring a Communist, Marxist-Leninist outlook? The RAPP method had sought to impose dialectical materialism upon the writer, said Rozental, without which he was bound in advance to create a faulty work of art. The only avenue of escape was thus to change his world view before he ever began writing.[7]

Here the cardinal error resided in the supposition that a world view carried over "mechanically" to artistic images. "Objective reality itself, its impact and influence upon an artist's work—all this vanishes," explained Rozental. Of course, he admitted, class played a role in the creative process. "The artistic image is in a specific way a reflection of reality passing (not mechanically, straightaway, or directly) through the prism of a writer's ideology." But to argue for complete accord

7. Mark Rozental, "Mirovozzrenie i metod v khudozhestvennom tvorchestve," *Literaturnyj kritik* 6 (1933): 12–16.

between world view, consciousness, and creative process was false; there was no mechanical nexus between outlook and method, said Rozental, whence arose "the possibility of a contradiction between a writer's ideological principles and his creative method" (17).

Here, in a nutshell, was the position of the *Voprekisti* (the "Inspitivists") and of Georg Lukács. These critics contended that great art could be created "in spite of" (*vopreki*) the artist's class ideology. To prove their point, they brought up the question of classic literature, their favorite example being Balzac, their pet quotation Engels's characterization of Balzac first published in March 1932: "That Balzac was forced to go against his own class sympathies and political prejudices, that he recognized the inescapability of the downfall of his beloved nobles and described them as people deserving no better fate, and that he saw the real men of the future—I consider this one of the greatest triumphs of realism, and one of the greatest features in old Balzac."[8] Two types of influences collided in the process of creation, reasoned Rozental: the influence exerted by world view and that exerted by "life itself," the substance of objective reality. Of course an artist's class ideology was ever present when he reflected reality in art, but "life itself" could lessen its impact upon literature when "living facts" convinced the artist that reality differed from his class's definition or understanding of it. The possibility of a contradiction therefore existed between class viewpoint and creative method if a great writer based himself on knowledge of reality and drew his images from life itself; this could "paralyze the influence of an incorrect world view and give him the possibility, in spite of his world view, to reflect profoundly several essential sides of reality."[9]

Rozental stressed that he was speaking primarily of past art. The historical development that had climaxed in the victory of the proletariat had changed things insofar as, in principle, the question of a contradiction between world view and creative method vanished for artists who possessed Communist, proletarian outlooks. But the issue retained its significance because of Soviet writers who had not changed their world view into a Communist one, yet were fighting for the construction of socialism. Historical experience had shown that the "realistic method of artistic creation" was not only a means of reflecting reality but also the road to procuring a correct world view. He thus reversed the old RAPP injunction: socialist realism did not call upon the writer to study the principles of Marxism-Leninism before writ-

---

8. Quoted here from *Die Linkskurve* 3 (1932): 11–14.
9. Rozental, "Mirovozzrenie," p. 24.

ing, without which there could be no reflection of "essential characteristics of our reality"; rather, the creative praxis itself, the sincere study
of facts connected with socialist construction and their truthful, sincere reflection would lead the way to an eventual Marxist-Leninist
standpoint.

Isaak Nusinov of the Institute of Red Professors took Rozental to
task. He reasoned that a world view determined completely the nature of a work of art and insinuated that Rozental, by invoking Engels's authority to claim that Balzac achieved his realism independently
of his reactionary world view, gave any nonproletarian Soviet author
the right to reject "a proletarian outlook as nothing more than an
insignificant plus for a writer's work." That, of course, was not what
Rozental had said. As for Balzac, Nusinov's ideas were at loggerheads
with those held by the *Voprekisti*. Yes, there were "contradictions" in
Balzac's work, but these sprang not from a conflict between class
ideology and realistic creative method; rather, they informed his method
and his world view.

For Nusinov, Balzac's "triumph of realism" resulted not from his
realistic creative method per se but from his "class praxis"; his own
class contradictions compelled him in a direction against his class
sympathies and political prejudices. "The contradictions in Balzac's
work are contradictions in reality itself, not contradictions between his
method and his world view," and they were not, as Rozental had
argued, grounded in the very nature of art. Nusinov summed up his
position: "The writer of genius reflects in his work with great profundity and thoroughness those sides of reality that his class recognizes.
But only those sides. . . . A writer capable of showing reality with
maximum profundity and thoroughness just as his class, but only his
class, sees it, is a genius."[10] Here was the quintessence of *Blagodarizm*,
the viewpoint that great art originated "thanks to" (*blagodarja*) a writer's class orientation. Nusinov stressed in conclusion that the struggle
for a Marxist-Leninist understanding of reality, for a socialist world
view, remained the central task of Soviet literature, and the success of
socialist realism depended on all Soviet writers acquiring a socialist
outlook.

Rozental in response went to the heart of Nusinov's argument, the
existence of contradictions in a writer's world view, and ridiculed the
practice of establishing countless "shades of world views" in order to
discount the possibility of a contradiction between class and creative

10. Isaak Nusinov, "Sotsialisticheskij realizm i problema mirovozzrenija i metoda," *Literaturnyj kritik* 2 (1934): 139–55.

method. Such arguments held that Gogol was a representative of "bourgeoisifying nobility," Balzac of "nobilifying capitalism," writer "x" a left bourgeois, writer "y" a right bourgeois, writer "z" a "right-left" or a "left-right." In spite of what "Nusinov and friends" argued, Rozental reaffirmed his conviction that the realistic method of expressing reality very often contradicted the subjective views of the writer. This remained the only real issue, and "Nusinov and friends" got around it by explaining away contradictions in writers like Gogol and Balzac through "halving" them, turning Balzac into a half-aristocrat, half-bourgeois and Gogol into a half-nobleman, half-capitalist.[11]

Rozental recognized clearly that the situation was different for Soviet literature, so he scored Nusinov for his "mechanical identification" of the role played by world view in the artistic endeavors of the bourgeoisie of the past and the proletariat of today. To apply the lessons of Balzac's realism directly to Soviet literature ignored completely the changed social conditions. The goals and aspirations of the proletariat not only did not contradict the historical pattern of laws governing social development, but the proletariat was also the only class under whose guidance working humanity could realize its historical mission. So of course a Soviet writer with a proletarian world view, unlike writers of other classes, could never come into contradiction with historical social tendencies.

The problem involved the "path of Soviet writers who had not freed themselves from the prejudices of their old world view to gain the world view of the proletariat." Here, said Rozental, the RAPPists had committed grave errors; as for Nusinov, he posed the question falsely of whether a Soviet writer needed a dialectical materialist outlook. Of course he did, but how to acquire one? It was a matter of socialist realism, of the artistic *method*. Nusinov's position was essentially identical with RAPP's, charged Rozental; socialist realism, on the other hand, called upon a nonproletarian Soviet writer to study socialist reality and reflect it correctly. The methods of truthful reflection of reality in connection with the serious study of Marxist-Leninist theory provided the only way for a writer to master a dialectical materialist world view. Nusinov cried out, "'Help! Save the world view!'" and repeated the mistakes of RAPP. But socialist realism was a militant slogan for all of Soviet literature; by teaching the specifics of a creative method, it provided guidance for all, including those who still had to overcome the vestiges of an old world view.

11. Mark Rozental, "Eshche raz o mirovozzrenii v khudozhestvennom tvorchestve," *Literaturnyj kritik* 5 (1934): 8–33.

The debate between the *Voprekisti* and the *Blagodaristi*, the two competing schools of literary criticism, continued on into 1936. Both sides purported to apply the lessons of past literature to Soviet literature while working toward a definitive explanation of socialist realism; but neither group had received an official stamp of approval, and their respective "creative methods" could not yet be imposed upon Soviet writers. In 1936 the situation began to change and the party's inclinations grew clearer. Socialist realism was outfitted with a set of new prescriptions and injunctions demanding "simplicity and plebeianism"[12] in art and excluding "formalism and naturalism." These were virtually all terms either invented by the *Voprekisti* (and already inherent in their literary theories) or simply given theoretical respectability by *Voprekisti* critics.

The term *plebeianism*, for example, was apparently first coined in November 1935 in an editorial printed in *Literaturnyj kritik*, a journal that, after a few years of neutrality, now became colored with *Voprekizm*. The idea of plebeianism, implicit from the outset in *Voprekizm*, described literature expressing the aspirations of the common people. All great writers of the past were plebeian if, in spite of class limitations, they had depicted "typical characters in typical circumstances," if they had observed reality and embodied in their work mankind's progressive tendencies and the forward course of history. The idea was alien, on the other hand, to the class analysis of the *Blagodaristi*—now more frequently called "vulgar sociologists"—who argued that great writers of the past depicted reality only as their class saw it. *Literaturnyj kritik* pointed out that only literature embodying the creative spirit of the people was genuinely plebeian literature. Soviet literature, because of its position in the land, was truly plebeian, for it had no interests running counter to those of the people. But plebeianism was not a quality only of Soviet literature, and *Literaturnyj kritik* announced its intention to devote future articles to show the historical development of plebeianism as it pertained to Soviet literature and to show how it differed in the past and present.[13]

Whether plebeianism was solely the invention of the *Voprekisti*, as it may well have been, is unclear; nor is it certain who in the party decided to turn it into the clarion call of socialist realism, which it now became. The appeal for "simplicity and plebeianism" in art was issued in a January 1936 *Pravda* attack on Dmitrij Shostakovich's recently

12. *Narodnost* in Russian and *Volkstümlichkeit* in German are translated throughout this chapter, for lack of a better term, as plebeianism or plebeian.
13. "Literatura i narod," *Literaturnyj kritik* 11 (1935): 3–9.

performed opera, *Lady Macbeth from Mtsensk*.[14] The *Pravda* article barred "formalism and naturalism" from all Soviet art and precipitated a round of heated discussions among Soviet composers, architects, sculptors, painters, and other artists. The campaign against formalism and naturalism, the obverse of the call for plebeianism, was also waged in the sphere of literature. On 3 March 1936 the *Literaturnaja gazeta* published an editorial on the meaning of *Pravda*'s pronouncements. The response of some literati revealed that they had not understood that a *"restructuring of all fronts of art"* was occurring under the banner of new demands for quality. "The new Soviet man demands from his artists a correct and plebeian art." Great themes that animated the masses, a profound and accurate understanding of Soviet reality, crystalline clarity of image, richness and purity of language, well-balanced composition—all these flowed from the insistence on simplicity and plebeianism in literature, from the need for a literature of socialist realism. But the triumph of simplicity and plebeianism required a defeat of formalism, which signified a writer's retreat from reality and the life of the people; naturalism also betrayed a writer's inability, or refusal, to penetrate to the heart of phenomena in the life he depicted. "Formalism, left-wing radical foolishness (*levatskoe urodstvo*), and crude naturalism" all trampled upon the wishes of the broad working masses.[15]

There followed a series of meetings and speeches from 10 to 26 March 1936 in the Home of Soviet Writers. Vladimir Stavskij set the tone. Formalistic attempts, the craving for originality at any price, affectation, left-wing radical foolishness, naturalism in its crudest form—these existed to an unsettling degree in Soviet literature. Among others, Stavskij attacked Boris Pilnjak, whose writing ostensibly flew in the face of the party's call for simplicity and plebeianism; it was impossible to understand what he was saying in *The Ripening of the Fruit*. This difficulty resulted from an irresponsible attitude toward his own work. Not to make oneself understood was "impolite" to the reader, claimed Stavskij, likewise flaying Gladkov and Nikiforov for being "disrespectful to their readers"; these people had "nothing in common with our literature." Simplicity and plebeianism was now the battle cry of Soviet literature, "perfect instances" of which were the works of Lenin and Stalin.[16]

14. "Sumbur vmesto muzyki," *Pravda*, 28 January 1936.
15. "Nuzhen otvet delom," *Literaturnaja gazeta*, 5 March 1936.
16. Vladimir Stavskij, "O formalizme i naturalizme v literature: Vstupitelnoe slovo Tov. Stavskogo na obshchemoskovskom sobranii pisatelej," ibid., 15 March 1936.

A few days later, *Literaturnaja gazeta* summed up the results of the continuing discussion.[17] No one had yet worked out a nexus between the elements of a naturalistic approach to reality and formalistic artistic means; this connection, said the editorial, existed in many works of Soviet literature. Incapable of penetrating to the essence of real phenomena, naturalist writers tended to play around formalistically with the external superficial side of real facts and processes. The result was a grey depiction of daily affairs, superficial factography, in which the development of a theme was obscured by unnecessary complication, formal literary techniques, and disconnected narration. These faults were all linked, said the *Literaturnaja gazeta*, with another manifestation of the same basic problem. There had been much talk of vulgar sociology (*Blagodarizm*) in literary criticism; but elements of vulgar sociology were also frequently encountered in Soviet works of art. In such works, the hero's sole purpose was to carry around crudely schematic ideological "baggage" and to represent oversimplified ideas and character types. Prevented by naturalism from creating the real image of a hero, the writer turned his intellectually pallid figure into a mouthpiece for great ideas that were simply excerpted from the Soviet press.

After the discussion meetings had ended, Aleksandr Shcherbakov summed up the results. He repeated the newly minted phrases and stressed that the objective of the seven meetings had been to raise the quality of Soviet literature for the millions of builders of socialism. The typical Soviet reader now read Balzac, a writer of an age when the bourgeoisie was still progressive; "from him there is much to learn." The typical Soviet reader rejected Joyce, a writer who reflected the decline of bourgeois culture; "from him there is nothing to learn." However, in a show of tolerance, Shcherbakov did reject Gronskij's politicized definition of formalism and naturalism as the "mask of the counterrevolutionary struggle against Soviet power." Of course, said Shcherbakov, there were enemies of socialist construction still in literature; but Gronskij's incorrect characterization led him to suggest "administrative measures" as a means of dealing with formalism and naturalism in Soviet literature. Shcherbakov hastened to assure the writers that these views were not in consonance with the party; they were, in fact, "harmful."[18] This went over well, but the time when literary prescriptions did not go hand in hand with "administrative measures," when offenses against Soviet literary formulas and codes were not

---

17. "Glavnaja zadacha pisatelskikh organizatsij," ibid., 20 March 1936.
18. Aleksandr Shcherbakov, "K itogam diskussii," ibid., 5 April 1936.

treated as crimes against the state, and the people, was rapidly running out.

The campaign against vulgar sociology paralleled the debate over formalism and naturalism, and by late summer it had ended with the rout of the *Blagodaristi*. The lead in the dispute over vulgar sociology was taken not by a party scribe or by a man of Stavskij's ilk but by a young philosopher from the Marx-Engels-Lenin Institute, Mikhail Lifshits, who compiled the first collection of remarks by Marx and Engels on literature and art and published his own study on Marx's philosophy of art. In early 1936 Lifshits sensed that the time was right for an all-out battle with vulgar sociological theories. Support came from the highest quarters when Mekhlis persuaded Stalin of the need to destroy vulgar sociology.[19] Lifshits began with an article in the *Literaturnaja gazeta* for 20 January 1936,[20] using "plebeianism" in great art of the past as an argument against the vulgar sociologists and backing himself up with references to Lenin's utterances about Tolstoy, namely, the remark that Tolstoy had portrayed in his work the broad mood of the masses oppressed by the existing regime. Could an artist who belonged to the aristocracy give expression in his writing to a popular movement? Lifshits asked. The vulgar sociologists said that he could not because all writers were the "lawful psychological product" of their environment.

Leninist criticism, on the other hand, said Liftshits, based itself on a Leninist theory of reflection and had nothing in common with the fatalism of the vulgar sociologists. Lenin had written of Tolstoy that through him there spoke the "masses of the Russian people in the millions who had *already* come to hate the masters of today but who had *not yet* come to the point of waging a conscious, consistent, definitive, irreconcilable struggle against them." Lifshits pointed out that conscious revolutionary thought, as well as conscious defense of reaction, existed always; but rarely were things so clear-cut; there was often "objective class confusion" expressing itself in the fact that millions hated their oppressors but were not ready historically for active rebellion. Such vacillations on the part of the masses, Lifshits believed, best explained the contradictions of great writers and thinkers of the past. These men, while observing reality and the masses and breaking with long-standing ideas and preconceptions, had been unable to orient themselves correctly and perceive perfectly the solutions to human

19. From a 1977 conversation between the author and Lifshits.
20. Mikhail Lifshits, "Leninizm i khudozhestvennaja kritika," *Literaturnaja gazeta*, 20 January 1936.

history. Thus their work exhibited both progressive and backward ideas.

Whereas the vulgar sociologists reduced great writers to mouth-pieces of various classes, degrading the long history of art, Lenin, said Lifshifts, taught how to weed out the unimportant from the valuable in past art. This was a genuine class analysis. The vulgar sociologists, on the other hand, although they talked much about class struggle and class analysis, isolated privileged groups of the bourgeoisie and nobility and presented the history of art as a "petty quarrel among parasites of various kinds over some piece of prey." Was that all there was to the class struggle? Where was the never-ending conflict be-tween the lower and upper strata of humanity? "Where are the peo-ple?" The "class struggle in literature" was the struggle of plebeian tendencies against all that obstructed historical progress, answered Lifshits; this was the only way to understand the great cultural heritage—its failures, contradictions, and successes.[21]

Isaak Nusinov, at a public discussion, came out forcefully against Lifshits, who reiterated and elaborated upon his ideas in another article in the *Literaturnaja gazeta*.[22] A writer's attitude toward the class struggle, as it revealed itself at the time, was never straightforward and uncontradictory, but full of various tendencies. Great art had to be viewed against a far broader historical backdrop than the vulgar sociologists were accustomed to doing. These theoreticians, Lifshits charged, actually rejected class analysis, for they failed to account for the *"artistic development of mankind,* especially in terms of the entire history of the class struggle." The works of vulgar sociologists were in fact the "crudest formalism," for, after they finished reducing a writer to a lackey of the bourgeoisie or of the gentry, they still sought to measure a writer's greatness by way of his artistic craftsmanship. But truly great writers from the aristocracy and the bourgeoisie had grown into "genuinely plebeian writers" irrespective of their class background; Lifshits qualified his remarks somewhat, admitting that the combina-tion of conservative and democratic traits in a writer grew less possi-ble as the class struggle intensified and the alignment of forces grew clearer. In today's day and age, conscious alliance with the fighting masses was required ("Gorky takes the place of Tolstoy"), but in the past ideological contradictions were still a normal part of great litera-ture.

Nusinov had only one opportunity to answer Lifshits publicly in the

21. Ibid.
22. Mikhail Lifshits, "Kriticheskie zametki," *Literaturnaja gazeta*, 24 May 1936.

Literaturnaja gazeta,[23] where he made light of Lifshits's phrase "objective class confusion" and referred instead to "objective class confusers." He accused Lifshits of denying the class nature of an artist, thereby placing the blame for contradictions inherent in the writings of bourgeois and aristocratic artists on the shoulders of the masses. He argued (as he had in 1934) that these contradictions between class position and literary work did not derive from the vacillations of the masses; rather, the great writers of the past mirrored contradictions of the propertied classes whose ideals and ideology they sought to depict. Nusinov went on to accuse Lifshits, as he had Rozental, of neglecting to distinguish between socialist literature and literature of past ruling classes, of not drawing a line between issues of plebeianism in socialist literature and those in ruling class literature. Lifshits accordingly saw literary history not as the history of class but as that of plebeian literature, the literature of the wavering masses. But the writers in question were not the ideologists of the masses at all; they represented the aristocracy and the bourgeoisie, said Nusinov. He concluded that the literary heritage needed to be carefully and critically appropiated, but it was false ("literary class confusion") to declare all great past writers spokesmen of the people's interests.

Nusinov was by now out of touch with the times, blind to the recognition of his own position as a frontal attack upon party-backed plebeianism. Acceptable theories now established a direct link between plebeianism in past art, the need for plebeianism in contemporary bourgeois literature (a task that devolved primarily upon Georg Lukács), and the supposedly perfect conditions for plebeianism existing in the USSR. The debate was really over, although it lasted a few more months. Lifshits answered Nusinov's article a few days later, stressing again that the immaturity of mass movements and their uncertain forward progress down through history lay at the heart of ideological contradictions in works of art by great writers.[24] The vulgar sociologists, Lifshits declared, were caught in a bind; either they had to maintain that all great elements in past art expressed the ideology of exploiters, or they had to grasp the fact that great artistic accomplishments emerged from the process of struggle against such exploiters, "as art came into closer contact with the people."

Thus far the party had remained silent, but on 8 August 1936 *Pravda* spoke, and the editorial made it clear that vulgar sociology no

23. Isaak Nusinov, "Ob 'obektivnoj klassovoj putanitse' i pretentsioznom putanike," ibid., 10 July 1936.
24. Mikhail Lifshits, "Kriticheskie zametki," ibid., 15 July 1936.

longer had any place in Soviet literary criticism.[25] It was time, the paper editorialized, to deny vulgar sociology and its theories entry into Soviet schools because of what such notions had done to students' appreciation of the literary heritage. A decisive struggle had to be waged against those "'theories'" that reduced the richness of Soviet and Western literature to "empty formulas." Great artists belonged to the people and had bequeathed to them everything of cultural value created by previous classes; it was not in "our interest" to turn such values into "historical rubbish." *Pravda* also called for an end to the protection of vulgar sociology in the People's Commissariat for Education. *Literaturnaja gazeta* took the cue and, introducing two last articles against vulgar sociology by Mark Rozental,[26] indicated that with them the discussion was over. One conclusion was clear, said the *Literaturnaja gazeta*; Leninist views on appropriating the cultural heritage profoundly contradicted vulgar sociology. The paper said that *Pravda*'s remark about denying vulgar sociology access to Soviet schools should become law "for all future work in the sphere of literary theory and for the propagation of the classics; the remark obligates both literary scholars and critics to proceed to a profound and concrete study of the work of great artists of world literature."[27]

Bearing in mind that Soviet critics voiced them, many *Voprekisti* views did not sound bad for the times—on paper. But seldom have literary debates been more meaningless than in 1936 in the Soviet Union. Of what value were admonishments to "study objective reality" and embody in literature the truth of life when the writing receiving Glavlit's stamp of approval had little to do with objective truth? These new *Voprekisti* theories existed in a vacuum with no connection between theory and practice. But the "triumph of realism," literature as a reflection of objective truth and of possible contradictions between a writer's subjective ideology and his creative method, plebeianism, even the injunctions against "formalism, naturalism, and left-wing radical foolishness"—all these features of *Voprekizm* and socialist realism were likewise developed in their relation to Western writers, chiefly the "anti-Fascist" writers of western Europe and of the German emigration. In the West there were possibilities for their practical application, and the man who sought to apply them was Georg Lukács.

25. "Privit shkolnikam ljubov k klassicheskoj literature" and, on the inside page, "Protiv vulgarnykh sotsiologov i ikh narkomprosovskikh pokrovitelej" (Against Vulgar Sociologists and their Protectors in Narkompros), *Pravda*, 8 August 1936.
26. Mark Rozental, "Protiv vulgarnoj sotsiologii v literaturnoj teorii," *Literaturnaja gazeta*, 10 and 15 September 1936.
27. Ibid.

Virtually all the underlying concepts in Lukács's essays and books of the thirties either existed first in the early ideas of the *Voprekisti*, among whose ranks Lukács counted his closest friends (Lifshits, for instance), or Lukács himself invented and helped make them a part not only of *Voprekizm* but of what passed for socialist realism from 1936 to 1939. Would Lukács try to obtrude socialist realism upon Western writers? From within the Soviet Union he unquestionably set out to thrust a creative canon upon Western "bourgeois" and revolutionary proletarian writers, but he regarded this canon as his own. Lukács naturally adapted himself to some extent to the emerging dogmas of socialist realism, but many of its tenets happen to have been present in Lukács's writing before they appeared as official Soviet dictates, the stigmatization of formalism and naturalism, for instance, or the "triumph of realism." These notions had already shown up in his *Linkskurve* essays. Did Lukács somehow anticipate, perhaps in 1933 to 1935, the future development of socialist realism or did he in fact use his ideas to guide its very formulation? His theories, I suggest, did not assume a fundamentally different form than they would have if he had not gone into Soviet exile; that his views came to fruition, survived, and indeed prospered in the thirties resulted either from Lukács's role in defining several key elements of what was called socialist realism or from an almost coincidental similarity between the new "creative method" and Lukács's aesthetic. But Lukács did not theorize on cue from above; there is not a single instance where he bent to the breaking point any one of his underlying ideas for the sake of adapting them to socialist realism. True, he was fortunate in never being ordered to revamp his notions completely to conform with some new line, but he passed several tests in exile of his commitment to his own principles, most notably during the 1939–40 campaign against the Lukács-Lifshits "Trend," when he defended his position without the slightest hesitation.

Lukács began by applying an abstract theory of art to literature past and present, Soviet and Western. His basic premise was the existence of an objective, external world that could be recognized and reflected artistically in literature. The problem of art was the reflection of objective reality. Lukács's essay "Kunst und objektive Wahrheit" (1934) sets forth this principle programmatically.[28] There was a dis-

---

28. This essay was first published, greatly abbreviated, as "K probleme obektivnosti khudozhestvennoj formy," *Literaturnyj kritik* 9 (1935): 5–23. I quote from "Kunst and objektive Wahrheit," *Probleme des Realismus I*, pp. 607–50. All the passages cited were contained in the original Russian version. Subsequent page citations appear in the text in parentheses.

crepancy between phenomena as they appear to be and their essence. The goal of all great art was to picture reality so as to resolve the conflict between appearance and essence. In any piece of literature this required a complete context; all characters, situations, and events had to be self-sustaining and justified within the work of art, for the unity of appearance and essence was produced only when the reader saw the processes involved in forming characters and events, not just the "finished results." "The original materialism of very great artists (irrespective of their often partially or completely idealistic world view) is expressed by the fact that they always clearly depicted those existential conditions and prerequisites within whose context the consciousness of the characters originates and develops" (617).

Art was to reflect accurately and in the correct contextual proportions those objective determinants governing the piece of life being portrayed. These determinants needed to be drawn into the work as personal traits of the characters and as specific features of the various situations, for, "by depicting individual human beings and individual situations, the artist creates the appearance of life. By depicting them as exemplary human beings, as exemplary situations (unity of the individual and the typical), by making the greatest possible wealth of life's objective determinants immediately evident as separate traits of individual human beings and situations, his 'own world' originates, one that therefore can reflect life in its eventful entirety, as a process and totality" (620). Great art was objective art; but, as Lukács defined it, such art still embodied a form of partisanship, though not one carried over arbitrarily into the external world by the "subject," the artist. Lukács's "partisanship of objectivity" was not a subjectively infused, subjectively "'attached'" tendency. Ideas themselves must not be copied in art because this was subjectivism, which, along with any imitation of life in terms of immediately evident *surface* details, endangered art's reflection of reality.

These subjective tendencies destroyed the dialectical unity of form and content, Lukács continued, explaining that "the artistic form is likewise a type of reflection of reality" (626), necessary for depicting a complete context. "Form is nothing but the supreme abstraction," he argued, "the supreme type of condensation of content . . . the establishment of correct proportions between separate determinants, the hierarchy of importance between separate contradictions in life" (632). Form could possess an objectivity independent of the artist's consciousness. The figures and plots of a work of art, though they originated in the artist's mind, had their own dialectic that the writer had to respect at the risk otherwise of destroying his own work. Basing himself on

Marx, Lukács then linked the emergence of forms to sociohistorical development, claiming that "every art form in its origin and growth is tied to certain social and ideological (*weltanschaulich*) preconditions provided by society; that only within the context of these preconditions . . . can those form elements originate that bring a certain form to its greatest bloom" (637).

Lukács turned to the past to explain the essence of great art as objective art. Profoundly realistic literature had been written through a "triumph of realism," he said. The greatness of a Balzac lay in the severe self-criticism of his own views and deepest convictions through an inexorable depiction of reality. Balzac counted himself among the aristocracy, wrote Lukács in his essay "*Die Bauern*,"[29] yet he depicted not only the downfall of the nobility but the inevitability of its fall as well, which, as an aristocratic royalist, he failed to comprehend. "His greatness," Lukács believed, "consists of the fact that—irrespective of his political and ideological prejudices—he observed with an unerring eye and depicted all palpable contradictions" (464). It was a matter of his "profound realism," his creative method. Balzac avoided the "'scientific character'" practiced by his literary successors, writers like Zola and Flaubert, said Lukács in another essay.[30] He developed problems of the material world only as they touched on the "individual passions of his heroes." Never moralizing about his figures, Balzac depicted the "objective dialectic of their rise and fall and motivated both through the totality of the character in interaction with the totality of objective circumstances" (477). This resulted in a unifying principle, Lukács said of *Verlorene Illusionen*, which was nothing less than the totality of social processes itself. But Balzac's human beings were never mere "'figures'" expressing a certain side of social reality; Balzac diffused all social determinants in the "maze of personal passions and coincidental happenings" (478), the secret to embodying simultaneously, without patterned schemes, the typical and the commonplace. Balzac's characters were both typical representatives of sociohistorical currents and individual human beings.

29. The essay was first published as the foreword to a 1935 Soviet edition of Balzac's novel and reprinted in Russian in Lukács's *K istorii realizma*, pp. 175–201. I refer to the German version published in Lukács, "*Die Bauern*," in *Probleme des Realismus III*, pp. 447–71; subsequent page citations appear in parentheses.
30. "*Verlorene Illusionen*" was first published as the foreword to a Soviet edition of Balzac's novel and later reprinted in *K istorii realizma*, pp. 243–331. This reference is to Lukács, "*Verlorene Illusionen*," in *Probleme des Realismus III*, pp. 472–89; subsequent page citations appear in parentheses.

Balzac's realism sprang in part from the existence in his lifetime of certain social processes and his involvement in them: the rise of the bourgeoisie, the emergence of capitalism as a progressive social force, and the decline of feudalism and the aristocracy. It also stemmed in part from his use of an objective art form, which emerged because of social processes and was alone capable of reflecting them realistically. These preconditions for great realism were destroyed by the development of bourgeois society after 1848, Lukács maintained. European writers of this period had increasingly become *"mere observers"* of social development rather than, as the great realists before them, *"experiencing"* the process of social development. The very possibility of experiencing, however, was an objective process and not an expression of a writer's inclinations. Whether there existed or came to exist between writer and society the type of relationship that engendered great realism depended on the presence of "one or more great, historically significant social and ideological currents to which the writer [could] devote himself with the entire pathos of his personality." Such currents, Lukács contended, grew rare as bourgeois society began to decline and entered the "apologetic phase of ideological development." As capitalism began to stagnate, great literary figures after 1848 turned away from life and from the development of their own class with disgust and hatred. Because they could find no social current to support, they had to assume the post of an observer of social phenomena.[31]

The period between the French Revolution and 1848 thus became the last great epoch of bourgeois literature.[32] The ensuing entry into the apologetic stage of bourgeois ideology did not mean, though, that all writers became apologists and certainly not "conscious apologists" (54). Nonetheless, the new age left an indelible imprint upon every writer. The realism of Flaubert and Zola, explained Lukács, was a battle against betrayed bourgeois ideals, but it was necessarily a subjective struggle, for objectively—"even if counter to the intentions of such significant poets"—this struggle met up with the apologetic current of general bourgeois ideological development. Why? Because at the heart of every apologia was the tendency to remain on the surface of phenomena, to ignore the more deeply rooted, essential, and decisive problems. For Flaubert and Zola, the subjective intention in making day-to-day reality their sole or predominant literary theme was to

31. Georg Lukács, "Leo Tolstoj und die Entwicklung des Realismus," *Internationale Literatur* 10 and 11 (1938): 115–38 and 112–45.
32. Georg Lukács, "Der Niedergang des bürgerlichen Realismus," *Das Wort* 6 (1936): 57–67. Page citations are given in parentheses in the text.

expose bourgeois hypocrisy. But to proclaim daily reality the norm of realism meant to renounce the treatment of social contradictions; the "new realism" (naturalism) of the Flauberts, Zolas, and Goncourts began under the "flag of a revolutionary renewal of literature. . . . The new direction of realism imagines that it provides a higher objectivity than earlier literature" (56). But this was only the "semblance of objectivity," for description could never discover anything new in themes dealing with the day-to-day, the commonplace.

Zola was never an apologist for capitalist society, but he made the transition from realism to naturalism. The transition was caused by social development that "degraded" writers, changing them from participants actively involved in the great struggles of their age to mere observers and chroniclers of daily life.[33] Zola's "naturalistic, 'experimental' novel is nothing more than an attempt to invent a method through whose help a writer degraded to the status of mere onlooker can be enabled to deal realistically with reality" (514). But in naturalism the dialectical unity of the typical and the individual was supplanted by a mechanical, statistical average; "epic situations and epic plots are replaced by descriptions," the action and interaction of human beings, at once individuals and representatives of important class tendencies, ceases. Zola was nonetheless an outstanding writer, but not as outstanding as past realists and then only because he failed to abide faithfully by his own literary program. Had there occurred in such cases a "triumph of realism"? No, said Lukács; Balzac's observation of reality was in continual contradiction to his *political* bias. This was a "triumph of realism": when Balzac's *artistic goals* did not stand in the way of picturing social truth. There existed for Zola no such abyss between his political views and the socially critical propensity of his writing. The contradiction endured instead in the artistic sphere. Zola's creative method, which was "for him and for an entire generation of writers insurmountable inasmuch as it derived from the social position of a lonely observer" (516), obstructed realistic writing. Zola's battle for realism was therefore fought, and by and large lost, within his own creative method rather than between reality and political bias, as in the case of Balzac.

Zola thus belonged to the large number of "artist tragedies" of the nineteenth century; he had been called to greatness but hindered from creating a genuinely realistic art by the "unfavorable circumstances of capitalism" (520). Was this unavoidable? Here Lukács is

33. Lukács, "Zum hundertsten Geburtstag Zolas," in *Probleme des Realismus III*, pp. 510–21; subsequent page citations appear in parentheses.

not entirely clear. He wrote in *Der historische Roman*, speaking of the period after 1848, that such artists could be as critical as possible of the ideological consequences of the historical situation, but the socio-political facts themselves, whose ideological consequences such writers battled, were unavoidably reflected in the content and form of their writing. Still, Lukács sought to modify his fatalism: the general nature of a historical trend did not influence uniformly the work of all writers active in this period, but "in view of the deep roots that this literary tendency has in the social reality of developing capitalism, and particularly in the age of imperialism, the writer's opposition to these tendencies must run deep to enable a successful artistic struggle against their literary manifestations." Such a struggle was possible, however, said Lukács, mentioning the names of Gottfried Keller, Anatole France, and Romain Rolland among "many examples."[34]

In "Erzählen oder Beschreiben" Lukács explained his aesthetic principles in terms of two styles of writing: narration corresponded to objectivity and description to subjectivity in imaginative literature.[35] In the writings of Scott, Balzac, or Tolstoy the reader learned of events significant because of their impact upon the destinies of the characters: "We experience these events" (11:104). The characters of Flaubert and Zola, on the other hand, were spectators of events: "We observe these pictures" (11:104). Whether a writer experienced or observed reality and therefore either narrated or described hinged on his social position. Balzac, Stendhal, Dickens, and Tolstoy pictured bourgeois society in the process of formation and involved themselves in the social transition; on the other hand, Flaubert and Zola began writing after 1848 within a developed, consolidated bourgeois society and could no longer actively participate and experience social life, which they found repugnant anyway. They loathed the political and social system and became critical observers of capitalist society. Both styles resulted from sociohistorical necessity; "to experience or to observe are therefore the socially determined responses of writers in two periods of capitalism; narration or description are the two fundamental creative methods of these periods" (11:106).

The "social disfavor" of the era after 1848 had distorted literary forms. In place of narration, which alone could depict realistically an

---

34. *Der historische Roman* was only published at the time in Russian in issues 7, 9, and 12 (1937) of *Literaturnyj kritik*, pp. 46–109. 27–54, and 118–47; and in issues 3, 7, 8, and 12 (1938), pp. 59–90, 11–52, 51–96, and 40–74. Quotes are taken from the German version in Lukács, *Probleme des Realismus III*, p. 291.

35. Georg Lukács, "Erzählen oder Beschreiben," *Internationale Literatur* 11 (1936): 100–118, and 12 (1936): 108–23. Subsequent issue and page citations in parentheses.

epic totality, there emerged description, a literary substitute for the missing epic whole. A "false objectivity" and a "false subjectivity" resulted, both of which wrought havoc upon the portrayal of human beings. The description of things had no attachment to the destinies of the characters; the writer composed in terms of inanimate objects, placing a complex of facts at the center of his novel. This "false objectivity" was related to an equally false form of subjectivity, for the tendency arose to construct a novel on the basis of a character's individual psychology. "But the series of subjective moods results just as little in an epic context as the series of fetishized clusters of objects" (11:117).

"This heritage has been taken over from the founders of naturalism by the different naturalistic and formalistic trends of the imperialist period" (12:111), said Lukács, applying his doctrine to the present; these were the underlying faults of modern writers and their literary forms in the age of bourgeois decline: the false, naturalistic objectivity of a series of fixed pictures existing independently of each other and a false, formalistic subjectivity, which set the human subject opposite the external world with no interaction between the two. Ideologically and poetically, the weakness of writers who practiced the descriptive method was thus their capitulation before what they described as completed results, unchanging, unchangeable products of capitalist reality. The question of intention was immaterial. The post-1848 French naturalists represented subjectively a protest movement against the degradation and deformation of man in a capitalist society; this subjective protest continued in later literary trends in declining capitalism, where significant representatives of different formalistic trends attempted to combat the meaninglessness of capitalist life. But such "revolts" were condemned beforehand to failure because of their objective inability to depict in a stagnating, dying society forward-moving forces of mankind's struggle for meaningful existence (12:116).

This was the theory to which Lukács adapted contemporary literature. He had little positive to say about Soviet belles lettres. Portrayal of the "richness" of Soviet life and of the new Soviet man had been hindered by "vestiges of bourgeois consciousness," for Soviet literature had not been immune to the influence of declining bourgeois culture and art. "A portion of our books are populated not by human beings but by a silhouette gallery of lifeless schemata," Lukács charged. There was serious need for a "culture of realism" that went beyond the pseudorealism of naturalistic inclinations and overcame the obsession with literary activism in the form of *agitka* styles of writing.

Soviet writers needed to learn this culture of realism from the classics, a realism necessarily lacking, for historical reasons, in the works of late bourgeois writers but unjustifiably missing in Soviet literature.[36] Naturalism and formalism in the West had trivialized the horror of capitalist society; remnants of naturalism and formalism, the style of observation and description, had equally trivialized the "process of mankind's greatest revolutionary transformation" in the Soviet Union, reasoned Lukács, adding: "This style must therefore be exterminated with the severest of criticism." Experience or observation, narration or description sprang from the writer's relation to life. "But what was a tragic situation for a Flaubert is here with us [in the Soviet Union] simply something mistaken—a vestige of capitalism yet to be overcome."[37]

Although the notion of bourgeois cultural decline served as the keystone to the literary doctrine that Lukács applied to the West, he by no means wrote off all bourgeois literature as decadent. Lukács also carried Engels's triumph of realism over to his interpretation of contemporary Western literature.[38] Yes, the paths of ideological development were socially necessary, he explained, but not (as the vulgar sociologists would argue) fatalistically for every individual.

Certain historically engendered class processes could be combated by rare individuals, though in an era of decaying capitalism profound intellectual and moral qualities were required to resist the forces of apologetic bourgeois ideology. Still, bourgeois writers could escape the snares of decadence through a triumph of realism. Neither subjective honesty nor the adoption of a certain world view, however, offered sure guarantees of realism. "There are instances where a politically and socially reactionary world view cannot hinder the creation of the greatest masterworks of realism, and there are instances where the very political progressiveness of a bourgeois writer takes on forms obstructing realism in his writing" (122). Literature, Lukács reasoned, could embody the contradictions, struggles, and conflicts of social life just as they appeared in the souls and in the lives of real

36. Lukács, "Die intellektuelle Physiognomie des künstlerischen Gestaltens," in *Probleme des Realismus I*, p. 184. The first two-thirds of this essay were published in German in *Das Wort* 4 and 6 (1936): 72–81 and 53–67; the third portion, which dealt with Soviet literature and was also scheduled for publication in *Das Wort*, was not printed in German. *Literaturnyj kritik* 3 (1936): 12–47 had already carried the entire essay in Russian.
37. Lukács, "Erzählen oder Beschreiben," *Internationale Literatur* 12 (1936): 123.
38. Georg Lukács, "Marx und das Problem des ideologischen Verfalls," *Internationale Literatur* 7 (1938): 103–43. Subsequent page citations appear in parentheses.

people; the knowledge imparted through such portrayals was a triumph of realism in literature. The authors of this literature need not realize that the portrayal of people caught up in social conflicts was the start of a rebellion against the ruling system, but inasmuch as prominent realists, whatever their world views might be, depicted the real dialectic between being and appearance in human existence, they spontaneously came into conflict with capitalism and its decadent ideology.

In *Der historische Roman* Lukács set forth in detail his views on "revolts and resistance" against general literary decadence; here he expounded his theory of popular front literature—the "humanistic literature of protest."[39] Lukács was enthralled by the popular front and by all talk of new "democracies," or, as he called the concept, "revolutionary democracy." Lukács was sincere; he seems honestly to have believed that the inception of popular front politics in France, Spain, and Germany betokened a new era for bourgeois writers, one that would change history and reverse the process of cultural disintegration.

"The triumph of Hitler fascism in Germany is a turning point in development not only for Germany but above all for the oppositional humanism of eminent *German* writers," Lukács avowed; "the formation of a popular front against fascism is not only politically an event of global-historical magnitude; it heralds in ideological and literary terms as well the onset of a new period of German literature" (319). The foremost humanist opponents of fascism had undergone a process of ideological clarification. Not that they had become Marxists; that was not the point. Lukács charged that it would be "petty and narrow-minded, a sectarian point of view" (320), to judge things in terms of a writer's conscious acceptance of Marxism and communism. The "spirit of *revolutionary democracy*" had reawakened under the influence of Hitler's rule, of popular front "successes" in France and in Spain, and of the "triumph of socialism" in the USSR, Lukács maintained. He insisted that the significance of great anti-Fascist writers ought not to be gauged by their ideological proximity to Marxism; but, on the other hand, this was not to argue that "their coming to terms with the problems of socialism is not an important touchstone for the validity and sincerity of revolutionary democracy in our time" (321).

Hitler fascism, the Spanish revolution, socialism in the Soviet Union, the heroic struggle of German workers—these were the events that

39. Lukács, *Der historische Roman*, in *Probleme des Realismus III*, p. 308. Subsequent page citations appear in parentheses.

strengthened the revolutionary democratism of prominent German writers. Socialism thus became a central question relating to the life of the people by touching on the material and cultural well-being of the broad working masses. Again, Lukács reiterated, to experience these questions as paramount, a writer by no means needed to be an adherent of socialism, to say nothing of Marxism. Of course the example of the Soviet Union played a large role and, needless to say, the appropriation of Marxism simplified the intellectual mastery of these questions for every "important, honest thinker." Still, Lukács repeated an idea that Rozental had expressed in 1934 in reference to Soviet fellow travelers: Marxism was not the beginning but, at best, the end of this path. First and foremost came the "honest, consistent, and lively concern with the burning issues" (322) of popular life in Germany.

However, this was all double-talk. Lukács was no different from any other undissembling Communist intellectual of the time, for whom the popular front was a mixture of myth and wishful thinking (the unified, fighting masses inside Germany) combined with a belief that it all truly represented something new. Had anything changed? Lukács and other Communist intellectuals saw clearly that a number of prominent writers had drawn close to communism with respect to their view of fascism and its "antithesis," the Soviet Union. In their elation over the popular front, though, the Lukács' actually came to believe that they, the Communists, had adopted a genuinely more moderate position. But what point was there in saying that the anti-Fascist writers did not have to be "Marxists" as long as the Communists still insisted, as Lukács did, that the intellectuals' antifascism conform with the Communist theory of National Socialism? As Lukács said, in the final analysis the question of "socialism" remained the touchstone of anti-Fascist validity and sincerity.

On this foundation Lukács constructed a theory centering on "plebeianism."[40] Germany's anti-Fascist intelligentsia had come to realize that the nation's renewal would occur through the strength of the German people. This understanding placed the historical novel at the center of attention within anti-Fascist German literature, for on the basis of knowledge about the great popular struggles of the past, such novels undertook to provide courage and consolation to men battling today. Although these novels counterbalanced the tendency in other historical novels to flee from the present, they still plainly displayed

---

40. *Der historische Roman,* written in the winter of 1936–37, was not the first of Lukács's works to speak of plebeianism. "Tolstoj und die Entwicklung des Realismus" (1936) developed the notion at length.

their "transitional character." Writers were passing from the liberalism of the Weimar era to revolutionary democracy, Lukács imagined, and this transitional period manifested itself in the historical novel in the fact that revolutionary democracy had not yet assumed concrete literary form. The writers longed for ardent bonds with the people; there was a recognition of the significance of the masses in a political sense, but this had not yet been followed up by the depiction of popular life itself as the basis of history.

Here was Lukács's *plaidoyer* for plebeianism in literature; where it was missing, the artistic creation experienced adverse thematic and formal effects: the literary principles of composition spawned by "bourgeois decadence" penetrated the works of prominent anti-Fascists. A genuine gift of fictional invention, the need for a plot, presupposed knowledge about the life of the people. Without such knowledge, writers stuck to surface facts and failed to see in fictional invention the supreme literary form of an accurate reflection of objective reality. The problem could only be solved through a writer's ties with the life of the people. The difference between a Marxist and a non-Marxist or pre-Marxist revolutionary democrat was the latter's unawareness of the social and cognitive factors that underlay the unity of his theory and practice; he achieved this unity, unlike a Marxist, on the basis of a false consciousness. "But the experience of literary history" (Lukács mentioned Balzac, Walter Scott, and Tolstoy) "proves that when a writer is deeply rooted in the life of the people, when he creates on the basis of his familiarity with the decisive questions of popular life, he can penetrate through to the genuine depths of historical truth even with a false consciousness" (336).

"Today the anti-Fascist emigration is the widely resounding voice of the struggle for liberation by millions of German toilers" (339), claimed Lukács; anti-Fascist literature had the task of bringing ideas of revolutionary democracy and militant humanism to the German people by treating them as the necessary, organic product of Germany's historical development. This could be the function of the historical novel in the anti-Fascist struggle, but it had yet to be carried out for reasons connected with its "transitional nature" and accompanying lack of true plebeianism. These problematical sides of the new historical novel were all linked to the circumstance that the political "transformation of anti-Fascist writers to revolutionary democrats" had not yet fully informed their artistic work; vestiges of "liberal and intellectualistic alienation" from problems of popular life were not yet wholly overcome, and these led to weakness in the basic conception of such novels.

The classic historical novel had been "historical" in the sense that it gave a *"concrete prehistory of the present"* (362), following the progress of the people through crises of past ages up to the present. Contemporary historical novels, on the other hand, although they worked out ties with the present, had thus far failed to write a prehistory of the present age; instead, they contained reflections in past history of contemporary problems, an abstract prehistory of the present. The role of popular destiny remained weak because the writers generally focused on historical characters belonging to the upper strata of society. Purely "symbolic tableaus" (366) resulted, and these could be left behind only when the spirit of democracy and plebeianism infused the literature. "There is nothing that can replace a concrete bond with the present or, the same thing, concrete familiarity with popular life" (415–16), Lukács stated. The existence of a popular front in Germany and the renewed spirit of revolutionary democracy had now made possible the depiction of the popular longing for liberation in positive literary characters. Only through a highly artistic realization of such literary figures could the "genuine deep longing of the broadest popular masses for a positive solution to the horrible crisis," which the German people had experienced in its "long, hard history" (416–17), be represented. The cardinal weakness of the anti-Fascist German historical novel was its inability to reveal the *"historical genesis"* of the present. "The foremost problem confronting anti-Fascist humanism is the task of unraveling those social-historical and human-moral forces whose interplay made the German catastrophe of 1933 possible" (420), argued Lukács.

Thus, through a literary aesthetic that interlocked prescriptions and proscriptions for anti-Fascist writers wishing to produce realistic literature, Lukács reached across the Soviet frontier in an attempt to impose his literary canon and the precepts of socialist realism upon Western writers. What does he call upon "non-Marxist" writers of "revolutionary democracy" to treat in their works? "Only a genuine understanding of these forces [whose interplay made the catastrophe of 1933 possible] in all their complexity and their entanglement can reveal how those forces concretely lie, and what directions of development they can take in order to lead to a revolutionary overthrow of fascism" (420). Only the question of how the Hitler regime became possible in Germany could lead aesthetically to a renewal of the classic type of historical novel such as that by Scott and Balzac. The future prospects of the historical novel thus hinged on the resumption of classic literary traditions, on the appropriation of the classical heritage. Both content and form were involved, for this heritage lay, on the one hand, in the plebeian, democratic, and therefore genuine and concrete "historical spirit" of the classical heritage and, on the other hand, in "artistic concreteness of form" (422).

How much substance was there to Lukács's insistence that revolutionary democratic writers need not be Marxists? Lukács's dogmatism was consummate; every aspect of his aesthetic theory sprang from the assumption that past history and present events were governed by Marxist laws; every side of his doctrine concerned either the manner in which past and present "objective" historical currents could be reflected accurately in literature or the nature of decadent, subjective, imperialist bourgeois trends whose influence ruined beforehand the chance for a "triumph of realism." As for Soviet writers, Lukács seems to have sensed the cynicism of calling upon them to depict objective reality, when anything of the sort would cost them their necks. For that reason, he wrote little about Soviet literature; after 1936[41] Lukács wrote almost nothing about Russian writers until 1939, when (for whatever personal reasons he must then have had) he again strongly criticized Soviet belles lettres.[42]

Lukács had no compunction, on the other hand, about telling Western writers the way to an accurate reflection of objective reality. What he utterly failed to fathom was that his own perception of reality in the West, which he used to formulate his demands upon bourgeois writers, bore little resemblance to the prevailing situation. The popular front was a hoax, and Lukács's notion of "revolutionary democracy," the inspiration for which came from the KPD's appeal for a "democratic republic" (even if Lukács had used a similar term in his 1928 *Blum-Thesen*), was a delusion. None of this existed as Lukács imagined it did. As for the cornerstone of his theory, plebeianism, a writer's bonds with the people, Lukács never figured in the factor of exile. Just how were writers supposed to draw sustenance and inspiration from the German people in order to write plebeian literature? How were they to know what was happening among the masses? Were they simply to read the Communist press? How would writers use their literature to influence the people, when Germany prevented the entry and dissemination of such literature? These simple facts alone severely damage extensive portions of Lukács's doctrine, which largely collapses of its own accord anyway in the absence of any real possibility

---

41. See notes 36 and 37.
42. Particularly in "O dvukh tipakh khudozhnikov," *Literaturnyj kritik* 1 (1939): 16–52 and in "Khudozhnik i kritik," ibid. 7 (1939): 3–32 (the passages pertaining to Soviet literature were omitted from the German version, "Schriftsteller und Kritiker," in *Internationale Literatur* 9/10 [1939]: 165–86).

for plebeianism in anti-Fascist writing. Because it was simply not true that "millions" in Germany were fighting heroically against Hitler, that inside Germany there was a historical popular front movement that made possible a plebeian literature, a good deal of Lukács's aesthetic was based on a false assumption. In 1942 and 1943 he finally realized that he had deluded himself, but never really took this into account in rethinking his literary principles.[43]

A new cult of facts had developed in the age of imperialism, Lukács explained in his view of modern literature in *Der historische Roman*. Particularly in naturalism and later in the literature of *Neue Sachlichkeit*, "pseudorealistic currents" had come into existence on the basis of a cult of isolated facts torn out of context, a cult that culminated in the theory of montage as art. But montage, an art substitute, was both the epitome of naturalism's false tendencies, because it did not even observe empiric reality as original naturalism had done, and the culmination of formalism, because the connection between details had nothing to do with the objective, inner dialectic of the characters and their fates.[44]

In such decadent literature there could be no triumph of realism, for this type of plotless writing was unable to test the validity of characters' emotions and experiences against the external world. "The inherent dialectic of their destinies can therefore no longer go beyond the writer's intentions, beyond his original prejudices, cannot refute this prejudice through the undaunting depiction of life's genuine process of development."[45] The less a writer was able to control his figures

43. See Chapter 12, pp. 404–7, for a description of Lukács's changing position. In *Deutsche Literatur im Zeitalter des Imperialismus*, written during his last years in Soviet exile and published immediately after the war, Lukács mentions the many illusions about National Socialism that had plagued exile writers. But he neglected to indicate that he had shared these same illusions. In writing about Fascist Germany, he said, the exiles had encountered tremendous objective difficulties. "The writers have been living outside of Germany for years. They are very limited in what they know about events inside the country. . . . Above all, the notion that fascism involves a tiny clique that has ruled over people the majority of whom oppose the tyrants has had a deleterious effect. . . . This idea, by no means restricted to literature, has been devastatingly refuted by the experience of the war. . . . Depicting through literature German society under fascism, the Nazi takeover, and Nazi rule, the writers viewed falsely and misunderstood the alignment of power in Germany and the depth of Hitlerism's infection of the people" (Lukács, *Deutsche Literatur im Zeitalter des Imperialismus*, pp. 63–65).
44. Lukács, *Der historische Roman*, in *Probleme des Realismus III*, pp. 306–8.
45. Georg Lukács, "Marx und das Problem des ideologischen Verfalls," p. 126. Subsequent page citations appear in parentheses.

and their actions arbitrarily, the greater the prospects for a triumph of realism, which could not occur as long as the "world of capitalism" was depicted in a static, final state. "The style of writing in the age of decline, the depiction of the finished results of capitalism's deformation of mankind in company with an elegiac or angry admixture of sentiment is nothing more than the literary immobilization of the surface plus commentary which does not touch, cannot touch, the essence of the matter" (129). Such was decadence: "false—because lifeless—objectivity, and false—because empty—subjectivity" (129). Nor did a writer's honest intentions, his belief that he was being politically and socially "'revolutionary'" change anything. The intentions of many writers who thought themselves sincere and passionate opponents of capitalism remained on the surface in an abstract political or abstract social tendency. Thus had great realism perished in a declining era. It was supplanted by openly reactionary, apologetic literature, and also by a long string of literary currents that "very 'radically,' very 'avant-gardistically' endeavored to liquidate realism by the roots" (142). Whatever the intention of representatives of such writing might be, Lukács concluded, objectively they aided the bourgeoisie in its fight against genuine realism.

That Lukács's assault on modernism—whether he called it naturalism, formalism, montage, reportage, surrealism, subjectivism, or simply decadence—broke out into the open over the issue of expressionism probably resulted from an initial coincidence. Back in 1932, in his article on Ottwalt, Lukács had brought up the issue of expressionism, which he saw as just one of many antirealistic currents. Then, in 1933, he wrote an essay devoted solely to expressionism, a literary form of advanced imperialism, Lukács said, easily put into the service of Fascist demagogy and fascism's combination of decadence and regression.[46] The subject then rested until September 1937 when Klaus Mann chanced to submit an essay to *Das Wort* dealing with Gottfried Benn's short-lived fascination with National Socialism.[47] This was the coincidence. But then Alfred Kurella "happened" to follow Mann in the same issue with an indictment of expressionism in general, which reaffirmed many of Lukács's utterances of 1933. This was no coincidence. *Das Wort* introduced both essays, announcing that the topic of expressionism was up for "discussion."[48]

46. Georg Lukács, "'Grösse und Verfall' des Expressionismus," *Internationale Literatur* 1 (1934): 153–73, first published in Russian in *Literaturnyj kritik* 2 (1933): 34–54.
47. Klaus Mann, "Gottfried Benn: Die Geschichte einer Verirrung," *Das Wort* 9 (1937), 35–42.
48. "Vorbemerkung der Redaktion," ibid., p. 35.

Kurella, writing as "Bernhard Ziegler," admixted to Lukács's 1933 arguments features of socialist realism, namely, plebeianism and formalism. Anti-Fascist literature had to clarify its position with respect to recent art history, the last significant movement of which was expressionism, said Kurella. He then made the provocative remark: "First, it is clear today what spirit begot expressionism and whither that spirit, consistently followed, leads—to fascism. Second, we . . . must honestly admit that all of us from those years have something stuck in our bones." Whether anti-Fascist literature was to be "more than a stage in the general decline of German literature or whether it could become the beginning of a great art that again took up the real traditions of national and international intellectual culture" depended upon the recognition and elimination of expressionistic residues. Claiming that expressionism had contributed to the "liquidation" of the classical heritage and offered nothing of value for the anti-Fascist struggle, Kurella demanded from émigré writers that they take a stand on three questions concerning the classics, formalism ("the main enemy of literature that truly aspires to great heights"), and plebeianism or popular appeal ("the basic criteria of any genuinely great art").[49]

There is no doubt that the intention in Moscow was to trigger controversy and use it to obtrude upon writers not living in the USSR a literary code mandatory for Soviet literati. The Muscovites were unquestionably counting upon a big response to Kurella's provocation; at the beginning, however, there was almost none. Ernst Bloch did inquire whether Ziegler's article had been written before or after Hitler's Munich speech defaming expressionism as "degenerate art," an embarrasing coincidence that nonetheless failed to prevent the Soviet exiles from proceeding with their discussion.[50] Erpenbeck answered that Ziegler's article had in fact been written before Hitler's speech and then asked Bloch to contribute an article.[51]

Bloch wrote two, together with Hanns Eisler, but he crossed up hopes in Moscow for a debate not only by sending them to *Die neue Weltbühne* instead of *Das Wort* but by avoiding the issue of expressionism altogether; Bloch and Eisler realized that Kurella's article on expressionism represented no more than a slightly roundabout way of restating Georg Lukács's views on realism and decadence while leaving Lukács, for the time being, out of the picture. In the first essay, "Avantgardekunst und Volksfront," Bloch and Eisler downplayed

49. Alfred Kurella [Bernhard Ziegler], " 'Nun ist dies Erbe zuende . . . ,' " ibid., pp. 42–49.
50. Ernst Bloch to Redaktion "Das Wort," 8 October 1937, TsGALI, 631/12/141/145.
51. Fritz Erpenbeck to Ernst Bloch, 15 October 1937, TsGALI, 631/12/141/144.

the need for continual experimentation in avant-garde art. "Today an artist remains an avant-gardist only if he succeeds in making the new artistic techniques practicable for the life and struggle of the broad masses."[52] The next essay, "Die Kunst zu erben," highlighted the battle to rescue the heritage from Fascist misuse. The task of the day outside of Germany was to help "select and prepare classical material suitable for such a struggle." As far as Lukács was concerned, Eisler and Bloch said that artists were not helped by remarks to the effect that all art produced at the present was necessarily decaying and would always be decaying; artists needed understanding and knowledge of the specific problems that they encountered in their writing. "For that reason, it would behoove the theoretician, who, moreover, comes across at times like a schoolmaster, to be cautious in his advice to modern artists," said Bloch-Eisler, adding: "What ignorance of modern art speaks from their [Lukács and his supporters] pronouncements; what bias, what abstract blindness! Everything that occurs in our time counts here as putrefaction pure and simple, summarily, a priori, without any difference." It was utterly absurd to send all writers back to the classics for models. "That is a new type of Don Quixotism and by no means a knightly kind."[53]

In mid-November 1937 Erpenbeck wrote Bloch to say that he was amazed to discover Bloch's article on avant-garde art in the *Neue Weltbühne*. He had heard that Bloch would contribute something of that nature to *Das Wort*, or did he still intend to? "That's entirely possible," said Erpenbeck, voicing his hope of having a manuscript by Bloch in his hands soon. But Bloch turned down the request, writing in late December that he preferred not to participate in the expressionism debate. Ziegler's essay had made an exceedingly bad impression in Prague, and they all ought to be happy that the "enemies have evidently overlooked it; what all the Schwarzschilds could have done with it! What kinds of 'parallels' could they have drawn from the private opinion of a Moscow writer with the extremely unfortunate pseudonym 'Ziegler,'" said Bloch, voicing his fear that the "Schwarzschilds," opponents of the Soviet Union, might have called attention to "parallels" between a Nazi art official named Ziegler, Nazi condemnation of "degenerate art," and the Soviet "Ziegler's" view of expressionism as decadence. The subject, said Bloch, ought to be laid to rest.[54]

52. Ernst Bloch and Hanns Eisler, "Avantgarde Kunst und Volkfront," *Die neue Weltbühne* 50 (1937): 1568–73.
53. Ernst Bloch and Hanns Eisler, "Die Kunst zu erben," ibid. 1 (1938): 13–18.
54. Fritz Erpenbeck to Ernst Bloch, 15 November 1937, TsGALI, 631/12/141/143;

But Bloch had other reasons for backing away from a discussion. He complained about the "congenial but reserved note" with which the editors had introduced his recent article, "Originalgeschichte des Dritten Reiches,"[55] in *Das Wort*. *Internationale Literatur* had likewise printed such an introductory comment to Bloch's "Rettung der Moral," but *Das Wort*, wrote Bloch, "if I am correctly informed, is a broad journal devoted more to the literary interests of the German popular front than the IL." He welcomed a discussion, but only on the condition that "it did not become schoolmasterish, as has unfortunately already been the case." Bloch continued: "The raised index finger, censorship, the mechanistic and schematic pronouncement: 'It is correct that . . . it is incorrect that . . .' (as in a press announcement)—all these forms of an arrogant (and on the basis of accomplishments not always proven) better-know-it-all attitude ought seriously to be stopped in this and other cases. Discussion is useful only if it is held fairly and impartially. I prefer not to expose myself to other types of discussions again." There were many being driven away by such an attitude, writers who, "though outside the party, like I am, do wish . . . to put their work at the disposal of the popular front." It was pointless to frighten away these circles of intellectuals by relapses into the tone of voice used during the "time of sectarianism."[56]

A full-blown debate soon broke out in the ensuing issues of *Das Wort* after all, though Bloch himself changed his mind and contributed to the discussion only several months later. In the meantime, *Das Wort* received and printed in the December 1937 issue and in the February, March, and May 1938 issues five different essays on expressionism before declaring the discussion closed with the publication of seven final essays in the June volume.[57] Almost certainly according to plan, Georg Lukács had remained silent until June. He had prepared an earlier response to Eisler and Bloch, entitled "Wozu brauchen wir das klassische Erbe," but he decided not to publish the essay. Here Lukács had been more blunt than usual, striking out at Bloch for viewing "figures like Dos Passos and Brecht" as representatives of contemporary art and for ignoring the "significant realists of our

Bloch to Erpenbeck, 22 December 1937, TsGALI, 631/12/141/142.

55. Ernst Bloch, "Originalgeschichte des Dritten Reiches," *Das Wort* 12 (1937): 54–73. Behind the "congenial but reserved" introductory note stood Lukács. He had been given Bloch's article for evaluation by Erpenbeck (Erpenbeck to Lukács, 8 October 1937, TsGALI, 631/12/143/303).

56. Ernst Bloch to Fritz Erpenbeck, 22 December 1937, TsGALI, 631/12/141/142.

57. The essays have been reprinted, although they are introduced by a poor foreword, in Schmitt, *Die Expressionismusdebatte*.

time"—Romain Rolland, Thomas Mann, and Heinrich Mann. Did the progressive currents of contemporary art consist solely in the destruction of old forms, "as Dos Passos in epic prose and Brecht in dramaturgy consistently carry out?" Did not the "'traditional'" narrative art of a Gorky, a Rolland, or a Thomas Mann tower above "form-destroying experiments," both artistically and in terms of the democratic-cultural tasks of the popular front? By no means did he reject contemporary art out of hand, said Lukács, he criticized only the influential "*antirealist* currents."[58]

Bloch and Eisler, Lukács went on to point out, had expressed pleasure in their essays with the struggle against vulgar sociology in the USSR, but they had ignored the major accomplishment of that struggle, "namely, the notion that a writer's political or ideological attitude for or against a certain social system offers no guarantee that his depiction of this society will be profound and truthful." Writers could be politically and socially very radical and fight against the reactionary tendencies of their time while still going along with inhuman artistic currents. Conversely, there were writers far less radical politically who in character portrayal put up stiff resistance to the barbaric currents of their age—Thomas Mann, for example. In his opposition to the barbarity that culminated in fascism, Mann was "much more radical, decisive, and consistent than any Brecht or Dos Passos." The issue was not an abstract pro or con but the "*how* of a realistic manner of writing." Lukács said this of Brecht:

> We are not speaking of a degree of talent. Brecht is an extremely gifted writer. But take a close look at what he made out of Maxim Gorky's wonderful, humanely mature, and profound *Mother*. Out of Gorky's profound portrait, so rich in perspectives, Brecht made a dry hour's worth of agitation in dialogue about certain theses lifted from *Das Kapital* and taken from Communist tactics. In character portrayal Brecht consciously submitted to those tendencies of recent development that suffocate all humanity and accept . . . the abstract reduction of man to a numeral as an unchangeable result, as "fate." Of course I realize: Brecht as a person and a politician is a passionate opponent of this development; but the entire theory and praxis of his "anti-Aristotelian" dramaturgy bases itself on the dogmatic, uncritical recognition of this social state of affairs.[59]

58. Georg Lukács, "Wozu brauchen wir das klassische Erbe?" Lukács Archivum.
59. Ibid.

Caught in the barbaric prejudices of an imperialist age, contemporary writers had lost virtually all standards of character portrayal; they accepted an accumulation of superficial, meaningless details for the truth of life or an abstract scheme for the quintessence of reality. The Gorkys and the Rollands, the Thomas and Heinrich Manns, Lukács explained, were different, for they had spent their lives fighting just such inhuman and uncritical tendencies. For that reason, "the great, living, and liberating spirit of the classical period infused their works." Bloch ought to think for a minute about the "plebeianism of classical art," which consisted of the fact that the classic writers depicted those human energies, inherent in the people, that needed only a triggering cause to become productive and formative in the life of society. Such was the goal of contemporary popular front literature: "to observe with a sharp eye and depict so thrillingly the reawakening of these forces in a German people enslaved by fascism that the portrayed picture becomes an activating example for the popular masses."[60]

Though this article was never published, Lukács still had the last word in the expressionism debate with another essay that followed Ernst Bloch's "Diskussionen über Expressionismus." Bloch had begun by announcing his intention to go back to the start of the entire debate, Lukács's 1933 essay on expressionism, which, said Bloch, underlay the articles by Ziegler and Franz Leschnitzer. Bloch repeated his amazement at Lukács's poor understanding of modern art, which "without further ado he consigned to capitalist putrefaction—and not only, understandably, to a certain extent, but in toto, wholesale." Bloch saw clearly the true thinking behind this either-or attitude: "It relegates almost all expressions of opposition against the ruling class that are not Communist from the outset, to the ruling class." During the era of the popular front, the continuation of a "black-and-white technique" was inappropriate, said Bloch. He likewise rejected Kurella-Ziegler's "three questions" by pointing out the disingenuousness of phrasing them so as to imply that all who answered in the negative or simply considered them falsely posed were concealing "'vestiges of expressionism.'"[61]

Then Lukács was given the floor for his essay "Es geht um den Realismus."[62] The difference of opinion concerned not modern literature as opposed to the classics, but this question: "Which writers, which literary currents, represent *progress* in contemporary literature?

---

60. Ibid.
61. Ernst Bloch, "Diskussionen über Expressionismus," *Das Wort* 6 (1938): 103–112.
62. Georg Lukács, "Es geht um den Realismus," ibid., pp. 112–38.

It is a matter of *realism*." Lukács went over the same ground covered in his other essays: literature as a reflection of objective reality; the dialectical unity of appearance and essence; the subjective, antirealist tendency of modern literary techniques to remain in the realm of immediate, surface reality; and the core ideas that, on the one hand, a writer need not be conscious of his role in uncovering the hidden tendencies of objective reality but that, on the other hand, the most impassioned desire to revolutionize art and create something "'radically new'" could not alone make a writer into an anticipator of the future path of development.

"The way to hell is paved with good intentions," wrote Lukács, and he proceeded to a discussion of plebeianism and the heritage. "To possess a living relationship with the heritage means to be a son of one's people, to be carried along by the current of development of one's people." Just the opposite was the avant-garde attitude toward the heritage; avant-gardists approached popular history as a "giant rummage sale," charged Lukács, mentioning Bloch's use of expressions like "usable pieces of the heritage." He criticized Hanns Eisler likewise, who suggested, according to Lukács, that one pick apart the classics and then paste the "suitable pieces together" for use in the anti-Fascist struggle. Lukács admitted that the plebeian-realistic development of contemporary German literature was not as strong as in other countries, but for that very reason attention ought to be focused on the "plebeian-realistic literature of Germany's past"; such literature did exist, and an outstanding example of it was Grimmelshausen's *Simplizissimus*. "It can be left to the Eislers to appraise the montage value of the battered pieces of this masterwork—for a living German literature it will continue to exist . . . as a vital and typical totality in all its greatness."

Works of his sort, by providing an understanding for progressive and democratic epochs of human development, prepared a fertile soil among the broad masses for "revolutionary democracy of a new type, represented by the popular front." The deeper anti-Fascist militant literature was rooted in this soil, the stronger its resonance would be among the people. "Popular front means: struggle for genuine plebeianism, many-sided bonds with the entire . . . life of one's own people; it means to locate guidelines and slogans that, on the basis of *this* popular life, awaken tendencies toward a new, politically effective life." The emigration and the struggle for a popular front in Germany had strengthened such tendencies, though there existed other antirealistic traditions that still had strong roots among politically progressive-minded, loyal adherents of the popular front.[63]

All along the Muscovites hoped that Bertolt Brecht would be provoked into a reply, which they no doubt intended, as in Bloch's case, to rebut with a suitable response by Lukács. The irony is that this all occurred in Brecht's journal! But he saw clearly the pointlessness of exchanging views with Lukács and his supporters publicly;[64] Lukács's approach to literature was so utterly opposed to Brecht's aesthetic that no amount of discussion would ever have led anywhere. Nonetheless, Lukács's essay "Es geht um den Realismus," particularly the rude remark about Eisler, had provoked Brecht's ire. Having seen the essay in manuscript form as part of the June issue of *Das Wort* ostensibly requiring his approval for publication, Brecht protested.[65] On 8 June 1938, Kurella, Erpenbeck's stand-in as de facto editor of *Das Wort*, wrote Erpenbeck in Yalta:

> Quickly a new intermezzo: the enclosed letter from Brecht just arrived. Tahu-tata! Now the cat sticks his head out of the bag. Especially in the postscriptum. (Incidentally: you had a good nose when you asked Lukács to soften the Eisler passage.) . . . To the point: as I already telegraphed, I think we have to give in out of formal considerations. Formally he is correct that articles can appear in the journal in the name of the editorial board only if none of the editors have any objections. . . . I hope you concur. I'll give a copy of the letter to Walter and will also speak with him and see how we should react. The crux of the matter is: at any rate he is now so "stimulated" that he will write for sure. And that is a gain however you look at it. How nicely the links we have long suspected in that theater wing are revealing themselves. Of course the Bloch-Eisler campaign (which is what it was, after all) did not spring from their empty bellies.[66]

Kurella concluded by expressing his eagerness to see "the 'most broadly minded' interpretation of realism that we can expect from

---

63. Ibid.
64. Brecht told Walter Benjamin that Lukács, Kurella, and others of their type ought not to be challenged theoretically (Benjamin, *Versuche über Brecht*, p. 130).
65. I have not seen this letter; whether it is extant in Moscow is an open question.
66. Alfred Kurella to Fritz Erpenbeck, 8 June 1938, TsGALI, 631/12/152/80.

that corner."[67] Brecht's protest, then, was ignored; Lukács's essay appeared against Brecht's wishes, and the mention of the name "Walter" (Ulbricht) points to the initial political nature and political origin of the discussion. A short time later, Brecht wrote Kurella again, evidently in response to a letter to Brecht mentioned elsewhere in Kurella's 8 June communication with Erpenbeck; he enclosed a brief note for publication in *Das Wort* concerning Lukács's remark "It can be left to the Eislers," and told Kurella that he, Brecht, would soon send along an essay, "Volkstümlichkeit und Realismus."[68] Kurella had been right: Brecht was so "'stimulated'" that he now wanted to contribute to the debate.

Brecht's was not the only voice raised in protest. On 20 August Hanns Eisler sent *Das Wort* an "Antwort an Lukács" and expressed his expectation that his rejoinder would be promptly published. It would be "absolutely inexcusable" were he denied the opportunity to respond to Lukács's "extraordinary abuse," the more so since "my friend Brecht writes me that you declined to print his statement on the subject."[69] But Erpenbeck refused to publish Eisler's "Antwort" either, telling him that it had been received too late; the expressionism debate was over. Had it arrived earlier, Erpenbeck assured Eisler, "we would of course have printed it. . . . It goes without saying that all of our contributors, like Lukács, have an equal right to express their opinions." Instead, Eisler was asked to contribute an essay on plebeianism or *Volksnähe*, for this was the direction in which the discussion would continue, and Eisler could polemicize much better with Lukács in such an article than in his "Antwort." Erpenbeck suggested that Eisler express his views along the lines that "one can set up this equation: realism equals plebeianism, but that this equation is schematic." He could use Lukács as a "negative example."[70]

Erpenbeck then lied: "With Brecht, who had the material with the Lukács essay in his hands on time but didn't read it carefully and therefore didn't protest against Lukács's phraseology, we have made the following agreement: we cannot publish his note (which he sent), since it is inappropriate for an editor to come out against an article

67. Ibid.
68. Bertolt Brecht to Alfred Kurella, 17 June 1938, Brecht-Archiv, Sig. 1395/32. It may be worth noting that the phrase "It can be left to the Eislers" was changed in the Russian version to "We will leave it to Eisler" ("Spor idet o realizme," *Internatsionalnaja literatura* 12 [1938]: 188).
69. Hanns Eisler (New York) to "Liebe Freunde," 20 August 1938, TsGALI, 631/12/152/66.
70. Erpenbeck to Eisler, 4 September 1938, TsGALI, 631/12/152/65.

after its publication in his own journal, an article which he *ought* to have seen beforehand."[71] But *Das Wort* would publish a series of "monographs" about prominent émigrés, beginning with one by Brecht about Eisler.[72] Moreover, said Erpenbeck, Brecht had promised an article on the "plebeianism discussion."[73] Erpenbeck's proposed solution still failed to placate Eisler. He would be happy to write an article on plebeianism, but this had nothing to do with a reply to Lukács, a "necessary response, once and for all, to an unacceptable way of discussing and twisting things." Needless to say, he could publish the "Antwort" in the *Neue Weltbühne* at any time; but that would give the appearance of differences between them, and he would do so only in an extreme case.[74] He ended up publishing it in the *Neue Weltbühne*.[75]

In the meantime, Lukács had made another derogatory remark about Brecht. In the July issue of *Internationale Literatur*, Lukács had printed the German version of "Marx und das Problem des ideologischen Verfalls." There he had written that antirealist writers might be "honest and impassioned opponents of capitalism" but that this sociopolitical tendency remained on the level of an abstract social and abstract political tendency. "In such cases—as in certain plays by Brecht or in novels by Ehrenburg—there ensues a literary abstract revolutionary utilitarianism."[76] On the heels of Lukács's essay in the June issue of *Das Wort*, this proved too much for Brecht to take. He wrote Willi Bredel in Paris that work on *Das Wort* was growing increasingly problematical; the journal seemed to be assuming a peculiar course in which a "small clique, evidently led by Lukács and Hay, is setting up a very specific form ideal implying opposition to everything that doesn't accommodate itself to this form ideal, which is derived from the bourgeois *romanciers* of the past century." The important struggle against formalism was thus itself becoming formalism. Brecht went on:

> In the *IL*, 7th issue, Lukács in fact lashed out at me again (and lumped me together with bourgeois decadence). . . . Now and then I receive a request from Erpenbeck to participate in the debate, but of course I have no interest in doing so since I

71. Ibid.

72. Brecht, in his letter of 17 June 1938, had suggested that *Das Wort* publish a series of monographs of well-known émigré artists.

73. Erpenbeck to Eisler, 4 September 1938, TsGALI, 631/12/152/65.

74. Eisler to Erpenbeck, 30 September 1938, TsGALI, 631/12/152/64.

75. Hanns Eisler, "Antwort an Lukács," *Die neue Weltbühne* 50 (1938): 1583–84.

76. Lukács, "Marx und das Problem des ideologischen Verfalls," *Internationale Literatur*

look at such debates as being very harmful and confusing, that is, just now, and then when every time at the end the opinion of the virtuous Lukács is praised (at least by Lukács himself) as the Marxist position. What value is there in proclaiming to the world that my portrayal of the Third Reich does not accord with reality . . . and that my convictions are not socialist? I don't know if these people represent thereby the opinions and sentiments of the emigration; if not, you and the Parisian comrades perhaps ought to take the opportunity to tell that to the *IL*.[77]

As things now stood, Brecht said, he received from *Das Wort* only material which had already been sorted out, and his objections were almost never taken into consideration. "I can assure you," he told Bredel, "I'll not let this go on much longer. It is important that we have this journal, after all, and it is extremely important to make it good. What can be done?"[78] Nothing was done, and none of Brecht's articles or notes was published—neither "Volkstümlichkeit und Realismus," the note about Eisler, nor Brecht's monograph on him, though it is unclear whether the plebeianism article was ever sent on to Moscow.[79] After Lukács's July article, Brecht may have decided that no further purpose would be served by forwarding it to Erpenbeck.

Brecht did respond to the affronts privately with several articles and with commentary in his *Arbeitsjournal*. Brecht had read the essays to Benjamin, who called them "camouflaged but vehement attacks,"[80] and asked his advice about publishing them. Since Lukács held an "important position" in Moscow, as Brecht explained it, Benjamin concluded that questions of power were involved; someone in Moscow needed to stand up and speak. "You have friends there, after all," Benjamin said to Brecht, who answered: "Actually I have no friends there. The Muscovites have none either—like the dead."[81] So the essays, with one exception, remained unpublished until 1966. In them Brecht repeats time and again one key idea. "To turn realism into a question of form, to tie it to one and only one form (and an old one at

7 (1938): 133.

77. Brecht to Bredel, no date (ca. July 1938), Bredel-Archiv, no archival signature.
78. Ibid.
79. Brecht's article on Eisler was sent to Moscow; in March Ruth Berlau passed on two additional sentences by Brecht, which were to form the conclusion of the article (Ruth Berlau to "die Redaktion," 4 March 1938, TsGALI, 631/12/154/16).
80. Benjamin, *Versuche über Brecht*, p. 133.
81. Ibid.

that), means: to sterilize it," he wrote in "Die Expressionismusdebatte."[82] He added in another article that "realism is not a question of form. One cannot take the form from one realist . . . and call it the realistic form. That's not realistic. . . . We ought to guard against formalism in criticism. It is a matter of realism."[83] In yet another essay he called upon critics to understand that they were practicing formalistic criticism as long as they declined to deal with formal questions in terms of conditions for the struggle for socialism.[84]

Though Brecht's essays were, as Benjamin said, "vehement," they still exhibited a sort of reserve and correctness; there were no derogatory references to Lukács at all. But the diary entries made in July, August, and September 1938, with one last comment in February 1939, were a different matter altogether.[85] Lukács, whose "significance consists of the fact that he writes from Moscow," was a "Murxist," said Brecht, writing sardonically: "In the literary treatises of journals published by Marxists the concept of decadence has surfaced again frequently. I have discovered that I too am part of decadence. Of course that greatly interests me." Reading Lukács's "Marx und das Problem des ideologischen Verfalls," Brecht criticized his notion of depiction (*Gestaltung*). Since Balzac and Tolstoy "depicted," they reflected reality; likewise the Sholokhovs and Thomas Manns. But, Brecht wrote, "There is no conflict between the realism of the bourgeoisie and that of the proletariat . . . in order to *depict* you don't need to know anything (for Th. Mann depicts and, after all, knows nothing). While depicting, these half-wits[86] give reality preference over their own prejudices, without knowing it. It is a direct process of experience: you get kicked, say ouch! He gets kicked, have him say ouch. Oh simplicity!" The class struggle, said Brecht, was a hollowed out, prostituted, plundered concept—for "the Lukács'" only an empty principle. Because the class struggle existed in reality, let the writer portray reality and it will be captured in his writing, Brecht mocked Lukács; class struggle supposedly involved everything, after all. "This obtuseness is gigantic."[87]

Brecht understood perfectly what Lukács meant with his distinction between narration and description, but he argued that the narra-

82. Brecht, "Die Expressionismusdebatte," in *Schriften*, 2:291.
83. Brecht, "Praktisches zur Expressionismusdebatte," in ibid., 2:296.
84. Brecht, "Über sozialistischen Realismus," in ibid., 2:380.
85. Brecht, *Arbeitsjournal, 1938 bis 1942*, pp. 12–39.
86. "Half-wits" is in English.
87. Brecht, *Arbeitsjournal, 1938 bis 1942*, pp. 12–39.

tive form of the Balzacs and Tolstoys had been broken apart by such "'spiritless' complexes of facts" as mine works, money, and so on—the subject matter of the Zolas. The admonitions of "the professors" could not paste back together the old narrative form of the realists, Brecht said, adding in English, "all the king's horses and all the king's men couldn't Humpty Dumpty put together again."[88] Brecht likewise understood clearly the proscriptiveness of Lukács's essays. The realism debate would block literary production if it continued along the same lines, he remarked to Benjamin in reference to Lukács, Gábor, and Kurella: "'These are enemies of production. Production is suspicious to them; it is the unforeseeable. You never know what will result. And they themselves don't want to produce. They want to play the apparatchik and have control over others. Every one of their criticisms contains a threat.'"[89]

As the summer of 1938 drew to a close, the expressionism debate, which the Muscovites tried to continue on the subject of "plebeianism," faded away, though in August Lukács published a review of Heinrich Mann's *Henri Quatre* in *Das Wort*, repeating the arguments for plebeianism that he had voiced in *Der historische Roman*. In the September issue he also printed an article on Tolstoy's plebeianism, which was excerpted from his long essay on the Russian writer.[90] The actual debate ended with a dissembling article by Kurella, who claimed that he had not intended to start a controversy when he wrote about Benn and then went on to deal with expressionism.[91] Erpenbeck then tried to launch a new discussion on "plebeianism," underscoring its pivotal role in anti-Facist art. "Precisely in this question there ought to be the broadest *agreement* within the anti-Fascist literary front. Otherwise we shall not move forward," he said.[92] But with the essays by Kurella and Erpenbeck, the expressionism and plebeianism debate broke off completely, probably for lack of interested Western discussants; there was hardly any point, after all, in a discussion in *Das Wort* or *Internationale Literatur* just between Muscovite German émigrés who could not or would not disagree on these issues anyway. The

88. Ibid.
89. Benjamin, *Versuche über Brecht*, p. 132.
90. Georg Lukács, "Die Jugend des Königs Henri Quatre," *Das Wort* 8 (1938): 125–32; "Der plebejische Humanismus in der Ästhetik Tolstois," ibid. 9 (1938): 115–21.
91. Alfred Kurella, "Schlusswort," *Das Wort* 7 (1938): 103–22.
92. Fritz Erpenbeck, "Volkstümlichkeit," ibid., pp. 122–28. There seems to have been some talk about publishing Erpenbeck's article under a pseudonym. Erpenbeck wired from Yalta: "Of course place my name under my article; I personally have no intention of identifying myself with Brecht's theoretical views" (TsGALI, 631/12/152/81).

matter did surface again briefly in May 1939, when *Internationale Literatur* published an exchange of letters between Anna Seghers and Lukács.[93] Then, after the war, many of the same issues were debated all over again in East Germany.

Beginning in late 1939, Lukács took part in the last literary debate of his Soviet exile. This time the tables were turned on him. The first sign that Lukács's exalted standing of the last three and a half years might be in jeopardy came in a *Literaturnaja gazeta* editorial for 10 August 1939. The editorial upbraided vulgar sociological notions as anti-Marxist and pernicious, "though it by no means follows that every vulgar sociological error makes one an enemy of the people." The paper added that vulgar sociology had used a class analysis to "expose" great artists of the past. Now, however, the opposite extreme was occurring: class analysis of any kind had been excluded from literary criticism and the concepts of "'humanism' and 'plebeianism'" were becoming meaningless through overuse; "vulgar sociology and vulgar humanism—these are two manifestations of one and the same weakness, the switch from one extreme to the other," said the paper.[94]

Five days later, Lukács published a short piece in the same paper on Joseph Roth's *Radetskymarsch* and made a remark soon used against him: "It is a curious phenomenon: the significant artistic merits of this work, if they do not derive from the author's ideological weaknesses, are in any case intimately bound up with them. If Roth had not suffered from his illusions, he would scarcely have succeeded in viewing so penetratingly the inner world of his civil servants and officers."[95] This was the main source of the charge that Lukács correlated an artist's *reactionary* outlook with his artistic mastery. V. Ermilov singled out this phrase for criticism in the first significant attack upon Lukács and the "pernicious views of *Literaturnyj kritik*."[96] Lukács contended

93. *Internationale Literatur* 5 (1939): 97–121. The publication had originally been planned for *Das Wort* in summer or fall 1938 (cf. the Seghers-Erpenbeck-Kurella correspondence for June, July, and September 1938, TsGALI, 631/12/141/22, 20, 19, 18, and 631/12/149/17, 16). In February 1939 Seghers received a letter from *Internationale Literatur* declaring its intention to publish the letters; Seghers told Erpenbeck that she had never understood why they had not appeared, as planned, in summer 1938 (Seghers to Erpenbeck, 13 February 1939, TsGALI, 631/12/155/4).
94. "Marksistsko-Leninskaja teorija i nauka o literature," *Literaturnaja gazeta*, 10 August 1939.
95. Georg Lukács, "*Marsh Radetskogo*," ibid., 15 August 1939.
96. V. Ermilov, "O vrednykh vzgljadakh *Literaturnogo kritika*," ibid., 10 September 1939.

that the more false illusions an author entertained, the more truthfully he depicted reality, charged Emilov. This, of course, was not
what Lukács had meant, at least not in such a vulgarized, oversimplified
form; but he had used a "dangerous phrase," as Lifshits called it in
1977, and had written too "carelessly, without considering the circumstances."[97] Not that the Lukács-Lifshits "Trend" would distinguish
itself with its polemical tactics. In fact, Igor Sats, the editorial secretary
of *Literaturnyj kritik*, called the ensuing debate so dirty that no one
could figure out the other side's position.[98]

The controversy really began over Lukács's *K istorii realizma*, which
contained essays all written and most published in 1934–36. Now the
ideas in those essays were suddenly suspect. Evgenija Knipovich attacked the volume and Lukács with the accusation that in his article
on Balzac and Stendhal, Lukács took the position that Stendhal's
"clearer, plainer, more progressive" world view, in comparison with
Balzac's, prevented Stendhal from being a genuine realist.[99] This was
the reverse of the argument that a writer's greater reactionary outlook benefited his realism. Lifshits responded to Knipovich in early
1940 in the *Literaturnaja gazeta*, which now carried the debate. "Enough,"
Lifshits called his article. He insisted that Knipovich was not interested
in a serious, sincere exchange of views at all. "Ungrounded political
accusations," said Lifshits, destroyed the basis of serious discussion.
Knipovich had earlier supported vulgar sociological views. But with
the defeat of those notions, she had changed her position by 180
degrees. Now, Lifshits charged, after the vulgar sociological class analysis had been discredited and "self-satisfied sectarianism" (Dimitroff)
with regard to Western writers overcome, there had emerged in its
stead a "non-Marxist vulgar democratic and liberal phraseology," which
adopted a noncritical attitude toward the French bourgeois revolution
and accused Lukács of being a "Thermidorian."[100]

After Knipovich had repeated her arguments,[101] V. Kirpotin, in the
same issue of *Literaturnaja gazeta*, accused Lukács of contending that
Tolstoy's "illusions and errors" were beneficial to his artistic work, an
anti-Leninist attitude.[102] Lukács acknowledged in some cases that a

97. From the author's 1977 conversation with Lifshits.
98. From the author's 1979 conversation with Igor Sats.
99. Evgenija Knipovich, "Novaja kniga G. Lukacha i voprosy istorii realizma," *Internatsionalnaja literatura* 11 (1939): 205–10; also in *Literaturnaja gazeta*, 15 November 1939.
100. Mikhail Lifshits, "Nadoelo," *Literaturnaja gazeta*, 10 January 1940.
101. Evgenija Knipovich, "Nichego ne podelaesh," ibid., 15 January 1940.
102. V. Kirpotin, "Mirovozzrenie i khudozhestvennaja literatura," ibid., 15 January
1940.

reactionary ideology was good for art, said Kirpotin, who then resurrected the old *Voprekisti-Blagodaristi* difference by saying that in other cases Lukács "simply ignored questions of the world view" in his analysis of literature. Unable to turn the clock all the way back to 1933–34, the former *Blagodaristi* now displayed their facility at appropriating *Voprekisti* arguments and twisting them for use *against* the original *Voprekisti*. Because Kirpotin and others had charged that Lukács correlated a reactionary ideology or world view with good literature, Kirpotin now attributed to Lukács a *Blagodaristi* position! But an artist did not create independently of his world view, said Kirpotin, repeating the old vulgar sociological-*Blagodaristi* argument that he still upheld. But—this is the switch in Kirpotin's position—if an artist who possessed a reactionary world view created great art, this occurred not "because of" his world view, as Kirpotin accused Lukács of maintaining, but "in spite of" it. Kirpotin was now the *Voprekist* and Lukács the *Blagodarist*.

Lukács's enemies now christened the Lukács-Lifshits and *Literaturnyj kritik* school of thought the "Trend" or the "New Trend" as the attacks mounted. None of the critics proved as adept at using Lukács's and Lifshits's tenets against them as N. N. Viljam-Vilmont, the title of whose article points to the nature of his argumentation: "The Enthronement of Oswald Spengler." Viljam-Vilmont spoke of the "*revision of Marxism-Leninism*, which for several years has been guided by M. Lifshits and G. Lukács." It was Lifshits whose theories resembled those of the "ideologues of decadence"; Lifshits was the "revisionist"; the irreconcilable enemies of everything "vulgarized," Lifshits and Lukács themselves understood the Leninist theory of reflection in a "vulgarized fashion"; only in terms of Spengler's thought was Lukács's and Lifshits's "prattle about the benefit of a reactionary world view," about the confluence of "the 'reactionary' with the 'plebeian'" understandable. Art, Viljam-Vilmont lectured, not only reflected the class struggle, but was also the "arena" of the class struggle. Finally, he concluded, the "lifeless scheme of representatives of the 'Trend'" not only suppressed and crippled the great heritage of the past, but these people also tried to "distort the impressions of Soviet readers about the path of development of contemporary Western literature." Spengler's philosophy had been swallowed up entirely by the "Marxism-Leninism" of Lifshits and Lukács.[103]

Bernhard Reich, Brecht's friend, added insult to injury in another

---

103. N. N. Viljam-Vilmont, "Vozvedenie na prestol Osvalda Shpenglera," *Internatsionalnaja literatura* 5/6 (1940), pp. 288–303.

sharp attack on Lukács. Reich characterized Lukács as an "objectivist" who revealed his "indifferent attitudes toward questions of the class struggle in literature." Realism for Lukács was an objectivist depiction of life as it was, and the subjective creative role of the writer was therefore belittled, reduced to a passive ability to perceive reality. Lukács's realism was "'abstract,'" said Reich, quoting from Eisler's "Antwort an Lukács"! These views had done severe damage to efforts aimed at attracting to the "side of the people" the most honest and progressive Western artists; the Trend, concluded Reich, had attempted to "revise and distort Marxist-Leninist views on art."[104]

Lukács fought back, but now the Brecht-Lukács roles of the expressionism debate were reversed: with one exception, the five essays Lukács wrote were never published. "There is a specter in our literary theory," said Lukács in "Prinzipielle Fragen einer prinzipienlosen Polemik": "Vulgar sociology, which was destroyed with arguments in the 1930 debates,[105] pretended cleverly to be dead, gave up its untenable positions, changed its terminology, yes, even appropriated those of its opponents with consummate mimicry. But its basic attitudes remained unchanged." What was most dear to the hearts of the vulgar sociologists? The "debates of 1930" had revealed this clearly: uncontradictory progress, starting specifically with the liberal bourgeoisie and proceeding "merrily along a straightaway thoroughfare" to socialism. This was the focus of Lukács's countercharges against the new vulgar sociologists: their proclivity to view the liberal progressive bourgeoisie uncritically and to denounce criticism of the bourgeoisie as an attack on progress in general, as pessimism, as reaction. "A strategic retreat is always preparation for a new offensive," said Lukács, "and thrusts by vulgar sociology have recently become more frequent." Knipovich's article was interesting as a "thrust" by reorganized vulgar sociology. In her criticism of Lukács's article on Balzac and Stendhal, she had resurrected ("contradicting Engels") the old argument about the supremacy of Zola over Balzac, of naturalism over genuine realism. In years past that argument, advanced by means of a "frontal assault," had ended in complete defeat. Now the tactics had been changed; Stendhal meant nothing to Knipovich; his "great name is misused by K. for a flank maneuver."[106]

104. Bernhard Reich, "Uroki literaturnoj diskussii," *Teatr* 6 (1940): 124–36.

105. Lukács refers here to the attacks on RAPP from the left, specifically the LITFRONT controversy. He leaves it unclear, however, that at the time his was very much an Averbakhian, RAPPist position.

106. From "Prinzipielle Fragen einer prinzipienlosen Polemik"; original is in Lukács Archivum.

In "Verwirrungen über den 'Sieg des Realismus'" Lukács defined again his understanding of Engels's notion of the triumph of realism. This triumph assumed changing forms with different writers of different epochs and classes. But a certain form of *trotzdem* ("in spite of it") was to be found among pre-Marxist representatives of every world view—"among *all* world views, *even* among *progressive* ones (in a bourgeois sense)." This was the key point of the present dispute, explained Lukács. Since the Trend's enemies refused to recognize the limitations, inexactitudes, illusions of progressive bourgeois world views—believing instead in a straightforward, noncontradictory historical line of development—they mechanically divided literature and writers into two groups: those with a progressive world view, which could *only* further literature, and those with reactionary views, which could *only* obstruct literature.[107] This, of course, clearly ran counter to Lukács's doctrine that reactionary views at times failed to hinder realistic portrayal and that progressive world views offered no guarantee in themselves of realism. "Comrades" Knipovich and Kirpotin saw no problem here, wrote Lukács, neither a dialectical contradiction between world view, reality, and literature, nor a set of artistic problems. They could think only in terms of a "'reactionary only'" or a "'progressivist only.'"[108]

His opponents all applied a "formal-democratic standard" to literature, which caused them to make central literary figures of Byron, Hugo, and Zola instead of Goethe, Pushkin, Shelley, Balzac, and Tolstoy.[109] These critics (Lukács called them "progressivists") still judged works in terms of a writer's world view. Kirpotin, for instance, began with the writer's intellectual outlook and his political convictions; he then searched for an expression of these convictions in the work and denied any direct influence of reality itself. Things had changed to a degree, said Lukács; "Kirpotin and Co." no longer had the courage to reject Shakespeare or Balzac wholesale for reasons of world view, as in the halcyon days of vulgar sociology; there had occurred a surface reconciliation with Marxism, but this had not changed the essence of how these critics evaluated literature.[110]

What had *Literaturnyj kritik* and its contributors really done? They

---

107. I refer to the German original, "Verwirrungen über den 'Sieg des Realismus,'" in the Lukács Archivum. This essay Lukács also published in Russian in *Literaturnaja gazeta* 13 (1940).

108. Georg Lukács, "Die Widersprüche des Fortschritts und die Literatur," Lukács Archivum.

109. Lukács, "Verwirrungen über den 'Sieg des Realismus,'" Lukács Archivum.

110. Georg Lukács "Warum haben Marx und Lenin die liberale Ideologie kritisiert?," Lukács Archivum.

had simply refused to make manifestations of literary decadence part of their aesthetic, even when particular writers in their "zigzag careers" had occasionally espoused views that enthralled the "progressivists." But Lukács was sure that this time too, "as in the RAPP debates," the unscrupulous methods of the vulgar sociologists would prove impotent against the truth of Marxism-Leninism.[111] Lukács summed up his position: the crude error of the "vulgarizers" lay in their perception of world views outside of time, space, and social circumstances; they saw only abstract "reactionary" or "progressivist" schemes and brought art works down to the same low level. But the progressive element of a Balzac or a Tolstoy was intimately bound up with limitations, backwardness, and so on, as was every progressive bourgeois current. This was necessary to stress, said Lukács, because his opponents proceeded from the axiom that progressive world views, in a bourgeois sense, had no such limitations and that Engels's "'triumph of realism', the victory of the truth of life over the prejudices of a writer, is only possible and necessary in the case of reactionaries (again in a bourgeois sense)." Lukács concluded by expressing his certainty that the mechanical application of "'formal-democratic' standards" had to be resisted, for it brought with it the "liquidation of Marxism-Leninism."[112]

The Trend, not Marxism-Leninism, was liquidated by a special Soviet Central Committee resolution dissolving *Literaturnyj kritik* with the March issue. The next month *Krasnaja nov* summed up all the "pernicious views of *Literaturnyj kritik*."[113] Under the "flag of combating vulgar sociological oversimplification," the journal had contended that the history of literature and art stood outside the class struggle. "The group around *Literaturnyj kritik* replaced classes and the class struggle in past history with abstract concepts of 'people' and 'plebeianism,'" wrote *Krasnaja nov*, stressing that everything written by Engels about Balzac and by Lenin about Tolstoy (Lukács's pet quotations) strictly contradicted the Trend's assertations. Mentioning Lukács's comment about Joseph Roth, the journal pointed out, as Ermilov had, that Balzac and Tolstoy wrote great literature not "thanks to" their reactionary views but "in spite of" them. This, of course, had been Lukács's position all along, but setting the record straight was not the purpose of the debate. The most serious charge leveled against the Trend, however, was that it had isolated itself from Soviet belles lettres

111. Ibid.
112. Lukács, "Die Widersprüche des Fortschritts und die Literatur," Lukács Archivum.
113. "O vrednykh vzgljadakh *Literaturnogo kritika*," *Krasnaja nov* (1940): 159–73.

and from the majority of Soviet writers; basing their ideas on a theory of decline, Lukács and Lifshits were said to view Soviet art as one of the manifestations of decadence.[114] *Literaturnyj kritik* and its contributors, *Krasnaja nov* concluded, held a "contemptuous attitude toward Soviet literature."[115]

There is no doubt about Lukács's influence within the German Section of the Soviet Writers' Union; he was the group's voice in all questions of literary theory. His essays likewise leave little room for speculation about his attitudes toward both Western and Soviet literature. But questions still remain concerning Lukács and the possibility of a connection between literary-political developments in the West and those in the Soviet Union. Was it coincidence that in the West the Soviet-backed literary and political popular front picked up momentum in 1936 just as a new literary-theoretical school of thought won out in the Soviet Union and eliminated many of the literary notions whose continued existence would have led to a contradiction between Soviet literary policy and popular front cultural politics? Would a literary popular front in the West, supported by the USSR, have been practicable as long as the prevailing Soviet view of classical and contemporary bourgeois literature sprang from vulgarized Marxist class analyses? There was a definite need in 1936 for a "creative method" that could be applied to Soviet literature *and*, mutatis mutandis, to bourgeois Western writers.

RAPP's dialectical materialist method, which had required a conscious Marxism from all writers, was clearly unsuitable for the West; in his 1931 and 1932 *Linkskurve* essays, Lukács was able to apply aesthetic standards virtually identical with RAPP's to revolutionary-proletarian writers, but he could never have carried these criteria over to Western fellow travelers. A new creative method, which could be interpreted as downplaying Marxism—"write the truth," "reflect reality"—was required. That socialist realism in the Soviet Union not only stressed moderate concepts like humanism and plebeianism but also spelled out taboos—formalism, naturalism, "left-wing radical foolishness"—only spotlights the new literary doctrine as just the two-

---

114. Lukács had written in "O dvukh tipov khudozhnikov," *Literaturnyj kritik* 1 (1939): 47, that socialism had exterminated all the economic and social bases of capitalist society. "And only bourgeois vestiges in the consciousness of [Soviet] artists, only the cultural backwardness makes the artists susceptible to the spreading influence of decadence and supports their interest in passing aesthetic 'innovations' and 'accomplishments' produced in the art of the imperialist West."
115. "O vrednykh vzgljadakh *Literaturnogo kritika*," *Krasnaja nov* 4 (1940): 159–73.

edged sword Soviet literary authorities needed: more tolerant in theory than RAPP's program through its emphasis on the heritage, plebeianism, and the triumph of realism, but equally decretory and censorial in its "antidecadent" practical side.

Is it also happenstance that within a short time after the Hitler-Stalin pact finally buried the popular front, Lukács, Lifshits, and the Trend came under fire for the very arguments that had official sanction between 1936 and 1939; that within a matter of months the Trend was routed, and that the entire controversy broke out suddenly over a book that contained essays from 1934 to 1936? Why had these ideas never been seriously challenged before 1939? None of this is a suggestion that Lukács had ever formulated his aesthetic doctrine in response to political directives. His theories were largely in place before socialist realism was precisely defined in 1936, and the relationship of Lukács's views with official socialist realism thereafter was symbiotic rather than synonymous. But if it is true that Lukács's theoretical ideas emerged independently of socialist realism, they nonetheless lent themselves perfectly for use in popular front cultural politics, and their precise application was probably worked out in political circles as strategy.[116] Here no Soviet or other Marxist literary critic could ever have taken Lukács's place. He was the right man at the right time. Had there been no Lukács in 1933 to 1939, he would have to have been invented.[117]

116. The mention of Ulbricht's name in connection with the expressionism debate will be recalled; then there is a curious handwritten and fragmentary piece of paper in TsGALI, at the top of which is written "Ulbricht, 23 April 1940. Old material." The page contains a list of several essays (the titles are given in German) pertaining to the 1939–40 controversy (TsGALI, 631/12/86/31). It is unclear what all this means, but it is obvious that Ulbricht was familiar with the 1939–40 debate.
117. The secret of Lukács's survival in the thirties may also lie ultimately in the importance that Comintern officials, Dimitroff, for instance, attached to the cultural-political ramifications of Lukács's work.

Chapter 11

The German *Ezhovshchina*: Stalin's Purge of Germans

The murder of Max Hölz, the first prominent German in the Soviet Union to fall victim to the developing purge, would be committed differently than later killings, but it was a murder nonetheless. After spending eight years in a German prison for his revolutionary military activity during the 1921 *März Aktion*, Hölz in 1929 went to the Soviet Union, where he traveled widely and, as a result of what he saw and experienced, soon became disillusioned. He quickly attracted the attention of the GPU.[1] In May 1933 Hölz's disenchantment with life in Soviet exile reportedly reached its zenith, and, after a confrontation with Soviet political figures who threatened to take measures if he failed to keep his mouth shut, Hölz is said to have suffered a nervous breakdown. Fearing arrest, he fled to the apartment of a German embassy official, pleading for permission to return to Germany. Then, afraid that he had walked into a trap, he ran from the apartment and barricaded himself in his hotel room in the Metropol. There he threatened to use his revolver's last sixty bullets to kill fifty-nine GPU men, should they try and take him, and then himself. Hölz was eventually calmed and convinced that no one wanted to do him harm. Soon after, he was sent from Moscow to the city of Gorky (Nizhnij-Novgorod).

In September 1933 the prominent old Bolshevik Osip Pjatnitskij told a number of leading German Communists to pack their bags for

1. The Soviet secret police bore the name Cheka from 1917 to 1922, GPU from 1922 to 1924, and NKVD from 1934 to 1943. Until 1953 the designation was MGB and from then to the present, KGB. My account of Max Hölz's murder is based on published and private sources. Karl Albrecht's book provides the most detailed account, which I have generally followed here, because, though this source must be used cautiously, Albrecht's treatment of Max Hölz conforms to other accounts as well as to what I have been told privately by those who knew Hölz in the early thirties. See Albrecht, *Der verratene Sozialismus*, pp. 314–18.

a trip to Gorky to attend Hölz's funeral. He had drowned on the sixteenth while swimming in the Oka or Volga River, Pjatnitskij said. Albrecht claims that at the funeral the coffin was surrounded by so many flowers that no one could get near it; nonetheless, severe facial and skull injuries were visible on Hölz's body. The day after the funeral, according to Albrecht, "several well-known Bolsheviks" made a secret trip to Gorky to look into the cause of Hölz's death. They managed to locate a pair of fishermen who had watched as two men beat up a third—all three of them in boats—in the middle of the Volga. The third man, "screaming in a foreign language," was finally shoved under water and kept there. So Hölz met his end. In the aftermath of his death, two "authorized" versions of the drowning were circulated in the Soviet Union. The official account, given in a pamphlet published in 1933 in honor of Hölz, claimed that he had spent the night with a family he knew before he drowned.[2] The next morning he had tried to cross the river by boat, but it tipped over in the waters of the Volga and the Oka, swollen by recent storms, and Hölz drowned.[3] The "unofficial" authorized version, which the GPU disseminated at the time, had it differently: Hölz invited a woman to go with him on the river. He was drunk and tried to assault her; she resisted, and the boat tipped over, drowning Hölz. The woman was produced shortly after the event to "confirm" what had happened.[4]

Thus began the purge of Germans in Soviet exile. Though in the next three years there were a number of other incidents involving German émigrés, arrests did not take place in significant numbers until 1936. By March of that year, however, political exiles were being picked up in the International Liaison Office (OMS) of the Communist International.[5] Trouble also arose in conjunction with the arrest of Alexander Emel (Moissej Lurye) and Fritz David (Ilja Krugljanskij), two Russians who had worked for years in the KPD apparat and were soon to become defendants in the August 1936 show trial. Dmitrij Manuilskij used the David affair, for instance, to attack Hermann Weber: instead of exercising self-criticism for his lack of vigilance in not spotting David earlier as an enemy of the people, Weber had claimed that "no one had any idea that David was a terrorist."[6]

On 9 August 1936, as part of the buildup in the Soviet press before

2. This much of the account, at least, is true.
3. *Max Hölz*, pp. 35–39.
4. Private information.
5. Private information.
6. Wehner, "Erinnerungen," p. 138.

the August trial, an article entitled "Learn to Unmask the Enemy" appeared in the *Deutsche Zentral-Zeitung*. It contained ambiguous references to German writers: "Even the comrades who have come to us from abroad and are working in the Soviet Union have not always shown sufficient Bolshevist vigilance. The liberals; those without eyes to see; the double-dealing, morally degenerate elements; the avaricious and the careerists—these types are a long way from being utterly exposed and driven out [of the party]. And this aids and abets the enemy in his insidious activity. Because of the insufficient vigilance of individual German writers, the enemy succeeded in burrowing into their ranks and exploiting their blindness and carefree attitude to its advantage."[7]

The identity of the enemy who had "burrowed" into the ranks of the German writers was not disclosed, but within a matter of days Soviet writers throughout the land were being unmasked as Trotskyists, Zinovievists, and Fascist agents. Vladimir Stavskij, secretary of the Soviet Writers' Union, announced the news in a spate of articles published in the *Literaturnaja gazeta*. On 15 August he revealed that a "certain Isaev," who had managed to pass an examination of his party documents, had been active within the party organization of the Writers' Union. He had even been recommended for work in the Home of Soviet Writers by the "former secretary of the party committee," Marchenko. But then it turned out that, documents or not, Isaev was an "infamous enemy, a Trotskyist," although the party organization had not taken a hand in Isaev's unmasking, not the first time this had happened. For, along with Isaev, "several enemies" were uncovered without the assistance of the party organization. There was something behind this, as Stavskij now explained: the former party committee secretary, Marchenko himself, had sponsored a number of discussion sessions dealing with Galina Serebrjakova's writing and had invited as one of the speakers a "certain Friedland," who turned out to be "our sworn enemy, now unmasked." Marchenko himself had introduced Serebrjakova, favoring her with the remark that she was a literary Stakhanovite worker. But Serebrjakova was soon after expelled from the party when it turned out that she had been closely associated for years with long-time enemies of the party. Stavskij raged, "What kind of vigilance is this! We have here both want of vigilance and rotten liberalism."[8]

7. "Lernt den Feind entlarven," *Deutsche Zentral-Zeitung*, 9 August 1936.
8. Vladimir Stavskij, "Usilit revoljutsionnuju partijnuju bditelnost," *Literaturnaja gazeta*, 15 August 1936.

Several days later, speaking again of Serebrjakova and Friedland, Stavskij revealed that Marchenko had now been "taken into custody." Still decrying the lack of vigilance, he noted: "We kicked out the likes of Tarasov-Rodionov, Serebrjakova, Grudskaja, Selivanovskij, and Troshchenko, who for years had ties with class enemies, the Trotskyists and Zinovievists."[9] In another article Stavskij told of the most recent development: Ivan Kataev, it turned out, had gone to visit Voronskij in exile in 1928 to obtain "directives," had collected money, and had sent it to exiled Trotskyists. Up to the last he had been associated with Trotskyists, said Stavskij.[10] The purge now claimed its first victim from among the German writers. Karl Schmückle had published an article in the *Literaturnaja gazeta* as late as 15 August,[11] but soon after he disappeared without a trace. The only hint of what had happened to him was a terse remark in the paper's editorial for 27 August, "The Will of the People": "Trotskyists Rodov, Schmückle, Troshchenko—this entire band of party enemies using the political myopia of the party committee and the Soviet Writers' Union . . . successfully masked their foul double-dealing."[12] They had now been taken care of. The editorial then mentioned the discovery of scores of enemies among writers everywhere—in Armenia, the Ukraine, Leningrad, Kiev, and so on. Before the worst of the terror subsided, some six hundred Soviet men of letters would be arrested. Most of them perished in the camps.[13]

On 21 August, Willi Bredel, speaking in front of a general assembly of Moscow writers on the subject "The Hand of German Fascism has been Severed,"[14] revealed the impact of the burgeoning purge on the German writers: "The enormous joy and profound satisfaction which

9. "Povysit revoljutsionnuju bditelnost." Iz rechi tov. Vl. Stavskogo na obshchem sobranii moskovskikh pisatelej 21 Avgusta 1936 goda, *Literaturnaja gazeta*, 27 August 1936.

10. Vladimir Stavskij, "Sdelat vse prakticheskie vyvody," *Literaturnaja gazeta*, 27 August 1936. See also *Pravda*'s description of Kataev's unmasking at a Soviet Writers' Union meeting: " 'Kataev, tell me,' asked Comrade Stavskij three times, 'what would you do with a party member if you learned that he had gone to a Trotskyist for directives, that this Communist gathered money and sent it to an exiled Trotskyist, that to this day he had retained his ties with Trotsky?' 'I would expell him from the party,' answered Kataev. The conclusion drawn by Kataev himself was approved by the party organization, which unanimously voted for his exclusion from the party" ("V partijnoj organizatsii Sojuza pisatelej," *Pravda*, 27 August 1936). Kataev died in a labor camp.

11. Karl Schmückle, "Vstrecha s asturijtsem," *Literaturnaja gazeta*, 15 August 1936.

12. "Volja strany," *Literaturnaja gazeta*, 27 August 1936.

13. Medvedev, *Let History Judge*, p. 231.

14. Willi Bredel, "Ruka germanskogo fashizma otrublena." Iz rechi t. V. Bredelja na obshchem sobranii moskovskikh pisatelej, 21 Avgusta 1936 g., *Literaturnaja gazeta*, 27 August 1936.

we German comrades living in the Soviet Union feel compells us to ask ourselves if we have done everything to keep the enemy from infiltrating our ranks. We are posing this question within our number and are checking out each one of us." David Schellenberg and Gustav Brand were now "kicked out of the Party after a check of their party documents."[15] Scrutiny by his peers must also have been the undoing of Karl Schmückle,[16] who was picked up from his room in the cooperative apartment building, Weltoktober. Anna Bernfeld-Schmückle's last words to her husband were, "Hold out, Karl."[17]

Hold out, Karl was the title of Béla Balázs's popular children's story about a young boy whose Communist parents were arrested by the Gestapo. The story was later filmed, but the picture is said to have been quietly prohibited because someone had claimed that Balázs's film was secretly based on the true story of "the Trotskyist Ruth Fischer's son."[18] Balázs later wrote a sequel to the book, *Karl Brunner*, which was also filmed, but officials of the Odessa Film Agency had evidently edited out portions of the picture. Balázs called this a "mutilation" and waged a long campaign to get the edited frames returned to him from Odessa. He wanted to resplice the film, which had "lost its politically most important and powerful episodes," show it to party authorities, and gain permission for its release.[19] The "mutilation" of the film also seems to have been criticized in the Soviet press, which led to the firing of the film makers in Odessa and their subsequent arrest. Balázs wrote a certain Shumjanskij that the Odessa officials

15. "Volja strany," ibid.
16. In the light of what Bredel said, there may be some truth to Gustav Regler's account of a conversation he had with Schmückle, who supposedly told Regler that some of his, Schmückle's, latest articles had been characterized as ideologically false and that J. R. Becher and Willi Bredel had been put in charge of interrogating him (Regler, *Das Ohr des Malchus*, pp. 336–37).
17. Beer, "Memoirs." Schmückle was in trouble earlier. In 1931 he and his wife had been purged—at that time it involved only the loss of his job—from the Marx-Engels Institute in connection with the Rjazanov affair (Huppert, *Wanduhr mit Vordergrund*, p. 300). Then, in 1935, he was having difficulties of some sort in his capacity as a high official in the German Commission of the IVRS and as editor of *Internationale Literatur*. "Karl is having certain difficulties, of which you have probably heard by now. Not only will he no longer be working in the German Commission, but he will likely also assume a function other than chief editor in the offices of the IL" (Willi Bredel to Peter Merin, 7 March 1935, TsGALI, 631/13/69/42). Sometime between then and his arrest Schmückle was also kicked out of the party, a fact Bredel mentioned in a different context (Willi Bredel, "Konsultation zu Theodor Pliviers *Das grosse Abenteuer*," in Bredel-Archiv, Sig. 334/8 [173]).
18. Sinko, *Roman eines Romans*, p. 399.
19. Balázs to Julja Annenkova, no date, MTA, Balázs Béla-Hagyaték, Ms. 5018/115.

had "lost their jobs, and some of them were expelled from the party and hauled into a courtroom." Now Balázs was trying to enlist the aid of sundry individuals in recovering the edited portions, "for the film became too superficial and simple through the absence of its important episodes! (This mutilation just may have been intentional wrecking activity.)"[20]

Balázs had no end of trouble with his *Karl* books. Just as he was about to be paid for a film script, the Hitler-Stalin pact was signed, and this "sudden change in world politics rendered it impossible to make an anti-Hitler film," Balázs complained to Aleksandr Fadjeev. The film agency had thereupon refused to pay Balázs, because the film could not be completed. He then filed suit, asking for Fadjeev's help in the matter.[21] Balázs, by the way, was not a man to cross—he knew how to protect himself and his interests. For example, when Hugo Huppert intentionally omitted mention in the *Deutsche Zentral-Zeitung* of Balázs's *Hold out, Karl* among new Russian children's films in the making, Balázs wrote him: "Of course [the omission] could be coincidence; but don't you think that this would strike me as so peculiar that it would also be obvious to any party authorities whose attention was called to it? I think the DZZ must make this good somehow immediately."[22] The implied threat was unmistakable.

Zenzl Mühsam, the wife of the German anarchist Erich Mühsam, was reportedly arrested for the first time as early as April 1936.[23] Her husband had been murdered by the Nazis in Oranienburg in 1934, and Zenzl Mühsam was afterwards invited to the USSR by Elena Stassova, the head of the International Red Relief agency (MOPR). In August 1935 Mühsam arrived in Moscow,[24] where she was given a room in the Novaja Moskovskaja Hotel. Her arrest probably came as the result of her inability to hold her tongue. She is said to have become rapidly disillusioned with the Soviet Union.[25] The charge lodged against her, however, was that she had been a Trotskyist courier for Erich Wollenberg, whom she had visited in Prague before entering the USSR. News of her arrest somehow leaked out to the West, triggering a campaign for her release in the Western press.[26]

20. Balázs to Shumjanskij, no date, ibid., Ms. 5018/117.
21. Balázs to Fadjeev, 19 April 1940, ibid., Ms. 5018/129.
22. Balázs to Huppert, no date, ibid., Ms. 5018/116.
23. Leonhard, *Gestohlenes Leben*, p. 71.
24. Ibid. Cf. also Buber-Neumann, *Als Gefangene*, p. 165.
25. Leonhard, *Gestohlenes Leben*, p. 71. See also Weissberg-Cybulski, *Hexensabbat*, p. 689.
26. Buber-Neumann, *Als Gefangene*, pp. 164–66. In a December 1936 letter to André Gide, which the French writer included in his second book on the Soviet Union, A.

Because of the publicity, Mühsam was released from jail after six months of imprisonment, according to one source,[27] and turned out onto the street in her prison pajamas. She went back to the hotel in which she had been living and then attempted to leave the Soviet Union. Buber-Neumann writes that Mühsam was actually given an American entry visa, but was arrested for the second time while awaiting a Soviet exit visa.[28] After a brief stay in the Butyrki prison, she was sentenced by a "special commission" to eight years in a corrective labor camp.

Carola Neher, the well-known stage and screen actress who played Polly in Bertolt Brecht's *Dreigroschenoper,* was evidently taken in August 1936.[29] She was charged with the same "crime" as Zenzl Mühsam: both were friends of Erich Wollenberg, and Neher too had visited him in Prague, where he had given her the address of a Moscow acquaintance. When the terror began in conjunction with the August show trial, Neher was arrested and accused of carrying messages to Moscow for the "Trotskyist" Wollenberg. She was sentenced to ten years in prison.[30] While still in the Lubjanka, she had opened her veins in an attempt to kill herself.[31] During her imprisonment she was tortured by being stuck in an isolator, was half-starved to death, and had a bout with typhus.[32] She was in prison for a time with Evgenia Ginzburg, who left this description: "I immediately recognized the German film star Carola Heintschke, the one who had hidden her gold rings in her hair during the first memorable search at Butyrki. She had changed greatly since then. The gold of her hair had lost its luster, and pathetic little wrinkles showed at the corners of the mouth.

Rudolf spoke of the fate of Zenzl Mühsam. See Gide, *Afterthoughts*, pp. 136–40. Thomas Mann knew about her arrest by July–August 1936 (see Mann, *Briefe, 1889–1936*, pp. 421–22).

27. Leonhard, *Gestohlenes Leben*, p. 71; see also Buber-Neumann, *Als Gefangene*, p. 165.

28. Buber-Neumann, *Als Gefangene*, p. 166. The interval between the two arrests seems to have been quite long. In December 1937, when he was interrogated in the Lubjanka, Herbert Wehner was asked about Zenzl Mühsam, who was free at the time (see Wehner, "Erinnerungen," p. 163). Mühsam apparently visited Theodor Plivier frequently as late as 1939, and, according to Hildegard Plivier, was arrested the second time just before the Hitler-Stalin pact. (Plivier, *Ein Leben gelebt und verloren*, pp. 103, 153–55).

29. Buber-Neumann, *Von Potsdam nach Moskau*, p. 447. Weissberg claims that Neher was taken in spring 1936, which is incorrect because she was mentioned in the *Deutsche Zentral-Zeitung* as late as July 1936. See Weissberg-Cybulski, *Hexensabbat*, p. 691.

30. Buber-Neumann, *Als Gefangene*, p. 164. According to Plivier, an agent provocateur played a role in her arrest (Plivier, *Ein Leben gelebt und verloren*, p. 140).

31. Buber-Neumann, *Als Gefangene*, p. 164.

32. Weissberg Cybulski, *Hexensabbat*, p. 691.

Yet she was even more fascinating than before. Her face was ivory-white, without the faintest trace of color. She had a childlike smile and sad, amber-colored eyes."[33]

Erich Wendt, who became a state minister in East Germany after the war, was the assistant director of VEGAAR. He was arrested as early as September 1936 on the basis of a denunciation from the Volga-German ASSR. Wendt had been sent to Engels to look into the possibility of setting up a German-language press. He had then returned to Moscow. Soon after, a typesetter—a Reich German brought to Engels because the locals could not do the job right—was arrested and subsequently denounced Wendt, who was taken into custody in Moscow and extradited to Engels. His arrest prompted a VEGAAR meeting during which everyone had to repudiate Wendt. Fritz Schälicke, a boyhood friend, was given a particularly rough time and was asked why he had not been more vigilant. Badgered repeatedly, Schälicke finally remarked, "Oh yes, now I do remember that he once made a certain comment."[34] Wendt's Russian wife is also said to have severed her ties with him.[35] Wendt was never sentenced because he refused to confess to any crime,[36] and a few years later the investigation against him was terminated. He was then released. However, when he returned to Moscow from the Saratov Prison in the Volga-German ASSR, he had no place to go and spent his first night somewhere off the side of the street in the shrubbery. Wendt soon returned to the Volga-German Republic. When it was dissolved in the summer of 1941, he was deported with the rest of the Volga Germans. Sepp Schwab, head of the German Section of Radio Moscow, later managed to bring Wendt back from Siberia to work at the station.[37]

Susanne Leonhard, the mother of Wolfgang Leonhard, was arrested at two or three in the morning on 26 October 1936. In the Lubjanka, she was taken to an interrogation four days later. There she was told that if she valued her life and ever wanted to see her son again she would admit that she came to the USSR as a Trotskyist courier and would sign a confession to that effect. She refused. At a later interrogation, in November 1936, she was read a long document that contained a so-called verbatim report of all conversations she had had in Moscow with her friend Hans Rodenberg, the German actor and

---

33. Ginzburg, *Journey into the Whirlwind*, p. 691.
34. From the author's conversation with Dr. Hans Goldschmidt, who worked for VEGAAR from 1932 until 1937 and attended this particular meeting.
35. Beer, "Memoirs."
36. This is Goldschmidt's account.
37. Beer, "Memoirs."

producer. The only difference was that all of the remarks in the report were attributed to her, including leading comments that Rodenberg had made to elicit what were said to be Leonhard's "anti-Soviet" opinions. On 17 June 1937 she was sent off to the camps.[38]

The real massacre of Germans occurred in the Ezhovshchina during the years following Jagoda's replacement as head of the NKVD by Nikolaj Ezhov in September 1936. There is ample evidence to indicate that the first large-scale round-up of foreigners in the USSR took place in early November 1936. Karlo Štajner, a Yugoslav Austrian, was arrested in his apartment on 4 November 1936. He had emigrated to the USSR in mid-1932 and worked in the publishing house of the International Agrarian Institute. Although he soon got into trouble for his inability to "adapt,"[39] he nonetheless became a member of the Soviet Communist party and a Soviet citizen. On 6 September 1937 he was sentenced to ten years according to section 58, articles 1a, 6, 8, and 9.[40]

Werner Hirsch was imprisoned on the same day, 4 November 1936. Hirsch, who together with Fritz David had been one of Wilhelm Pieck's ghost writers and who was also known in party circles as Ernst Thälmann's *Füllfederhalter,"* ("fountain pen"), had been arrested by the Nazis with Thälmann on 3 March 1933. Hirsch then spent eighteen months in various Gestapo prisons and concentration camps.[41] One source claims that Hirsch was released after about a year due to Emmi Göring's intervention and his mother's connections, another that Hirsch's release was the result of his mother's friendship with General von Hammerstein, who was commanding general of the Reichswehr until 1934. Hirsch is said to have "converted" the general's two daughters to communism, after which they supplied Hirsch with information from their father's desk. The main points of the accusation against him after his arrest in Russia were reportedly his relationship with Hammerstein's daughters and the very fact that he had been freed from the Nazi concentration camps with the help of von Hammerstein (Hirsch was said to have been a spy for the Reichswehr). An NKVD troika dictated a sentence of ten years to him.[42]

Hans Günther and Trude Richter were likewise picked up on 4

38. Leonhard, *Gestohlenes Leben*, pp. 45, 56, 90.
39. Štajner, *7000 Tage in Sibirien*, pp. 50–52.
40. Ibid., p. 46. That is, treason, espionage, terrorism, and sabotage.
41. Hirsch, *Sozialdemokratie und kommunistische Arbeiter im Konzentrationslager*, p. 19.
42. Poretsky, *Our Own People*, p. 181; *Pattern for World Revolution*, pp. 166–68; Štajner, *7000 Tage in Sibirien*, p. 73.

November 1936.[43] They were arrested by the NKVD at two in the morning in their room in the Kievskaja Hotel and taken to the Lubjanka, where they waited in the basement in the company of dozens of other newly arrested unfortunates. At seven in the morning the pair was separated. Richter was then brought to a communal cell in the Butyrki, which she shared during her stay (apart from Russians) with four other Germans, one of whom was Waltraut Nicolas, the wife of Ernst Ottwalt.[44] Ten months passed before Richter's first interrogation in August 1937; it lasted a quarter of an hour. At later questioning sessions she was accused of the following: in 1935 she and Günther had gone to one of the frequent literary gatherings in the headquarters of the IVRS. Well after the meeting had started, someone arrived late. It was Moissej Lurye, who took the only seat left, next to Richter. Following the discussion, the meeting broke up and everyone left. Outside the building Richter and Lurye shook hands. She was confronted with that episode during her interrogation, long after Lurye had been tried and convicted in the August show trial, and it formed the basis of the charge of Trotskyism raised against her. There was another accusation. In 1935 Richter went to the German embassy to have her passport extended and was told that it would be done on the condition that she work for the Germans. Richter immediately notified the party of the attempt to recruit her, and she then applied for Soviet citizenship. After her arrest she was accused of being a double agent, probably by dint of the fact that she had set foot in the German embassy.[45] During one of the mass dispatches of prisoners to the camps, Richter was told that she had been sentenced to five years of corrective labor according to article 58, section 10 (Anti-Soviet Propaganda and Agitation).

Der Herren eigener Geist was at least partially responsible for Günther's arrest. He had drawn on substantial quantities of Nazi periodicals, newspapers, and books in research for *Der Herren eigener Geist*, among them Rosenberg's *Mythos des 20. Jahrhunderts*, sent to him by his moth-

---

43. The following account is drawn from Trude Richter's unpublished memoirs, which she showed the author in 1977 in Leipzig; it is also based on the 1977 conversations between Richter and the author.

44. Richter shows up, under a different name, in Nicolas's memoirs (Nicolas, *Die Kraft*, p. 34).

45. Beck and Godin write that "foreigners on the political blacklists in their own countries were as a rule disinclined to go anywhere near their own consulates, because visits to them were regarded as serious crimes by the Soviet authorities, including the NKVD. Nonpolitical specialists avoided their consulates for the same reason" (Beck and Godin, *Russian Purge*, p. 119).

er. In summer 1935, while vacationing in Malejevka at a sanatorium belonging to the Soviet Writers' Union, Günther was approached by Moissej Lurye, who had worked with Günther in the KPD's agitation and propaganda department. From 1933 to 1935 Lurye had been lecturing on Germany and fascism at Moscow State University, and he asked Günther to lend him his copy of Rosenberg's *Mythos*. But in the summer of 1936, Lurye was arrested and charged with accepting an assignment from Trotsky, Ruth Fischer, and Arkadij Maslow to assassinate Stalin; he was tried as one of the prominent defendants in the first Moscow show trial in August 1936, found guilty, and shot. When the NKVD arrested Lurye, Rosenberg's book was found in his library. Asked how he had come by it, Lurye told the police that it belonged to Günther. This provided the basis for one of the charges lodged against Günther. Like Richter, he received an initial five-year sentence, though he survived only the first two.[46]

While walking around Red Square on the evening of 6 November 1936, Ernst Ottwalt and Waltraut Nicolas were duped into accompanying an NKVD man to a nearby police station. There an officer checked their passports and asked if Ottwalt was the German writer of the same name. They were then taken to the Lubjanka and placed under arrest the next day.[47] Nicolas eventually received five years; the charge of espionage, which had been raised before sentencing, was dropped. Ottwalt too received an original sentence of five years. He seems not to have been charged with spying either, although rumors abounded after his arrest (deliberately spread by the NKVD) that he had been picked up as a Gestapo spy. He was sentenced, however, for "anti-Soviet agitation."[48]

So the arrests continued. In late 1936 an article appeared in the *Deutsche Zentral-Zeitung*, "The Criminal Activity of German Fascists in the USSR,"[49] announcing that in early November there had been a number of Germans arrested in Leningrad and Moscow and charged with activity hostile to the state. The arrested had allegedly tried to "form Fascist cells, involving the recruitment of Soviet citizens. Among the latter, the Germans engaged in Fascist propaganda, disseminated

46. Richter, "Memoirs." Richter writes that Günther rushed immediately to Wilhelm Pieck upon hearing that Lurye had been arrested. Pieck told Günther, " 'Don't worry, Comrade Hans, we in the Comintern were also thunderstruck; we were just about to entrust EMEL with a new post. There was no reason to suspect him.' "
47. Nicolas, *Die Kraft*, p. 20–22.
48. Nicolas, *Viele tausend Tage*, p. 20.
49. "Verbrecherische Tätigkeit deutscher Faschisten in der UdSSR," *Deutsche Zentral-Zeitung*, 18 November 1936.

illegal Fascist literature, carried out military espionage in the interests of a foreign state, and tried to obtain information relating to a particularly sensitive state secret."[50] The Germans were furthermore charged with sabotage against Soviet industry and acts of terrorism against the "leaders of the Soviet government." The article listed the surnames of some of those arrested: Parti, Klein, Futerknecht, Demisch, Trinkaus, Fischle, Oberberg, Moche, Niedermaier, and Goldschmidt.

On 1 March 1937 a follow-up story appeared in the *Deutsche Zentral-Zeitung* in which more names were included: Tilo, Melchior, Pfeiffer, Walter, Paul and Tatjana Beerwald, and Larisch. It was reported that on 16 February 1937 the People's Commissariat for Internal Affairs (the NKVD) had decided merely to expel a number of the arrested, "in spite of the fact that they have confessed to counterrevolutionary agitation and to espionage activity." The *Deutsche Zentral-Zeitung* reported that there had been a meeting between representatives of the German embassy, which had taken an interest in the case since the accused were German citizens, the NKVD, and the Commissariat for Foreign Affairs to discuss the fates of Tilo, Goldschmidt, and Pfeiffer, all three of whom had been ordered deported. Tilo and Pfeiffer told the embassy official that they refused to go back to Germany, and Pfeiffer declared, according to the *Deutsche Zentral-Zeitung*, that he wanted to remain in the USSR at all costs and that he was prepared to accept for his "crimes" any punishment as long as he was not forced to return to Germany. The *Deutsche Zentral-Zeitung* continued: "At the same time, Pfeiffer threatened, should he be expelled, to kill himself at the border." Tilo also reportedly asked that he be deported to any country but Germany. Pfeiffer, as it turned out, was the only one not expelled; his deportation was postponed, the *Deutsche Zentral-Zeitung* wrote, until he obtained a visa for a third country.[51]

50. Ibid. The Paris *Deutsche Volkszeitung* also picked up the "sensational" story, mentioning other names and noting that as of 22 November twenty-three "agents and spies" had been rounded up in Moscow, Leningrad, and other cities ("Nazi-Verschwörung in Moskau" and "Die Nazi-Spionage in der Sowjetunion," *Deutsche Volkszeitung*, 15 and 22 November 1936). The atmosphere was being readied for the second show trial in January.

51. "Ausweisung von neun deutschen Staatsangehörigen aus der UdSSR," *Deutsche Zentral-Zeitung*, 1 March 1937. There is reason to believe that this Pfeiffer was the Leningrad correspondent of the *Deutsche Zentral-Zeitung*. Pfeiffer's last article in the *Deutsche Zentral-Zeitung*, for which he wrote quite regularly, appeared on 9 October 1936, which at least gives an approximation of the date of his arrest. That Max Pfeiffer was arrested (regardless of whether he was identical with the Pfeiffer mentioned in the *Deutsche Zentral-Zeitung*) is confirmed by Karlo Štajner, who was together with him in the Solovki Islands. See Štajner, *7000 Tage in Sibirien*, p. 75.

Another story connected with citizenship concerns "Anna," a German Communist from Hamburg. After Hitler came to power, she joined her husband, who had also fled to the USSR and was working as a mechanic in Siberia. Anna was unable to adjust, and her husband decided to send her home. But in the meantime both had become Soviet citizens. He turned to the German representative in the Comintern, who promised to look into the matter. Then, in 1937, Anna's husband was arrested. She sold her possessions, moved back to Moscow, and, after waiting one day in a long line, got in to see the German representative. As soon as the word "arrest" came up, she was shown the door. She then went to the German embassy, where she was told: "You have become a Soviet citizen. . . . We can get you home only if the Soviet authorities release you from your Soviet citizenship." She was then sent to the Soviet office responsible for such matters and informed there that, "if you bring . . . a statement that the German consulate is willing to restore your German citizenship, we will release you from Soviet citizenship."[52] She went back to the consulate, filled out the necessary forms, and was told to come back the next day. That night the NKVD arrested her and charged her with being a spy.

The arrests continued through 1936 and 1937, when numerous eminent Communists disappeared. Leo Flieg, organizational secretary of the German party's Central Committee, was called to Moscow from Paris during Easter 1937.[53] His friend Willi Münzenberg, who was bombarded throughout 1937 with demands from Moscow that he too return to the Soviet Union to answer the charge of "Trotskyism," pleaded with him not to go. Flieg responded: "I've done nothing wrong; I won't try to wiggle out of it."[54] Flieg is said to have been arrested as he stepped off the train in Moscow.[55] The venerable old Spartacist Hugo Eberlein, who had been in attendance when the Comintern was founded, was still at liberty at the end of April 1937, but was arrested sometime thereafter. A friend of Liebknecht and Luxemburg, Eberlein at various stages in his political career had been

52. Lipper, *Eleven Years in Soviet Prison Camps*, p. 63.
53. Weber, *Die Wandlung*, 1:121.
54. Gross, *Willi Münzenberg*, p. 303.
55. Conquest, *The Great Terror*, p. 578. Wehner, however, writes that Flieg was arrested "after a few weeks." Cf. Wehner, "Erinnerungen," p. 152. Whether it was Flieg or not, in Ivanov's *Memoirs* there is a curious description of a German Communist, fresh off the train from Paris, entering cell no. 45 in the Butyrki wearing "a smart suit the likes of which Soviet citizens had not seen for many a long day" (Ivanov, *The Memoirs of Ivanov-Razumnik*, pp. 306–7).

a member of the German Central Committee and of the Comintern's Central Control Commission. While there had been rumors in the Western press as early as October 1936 that Eberlein and Münzenberg had been arrested, the same rumors are said to have surfaced somewhat later, this time in a Swiss socialist newspaper. A press conference was held in Moscow at which Eberlein laughingly described the "lies and fairy tales circulated by the foreign press" concerning his arrest.[56] The NKVD picked him up the next day. He was reportedly brutally interrogated and tortured in the Lefortovo Prison. He received a sentence of twenty-five years. A day after Eberlein's disappearance, at a general meeting of the workers and employees in the Comintern's Executive Committee, the candidacy of Jule Gebhard for a position on the ECCI's trade union committee was being discussed. Gebhard had worked under Eberlein and the day before had sat next to him in a meeting. He was now mercilessly cross-examined and pressured into admitting his want of vigilance with respect to Eberlein. He himself was not arrested, but a few days later his wife was, and Gebhard was forced to give up his job and his apartment, moving into the ramshackle house back of the Hotel Lux.[57]

Heinz Neumann disappeared during the early morning hours of 27 April 1937, when he was taken from his room in the Lux by three NKVD men and the commandant of the hotel, Gurevich, who forced their way into his room and told him that he was under arrest.[58] He was never seen or heard from again. Margarete Buber-Neumann's arrest warrant had been drawn up as early as 15 October 1937, but she was not taken into custody until 19 June 1938.[59]

Hermann Schubert, who had worked in the executive council of MRP since his expulsion from the KPD's leadership in 1935, was preparing to speak at a meeting of the presidium of the ECCI when the Italian Ercoli (Palmiro Togliatti) demanded to know if it was true, as the Austrian MRP functionary Malke Schorr had claimed, that Schubert had said that the Moscow trials and Trotsky's connections with German fascism could not be used for foreign propaganda because the Communists' enemies would then argue that Lenin too had collaborated with the enemy by traveling through Germany in a sealed train car with the permission of the authorities. Schubert's attempt to

56. Beck and Godin, *Russian Purge*, p. 122.
57. Wehner, "Erinnerungen," p. 149.
58. Buber-Neumann, *Von Potsdam nach Moskau*, p. 463.
59. Buber-Neumann, *Als Gefangene*, p. 11.

answer Ercoli was cut short, and he was arrested a short time later.[60] Hermann Remmele was arrested in 1937, as was his wife and their son Helmuth, a functionary of the Communist Youth Organization.[61]

In 1939 Hermann Weber and August Creutzburg were arrested in the Volga-German ASSR, the latter along with his wife, Klara Vater, and child. One account has it that Creutzburg was accused of collaborating with the Gestapo in the arrest of Ernst Thälmann in 1933. It was rumored that Creutzburg was asked by the NKVD how much money he got for betraying Thälmann. When he answered "twenty-five marks," his interrogators insisted that this was impossible. So Creutzburg changed his story: "Well then, write down three hundred marks."[62] Herbert Wehner has written that droves of German Communists arrested during the purges were accused of being responsible for Thälmann's arrest.

Erich Birkenhauer, Theodor Beutling, Max Strötzel, Willi Leow, Willi Koska, Roberta Gropper, Heinrich Meyer, Fritz Schulte, Kurt Sauerland—all were arrested, most of them in 1937 and most in the Hotel Lux, which was home in Moscow for hundreds of foreign Communists.[63] The purge was almost as severe in a variety of buildings housing foreigners, the cooperative apartment house Weltoktober, for instance. Weltoktober was a building made available for occupancy in April 1936. All sorts of people from a variety of different countries lived there: doctors, teachers, workers, engineers, journalists, politicians, and so on. "For a time in 1937 and also in 1938, there were arrests in Weltoktober every night," wrote Lilli Beer, who lived in the building; "they came in waves, according to country, for instance: 'all' Germans, 'all' Hungarians, 'all' Estonians or Latvians, and so on; and also all the Poles, this time without the quotation marks. Or they took place according to professions, and the next morning talk in Weltoktober revolved around who had been arrested the night before."[64] The

60. Wehner, "Erinnerungen," p. 150. Grete Wilde allegedly told German students at the Lenin School that Schubert had engaged in terrorist and provocational activity as early as 1934 in the Saar (ibid., p. 160).

61. Weber, *Die Wandlung*, 1:256. See also the (genuine?) description of Remmele's arrest in *Pattern for World Revolution*, pp. 244–45.

62. Wehner, "Erinnerungen," p. 153.

63. See Mayenburg's *Hotel Lux*.

64. Beer, "Memoirs." Medvedev (*Let History Judge*, p. 222) writes that by April 1938 the arrests of 842 German anti-Fascists had been recorded by the German representative to the Executive Committee of the Comintern. Medvedev told the author that most of these came from one émigré hotel.

arrests—during one night in particular fourteen people disappeared —reportedly followed a wave of deportations. The inhabitants of only a few apartments were spared either arrest or expulsion from the country.

The Ernst Thälmann Club in Moscow had originally been organized, before 1933, for the foreign workers in the Soviet Union. Later on it became a meeting place where various political and cultural functions were held: musical productions, plays, political discussions and presentations, literary lectures, and so on. The club had two thousand members.[65] The NKVD raided it as well, particularly the leadership. In mid-1937 the *Deutsche Zentral-Zeitung* carried an article by Alois Ketzlik entitled "Criticism and Self-Criticism in the Ernst Thälmann Club,"[66] which hinted at some of the problems. According to Ketzlik, a "new leadership" had taken over in December 1936, a reference, it would seem, to the arrest in late 1936 of the previous head of the club, the Communist trade-union official Erich Steffen, and his wife.[67] Herbert Wehner wrote that the German representative of the Comintern at one time washed his hands of the club, trying to get Wehner to assume responsibility for it. Wehner refused, justifying his unwillingness by pointing out that he had been deprived of his party functions and that a party investigation of him was in progress. After Steffen and his wife disappeared, the leadership of the club was assumed by Paul Schwenk, a former deputy in the Prussian Diet, his wife Martha Arendsee, and Albert Zwicker. Ketzlik's article highlights the atmosphere at meetings of the club's officials:

> At the second meeting Comrade Rose . . . participated in exercising self-criticism. . . . An element of the old club leadership, on the other hand, a class-enemy type . . . who for a long time had tried to gather comrades around him, expressed hostile, vindictive criticism of the new club leadership; in so doing he gave ample warning of how insufficient class vigilance can permit class-enemy elements to use the Bolshevist criticism and self-criticism demanded by the party for their own sinister purposes. Those in attendance at the three meetings of the German Section [of the club] saw through those intrigues. For the first time, the German Section engaged in Bolshevist criticism and self-criticism.

65. Barck, *Johannes R. Bechers Publizistik*, p. 55.
66. Alois Ketzlik, "Kritik und Selbstkritik im Ernst-Thälmann-Klub," *Deutsche Zentral-Zeitung*, 15 May 1937.
67. Wehner, "Erinnerungen," p. 148.

Above all else, these meetings were a signal to all comrades to practice Bolshevist class vigilance. The participants learned from one meeting to the next and established the basis for a new functioning of the club under the precepts of real Bolshevist self-criticism.

Whether before or after the article in the *Deutsche Zentral-Zeitung*, the "new leadership" of Schwenk, Arendsee, and "several younger members" was arrested.[68] In 1938 the club was dissolved and its rooms were closed.[69] Toward the end of 1937, the German club in Kharkov was stormed by NKVD troops and the walls of the building were smashed in during a futile search for "weapons."[70] Neither were the schools spared. The German Rabfak (*Rabochij fakultet*), a sort of night school visited by German workers, Austrian *Schutzbündler*, Russian Germans from the provinces and the Volga-German ASSR, and others for the purpose of raising the level of their education, was shut down in 1938.[71] The Karl Liebknecht School, which was attended by the children of German and Austrian émigrés in Moscow, witnessed the arrests of many of its teachers. Wolfgang Leonhard writes that, beginning in March 1937, one teacher after another was picked up. He mentions the names of his German teacher Gerschinski, a Communist who attended the Karl Marx School in Neukölln as a youth and who had come to the USSR in 1933; Heinz Luschen, a history and geography teacher; and Kaufmann, who taught math and chemistry. That included arrests just in Leonhard's class. The pattern repeated itself throughout the rest of the school, leaving behind a depleted, exhausted, and terrorized teaching staff.[72] Like the Thälmann Club, the Karl Liebknecht School was also dissolved (in January 1938, according to Susanne Leonhard).[73]

Nor was the German Children's Home safe. Home no. 6 was originally a building intended for the children of the *Schutzbündler*, some three hundred of whom had emigrated to the USSR following the aborted uprising of February 1934 in Austria. But the children of

---

68. Ibid.
69. According to Susanne Leonhard, that had happened as early as January 1938. (Leonhard, *Gestohlenes Leben*, p. 140).
70. Beer, "Memoirs."
71. Ibid.
72. Leonhard, *Die Revolution entlässt ihre Kinder*, p. 23.
73. Leonhard, *Gestohlenes Leben*, p. 140. Liebknecht's prominence may have been enough to have a school named after him, but it provided his family with no protection in Soviet exile. Medvedev writes that Liebknecht's son was expelled from the party, and his nephew Kurt was arrested (Medvedev, *Let History Judge*, p. 222).

other German-speaking Communists were also housed in Home no. 6. Leonhard describes arrests in 1938 among the children. At one time orders were given from above that those whose parents had been arrested by the NKVD, and there were many of them, were to be taken from the home and put into an NKVD orphanage. The order, however, was rescinded. In the wake of the Hitler-Stalin pact in 1939, a certain "reorganization" took place, and the house was dissolved in line with the "new demands of foreign policy."[74]

VEGAAR was decimated. Vali Adler, the daughter of the famous Viennese psychologist Alfred Adler, was arrested in January 1937 while working for VEGAAR. The charge against her was that her parents had met Trotsky abroad and that she was in contact with him through her parents.[75] The VEGAAR directors disappeared. Erich Wendt had been picked up in September 1936. Krebs disappeared in 1937 along with his crippled wife.[76] Otto Bork was arrested in 1937 during the November festivities.[77] Another editor who knew Bork, hearing of his arrest, remarked in the firm's office that Bork was a decent man. She was fired immediately and given a severe reprimand. Richard Sorger, a Hungarian who supervised translations of Lenin and Stalin into German, was also arrested.[78] Felix Wolf (Rakov), who had been expelled from the party in 1933 with Erich Wollenberg, was arrested while employed by VEGAAR.[79] How many more disappeared from the German section of VEGAAR (to say nothing of the other national sections) is not known, but there is reason to believe that most Germans who worked there had been arrested by late 1938. All of the proofreaders in the printing press Iskra revoljutsii, which did much of the foreign-language printing in Moscow, were picked up on one day.[80]

The Foreign Language Institute in Moscow had numerous German émigrés on its staff, many of whom were arrested. Lev Kopelev, a former student who studied under Herwarth Walden and Trude Richter, said that most of the arrests of the Germans came in the course of one month or so; there was a time, he said, when there were scarcely any Germans left in the school.[81] Richter had been arrested in

74. Leonhard, *Die Revolution entlässt ihre Kinder*, pp. 17–18, 28, 38–40, 47–48.
75. Buber-Neumann, *Als Gefangene*, p. 170.
76. Private information, and Margarete Buber-Neumann in a letter to the author.
77. Private information.
78. Private information.
79. Dr. Hans Goldschmidt in a letter to the author.
80. Beer, "Memoirs."
81. From the author's 1977 conversations with Lev Kopelev.

late 1936, and Kopelev recalled conversations with a number of unidentified men who were trying to gather information about her and Heinrich Spaan, who was also arrested (Spaan was a philologist who published a number of language and grammar books in the Engels Deutscher Staatsverlag in 1935). When the others in the institute were taken into custody is not known. Fritz Platten, the celebrated Swiss revolutionary who had helped arrange Lenin's trip in the sealed train car and who had also saved Lenin in 1918 from an assassination attempt, worked for the institute and was arrested. His picture was afterwards removed from the Lenin Library, where it had been displayed.[82] One story has it that Platten was accused of being a German spy in 1917 and was badly tortured. But he refused to sign a deposition, and he and his interrogator eventually agreed that he would admit to having spied for some other country, either America or Argentina, but not for Germany.[83] Other Germans apparently taken from the Foreign Language Institute were a certain Weiss; Lieben, who, according to Kopelev, was the author of sea stories; and Gustav (?) Fischer, who wrote short plays.[84]

One curious incident in 1937 involved the arrest of children of prominent Communists. Among the young people picked up were the son of Gustav Sobottka, cofounder of the Red Trade Union Organization; Max Maddalena's son; the son of Hans Beimler, of Spanish civil war fame; and both sons of the Revolutionary Socialist Max Seydewitz, Frido and Horst. The five were first accused of forming an illegal Hitler Youth group in the Ernst Thälmann Club, then of planning to blow up a factory, and finally of plotting Stalin's assassination.[85]

To Georg Born goes the dubious distinction of being the only German writer publicly denounced in the Soviet press; he was accused of being a spy. Born seems to have been arrested before V. Kolbanovskij attacked him in *Krasnaja nov* in a vicious article entitled "Several Methods of Ideological Diversion Used by Japanese-German Fascism: The Writer-Spy Georg Born."[86] Kolbanovskij began by pointing out that an important role in the many types of "diversionary spy activity of the agents of Japanese and German fascism" was played by the "different

82. From the author's 1977 conversations with Lev Kopelev.
83. Medvedev, *Let History Judge*, p. 283.
84. From the author's 1977 conversations with Lev Kopelev.
85. Wehner, "Erinnerungen," p. 166.
86. V. Kolbanovskij, "O nekotorykh prijemakh ideologicheskoj diversii japansko-nemetskogo fashizma (O literaturnoj dejatelnosti pisatelja-razvedchika Georg Born)," *Krasnaja nov* 7 (1937): 196–98.

methods of ideological diversion." For the leaders of Japanese-German espionage knew that in the Soviet Union it was impossible to show up openly with Fascist propaganda; that would meet with the merciless and unrelenting opposition of the entire Soviet people. Hence, the enemies of the union were forced to adopt different methods, masking their "pitiful ideas" in a form that was incomprehensible to people who suffered from the "idiotic sickness of carelessness and political myopia and that was wholly beyond the ken of politically and morally vacillating elements." Such an example of fascism's ideological diversion in Soviet literature, wrote Kolbanovskij, was the activity of a "certain" Georg Born. With his first two novels, Born had acquired the reputation of an anti-Fascist writer. But, Kolbanovskij elaborated, one was justified in expecting from an anti-Fascist writer an exposure of the Fascist secret police. That did not occur in Born's writing. Instead, he portrayed the Gestapo in an altogether false light; in his latest novel he told the reader "nothing new" about the Gestapo, compared with what had already been published in the periodical press. Gestapo agents in Born's novel, it was said, were very primitive and underdeveloped psychologically. This type of portrayal of the activity of the German secret police, which in reality made use of "far more complicated methods of espionage and provocation," could only serve as a means to "disorient" the reader. Georg Born disappeared without a trace.[87]

Almost as fantastic were the charges evidently filed against the German Jewish composer, Hans W. David. David, it seems, was warned not to seek refuge in the USSR; "he simply didn't fit in."[88] But he went anyway, with his wife Li David, an actress who may have been invited to the USSR by the Deutsches Staatstheater in Engels. In April 1937, David, by then the main conductor and artistic director of the Engels State Choir, wrote an article for the *Deutsche Zentral-Zeitung* in which he praised the USSR as a true land of asylum. He contrasted it with Paris, where he had been compelled to buy his daily copy of *L'Humanité* in a different part of the town "to avoid being spotted as a regular reader of the Communist newspaper." That "would have led to our expulsion." In the USSR, on the other hand, wrote David: "I don't live

---

87. During a German test in the Karl Liebknecht School in June 1937, the teacher prepared to read a selection from a book by the "anti-Fascist writer" Georg Born. Before he could begin, one of the students told him that Born had been arrested a few days earlier as an "enemy of the people." The teacher, ashen-faced, put the book away and read instead from a piece of reportage by Egon Erwin Kisch (see Leonhard, *Die Revolution entlässt ihre Kinder*, p. 24).
88. Greid, "Als Fremder drei Jahre," p. 34.

the life of an émigré, here on the Volga; instead, in the land of socialism I have found a new home."[89] David's date of arrest has not been determined, but in 1938 Li David turned up in Brussels, where she worked for a time with Martin Esslin. Although she had evidently been deported, her husband, she told Esslin, had been arrested for writing and sending a birthday "hymn" to Stalin—in twelve-tone music.[90]

Many of the exiled German Communists—editors, journalists, actors, and so on—had been sent to work in the Volga-German ASSR. The toll of the terror there is largely unknown, but there are indications that it was brutally high. How many Volga-German writers perished in these years is also cloaked in obscurity, but the following comments from a long article in the *Deutsche Zentral-Zeitung* portray the atmosphere there in 1938:

> The vile Trotskyist-Bukharinite enemies of the people, who managed for a time to sneak into the art institutions of the Volga-German ASSR and carry out their filthy work, did much to retard the development of national art. Thus, not only were the party's policies in the area of art distorted, there were also obvious acts of wrecking. For instance, the German State Philharmonic and the Musical Comedy Theater, both of which were extremely popular beyond the frontiers of the republic, were liquidated. That was not only a blow to art; much more than that, it resulted in a loss of more than half a million rubles. Presently the consequences of the wrecking activity are being dealt with. Even the German State Philharmonic has been rebuilt.[91]

What probably happened is that the "art institutions" of the Volga-German Republic were first decimated by the NKVD. The ranks of the Musical Comedy Theater and the orchestra were probably so thinned out that both had to shut down, or they were closed by the NKVD. By mid-1938, following the third and largest show trial, a whole new batch of "wreckers" had to be found, and the havoc wrought earlier by the NKVD was then blamed on the newly unmasked "enemies."

The sheer horror of it all—here just one fate in millions—is cap-

89. H. W. David, "Wahrhaftes Asylrecht," *Deutsche Zentral-Zeitung,* 9 April 1937.
90. Personal information from Martin Esslin.
91. S. Fedulkin, "Kunst und Künstler in der Republik der Wolgadeutschen: Rückblick und Vorschau," *Deutsche Zentral-Zeitung,* 14 August 1938.

tured in this montage of passages from eight letters written by Friedrich Wolf over a fourteen-month period. His letters concern a close friend, Lotte Raiss, in Engels:

> Four days ago I met Lotte in Engels. She is expecting a child by Lorenz. . . .[92] Lotte is having a damn difficult time. I had just seen her husband, and then, the very next day, he went the way so many are going today. For L. that is doubly difficult. If she should lose her job in the publishing house, with the two kids . . . but since she's divorced there is really no reason for that to happen. . . . What a life. Lotte's youth is ruined. . . . The fact is, she is now sitting alone with her two children. . . . For the time being she'll have to stay in Eng. [els], as hard as it is for her; but she can't get a residence permit in M. [oscow] without a job contract. . . . According to the new regulations in the USSR, L. will again receive work. It was high time for the change, in every respect. . . . L. also seems, in the meantime, to have "fallen ill" [that is, she was arrested]. Hilda should *not* send any more letters; it can only harm [Lotte]! Else [Wolf] is now fighting to get at least Lena to Moscow. Tell Hilda to write and tell me when and if she last heard anything from L. . . . Else just wrote that she is going to fetch Lena. She really pulled out all stops . . . since, after Lorenz, Lotte too was "secured." Unfortunately I couldn't do anything from here, but Else at least got Lena out of there. . . . Two days ago Else wrote that she had word for the first time from Lotte. Larissa, Lotte's child by Lorenz, died. Just imagine what L. must have gone through.[93]

In mid-November 1937 the prominent actor Alexander Granach was taken into custody in Kiev. What probably led to his arrest was his decision to leave the country. As late as September 1935 he was convinced that his "place was in the red sixth of the world,"[94] and he had decided to accept Soviet citizenship. But in early 1937, perhaps as a

---

92. Lotte's first daughter, Lena, was by Wolf; Larissa, about to be born, was by Lorenz.
93. Wolf (Moscow) to Walter and Margret Strub (Basel), 6 January 1937; Wolf (Engels) to Else Wolf (Moscow), 25 October 1937; Wolf (Engels) to Else Wolf (Moscow), 26 October 1937; Wolf (Helsingfors) to the Strubs, 4 January 1938; Wolf (Paris) to the Strubs, 26 January 1938; Wolf (Sanary-sur-mer) to Strub, no date; Wolf (Sanary) to M. Strub, 14 August 1938; Wolf (Paris) to M. Strub, 10 December 1938 (Wolf-Archiv, Mappen 280 and 332/1).
94. Granach to Lieven-Stiefel, 24 September 1935. Granach's letters are in the Alexander-Granach-Archiv, AdK (West Berlin).

result of the August 1936 and January 1937 show trials, Granach decided to leave the USSR, although he wrote Lotte Lieven-Stiefel that "there is a tendency 'from above' not to let me go—as a well-known anti-Fascist actor—and perhaps to involve me in films or in the Russian or Ukrainian theater."[95] Toward the end of 1937, Granach broke off his contacts with the theater in Kiev, where he had had differences with the management. His last letters to the West, on 2 and 9 November 1937, indicate that he wanted to go either to Paris to join Erwin Piscator or to southern France to work with Lion Feucht-wanger on a film project. Granach must have been arrested shortly afterwards. Julius Hay wrote in his memoirs that he heard about Granach's arrest only after the actor was free again; his detention evidently lasted only a few weeks. Granach seems to have been re-leased because he had with him a letter from Lion Feuchtwanger asking for Granach's participation in work on the film in France. The letter was in Granach's pocket when he was arrested.[96] According to Hay, Granach—pale, thin, and shorn of his hair—told him that the interrogator found the letter and at first wanted to charge him with correspondence with foreigners. Granach was beaten. "Finally it dawned on him that it wouldn't do to beat to death someone who got letters from a man who drank tea in a parlor with Stalin."[97] Granach left the USSR on 16 December 1937 and, after a short time in Zurich, emi-grated to the United States.

Bernhard Reich and his wife Asja Lazis were arrested sometime in 1937 or 1938. Reich was later released for a while, probably during the Ezhov-Berija transfer of power in December 1938, and was able to meet with Bertolt Brecht when the latter passed through Moscow in May 1941.[98] Reich was evidently banished from the capital sometime after that. Asja Lazis was in a camp until well after the war.

Wives and families of the arrested suffered a special fate. Many of the wives of "enemies of the people" automatically lost their apart-

95. Granach to Lieven-Stiefel, 3 February 1937.

96. Hay, *Geboren 1900*, pp. 228–29. Cf. also Granach to Lieven-Stiefel, 9 November 1940 (writing from Hollywood): "I am especially pleased with my savior Feuchtwanger." What worked for Granach failed to help Hans Günther. He had the arresting NKVD officers lug away two huge bundles containing Günther's manuscripts and correspon-dence, including complimentary letters from Lion Feuchtwanger and Heinrich Mann about *Der Herren eigener Geist*. Günther hoped to free himself with those two letters (from the author's 1977 conversations with Trude Richter). Heinrich Mann's letter, quoted in Chapter 3, p. 118, was a typewritten copy.

97. Hay, *Geboren 1900*, p. 229.

98. See Reich, *Im Wettlauf mit der Zeit*, p. 377. Brecht promised to intervene on behalf of Lazis with a "Russian ambassador" whom he knew.

ments and jobs. If they were party members, they were often expelled and banished from Moscow. No small number was also arrested, and many were put into working camps with a regimen only a notch above that of the regular forced labor camps. The Hotel Lux had a run-down building in the back that was set aside for the families of arrested Communists. Some of the wives reportedly tried once to obtain help from the International Red Relief agency (MOPR) but were thrown out of the building. To keep them from trying to get into the Comintern building itself, a separate office was set up in the center of town, headed first by Dittbender and, after his arrest, by Paul Jaeckel. Its purpose was to take care of matters pertaining to ordinary German Communists in the USSR, including the problems of wives whose husbands had disappeared. The actual German representative to the Comintern is said to have gone to great lengths to limit his contacts with the many German Communists in Russia and reputedly notified some one thousand party members *outside* of Moscow that they were no longer permitted to consider themselves party members.

Lotte Thiele had come to the USSR with her child and worked for the International Liaison Office (OMS) of the Comintern. Fired from that job, she was ordered to appear before the Comintern's International Control Commission to respond to charges that her husband had freed himself from a German concentration camp by agreeing to supply the Gestapo with information. Upon his release, he informed the party about the matter because he had had no intention of fulfilling his promise to the Gestapo, but he was still considered a traitor. A functionary by the name of Naujoks, whose husband was also in a Nazi camp, was interrogated by the ICC and expelled from the party for "supporting Trotskyists." She had remained in contact with her parents, who belonged to the Leninbund, and had sent them money in the West because they were in financial straits. After she was deprived of her party card, she visited the German representative to the Comintern, Philipp Dengel, who threw her out of his office, saying that one should not even talk with "such people" and that she ought to have been arrested.[99]

Carola Neher was snubbed repeatedly following the arrest of her husband.[100] Lilli Beer was fired from her job in the *Deutsche Zentral-Zeitung* because of the arrest in early 1938 of her close friend Franz Roscher. Felix Halle's wife was ignored by former friends; forced to

---

99. The above comments are based on Wehner, "Erinnerungen," p. 147.
100. Hans Rodenberg, a friend of Neher, remarked to another actress (Ada von Bastineller, also arrested later), "Carola? I scarcely know her" (*europäische ideen* 14/15 [1976]: 60).

vacate her large apartment, she was virtually thrown out on the street. She drowned herself in the Moscow River.[101] The wife of Ludwig Birkenfeld, who had been arrested in 1937, was told that she was "no longer worthy" of teaching children (she was employed in the Karl Liebknecht School) and not entitled to live in Moscow. She was made to take up residence a minimum of two hundred kilometers outside Moscow. The wives of many leading Communists—Remmele, Kippenberger, Creutzburg, to name a few—were arrested, the charge in almost every case being the crime of belonging to "the family of an enemy of the people."

In some other cases, wives were told that they could not live in any of the country's five, ten, or fifteen largest cities. Often the family's children were expelled from school, and even the youngest occasionally lost its place in a kindergarten. Most of the wives of the *Deutsche Zentral-Zeitung* editors arrested in early 1938 were deprived of their rooms in a dacha that belonged to the paper. The Austrian Communist party (KPOe) evidently did what it could for the wives of arrested *Schutzbündler* and members of the KPOe. Johann Koplenig reportedly watched out for a group of *Schutzbündler* wives, and these women were given financial help from a fund of contributions from other Austrian party members. A few other cases: Ella Müller, the wife of the KPD cadre director, was forced to work in a mine following the disappearance of her husband. Nora Auerbach was expelled from Moscow, but attempted to sneak back in several times. She was warned repeatedly before being arrested and sent to a labor camp; her two children were put in an orphanage. She later tried to escape from the camp to find her children and froze to death outside the compound. Anna Bernfeld-Schmückle was unable to deal with conditions during the evacuation of Germans from Moscow after the outbreak of war and committed suicide in central Asia.[102]

The year 1938 began with a devastating NKVD attack on the *Deutsche Zentral-Zeitung*.[103] Not that there had been no arrests within the *Deutsche*

101. Greid, "Als Fremder drei Jahre," p. 30.
102. Beer, "Memoirs," and personal information from Mrs. Beer.
103. Ibid. Many of the facts concerning the attack on the *Deutsche Zentral-Zeitung* are taken from Lilli Beer's "Memoirs." She went to the USSR in 1928 and remained for eighteen years, working at various times for the *Nachrichten* and the *Rote Jugend* in the Volga-German ASSR; for the Verlag für nationale Minderheiten in Moscow; in the German section of Utschpedgis, a pedagogical publishing house, under Jolan Kelen-Fried (who was arrested later); in the *Deutsche Zentral-Zeitung* until February 1938; and for the German section of Radio Moscow after the war broke out.

Zentral-Zeitung before: in late 1933 or early 1934, the chief editors, headed by the Soviet-German Frischbutter, were arrested. The new editor in charge was Julja Annenkova, a Soviet citizen of Lithuanian parentage. Arrests also took place in 1936. In 1936 or 1937 the editor Schumann vanished, only to reappear several months later, reluctant to talk about what had happened to him. Others taken before 1938 include Günther Auerbach, a translator, and Ladislaus (Johann?) Fodor, an editor. Leopold Forst had left the *Deutsche Zentral-Zeitung* for other work and was later arrested. Paul Klein, a translator who had been a member of the Soviet Communist party since 1920, was arrested in 1937. Hans Bloch disappeared (his last article in the *Deutsche Zentral-Zeitung* was published on 24 August 1937), as did Rudolf Haus, who wrote frequently for the paper in 1935. Haus last published in the *Deutsche Zentral-Zeitung* on 22 April 1936, which gives a rough idea of when he was arrested. His wife, Hilde Löwen, was also picked up,[104] although she seems to have been arrested at a later date. Buber-Neumann says that Haus was in the Vorkuta Camp before Hilde Löwen was arrested.[105] Bernhard Richter, a proofreader, was arrested.[106] Ernst Fabri spent some fourteen days in jail in early 1938. Upon returning to the *Deutsche Zentral-Zeitung* office, however, he claimed that he had merely been unable to get a pass to enter the building.

The most hazardous job in the paper was that of chief editor. On 1 June 1937 Julja Annenkova's name appeared for the last time as *Deutsche Zentral-Zeitung* editor. Annenkova, perhaps (according to Lilli Beer) married to Central Committee member Ljubimov, turned up soon after her arrest in a cell with Evgenia Ginzburg, to whom she explained that "traitors" had worked their way into "every branch of the government and party organization."[107] Her arrest, she claimed, had of course been a judicial error. Annenkova was replaced as chief editor by Karl Kürschner (Karcsi Garai), who lasted five months before his name disappeared from the *Deutsche Zentral-Zeitung* on 26 October 1937. In 1939 an NKVD court declared him innocent and released him, but the next year, while Kürschner was working in the Hungarian section of Radio Moscow, the state prosecutor protested against his release, and he was picked up again directly from the radio station, this time never to return. His place in the *Deutsche Zentral-Zeitung* was taken by a Hamburg Communist, Richard Greve, though by now the

---

104. Hay, *Geboren 1900*, p. 225.
105. Buber-Neumann in a 1978 letter to the author.
106. Wehner, "Erinnerungen," p. 150.
107. Ginzburg, *Journey into the Whirlwind*, p. 154–55.

name of the head editor was replaced in the newspaper by the designation "editorial collegium." Greve gave his interpretation of the arrests that had gone on around him at a political meeting of the paper, where he was heard to say: "Where wood is being cut, there are bound to be splinters."[108] He soon vanished. His wife, Traute Bernier, first a typist and then a secretary for the paper, was arrested and given a sentence of three years in camp as a "member of the family of an enemy of the people," the Soviet equivalent of *Sippenhaftung*. Greve was replaced by a Russian, Sobolevich, who spoke scarcely any German. He too lasted only briefly. The last chief editor of the *Deutsche Zentral-Zeitung* was probably Karl Hoffmann, a Latvian who spoke German as his native language. He stayed until July 1939, when the *Deutsche Zentral-Zeitung* ceased publication.

In the course of three days in February 1938, virtually the entire editorial staff of the *Deutsche Zentral-Zeitung* was liquidated, one after the other. The assault began on 11 or 12 February. The first morning Alois Ketzlik, the trade-union editor, failed to show up for work; nor did his close friend and companion Margret Mengel, who was part of the paper's editorial staff. Mengel's son Hannes had been told that he was to go immediately to family friends in the event of her arrest. He never appeared. During the next three days, the rest of the staff was led away; left behind, apart from one or two of the editors, were the typists and the technical help. One by one, while the remainder waited upstairs, the editors were called down to the office of the administrative director, Kuznetsov, to be taken into custody by the NKVD. Only a few were ever heard from or seen again. Some of the arrested included: Hermann Paul, a Sudeten German writer; Oskar Deutschländer, the editorial secretary; Franz Falk (real name, Geza Reitmann; party name, Franz Kunert), editor; the Galician Fedja, editor; Martin Jährig, assistant editorial secretary; Georg Metzger (or Georg Wegener, the name he used in the paper), foreign editor and work council spokesman; Jack Nawrey (Nussbaum), who reported mostly from the Volga-German ASSR; Schumann, for the second and last time; and Paul Stern (Ladislaus Csillag), agricultural editor.

What might have precipitated the raid, if indeed there was a specific "cause"? It is certainly possible, because every organization and institution (every collective of whatever size and importance) was said to have its share of wreckers and enemies of the people, that the NKVD in the three-day raid merely picked up the quota of "enemies" that had been established for the *Deutsche Zentral-Zeitung* somewhere in an

108. Beer, "Memoirs."

NKVD office building. The paper's time may simply have come. Something else, though, seems to have been in the air in the weeks before and, most importantly, during the arrests. On 21 January 1938 an article appeared in the paper entitled "The *DZZ* Must Reflect our Magnificent Soviet Reality." It was signed by D. H. Rosenberger, chairman of the central executive committee of the Volga-German ASSR, deputy member of the Supreme Soviet of the USSR. Rosenberger wrote:

> I would like to say something about the relationship between the *Deutsche Zentral-Zeitung* and the toiling masses of the Volga-German ASSR. In our republic I have frequently heard opinions of the newspaper that are not particularly high. It must be said that the *DZZ* is insufficiently disseminated in our republic. What was the cause of the poor relationship of the newspaper with the toiling masses of the Volga-German ASSR and of the low opinion of the newspaper? The cause was that enemies of the people were in the paper; that these Fascist enemies of the people undertook everything to see that our magnificent Soviet reality was not reflected or was reflected incorrectly.[109]

A few days later, a long, denunciatory article appeared in *Pravda* concerning the "shortcomings" of the Soviet Writers' Union; it was signed by Aleksej Tolstoj, A. Kornejchuk, Valentin Kataev, and A. Koralaeva.[110] The gist of the article was that the Soviet Writers' Union had become an utterly bureaucratized organization that placed belles lettres and the writing of creative literature at the bottom of its list of priorities. *Pravda* and the four coauthors of the article charged that the Soviet Writers' Union had become wholly cut off from creative literature, from the critical journals, and from the publishing trade. What is important about the *Pravda* upbraiding of the Writers' Union and its head, Stavskij,[111] to German matters is that the charges were mimicked a short time later in the *Deutsche Zentral-Zeitung*. However, there was one significant change: the accusations were leveled at the

109. D. H. Rosenberger, "Die *DZZ* muss unsere herrliche Sowjetwirklichkeit widerspiegeln," *Deutsche Zentral-Zeitung*, 21 January 1938.
110. Aleksej Tolstoj et al., "O nedostatkakh v rabote Sojuza pisatelej: Pismo v redaktsiju," *Pravda*, 26 January 1938.
111. Vladimir Stavskij, who had taken the lead in attacking other writers in 1936, was singled out for harsh criticism. Articles critical of the Soviet Writers' Union and of Stavskij continued to appear in *Literaturnaja gazeta* for several more months, though Stavskij escaped arrest. He died in the war.

German Section of the Soviet Writers' Union. On 10 February, no more than a day or so before the NKVD was launched against the paper's editors, a long article appeared in the *Deutsche Zentral-Zeitung* entitled "The German Section of the Writers' Union: The Way It Is," under the by-line of a certain Karl Stürmer, an obvious pseudonym. The *Deutsche Zentral-Zeitung* invoked the authority of the *Pravda* article and wrote that the paper's criticism was currently being discussed "animatedly" in all circles of Soviet writers. There was only one section of the Writers' Union that had refused to take a position on the article, and that was "the *German Section* of the Writers' Union and its supervisory board, the *German Commission*."[112] And, the *Deutsche Zentral-Zeitung* argued, *Pravda*'s strictures actually fit the German Section much better. "Karl Stürmer" charged the German Commission with utterly neglecting Soviet-German culture and its florescence in areas inhabited by Russian Germans.[113] But the atmosphere within the German Section itself bore the brunt of Stürmer's attack:

> What the German Section of the Writers' Union lacks, especially the German Commission, is a spirit of camaraderie. It is hard to imagine poorer relationships than those between the individual German anti-Fascist authors, the members of the German Section of the Writers' Union. The atmosphere that rules among these writers is not one that will further their desire to work and nurture their creative energy. Instead of working creatively and using their artistic endeavors to help the toiling masses with the construction of Soviet-German culture in the battle against fascism, valuable time and energy is wasted on nasty quarrels, malodorous gossip, petty hostilities, and intrigues.[114]

Printed beneath the article was an "editorial request" that the German writers respond to the charges. J. R. Becher, Andor Gábor, Georg Lukács, Hugo Huppert, Julius Hay, Theodor Plivier, Adam Scharrer, Berta Lask, and other "interested comrades" were asked for their opinions.

With the publication of Stürmer's article in the *Deutsche Zentral-*

---

112. Karl Stürmer [pseud.], "Die deutsche Sektion des Schriftstellerverbandes, so wie sie ist," *Deutsche Zentral-Zeitung*, 10 February 1938.
113. Ibid. ". . . there is no concern for the plans, difficulties, and success of the writers, who are given no concrete help, even though there are large numbers of comrades, not only in all the Soviet-German districts and cantons but also in Moscow proper, who have literary ability and are urgently in need of creative advice."
114. Ibid.

Zeitung, the long-standing feud between the German Section of the Soviet Writers' Union, particularly certain of its leaders (the German Commission), and the *Deutsche Zentral-Zeitung* came out in the open. The exact cause of the dissension is hard to pin down because it was no doubt rooted in intense personal rivalries; these were abundant to begin with among the figures involved and were only exacerbated by the atmosphere of the times. The animosity perhaps sprang from a *Deutsche Zentral-Zeitung* refusal to offer itself, to the extent the German Commission desired, as a publishing forum to German writers in the USSR. But the opposite may have been the case: certain editors in the *Deutsche Zentral-Zeitung* may have been offended that some writers chose to ignore the *Deutsche Zentral-Zeitung* because they took the view that it was beneath them to publish in a tabloid printed largely for the Soviet-German population. In any case, what then happened was this: a cryptic notice appeared in the 17 February 1938 issue of the *Deutsche Zentral-Zeitung*; it was signed by Alexander Barta, Johannes R. Becher, and Fritz Erpenbeck in the name of the German Section's directorate. The notice informed the paper's readers that on 14 February, at a meeting of the German Section attended by "members of the editorial board of the *DZZ*," consensus had been reached following a talk by Barta that the 10 February article had been "based on insufficient information" and had given a false impression of the activity of German anti-Fascist writers in the USSR. The notice claimed that in actual fact there was a "healthy" atmosphere within the German Commission and that no efforts were being spared to help and assist other writers. The article concluded: "Unprincipled attempts to answer justified criticism with unworthy means, such as Comrade Hugo Huppert undertook repeatedly, were unanimously and sharply condemned. All those present agreed that the meeting contributed to a good relationship of cooperation between the writers and the *Deutsche Zentral-Zeitung*."[115]

That reply from the German Section was followed by an editorial comment stating that the *Deutsche Zentral-Zeitung* regretted its publication of the incorrect article of the tenth; the discussion on the fourteenth, the paper wrote, had led to an airing of the relationship between the German Commission and the editorial board of the newspaper.[116] But the nature of the "airing" was the NKVD's annihilation

---

115. "Die Antwort der deutschen Sektion des Sowjetschriftstellerverbandes; Ammerkung der Redaktion," *Deutsche Zentral-Zeitung*, 17 February 1938.
116. Actually, even after February 1938 there was no noticeable increase in the number of contributions by German writers to the *Deutsche Zentral-Zeitung*.

of the editorial board, and the question that poses itself is whether or not the NKVD assault on the *Deutsche Zentral-Zeitung* was in any way connected to the altercation between the newspaper and the important figures of the German Section. Who was Karl Stürmer? Could it have been Hugo Huppert hiding behind the pseudonym? He was involved in matters pertaining to Soviet-German literature,[117] matters that the article of the tenth had raised. Huppert also had frequent dealings with the German Section, for whose leaders he harbored—and harbors—a hatred bordering on the pathological. And many members of the German Section felt the same way about Huppert. Consider, to take one example, the description given by Herbert Wehner of the writers' response to the news of Huppert's later arrest. He was promptly denigrated as the "incarnation of all filth and anti-Sovietism, as a clique former, and as having secret ties with fascism."[118] He was made responsible, according to Wehner, for everything bad that had happened in the previous year, for vicious reviews, cancelled publishing contracts, character assassinations, and so on.

The article of the tenth appeared in the cultural section of the *Deutsche Zentral-Zeitung*, which was headed by Huppert. None of the other *Deutsche Zentral-Zeitung* correspondents who published periodically in the paper had the slightest connection with the German Section and none would have been in a position to report in any fashion on its activities. Huppert, on the other hand, attended the meetings of the German Section regularly and was present at the meeting of the fourteenth. It could well be that Huppert tried to exploit *Pravda*'s censure of the Soviet Writers' Union to settle accounts with his many real and imaginary enemies in the German Section. This is the only scenario that accounts adequately for the 17 February reference to Huppert's "unprincipled attempts to answer justified criticism with unworthy means," an allusion, it seems, to an attempt Huppert probably made at the meeting of the fourteenth to ward off countercriticism against "Stürmer" and the *Deutsche Zentral-Zeitung*.

Huppert claims that he was arrested on 12 March 1938 (that is, one month after the editorial board of the *Deutsche Zentral-Zeitung* was decimated) and that he was freed from prison fourteen months later. But if Huppert's statements are true regarding the date of his arrest,[119] he must somehow have escaped the fate of the other editors

---

117. Huppert, *Wanduhr mit Vordergrund*, p. 491; see also his remarks at the 1934 Soviet German Writers' Conference cited in Chapter 6, pp. 131–32.
118. Wehner, "Erinnerungen," p. 160.
119. See Huppert, *Wanduhr mit Vordergrund*, p. 537.

during the three days in February. Yet something had certainly happened to him in February: his last article in the *Deutsche Zentral-Zeitung*, for which he had written regularly every few days in the preceding four years, appeared on 1 February, and his name disappeared from the cover of *Internationale Literatur*, of which he was a coeditor, in the February issue. In other words, if Huppert was not arrested along with the *Deutsche Zentral-Zeitung* editors shortly after 14 February, his position in the newspaper and in *Internationale Literatur* had at least undergone a radical change—in February, not in March, when one would have expected the changes to have occurred if he had been arrested at the later date.

In conversation with the author and by letter, Huppert lay all blame for his arrest on the shoulders of Lukács, Becher, and Barta, whom he accused of making "malicious, mendacious denunciations" of him. He, on the other hand, had made statements against no one, either before, during, or after his arrest, although he "could have destroyed the swine Becher with one sentence." As Huppert explained it, the "Lukács clique" (Erpenbeck, Becher, Gábor, and Barta) was infinitely jealous of him because he held down two posts, chief of the *Deutsche Zentral-Zeitung*'s cultural section and "vice-chief editor" of *Internationale Literatur*. Because of his membership in the Soviet Communist party, and because he had "married into power" (Huppert's wife was Russian), the Lukács clique had come to believe that "higher authorities had placed Huppert[120] in their midst, that he had certain responsibilities, perhaps even secret mandates; in other words, he was the 'commissar' in their midst!" The Lukács clique was thus determined to "topple Huppert, to do away with him, at all costs, to deprive him of his power." For all that, Huppert denied "a thousand times" that he had anything to do with the Stürmer article and claimed that he had no idea who Stürmer might have been, in spite of the fact that all articles destined for the cultural section of the newspaper had to cross Huppert's desk.[121]

In March, Herwarth Walden, former editor of the expressionist journal *Der Sturm*, was named by the German Section to be "language consultant" to the *Deutsche Zentral-Zeitung*. The April issue of *Das Wort* carried an article on stylistics by Walden, in which the following para-

---

120. In his letter to the author (27 October 1979), Huppert continually referred to himself in the third person.

121. In his October 1979 letter to the author, again referring to himself in the third person, Huppert wrote about the determination of German Section leaders to get him: "Huppert felt the hateful, angry 'encirclement' clearly and even put up resistance to superior power. He did not allow himself to be intimidated outrightly . . . and since the

graph sticks out: "Those who involve themselves with literature . . . must be aware of the fact that they do so in the interests of progress and the development of the entire collective. If they are unwilling or unable to do that, then their pen or their typewriter must be taken away from them. By the use of whatever means necessary."[122] Let Walden's words stand as a Soviet epitaph to the *Deutsche Zentral-Zeitung* editors.

Mikhail Koltsov, back from Spain and enjoying the immense success of his just published *Spanish Diary*, was elected a deputy to the Supreme Soviet in the summer of 1938. This responsibility was added to his work as an editor of *Pravda*, supervisor of the publishing firm Zhurgaz, head of the foreign office of the Soviet Writers' Union, and editor of the periodicals *Krokodil*, *Ogonek*, and *Za rubezhom*. Then his star began fading rapidly. He told his brother Boris Efimov, the political cartoonist, that "there was an ominous, hostile breeze blowing from somewhere." He noticed it in the behavior of Mekhlis, who

DZZ editorial board did not fire him, the entire rivalry between the group of authors and the _DZZ_ was concentrated in hatred toward the _DZZ_ representative Huppert." He added: "The Lukács clique, thanks to the support of Becher, had thoroughly scared the already intimidated chief editors of the _DZZ_ so that, by February, I had been ostracized and sacked in the _DZZ_ and my name, owing to the machinations principally of Barta, was in disrepute (I thought only temporarily); every perfidious method was employed . . . by Barta and the unscrupulous Gábor and others to bring about my hoped-for demise as rapidly as possible, though they didn't succeed until mid-March 1938 and this success only lasted until 28 April 1939. Then came my total and absolute rehabilitation. I regarded and regard the machinations of the entire Lukács-Barta clique as totally criminal." Huppert also noted that the "Lukács clique (Alexander Barta, Andor Gábor, Erpenbeck, and, unfortunately, Gustav and Inge von Wangenheim and others) conspired against my life and, regrettably, involved Becher too in the net of their intrigues." Much of this may well have been true in some form or other because the men involved were certainly capable of it; but Huppert's private account to the author (his autobiography published in East Germany mentions none of this) is one-sided, contradictory, and misleading—he failed to devote a single line in his letter to the arrest of his fellow _Deutsche Zentral-Zeitung_ editors or to explain the connection between the arrests and the Stürmer article. Huppert depicted himself as altogether guiltless in all matters connected with his association with the German Section. Witness this bit of bathos: "The situation not only disturbed and oppressed him [Huppert], but deeply pained him inwardly. For he was naive enough to expect friendship, goodness, and helpfulness, in short, solidarity among those sharing a common fate [exile]. He was almost sentimental, like many lyric poets." Huppert also claims that he was the only one of the writers to "fall under the wheels," when in fact Alexander Barta disappeared forever not long after Huppert's arrest. In a later letter (9 May 1980), after I had questioned him about several contradictions, Huppert told me he had "nothing to add" to his earlier remarks.

122. Herwarth Walden [Walter Sturm], "Das kleine Einmaleins des Schreibens," _Das Wort_ 4 (1938): 93–101. Walden occasionally wrote under the pseudonym Walter Sturm.

before had always treated him as a brother. Koltsov believed deeply, "fanatically," in the wisdom of Stalin; everything about him appealed to Koltsov, wrote Efimov in 1965; but for some reason, or probably without any, Stalin suddenly turned against Koltsov. During one private talk with the "boss," Stalin asked Koltsov if he had a gun and had ever thought of killing himself.

Later there came news of Ezhov's downfall as head of the NKVD and his replacement, on 8 December 1938, by Lavrentij Berija. This was good news, it seemed; perhaps it signaled an end to the *Ezhovshchina*, Efimov told his brother. But Koltsov pointed out, "Perhaps suspicion will now fall upon those whom Ezhov left untouched." Shortly after, Koltsov was intentionally not invited to a Kremlin reception given by Stalin for the visiting Spanish Republican General Cisneros, a friend of Koltsov, and on 12 December he disappeared without a trace. Koltsov had spent the evening of the twelfth at the Home of Writers, speaking there in connection with the recent appearance of Stalin's *Short Course History of the Party*. Late at night he had left to take care of some last-minute business in the editorial offices of *Pravda* and was picked up during the night.[123]

Maria Osten was still in Paris at the time. After hearing of his arrest, news of which spread rapidly, she went to the Soviet embassy to obtain an entry visa for the Soviet Union—against the advice of friends. According to Efimov (who, incidentally, dismissed as inaccurate Hemingway's portrait of Maria Osten in *For Whom the Bell Tolls*), Osten arrived in Moscow from Paris in hopes of clearing up the "slander" of Koltsov. "But the noble deed led only to the result that Maria Osten shared Koltsov's tragic fate; she, like him, was rehabilitated posthumously."[124] Osten was not arrested immediately. She had gone straight to her old three-room apartment, where she expected to find her son Hubert waiting for her. Hubert Lohtse, the son of a mine-worker family in the Saar, had been adopted by Koltsov and Osten in 1935 when the pair was in the area during the Saar plebiscite. They had brought him back to the USSR, where the Soviet press picked up the story and spilled gallons of ink on it, publishing countless pictures and articles. Hubert's experiences and impressions were also compiled in a book by Osten and Koltsov entitled *Hubert in Wonderland*, and he was even received in the Kremlin by Marshalls Tukhachevskij and Budennyj.[125]

Osten arrived at the door of her apartment in the company of

123. *Mikhail Koltsov, kakim on byl*, pp. 69–76.
124. Ibid., pp. 48–49.
125. Leonhard, *Die Revolution entlässt ihre Kinder*, pp. 137–40.

another adopted son, a five-year-old Spaniard named Jose. But Hubert and his new wife refused to let them in. There were, he told Osten, social interests that overshadowed the private interests of a "Komsomol member," and he did not intend to "besmirch" his name. Hubert's wife then spoke up, telling Osten that personally they respected her, but they had "just begun to live." In other words, Hubert refused to have anything to do with his mother because of her connections with the arrested Koltsov. "A son is not held responsible for his father," Hubert told Osten, but he knew that he would jeopardize himself by associating with Osten. "Do you really believe for a minute that nightmare about Mikhail," she asked Hubert, and he responded: "So do you think everyone around you is mistaken? How can an individual be more intelligent and correct than everyone else?" Osten and the five-year-old left, taking a room in a cheap hotel.[126] She was still at liberty when Bertolt Brecht and his entourage passed through Moscow in May 1941 on the way to California via Vladivostok. After Brecht, Helene Weigel, their children, and Ruth Berlau had left the Soviet capital by train, Osten watched over Brecht's friend and collaborator Margarete Steffin, who was dying from tuberculosis in a Moscow hospital. On 5 June Osten telegraphed Brecht the news of Steffin's death and was probably arrested before the month was out. She had recently taken Soviet citizenship, which may have sealed her doom, but when she was arrested and when she died is unknown.[127] Nor is it clear whatever became of Jose.

By late 1938, however, the worst of the *Ezhovshchina* had in fact passed. The terror subsided, and only a handful of Germans were thereafter arrested. Alexander Barta disappeared sometime before July 1939.[128] Josef Schneider, who had fled to the USSR following the 1921 *März Aktion*, during which he was a political commissar for Max Hölz, joined the Soviet Communist party in 1934 and became a Soviet citizen a year later. He evidently disappeared in 1939.[129] In October 1940 two French hunters discovered a corpse in the forest of Caugnet. It was Willi Münzenberg, who had last been seen fleeing on

126. Okljanskij, *Povest o malenkom soldate*, pp. 215–19.
127. Ibid., p. 221. Hubert too met a sad end. Wolfgang Leonhard ran across him in 1941 in Karaganda, down-trodden and dressed in rags, scarcely able to speak German anymore. That was the last to be heard of Hubert, who then disappeared in the Soviet "Wonderland" (Leonhard, *Die Revolution entlässt ihre Kinder*, pp. 137–40). Who knows what became of his wife.
128. Hay, *Geboren 1900*, p. 225.
129. *Lexikon sozialistischer deutscher Literatur*, p. 447.

foot from a French internment camp as German troops neared the area. There is no incontrovertible evidence that the NKVD got to Münzenberg; there are only "indirect clues," to use a phrase by Arthur Koestler, "all pointing in one direction like magnetic needles to the pole."[130]

The purge reached beyond the Soviet frontier in another bizarre fashion: wayward Communists still inside Germany were occasionally denounced to the Gestapo by the KPD.[131] In variation of that tactic, "disloyal" Communists outside Germany were sent into the Third Reich, ostensibly for underground work. The party then saw to it that the Gestapo knew the time and place of the man's border crossing. Another related trick was to denounce recalcitrant Communists living abroad to the local authorities. Karl Retzlaw, for instance, was working on the republication of Ignazio Silone's novel *Fontamara*. The office of the Central Committee of the Swiss Communist party found out about Retzlaw's plans and called him to account for bringing out the book of the "Trotskyist" Silone. Later, Retzlaw told Silone about the incident. Silone remarked: "You'll now be denounced to the police as a foreigner," which is exactly what happened. The Swiss Communist party caused a circular stating that Retzlaw was engaged in "Trotskyist activity" to fall into the hands of the Swiss police. He was asked to leave the country.[132]

In an open letter dated 25 April 1939, which he sent to a number of literary figures as well as to eleven newspapers and journals, Kurt Hiller inveighed against KPD tactics like these, charging that the Communists had not been above "slandering Communists and socialists who had fallen out of favor with the party by informing the police in Prague and Paris that these men were accomplices of Hitler. The result was house searches, interrogations, some arrests, and some

130. Crossman, *The God that Failed*, p.71.
131. Hans Kippenberger, who prior to 1933 had been the head of the KPD's military M-Apparat, was allegedly called to Moscow "to report" after ignoring Walter Ulbricht's demand that Kippenberger denounce to the Gestapo oppositional Communists and Trotskyists in Germany (see Wollenberg, *Der Apparat*, pp. 17–18). Kippenberger, by the way, was arrested during that busy first week in November 1936, on the fifth. One source records that he was accused of being in contact with the German General Bredow, another that he was charged with having been a Reichswehr agent for years (see Poretsky, *Our Own People*, p. 182, and *Pattern for World Revolution*, p. 167). Kippenberger was shot on 3 October 1937 after a secret trial (Wollenberg, *Der Apparat*, pp. 17–18). His wife Thea was arrested in February 1938 and died in 1939 (Weber, *Die Wandlung des deutschen Kommunismus*, 2:182.
132. Retzlaw, *Spartakus*, pp. 369–72.

expulsions. Among the victims of these filthy machinations were close friends of mine, as well as myself. That the denunciations (mendacious! and—to bourgeois authorities!) came from Communists is proven not just by circumstantial evidence but, in the most blatant instances, by witnesses."[133]

Some of the later arrests of Germans in the USSR are more difficult to understand because the incidence of arrests had fallen markedly by 1940 and 1941. A few of the Germans who disappeared during the first week or two of the war were perhaps picked up because of the panic that ensued when the Wehrmacht invaded Russia. And yet some were taken well before war broke out. On 13 March 1941 Herwarth Walden had his typewriter taken from him "by the use of whatever means necessary."[134] Gregor Gog, who had emigrated to the Soviet Union following a stint in a Nazi concentration camp, was arrested in 1940 and banished to Siberia. Released in 1944, he was made to stay in Tadzhikistan and died of tuberculosis in Tashkent in October 1945. The writer Albert Hotopp was arrested in 1941, shortly after the war began, and never seen again.[135] Heinrich Vogeler, the noted painter, died in Kazakhstan in 1942 during the forced evacuation of Germans from Moscow.

A similar fate befell Georg Lukács, rumors and accounts of whose arrest and narrow escapes are legion. In 1957 Lukács told George Steiner that in 1939, just after the Hitler-Stalin pact, he and J. R. Becher were given to understand that they would *not* be handed over to the Gestapo according to the stipulations of the pact. Instead, they were to be "liquidated internally," dealt with inside the USSR. The story goes that, after being informed of this in a conversation at the Hotel Lux, Lukács and Becher walked up Gorky Street past Majakovskij Square. The wind was blowing strongly, and the two were not walking close together. Then Becher said in a loud voice, "One of us has to survive, survive, survive."[136] Both did, of course, though Becher, sometime after Stalingrad, slashed his wrists in one of his many attempts to kill himself during his years in the USSR.[137]

The facts of Lukács's actual arrest are these: he was picked up on 29 June 1941 and remained in the Lubjanka until 26 August 1941,

133. Quote taken from the copy in the Akademie der Künste in West Berlin.
134. Walden seems to have brought the entire archive of *Der Sturm* to the USSR, where it disappeared with him.
135. Leonhard, *Die Revolution entlässt ihre Kinder*, p. 128.
136. George Steiner told the story to me.
137. Private information.

when the NKVD released him and closed the case.[138] Why was he arrested? During a 1977 conversation with the author, Mikhail Lifshits claimed that the NKVD was searching for a man named Lukács connected with the Yugoslavian embassy; Georg Lukács's arrest, occurring as it did during the first chaotic days of war, had been a genuine judicial error. Evidently, this was the story that Lukács told acquaintances at the time. But, for one thing, another prominent Hungarian politician, László Rudas, was picked up the same day as Lukács (both, by the way, were taken from their apartments in Weltoktober) and also released with him. This could scarcely have been a coincidence. Moreover, Lukács changed his party membership from the KPD, to which he had belonged from mid-1931 to April 1941, to the Hungarian Communist party just a few months before his arrest.[139] Those who knew Lukács in Moscow suspect that his troubles were in some way connected with Hungarian party factions. There is likewise no absence of accounts about his release. Lev Kopelev recalled hearing stories of Isaak Nusinov, once Lukács's most bitter Russian enemy in literary matters, making the rounds collecting influential signatures to be presented to the Central Committee in a petition for Lukács's release.[140] Whether that really happened is uncertain; Lukács himself gave this rendition: after his arrest, J. R. Becher, Ernst Fischer, and Joszef Révai turned to Dimitroff with the request that he intervene on Lukács's behalf.[141] He did successfully with Stalin.

In the years following the Hitler-Stalin pact and on into 1941, a large contingent of German exiles (both prisoners and nonprisoners, Soviet nationals and nonnationals) were handed over to the Gestapo. Herbert Wehner maintains that, toward the end of 1939 and during 1940, the organs of the NKVD were actually forcing German refugees to go to the German consulate to obtain formal permission to leave the USSR.[142] There are no final statistics concerning the total number of Germans involved in this campaign of forced repatriation. In 1939 several hundred German prisoners, most of them Commu-

138. Private information. Igor Satz told the author that the NKVD confiscated the manuscript of a Goethe monograph Lukács had written.
139. Georg Lukács, "Autobiographie," in Lukács Archivum.
140. From the author's 1977 conversations with Lev Kopelev.
141. Georg Lukács, "Tonbandgespräch," Becher-Archiv.
142. Wehner, "Erinnerungen," p. 167. The fact that many needed permission from the German authorities to return to Germany would seem to indicate that those involved were by this time Soviet citizens or, at least, lacked valid passports.

nists, were assembled in the Butyrki from dozens of Soviet prisons and camps. In this particular operation, 570 Germans are said to have been placed in a separate wing of the prison.[143] Some were then released to German authorities at the Polish-Soviet border, while others remained in the Soviet Union and were sent back to the camps. The criteria used for determining who was to be expelled and who was not are a matter of pure conjecture. Margarete Buber-Neumann was brought to Moscow, along with August Creutzburg's wife Klara Vater, from a camp in Karaganda. The cell contained only Germans, among them Roberta Gropper, the former Reichstag deputy; Hilde Löwen; Zenzl Mühsam; Carola Neher; Vali Adler; and Betty Olberg, the wife of Valentin Olberg, one of the chief defendants at the first show trial in 1936.[144] The women were assembled in early 1940. While in the Butyrki an attempt was made to recruit Carola Neher for the NKVD, but she refused.[145] She was not repatriated, and Buber-Neumann was the last one to see her. She was reportedly shot on 28 June 1942.[146] Zenzl Mühsam, who was also scheduled for expulsion, disappeared for many years in the Soviet Union instead. She survived somehow. A mental and physical wreck, she was allowed to return to East Germany in the mid-fifties. Vali Adler was likewise sent back to the camps, where she died.[147]

Buber-Neumann, Vater, and Olberg were put on a transport and taken to Brest-Litovsk. Twenty-eight male German prisoners were in the same group. At the Polish-Soviet border Buber-Neumann was handed over to the Gestapo. They knew exactly who she was. Others taken into German custody at the same time were Hans Bloch, the *Deutsche Zentral-Zeitung* editor, a Jew who tried to resist at the border; and Hans Drach, the young German actor who had worked at the

143. Herling, *A World Apart*, pp. 62–63.
144. Buber-Neumann, *Als Gefangene*, p. 161.
145. Ibid., p. 171.
146. *europäische ideen* 14/15 (1976): 59. Neher's husband was shot as early as 1937. In 1968 Carola Neher's son, Georg Becker, was located in Odessa, unaware until then of who his mother was. After the arrest of his parents in 1936, Becker was taken care of by a German couple, but they failed to escape the purges either. Hermann Taubenberg was shot in the thirties, and his wife Else was banished to Siberia. Only in 1972 was she allowed to leave Russia for West Germany, where she died a few months later. In 1975 Georg Becker was allowed to leave the USSR. Shortly before her arrest in Moscow, the Prague *Arbeiter-Illustrierte Zeitung* (see the photographic reproduction of the issue in *Exil in der Sowjetunion*, between pages 320 and 321) carried a picture of Carola Neher and her son with this caption: "I had long wished to have a child, but over there [in the West] I didn't have the courage; only in the USSR could I see my wish fulfilled."
147. Leonhard, *Gestohlenes Leben*, p. 345.

Deutsches Staatstheater in Engels. Alexander Weissberg seems to have been expelled on a later transport. Hans David, the German composer arrested for composing birthday greetings to Stalin in twelve-tone music, was expelled two months after Weissberg. He was released from a Gestapo prison in Lublin, Poland, in May 1940 and became an official in the city's Jewish council. In 1942 he was arrested and gassed in the Maidanek concentration camp.[148] Waltraut Nicolas, Ottwalt's wife, was deported 1941.[149]

The number and size of transports and deportation operations similar to the one described by Buber-Neumann is unknown;[150] nor is it clear how many of those deported were taken immediately into custody by the Gestapo and placed in concentration camps. At least some of the women seem to have been released and given receipts stating that they were obligated to return to their home town in Germany and to register with the Gestapo.[151] Some of the Jews, like David, were released into the Lublin ghetto, and there is obviously no reason to assume that any Jewish repatriates were freed within Germany proper. The more prominent political prisoners ended up in concentration camps; Buber-Neumann, for instance, spent the war years in Ravensbrück and survived to write her memoirs.

Only ten percent of those arrested between 1936 and 1938 in the Soviet Union are thought to have survived the camps.[152] The bulk of the Germans known to have been arrested perished, a fate surely shared by the hundreds and perhaps thousands of low-level party functionaries and ordinary party members, the remnants of the German specialists, the *Schutzbündler*, families of arrested Germans, and so on, whose names were never known. Those about whom some sketchy details are available include Fritz Platten, who "died in Kargopollag, a camp for invalids, making shingles and weaving baskets";[153] Hermann Remmele, who reportedly went mad in camp, fighting with guards and inmates;[154] and Hugo Eberlein, who had received a

---

148. Weissberg-Cybulski, *Hexensabbat*, p. 696–97.

149. Nicolas, *Viele tausend Tage*, p. 32–45. These pages describe Nicolas's return to Germany and her treatment there by Nazi officials.

150. Buber-Neumann, in a letter to the author, mentioned an approximate figure of nine hundred Germans who were handed over to the Nazis.

151. Buber-Neumann, *Als Gefangene*, p. 190.

152. Conquest, *The Great Terror*, p. 496.

153. Medvedev, *Let History Judge*, p. 201.

154. Conquest, *The Great Terror*, p. 577.

twenty-five-year sentence, but died in 1944.[155] Max Pfeiffer of the *Deutsche Zentral-Zeitung* was in the same cell as Karlo Štajner in the Butyrki in 1938. Werner Hirsch was also in a cell with Štajner from March to December 1938, where Hirsch went on a hunger strike.[156] In 1941, in prison with the *Schutzbündler* Gustl Döberl (who had been given a sentence of fifteen years, which he lived through), Hirsch again went on a hunger strike, this time for ninety-two days. He died in the prison hospital.[157] Franz Falk, one of the few *Deutsche Zentral-Zeitung* editors to survive, returned to Vienna in 1948. Julja Annenkova ended her life in a camp in Magadan; she reportedly hung herself after learning that her ten-year-old son had repudiated her. Jack Nawrey of the *Deutsche Zentral-Zeitung*, was last seen in the gold fields of Kolyma before he was transported because his physical strength had deteriorated.[158] Ernst Ottwalt breathed his last in a camp in the north in 1943, and Herwarth Walden met his end in Saratov in October 1941.[159] These few fates typify those of thousands, the many German actors, writers, journalists, Austrian *Schutzbündler*, and political figures of the KPD and Austrian Communist party who finished their lives in Soviet prisons and camps.

After being separated in Moscow, Hans Günther and Trude Richter happened to meet again in a transit camp in Vladivostok.[160] By then Günther's health had deteriorated, and he was not shipped out to a camp because he was incapable of working. Richter later learned that Günther died in October 1938 during a typhus epidemic in the camp, the same outbreak that took the life of the Polish writer Bruno Jasienski. From Vladivostok Richter was sent to one of the worst areas in the Soviet camp system, the Elgen-Kolyma region, where she was put in a women's camp containing between six and eight-hundred inmates. She spent her entire original sentence of five years there, until September 1941, when she was scheduled to be released. But she was forced to sign a declaration, a result of the outbreak of war,

155. Beck and Godin, *Russian Purge*, p. 121–22; Conquest, *The Great Terror*, p. 577. Aino Kuusinen (*Der Gott stürzt seine Engel*, pp. 217–18), the arrested wife of the Finnish Communist, seems to have been the last one to see Eberlein. Kuusinen met him briefly in early summer 1939 in Archangelsk.

156. Štajner, *7000 Tage in Sibirien*, pp. 72–74.

157. Personal information from Lilli Beer, who heard the story from Gustl Döberl.

158. He was seen by Erich Wronke. Wronke told the story to Lilli Beer, who passed it on to me.

159. Sina Walden, "Nachrichten über meinen Vater," *europäische ideen* 14/15 (1976): 14–15.

160. This account is again based on Trude Richter's unpublished memoirs.

according to which she would remain in custody "for the foreseeable future."[161] In fall 1946 Richter was finally released and allowed to settle in Magadan, where she worked as a hatcheck lady in a theater. But in August 1949 she was rearrested and imprisoned. After an "investigation" of four months—the NKVD tried to get her to confess that the BPRS had been financed by the Nazis!—she was sentenced to "eternal exile" in Ust-Omchug, 350 kilometers north of Magadan, where she taught English in various institutes until 1957. Only then, with the help of Anna Seghers, was she allowed to return to East Germany.

There are a few recorded cases where top KPD officials attempted to intercede with the NKVD on behalf of arrested Germans, though this happened rarely[162] and certainly never involved those former party leaders who at one time or other had been purged politically (such as Neumann, Remmele, Schulte, or Schubert).[163] Only on rare occasions was anyone released after arrest and, when that happened, the prisoner was generally forced to sign a statement that he would say nothing about his imprisonment.[164] In 1939 Bernhard Koenen, who had been arrested in 1937, was freed and contacted Wilhelm Pieck.[165] Koenen complained to Pieck in general terms about the NKVD, mentioning specifically certain NKVD officers who had used torture to extract confessions. Pieck, writes Wehner, "agreed" that the accusations should be passed on to Stalin, and the initial result of the complaint was Koenen's rearrest and incarceration for several more months.

In connection with the Koenen matter, Wilhelm Florin and Walter Ulbricht are said to have undertaken to do something for a small number of Germans. They tried to obtain information about Bernhard Richter, Paul Kerff, Datten, the two sons of Max Seydewitz, and the son of the Social Democrat Otto Brass. It was assumed that Brass had been arrested because his father corresponded through him with Hermann Remmele. Stalin's office was informed that the elder Brass

---

161. It was not unusual after war broke out for Germans to receive extensions of their sentences.

162. Palmiro Togliatti, the head of the Italian Communist party, remarked when asked to intervene on behalf of a German friend: "I can't even do anything for the arrested Italians." Personal information.

163. The extent to which certain KPD figures were involved in using the NKVD to do away with former and current political rivals cannot be documented.

164. For instance, in the case of Kassler, a former Communist Reichstag deputy (cf. Wehner, "Erinnerungen," p. 167). This is perhaps the reason why Lukács lied to Lifshits about his arrest.

165. The following comments are drawn from ibid., pp. 162–67.

was working illegally in Germany on party business and that the correspondence between father and son had the KPD's sanction. The NKVD reportedly released Brass's son after several months. All that was offered in support of Datten and Richter was proof of their many years of loyal party service. Pieck's repeated attempts to obtain information concerning certain prisoners eventually led to a confrontation with Dmitrij Manuilskij, who called Pieck to task, telling him that he failed to understand why Pieck was so concerned about the arrested. "Almost all" of the prisoners had confessed and had signed depositions that they were working in the pay of the Gestapo; and since "no one," Manuilskij said, would maintain that these confessions had been forced from those concerned, it was obvious that one became involved with "dubious elements" when dealing with the arrested Germans.

No news was ever obtained about Datten and Richter, but the NKVD said that Paul Schwenk had signed a confession according to which the Gestapo ordered him to participate in Trotskyist acts against the Soviet state. Schwenk, in spite of his "confession," was released after three years, although this was an exception to the rule that chances for release were largely nil when a prisoner gave in to NKVD torture and signed a deposition. Kerff, a former member of the Prussian Diet who had spent a few years in a Nazi concentration camp before fleeing to the USSR, had refused to sign anything. After his arrest, he was confronted during his interrogation with Walter Dittbender, who had also served time in a Nazi camp and had behaved courageously during the Reichstag Fire Trial in Leipzig. Under NKVD pressure Dittbender charged that he had recruited Kerff for a "Trotskyist" organization planning to carry out wrecking activity in the USSR. An NKVD prosecutor later told Wilhelm Pieck that he wanted to release Kerff and that the latter had not signed a confession. But matters were complicated by the accusation made by Dittbender, who had been condemned and shot in the meantime. Kerff was eventually released after about three years in prison and emerged, white-haired and stoop-shouldered at the age of forty-two.

Following the arrests of the sons of Seydewitz, Beimler, Sobottka, and Maddalena, word leaked out that they had been given sentences of five years. Sobottka and his wife did everything they could to obtain information about their son. After two years, they were told that he would be released on a certain day. When he was not, his mother lost her sanity. Sobottka found out a year later that his son had in fact died in a punitive camp well before they had been told that his release was imminent. Beimler and Maddalena were freed after about nine months.

Ulbricht claimed to have been told at the time that the two made accusations against their comrades and were released in exchange for a promise to supply the NKVD with periodic reports. They had been commissioned by the NKVD to spy on Florin and Pieck. The Seydewitz brothers returned to the eastern zone of Germany well after the war.

What set apart the purge of Germans from the terror in general? For one thing, their very nationality made Germans particularly susceptible to arrest; they could more readily be charged with espionage or with links to the Gestapo than could ordinary Soviet citizens. In addition, virtually all Germans in the USSR were "political" in one way or another by 1936. Almost all were members of the KPD, KPOe, or the Soviet Communist party; and a sizable percentage of them worked in the Comintern apparat. These factors acted against them, for the purge hit hardest in the ranks of party cadres and functionaries. The standard charge against Germans was affiliation with the Gestapo or with Fascist Germany. Such accusations were generally shorn of all vestiges of credibility. Alexander Weissberg's wife was charged with having secretly incorporated the swastika into the patterns of her ceramics.[166] Hedi Gutmann, who worked for a time in the Marx-Engels Institute before becoming a German teacher, was denounced by an NKVD man who had slipped into her circle of friends. She was said to have organized the Moscow Central of the Gestapo in her apartment.[167] In many cases, however, there was an actual "pretext" that supplied the NKVD with a factual basis (naturally distorted beyond

---

166. Weissberg-Cybulski, *Hexensabbat*, p. v.

167. Beer, "Memoirs." Another way of getting at writers was to denounce a specific work. In early March 1937 Friedrich Wolf complained in a letter to the Leningrad Art Committee (Wolf to Tscherbakov, 24 March 1937, Wolf-Archiv, Mappe 300/3) that his play *Die Matrosen von Cattaro*, after hundreds of performances, had been pulled from the stage in Leningrad. "The taking down of the red flag [at the end of the play] supposedly makes a defeatist impression today." Wolf explained that the ending of the play was in fact "*optimistic*." A few months later Wolf was again forced to defend himself after S. Dreiden wrote in *Izvestija* ("Department iskusstv," *Izvestija*, 4 July 1937), in connection with an attack on a certain Rafael, head of the Leningrad Art Committee, that the play was "defeatist and politically harmful"; it had been struck from the repertory "at the demand of the Leningrad public." Wolf wrote *Izvestija*, the art committee, and the Soviet Writers' Union (5 July 1937, Wolf-Archiv, Mappe 300/3) and complained about Dreiden's attack. He charged that Dreiden was again spreading "tendentious and false statements," as he had done earlier in the Leningrad *Literaturnaja gazeta*. At that time, the Soviet Writers' Union had met and rejected Dreiden's accusations on the strength of evaluations written by Zalesskij, Shklovskij, Brik, and Glebov. Wolf was now compelled to ask again for an investigation of Dreiden's charges.

recognition) for an arrest. Trude Richter's handshake with Moissej Lurye and her visit to the German embassy, for example, or Carola Neher's and Zenzl Mühsam's contact with Erich Wollenberg served as justification for their arrests.

In most cases where the nature of the accusation against a German has been recorded, it is evident that the NKVD disposed of a wealth of information about individual Germans and that most of those arrested were, at least at the start of the purge, *not* picked up immediately after some sort of "incriminating evidence" had come to the attention of the police. Neher and Mühsam had spoken with Wollenberg well before emigrating to the USSR, and they led uneventful existences in Moscow until 1936. Richter had visited the German embassy in 1935, at least one year before that visit was used to accuse her of being a double agent. This type of circumstance points to the fact that the NKVD compiled dossiers on all the Germans in the USSR, and "evidence" or denunciations were simply held back until a person happened to be arrested. The NKVD files on the Germans were clearly the result, then, of a massive system of surveillance and information-gathering based on the work of informants. These informants generally belonged to one of two categories: those who informed willingly, out of pure maliciousness or misguided idealism, and those who were pressured into informing in the hope of saving their own lives or the lives of arrested family members. Because they themselves were continually pressed by the secret police for information that would help feed the purges by filling the quotas, the willing informants no doubt supplied the NKVD with anything that could possibly be construed as anti-Soviet. The worse the purge became, the more tenuous the factual basis of such information; finally, outright fabrication prevailed as more and more people disappeared and it became harder to obtain "credible" evidence.

In the thirties in the USSR, personal animosities, whether in the sphere of literature or politics, were potentially lethal. For whatever motives—careerism, NKVD pressure, fear for their own lives, perverted loyalty, or natural inclination—a handful of Germans gained notorious reputations within the German community as NKVD stool pigeons and police operatives. Alfred Kurella's name is one of several usually mentioned in this connection. Those who knew him in the USSR refer to him as a "guillotine," one who "denounced as a matter of routine."[168] There is one instance where Kurella, after the arrest of

168. Private information.

a former close friend, is known to have acted with the secret police in providing "evidence" against his friend in a confrontation with him at police headquarters.[169] The case of Hans Rodenberg, which Susanne Leonhard outlines in her memoirs, is indicative of how the system of informing functioned. Rodenberg merely wrote down the substance of all the conversations he had with Leonhard, extemporizing and embellishing freely, and passed the reports on to the NKVD. They then disappeared into Leonhard's file until she was picked up.[170] There is no reason to think that Rodenberg's work was restricted to Leonhard.

On the other hand, it would be a misreading of the situation to fashion an elaborate theory about the German *Ezhovshchina* based on speculation about who might have denounced whom. Matters were generally more complicated. Denunciations were surely rampant and no doubt often sufficed to lead directly to an arrest, especially later in the purge. But the bits and pieces of information gathered from denunciation and from informants were probably used initially to fill up the files until a decision was eventually made to pick someone up. Then the "evidence," which might go back several years, was ready at hand. The NKVD surely had evidence in ample amounts to arrest virtually every single German in the USSR, regardless of party rank. Why some survived and others perished is often an impossible riddle to solve.

Some informants provided information because of NKVD pressure, perhaps in the hope of obtaining the release of arrested family members. Without exception the NKVD seems to have approached the wives of arrested Germans and Austrians in an attempt to recruit them. Nora Auerbach was picked up and at NKVD headquarters was given a piece of paper to sign in which she agreed to "watch" certain people. She refused and was forced to remain standing on her feet for hours until she gave in, but she supplied nothing of use and was eventually left alone. Gustl Döberl's wife avoided having conversations with more than one person so that she could not be asked later to provide an account of private talks. The NKVD finally left her alone too because she had denounced no one.[171] Pathetic was the case of Heinrich Meyer's wife, who tried insanely to gather information of any kind about anyone to use in obtaining her husband's release.[172]

169. Private information. Heinrich Kurella perished in the camps. Inmates who spent time with him and survived reported later that he had charged his brother Alfred with responsibility for his arrest.
170. Leonhard, *Gestohlenes Leben*, pp. 33, 56–8.
171. Personal information from Lilli Beer.
172. Wehner, "Erinnerungen", p. 169.

Prisoners were occasionally freed for the express purpose of shadowing and informing on others. Such information filled dossiers. The NKVD files on those yet to be arrested were also thickened by the confessions and revelations of German prisoners who had fictitious information tortured out of them. The newly arrested were invariably asked about accomplices and friends and forced to compile lists of other "counterrevolutionaries." [173] Presumably, Julja Annenkova testified willingly against the luckless *Deutsche Zentral-Zeitung* editors. When the decision was made to pick them up, Kuznetsov, the paper's administrative director, was asked by the NKVD to draw up his own list of enemies. Ernst Fabri, it seems, also helped. He had been held in detention for fourteen days just prior to the main assault on the paper, and he reportedly knocked on the prison door every ten minutes to make another denunciation or to provide the NKVD with more information. [174]

But if virtually every German could have been arrested, why were some taken and others not? Occasionally, as regards important personages in both politics and literature, personal "protectors" in the upper echelons of the KPD or the Comintern apparat were of some help in keeping one out of the hands of the NKVD, at least as long as one's own protector was in good standing. There were also Germans who had ties to the NKVD; such ties offered the best protection, even though these liaisons were fraught with another danger: with the various changes in the NKVD leadership and the periodic purging of NKVD officers, personal contacts there could quickly become a liability rather than an asset. What then might have determined why some Germans survived while others perished? As one NKVD officer (who was himself arrested) noted, the largest factor seemed to be "chance. People are always trying to explain things by fixed laws. When you've looked behind the scenes as I have you know that blind chance rules a man's life in this country of ours." [175]

The reaction of Germans in the USSR to the terror that affected them all is difficult to describe. There were relatively few survivors, of

173. Hans Günther told Trude Richter in the transit camp at Vladivostok that the NKVD had tried to get information from him to make a case against Andor Gábor, who, as it turned out, was never arrested (Richter, "Memoirs").

174. Beer, "Memoirs," and personal information from Mrs. Beer. The story was passed on by Franz Falk, who was with Fabri in the cell.

175. Conquest, *The Great Terror*, p. 627. Lilli Beer told me of the cases of two *Schutzbündler* in which chance played a decisive role. Josef Schneider was scheduled to be picked up in the apartment building "*Schutzbündler.*" Everything on his arrest order was correct except the first name of Schneider's father. While in the process of arresting Schneider,

whom the majority returned to East Germany, where they have never given an honest appraisal of their experiences. To understand the German response to the terror, a distinction must be made between the outward manifestations of the purges—the show trials and the general public campaign against spies, wreckers, and saboteurs—and the mass terror against the population at large, which was never really publicized in the press. In the *Deutsche Zentral-Zeitung* between 1936 and 1938, for instance, there was full-issue coverage of the public show trials, but only sporadic references to the arrest of an occasional "spy" or to the unmasking of a "Trotskyist"; and these brief reports were generally published only in the weeks just before and after one of the three show trials. Most of the Germans in the USSR were thus easily duped by the trials, which is not surprising in light of the lack of outside information. After all, countless intellectuals in the West also failed to question the legitimacy of the trials.

The mass terror was a different issue. As long as the campaign of arrests among the general citizenry was in its infancy, it was easy to explain away occasional incidents. Only as the purge acquired momentum did Germans begin to doubt privately the official justification for what was happening. They first began to question the lawfulness of the arrests of "Gestapo agents" in connection with the disappearance of their own friends and acquaintances. Lotte Schwarz recalls her reaction to the arrest of Karl Schmückle: "His disappearance was the first profound shock. Until then I had always told myself: there has to be some truth to the charges if they arrested so-and-so."[176] The arrest of a close acquaintance thus often led to the realization that, at best, the NKVD was making bad mistakes and, at worst, was arresting innocent people.

At least during the beginning of the purge, given the atmosphere in the USSR and the threat of Nazi Germany, it was understandable that many Germans did not doubt that Nazi spies might have infiltrated the ranks of Germans in the USSR. That was one of the most frequent explanations for the arrests of Germans until their numbers acquired such proportions that the credibility of that explanation was threatened. Then there were those, probably many, who accepted the validity of the arrests throughout the purge. In answering a letter from a German exile in the West who had asked Erpenbeck about the

the NKVD officers discovered the discrepancy, so they left without him and never came back. In Gorky (Nizhnij-Novgorod) the NKVD arrived to take the *Schutzbündler* Wassermann. He happened not to be at home, so the officers left, giving the time they expected to return. They never showed up again, and Wassermann escaped arrest.
176. Lotte Schwarz in a 1977 letter to the author.

possibility of asylum in the USSR, Fritz Erpenbeck wrote: "As to your . . . question of whether we can help you from here [that is, from Moscow], I unfortunately have to say no. At least not for the foreseeable future. At the moment the political situation is too tense, as you yourself can see, and the experiences the USSR has had in the past with its thoroughly broad-minded assistance were not exactly encouraging."[177] Erpenbeck was simply saying that the USSR had made a mistake in allowing so many Germans to take refuge in the Soviet Union, for many had later been exposed as spies and saboteurs.

Some also thought that Gestapo agents had ensconced themselves within the apparat of the NKVD and were using false denunciations to decimate the German exile community.[178] That too was an understandable attempt to find a rational explanation for something whose real cause escaped most people. Such an interpretation was a cut above the acceptance of an actual Gestapo presence among the Germans in Russia, for imagining the existence of traitors in the NKVD at least assumed, as a starting point, the general lawlessness of the terror. After 1939, Julius Hay had another explanation for the arrests, which differed from the one given in his play *Tanjka macht die Augen auf.* He was reportedly so embittered by the Hitler-Stalin pact that he interpreted the purges of 1936 to 1938 as Stalin's means of eliminating all possible future resistance in the USSR to his upcoming agreement with Hitler.[179] Yet whatever the explanations that Germans came up with in private, it became obvious to a good many of them in 1937 and 1938, when even wives and children were being picked up, that something was wrong. Still, they had no choice but to feign enthusiasm for the purge while they feared for their lives.

Some news of what was going on in the Soviet Union trickled out to the West, where it was generally downplayed by fellow-traveler types and publicly rejected as slander or privately disbelieved by Communists. On 17 August 1936 Wieland Herzfelde wrote to Bredel, "I read in the *DZZ* about the insufficient vigilance of Ge[rman] wri[ters]. What's going on?"[180] Then, in a letter of 9 November 1936, a date that

177. Fritz Erpenbeck to Walter Schenk, 22 August 1938, TsGALI, 631/12/141/61.
178. Lev Kopelev, in a 1977 conversation with the author, attributed that reasoning to Willi Bredel. Kopelev and Bredel knew each other well. In her poem, *Mit meinem Trotz*, Klara Blum had written of a Nazi spy among the Germans, slandering innocent exiles.
179. This is Kopelev's report to the author; it was taken from conversations he had with Hay after 1939.
180. Herzfelde (Prague) to Bredel (Moscow), 17 August 1936, TsGALI, 631/12/143/85. The reference was to the 9 August issue.

corresponds with the first large wave of arrests of Germans, Herzfelde, in Prague, wrote Bredel: "The wildest rumors are making the rounds here (in part in the press): Zensi has been shot, Willi M. [ünzenberg] arrested, ditto Hugo [Eberlein], ditto Carola Neher. As for us? What can we answer? That we don't believe it; but that is not very convincing of course. I don't understand why false reports, at least when they are carried in the papers, are not consistently and immediately denied by the responsible [Soviet] authorities. Evidently it is not understood that this is hurting us and causing mistrust."[181] Bredel, of course, could say nothing to Herzfelde in reply, for the "false reports" were inaccurate only in certain details: Zenzl Mühsam had not been shot, only arrested; Eberlein was to remain at large for another six to eight months; the NKVD, presumbably, only got to Münzenberg in France in 1941; and so on. Otherwise, only Zenzl Mühsam was to survive, if her condition after release can be characterized as survival.

In some cases attempts to intervene on the behalf of arrested Germans were made from outside the USSR. Albert Einstein, for instance, wrote Stalin personally on behalf of the Austrian physicist Alexander Weissberg; so did the French Nobel Prize-winning physicists Irene and Frederic Joliot-Curie,[182] but it did no good. All Einstein managed in another case, that of Vali Adler, was to obtain in 1952 information about the date of her death.[183] Bertolt Brecht was well-informed about the arrests of his friends and acquaintances in Russia, and he seems to have done what he could. In the case of Carola Neher, he wrote Feuchtwanger during the latter's two-month stay in Moscow, asking if Feuchtwanger could do anything for the actress, who was "said to be in prison in M." Brecht had no idea what the charges were, "perhaps she got involved in some female affair," he speculated. In another letter Brecht wrote: "Do you have any chance . . . to ask about Neher? In connection with the very justified action being taken against Goebbels's organizations in the USSR mistakes can naturally take place. . . . If Neher indeed got mixed up in treasonous activities she can't be helped; but perhaps the investigation can be expedited and her case resolved separately through a reference to her great artistic abilities. . . . I would appreciate it if you would treat the matter confidentially because I want neither to spread mistrust about the practices of the Union nor give anyone the opportunity to claim that I am." In May Feuchtwanger wrote back to Brecht, "Carola Neher was in jail while I

181. Herzfelde to Bredel, 9 November 1936, TsGALI, 631/12/143/63.
182. See the facsimiles in Weissberg-Cybulski, *Hexensabbat*, pp. xiii–xvi.
183. Leonhard, *Gestohlenes Leben*, p. 345.

was in Moscow. She is said to have been involved in a treasonous conspiracy of her husband's. I don't have any details."[184] Thomas Mann wrote Mikhail Koltsov in early August 1936 to express his concern about the arrest of Zenzl Mühsam and his fear that Soviet asylum might be acquiring the form of a prison cell.[185]

Then there were those who did nothing. Alfred Kantorowicz and Gustav Regler were in Moscow during the summer and fall of 1936 just as the arrests were mounting.[186] They must have known what was happening. Yet, as loyal party members, they failed to publicize the plight of their countrymen upon returning to the West in late 1936.

The number of German victims of the great purges has yet to be established. Of the approximately 130 Germans who might reasonably be assigned to the cultural sphere of the German exile community —this includes journalists and editors such as those who worked in the *Deutsche Zentral-Zeitung* and in the German-language publishing houses—close to 70 percent of them, according to my reckoning, were arrested in the purge. The percentage is higher if those who were absent from the USSR for most or all of the period between 1936 and 1939 (Bredel, Weinert, Wolf, Piscator, Ernst Busch, Otto Heller, Hermann Greid, or Peter Kast, for instance) are subtracted from the list of 130. And these figures make hardly any allowance for the families of the arrested or for the dozens of other ordinary German office workers and staff members of the *Deutsche Zentral-Zeitung*, VEGAAR, *Internationale Literatur*, or *Das Wort*. Should additional information ever come to light, it seems probable that the percentage of Germans who were living in Soviet exile and lost their lives in the *Ezhovshchina* would rise.

184. Brecht's letters evidently failed to get through to Moscow; Feuchtwanger told Brecht that he had received no mail from him in Moscow. Brecht to Feuchtwanger, no date (December 1936 or January 1937); Brecht to Feuchtwanger, no date; Feuchtwanger to Brecht, 30 May 1937, Brecht-Archiv, Sig. 478/67–68, 76. Feuchtwanger reportedly told Egon Erwin Kisch that, according to what Stalin told Feuchtwanger during their meeting, Ernst Ottwalt was a Gestapo agent (Mytze, *Ottwalt*, p. 69). If Feuchtwanger asked after Ottwalt in speaking with Stalin, one wonders why he did not bring the matter of Neher to Stalin's attention. Feuchtwanger, by the way, up to his death in 1957, seems never to have discounted the story of Neher's complicity told him in Moscow.
185. Mann, *Briefe, 1889–1936*, pp. 421–22.
186. See Willi Bredel to Oskar Maria Graf, 8 August 1936, TsGALI, 631/12/154/152 ("Yesterday Gustav R. and Kanto arrived here in Moscow."); "Ein wahrhaft internationales Treffen: Begegnung mit Gustav Regler und Alfred Kantorowicz," *Deutsche Zentral-Zeitung*, 4 September 1936; and also "Nemetskie revoljutsionnye pisateli v Moskve (Beseda s Gustavom Reglerom; Beseda s Alfredom Kantorovichem)," *Literaturnaja gazeta*, 10 August 1936.

Chapter 12

War

On the evening of 23 August 1939, Stalin drank the health of Hitler, signed the Pact of Nonaggression, and dispensed with Soviet support of antifascism for the next two years. In one of the first Soviet post-pact pronouncements, Foreign Minister Molotov scored certain "short-sighted people" in the USSR who "let themselves be carried away by an oversimplified anti-Fascist agitation"; this, Molotov charged, played into the hands of Soviet enemies who wanted, as Stalin had put it, "'to provoke a needless conflict with Germany.'"[1] "Oversimplified" antifascism in the USSR promptly passed from sight. Anna Segher's novel *Das siebte Kreuz* and Feuchtwanger's *Exil*, for instance, both in serialization in *Internationale Literatur*, were broken off, and the journal's notes and comments on affairs in Germany vanished. Likewise inopportune now were anti-Fascist demonstrations and gatherings. An appearance of German émigré writers in the Kremlin, planned for months, was cancelled.[2] The *Deutsche Zentral-Zeitung* had already ceased publication in July, whether in anticipation of the pact or not is uncertain. At the end of 1939, the German Section summed up the new circumstances; it had been particularly active in August 1939, the section reported, until "objective considerations compelled all of our writer-émigrés to rearrange their activity." But thanks to the "comradely help and work of the leadership of the Soviet Writers' Union," everyone had been able to go on to "deal with new topics,"[3] the "new topics" being, in many cases, nonpolitical translations.

The Hitler-Stalin pact ushered in one of the most cynical periods in Comintern history. After war broke out in September, the Comintern

1. W. M. Molotov, "Zur Ratifizierung des sowjetisch-deutschen Nichtangriffspaktes," *Rundschau*, 7 September 1939, pp. 1349–53.
2. Personal information from Lev Kopelev, who had been invited to participate in the evening.
3. Barck, *Johannes R. Bechers Publizistik*, p. 245.

announced that the fighting had nothing to do with a struggle between the Western democracies, France and England, and Hitler's fascism; the war was unjust, imperialist. Wilhelm Pieck explained that the European war was being waged between English and French imperialism, on the one hand, and German imperialism on the other; although the French and English fostered the impression that democracy, national freedom, and a just and lasting peace were at stake, such explanations merely hid from the masses the imperialist and reactionary designs in furtherance of which the British continued the fighting. English imperialism had always traveled "hidden paths" in its foreign policy in order to conceal its true ambitions and to let other peoples shed their blood for its expansion of power, said Pieck. The true goal of English imperialism was really the "subjugation of the German people and the formation of a 'conservative' regime in Germany that would fulfill its obligation as the gendarme of capitalism against the Soviet Union. . . . The war between England, France, and Germany is an imperialist war waged by the capitalist powers of these lands for the redivision of the world."[4]

Dimitroff vented similar feelings. The war was leading to an acute sharpening of all the basic contradictions of the capitalist world, laying bare the class relations in bourgeois society and taking to the uttermost limits the contradictions between the proletariat and the bourgeoisie, between the "whole world of the exploited and the handful of exploiters." The war was generating a profound crisis of capitalism. It made little difference who attacked first and in whose land enemy troops were to be found; what mattered was which class waged war and whose politics were being furthered. The past tactics of the popular front were now rejected, for "the unified popular front presupposed joint action between Communist parties and Social Democratic, petty bourgeois, 'democratic,' and 'radical' parties against reaction and war. But the heads of these parties have now gone over to the positions of active support of imperialist war." Thus Dimitroff explained the latest Communist "abrupt turn."[5]

Walter Ulbricht's pronouncements infuriated many anti-Hitler Germans who had previously cooperated with the Communists. The "German" (not Fascist) government had come out in favor of peaceful relations with the USSR, while the "English-French military bloc"

4. Wilhelm Pieck, "What is the War all About," *The Communist International* 12 (1939): 1182–87.
5. Georgi Dimitroff, "The War and the Working Class of the Capitalist Countries," *The Communist International* 11 (1939): 1100–1110.

wanted war against the Soviet Union. "He who intrigues against the friendship of the German and Soviet peoples is an enemy of the German people and must be stigmatized as an accomplice of English imperialism," Ulbricht charged. The reactionary nature of English imperialism had proven itself anew by refusing a German proposal, backed by the Soviet government, for an end to the fighting; by continuing the "offensive against the workers"; by surpassing itself in its anti-Bolshevist "slander campaign"; and above all by "organizing the concentration of all reactionary forces for a war against the Soviet Union."[6]

In rushing to the defense of Soviet military expansion, the Communists outdid themselves in cynicism and hypocrisy. In the secret portions of the "nonaggression" pact, Hitler and Stalin had divided the whole of eastern Europe into spheres of influence. With no fear of a Soviet military response, Hitler launched his attack on western Poland while the Red Army invaded Finland, moved into the three Baltic states, and took over the eastern half of Poland. Comintern propagandists sprang into action, for instance, in an article entitled "The Disappearance of a Bastard State."[7] To protect Ukrainian and Bjelo-Russian "blood brothers" in previously Polish regions and to "reunite them with the Soviet fatherland," the USSR had occupied these territories. Not an inch of Polish soil had been taken. Moreover, the Soviet Union had gone on to rectify a "twenty-year-old injustice" by generously returning Vilna and the Vilna territory to Lithuania. "The extraordinary joy with which the Red Army was greeted everywhere and received as a liberator from misery and suffering and unprecedented oppression was one more proof that the Poland of the Pans had thoroughly deserved to disappear." By its "resolute deed" the Soviet Union had done a service to world peace and the world proletariat. With the disappearance of "imperialist Poland," one of the most dangerous breeding grounds of unrest in Europe had been liquidated.

A scant two years after he raised his glass to Hitler, Stalin's German policy was shattered by Wehrmacht planes, tanks, and infantry divisions. As suddenly as it had disappeared, Soviet antifascism again became the order of the day. Fascism, not English imperialism, was the enemy after all. Overnight the imperialist war became a "just war

6. Ulbricht's article is reprinted in Weber, *Der deutsche Kommunismus*, pp. 364–67.
7. Franz Schneider, "The Disappearance of a Bastard State," *The Communist International* 12 (1939): 1201–8.

of the fatherland," as Molotov called it in the first public Soviet response to the invasion.[8] Molotov set the tenor for all subsequent Soviet and German Communist explanations in his statement that this war had been forced upon the USSR not by the German people, not by the "German workers, peasants, and members of the intelligentsia," but by a "clique of blood-thirsty Fascist rulers."[9] Similar strains were heard in the first KPD pronouncement after the outbreak of war (with the Red Army in utter disarray). "Toilers of all occupations! It is our cause that the Red Army is triumphantly defending." The victory of the Red Army would be the triumph of the German people as well, the KPD proclamation of 24 June announced. The war had been started by the "leaders of the National Socialist party," who had ignored the traditions of German-Russian friendship and the "satisfaction of the German people over the German-Soviet Pact of Nonaggression." Now the "fate" of the German nation lay in the hands of the "toiling German people," who were called upon "to affirm by deed the friendship between the German and Soviet people." The statement concluded with a call to "forge the unity of the working class. . . . The toiling German people fight at the side of the Red Army and the peoples of occupied lands battling for their national liberation against the enemy of civilized mankind—fascism."[10] Several days later Wilhelm Pieck added that an "infinite chasm yawns between Hitler, his clique of criminals, and the German people."[11]

As absurd as it sounds, this was a perfectly logical though chimerical response. For years the Communist theory of fascism had fostered the belief that Hitler's hold over the German people was based overwhelmingly on terror. Now that German Fascist imperialism had finally culminated in open warfare, it was logical for the Communists to assume that this act would expose Hitler to the German people for what he was. Nor was this thinking confined to the German Communists. Stalin himself, when he finally addressed the nation on 3 July, stated that the "best people in Germany" joined in condemning the perfidious actions of the Fascists and that in the war the Soviet Union

8. Quoted in Fischer, *Sowjetische Deutschlandpolitik*, p. 15. Stalin himself was silent until 3 July 1941; he seems to have disappeared inside the Kremlin for days, and there are many indications that he suffered a collapse bordering on a nervous breakdown when he received news of the invasion.

9. Ibid., p. 14.

10. Sywottek, *Deutsche Volksdemokratie*, pp. 113–14; *Geschichte der deutschen Arbeiterbewegung*, 5:547–8.

11. Pieck, "Im Sieg der Roten Armee liegt die Rettung des deutschen Volkes," in *Gesammelte Reden und Schriften*, 6:77.

would have the "peoples of Europe and America, among them the German people," as loyal allies.[12] Wilhelm Pieck wrote that Stalin's speech—it would "survive centuries"—showed German workers, farmers, and the intelligentsia that the USSR and the Red Army were the true friends and saviors of the German people. Stalin's words filled all Germans loyal to the interests of their people with gratitude, Pieck imagined, adding confidently that in every segment of the population, including the army, all contradictions and conflicts would grow deeper and more acute in light of the heroic struggle of the Soviet people. "With each passing day, all those elements dissatisfied and outraged with the Fascist regime will gain confidence, courage, daring." For the first time, the German masses saw before them the real prospect of liberation from the claws of the Hitler regime in combining their forces with the forces of the Red Army.[13]

The émigré writers sent the Red Army into battle with certainty of victory and fervent words of exhortation. "Hitler isn't Germany," wrote J. R. Becher a few days after the outbreak of war; "Hitler and his Fascist clique are acting against the clearly expressed will of the German people, for whom friendship with the Soviet Union is as necessary as air." Friedrich Wolf added that the "socialist republic of workers and peasants is passionately loved by us, by the toilers of the entire world, loved by many, many German workers and peasants. Remember: Hitler is not the German people." While Willi Bredel cried out, "Forward, heroic, beloved Red Army! Forward for the cause of Lenin and Stalin! Annihilate the Fascist enemies of the people," Erich Weinert sent his "flaming greetings to our Red Army! Long live the Soviet nation!" Wolf urged the men on: "Down with Hitler and the instigators of this war! Long live the Red Army and the Red Fleet! Long live the Soviet pilots! Long live our Soviet homeland! Long live the party of Lenin-Stalin! Long live Stalin!"[14]

Three days after war broke out, the Soviet Central Committee formed the Central Political Administration of the Workers' and Peasants' Red Army (GlavPURKKA), the organization in charge of political propaganda during the war.[15] The "seventh section" of GlavPURKKA, run by M. I. Burtsev, had direct responsibility for propaganda among enemy troops and POWs, and the section's "German subdivision,"

12. Stalin, "Vystuplenie po radio (3 July 1941)," in *O Velikoj otechestvennoj vojne Sovetskogo sojuza*, pp. 12 and 16.
13. Pieck, "Im Sieg der Roten Armee liegt die Rettung," pp. 80–82.
14. *Nemetskie antifashistskie pisateli—bojtsam Krasnoj Armii*, pp. 2–8.
15. The initials stand for Glavnoe politicheskoe upravlenie raboche-krestjanskoj Krasnoj Armii.

headed by Captain Braginskij, employed German émigré writers. The seventh section was headquartered in the Marx-Engels Institute until that building was bombed out. It then moved into the newly built Red Army Theater, where work during the first chaotic months of the war revolved mainly around the evaluation of enemy radio broadcasts, captured German documents and private letters, and reports of POW interrogations. Many of the prominent literary and political émigrés continued to write texts for German-language programs transmitted by Moscow Radio's foreign broadcasts (Ino-Radio), which had been used by the exiles in the USSR since 1933, and by the Deutscher Volkssender, which began transmitting in September 1941.[16] The absence of program records for these radio stations makes it impossible to document the extent of émigré involvement in their broadcasting, but in late 1941 Willi Bredel wrote Ino-Radio with suggestions for improving German-language broadcasts. He argued in favor of a greater number of "anti-Fascist literary programs" and pointed out that six months earlier the German writers had sent a "collective petition" to the administration of Ino-Radio proposing that literary broadcasts be introduced on a regular basis. "We had pledged ourselves at the time," Bredel wrote, "to prepare suitable radio programs." But the petition went unanswered and nothing more came of it. Bredel added that the émigré writers all realized how important regular radio work was and that "deficiencies" in the administration of Ino-Radio had hampered the activity of the émigrés on a regular basis.[17]

The first large-scale propaganda operation against the Wehrmacht was the publication of German-language newspapers for the front. Part of the Soviet prewar contingency plans, these papers began to show up at the front within a few days after the invasion: *Soldatenfront-Zeitung* on the Volkhov front, *Die Wahrheit* on the west front, *Soldatenstimme* on the Brjansk front, *Soldatenwahrheit* on the southwest front, *Soldaten-Zeitung* on the south front, and so on. In the beginning the papers were prepared by German-speaking Soviet journalists, but because the texts were continually plagued by embarrassing and damaging linguistic and stylistic gaffes, German émigrés were soon asked to help edit and evaluate the papers.

16. Cf. Luise Kraushaar, "Der 'Deutsche Volkssender' (1941–1945)," *Beiträge zur Geschichte der deutschen Arbeiterbewegung* 1 (1964): 116–33; Richard Gyptner, "Über die antifaschistischen Sender während des zweiten Weltkrieges," ibid. 5 (1964): 881–84.
17. Willi Bredel, "An das Ino-Radio, Genosse Polikarpow: Vorschläge für eine regelmässigere, intensive Mitarbeit am Ino-Radio, besonders an den Sendungen in deutscher Sprache," [1941–42 archive date], Bredel-Archiv, Sig. 1501.

In August 1941 Erich Weinert reviewed issues of several front papers and noted the absence of any information in them about the Soviet Union; he concluded: "No doubt the soldiers want to know something about the world against which they are being hurled and about which so many infamous lies are being spread daily in their newspapers."[18] Weinert's notion of effective propaganda was, of course, wholly out of touch with reality, but his rationale was characteristic of the thinking within GlavPURKKA. He was suffering from the same illusions a month later when he reviewed *Soldatenfreund*. He suggested that each issue ought to contain news about Fascist atrocities, for he felt that it would be beneficial if the soldiers found out that Wehrmacht crimes were known to the Soviet public. Weinert was oblivious to the fact that such a propaganda line was completely ineffectual; the German soldiers either discounted claims of atrocities as enemy propaganda or, when they knew the charges were true, passed them off as a part of war. Besides, as far as the German soldiers were concerned, it was a case of the pot calling the kettle black. They knew well that the Red Army had already committed its share of atrocities.

Weinert repeated his suggestion that issues of the front papers include information about the USSR; he proposed "simple, easily understood articles that impart at least an elementary knowledge about the history of the Soviet Union and its socialist societal structure." This Weinert thought particularly important in view of the "fantastic misconceptions" of the German soldiers, as reflected in their letters, interrogations, and diaries. The soldiers ought to be told what "real socialism" was as contrasted with the "socialism" of the Nazis. Weinert's tenuous grasp of reality was just as evident in his suggestion that statements, addresses, appeals, and accusations be issued by "German anti-Fascist personalities (politicians, writers, etc.) whose names are not unknown to the Germans." But who, after nine years of Hitler, remembered or had ever heard of the names Becher, Bredel, Ulbricht, or Pieck? Many of the common soldiers were not even in their teens when the Communists packed their bags in 1933. Just as fanciful was the suggestion that "Soviet workers and peasants explain to the German workers and peasants in soldiers' uniforms why they were defending their fatherland, explain the disgrace of Hitler's invasion, and awaken the subliminal sense of class solidarity."[19]

---

18. Erich Weinert, "Kritische Bemerkungen zu den Frontzeitungen *Soldatenwahrheit, Soldatenfreund, Soldaten-Zeitung*," Moscow, 19 August 1941, Weinert-Archiv, Sig. 815.
19. Erich Weinert, "Kritische Bemerkungen zu der Frontzeitung *Soldatenfreund*," 20 September 1941, ibid., Sig. 817. Weinert soon tried his own hand at writing propa-

On 6 October 1941 the Central Committee of the KPD again turned to the German people: "We Communists warned you repeatedly about the acute danger that Hitler represented for our people and our country. We summoned you to fight against the Hitler beast. We told you that Hitler meant infinite suffering, unparalleled disgrace, and unending war." The appeal went on to conjure up a vision of Germans entering the third winter of the war "worn out by exhausting work, hungry, without shoes and clothes, trembling in fear for the lives of their sons, filled with deep unrest." The only salvation for the German people was to put an end to the war, and the only way to stop the war was to bring down Hitler, for "the war will continue as long as Hitler and his band rule Germany." The proclamation added a note of warning: "And woe unto our people if it ties its fate to the end with Hitler, if we Germans do not establish order ourselves but leave it instead to other peoples to purge Europe of the Fascist plague."[20]

The propaganda work of the exiles in Moscow came to an abrupt halt when, with the Wehrmacht on the outskirts of the Soviet capital, the decision was taken to "evacuate" all Germans from the city. Wolfgang Leonhard described the chaotic scene. On the evening of 14 September 1941, a policeman knocked on his door to tell him that he had to appear the next day at the police station; all the less prominent émigrés were apparently similarly notified. Early on the fifteenth Leonhard arrived at the station, which overflowed with some 150 people, mostly German émigrés, who were having their passports stamped with permits restricting their movements to the Kysil-orda region of Kazakhstan. They were then taken there by freight train in a trip lasting twenty-two days. When the train finally stopped, virtually in the middle of nowhere, the evacuees were assigned to various nameless ("no. 5, no. 12") "settlements" and collective farms. The lack

---

ganda leaflets. Here is an excerpt from one addressed to German soldiers at the Leningrad front: "Do you know what LENINGRAD means? HERE stood the cradle of the greatest revolution in world history! HERE the Russian plutocracy was toppled and destroyed! . . . This powerful city, which was once called Petersburg and Petrograd—it was renamed LENINGRAD! Do you know who LENIN was? . . . LENIN was one of the most noble and illustrious of men. . . . HE LOVED THE GERMAN PEOPLE! . . . THE CITY OF LENINGRAD is what you are being urged on against, which you are to rob and destroy! . . . DON'T LET yourselves be misused in this unworthy act of disgrace. . . . THE CITY OF LENINGRAD CALLS TO YOU GERMAN BROTHERS, WORKERS, SOLDIERS! THIS IS SACRED SOIL! DON'T DEFILE IT WITH YOUR BLOOD!" Weinert's leaflet is reprinted in Erich Weinert, *Um Deutschlands Freiheit* (Berlin: Aufbau Verlag, 1958), pp. 343–44.
20. "Aus der Erklärung der KPD vom 6. Oktober 1941," in *Geschichte der deutschen Arbeiterbewegung*, 5:550–53.

of firm figures regarding the number of Germans living in the USSR at any given time makes it impossible to say either how many were "evacuated" or how many managed to survive the harsh living conditions to return to Moscow a year or two later.[21] Of some fifty Germans who attended an "émigré conference" held in Karaganda in December 1941, Leonhard happened to see only one of them in the Soviet occupation zone after the war.[22] Many undoubtedly shared the fate of the painter Heinrich Vogeler.[23]

The prominent politicians and writers were handled differently. Most of the party elite were evacuated to Kuijbyshev, along with various Soviet governmental agencies and ministries; the Comintern staff went to Ufa in the Bashkir Republic. The writers were evacuated by the Soviet Writers' Union and sent first to Kazan, where Kurella, Bredel, and Weinert remained for the next few months while the others left for Uzbekistan after three weeks. There, in Tashkent. Becher, Plivier, Scharrer, Wangenheim, Lukács, Leschnitzer, and Gábor spent the next several months.[24] Béla Balázs was sent to Alma Ata along with Soviet film makers, Friedrich Wolf, likewise.[25]

Shortly before the evacuation, the German Communists began trying out a new method of propaganda—the political "reeducation" of POWs. This reeducation was called Antifa, although it was nothing more

21. Cf. Leonhard, *Die Revolution entlässt ihre Kinder*, p. 131: "[The evacuees] were humiliated by Kolkhos bosses and brigade leaders, scorned and scolded as Germans. Words of insult were shouted after them; occasionally they were even physically assaulted. In many instances they were intentionally assigned a lower level of food provisions. . . . Many of the German emigrants had been given the worst quarters in the villages, with holes and cracks in ceilings and walls, which exposed them without protection to the icy wind, the *buran*."

22. Ibid., pp. 106–45.

23. The staff of the Verlag für Fremdsprachen was evacuated under the direction of Wilhelm Zaisser, who in 1950 took over the East German ministry of state security. One of the editors, after Zaisser told her she would be assigned to a collective farm, answered that her health would not withstand the rigors of such conditions. Zaisser responded by telling her cynically that she would then not be the "first victim of fascism." Private information.

24. Never one for understatement, Andor Gábor characterized this group of notables, arriving in the capital of "an Uzbekistan liberated by the Soviet government," as the "most significant group that today's anti-Fascist literature—and it is large and branched out in countless countries, just not Germany!—can present." (Andor Gábor, "Deutsche antifaschistische Schriftsteller in Tashkent," MTA, Gábor-Andor Hagyaték, Ms. 4479/114).

25. See Wolf's evacuation orders, "Spravka" (Sojuz sovetskikh pisatelej), which were issued by Kirpotin on 13 October 1941, and the specific orders to Alma Ata given him the next day by the "Tsenarnaja Studija Komiteta po delam Kinematografii pri SNK SSSR" (Wolf-Archiv, Mappe 248/5–7).

than political indoctrination. In July, Walter Ulbricht commissioned an initial study of the problems of Antifa among POWs; this study revealed the thinking behind all such future work. The conflict between Germany and the USSR, which would end with the "collapse of the ruling capitalist classes in several countries, and particularly the conflict between the working class and the bourgeoisie in Germany," resulted in a special task for the Communists of carrying out education work in the POW camps of the USSR so as to have ready the cadres when the "revolutionary confrontation in Germany begins."[26] Ulbricht voiced similar ideas in "diary entries." Work among the German soldiers and officers both at the front and in POW camps was a means, he said, to accelerate the military defeat of Hitler fascism and to "enlighten" the German men and officers in Soviet captivity in such a manner that they would work "as confirmed anti-Fascists for the construction of a new Germany after the collapse of Hitler fascism."[27]

In July and August 1941 an "anti-Fascist activist group" (*Antifa-Aktiv*) was formed in Camp 58 (Temnikov) by the émigré Communist functionary, Heinz Ewers. Then, in September, Ulbricht himself paid his first visit to Temnikov, a camp that soon became something of a collection point for POWs who had shown some inclination to lend their support to an anti-Fascist movement or at least were less openly antagonistic toward one. The recalcitrant POWs had been shipped out to other camps. Still, little progress was made. In a camp of five hundred to a thousand men, Ewers managed to gather no more than twenty-one signatures to use on leaflets calling for an end to the war. In October Ulbricht arrived once again in Temnikov, this time with a statement prepared by the KPD Central Committee, an "Appeal to the German People." He sponsored a two-day conference scheduled to conclude with a mass expression of support for the document, which would be presented as the work of the POWs.[28] Eventually, 158 of them, all ordinary soldiers, signed it. The first manifestation of a new brand of united front (although it was not designated as such), the appeal began by noting that the 158 soldiers represented all strata of the German people. "Industrial workers from Berlin sat side by side [at the conference] with peasants from Bavaria; clerks formerly employed at the Siemens-Schuckert Works sat beside artisans from

---

26. Quoted in Sywottek, *Deutsche Volksdemokratie*, p. 115.
27. Ulbricht, "Erinnerungen an die ersten Kriegsjahre," in *Zur Geschichte der deutschen Arbeiterbewegung*, 2:259.
28. Cf. Robel, *Die deutschen Kriegsgefangenen in der Sowjetunion*, pp. 30–42; Fischer, *Sowjetische Deutschlandpolitik*, pp. 22–27; *Geschichte der deutschen Arbeiterbewegung*, 5:317–19.

Saxony; and by the side of a miner from the Ruhr sat a student from Frankfort. Ex-members of Hitler's Youth League, ex-members of the Socialist Labour Youth League, Communists and non-party workers, and former members of the free trade unions of Germany, as well as those now belonging to the 'Labour Front'"—all were inspired, the appeal said, by the idea of putting a stop "to Hitler's war madness."[29]

The document contained the long-standing Communist definition of fascism: "The most reactionary and barbarous political system in the world" was Nazi rule, which "serves the brutal and avaricious German capitalist plutocracy." The appeal also contained encomiums to the Red Army and the Soviet people: "The unexampled staunchness of the Russian workers and peasants amazes us Germans. Their indomitable determination to fight springs from the ardent patriotism of a people fighting to defend their country. It is the almost superhuman will of a people fighting to defend their socialist system under which the land, factories, and mines belong not to landlords and capitalists, but to the workers and peasants. Such a people are invincible."

But the main message of the appeal was an expression of belief in the existence of two Germanies. "If the majority of our people could openly express their thoughts, they would loudly declare in one voice that Hitler and his Nazi party must not be identified with Germany." The appeal continued:

> There are two Germanies: the Germany of the Nazi parasites and the Germany of the working people; the Germany of brutal robbers and murderers and the Germany of honest and industrious people. There is a Germany of fascist barbarians and the Germany of great thinkers, scientists and poets whose labours have enriched the world's culture. There is the Germany of insane rulers suffering from megalomania who want to maintain their rule in a hopeless fight to the last German soldier, and there is another Germany which curses Hitler and his terror. There is a Germany of the German people which is demanding the immediate cessation of the war.[30]

Between these two Germanies lay an impassable gulf, the appeal added. Only the overthrow of Hitler could save Germany from an-

29. *First Conference of German Prisoner of War Privates and Non-Commissioned Officers in the Soviet Union*, p. 5.
30. Ibid., p. 20.

other Versailles and lead to a just peace, but to win such a peace the German people had to launch a nation-wide struggle against Hitler's rule and against the war. Only in this way could the country win the respect of other nations that had fallen victim to Hitler. It was up to the German nation to prove not by words but by deeds that it had nothing in common with Hitler. The document then added the same note of warning contained in the KPD appeal of 6 October 1941: "Woe to us Germans if Hitler is defeated without our aid, without our participation, and without our active cooperation." The appeal closed with a vision of the "new Germany" to come, a nation based on a "really democratic constitution" that guaranteed the people "all their rights and liberties."[31]

Soon after the Temnikov conference and the issuance of the appeal, great successes were registered in other POW camps: in Camp 98, 80 percent of the prisoners were said to have affixed their signatures to the appeal, while *Pravda* reported massive support in other camps, 765 POWs signing in Camp 78 in January 1942 and 805 in Camp 74 in April. But without denying the existence of some true Antifa converts, such statistics, even when genuine, were generally unreliable and often totally meaningless as a gauge of the real strength of the Antifa movement in the camps. The psychological frame of mind of freshly captured POWs, horrendous living conditions, stifled discussions, hunger, cheap blackmail (kasha for a signature), all this conspired to cast doubt on the significance of the Antifa recruitment drives. In March 1942 a "noncommissioned officers conference" in Camp 95 (Elabuga) met after a "delegate vote" in various camps in which 1,242 POWs participated, a figure that probably reflected the total strength of the Antifa movement. At the time 30,000 Germans had been taken captive, so that the 1,242 represented a scant 5 percent of the prisoner population either talked or browbeaten into voting for delegates to attend the conference.[32]

In December 1941, in Elabuga, another signature-gathering campaign had been started up in support of the appeal. After only twenty-five POWs cooperated, the senior German officer in the camp, along with twenty-four noncommissioned officers thought to be obstructing the Antifa process, were taken from camp and thrown into the Elabuga city prison. The German Communist in charge of the campaign, Otto Braun, in the presence of the Russian Pavel Judin, accused the senior officer Herrfurth: "You are guilty of Fascist propaganda, you are

---

31. Ibid.
32. Robel, *Die deutschen Kriegsgefangenen in der Sowjetunion*, pp. 42–43.

guilty of sabotaging camp work, you are guilty of sabotaging cultural work, you are guilty of threatening German POWs [that is, the Antifa activists] who are in our custody! You are a Fascist!" There followed month-long interrogations culminating in a twenty-five point indict-ment that called for the death penalty for four of the men, Herrfurth included. In December 1942 the four were finally taken from their death cells, pardoned, and in September 1943 returned to the camp. The twenty-one other men apparently died in prison.[33]

Early in 1942 three of the German writers returned to Moscow from their cities of evacuation. Willi Bredel arrived first from Kazan on New Year's Day, and Erich Weinert soon followed.[34] Friedrich Wolf had been in Alma Ata for only three weeks before he was called back to Moscow, on 25 December 1941, by the ministry of defense to work in GlavPURKKA.[35] He reached Moscow in early January. The writers were again asked for advice on how to raise the quality of front pro-paganda, which had thus far been completely ineffectual. In a critique of the paper *Die Wahrheit* in January 1942, Erich Weinert complained about the lack of "artistic propaganda." This was a point he raised continually, probably because Weinert himself produced this type of propaganda—poems, sketches, and the like. Because the papers were prepared by German-speaking Russians right at the front, to make them as up-to-date as possible, Weinert's call for more artistic propa-ganda was his way of arguing for the need to send the writers to the front lines. Weinert insisted in his critique on the need for short stories, ardent or satirical poems, witty epigrams, satire, and so on. It could be, he said, that the lack of such propaganda in the front pages was connected with the absence of material. "But the German-speaking poets and writers really ought to be drawn more systematically into this work." To come up with "passionate appeals" rather than lifeless and sober editorials, "the writers ought to be sent to the front!"[36]

In a report he sent Wilhelm Pieck concerning his propaganda activ-ity from 1 January to 13 April 1942, Bredel also pointed out that material prepared by the writers was not being used effectively.[37] Bredel

33. Ibid., pp. 49–51.
34. Willi Bredel, "Brief aus Moskau," *Freies Deutschland* (Mexico City) 10 (1942): 16–17.
35. "Komandirovochnoe predpisanie" issued by the ministry of defense (Mekhlis!) on 25 December 1941, Wolf-Archiv, Mappe 248.
36. Erich Weinert, "Kritik an den Nr. 1–7 und 11–13 der Soldatenzeitung *Die Wahrheit*," 25 January 1942, Weinert-Archiv, Sig. 811.
37. Willi Bredel, "An das ZK der Kommunistischen Partei Deutschlands z. Hd. Gen. W. Pieck," 13 April 1942, Bredel-Archiv, Sig. 74.

drew up a list of the leaflets, newspaper articles, and other material that he had written. Of seventeen leaflets, only one had even been printed, and of seven articles for front papers, six were never used. Bredel had more luck with his radio broadcasts; several texts written for Ino-Radio and for the Deutscher Volkssender had either been transmitted or telegraphed to London for use by the BBC, while Bredel's articles prepared for *Izvestija* and for *Internationale Literatur* had been published. Things later improved, and by mid-August 1942, Bredel was able to provide a list of ten articles that had found their way into various front papers.[38]

In June 1942 both Bredel and Weinert evaluated propaganda leaflets. Bredel examined forty that had been prepared for the Brjansk front and criticized them thoroughly. For one thing, the language was unacceptable: "It is particularly bad when, as in several cases, supposedly original German texts are involved, ostensibly written by German soldiers." Everyone could see, Bredel wrote, German soldiers too, that these were translations from the Russian.[39] Then there were gaffes such as the use of the word *Mordskerle* in reference to the Fascists. This word, of course, did not mean "murderers," as the leaflet's author thought, but was more accurately translated as "real men." Another leaflet told the story of 250 German soldiers surrendering to *one* Red Army guard because the Germans had recognized the strength of the Red Army! Still another pictured a stack of corpses with the heading, "Here is where you'll find your end!" And on the reverse side, "Those who don't surrender will be annihilated!" This, Bredel pointed out, merely spurred Germans on to fight to keep from being annihilated. Then there was a leaflet promising every POW a daily ration of "bread, lard, plant oil, flour, barley, fish, salt, vegetables, potatoes, tomato paste, tea, sugar, as well as spices, bay leaf, pepper, vinegar, and soap." Bredel remarked sardonically, "I'd like to have that every day myself. Of course not a *single* German soldier believes that he will really receive all this *daily* in captivity. And he is right to doubt it."[40]

38. Willi Bredel, Report and letter to Braginskij, 9 August 1942, Bredel-Archiv, Sig. 74. Bredel mentioned that he had written some six articles with strong nationalistic and historic overtones (von Clausewitz, York, Bismarck, Russian-German friendship); Braginskij had liked them, but Aleksandr Shcherbakov reportedly remarked that the time was not yet right to try and influence the soldiers ideologically in this manner.

39. The Soviets had made it a practice to print up leaflets with texts allegedly written and signed by POWs, but there were cases where photographs and facsimile signatures of POWs were gained and used by trickery. See Robel, *Die deutschen Kriegsgefangenen in der Sowjetunion*, pp. 36–37.

40. Willi Bredel, "Rezension über die Flugblätter des Brijansker Frontabschnittes," 21 June 1942, Bredel-Archiv, Sig. 153.

Weinert's opinion of leaflets prepared at the Leningrad front was somewhat higher than Bredel's. The language was relatively free of the stylistic errors that had given leaflets at other fronts a "comical and thus harmful tinge." But Weinert complained about the lack of "operationalism," namely, the tailoring of propaganda to a specific situation. An example would be the addressing of leaflets to individual platoons, officers, front sections, and so on with up-to-the-minute accuracy. Weinert thought that the Leningrad leaflets were deficient on this score because none of them even said anything about the Leningrad front. In his criticism of the *Soldatenzeitung* in Leningrad, Weinert made the same point. There was nothing in the paper to remind its readers of the battle of Leningrad. "The paper smells not of the front but of an editorial office," he said. Reaffirming his interest in seeing more material by the German writers, he called for greater use of "artistic propaganda": short stories, slogans in rhyme, poems, dialogues, scenes, anecdotes, caricatures, and so on. What was also missing, added Weinert, was the "voice of personalities: articles by representatives of the Soviet intelligentsia, German politicians and writers." It had still not dawned on him that the names of Soviet intellectuals or German Communist émigrés meant absolutely nothing to the ordinary Wehrmacht fighting man.[41]

A month later, Weinert found out how useless the propaganda had been. In July 1942 he spent three days in the Krasnogorsk camp near Moscow, where POWs told him that the leaflets were being found everywhere behind the lines and that in some cases village children were made to collect them for burning. But no one believed the claims made in them. Front papers apparently never reached the troops. Weinert's real education should have come when he discovered the extent to which his perception of reality differed from that of the POWs. He included in his report this account of a conversation with a POW:

WEINERT: Can you deny that Hitler perfidiously invaded the Soviet Union?

POW: He didn't invade the Soviet Union, he merely anticipated an invasion by the Soviet Union. . . .

WEINERT: And what interest does the Soviet Union have in invading Germany?

41. Erich Weinert, "Rezension über Flugblätter und Propagandaschriften des Leningrader Frontabschnittes," 21 June 1942, Weinert-Archiv, Sig. 842; "Kritik an den Nummern 44–58, 1942 der *Soldatenzeitung* (Leningrad), 10 July 1942, ibid., Sig. 812.

POW: To introduce bolshevism in Germany. The goal of the
             Communists, after all, is world revolution.
WEINERT: Has the Soviet Union in twenty-five years of existence ever
             given any proof that it would invade another country in
             order to set up its form of state system? Did it not even
             leave Finland's independence and internal constitution
             untouched after defeating it?
POW: But the Soviet Union used force to take over Bessarabia
             and the Baltic states.
WEINERT: Don't you know that Bessarabia had been torn violently
             from Russia by the peace treaty [Versailles] and that the
             Soviet Union has corrected an old injustice there? With
             Bessarabia the case is no different than with the Saar and
             Germany.
POW: I didn't know that. But how about the Baltic states?
WEINERT: Aren't you aware that the Baltic states were annexed by
             the Soviet Union only after the people of those countries
             came out overwhelmingly in favor of it in a plebiscite?:
POW: We were never told that. No one in Germany knows
             anything about that.[42]

And so on. Weinert, apart from his activity in Spain, had spent the
years 1935 to 1942 in Soviet exile; the POW had lived the last nine
years of his life in Hitler's Germany. But who displayed here the
greater capacity for critical thought? Because the main objective of
Soviet propaganda had thus far been to convince Wehrmacht soldiers
to surrender, Weinert's report included an analysis, based on conversations with the men, of the lack of response to calls for desertion.
"Propaganda about the shooting of prisoners is still effective almost
everywhere," said Weinert.[43] "Our explanation that the POWs themselves appeared in print in leaflets and front papers by way of their
signatures, home addresses, and pictures" was dismissed by many

42. Erich Weinert, "Bericht über Gespräche mit neuen Kriegsgefangenen im Lager
Krasnogorsk, 19. bis 21. Juli 1942," Weinert-Archiv, Sig. 691.
43. Ibid. The German high command had always adhered to the line that the Red
Army took no prisoners. Though this was a lie, by and large, there had been some truth
to it in the opening weeks and months of the war, as the advancing Wehrmacht well
knew. Cf. Robel, *Die deutschen Kriegsgefangenen in der Sowjetunion*, pp. 27–30. In order to
combat this generally accepted notion, Stalin made a point of mentioning, in his famous order no. 55, that the "Red Army shall take prisoner German soldiers and
officers who surrender to captivity and will protect their lives" (Stalin, *O Velikoj otechestvennoj vojne*, p. 48). That paragraph was printed on countless Red Army propaganda
leaflets.

with the argument that soldiers at the front assumed that POWs were forced to draw up such leaflets before being shot, or they were simply invented. But the POWs had other reasons for their refusal to surrender, even in hopeless situations. The assumption was widespread both in the camps and at the front that "whoever gives up is doomed one way or another, even if the Russians don't shoot their prisoners; for if Germany emerges triumphant, no POW will be left alive in Russia; if Russia wins, it will allow no POWs to return home because they will have to rebuild here." Other POWs, Weinert added, "were simply afraid that after the war the homeward-bound POW transports could well take years."[44] Weinert suggested that these fears be taken into account in the propaganda, which they were; future leaflets and appeals assured German POWs of a swift return home after the war. But the fears expressed by the POWs in talking with Weinert were an accurate forecast of the fate that lay in store for German POWs. Here too the men had a better grasp of reality than Weinert.

Willi Bredel was the first German writer to whom GlavPURKKA assigned duty at the front; on 13 September 1942 he received orders that took him to the Voronezh front for two months. This first experiment with writers working right at the front lines proved to be a disappointment for Bredel. He ended up spending most of his time sitting around doing nothing. On 13 October he wrote in his diary: "A month ago I received my orders. So far in about three weeks I've written about a dozen pieces; *one* leaflet has been printed. Is my stay here worth this work? . . . It's not really Kirs. [anov's] fault or that of any individual, rather the fault lies with the system of doing things." A few weeks later, Bredel still complained that he saw no prospects for a chance to be sent up to the front lines to speak by loudspeaker to German soldiers, and in mid-November he returned to Moscow without making a single propaganda broadcast across the lines.[45]

That opportunity came shortly afterwards when the German Sixth Army (twenty-two divisions) was encircled in and around Stalingrad in late 1942. As the net was drawn daily tighter around the Germans, the Red Army began warning them repeatedly that further resistance was useless. At this point, according to Erich Weinert, "we—several Germans living in Moscow—suggested to the Red Army high command

44. Weinert, "Bericht über Gespräche mit neuen Kriegsgefangenen," Weinert-Archiv, Sig. 619; also see note 39.
45. Willi Bredel, "Tagebuch: Aufzeichnungen einer Front-Kommandierung in Stichworten," Bredel-Archiv, Sig. 20.

that we be allowed to speak directly to our misled compatriots, German to German; perhaps they wouldn't dismiss *our* warnings simply as 'enemy propaganda.'"[46] The request was granted, and Weinert, Bredel, and Walter Ulbricht set out from Moscow for Stalingrad. Here all past experience in front propaganda was brought to bear and new techniques were developed to meet the unusual situation. Never before had such an enormous army been trapped in a pocket. At stake were the lives of close to three hundred thousand men and officers, who had to be convinced that surrender was their only hope of remaining alive. Bredel's diary entries capture in telegraph style some of the urgency and excitement of front line propaganda broadcasts, POW interrogations, POW missions back across the front lines in attempts to convince Wehrmacht soldiers to surrender, and the last days of the Sixth Army:[47]

11.30. Ordered to the Stalingrad front: Don section (Weinert a. Ulbricht to the Volga section)

12.7. In the night of 7–8 *first* front broadcast. In the morning there had still been fierce fighting.

12.8. Again in the evening. Snow storms. Impossible to speak. Return towards morning.

12.13. Broadcasts on the outskirts of Marinovka. 3 transmissions.

12.20. 4 transmissions (22 transmissions)

12.26. With the 25th [?] evening in snow suits up to the front line and 4 *talks*.

12.27. In the evening again to the front lines. Got lost. Within an inch of driving over to the Germans. Spoke *4 times*.

1.8. The prisoner *Karl Fuchs*. Conversation with him. He'll return [to the German lines]. Wants letter . . . from me. . . . Went back over during the night.[48]

1.9. Preparations for battle. Tank hulks. Ultimatum.[49]

1.10. Attack begins. Preparations. On 1.9: morning, 4;

46. Erich Weinert, "An der Stalingrader Front," Weinert-Archiv, Sig. 674.

47. Bredel, "Tagebuch," Bredel-Archiv, Sig. 20. Bredel generally made an entry in his diary every day; these excerpts I have culled from the entire diary without indicating omissions between each day's entries. Bredel's diary was written by hand in a Russian *tetrad*.

48. Cf. Bredel's post-Stalingrad report on pp. 380–81, where he tells in more detail the story of Karl Fuchs.

49. On 8 January 1943 Voronov and Rokossovskij issued the ultimatum to Paulus to surrender. Erich Weinert spent most of the night of 8 January broadcasting it by radio

evening, 6 deserters on the basis of my letter—Karl Fuchs arrested by officers. POWs interrogated. 2 came over with my leaflet in their hands.

1.14. On 1.13. end *of the first phase* of this mission / 50 broadcasts 18 deserters using my name.

1.16. Drove around in ice and cold. . . . Rapid progress. Impossible to broadcast. 5 prisoners. Conversations. All five will return.

1.17. Drove around again senselessly and uselessly. . . . Ruins everywhere. Erich will stay, Ulbr. returning [to Moscow].

1.25. Marvelous progress in the pocket battle.

1.27. Advancing through snow and ice, bodies and ruins to Belo-Front headquarters.

1.29. On to Stalingrad. During the night 5 talks. Samoilov wounded.[50]

Two days later Bredel looked on as Paulus surrendered officially in the Stalingrad Univermag.[51] Ulbricht had returned to Moscow on 23 January while Weinert flew back on 2 February. Bredel was ordered to the Southwest Front, where he spent another month in and around Slavjansk. Efforts there met with as little success as in Stalingrad. The attempt to induce German soldiers to desert to the Red Army had failed utterly. The Germans fought until they could fight no more, and over two hundred thousand soldiers preferred to die fighting rather than surrender to the Red Army; moreover, the ninety thousand who were captured more dead than alive would probably have continued to fight had they been so ordered. In spite of what Weinert called their "passionate efforts,"[52] only small numbers of soldiers had

---

to the Germans. It was rejected, of course, and the final Soviet offensive began. Cf. Weinert, *Memento Stalingrad*, pp. 99–103.

50. Bredel, "Tagebuch," Bredel-Archiv, Sig. 20. Samoilov, who had directed a number of the front broadcast missions in which Weinert participated, had been severely injured by a shot in the stomach when a brigade made up of himself, a technician, a truck driver (the broadcast equipment was mounted on the truck), a German Antifa activist, and a Soviet first lieutenant had been forced by heavy snowfall to drive to the front using headlights. The truck suddenly came under heavy enemy fire, which killed the technician and badly wounded Samoilov and the driver. Weinert had planned on participating in the mission but remained in the camp because of a hoarse voice. See Weinert, *Memento Stalingrad*, pp. 124–29.

51. Bredel's depiction of the surrender is given in Weinert, *Memento Stalingrad*, pp. 262–64, and in Bredel's unpublished "Stalingrad" novel, "Die Wolga hat nur ein Ufer," Bredel-Archiv, Sig. 3.

52. Weinert, *Memento Stalingrad*, p. 130.

paid attention to the front propaganda or responded to the entreaties of comrades who had returned from Russian lines to persuade the troops to desert.

But by what standards should the efforts of Bredel and Weinert be judged? Their commitment to saving the lives of German soldiers was definitely serious, sincere, and often courageous.[53] What casts a pall over their attempts to convince German soldiers to "save their lives by surrendering" to the Red Army is the fact (unknown, by and large, to Bredel and Weinert) that the POWs chances for survival in Soviet captivity were often as bad or even worse than for those who chose to fight every battle to the end. From the outbreak of the war, most German soldiers firmly believed that the Red Army took no prisoners; Bredel and Weinert tried to counteract that fear in their front broadcasts,[54] and their motives were unimpugnable. What they told the soldiers, however, was false and misleading. In one of Bredel's front broadcasts, for instance, he argued against Nazi claims that POWs would be tortured and killed in Russian captivity or sent off to the coldest regions of Siberia. "You are supposed to fear captivity more than death," said Bredel. "I, a compatriot of yours, tell you that these are lies and calumnies. No one even thinks of violating the German people once Hitler and his criminal accomplices have been toppled. Germany will never be cut up,[55] and Germans will not be abducted or profaned."[56] In another front broadcast Bredel appealed

53. Willi Bredel has described an emotional scene in which he watched Erich Weinert, late at night, wandering in tears among burned-out tanks and frozen corpses and talking with the dead German soldiers—eighteen- and nineteen-year-olds. Weinert was depressed and upset at the failure to convince them to cease fighting and surrender (Willi Bredel, "An der Wolga," Bredel-Archiv, Sig. 245/9).

54. Some of the methods used were terribly primitive. Compare this excerpt from one of Bredel's front broadcasts. It is a recreation of a conversation between two Germans, one in Russian captivity, the other still on the German side of the front: "Fritz: Hello Franz! I'm in Russian captivity! Franz: Oh my God! What bad luck! When are they going to shoot you? Fritz: Why bad luck? And as far as being shot is concerned, you ought to watch out they don't get you. I've escaped that danger. Franz: How about that, Fritz, I don't understand that at all. You can hear me, they evidently haven't cut off your ears? Do you still have your eyes? Fritz: Why shouldn't I still have my eyes? Franz: What? The Russians haven't poked your eyes out?" And so on. "Fritz" went on to add that he was being treated capitally and that for the first time in ages he had been able to "eat his fill" (Willi Bredel, "*Material zur Lautsprecherpropaganda an der Front:* Fritz und Franz— eine Unterhaltung über die Frontlinien." Bredel-Archiv, Sig. 152.

55. Actually, Stalin had been one of the first of the Big Three to propose dismemberment of Germany after the war. Cf. Meissner, *Russland, die Westmächte und Deutschland*, p. 23.

56. Willi Bredel, "*Programm für eine Lautsprecher-Sendung an der Front:* Vor dem zweiten Russenwinter," Bredel-Archiv, Sig. 170.

to the men: "GERMAN SOLDIERS, PUT AN END TO THIS ACCURSED WAR OF HITLER'S! DON'T ALLOW YOURSELVES TO BE INTOXICATED ANY LONGER BY NAZI PHRASES! LAY DOWN YOUR ARMS! SURRENDER TO RED ARMY MEN! We guarantee you good treatment, sufficient food, winter quarters and, after the war, immediate return to your homes. It is your choice!"[57]

But was it? The POWs certainly were not shot out of hand; but no one, least of all the émigrés, was able to keep the promises made in the propaganda. There was insufficient food and little or no protection from the elements. The POWs were not returned to Germany right after the war; many waited long years—well into the fifties— before they were sent back.[58] Ninety-five percent of all POWs captured in 1941 and 1942 died in captivity; of the 90,000 Stalingrad survivors, most died in Russia. Only 18,000 of them even managed to survive the trip to their initial Soviet camp destinations, whereas a mere 30 percent of all POWs captured during the first quarter of 1943 survived the hunger and cold of the camps.[59]

Both Bredel and Weinert gave written accounts afterwards of their work at Stalingrad. Weinert drew the following conclusions: leaflets remained the most important and effective method of propaganda; far more men could be reached by leaflets than by oral propaganda. But talks with POWs had shown him that most leaflets did not reach the forward positions, where they alone could do any good, but instead ended up far behind the lines among artillery units and camp followers. As for oral propaganda, hundreds of POW interrogations proved that "radio [that is, amplified oral] broadcasts are heard by very few soldiers. . . . Of a hundred men, only two or three say that they ever heard anything from across the lines." Weinert suggested that greater use be made of broadcast recordings, which, when amplified, were much louder than the human voice and indistinguishable from it as well. The problem was that none of the army units in which Weinert had worked had on hand any of the "countless records prepared by GlavPURKKA (speeches of prominent Germans, poems, song parodies, etc.)." Weinert also pointed out that front propagandists had good experiences with the POWs who were utilized as speakers in front broadcasts after being tested for their suitability. However, the use of "prominent persons (Reichstag deputies, writers, etc.) from the

57. Willi Bredel, "Program für mündliche Propaganda," Bredel-Archiv, Sig. 99.
58. See Böhme, *Die deutschen Kriegsgefangenen in sowjetischer Hand.*
59. Ibid., p. 53. See also Ratza, *Die deutschen Kriegsgefangenen in der Sowjetunion,* pp. 205–15.

German emigration as speakers in radio transmissions has not had an appreciable effect." [60] Few soldiers heard the broadcasts without disruption; fewer still understood or even knew the names of the prominent émigrés anyway (this was finally brought home to Weinert), and their broadcasts therefore were not more important than those by any other speaker.

Weinert provided a thorough report on the technique of sending freshly captured Germans back across the lines to their troops. This tactic was experimented with because the "encircled troops, in spite of intensive oral and printed propaganda, showed no inclination to lay down their arms." Talks with POWs had shown that they would have surrendered only under certain conditions: (1) had they been convinced of the utter hopelessness of the pocket being liberated; (2) had they known for sure that they would not be shot, maltreated, starved, or sent to Siberia, had they been given assurances of a rapid return home after the war instead of being used for forced labor in reconstruction work, and had they been guaranteed the chance to send news to their relatives; (3) had their officers tolerated or ordered a capitulation. Weinert reported that the propaganda had been unable to counteract claims by the German high command that the Stalingrad ring would be broken. It was clear, said Weinert, "that the desperate soldiers, fearing captivity, still preferred to await a miracle rather than surrender." The risks involved in desertion also held them back. The POWs told Weinert that, if they had spoken to their comrades about giving up, they would have been handed over to the Gestapo immediately. Soldiers who had deserted to the Red Army explained that this was a life-and-death situation. "For, (1) it can happen that if a small group agrees [to desert], one of them, an informer or a person acting out of cowardice, will squeal on the plans at the last moment and all will be lost; (2) it can happen that an individual deserter or several on their way to the Russians will be seen by a rear machine gunner and shot at; (3) it can happen that, being unfamiliar with the terrain occupied by the Red Army, they might wander into a mine field; (4) it can happen that during the night they might be shot at by Red Army sentries who think that the hands in the air is a trick (which has happened often enough)." [61]

60. Erich Weinert, "Bericht über meine Propagandaarbeit und die dabei gemachten Erfahrungen an der Stalingrader Front und an der Donfront in der Zeit vom 1. Dezember 1942 bis 31. Januar 1943," Weinert-Archiv, Sig. 846. Weinert, by the way, worked for a time at Stalingrad under Nikita Khrushchov (see Weinert's unpublished diary notes in the Weinert-Archiv).
61. Ibid.

It was thus decided to send prisoners back across the lines. The front situation would be explained to a fresh POW, who was told "the meaning of Hitler's predatory war, the impossibility of Hitler's victory . . . and the hopelessness of the encircled troops in Stalingrad." He was then charged with the "moral responsibility" of saving his fellow soldiers from a senseless and certain death by going across the lines to talk with them personally. The "returnees," Weinert explained, received papers from the Red Army command. They were to show these papers to the first Red Army sentry when they returned either alone or with a group of German soldiers. "Many positive results connected with the returnees came in from different segments of the front," wrote Weinert. "A portion came back to us with smaller or larger groups."[62] But he indicated that he personally had not had the chance to speak with the returnees about their experience. In any case, he said, the return of the POWs ought to destroy the legend that the Red Army took no prisoners.

Bredel mentioned in his report a total of seventy-six loudspeaker broadcasts that he had given at Stalingrad, each lasting ten to fifteen minutes and dealing with three general topics: (1) the situation of the German troops in the pocket; (2) the international situation (Africa, the Allied bombing of Germany, the Red Army offensive; (3) the guarantee of protection of life in captivity, sufficient rations, no deportation to Siberia, and return home at war's end.[63] Like Weinert, he dealt with the propaganda tactic of sending POWs back to their units and recounted the story of Karl Fuchs, whom in this report he called Karl Fink. After a long amiable conversation with Fink, newly captured, the POW suddenly expressed his desire to return to his comrades and persuade them to surrender. Fink asked Bredel to write a letter to the men, which Bredel did.[64] That night Fink went over, and the next morning four soldiers crossed the lines to Soviet positions. Fink, they told Bredel, had read them his letter and explained his own impressions of the Russians and the front situation. They then fol-

---

62. Ibid.

63. Willi Bredel, "Bericht von meiner Front-Kommandierung, Dauer: vom 30.11. 1942—3. 3. 1943, Tätigkeitsgebiet: Don-Armee bei Stalingrad und Südost-Armee," Bredel-Archiv, Sig. 73.

64. Bredel repeated the promises that would not be kept: "Lay down your arms! Give yourselves up! Don't be afraid of Russian captivity. I have visited numerous POW camps, which are all in European Russia. Not a single German POW is being sent to Siberia, which is the lie you are being told, and I assure you that if you give yourselves up, you will not need to fear for your lives, you will have enough to eat, and you will be able to return to your homes immediately after war's end" (ibid).

lowed Fink's advice and surrendered. The next night six more soldiers deserted, bringing news, however, of Fink's death. While reading Bredel's letter, Fink had been arrested by an officer and promptly
shot. Later Bredel sent five of the deserters back across the lines and
afterwards found out that a total of forty more Germans had given
themselves up. He had had no news of the five, though, nor of the
outcome of another similar operation because he had left for duty
elsewhere the next day.

Well-prepared and organized oral propaganda, Bredel concluded
his report, was extremely important, although organization of the
activity "left much to be desired." The equipment was often in faulty
condition, and repairs were made slowly. Frequently the broadcast
equipment was not carried far enough forward so that the Germans
could understand what was being said, all the work and danger then
going for naught. Bredel also claimed that the Russian speakers often
had too poor a grasp of German and that the work was frequently
done by the Soviets to fulfill the plan and file reports rather than to
achieve results. Bredel added that, however important the oral propaganda was, its effectiveness ought not to be exaggerated. "The ex-
penditure of time, energy, and work, and the risk, is generally high.
Compared with that, the results are usually very meager."[65]

At Stalingrad the refusal of German men and officers to lay down
their arms voluntarily under any conditions highlighted the lame
effect of all GlavPURKKA front propaganda. This failure, combined
with deteriorating relations between the Soviet Union and the western
Allies, prompted a major reassessment of propaganda tactics. In July
and September 1943, at Stalin's urging, the National Committee for a
Free Germany (NKFD) and the League of German Officers (BdO)
were formed out of a group of German POWs and émigré politicians and literati.[66]

---

65. Ibid. Friedrich Wolf too had worked at the front beginning in early 1943, but there
are few extant materials to document the nature of his work. On 12 February 1943 he
had been sent by GlavPURKKA to the southwest front to work there in the seventh
section of PURKKA. About a month later, he was ordered back to Moscow. (See his
travel documents, "Vremennoe udostoverenija" [issued by GlavPURKKA at the southwest front on 12 February] and the "Komandirovochnoe predpisanie" from 13 March
1943 authorizing his return to Moscow, Wolf-Archiv, Mappe 248.) He had also been in
the Stalingrad region in January 1943, working on the western portion of the ring, but
facing west rather than towards Stalingrad (Pollatschek, *Friedrich Wolf*, p. 286).
66. What follows is not a thorough account of the convoluted history of the NKFD and
BdO. The standard work, on which I draw heavily, is Scheurig, *Freies Deutschland*. A

The NKFD and the BdO were created at a time when relations between the Soviet Union and the Western powers had reached their nadir, and they thus had more to do with foreign policy considerations than with an attempt to upgrade the quality of front propaganda. Early in the war in talks with Anthony Eden and Lord Beaverbrook, Stalin had demanded that the Soviet annexation of the Baltic states, Karelia, eastern Poland, Bessarabia, and various other areas that had become part of the Soviet Union in 1939 and 1941 be recognized as legitimate. The Allies' refusal to acquiesce and give their stamp of approval to Soviet territorial claims and the continuing delays in establishing the promised second front in France fostered Russian suspicion about Allied intentions in the war against Germany. Stalin accordingly began to look for ways to pressure the Allies by playing off Germany and the threat of a separate peace against them. First, the Soviet Union put out peace feelers to Germany through the Soviet embassy in Stockholm. The initial conversations between Peter Kleist of the Ostministerium and foreign office and Soviet middleman Edgar Clauss took place in mid-December 1942, when Kleist was informed that the Soviet Union was interested in an accord with Germany. Clauss reportedly told him, "I can guarantee you that if Germany pulls back to its borders of 1939, you can have peace in eight days." More talks were held the following summer when Clauss explained that the USSR was not about to continue fighting for British and French interests so that, once victory over Germany was won, an exhausted Russia would be left facing the fresh military might of the West. But Germany rejected the overtures, seeing in them a palpable effort by the USSR to pressure its Allies into complying with its wishes. In late September 1943 the Soviet representative told Kleist that Germany had thrown away her last chance in the East by rejecting the Soviet offer.[67]

The formation of the National Committee for a Free Germany in mid-July 1943, followed a month later by the League of German Officers, ran directly counter to the Allied policy of unconditional surrender adopted at Casablanca in that it exhibited Soviet readiness to cooperate politically with a future non-Hitler German state. By threatening to work for a modus vivendi with Germany that excluded the Allies, the Soviet Union was able to use the NKFD to pressure the

---

thoroughgoing, if very slanted, rendition of the work of NKFD "front delegates" may be found in Wolff, *An der Seite der Roten Armee.*

67. Cf. Fischer, *Sowjetische Deutschlandpolitik,* pp. 38–45; Meissner, *Russland, die Westmächte und Deutschland,* pp. 11–21.

West into demonstrating a greater willingess to consider various So-viet demands.[68] The connection between the NKFD and Soviet-Allied relations became much more evident in late 1943. But for the time being, the NKFD and BdO also had the task of improving Soviet front propaganda, which had achieved only negligible results after more than two years of fighting.

The organizations were made possible by Stalingrad. During the months following the defeat of the Sixth Army, top Soviet representa-tives and German émigrés had set out to win POW support for the planned NKFD. They argued that after Stalingrad, where Hitler had unscrupulously and pointlessly sacrificed an entire army, Germany could never win the war and that patriotism now demanded of all Germans a supreme effort to overthrow Hitler and prevent Germa-ny's total collapse. Qualms on the part of POWs about Communism and about propagandizing against the Wehrmacht and the homeland from enemy soil were smoothed over with the argument that the proposed National Committee would not be a Communist organization at all but an alliance of those Germans who sensed the urgency of overthrowing Hitler before it was too late. As for the feeling that such collaboration from behind barbed wire smacked of treason, it was pointed out that fascism and Hitler were the ones betraying Germany —Nazi callousness at Stalingrad had shown that. True patriots op-posed Hitler in Germany's national interest. To create an atmosphere of nationalism within the committee, the old colors of the monarchy (black, white, and red) were adopted as its symbol instead of the black, red, and gold of the Weimar Republic. After a few months of prepa-ration, the National Committee became reality at Krasnogorsk on 12 and 13 July 1943. During the meetings, members approved unani-mously the choice of Erich Weinert as president and Major Karl Hetz and Lieutenant Heinrich von Einsiedel as first and second vice-presidents.

The NKFD manifesto, addressed to the German people and to the Wehrmacht, was likewise accorded unanimous consent at the constit-uent assembly. The document claimed that "the weakened German Wehrmacht, surrounded ever more closely by vastly superior ene-mies, cannot and will not withstand this pressure in the long run. The day of collapse is near!" For Germany the war had been lost; contin-ued fighting would serve no other purpose than to draw out the

---

68. Meissner, *Russland, die Westmächte und Deutschland*, pp. 11–21. See Scheurig, *Freies Deutschland*, pp. 71–79, for the Allied and German reactions to the formation of the NKFD.

suffering and lead to conditions spelling Germany's demise. "If the German people continue to allow themselves to be led to their doom without resistance or a will of their own, they will not only become weaker and more helpless with every day of the war but also more guilty," the manifesto charged, "because Hitler then will be brought down only by the weapons of the coalition. That would mean the end of our freedom as a nation and as a state; it would mean the partitioning of our fatherland. And we could then accuse nobody but ourselves." The German people had to show the world that they were through with Hitler; all sections of society were to rise up and resist, for that alone would assure Germans the "right to decide about their future and to be heard in the world." A new German government had to be formed. This government would be born out of the "fight for freedom of all sections of society and would be based on the activist cadres that united to overthrow Hitler." Such a government needed to stop the war immediately, pull back the Wehrmacht to the frontiers of the Reich, and initiate peace talks. This was the only means by which the German people could create for themselves the possibility of "expressing their national will freely and in peace and of shaping Germany's destiny as a sovereign nation."[69]

The manifesto had little immediate effect in the POW camps. Many remained convinced that collaboration with the NKFD was impossible as long as no high-level officers involved themselves, and thus far neither the previous Antifa camp groups nor the newly-formed NKFD could boast any notable officer participation. The indifference and rejection in the camps made it paramount to win support for the committee from some well-known officers, a group of whom had been brought to Krasnogorsk to observe the founding ceremonies.[70] The officers, however, had generally been put off by the aspect of the program that called for subversion of the Wehrmacht as a principal goal. This they rejected out of hand, though otherwise they accepted the substance of the manifesto and the military analysis. Because all that seemed necessary to convert this particular group of officers was timely concessions concerning the nature of the propaganda, Soviet representatives suggested that they form an initiating group existing and functioning independently of the NKFD, a league of officers that would develop in accordance with its own ideas. The group was set up

---

69. The manifesto is reprinted in Weinert, *Das Nationalkomitee "Freies Deutschland," 1943–1945*, pp. 19–23.
70. Scheurig, *Freies Deutschland*, pp. 50–66.

and moved from Krasnogorsk to Lunjovo, outside of Moscow (the home of the NKFD), to prepare the Officers' League.

In the meantime, recruitment delegations were dispatched to officer POW camps. One of the groups included Friedrich Wolf and Heinrich von Einsiedel, who spent time in Elabuga trying to win converts to the NKFD and the planned Officers' League.[71] Elabuga had acquired a notorious reputation for its staunch resistance to past Antifa proselytism, and Einsiedel and Wolf ran squarely into the opposition of hardcore Nazi officers.[72] After their one-month stay, Wolf filed a report that recounted some of the difficulties they had encountered. A certain "not insignificant" group of officers, Wolf said, was incorrigible. These officers were simply unable to fathom the fact that the German armed forces could be defeated in battle. "'*Deutschland über alles*' is deeply ingrained in these officers," Wolf remarked. As for Germany's political situation, Wolf reported that many of the officers opposed overthrowing Hitler by arguing that a military defeat would lead to the "political disintegration of Germany and the demise of the German people." England and the other allies like France, Czechoslovakia, Poland, and Yugoslavia would demand the complete occupation of Germany "for decades," while France, Poland, and Czechoslovakia would advance their borders far into German territory. "Military defeat would mean political and economic ruin for Germany. Therefore, there *must* not be a defeat for us. We must fight to the last man and take advantage of the last chance!"[73]

The opposition was thus considerable. During a "Heine Evening," for instance, a musical and informational program put together by Wolf,[74] one of the officers sang Heine's "The Grenadiers" to Schumann's music. The applause after the line "Then my emperor will ride over my grave" turned into a pro-Hitler demonstration.[75] Nonetheless, after the initial speeches by Einsiedel and Wolf, fifty officers decided to join the BdO group, and officers who had previously ignored the camp's Antifa circle became more open to discussion. Wolf's

71. See Wolf's travel document (*Predpisanie*) issued by GlavPURKKA on 29 July. It was valid for a stay from 29 July to 25 August 1943 (Wolf-Archiv, Mappe 248). Wolf had already been in Elabuga in June and July.

72. Cf. Einsiedel, *Tagebuch der Versuchung*, pp. 64–75.

73. Friedrich Wolf, "Erfahrungen aus dem Offizierslager Nr. 97 Jelabuga," Wolf-Archiv, Mappe 234/8.

74. Cf. the program given in mid-July, which was probably identical to the one given during Wolf's visit with Einsiedel ("Literarisch-musikalischer Abend: Heinrich Heine und die deutsche Romantik," Wolf-Archiv, Mappe 234/2).

75. Einsiedel, *Tagebuch der Versuchung*, p. 74.

report mentioned that many of the talks lasted well into the night, and "when we entered the camp at eight in the morning, between six and ten officers were invariably waiting for us" with questions. As a result of the visit to Elabuga, Wolf claimed these final figures: by 22 June, only five officers and no soldiers (out of 1,000 officers and 130 men!) had belonged to the Antifa group; by 14 July, the figures stood at only 19 and 12; by 18 August, 197 more officers and 96 men joined the NKFD and BdO.

While Wolf and Einsiedel were recruiting in Elabuga, the League of German Officers had been formed on 11 and 12 September 1943. Final objections on the part of some men, who were otherwise convinced that something indeed had to be done to ward off a national catastrophe of unprecedented proportions, were overcome when a Soviet NKVD general promised, in the name of the Soviet government, that, if the Officers' League was able to get the Wehrmacht leadership to act against Hitler and to end the war before fighting took place on German soil, the Soviet government would be prepared to ensure a Reich with the frontiers of 1937 (including Austria!). The only stipulation was that the new German government be liberal, democratic, and aligned with the USSR through treaties of friendship. General Walter von Seydlitz and a handful of other prominent officers were won over. However, this was still anything but a mass movement, and most of the Stalingrad generals boycotted the organization. After the question of a propaganda slogan had been solved—the BdO continued to reject any propaganda aimed at subverting the Wehrmacht by calls for desertion, accepting only a line intended to convince the German high command to lead the army back to Germany's frontiers—the National Committee and the League "merged." Erich Weinert remained president, and General Seydlitz and four other officers served as vice-presidents.

The new propaganda line, "orderly withdrawal to the Reich frontiers," was immediately tested at the front. The first five National Committee "front delegates" (*Frontbevollmächtigte*) began to arrive at various areas of fighting in mid-July; a few weeks later, eight more NKFD delegates were sent to different fronts, followed on 17 September by an additional four. The seventeen delegates were assisted in their work by a large number of "army delegates" and "division assistants," who brought the number of Germans involved in the NKFD front organization to a total ranging between 350 and 400.[76] Von

76. According to Wolff, *An der Seite der Roten Armee*, p. 35. In spite of the non-Communist emphasis, all front delegates were Antifa graduates and thus by this time

Einsiedel was the delegate to the south front, accompanied by Friedrich Wolf.[77] They arrived in late September and, after talks with the NKFD representative Herbert Stresow, who had preceded them by a few weeks, discovered that the National Committee's manifesto had thus far been announced to the German troops only by loudspeaker because of a severe shortage of NKFD propaganda materials (copies of the paper *Freies Deutschland*, leaflets, pamphlets, and the like). In particular, the NKFD material appealing directly to the Wehrmacht leadership had been unavailable, and consequently the slogan "orderly withdrawal" had not been made known to German officers. Wolf, as he said in his first status report, ascertained from talks with fresh POWs that they "so far knew very little from leaflets about the existence of the National Committee."[78]

Wolf's next report dealt with the results of his and Einsiedel's efforts between 9 and 25 October. They explained to NKFD headquarters in Moscow how loudspeaker broadcasts were made across the front lines. "First, von Einsiedel gave a speech as vice-president of the National Committee, during which he explained the formation, purpose, and goals of the National Committee; afterwards Dr. Wolf spoke as a member of the National Committee." Wolf then explained the hopeless situation of the Wehrmacht and pointed the way to escape from catastrophe. Einsiedel and Wolf then told the troops: "If you've heard our words and agree with them, answer us with three salvos into the air. Right after the broadcast, the German soldiers indeed answered with the three bursts of fire. . . . Not until ten minutes later, after the final broadcast, did the enemy spray the area with poorly aimed shellfire."[79] The front delegation also tried sending newly captured POWs back across the lines. The first such POW failed to return. According to Wolf, however, it was unclear whether this had been the result of a sudden outbreak of fighting and of shifting positions, which may have prevented his return. Another POW was sent over and returned, but it was discovered that he had thrown the leaflets and other propaganda materials away without ever talking to his fellow soldiers. Three others were likewise sent across the lines

generally convinced Communists. Cf. Robel, *Die deutschen Kriegsgefangenen in der Sowjetunion*, pp. 87–94.

77. See Einsiedel's account in *Tagebuch der Versuchung*, pp. 86–104.

78. Friedrich Wolf, "Erster Bericht der Bevollmächtigten des Komitees an der Südfront (An den Präsidenten des 'National-Komitees/Freies Deutschland' Erich Weinert)," Wolf-Archiv, Mappe 233/3.

79. Friedrich Wolf, "2. Bericht der Bevollmächtigten des National-Komitees an der Südfront, Zeit: 9.-25. X. 43," ibid.

without returning, but in these cases too Wolf thought that fresh outbreaks of fighting may have kept them from coming back to the Russians.

One of the major problems encountered in this tactic was the reluctance of Red Army officers to permit it. Wolf indicated in his report that it was virtually impossible to convince the soldiers and the lower-level Soviet commanders to allow POWs to be used by the NKFD representatives and that for behind-the-lines work Antifa POWs ought to be trained and equipped in Moscow rather than at the front. As for attempts to influence German officers, Wolf and Einsiedel discovered, after talking with a POW, that German commanders could only be reached with any effect if POW officers were sent across the line in attempts to persuade them to follow the NKFD appeals. "If a German officer . . . would take a personal letter to a Wehrmacht general with whom he was acquainted and personally hand it to him, this would have today a real, perhaps decisive impact upon the general," Wolf thought. Otherwise, German officers discounted appeals to the army leadership as "enemy propaganda." The Wolf-Einsiedel "front delegation" met with little success in contacting, much less influencing, German officers—the focus, after all, of the NKFD propaganda line.

In his postwar memoirs, Einsiedel explained the nature of the problems encountered at the front. The major difficulty was the continuance, independent of the NKFD, of Red Army propaganda in the form of leaflets containing the same type of crude distortions and calls for desertion used in the opening months of the war. It had been illusory, wrote Einsiedel, to think that the common German soldier could differentiate between Red Army leaflets promoting desertion and trying to demoralize the German armed forces and NKFD leaflets appealing for political action by Germans and the Wehrmacht against the Hitler regime. The continued Red Army emphasis on desertion acted against the NKFD appeals for organized withdrawal from occupied territory and for opposition to Hitler. Under the barrage of conflicting and contradictory propaganda, German soldiers, who had never had positive impressions of Soviet Red Army propaganda during the past two years, now transferred their opinions to the leaflets of the NKFD without giving further thought to the "new" message. Moreover, working by plan created a situation where the Russians in charge of the NKFD operatives at the front were often more interested in reporting to their superiors that a certain number of "German anti-Fascists" had been sent behind the lines for illegal work, regardless of whether anything ever came of it. Nor was there any real incentive for the German troops to surrender, wrote Einsiedel, for often enough, after a German counterattack, POWs had been found murdered. One of the NKFD propaganda officers had told Einsiedel of watching a drunken Russian shoot down three German soldiers who had crossed over to the Russian side after listening to a front broadcast. Every POW with whom Einsiedel had spoken reported severe cases of POW maltreatment.[80]

Willi Bredel's experiences at the front were not much different from those of Wolf and Einsiedel. In the company of NKFD delegate Lieutenant Bernd von Kügelgen, Bredel set out for the Voronezh front on 17 September, like Wolf and Einsiedel. He reported on his stay at the front to Manuilskij in GlavPURKKA[81] and to Weinert at NKFD headquarters in Moscow. Bredel was a living illustration of Einsiedel's criticism of mixing Red Army and NKFD propaganda. In October and November 1943 he had given fourteen broadcasts about the National Committee. "Each program," he explained, "consisted of three transmissions lasting about an hour." Bredel had first given his name and provided information about the creation of the NKFD and BdO, describing the tasks and goals of both organizations. He then read the manifesto, an appeal to the German people and the Wehrmacht, or the BdO appeal, followed by the latest news from the front and from Germany. He concluded his broadcast with a personal appeal, which evidently consisted, as of old, of calls for desertion because Bredel mentioned that two POWs had surrendered voluntarily after hearing his broadcasts. In his written propaganda too Bredel mixed his message. He had written a total of eighteen leaflets, he said; "three leaflets I wrote at front headquarters as a member of the National Committee, three others I wrote anonymously for the Red Army and called for desertion. At army headquarters I wrote one leaflet as an NKFD member and eleven anonymously for the Red Army." These last eleven, Bredel indicated, were concise, operative leaflets referring to recent events among the German troops, which "I didn't want to tie in with the program and goals of the NKFD, particularly because I continually called for desertion in the form of surrender in the interests of expediency."[82] Bredel was clearly oblivious to the fact that he was depriving the NKFD appeal of any possibility of acceptance by the troops by reverting to a form of propaganda that had never worked previously.

80. Einsiedel, *Tagebuch der Versuchung*, pp. 98–99.
81. Manuilskij, the former head of the Comintern, was the representative of the Soviet Central Committee in the GlavPURKKA.
82. Willi Bredel, "An den Genossen Manuilski, GPKK, An den Genossen Weinert, Präsi-

Like Wolf, Bredel reported difficulties with Red Army commanders who "categorically refused" to allow German POWs to be sent back across the lines, but he also pointed out that in this case he could see the rationale. The POWs had had a good look at the Soviet emplacements; it was therefore feared that they would provide the Germans with detailed intelligence about the positions of the Red Army if they were sent back to their original units. As for letters to German commanders explaining the NKFD position, Bredel had written two letters by hand to German officers. They were to be sent on to the officers by partisans along with NKFD and BdO material. He received no answer.

After talking with some 180 POWs, Bredel concluded that only 10 percent had even known of the National Committee, half of them not because of front propaganda but because of NKFD radio broadcasts heard, in part, while on leave in Germany. In other words, a miniscule 5 percent of the 180 had been reached by front propaganda. Bredel did indicate that NKFD leaflets seemed recently to have found their way to the Wehrmacht; the leaflet containing the manifesto was known to some of the POWs. Bredel also discovered, like Wolf before him, that captivity did wonders for the men's readiness to associate themselves with the committee. "All the prisoners" but one agreed with the goals of the NKFD. But such immediate postcapture conversions to the cause of the NKFD were questionable, and it was clear anyway that, to do any good, the soldiers had to become NKFD converts while still fighting in the Wehrmacht.

Einsiedel's conclusions about this first phase of NKFD activity during the second half of 1943 sum up the overall ineffectiveness of the entire strategy.[83] The central NKFD appeal called for Hitler to be overthrown and for the Wehrmacht officers to withdraw the army to the Reich frontiers. The main slogan, then, was an appeal to Wehrmacht officers and generals, for there could obviously be no orderly withdrawal without the approval and direction of the Wehrmacht leaders. Thus, the point of the propaganda was generally lost on the common soldiers at the front—precisely the ones, of course, reached by loudspeaker broadcasts and by soldiers sent back across the lines. The only advice the NKFD front delegates could really give the soldiers, particularly in encircled positions, was to surrender in order to save lives. Only if desertions and surrenders reached mass proportions would

---

dent des Nationalkomitees: Tätigkeitsbericht von meiner Frontkommandierung in die 1. ukrainische Armee," Bredel-Archiv, Sig. 24.
83. Einsiedel, *Tagebuch der Versuchung*, pp. 106–9.

the generals be compelled to follow the NKFD call for withdrawal. In essence, then, the National Committee, whose front propaganda was geared to reaching front-line soldiers, was back where GlavPURKKA had started in 1941—calling upon German troops to desert.

According to Einsiedel, news that the situation had more or less compelled the front delegates to appeal to German soldiers to desert horrified the right wing of the NKFD-BdO organization—the members of the Officers' League around Seydlitz, who had always been adamantly opposed to suggestions for subversion and disruption of the German armed forces. But the military and political situation was rapidly changing, and through continued Red Army victories the BdO officers were losing whatever bargaining chips they may originally have had. After heated discussions with the BdO officers in late 1943, the slogan "Cease Fighting! Save Yourself by Going Over to the Side of the National Committee!" replaced calls for a military withdrawal to the Reich frontiers. This rejection of the initial NKFD slogan represented, in effect, an admission that the original propaganda had been a total failure. However, the fact that the line was changed so swiftly—the front delegates, in small numbers, had been active for only a few months—indicated that other motives were involved in the choice of the new line, "Save Yourselves by Joining the Cause of the National Committee." It was announced by Weinert at a 5 January 1944 plenary session of the NKFD-BdO.

During the Moscow foreign ministers' conference in October and at the Teheran meeting of the Big Three in November and December 1943, decisions had been reached and policies approved that pulled the rug from the NKFD.[84] If Stalin from the outset had viewed the operation primarily as a means of pressuring the western Allies into greater acceptance of Soviet demands by threatening to use the NKFD as the core of a possible post-Hitler government to be set up after a separate Soviet-German accord, then the strategy, combined with Soviet military advances, had worked. At Teheran Stalin was given assurances that France would be invaded and that the long-desired second front would be established in May 1944. The Allies announced their recognition of the "Curzon line" as the new Soviet-Polish border, sanctioning Russian territorial gains between 1939 and 1941. Poland was to be repaid at the expense of Germany, which would lose vast regions of eastern Prussia when the Oder-Neisse line became the new German-Polish border.

---

84. Cf. Fischer, *Sowjetische Deutschlandpolitik*, pp. 53–59; Scheurig, *Freies Deutschland*, pp. 113–24.

From here on out, the National Committee for a Free Germany, though it survived until November 1945, existed for reasons different from those that had led to its creation. Through 1943 the organization operated in the hope that Germany still had a chance for a tolerable peace if the Wehrmacht retreated and Hitler was replaced by a German uprising. By the beginning of 1944, that hope was gone; total military victory was now a certainty for the Soviet Union, and the NKFD was reduced to a group calling for little more than a popular uprising with no guarantees and attempting to shorten the war and save lives by subverting the Wehrmacht.[85] Here too the NKFD met with failure. The new line of appeals for desertion were tried out in the Cherkassy region, where some seventy-three thousand German troops were trapped at the end of January 1944. A major National Committee effort was undertaken to stop the fighting and avoid a second Stalingrad. Propaganda leaflets with appeals to desert and surrender voluntarily were dropped by the thousands on German positions and personal letters written by Seydlitz and other BdO officers were addressed to Wehrmacht generals, but all the appeals went unanswered. Instead of surrendering in an orderly fashion, the Germans tried desperately to break out; several thousand did fight their way through the Soviet lines, but many died or fell prisoner with NKFD leaflets still in their pockets.[86]

With rare exceptions, all the imaginative literature published by German exiles between 1941 and 1945 betrays a thoroughly deficient grasp of reality, exhibiting the extent to which the writers had become prisoners of their own rhetoric about the existence of two Germanies. In working that theory into their creative literature, the writers produced a picture of Germans at home and at the front that bore no resemblance at all to the truth of the situation. They simply perpetuated under new conditions the myths of the stories published between 1933 and 1939.

At a German military air field in western Europe in June 1941, a Junkers 88 crew has just received word of its transfer to the as yet nonexistent "eastern front." War with Russia, the men are given to understand, is imminent. One of the crew asks in amazement, "but we have a treaty with the Russians," and there is even talk of the Russians as "friends." The men clearly do not want war with the Soviet Union ("Have we even declared war on them?") and thoughts of a

85. Scheurig, *Freies Deutschland*, pp. 113–36.
86. Ibid., pp. 124–31.

possible feigned forced landing and surrender to the Russians enter their minds immediately . During the flight to the East, the move is discussed. When one of the crew objects, charging that the others want to desert to the enemy, he is answered: "To the enemy? No. . . . But perhaps to the Red Army!" Another explains: "Against Russia, to top it all off! I'm not a Communist. . . . But Russia, that's something else . . . something new. They've had a revolution after all." "Naturally" reckoning with decent treatment by the Russians, the final decision is taken: the Junkers banks away from the other planes and lands on Soviet soil. "The four German flyers climb out of the plane, the radio man in the lead. With raised hands he heads toward the farmers, crying out loudly, as if jubilant, 'To-va-rishchi! . . . To-va-rishchi!'" Such was Willi Bredel's literary perception of the outbreak of war between Russia and Germany.[87]

Johannes R. Becher's play *Schlacht um Moskau* tells a tale of two German families with sons participating in the eastern campaign. The play's characters include staff sergeant Gerhard Nohl, fighting on the outskirts of Moscow, and his proletarian father at home, and Gerhard's friend Johannes Hörder, whose father, Karl Hörder, is an SS judge. At the front Gerhard deserts to the Red Army, after which Johannes returns home on leave for Christmas to discover that his mother has become an anti-Nazi. In the meantime, Karl Hörder has the elder Nohl arrested. Torture is unable to force a confession from him regarding his anti-Nazi attitude, but when the SS judge shows him a propaganda leaflet written by his son in Soviet captivity, his resistance is broken. Gerhard writes: "There is a Germany of megalomaniacal rulers, and there is another Germany, a Germany of the people." The leaflet closes with this poem:

> The honor of the people shall be redeemed by those
> Who rise up and proclaim the truth,
> And by their deed prove to the world
> That the entire people do not share in this guilt of blood.[88]

As the play reaches its denouement, Karl Hörder is murdered by his wife when she learns that he had personally shot and killed his elder son because of his opposition to Hitler (he had "begun to dream of another Germany"). Johannes returns to his unit at the front, where he is executed for refusing orders to shoot two Russian parti-

---

87. Bredel, "Der grosse Entschluss," in *Der Moorbauer*, pp. 46–67.
88. Johannes R. Becher, *Schlacht um Moskau, Internationale Literatur* 1/2, 3/4, 5/6 (1942), pp. 31–55, 9–52, 32–82.

sans. The play ends with the Germans retreating before the glorious Red Army, one of whose commanders arrives at the scene to proclaim, as the curtain falls, the idea of two Germanies. A Wehrmacht full of men who have profound doubts about nazism and the justification for war with Russia; praise of the Russians; a German population seething with rebellion—all the staples of KPD propaganda are there. Five of the six major characters are or become anti-Nazis. There is a succession of improbable scenes, and one schematic comical character follows another. For instance, the Russian "émigré" prince (of late a "chauffeur" in Paris) accompanies the Wehrmacht across Russia pining for his estate that was liberated now from the "bloody rule of Bolsheviks." Also included is the theme of the capitalist aspect of the war, here with a strong admixture of the nationalism that informs all of Becher's poetry:

> German nation! How magic the sound!
> How bold the cry contained therein!
> How impudently misused is this proud name
> By rulers who appeal to it.
> They have usurped the people's will
> To fulfill their own foolish greed for power,
> Confusing "German Calling" with business
> Which profits the concerns but not the people.

Only one of the exiled writers, Theodor Plivier, reached the level of good literature in his depiction of the war. In *Der Igel*[89] Plivier portrays the annihilation of a German infantry company in a tiny, burned-out Russian village. The persuasiveness of the story derives from Plivier's compelling description of events from the vantage point of both the few surviving Russian locals and the individual German soldiers. On the one hand, he uses the seemingly guileless actions and perceptions of an old Russian peasant to fill in the background to the story: The Germans pass through the village on their way to Moscow, murdering, pillaging, and burning, and then, a few months later, return the same way in tattered uniforms and depleted numbers. By reproducing the simple workings of the old peasant's mind, Plivier evokes with a minimum of effort the cruelty of the Wehrmacht's scorched-earth policy, and he does so without recourse to the moralizing that vitiates the writings of the other émigrés.

But Plivier also shows events through the eyes of the Germans, who take a hedgehog position when passing back through the village. While

89. Plivier, *Der Igel*.

entrenched there, a German plane passes over to make a mail drop to the men. These messages Plivier "quotes," blending in the soldiers' thoughts as they read about homes and relatives. Each soldier thus assumes a personality, becoming a genuine flesh-and-blood human being rather than a mindless murderer. Here Plivier shows the German side of the war at the level of the common man. There is no obtrusive ideology; Plivier concentrates, to be sure, on the Russian-German confrontation, but this is seen more as an elemental struggle between a marauding, invading army and simple local villagers than as a grandiose confrontation between fascism and socialism. As he did with the Russian peasant, Plivier recreates empathetically the feelings and impressions of the soldiers, whose human qualities are meant to contrast with the way in which the Wehrmacht wages war. Through these vignettes of the soldiers reading letters from wives and families, the reader gets to know the men, increasing the shock when the surviving villagers, who had taken to the woods, return with partisans and wipe out the German unit.

This empathetic talent, the ability to understand the Germans and their psychology, is entirely missing in Bredel's writing. His *Das Vermächtnis des Frontsoldaten*[90] has all the familar components: a Wehrmacht retreating in the face of staunch Red Army men, front-line German soldiers transformed into anti-Nazis, and German civilians who oppose the war. Bredel ostensibly hears the story of Hans Sperber and his fiancée Elfriede Walsrode, in a Russian POW camp from Hans's surviving friend, Franz Uschert. This is the story Uschert tells: Under the influence of his experiences at the front, where he was revolted by German atrocities, and of the letters he receives from Elfriede, Sperber, who had a "clear, firm class consciousness," decides to oppose the war while participating in the march on Moscow in late 1941. Elfriede too had originally backed Hitler, but she gradually realized that the entire war was only meant to profit big business. She also harbors an innate admiration for Soviet Russia, a country that "for several decades had done everything to eradicate illiteracy." Her convictions infect Sperber, who eventually ignores an order to execute a twenty-year-old Russian partisan and is arrested.

Much of Germany—this is the impression Bredel gives—was enveloped in an atmosphere of opposition to war with Russia. "Never had Berlin been so quiet as in these summer days of 1941. The people passed by each other wordlessly and apprehensively. No one dared look another in the eyes. Everywhere one met fear and dismay. . . .

90. Bredel, *Das Vermächtnis des Frontsoldaten.*

The bleak conditions in Berlin, the depressed mood of the people, the frankly expressed opposition to the war. . . ." And so on. Elfriede finally learns that Hans has been murdered by his commanding officer for insubordination. She then begins to resist, joining the Bekenntnis- kirche and wearing the Jewish yellow star out of a sense of solidarity. One day she goes to the train station in Berlin to read aloud from Hans's antiwar diary. This prompts a group of soldiers' wives to lie down on the tracks and block a departing train carrying their hus- bands to the eastern front. A fight breaks out with the police; sixty women are arrested and four wounded by gun shots. Elfriede now fosters the hope that Germans would "find the strength to mount a national revolution, drive Hitler and his accomplices to hell, and show the people of Europe and the entire world: See, we don't want to bear the guilt of the crimes of these villains. . . . In such a way, she thought, Germany could still be saved."[91] The story ends with Uschert's return to the front, where he deserts directly to the Russians (the officer who had murdered Hans has, in the meantime, been shot in the back by his own men). In captivity Uschert discovers that Hitler's war is "an imperialist war."

Friedrich Wolf's *Der Russenpelz*, written in mid-1942, is a similarly unrealistic portrayal of "two Germanies." It conjures up a vision of thousands of Germans on the brink of open rebellion against Hitler. Unemployment, death at the front, pockets of civilian resistance ev- erywhere, low morale, industrial sabotage, lack of food, suicides—this is Wolf's Germany in 1941. "The people seemed . . . suddenly to resemble a wild, angry animal kept in check . . . with pistols and iron rods. At the slightest turn they could rise up," Wolf writes.[92] Bredel, in another vignette of life in Germany, speaks of machine-gun towers erected on street corners to prevent "disturbances."[93] Elsewhere he has a front-line soldier return to Germany on leave to find that his wife has been thrown in a concentration camp for "activity hostile to the state."[94] Large segments of the population agree that an end must be put to the war. The soldier goes to Gestapo headquarters to protest the incarceration of his wife, shoots down three Gestapo officers, and, as the story closes, is led away to an unspecified fate.

The serialization in *Internationale Literatur* of Theodor Plivier's *Stalingrad*, the one genuinely fine piece of literature produced by the German

91. Ibid.
92. Wolf, *Der Russenpelz*.
93. Bredel, "Der Blockwart," in *Kurzgeschichten aus Hitlerdeutschland*, p. 60.
94. Bredel, "Heimaturlaub," in ibid., p. 31.

emigration in Russia, was preceded in October 1943 by "In der Bresche," which was "the first chapter from an unpublished novel" to be continued in later issues.[95] This chapter, which is not part of *Stalingrad* but a story fleshed out after the war to form Plivier's novel *Moscow*, contains a story within a story. The outer frame is formed by scenes from the initial assembly of the National Committee for a Free Germany, as witnessed by Second Lieutenant Riederheim, who has recently gone over to the Russians. Between fleeting glimpses of the NKFD meeting, the story is told of Riederheim's close friend August Gnotke, one of the recurrent characters in *Stalingrad*. The story includes his entry into the SA in 1932, his involvement in storm trooper terror in 1933 and 1934, the beginning of the war against Russia, Gnotke's gradual disillusionment with the fighting, and, finally, his refusal to obey orders at the front. These events, brought to life through flashbacks as Riederheim's mind drifts in and out of focus during the NKFD constituent assembly, culminate in Gnotke's assignment to a penal division at the front. This is Gnotke's predicament when Stalingrad begins. The next issue of *Internationale Literatur* then contained the first installment of *Stalingrad*, the actual text of which opens with the well-known phrase, "And then there was Gnotke."[96]

Plivier's characters, the grave diggers Gnotke and Gimpf, for instance, are powerful in their simplicity. The standard, psychologically stereotyped "Nazi" ever present in other émigré writings is absent in *Stalingrad*. Where Plivier does allude to the political convictions of this or that character, it is done in a style of moderation, not with the schematization of Wolf, Bredel, or Becher. There are no real heroes in *Stalingrad*, only tragedians; its collective protagonist is the German Sixth Army, which is described in countless fragmentary scenes, bits of recreated conversations, death throes, screams of agony, acts of unthinking (and pointless) bravery, and degrading images of wasted, dismembered bodies, spiritual and physical dissolution, and stolid obedience to senseless and suicidal orders. So Plivier's protagonist is in no way glorified; he shows the battle of Stalingrad as a horrible, filthy, stinking, gory chaos, with the Sixth Army having degenerated into an inhuman state: "This thin ring of infantry troops [on the

---

95. Theodor Plivier, "In der Bresche," *Internationale Literatur* 10 (1943): 40–56.

96. All page references to *Stalingrad*, given in the text, are from the first definitive edition published in East Berlin in 1945; this version, which Plivier had reworked while still in Soviet exile, was not identical to the text serialized in 1943 and 1944 in *Internationale Literatur* (see bibliography). The English translation is by Richard and Clara Winston.

periphery] had to hold. It served the same function as the shell of an egg; if it broke, the contents would instantly spill out and there would be nothing left but pus and blood and stench, for the egg was rotten" (125).

Stalingrad also lacks a genuine antagonist. The Red Army, the logical pendant to the trapped Germans, is curiously unapparent. Certainly, as the novel progresses, the noose tightens around the destroyed city and the omnipotence of the Russians is sensed; but there is almost an impression of the Germans as victims of the elemental forces of cold and hunger. Even the horrific wounds suffered by the ordinary soldiers and described in photographic detail seem less injuries caused by Russian grenades, shellfire, bayonets, and bullets than festering sores that are somehow part of the preternatural situation. There are no epic battle scenes between Hitler's Wehrmacht and Stalin's Red Army; nor could there be, really. By the time the novel begins, no real fighting took place any more, just slaughter inside the ring. *Stalingrad* is thus a novel about the German army, and the reader is trapped for its duration in the pocket with the men. The prison is left only on the few occasions when Plivier switches his narrative to Germany.

Compared with the war writings of the other émigrés, the strength of *Stalingrad* emanates from Plivier's elimination of heavy-handed preaching or editorialization. *Stalingrad* is anything but a confrontation between ideological forces. There is no real praise of the glorious Red Army defending its homeland, no mention of the difference between a just and unjust war or between wars of imperialism and wars of national liberation, and no talk of capitalist plutocracies. Just as Plivier takes his reader inside the Stalingrad pocket, so too he questions the war only within the context of the men fighting inside the ring; he refuses to impose alien ideas (that is, any sort of intuitive Marxism-Leninism) upon the men he describes. He plainly points out the criminality of the war, but he does it through men like Vilshofen, who puts things in nonideological terms. Of course the campaign in Russia was criminal, and Plivier sees the German defeat as inevitable, but not for the schematic reasons given by German Communists. A dying captain asks himself, "Have I set fire to a house? No. Have I taken away a peasant's cow? No. Did I have any need of the Volga? No, no, no. But others needed it and others set fire to houses, stole cattle, filched bread from widow's cupboards. . . . Captain Steiger, Coppersmith Steiger, you went along with it. . . . You are dying . . . not for Bopfingen, not for Germany, but for the land of the Kalmucks. There is the guilt" (147).

The notion of two Germanies is absent from *Stalingrad*; just the opposite is true, in fact: "How heavy is the guilt? . . . Children shot, women shot, old men, helpless prisoners shot—according to orders, 'as the law provides.' What sort of law is that? . . . Is it the law of the German people, the same people who brought forth a Gutenberg, a Matthias Gruenewald, a Martin Luther, a Beethoven, an Immanuel Kant?" Plivier asks, "Did the German people have no other political face to show the world? What a contorted countenance! . . . The catastrophe was not only a military catastrophe, the collapse not only a physical collapse. It was not only the typhus foam on the lips that counted. German people, what madness is being sweated away here, and whose madness!" (375–76).

Plivier is careful in apportioning responsibility. Though he often indicates that the soldiers should have ignored the suicidal orders of their officers, he also answers in his novel the riddle of why they did not. This is one of Stalingrad's enigmas, and there is no simple solution to it. Nor does Plivier have a pat response; his explanation is embedded in the totality of the narrative, in the thoughts and actions of every soldier described in *Stalingrad*. The true guilt for the slaughter lay with the generals who allowed the senselessness to continue. "Good God," Vilshofen asks in one scene, "where was the commander-in-chief, where was the general, where was the officer who would put a stop to this shameful spectacle, who would give the signal for disobedience?" (184). That officer never stepped forward; "where the need of the hour had been courageous defiance of the rulers, four and twenty generals had clicked their heels as one man" (311). For Plivier a war that is criminal to begin with is matched by the crime of continuing a useless massacre. It was equally evil to apply the term sacrifice to what was taking place in Stalingrad, as Hitler tried to do even before the Sixth Army had finally ceased to exist. "Sacrifice is conceivable . . . only when it is done for the sake of one's own soil, for the preservation of one's own people," writes Plivier. "But it was impossible to try and glorify an unsuccessful marauding expedition by making an idealistic sacrifice. It was absurd, it was grotesque" (367).

Willi Bredel, who was there, should have known Stalingrad better than Plivier, but produced only a clumsy story entitled *Der Sonderführer*.[97] With its maladroit attempt to capture in print the psychology of the Nazi war correspondent Otzhausen, who is trapped in the pocket, it ends up as a caricature of everything Bredel depicts. What he wrote betrays an appalling ignorance of events taking place inside the ring and inside the minds of the soldiers. Bredel delivers himself of this

97. Bredel, *Der Sonderführer*.

characterization of morale: "Rebellions, insubordination, desertions had increased to startling proportions. . . . Death sentences, desertions, insubordination, mutinies, plundering of military stores were daily occurrences. . . . Crossing the lines to surrender was becoming a mass phenomenon. Two days earlier an entire regiment along with its officers had gone over to the Russians."[98] Like most of the émigré war writers, Bredel produced here a literature of wishful thinking. With the exception of Plivier, all of the émigrés wrote and thought in their poetry and prose in the language and hypotheses of leading editorials, although one wonders, in the case of the above story, why Bredel wrote what he did. Here he knew better, having seen with his own eyes that German soldiers refused to surrender in Stalingrad and that they largely remained obedient to the end to the officer corps.

Friedrich Wolf's second long story, *Die Heimkehr der Söhne* (written during the first half of 1944),[99] is a notch or two above his earlier *Der Russenpelz*; it is also of higher quality, say, than Bredel's wartime vignettes of life in Germany. Somewhat less infused with a political editorial line on every page (though the political commentary is there nonetheless), a few of the characters have contours and minds of their own, and occasionally even possess persuasive personalities. Wolf tells the story of a German family visited by the two elder sons who are home on leave from the eastern front. During their stay, all are caught up in an air raid on Berlin, which leaves one of the sons dead. This is the unusual aspect of the story because rarely are there detailed passages concerning the Allied contribution to the war effort in the literature written by Germans in the USSR. Wolf's purpose in focusing on the effect of the bombing is to show that time was running out for Germany; Germans were trapped between the military forces of both East and West, and the country would soon be faced with a final settling of accounts. If the story has any lasting artistic value, it is due to Wolf's occasional success in describing a family that has simply had enough of war and bloodshed and is ready to stand up and say so, without KPD slogans and rhetoric. But the overall effect of the story is nonetheless vitiated by the impression that opposition to the war was growing throughout Germany ("by the hundreds, by the thousands") and by a foolish ending that ruins whatever ambience the story had possessed up to then.

Here and there, mostly in the poetry, a sense of despair at the absence of rebellion within Germany does manage to break through

98. Ibid., pp. 39 and 73.
99. Wolf, *Die Heimkehr der Söhne*.

to the surface, revealing perhaps the real feelings of the exiles about the situation in Germany.[100] Erich Weinert's poem "Genug des Jammerns und der Schande" is just one example:

> My heart bleeds at the thought:
> How you have defiled Germany!
> And is there no one to set bounds to the crimes
> That cover our name with shame and disgrace?
>
> An entire people permits itself to be plunged into catastrophe?
> It endures the contempt of the world?
> Will no one do away with the rabble
> Besmirching and distorting the image of Germany?
>
> The people bled to death, the land laid waste
> In a war with no end!
> Are you so deluded and devoid of sense,
> Blind to the abyss before you?
>
> Is there no one to withstand the unseeing hordes
> Being led to their demise?
> What a cowardly people you've become,
> Dying rather than rising in rebellion![101]

. . . .

In February 1942 Stalin had made his celebrated remark, "It would be ridiculous to identify the Hitler clique with the German people, with the German state. History teaches that the Hitlers come and go, but the German people, the German state remains."[102] Stalin's pronouncement confirmed that the notion of two Germanies, which had been the cornerstone of the KPD-Comintern view of Germany since the day Hitler came to office, would continue to dominate Communist propaganda. However, this would have been a very difficult if not impossible theory to disavow suddenly, embedded as it was in the Communist theory of fascism. If Hitler was a mere marionette of the Fascist bourgeoisie, a puppet of the capitalists and industrialists who enslaved the people, then he was clearly acting against popular interests, and that would sooner or later lead to an uprising. Without altering some basic elements in this theory, the notion of two Germanies

100. Becher's poetry, for instance, is full of such sentiment.
101. Weinert, "Genug des Jammerns und der Schande," in *An die deutschen Soldaten*, p. 19.
102. Stalin, *O Velikoj otechestvennoj vojne*, p. 46.

could not really be touched. But after war broke out, "Hitler fascism" was in fact still described in the rhetoric of the twenties. In 1942 Wilhelm Pieck repeated the penny catechism that the Hitler clique was a band of thieves and liars and deceivers, corrupt and degenerate scoundrels who maintained a bloody, terroristic dictatorship over the toiling people and who robbed them of all rights and liberties. "The Hitlers, Görings, Himmlers, Leys, Goebbels, Ribbentrops, and their consorts were bought with millions of marks by that plutocratic upper level of German finance capital, which encompasses the most reactionary and most chauvinistic and imperialistic elements. They were entrusted with beginning this new imperialist predatory war and with preventing by deception and terror all resistance by the toiling masses."[103]

Throughout the war the Communists kept up their incessant barrage of appeals to the German people to rise up against Hitler, liberate themselves, and stop the war. None of the German-language radio broadcasts of Radio Moscow or of the Deutscher Volkssender, given by Pieck or Ulbricht, for example, or by various émigré writers, lacked such calls. Willi Bredel's numerous broadcasts invariably ended on the same note:

> Only when Hitler has lost his position of leadership of the German people will this war come to an end, and only when the German people themselves overthrow this blood-stained . . . "Führer" and drive him out will it have taken the first, decisive step toward its salvation and rebirth. . . . If Germany is to live—Hitler must fall. . . . It would be disastrous if Germans were to wait until Hitler and his accomplices are annihilated once and for all by Hitler's military opponents, for then there would be no evidence to use in argument against the total complicity of the German people. The Hitler regime has to be done away with by the German people themselves. . . . That is the only way they can save themselves and create the basis for reconstruction of a free and peaceful Germany working toward a happy future. . . . Hitler and his bankrupt band of criminals have to be done away with! Before this occurs, bombs will continue to fall on German cities . . . until, yes, until Germany is laid waste and bled to death! Don't let things come to this! Overthrow Hitler

103. Pieck, *Der Hitlerfaschismus und das deutsche Volk*, pp. 4–5.

and his Nazi pack and save Germany! . . . Don't wait until
Hitler escapes responsibility by a pistol shot; then it will be
too late for you too.[104]

The appeals all fell on deaf ears. Johannes R. Becher's pamphlet
Deutsche Sendung betrayed in 1943 a sense of growing urgency that was
already combined with despondency at the lack of any echo in Germany. Addressing the German people, Becher began: "You have been
silent long enough, so I am speaking. You continue to be silent, so I
am speaking." He called passionately upon Germans to open their
eyes before it was too late. Didn't they see the way they were headed?
Didn't they see the sign posts, the warnings, the ruins of bombed-out
cities, the forests of birchwood crosses on both sides of the road?
"Don't you see where the road leads, endlessly but inexorably toward
the end—disaster!" There was only one solution: the war must be
ended as quickly as possible, for Germany's salvation could only be
achieved through Hitler's downfall. "To shorten the path of suffering
of the German people, to take the lead for the people in their struggle
for liberation from the Hitler regime, this is our calling, this is the
'German calling' of our time."[105]

Becher's pamphlet is dotted with expressions of disbelief and dismay that the German people had done nothing to stop Hitler. Was it
possible, he asked, that the Germans by and large approved of the
crimes of their government and participated in them voluntarily? Was
it thinkable that the German people had in the majority become a
people of criminals and executioners? "No, that is not the case," Becher
answered, "that's not possible. That's not conceivable. . . . Hitler is *not*
Germany; Hitler and the German people are not one and the same; *by
no means* is Hitler Germany." But Becher seemed to be trying to
convince himself as much as the German people. Did they want to go
down in history as a people of executioners, cowards, and wretches, as
a people unable to deal themselves with the criminals and the enemies of mankind in their midst? "Do you want to go down in history,"
Becher asked imploringly, "as the tragic example of a nation that was
unable to take its destiny in its own hand and that, in its political
immaturity, fell victim without resistance to a Hitler? . . . No, you don't
want that, no, you can't want that. . . . German people—where are
you?"[106]

104. These remarks have been culled from a number of Bredel's radio broadcasts
(Bredel-Archiv, Sig. 281–82, 284, 288, 290, 295/1, 264–65).
105. Becher, *Deutsche Sendung*, pp. 3–4, 18.
106. Ibid., pp. 23–25.

Others, though they were few in number, expressed their doubts about the existence of "two Germanies" more explicitly. Theodor Plivier had hinted clearly in *Stalingrad* that there were not two Germanies, and in a number of articles published in *Internationale Literatur* he grew more outspoken. In a lengthy piece published in the November 1944 issue of *Internationale Literatur*, "Zur deutschen Katastrophe," Plivier made an eloquent statement about the causes and course of the war. He did not question the standard party view of fascism as a product of German big business and heavy industry, because he spoke often of "a group of about forty representatives of heavy industry against the entire nation" and of the "[absolute] rule of industrial capital." But he expressed his views in more persuasive terms than those used by the ordinary party theoreticians and went beyond a parroting of the definition of fascism as the most reactionary and chauvinistic elements of trust capital. Whether one accepts this underlying thesis or not, Plivier's moral indictment of the war and his stress on the guilt of the German people is forcefully put. Plivier wrote: "Close at hand too were the people, able to forget their cultured past, ready to let themselves be led to barbaric cruelty and transformed into an instrument for use by cool, calculating robbers and insidious criminals. . . . Hitler would not have been possible without the arrogance and exaggerated opinion as the reverse side of the servility and slavishness present in large numbers of our people." [107]

Lukács was another who, abandoning the most important and indispensable premise of his notion of popular front literature, now discounted the existence of strong internal opposition to Hitler. During his 1941 and 1942 evacuation to Tashkent, he published a seventy-page booklet in Russian entitled *The Struggle of Humanism against Barbarism*. He closed his analysis of fascism with the remark that Abraham had implored Jehovah to spare Sodom and Gomorrah if even one righteous man were to be found, the allusion being that no righteous men were left in Germany. Lukács went on to say that "real history" was not a religious legend but a "harsh, pitiless world court that knew no mercy," and the German people still needed some "bloody lessons" before they would dissociate themselves from the political and social insanity that had firm control over them. Only after Hitlerism had been swept aside would the German people begin the process of awakening, self-healing, and self-control. [108]

107. Theodor Plivier, "Zur deutschen Katastrophe," *Internationale Literatur* 11 (1944): 62–63, 66–67.
108. Lukács, *Borba gumanizma i varvarstva*, pp. 67–68.

The means by which Hitlerism had acquired a hold on the people is the paramount question for which Lukács sought an answer in another long (unpublished) manuscript on National Socialist ideology written in Tashkent in 1942 or 1943.[109] Lukács accepted all the major points of the party theory of fascism. Hitler, for instance, possessed no special qualities and no role that he alone was suited to play. "Had Hitler not done it [used violence to protect the endangered interests of the bourgeoisie], some other 'genius' of extreme reaction would have taken his place" (121). Nor was fascism any sui generis political-ideological movement; it differed from other reactionary parties only in the "logical consistency of its reactionary essence, in the decisiveness with which it . . . passed state power into the hands of the most reactionary Junkers and big capitalists" (134). Fascism had not sprung up out of nowhere; it had grown organically out of all past German reactionary tendencies (Spengler, Nietzsche) and was no more than a clever, demagogic application of this development to the needs of the broad masses in an era of crisis. Hitler's achievement was to give concrete political expression to a large body of reactionary thought and impart it to the masses in a simplified and vulgarized form. By way of nationalist and socialist demagogy, nazism had infected the minds and souls of the German masses, and the "Hitlerist pseudo-revolutionary mass hypnosis intended to involve [them] by the millions in this barbarism" (150), said Lukács. He then added: "To the disgrace of the German people, it has to be said that fascism's nationalist and socialist demagogy has succeeded here on a far-reaching scale. Above all it contrived to found a large mass party whose members have been swept along by this hypnosis and, believing in it, commit the most horrible acts without scruple, indeed, even take the initiative in them. The Fascist mass party has cleverly drawn different social classes . . . into this practical barbarization and turned them into "accomplices" (150). Such remarks have only to be compared with Lukács's pronouncements in, say, *Der historische Roman* to reveal the completeness of his volte-face.

The thrust of Lukacs's elaborations clearly contradicted the official notion of two Germanies, "One hated, one loved! / One sworn to the Hitlers / The other true to itself," as Erich Weinert put it.[110] It also dispelled the notion of the presence of large numbers of Germans on the verge of rebellion against Hitler, thus far kept in check only by

109. Lukács, "Wie ist Deutschland zum Zentrum der reaktionären Ideologie geworden?," Lukács Archivum. Subsequent page citations in the text appear in parentheses.
110. Weinert, "Für welches Deutschland?," in *An die deutschen Soldaten*, p. 29.

Gestapo terror. But Lukács evidently became apprehensive about his categorical interpretation of the impact of Nazi ideology upon the overwhelming majority of Germans; all along he had interlarded his comments with assertions that Fascist ideology had taken complete control of the minds of the masses; the point of his entire analysis had been to reveal the means by which this had been accomplished. But toward the end of his manuscript, he raised an already answered question: "How deeply has this subversion of morality penetrated the entire people? How powerful and how widespread are the counter-tendencies that resist this poisoning of the German people?"[111] An answer, he said, could not be given with "apodictic certainty." In one breath he noted that "by no means" had the entire German people been drawn into Fascist barbarism, but in the next breath he added that the poison had found its way into "very large segments of the population."

In contradiction to the substance of his previous remarks, Lukács then supplied a theory of two Germanies after all. The "increasingly intensifying terror of fascism" showed that the number of its irreconcilable enemies had to be considerable; speaking of "tens of thousands" of German workers and intellectuals fighting a heroic underground battle and of the underground "popular front movement," Lukács explained that for ten years "we have been hearing uninterruptedly" of the best sons and daughters of the German people being executed and martyred for their staunch stand against fascism. The trouble was, and it seems to have dawned on Lukács by now, that all this had been heard of only in the Communist press and afforded a poor impression of the overall situation in Germany. Lukács then continued his discussion of underground resistance, contradicting virtually everything he had said before. He even pointed out that it was very difficult anymore to determine the number of truly convinced Fascists, whose number was diminishing.

But it seems to have become clear to Lukács that his remarks following the question about the pervasiveness of moral degradation in Germany, which he had probably tacked on to his text in the first place only because he knew it to be part of the party canon, contradicted what he had been explaining all along. In his manuscript he crossed out the entire section, replacing it with a brief statement to the effect that, however large the resistance movement, Germany's future fate would in any case be decided by the extent to which the

111. Lukács, "Wie ist Deutschland zum Zentrum der reaktionären Ideologie geworden?," p. 169; subsequent page citations appear in parentheses.

military defeats triggered a social movement inside Germany, a movement that would culminate in Hitler's collapse. About the possibility of that happening, though, Lukács was profoundly pessimistic. German history had shown, he explained in the continuing paragraphs not crossed out, that all past progress toward the liberation of the German people had come as the result of military collapse and not on the basis of internal German resolve. Lukács then provided this general assessment (the bracketed portions were crossed out in the manuscript or were replaced by the preceding word or phrase): "Events show that military defeat is unavoidable [and that realization is growing in increasingly broad segments of the German people]. Now everything depends on whether any [growing] dissatisfaction with the Hitler regime, any [growing] outrage against Fascist barbarity, comes into existence [will be capable of], leading to a genuine, internal storming of the Bastille" (172).

Lukács went on to quote Stalin's comment to the effect that the Hitlers come and go but the German people remain, and then crossed that out too. He had set out to explain how National Socialism won the minds of the masses through a demagogic ideology and had unraveled a theory with no room in it for claims about the existence of a large force of Germans opposed to Hitler. That Lukács originally incorporated into his manuscript such assertions points probably to his intention of bringing his analysis into rough conformity with party mythology, a mythology in which he had earlier believed. By crossing it out in his private typescript, Lukács now underscored his rejection of the myth of two Germanies that he had helped create.

Almost to the day of surrender the German Communists stuck by their insistence that Hitler was not the German people; the people would soon rise up, they claimed, and overthrow him. The appeals for a German uprising continued through late 1944 and on into 1945 in radio broadcasts by, among others, Pieck and Ulbricht.[112] Time and again the Communists warned their people that only by toppling Hitler themselves would they have a say in forming the post-Hitler government. Pieck wrote in November 1944, "For dealing with the *situation* and the *future* of the German people there is a *big difference* whether the *end of war* and *peace* have to be forced upon the German people by *violence*."[113] But did it really make a difference to the Com-

---

112. See, for instance, selections from Pieck's addresses, in Pieck, *Gesammelte Reden und Schriften*, 6:270, 273, 326, 371; and Ulbricht, *Zur Geschichte der deutschen Arbeiterbewegung*, 2:371, 383, 394.

113. Pieck, "Das Aktionsprogramm der KPD: Rededisposition für eine Lektion an der Parteischule der KPD Nr. 12 in Nagornoje," in *Gesammelte Reden und Schriften*, 6:283.

munists? What did they know at this time of the role they would be allowed to play in a defeated and occupied Germany? The irony of KPD propaganda is that the political program the Communists now began to develop for Germany, even as they professed to believe that the nation would yet rise up, was identical to the one they began to institute in the summer of 1945 in the Soviet Occupation Zone, in spite of the fact that Germans backed Hitler to the end.

Had the Communists genuinely expected that Germans would revolt during the last months of the war? According to all their public pronouncements, they did. In a speech at a KPD party school in December 1944, Pieck actually claimed: "It is possible that the Nazi band will force the German people *for a time yet* to follow along, but the *uprising* against this band of criminals will *come all the more suddenly, the more so because unrest* and anger are on the increase *not only in the upper levels* of the German bourgeoisie but in large measure among the *working masses of people.*"[114] December 1944! Did Pieck really believe it? Fritz Erpenbeck, in March 1945 no less, was still pointing out that there was an active opposition in Germany.[115] The first semipublic admissions that the German people largely backed Hitler to the hilt were not forthcoming until late in March when Germany was on the brink of defeat. Yet Pieck himself made a remark much earlier that seems to have been repeated nowhere else at the time. In early November 1944, in his speech at the party school, he had noted, "Our people are sick *to the depths of their souls,* poisoned by the Nazi pestilence."[116] How does that square with professions of belief in the existence of two Germanies? It does not. Since Pieck immediately proceeded to point out that Communists must not lose faith in their people ("because we could otherwise just as well cease our work as Communists") and must begin a *"large process of politicization and democratization"* so as to "exterminate what *reaction, fascism,* imperialism, and the reactionary Prussian spirit have pumped into our people through a thousand canals,"[117] it is tempting to argue that by late 1944 all the talk of two Germanies and expectations of a popular revolt—coupled with dire warnings of things to come if the revolt failed to materialize—were intended to be used after the war to justify

---

114. Pieck, "Die KPD—ihr Aufbau und ihre organisationspolitischen Probleme: Aus der Rededisposition für eine Lektion an der Parteischule Nr. 12 in Nagornoje," in ibid., 6:324.
115. Fritz Erpenbeck [Hannes Waterkant], "Unsterbliche Opfer," *Internationale Literatur* 3 (1945): 79.
116. Pieck, "Das Aktionsprogram der KPD," p. 288.
117. Ibid.

draconic political and economic measures taken without popular approval.

Could this have been true? It must certainly have occurred to German Communists, and yet to assume that the propaganda line by late 1944 and early 1945 was intended for postwar justification of a communization of Germany would presuppose that the German Communists knew what shape the country would be taking under Allied occupation in the immediate postwar months and years. This was certainly not the case at the time the KPD began formulating its plans for political life in the "new, free, democratic Germany.

What, according to the German Communists, was to be the nature of the government that would replace Hitler once he had been overthrown in a popular uprising? Pieck wrote in his 1942 pamphlet that, to ward off castastrophe for Germany and the German people, it was the urgent task of all Germans to create a unified fighting front for the rapid end of the war (to bring down the Hitler regime and the Hitler dictatorship) and for the formation of a new, free Germany. "All truly German men and women who oppose the Hitler war and the Hitler dictatorship; all workers, employees, and civil servants, all farmers, manual workers, business men, and intellectuals must unite themselves in this fighting front and take up the struggle against the war and the Hitler dictatorship." The Hitler clique had to be swept away by a "genuine people's revolution," and all "honest elements of the German people" had to come together in this national deed. For this was the only way that the German people could achieve a "new, free Germany, in which a fascist-plutocratic band of adventurers and thieves no longer rule, in which bags of money no longer have control, in which, rather, the honest, working German people are masters of their own houses, in which all rights and liberties are assured through a genuine democratic constitution. . . . The struggle of the German people involves a great national goal—ending the war quickly, liberating Germany from Hitler barbarism, and creating a new, free Germany. . . . Long live the people's revolution for a new, free Germany."[118] The National Committee for a Free Germany had likewise called for a "strong democratic state that has nothing in common with the impotent Weimar regime, a democracy that will ruthlessly smother any attempt to revive conspiracies against the people's right to freedom or against the peace of Europe."[119]

Then, in early 1944, the German Communists in Moscow began

118. Pieck, *Der Hitlerfaschismus und das deutsche Volk*, pp. 89, 100–110.
119. Weinert, *Das Nationalkomitee "Freies Deutschland,"* p. 21.

work on a political program that they planned to put into effect in postwar Germany. In February the KPD Politburo formed a twenty-member commission,[120] which met some eighteen times between March and August to formulate what was summed up in October 1944 in the "Action Program for a Bloc of Militant Democracy."[121] The "militant democracy" was characterized in terms reminiscent of the KPD's "democratic republic" of 1936 to 1939. However, even though democracy had supplanted proletarian revolution, the analysis of social conditions in Germany and the steps that were necessary to deal with them were still based on the reduction of fascism to monopoly capitalism. Fascism, the action program explained, was the "imperialist path [taken] under the dictatorship of German finance capital and monopoly capital, which wanted to attain the status of a world power through imperialist predatory war, intensified exploitation and terroristic suppression of the toiling masses, and the subjugation of other peoples." Germany's salvation could only be achieved by breaking the "omnipotence of Fascist-imperialist monopoly capitalism" and by setting up a "strong, democratic people's regime." The economy was to be put in the service of the people; all the roots of fascism and imperialism were to be exterminated; and the entire German people were to be "reeducated for democracy."[122] The initial steps would be taken, under the conditions of military occupation, by organizing a mass movement for creation of a "bloc of militant democracy," which would encompass all organizations, parties, groups, and persons who wished to fight for the salvation of Germany by destroying Fascist-imperialist reaction and by forming a democratic people's regime.

The way was clear: certain peace, freedom, and the prosperity of the people could be achieved only by removing power from armaments capital and monopoly capital, "with all their Junker, military, and bureaucratic trappings. . . . They put Hitler and the NSDAP into the saddle, for he was their tool used to suppress the people, to prepare and unleash the war with which they intended to erect their imperialist world power!" Germany had to be purged of parasitic monopoly capitalism, of the reactionary Junkers' caste, wild militarism, and calcified bureaucracy. "Only then will accursed Hitlerism

---

120. Among the members were Pieck; Florin, Ulbricht, Ackermann, Weinert, Kurella, Winzer, Sobottka, and Becher. For the complete list, see Laschitza, *Kämpferische Demokratie gegen Faschismus*, p. 91.
121. Cf. Sywottek, *Deutsche Volksdemokratie*, pp. 150–83; Fischer, *Sowjetische Deutschlandpolitik*, pp. 83–119; Laschitza, *Kämpferische Demokratie gegen Faschismus*, pp. 88–183.
122. Laschitza, *Kämpferische Demokratie gegen Faschismus*, pp. 193–209.

have been exterminated by the roots and the way paved for the democratic renewal of Germany." [123]

In retrospect all this sounds like a program for a Soviet Germany, in a nineteen-twenties sense, called now by a different name. But the fact that this "Bloc of Militant Democracy" became just that in 1945 to 1949—a euphemism for a sovietized Germany—does not mean that it was intended to be so from the outset. In late 1944 the German Communists were still guessing about what postwar Germany would look like under Allied occupation. Wilhelm Pieck interpreted the action program as the "further development of the politics of the popular front, of the "national peace movement," [124] of the Free Germany Committee and movement." [125] In other words, in the beginning Communists were not going to have total control in Germany, or in part of it, and would have to gain power by democratic processes. The Communists knew that the country would be occupied; they also realized, in spite of all the rhetoric about last-minute uprisings, that the German people "would *to begin with lose the right of self-determination* with respect to the internal regime" and that all important measures pertaining to governmental questions would be taken by occupation authorities; finally, they knew that a "part" of Germany would be occupied by the Red Army and that the length of any occupation depended on the nature of civilian cooperation with the authorities in establishing a new, free Germany. [126] Now, Pieck explained, a broad "*antiimperialist, democratic mass movement*" had to be called to life to "save" the nation, and the concept of a militant democracy was to be the core ingredient. the "*central, political program*" of the movement to reshape Germany. [127]

And the KPD? "*With the fall of Hitler* and the *shattering of the Nazi party*, the question will arise in Germany of how the *future configuration of parties* will look and with *what possibilities* we have to reckon." [128] It was assumed by the KPD at this time that under Allied military occupation there would be no elections, no parliament, no government. Pieck

123. The "action program" is reprinted in ibid.
124. The so-called national peace movement was another meaningless Communist stunt. In late 1942 the KPD leadership in Moscow drew up a "Peace Manifesto to the German People and the German Wehrmacht," which was passed off as the result of an "illegal meeting" of a national peace movement in western Germany (see Pieck, *Gesammelte Reden und Schriften*, 6:402–3).
125. Pieck, "Das Aktionsprogramm der KPD," 6:299.
126. Ibid., 6:284.
127. Ibid., 6:290.
128. Pieck, "Die KPD—ihr Aufbau und ihre organisationspolitischen Probleme," 6:301.

mentioned, however, that the Allies had reached no final decisions with respect to political measures under the occupation. But, referring to a London broadcast of October 1944, Pieck noted that political parties would evidently be allowed, apart, of course, from the NSDAP. He pointed out that this announcement was not based on an agreement between the three big powers—the USSR, England, and the United States. He believed, however, that if the German people reacted accordingly, the Communists could count on an amelioration of the restrictions for anti-Fascist political life within the Allied process of exterminating the Nazi political apparatus.

Pieck went on to cite remarks made in an American newspaper in August 1944, comments, Pieck thought, that gave the Communists a cue as to what conditions they could expect for reconstructing their party in Germany. The article hinted that Germany would be divided up, according to the government in charge of each occupation zone, among the three large parties—KPD, Center (the Catholic party), and the SPD. But Pieck added, "This is an opinion based on *political speculation. Reality will be completely different.*"[129] Pieck evidently believed at this time that things would have to be done democratically, assuming, as he seems to have done, that some sort of uniform Allied regulations would be in force for all of occupied Germany. Here, of course, he was wrong; but in December 1944 he probably never dreamt that the German Communists would be given control of Germany, if only a portion of it, without ever having to engage in a fair political process of acquiring popular support.

At this point he had to assume that the political configuration in Germany, with respect to German parties, would depend largely on the mood of the people and their political orientation and would hinge on which party acquired the trust of the masses. On the basis of extant documents, this seems to have been the original intent of the KPD Action Program for a Bloc of Militant Democracy. It was a program designed to allow the Communists the greatest possible room for political maneuvering within an essentially democratic framework. For "we of course *cannot* count on the *KPD being the only party*, regardless of how daringly we approach *our work* in order to become the *large mass party* of the working people."[130] Pieck assumed that there would be a Communist party, an SPD, and some form of German demo-

---

129. Ibid., 6:303–05. Pieck's manner of phrasing his arguments seems to indicate that the KPD leadership was not privy to high-level Soviet policy thinking on the question of immediate postwar Germany.
130. Ibid.

cratic party, all of which would try to "distract attention" from their responsibility for the rise of Hitler and the war by taking up an anti-Fascist stance and by coming out in favor of a "new, democratic, peaceful Germany," making all sorts of promises to acquire a mass following. The KPD would have the task of forcing these parties to adopt clear positions with respect to the extermination of fascism, the thorough settling of accounts with imperialism and militarism, and the development of a "genuine *militant* democracy."

The KPD would present these parties with the action program, making them take a stand on the "vital questions" of the German people, and would do everything possible to create the broadest fighting front and a *"firm working people."* The KPD had to come forth as the *"large unifying national force"* in the eyes of the masses and compel the other parties either to work in this bloc or to place themselves in opposition to the interests of the masses and thus isolate themselves from the people.

It all happened much differently, of course; the German Communists, who had always spoken in the name of the people, would end up making the only revolution of which they were capable, one from above backed by the Red Army. But that was still several months away. In March 1945 the Communists finally relinquished their theory of two Germanies, if only reluctantly, and admitted that the German people were responsible for Hitler. On 29 March 1945, in the fifteenth plenary session of the National Committee, Erich Weinert explained that things had finally come to the point where the people had degraded themselves into accessories of Hitler.[131]

Anton Ackermann, in an April article published in *Internationale Literatur*, spelled things out clearly: "No one will argue that the Hitlers, Himmlers, Keitels, and Guderians could still be waging war without the obedient following of masses of millions of Germans." He neglected to mention that Communists had argued along similar lines for years. But now the analysis changed. "Himmler's terror certainly makes matters hard and explains much, but not everything," said Ackermann. Against the will of an entire people terror could accomplish nothing. Ackermann added that Hitler and Goebbels had managed to lead the German people in their entirety into a "criminal war of conquest because they succeeded in poisoning the mass of the German people with an imperialist robber ideology."[132]

Wilhelm Pieck concurred in an April speech: *"It is true, our people in*

131. Weinert, *Das Nationalkomitee "Freies Deutschland,"* pp. 96–97.
132. Anton Ackermann, "Zur Krimkonferenz," *Internationale Literatur* 4 (1945): 3.

the great majority are sick, very sick of soul and intellect. They are suffering from this *terrible pestilence* with which the Hitler band has poisoned the *hearts and minds* of our people and which has *apparently deprived them of their own resolve* to free themselves of this *mental illness.*" The Germans bore a great responsibility, Pieck went on, for, by supporting Hitler's war, they had made themselves guilty of the horrible crimes that the Hitler band had perpetrated upon other peoples, "especially on the *Soviet people.*" No one could claim that the Germans had known nothing of these crimes; they had been "committed before the *eyes* of our people and supported by them." Pieck added, however, that "*as much as* our people have been infected by Nazi ideology . . . *we still have confidence in them and believe* that under our influence and on the basis of their bitter experience they will *turn* from nazism, no longer allowing themselves to be misused *by other reactionary forces*, but instead will take *the way of militant democracy* to a new, peaceful, democratic *Germany.*"[133] What else could he have said? He had already pointed out in November 1944 that without confidence in the people the party might as well cease its work. Because they had no intention of doing that, the German Communists now set out to return to Germany and replace National Socialism's sound popular instinct (*gesundes Volksempfinden*) with class consciousness.

133. Pieck, "Zum Abschluss des 6. Kursus an der Antifa-Schule für deutsche Kriegsgefangene in Krasnogorsk (17. April 1945)," in *Gesammelte Reden und Schriften*, 6:382, 385, 395.

Bibliography

Archives

Akademie der Künste der DDR (East Berlin)
  Johannes-R.-Becher-Archiv
  Bertolt-Brecht-Archiv
  Willi-Bredel-Archiv
  Erich-Weinert-Archiv
  Friedrich-Wolf-Archiv
Akademie der Künste (West Berlin)
Magyar Tudományos Akadémia (Budapest)
  Balázs Béla-Hagyaték
  Gábor Andor-Hagyaték
Lukács Archivum és Könyvtár (Budapest)
Tsentralnyj gosudarstvennyj arkhiv literatury i iskusstv (Moscow)

Unpublished Manuscripts

Beer, Lilli. "Memoirs."
Bredel, Willi. "Die Wolga hat nur ein Ufer: Nach Aufzeichnungen aus zwei Front-Tagebüchern." Bredel-Archiv, Sig. 3 (page proofs).
Greid, Hermann. "Als Fremder drei Jahre—1933 bis 1936—in Schweden und in der Sowjetunion." Akademie der Künste, West Berlin.
Lukács, Georg. "Die Erbschaft dieser Zeit." Lukács Archivum.
———. "Grand Hotel 'Abgrund.' " Lukács Archivum.
———. "Marxismus oder Proudhonismus in der Literaturgeschichte?" Lukács Archivum.
———. "Prinzipielle Fragen in einer prinzipienlosen Polemik." Lukács Archivum.
———. "Verwirrungen über den 'Sieg des Realismus.' " Lukács Archivum.
———. "Warum haben Marx und Lenin die liberale Ideologie kritisiert?" Lukács Archivum.
———. "Die Widersprüche des Fortschritts und die Literatur." Lukács Archivum.

————. "Wie ist Deutschland zum Zentrum der reaktionären Ideologie geworden? (IV. Der Faschismus als theoretisches und praktisches System der Barbarei)." Lukács Archivum.

————. "Wozu brauchen wir das klassische Erbe." Lukács Archivum.

Richter, Trude. "Memoirs."

Wehner, Herbert. "Erinnerungen."

Contemporary Periodicals and Newspapers

Arbeiter-Zeitung (Basel)
The Communist International (New York)
Deutsche Volkszeitung (Paris)
Deutsche Zentral-Zeitung (Moscow)
Freies Deutschland (Mexico City)
Die Internationale (Prague)
Internationale Literatur (Moscow)
Das internationale Theater (Moscow)
Izvestija (Moscow)
Der Kämpfer (Engels)
Krasnaja nov (Moscow)
Die Linkskurve (Berlin)
Literaturnaja gazeta (Moscow)

Literaturnaja ucheba (Moscow)
Literaturnoe obozrenie (Moscow)
Literaturnyj kritik (Moscow)
Neue Deutsche Blätter (Prague)
Das neue Tage-Buch (Paris)
Die neue Weltbühne (Prague-Paris)
Neuer Vorwärts (Karlsbad)
Pravda (Moscow)
Die Rote Fahne (Berlin)
Rundschau (Basel)
Der Sturmschritt (Kharkov)
Das Wort (Moscow)
Die Zukunft (Paris)

Primary Literature

Aktionen Bekenntnisse Perspektiven: Berichte und Dokumente um die Freiheit des literarischen Schaffens in der Weimarer Republik. Berlin-Weimar: Aufbau-Verlag, 1966.

Albrecht, Karl I. *Der verratene Sozialismus: Zehn Jahre als hoher Staatsbeamter in der Sowjetunion.* Berlin-Leipzig: Nibelungen-Verlag, 1942.

Balázs, Béla. *Der mächtige Verbündete: Erzählung.* Moscow: Mezhdunarodnaja kniga, 1941.

Becher, Johannes R. *Die Bauern von Unterpeissenberg und andere Gedichte aus dem bäuerlichen Leben.* Engels: Deutscher Staatsverlag, 1938.

————. *Dank an Stalingrad.* Moscow: Verlag für fremdsprachige Literatur, 1943.

———. *Deutsche Sendung: Ein Ruf an die deutsche Nation.* Moscow: Verlag für fremdsprachige Literatur, 1943.

———. *Deutschland: Ein Lied vom Köpferollen und von den "nützlichen Gliedern."* Moscow-Leningrad: Verlagsgenossenschaft ausländischer Arbeiter in der UdSSR, 1934.

———. *Gedichte, 1936–1941.* Berlin-Weimar: Aufbau-Verlag, 1966.

———. *Gewissheit des Siegs und Sicht auf grosse Tage: Gesammelte Sonette, 1935–1938.* Moscow: Mezhdunarodnaja kniga, 1939.

———. *Der Glücksucher und die sieben Lasten: Ein hohes Lied.* Moscow: Verlagsgenossenschaft ausländischer Arbeiter in der UdSSR, 1938.

———. *Die hohe Warte: Deutschland-Dichtung.* Moscow: Verlag für fremdsprachige Literatur, 1944.

———. *Der Mann, der alles glaubte: Dichtungen.* Moscow-Leningrad: Verlagsgenossenschaft ausländischer Arbeiter in der UdSSR, 1935.

———. *Publizistik I, 1912–1938.* Berlin-Weimar: Aufbau-Verlag, 1977.

———. *Publizistik II, 1939–1945.* Berlin-Weimar: Aufbau-Verlag, 1978.

———. *Der verwandelte Platz: Erzählungen und Gedichte.* Moscow-Leningrad: Verlagsgenossenschaft ausländischer Arbeiter in der UdSSR, 1934.

Die Berner Konferenz der KPD (30. Januar 1. Februar 1939). Edited and introduced by Klaus Mammach. Berlin: Dietz Verlag, 1974.

Blum, Klara. *Die Antwort: Gedichte.* Moscow: Mezhdunarodnaja kniga, 1939.

———. *Donauballaden.* Moscow: Verlag für fremdsprachige Literatur, 1942.

———. *Erst recht!* Kiev: Staatsverlag der nationalen Minderheiten der USSR, 1939.

———. *Schlachtfeld und Erdball: Gedichte.* Moscow: Verlag für fremdsprachige Literatur, 1944.

———. *Wir entscheiden alles: Gedichte.* Moscow: Mezhdunarodnaja kniga, 1941.

Born, Georg. *Edinstvennyj i gestapo.* Moscow: Sovetskij pisatel, 1937.

———. *Gulliver u Arijtsev.* Moscow: Molodaja gvardija, 1936.

———. *Tagebuch des SA-Mannes Willi Schröder.* Moscow: Verlagsgenossenschaft ausländischer Arbeiter, 1936.

Brecht, Bertolt. *Arbeitsjournal, 1938 bis 1942.* Frankfurt/Main: Suhrkamp Verlag, 1973.

———. *Gesammelte Werke. Schriften: Zur Literatur und Kunst; Zur Politik und Gesellschaft,* vol. 2. Frankfurt/Main: Suhrkamp Verlag, 1967.

Bredel, Willi. *Der Auswanderer; Der Tod des Siegfried Allzufromm: Zwei Erzählungen über die Judenverfolgungen im faschistischen Deutschland.* Moscow: Mezhdunarodnaja kniga, 1941.

———. *Dokumente seines Lebens.* Berlin: Aufbau-Verlag, 1961.

———. *Kurzgeschichten aus Hitlerdeutschland.* Moscow: Verlag für fremdsprachige Literatur, 1942.

————. *Der Moorbauer: Antifaschistische Kurzgeschichten.* Moscow: Mezhdunarodnaja kniga, 1941.

————. *Nach dem Sieg: Erzählung.* Moscow: Mezhdunarodnaja kniga, 1939.

————. *Pater Brakel und andere Erzählungen.* Kiev: Staatsverlag der nationalen Minderheiten der USSR, 1940.

————. *Die Prüfung: Roman aus einem Konzentrationslager.* Moscow-Leningrad: Verlagsgenossenschaft ausländischer Arbeiter, 1935.

————. *Der Sonderführer: Erzählung.* Moscow: Verlag für fremdsprachige Literatur, 1944.

————. *Spanienkrieg.* 2 vols. Vol. 1, *Zur Geschichte der 11. Internationalen Brigade.* Vol. 2, *Begegnung am Ebro Schriften Dokumente.* Berlin-Weimar: Aufbau-Verlag, 1977.

————. *Der Spitzel und andere Erzählungen.* Moscow-Leningrad: Verlagsgenossenschaft ausländischer Arbeiter, 1936.

————. *Das Vermächtnis des Frontsoldaten: Novelle.* Moscow: Verlag für fremdsprachige Literatur, 1942.

Die Dritte Säule der kommunistischen Politik—IAH. Dargestellt nach authentischem Material. Berlin: Verlagsanstalt des Deutschen Holzarbeiter-Verbandes, 1923.

Erpenbeck, Fritz. *Deutsche Schicksale: Erzählungen.* Kiev: Staatsverlag der nationalen Minderheiten der USSR, 1939.

————. *Kleines Mädel im grossen Krieg: Erzählung.* Moscow: Mezhdunarodnaja kniga, 1940.

————. *Musketier Peters: Erzählung.* Moscow: Verlagsgenossenschaft ausländischer Arbeiter, 1936.

Feuchtwanger, Lion. *Erfolg: Drei Jahre Geschichte einer Provinz.* Berlin: Gustav Kiepenheuer Verlag, 1930.

————. *Moscow 1937: My Visit Described for My Friends.* New York: The Viking Press, 1937.

————. *Moskva 1937. Otchet o poezdke dlja moikh druzej.* Moscow: Gosudarstvennoe izdatelstvo "Khudozhestvennaja literatura," 1937.

First Conference of German Prisoner of War Privates and Non-Commissioned Officers in the Soviet Union. Moscow: Foreign Languages Publishing House, 1941.

Fischer, Ernst. *Die faschistische Rassentheorie.* Verlag für fremdsprachige Literatur, 1941.

————. *Freiheit und Diktatur.* Verlagsgenossenschaft ausländischer Arbeiter, 1935.

————. *Vernichtet den Trotskismus.* Strasbourg: Editions Prométhée, 1937.

Gábor, Andor. *Die Rechnung und andere Erzählungen aus dem Dritten Reich.* Moscow: Verlagsgenossenschaft ausländischer Arbeiter, 1936.

————. *Souper im "Hubertus": Erzählung.* Moscow: Verlagsgenossenschaft ausländischer Arbeiter in der UdSSR, 1936.

————. *Die Topfriecher und andere Erzählungen.* Engels: Deutscher Staatsverlag, 1935.

Gide, André. *Afterthoughts: A Sequel to Back from the USSR.* London: Martin Secker and Warburg Ltd., 1937.

————. *Back from the USSR.* London: Martin Secker and Warburg Ltd., 1937.

————. *The Journals of André Gide.* Vol. 3, *1928–1939.* New York: Alfred Knopf, 1949.

————. *Litterature engagée.* Paris: Gallimard, 1950.

Gles, S. *Deutschland erwacht! Geschichten aus dem "Dritten Reich."* Engels: Deutscher Staatsverlag, 1935.

————. *Deutschland gestern und heute: Erzählungen.* Kiev-Kharkov: Staatsverlag der nationalen Minderheiten der USSR, 1935.

————. *Verboten: Maischauspiel in 3 Akten.* Kiev-Kharkov: Staatsverlag für nationale Minderheiten, 1935.

Graf, Oskar Maria. *Der Abgrund: Ein Zeitroman.* Moscow: Verlagsgenossenschaft ausländischer Arbeiter, 1936.

————. *Reise in die Sowjetunion 1934.* Darmstadt: Sammlung Luchterhand, 1974.

Günther, Hans. *Der Herren eigener Geist: Ideologie des Nationalsozialismus.* Moscow-Leningrad: Verlagsgenossenschaft ausländischer Arbeiter, 1935.

————. *In Sachen gegen Bertram.* Kiev-Kharkov: Staatsverlag für nationale Minderheiten der UdSSR, 1936.

Heckert, Fritz. *Was geht in Deutschland vor: KPD und Hitlerdiktatur.* Moscow-Leningrad: Verlagsgenossenschaft ausländischer Arbeiter, 1933.

Hiller, Kurt. *Profile: Prosa aus einem Jahrzehnt.* Paris: Editions Nouvelles Internationales, 1938.

Hirsch, Werner. *Hinter Stacheldraht und Gitter: Erlebnisse in Konzentrationslagern und Gefängnissen Hitlerdeutschlands.* Zurich-Paris: Mopr-Verlag, 1934.

————. *Sozialdemokratische und kommunistische Arbeiter in Konzentrationslagern.* Strasbourg: Prometheus-Verlag, 1934.

Hoernle, Edwin. *Bauern unterm Joch: Erzählung.* Moscow: Verlagsgenossenschaft ausländischer Arbeiter, 1936.

————. *Wie lebt der deutsche Bauer.* Moscow: Verlag für fremdsprachige Literatur, 1939.

Hotopp, Albert. *Die Unbesiegbaren. Kurzgeschichten aus Hitlerdeutschland.* Engels: Deutscher Staatsverlag, 1935.

Huppert, Hugo. *Flaggen und Flügel: Skizzen / Reportagen / Geschichten.* Engels: Deutscher Staatsverlag, 1939.

————. *Jahreszeiten: Gedichte.* Moscow: Mezhdunarodnaja kniga, 1941.

————. *Vaterland: Gedichte.* Kiev: Staatsverlag der nationalen Minderheiten der USSR, 1940.

Kast, Peter. *Der Birnbaum.* Moscow: Mezhdunarodnaja kniga, 1938.

———. *Kampf an der Grenze: Kurzgeschichte.* Moscow: Verlagsgenossenschaft ausländischer Arbeiter, 1937.

Knorin, Valdemar. *Faschismus, Sozialdemokratie, und Kommunismus.* Moscow-Leningrad: Verlagsgenossenschaft ausländischer Arbeiter, 1934.

Kurella, Alfred. "Briefe." *Sinn und Form* 2 (1979): 244–81.

———. *Kleiner Stein im grossen Spiel: Roman.* Berlin: Verlag Kultur und Fortschritt, 1963.

———. *Wo liegt Madrid? 7 Erzählungen.* Kiev: Staatsverlag der nationalen Minderheiten der USSR, 1939.

———, ed. *Dimitroff: Briefe und Aufzeichnungen aus der Zeit der Haft und des Leipziger Prozesses.* Moscow-Leningrad: Verlagsgenossenschaft ausländischer Arbeiter in der UdSSR, 1935.

Lask, Berta [Gerhard Wieland]. *Ein Dorf steht auf; Johann der Knecht: Erzählungen aus Hitlerdeutschland.* Kiev-Kharkov: Staatsverlag der nationalen Minderheiten der UdSSR, 1935.

———. *Januar 1933 in Berlin.* Kiev-Kharkov: Staatsverlag der nationalen Minderheiten der UdSSR, 1935.

———. *Junge Helden: Erzählung aus den österreichischen Februarkämpfen.* Engels: Deutscher Staatsverlag, 1934.

Lenin, V. I. *Selected Works.* Vols. 1 and 3. Moscow: Progress Publishers, 1975.

Leschnitzer, Franz. *Verse.* Kiev: Staatsverlag der nationalen Minderheiten der USSR, 1939.

Lukács, Georg. *Borba gumanizma i varvarstva.* Tashkent: Gosudarstvennoe izdatelstvo UzSSR, 1943.

———. *Deutsche Literatur im Zeitalter des Imperialismus: Eine Übersicht ihrer Hauptströmungen.* Berlin: Aufbau Verlag, [1945].

———. *Deutsche Literatur in zwei Jahrhunderten.* Neuwied-Berlin: Luchterhand Verlag, 1964.

———. *Frühschriften.* Vol. 2, *Geschichte und Klassenbewusstsein.* Neuwied-Berlin: Luchterhand Verlag, 1968.

———. *K istorii realizma.* Moscow: Gosudarstvennoe izdatelstvo "Khudozhestvennaja literatura," 1939.

———. *Literaturnye teorii XIX veka i Marksizm.* Moscow: Gosudarstvennoe izdatelstvo "Khudozhestvennaja literatura," 1937.

———. *Probleme des Realismus I: Essays über Realismus.* Neuwied-Berlin: Luchterhand Verlag, 1971.

———. *Probleme des Realismus II: Der russische Realismus in der Weltliteratur.* Neuwied-Berlin: Luchterhand Verlag, 1964.

———. *Probleme des Realismus III: Der historische Roman.* Neuwied-Berlin: Luchterhand Verlag, 1965.

Lunacharskij, A. V. *Neizdannye materialy.* Moscow: Izdatelstvo "Nauka," 1970.

Mann, Heinrich. *Der Hass: Deutsche Zeitgeschichte*. Amsterdam: Querido, 1933.

———. *Verteidigung der Kultur: Antifaschistische Streitschriften und Essays*. Hamburg: Claasen, 1960.

Mann, Klaus. *Briefe und Antworten*. Vol. 1, *1922–1937*. Munich: Ellermann-Verlag, 1975.

Mann, Thomas. *Briefe, 1889–1936*. Frankfurt/Main: S. Fischer, 1961.

———. *Tagebücher 1933–1934*. Frankfurt/Main: S. Fischer, 1977.

———. *Tagebücher, 1935–1936*. Frankfurt/Main: S. Fischer, 1978.

Manuilsky, Dmitrij Z. *The Communist Parties and the Crisis of Capitalism (XI Plenum)*. New York: Workers Library Publishers, 1931.

———. *Problems of the Revolutionary Crisis and the Tasks of Sections of the Communist International: Concluding Speech at the Eleventh Plenum of the ECCI*. New York: Workers Library Publishers, 1931.

Max Hölz: Ein Deutscher Patriot. Moscow-Leningrad: Verlagsgenossenschaft ausländischer Arbeiter, 1933.

Mezhdunarodnyj kongress pisatelej v zashchitu kultury: Parizh, ijun 1935; Doklady i vystuplenija. Edited and with a foreword by I. Luppol. Moscow: Gosudarstvennoe izdatelstvo "Khudozhestvennaja literatura," 1936.

Miles [pseud.]. *Neu beginnen! Faschismus oder Sozialismus: Als Diskussionsgrundlage der Sozialisten Deutschlands*. Karlsbad: Graphia [1933].

Münzenberg, Willi. *Fünf Jahre Internationale Arbeiterhilfe*. Berlin: Neuer Deutscher Verlag, 1926.

———. *Solidarität: Zehn Jahre Internationale Arbeiterhilfe 1921–1931*. Berlin: Neuer Deutscher Verlag, 1931.

Nemetskie antifashistskie pisateli—bojtsam Krasnoj Armii. Moscow: Voennoe izdatelstvo Narodnogo komissariata oborony Sojuza SSR, 1941.

Ottwalt, Ernst. *Deutschland erwache! Geschichte des Nationalsozialismus*. Vienna-Leipzig: Hess and Co. Verlag, 1932.

———. *Put Gitlera k vlasti: Istorija natsional-sotsializma*. Moscow: Gosudarstvennoe sotsialno-èkonomicheskoe izdatelstvo, 1933.

Perepiska A. M. Gorkogo s zarubezhnymi literatorami. Moscow: Izdatelstvo Akademii Nauk SSR, 1960.

Pieck, Wilhelm. *Aufgaben und Zielsetzung der Einheitsfront: Zur Plattform eines Arbeitskreises revolutionärer Sozialisten*. Strasbourg: Prometheus-Verlag, 1935.

———. *Gesammelte Reden und Schriften*. Vol. 5, *Februar 1933 bis August 1939*. Berlin: Dietz Verlag, 1972.

———. *Gesammelte Reden und Schriften*. Vol. 6, *1939 bis Mai 1945*. Berlin: Dietz Verlag, 1979.

———. *Der Hitlerfaschismus und das deutsche Volk*. Moscow: Verlag für fremdsprachige Literatur, 1942.

———. *We are Fighting for a Soviet Germany*. Report to the Thirteenth

Plenum of the ECCI, December 1933. New York: Workers Library Publishers, 1934.

———. *Der neue Weg zum gemeinsamen Kampfe für den Sturz der Hitlerdiktatur. Referat und Schlusswort auf der Brüsseler Parteikonferenz der Kommunistischen Partei Deutschlands, Oktober 1935.* Moscow-Leningrad: Verlagsgenossenschaft ausländischer Arbeiter, 1936.

Plivier, Theodor. *Der Igel: Erzählungen.* Moscow: Verlag für fremdsprachige Literatur, 1942.

———. *Im letzten Winkel der Erde.* Moscow: Mezhdunarodnaja kniga, 1941.

———. *Die Männer der "Cap Finisterre": Roman.* Kiev: Staatsverlag der nationalen Minderheiten der USSR, 1940.

———. *Nichts als Episode.* Moscow: Mezhdunarodnaja kniga, 1941.

———. *Stalingrad: Roman.* Berlin: Aufbau-Verlag, 1945.

———. *Stalingrad.* In *Internationale Literatur* 11, 12 (1943); 1, 2, 4, 5, 6, 7, 8, 9 (1944).

Program of the Communist International. New York: Workers Library Publishers, Inc., 1929.

Protokoll der Verhandlungen des 12. Parteitages der Kommunistischen Partei Deutschlands. Berlin: Internationaler Arbeiter-Verlag, 1929.

Protokoll: Fünfter Kongress der Kommunistischen Internationale. Hamburg: Verlag Carl Hoym Nachfolger, 1924.

Protokoll des 6. Weltkongresses der Kommunistischen Internationale. Vol. 1. Hamburg-Berlin: Verlag Carl Hoym Nachfolger, 1928.

———. Vol. 4. Hamburg-Berlin: Verlag Carl Hoym Nachfolger, 1929.

Protokoll des VII. Weltkongresses der Kommunistischen Internationale. Vol. 2. Stuttgart: Verlag Neuer Weg, 1976.

Resolution der Maitagung 1938 des Zentralkomitees der KPD. Mit einer Einleitung von Wilhelm Pieck. Paris: Editions Prométhée, 1938.

Rudolf, A. [Raoul László]. *Der Moskauer Prozess: Seine Hintergründe und Auswirkungen.* Prague: Druck Buchdruckerei "Pokrok," 1936.

Scharrer, Adam. *Abenteuer eines Hirtenjungen und andere Dorfgeschichten.* Moscow-Leningrad: Verlagsgenossenschaft ausländischer Arbeiter, 1935.

———. *Die Bauern von Gottes Gnaden: Geschichte eines Erbhofes.* Engels: Deutscher Staatsverlag, 1935.

———. *Erlebnisroman eines jungen Proletariers.* Kiev: Staatsverlag der nationalen Minderheiten der USSR, 1940.

———. *Familie Schuhmann: Ein Berliner Roman.* Moscow: Mezhdunarodnaja kniga, 1939.

———. *Die Hochzeitsreise: Erzählung.* Moscow: Mezhdunarodnaja kniga, 1940.

———. *Der Krummhofbauer und andere Dorfgeschichten.* Kiev: Staatsverlag der nationalen Minderheiten der USSR, 1939.

———. *Der Landpostbote Zwinkerer und andere Erzählungen.* Moscow:

Verlag für fremdsprachige Literatur, 1944.

―――. *Der Landsknecht: Biographie eines Nazi.* Moscow: Verlag für fremdsprachige Literatur, 1943.

―――. *Wanderschaft: Erlebnisroman eines jungen Proletariers.* Kiev: Staatsverlag der nationalen Minderheiten der USSR, 1940.

―――. *Zwei Erzählungen aus dem Leben deutscher Bauern.* Moscow: Mezhdunarodnaja kniga, 1938.

Schmitt, Hans-Jürgen, ed. *Die Expressionismusdebatte: Materialien zu einer marxistischen Realismuskonzeption.* Frankfurt/Main: Suhrkamp Verlag, 1973.

Seydewitz, Max. *Stalin oder Trotzky.* Prague: Malik-Verlag, 1938.

VII. Kongress der Kommunistischen Internationale: Gekürztes, stenographisches Protokoll. Moscow: Verlag für fremdsprachige Literatur, 1939.

VII. Kongress der Kommunistischen Internationale: Referate und Resolutionen. Berlin: Dietz Verlag, 1975.

VII Kongress Kommunisticheskogo Internatsionala i borba protiv fashizma i vojny. (Sbornik dokumentov). Moscow: Izdatelstvo politicheskoj literatury, 1975.

Sozialistische Realismuskonzeptionen: Dokumente zum 1. Allunionskongress der Sowjetschriftsteller. Edited by H.-J. Schmitt und G. Schramm. Frankfurt/Main: Suhrkamp Verlag, 1974.

Stalin, Iosef. *O Velikoj otechestvennoj vojne Sovetskogo sojuza.* Moscow: Voennoe izdatelstvo, 1949.

Thälmann, Ernst. *Im Kampf gegen die faschistische Diktatur. Rede und Schlusswort des Genossen Ernst Thälmann auf der Parteikonferenz der KPD. im Oktober 1932; Die politische Resolution der Parteikonferenz.* Hg. von der Kommunistischen Partei Deutschlands, 1932.

―――. *Reden und Aufsätze zur Geschichte der deutschen Arbeiterbewegung.* Vol. 2. Berlin: Dietz Verlag, 1956.

―――. *Volksrevolution über Deutschland: Rede des Genossen Ernst Thälmann auf dem Plenum des ZK. der KPD. 15–17. Januar 1931.* Hg. vom ZK. der KPD., 1931.

―――. *Vorwärts unter dem Banner der Komintern: Rede des Genossen Thälmann auf der Tagung des ZK. der KPD. am 14. Mai 1931.* Hg. vom ZK. der KPD., 1931.

Thesen und Resolutionen des V. Weltkongresses der Kommunistischen Internationale. Hamburg: Verlag Carl Hoym Nachfolger, 1924.

Tretjakov, S. M. *Ljudi odnogo kostra. (Literaturnye portrety.).* Moscow: Gosudarstvennoe izdatelstvo "Khudozhestvennaja literatura," 1936.

Trotsky, Leon. *Literature and Revolution.* Ann Arbor: University of Michigan Press, 1975.

―――. *The Struggle against Fascism in Germany.* New York: Pathfinder Press, 1971.

―――. *Writings of Leon Trotsky* [1933–34]. New York: Pathfinder Press, 1975.

Ulbricht, Walter. *Zur Geschichte der deutschen Arbeiterbewegung; Aus Reden und Aufsätzen. Vol. 2, 1933–1946.* Berlin: Dietz Verlag, 1955.

"Ulbricht und die Volksfront." *SBZ-Archiv* 1/2 (January, 1963): 148–53.

Von Wangenheim, Gustav [Hans Huss]. *Helden im Keller.* Kiev-Kharkov: Staatsverlag für nationale Minderheiten der UdSSR, 1935.

Weber, Hermann, ed. *Der deutsche Kommunismus: Dokumente 1915–1945.* Cologne: Kiepenhauer und Witsch, 1973.

Weinert, Erich. *An die deutschen Soldaten.* Moscow: Verlag für fremdsprachige Literatur, 1942.

———. *An die deutschen Soldaten.* Moscow: Nationalkomitee "Freies Deutschland," 1944.

———. *Es kommt der Tag: Gedichte.* Moscow-Leningrad: Verlagsgenossenschaft ausländischer Arbeiter, 1934.

———. *Gedichte 1933–1941.* Berlin-Weimar: Aufbau-Verlag, 1975.

———. *Gedichte 1941–1953.* Berlin-Weimar: Aufbau-Verlag, 1976.

———. *Gegen den wahren Feind: Gedichte und Verse.* Moscow: Verlag für fremdsprachige Literatur, 1944.

———. *Kapitel II der Weltgeschichte: Gedichte über das Land des Sozialismus.* Berlin: Dietz Verlag, 1954.

———. *Lieder um Stalin.* Potsdam: Potsdamer Verlagsgesellschaft, 1949.

———. *Memento Stalingrad.* Berlin: Verlag Volk und Welt, 1960.

———. *Das Nationalkomitee "Freies Deutschland," 1943–1945: Bericht über seine Tätigkeit und seine Auswirkung.* Berlin: Rütten und Loening, 1957.

———. *Rot Front: Gedichte.* Kiev: Staatsverlag der nationalen Minderheiten der USSR, 1936.

———. *Um Deutschlands Freiheit.* Berlin: Aufbau-Verlag, 1958.

Weiss, Helmut [Hans Wendt]. *Heer im Dunkeln: Geschichten aus Hitlerdeutschland.* Kiev: Staatsverlag der nationalen Minderheiten der USSR, 1937.

Wentscher, Dora. *Flosstelle Iskitim: Sibirisches Tagebuch 1941/42.* Weimar: Volksverlag, 1962.

———. *Der Landstreicher: Erzählung.* Moscow: Mezhdunarodnaja kniga, 1940.

———. *Die Schule der Grausamkeit.* Moscow: Mezhdunarodnaja kniga, 1941.

———. *Zwei Erzählungen: Der Kamerad des Heldenjungen; Die Milch ist eingeteilt.* Moscow: Mezhdunarodnaja kniga, 1939.

Wolf, Friedrich. *Doktor Mamlocks Ausweg: Tragödie der westlichen Demokratie.* Moscow-Leningrad: Verlagsgenossenschaft ausländischer Arbeiter der UdSSR, 1935.

———. *Floridsdorf: Ein Schauspiel von den Februarkämpfen der Wiener Arbeiter.* Moscow-Leningrad: Verlagsgenossenschaft ausländischer Arbeiter in der UdSSR, 1935.

———. *Heimkehr der Söhne: Eine Novelle.* Moscow: Verlag für fremdsprachige Literatur, 1944.

———. *Der Russenpelz: Eine Erzählung aus Deutschland 1941–42*. Moscow: Verlag für fremdsprachige Literatur, 1942.

———. *Sieben Kämpfer vor Moskau*. Moscow: Verlag für fremdsprachige Literatur, 1942.

———. *Das trojanische Pferd: Ein Stück vom Kampf der Jugend in Deutschland*. Moscow: Verlagsgenossenschaft ausländischer Arbeiter in der UdSSR, 1934.

Zinner, Hedda. *Geschehen: Gedichte*. Moscow: Mezhdunarodnaja kniga, 1939.

———. *Unter den Dächern: Gedichte*. Moscow: Verlagsgenossenschaft ausländischer Arbeiter in der UdSSR, 1936.

"Zwei richtungsweisende Beiträge Walter Ulbrichts zur Entwicklung der Strategie und Taktik der KPD in den Jahren 1935–1937." *Beiträge zur Geschichte der deutschen Arbeiterbewegung* 1 (1963): 75–84.

Secondary Literature

Angress, Werner T. *Stillborn Revolution: The Communist Bid for Power in Germany, 1921–1923*. Princeton: Princeton University Press, 1963.

Bahne, Siegfried. "Die Kommunistische Partei Deutschlands." In *Das Ende der Parteien 1933*, edited by Erich Matthias and Rudolf Morsey. Düsseldorf: Droste Verlag, 1960.

———. " 'Sozialfaschismus' in Deutschland." *International Review of Social History* 10, pt. 2 (1965): 211–45.

Barbusse, Henri. *Stalin: A New World Seen Through One Man*. New York: Macmillan Company, 1935.

Barck, Simone. *Johannes R. Bechers Publizistik in der Sowjetunion, 1935–1945*. Berlin: Akademie-Verlag, 1976.

Baumgart, Hans. *Der Kampf der sozialistischen deutschen Schriftsteller gegen den Faschismus (1933–1945)*. Institut für Gesellschaftswissenschaften beim ZK der SED, 1962.

Beck, F., and Godin, W. *Russian Purge and the Extraction of Confession*. New York: The Viking Press, 1951.

Böhme, Kurt W. *Die deutschen Kriegsgefangenen in sowjetischer Hand: Eine Bilanz*. Munich: Verlag Ernst und Werner Gieseking, 1966.

Borkenau, Franz. *European Communism*. New York: Harper and Brothers, 1953.

———. *World Communism: A History of the Communist International*. Michigan: University of Michigan Press, 1962.

Brown, Edward J. *The Proletarian Episode in Russian Literature 1928–1932*. New York: Columbia University Press, 1953.

Buber-Neumann, Margarete. *Als Gefangene bei Stalin und Hitler: Eine Welt im Dunkel*. Stuttgart: Deutsche Verlags-Anstalt, 1958.

———. *Kriegsschauplätze der Weltrevolution: Ein Bericht aus der Praxis der*

Komintern 1919–1943. Stuttgart: Seewald Verlag, 1967.

———. *Von Potsdam nach Moskau: Stationen eines Irrweges*. Stuttgart: Deutsche Verlags-Anstalt, 1957.

Carr, Edward Hallet. *A History of Soviet Russia. Vol. 3, The Bolshevik Revolution, 1917–1923*. London: Macmillan and Co., Ltd., 1953.

Cohen, Stephan F. *Bukharin and the Bolshevik Revolution: A Political Biography, 1888–1938*. New York: Alfred A. Knopf, 1973.

Conquest, Robert. *The Great Terror: Stalin's Purge of the Thirties*. New York: Collier Books, 1973.

Crossman, Richard, ed. *The God That Failed: Six Studies in Communism*. London: Hamish Hamilton, 1950.

Damerius, Helmut. *Über zehn Meere zum Mittelpunkt der Welt: Erinnerungen an die "Kolonne Links."* Berlin: Henschelverlag, 1977.

Degras, Jane. "United Front Tactics in the Comintern." In *International Communism*, edited by David Footman. St. Antony's Papers, No. 9. London: Chatto and Windus, 1960.

Deutscher, Isaac. *The Prophet Outcast. Vol. 3, Trotsky: 1929–1940*. New York: Vintage Books, 1963.

———. *Stalin: A Political Biography*. New York: Vintage Books, 1960.

Dialog und Kontroverse mit Georg Lukács. Der Methodenstreit deutscher sozialistischer Schriftsteller. Leipzig: Verlag Philipp Reclam jun., 1975.

Diezel, Peter. *Exiltheater in der Sowjetunion, 1932–1937*. Berlin: Henschelverlag, 1978.

Duhnke, Horst. *Die KPD von 1933 bis 1945*. Cologne: Kiepenheuer und Witsch, 1972.

Edinger, Lewis J. *German Exile Politics: The Social Democratic Executive Committee in the Nazi Era*. Berkeley and Los Angeles: University of California Press, 1956.

Einsiedel, Heinrich Graf von. *Tagebuch der Versuchung*. Berlin-Stuttgart: Pontes-Verlag GmbH., 1950.

Ermolaev, Herman. *Soviet Literary Theories, 1917–1934: The Genesis of Socialist Realism*. Berkeley and Los Angeles: University of California Press, 1963.

europäische ideen, 14/15 (1976) and 45/46 (1979).

Fetscher, Iring. "Brecht und der Kommunismus." *Merkur* 9 (1973): 872–86.

Fischer, Alexander. *Sowjetische Deutschlandpolitik im Zweiten Weltkrieg, 1941–1945*. Stuttgart: Deutsche Verlags-Anstalt, 1975.

Fischer, Ruth. *Stalin and German Communism: A Study of the Origins of the State Party*. Cambridge: Harvard University Press, 1948.

Flechtheim, Ossip K. *Die KPD in der Weimarer Republik*. Frankfurt/Main: Europäische Verlagsanstalt, 1976.

Gal, N., and Kratova, S. *Antifashisty v podpole: O tvorchestve V. Bredelja*. Moscow: Gosudarstvennoe izdatelstvo khudozhestvennoj literatury, 1941.

Gallas, Helga. *Marxistische Literaturtheorie: Kontroversen im Bund proletarisch-revolutionärer Schriftsteller.* Neuwied-Berlin: Sammlung Luchterhand, 1971.

Geschichte der deutschen Arbeiterbewegung: Biographisches Lexikon. Berlin: Dietz Verlag, 1970.

Geschichte der deutschen Arbeiterbewegung. Vol. 4, *Von 1924 bis Januar 1933.* Vol. 5, *Von Januar 1933 bis Mai 1945.* Vol. 6, *Von Mai 1945 bis 1949.* Berlin: Dietz Verlag, 1966.

Ginzburg, Evgenia. *Journey into the Whirlwind.* New York: Harcourt, Brace and World, Inc., 1967.

Gross, Babette. "Die Volksfrontpolitik in den dreissiger Jahren: Ein Beitrag zum Verständnis der kommunistischen Taktik." In *Aus Politik und Zeitgeschichte,* supplement to *Das Parlament,* 24 October 1962.

—————. *Willi Münzenberg: Eine politische Biographie.* Stuttgart: Deutsche Verlags-Anstalt, 1967.

Die Grosse Sozialistische Oktoberrevolution und Deutschland. Vol. 2. Berlin: Dietz Verlag, 1967.

Grossman, Kurt R. *Emigration: Geschichte der Hitler-Flüchtlinge, 1933–1945.* Stuttgart: Europäische Verlagsanstalt, 1969.

Gyptner, Richard. "Über die antifaschistischen Sender während des zweiten Weltkrieges." *Beiträge zur Geschichte der deutschen Arbeiterbewegung* 5 (1964): 881–84.

Halfmann, Horst. "Bibliographien und Verlage der deutschsprachigen Exil-Literatur, 1933 bis 1945." In *Beiträge zur Geschichte des Buchwesens, Vol. 4.* Leipzig: VEB Fachbuchverlag, 1969.

Halperin, S. William. *Germany Tried Democracy: A Political History of the Reich from 1918 to 1933.* New York: W. W. Norton and Company, Inc., 1965.

Harris, Frederick John. *André Gide and Romain Rolland: Two Men Divided.* New Brunswick: Rutgers University Press, 1973.

Hay, Julius. *Geboren 1900: Erinnerungen.* Hamburg: Christian Wegner Verlag, 1971.

Herling, Gustav. *A World Apart.* New York: Roy Publishers, 1951.

Hofer, Karl-Heinz. *Willi Bredel.* Leipzig: VEB Bibliographisches Institut, 1976.

Huppert, Hugo. *Wanduhr mit Vordergrund.* Halle: Mitteldeutscher Verlag, 1977.

Istorija nemetskoj literatury: Tom pjatyj, 1918–1945. Moscow: Izdatelstvo "Nauka," 1976.

Istorija russkoj sovetskoj literatury. Vol. 2, 1930–1941. Moscow: Izdatelstvo "Nauka," 1967.

Ivanov, R. V. *The Memoirs of Ivanov-Razumnik.* London: Oxford University Press, 1965.

Iz istorii Mezhdunarodnogo objedinenija revoljutsionnykh pisatelej (MORP). Moscow: Izdatelstvo "Nauka," 1969.

Jahrbuch für Geschichte der UdSSR und der volksdemokratischen Länder

428   Bibliography

Europas. Vol. 11. Berlin: VEB Deutscher Verlag der Wissenschaften, 1967.

Jarmatz, Klaus et al. *Exil in der UdSSR.* Leipzig: Verlag Philipp Reclam jun., 1979.

Kantorowicz, Alfred. *Deutsches Tagebuch.* Munich: Kindler Verlag, 1959.

———. *Exil in Frankreich: Merkwürdigkeiten und Denkwürdigkeiten.* Bremen: Schünemann Universitätsverlag, 1971.

———. *Politik und Literatur im Exil: Deutschsprachige Schriftsteller im Kampf gegen den Nationalsozialismus.* Hamburg: Hans Christians Verlag, 1978.

Kersten, Kurt. "Das Ende Willi Münzenbergs: Ein Opfer Stalins und Ulbrichts." *Deutsche Rundschau* 5 (1957): 484–99.

Klein, Wolfgang. *Schriftsteller in der französischen Volksfront: Die Zeitschrift "Commune."* Berlin: Akademie-Verlag, 1978.

Koestler, Arthur. *The Invisible Writing.* London: The Macmillan Company, 1969.

Kraushaar, Luise. "Der 'Deutsche Volkssender' (1941–1945)." *Beiträge zur Geschichte der deutschen Arbeiterbewegung* 1 (1964): 116–33.

"Gespräch mit Alfred Kurella." *Sinn und Form* 2 (1975): 221–43.

Kuusinen, Aino. *Der Gott stürzt seine Engel.* Vienna-Munich-Zurich: Verlag Fritz Molden, 1972.

Langkau-Alex, Ursula. *Volksfront für Deutschland? Vorgeschichte und Gründung des "Ausschusses zur Vorbereitung einer deutschen Volksfront," 1933–1936. Vol. 1.* Frankfurt/Main: Syndikat, 1977.

Laschitza, Horst. *Kämpferische Demokratie gegen Faschismus: Die programmatische Vorbereitung auf die antifaschistisch-demokratische Umwälzung in Deutschland durch die Parteiführung der KPD.* Berlin: Deutscher Militärverlag, 1969.

Lazitch, Branko, and Drachkovitch, Milorad M. *Lenin and the Comintern.* Vol. 1. Stanford: Hoover Institution Press, 1972.

Leonhard, Susanne. *Gestohlenes Leben: Schicksal einer politischen Emigrantin in der Sowjetunion.* Herford: Nicolaische Verlagsbuchhandlung, 1968.

Leonhard, Wolfgang. *Die Revolution entlässt ihre Kinder.* Frankfurt/Main: Ullstein Verlag, 1976.

Lexikon sozialistischer deutscher Literatur: Von den Anfängen bis 1945. Leipzig: VEB Bibliographisches Institut, 1964.

Lipper, Elinor. *Eleven Years in Soviet Prison Camps.* Chicago: Henry Regnery Company, 1951.

Literatur der Arbeiterklasse: Aufsätze über die Herausbildung der deutschen sozialistischen Literatur (1918–1933). Berlin-Weimar: Aufbau-Verlag, 1976.

Literaturnaja èntsiklopedija. Moscow: "Sovetskaja èntsiklopedija," 1934.

McKenzie, Kermit E. *Comintern and World Revolution, 1928–1943: The Shaping of Doctrine.* New York: Columbia University Press, 1964.

———. "The Soviet Union, the Comintern and World Revolution: 1935." *Political Science Quarterly* 2 (1950): 214–37.

Maguire, Robert A. *Red Virgin Soil: Soviet Literature in the 1920's.* Princeton:

Princeton University Press, 1968.

March, Harold. *Gide and the Hound of Heaven.* Philadelphia: University of Pennsylvania Press, 1952.

Marcuse, Ludwig. *Mein 20. Jahrhundert: Auf dem Wege zu einer Autobiographie.* Munich: Paul List Verlag, 1960.

Matthias, Erich, ed. *Mit dem Gesicht nach Deutschland: Eine Dokumentation über die sozialdemokratische Emigration.* Düsseldorf: Droste Verlag, 1968.

Mayenburg, Ruth von. *Blaues Blut und rote Fahne: Ein Leben unter vielen Namen.* Vienna-Munich: Molden Taschenbuch-Verlag, 1977.

————. *Hotel Lux.* Munich: C. Bertelsmann Verlag, 1978.

Medvedev, Roy A. *Let History Judge: The Origins and Consequences of Stalinism.* New York: Vintage Books, 1973.

Meissner, Boris. *Russland, die Westmächte und Deutschland: Die sowjetische Deutschlandpolitik, 1943–1953.* Hamburg: H. H. Nolke Verlag, 1954.

Melzwig, Brigitte. *Deutsche sozialistische Literatur, 1918–1945: Bibliographie der Buchveröffentlichungen.* Berlin-Weimar: Aufbau-Verlag, 1975.

Michev, Dobrin. *Mezhrabpom—Organizatsija proletarskoj solidarnosti, 1921–1935.* Moscow: Izdatelstvo "Mysl," 1971.

Mikhail Koltsov, kakim on byl. Sovetskij pisatel, 1965.

Mittenzwei, Werner. *Exil in der Schweiz.* Leipzig: Verlag Philipp Reclam jun., 1978.

Moore, Barrington, Jr. *Soviet Politics—The Dilemma of Power.* New York: Harper and Row, 1965.

Motyleva, T. *Nemetskaja literatura v borbe protiv fashizma.* Tashkent: Gosudarstvennoe izdatelstvo UzSSR, 1942.

Mytze, Andreas W. *Ottwalt.* Berlin: Verlag europäische ideen, 1977.

Nicolas, Waltraut. *Die Kraft, das Ärgste zu ertragen: Frauenschicksale in Sowjetgefängnissen.* Bonn: Athenäum-Verlag, 1958.

————. *Viele tausend Tage: Erlebnisbericht aus zwei Ländern.* Stuttgart: Steingruben Verlag, 1960.

Nollau, Günther. *International Communism and World Revolution: History and Methods.* New York: Frederick A. Praeger, 1951.

Okljanskij, Jurij. *Povest o malenkom soldate.* Moscow: Izdatelstvo "Sovetskaja Rossija," 1978.

Pattern for World Revolution [Julian Gumperz and Johann Rindl]. Chicago: Ziff-David Publishing Company, 1947.

Petrova, Zoja. "Zhurnal *Das Vort*—organ nemetskoj antifashistskoj literaturnoj emigratsii." Dissertation, Moscow State University, 1973.

Pirker, Theo. *Komintern und Faschismus, 1920–1940: Dokumente zur Geschichte und Theorie des Faschismus.* Stuttgart: Deutsche Verlags-Anstalt, 1965.

Plievier, Hildegard. *Ein Leben gelebt und verloren: Roman.* Gütersloh: Bertelsmann, 1966.

Pollatschek, Walter. *Friedrich Wolf: Eine Biographie.* Berlin: Aufbau-Verlag, 1963.

Poretsky, Elisabeth K. *Our Own People: A Memoir of "Ignace Reiss" and His*

Friends. Ann Arbor: University of Michigan Press, 1969.

Preuss, Werner. *Erich Weinert: Sein Leben und Werk.* Berlin: Volk und Wissen, 1971.

Ratza, Werner. *Die deutschen Kriegsgefangenen in der Sowjetunion: Der Faktor Arbeit.* Munich: Verlag Ernst und Werner Gieseking, 1973.

Ravines, Eudocio. *The Yenan Way.* New York: Charles Scribner's Sons, 1951.

Regler, Gustav. *Das Ohr des Malchus: Eine Lebensgeschichte.* Cologne-Berlin: Kiepenheuer und Witsch, 1958.

Reich, Bernhard. *Im Wettlauf mit der Zeit: Erinnerungen aus fünf Jahrzehnten deutscher Theatergeschichte.* Berlin: Henschelverlag, 1970.

Retzlaw, Karl. *Spartakus.* Frankfurt/Main: Verlag Neue Kritik, 1972.

Richter, Trude. *Die Plakette: Vom grossen und vom kleinen Werden.* Halle: Mitteldeutscher Verlag, 1972.

Robel, Gert. *Die deutschen Kriegsgefangenen in der Sowjetunion: Antifa.* Munich: Verlag Ernst und Werner Gieseking, 1974.

Roder, Werner. *Sonderfahndungsliste UdSSR.* Erlangen: Verlag für zeitgeschichtliche Dokumente und Curiosa, 1977.

Rudenko, Roman. *Die Gerechtigkeit nehme ihren Lauf: Die Reden des sowjetischen Hauptanklägers Generalleutnant R. A. Rudenko im Nürnberger Prozess der deutschen Hauptkriegsverbrecher.* Berlin: SWA-Verlag, 1946.

Scheurig, Bodo. *Freies Deutschland: Das Nationalkomitee und der Bund Deutscher Offiziere in der Sowjetunion, 1943–1945.* Munich: Nymphenburger Verlagsbuchhandlung, 1960.

Schleimann, Jorgen. "The Organization Man: The Life and Work of Willi Münzenberg." *Survey* 55 (1965): 64–91.

Schweyer, Marc. "Theodor Plivier im Exil: Bibliographie seiner Schriften (1933–1945)." *Recherches Germaniques* 2 (1972): 167–203.

Serge, Victor. *Memoirs of a Revolutionary, 1901–1941.* New York: Oxford University Press, 1963.

Sinko, Erwin. *Roman eines Romans: Moskauer Tagebuch.* Cologne: Verlag für Wissenschaft und Politik, 1962.

Sovetskoe literaturovedenie za pjatdesjat let: Sbornik statej. Moscow: Izdatelstvo Moskovskogo universiteta, 1967.

Stadler, Karl R. *Opfer verlorener Zeiten: Geschichte der Schutzbund-Emigration 1934.* Vienna: Europaverlag, 1974.

Stahlberger, Peter. *Der Zürcher Verleger Emil Oprecht und die deutsche politische Emigration, 1933–1945.* Zurich: Europa Verlag, 1970.

Štajner, Karlo. *7000 Tage in Sibirien.* Vienna: Europaverlag, 1975.

Sywottek, Arnold. *Deutsche Volksdemokratie: Studien zur politischen Konzeption der KPD, 1935–1946.* Düsseldorf: Bertelsmann Universitätsverlag, 1971.

Sziklai, László. *Zur Geschichte des Marxismus und der Kunst.* Budapest: Akadémiai Kiadó, 1978.

Tupitsin, A. *Oblik fashistskogo zverja: Nemetskie pisateli-antifashisty o gitlerizme.*

Molotovskoe oblastnoe izdatelstvo, 1942.

Ulam, Adam B. *Expansion and Coexistence: Soviet Foreign Policy, 1917–73.* New York: Praeger Publishers, 1974.

Vietzke, Siegfried. *Die KPD auf dem Wege zur Brüsseler Konferenz.* Berlin: Dietz Verlag, 1966.

Walter, Hans-Albert. *Deutsche Exilliteratur, 1933–1950. Vol. 1, Bedrohung und Verfolgung bis 1933.* Darmstadt: Luchterhand, 1972.

———. *Deutsche Exilliteratur, 1933–1950. Vol. 4, Exilpresse.* Stuttgart: J. B. Metzlersche Verlagsbuchhandlung, 1978.

Weber, Hermann. "Die Parteitage der KPD und SPD." In supplement to *Das Parlament,* 9 January 1963.

———. *Die Wandlung des deutschen Kommunismus: Die Stalinisierung der KPD in der Weimarer Republik.* 2 vols. Frankfurt/Main: Europäische Verlagsanstalt, 1969.

Weingartner, Thomas. *Stalin und der Aufstieg Hitlers: Die Deutschlandpolitik der Sowjetunion und der Kommunistischen Internationale, 1929–1934.* Berlin: Walter de Gruyter und Co., 1970.

Weiss, Edgar. *Johannes R. Becher und die sowjetische Literaturentwicklung.* Berlin: Akademie-Verlag, 1971.

Weissberg-Cybulski, Alexander. *Hexensabbat: Russland im Schmelztiegel der Säuberungen.* Frankfurt/Main: Verlag der Frankfurter Hefte, 1951.

Wolff, Willy. *An der Seite der Roten Armee: Zum Wirken des Nationalkomitees "Freies Deutschland" an der sowjetisch-deutschen Front, 1943 bis 1945.* Berlin: Militärverlag der Deutschen Demokratischen Republik, 1975.

Wollenberg, Erich. *Der Apparat: Stalins Fünfte Kolonne.* Bonn: Hg. vom Bundesministerium für gesamtdeutsche Fragen, 1951.

Das Wort: Bibliographie einer Zeitschrift. Berlin-Weimar: Aufbau-Verlag, 1975.

Das Wort: Registerband. Berlin: Rütten und Loening, 1968.

Zinner, Hedda. *Auf dem roten Teppich: Erfahrungen, Gedanken, Impressionen.* Berlin: Buchverlag Der Morgen, 1978.

Zur Aktualität Walter Benjamins. Frankfurt/Main: Suhrkamp Verlag, 1972.

Zur Tradition der sozialistischen Literatur in Deutschland: Eine Auswahl von Dokumenten. Berlin-Weimar: Aufbau-Verlag, 1967.

Zur Tradition der deutschen sozialistischen Literatur. Eine Auswahl von Dokumenten, 1926–1935; Eine Auswahl von Dokumenten, 1935–1941; Eine Auswahl von Dokumenten, 1941–1949; Kommentare. Berlin-Weimar: Aufbau-Verlag, 1979.

Index